BOOKS BY EDMUND WILSON

THE THIRTIES

Edmund Wilson, 1930

EDMUND WILSON

The Thirties

From Notebooks and Diaries of the Period

Edited with an Introduction by
Leon Edel

FARRAR, STRAUS AND GIROUX

NEW YORK

Library of Congress Cataloging in Publication Data
Wilson, Edmund, 1895–1972. The thirties.
Includes index.
1. Wilson, Edmund, 1895–1972—Biography.
2. Authors, American—20th century—Biography.
I. Edel, Leon, 1907–   II. Title.
PS3545.I6245Z535   1980   818'.5209 [B]   79–28700

CONTENTS

ILLUSTRATIONS

Acknowledgment is made to the Collection of American Literature, Beinecke Rare Book and Manuscript Library, Yale University, for permission to reproduce the facsimiles facing pages 318 and 508

EDITOR'S FOREWORD

The text of Edmund Wilson's *The Thirties* is based on his own typewritten manuscript and certain of the typed and holograph journals in the Beinecke Rare Book and Manuscript Library at Yale University. Mr. Donald Gallup, the curator of American manuscripts, has had these journals conveniently sorted and numbered and I am much indebted to him for his help with this and other material in the Wilson archive. The Wilson typescript contains holograph insertions, corrections, explanations, and comments. It is clear from the condition of the typescript that he intended to do much more work on this book. Where necessary, I have verified the text of his manuscript against the Yale originals. As I explained in *The Twenties*, Wilson intended his journals to be edited as "trade" books, not as scholarly editions; he wanted no scholarly apparatus and in particular no treatment of his text as if it were sacrosanct. Journals are written in the rough; and he knew journal keepers repeat themselves. He wanted his slips of the pen silently corrected without the inevitable *sic* and explanatory notes.

In one respect I have not followed Wilson's instructions. He would have preferred fewer footnotes and would have explained his material and references in interpolated passages, as in his manuscript of *The Twenties*. In the absence of interpolations, and with a new generation requiring considerable guidance to the personalities and incidents involved, I have used brief footnotes where necessary. As before, the reader can distinguish between such interpolations as Wilson made and mine by his use of the first person. Mine are all in the third person. The sections and chronological headings are mine, as are the headnotes. Repetitions have been edited out and redundancies eliminated, as well as material already included in *The Twenties*. Wilson was very clear about wanting this manuscript as tidy as he would have made it himself.

A grant from the National Endowment for the Humanities proved of great help in my bringing this volume to completion. I am indebted to Elena Wilson and Daniel Aaron for a discussion of the material; to Allan Taub, Malcolm Cowley, John Hammond, the late Quincy Howe and Matthew Josephson for verification of certain facts relating to Wilson's adventure on the "barricades" early in the 1930s in the Kentucky mine fields. Rosalind and Reuel Wilson generously answered certain questions about their father, and James Canby, of Santa Barbara, gave me his recollections of his boyhood in Provincetown with his mother, Margaret Canby, and his stepfather. Malcolm Cowley and Bruce Bliven (the latter shortly before his death) clarified some of the *New Republic* background for me, and Dr. Gordon N. Ray, president of the John Simon Guggenheim Memorial Foundation, provided me with valuable data concerning Wilson's fellowship which took him to Russia in 1935. Robert Penn Warren responded to questions about Wilson's visit early in the 1930s to the "Agrarians" in the South. Finally, my former student, Louise Hazlett, gave me considerable assistance in identifying persons, places, and events which have faded into the past since Wilson kept these journals.

Although Wilson expanded and printed his Russian journal in two different volumes, *Travels in Two Democracies* and *Red, Black, Blond and Olive,* and drew on it in writing *To the Finland Station,* I have included it here in the belief that it will be useful for readers to have the text of his original notes and jottings.

L.E.

EDMUND WILSON
IN THE THIRTIES

How is one to speak of the plunge from the 1920s into the 1930s—the toboggan slide, as it seemed, from affluence to penury? The words used in common talk are "crash" and "slump" or "boom" and "bust" or simply "crisis" and "depression." How can such words begin to suggest shabby gentle men and women selling apples on the streets? or the shantytown that sprang up below Riverside Drive? or the millions of idle across a continent? New generations cannot begin to feel the strange nightmare shocks as we turned into the 1930 decade, fifty years ago. A thick curtain seemed to fall between the moment of the Wall Street panic in 1929 and the beginning of the second war in 1939. Looking backward, Edmund Wilson wrote that it was difficult for those born late "to believe that it really occurred, that between 1929 and 1933 the whole structure of American society seemed to be going to pieces." Seeking for a word in 1932, he spoke of "the American jitters" and published a volume with that title. There was indeed a state of the jitters. But later the word seemed a euphemism for disaster, and in the full light of history Wilson renamed his book, when it was revised and reprinted, *The American Earthquake*.

Now assembled for the first time, the 1930 journals of Edmund Wilson offer a vivid episodic picture; yet the totality of his kaleidoscopic reporting is highly documentary. A national mosaic takes shape: the desolation of factory shutdowns; the sharecroppers in the South; the insurgent movement of labor to the left; the word "solidarity" emerges—and one is conscious of poverty and suffering, threaded with trivial scenes, and popular songs—*No more money in the bank*—the catchy Depression hit keeps running through Wilson's mind. There was no money in the bank: and the banks at a given moment, like the huge industrial plants, closed their doors. And then, in the midst of the 'quake, personal life also had its endings. He divorced his actress wife; he bade farewell to poetry; his books did not sell; his play failed. But he was in love with Margaret Canby, a friend of some years. She was a lively laughing unliterary down-to-earth drinking companion, a woman of warmth and dignity. They married. Their domesticity would be erratic, tempestuous, passionate.

1

At the beginning of the decade Wilson completed *Axel's Castle,* his book on the literary moderns, showing how they descended from the French symbolists. He dealt with Yeats, Joyce, Proust, Valéry, Eliot, Gertrude Stein, anticipating the stature these writers now have. The book was praised, but, given the temper of the times, sold modestly (it would have a wide success in the later decades). Even as he read the proofs Wilson asked himself whether it wasn't obsolete. The "high aesthetic" in literature was yielding to the leftist insistence that novelists must concern themselves with the proletariat and poetry proclaim the clenched fist. Wilson understood the mood, even if he had other views. To his friends he jauntily remarked how invigorating it was "to find ourselves still carrying on while the bankers are taking a beating." He liked this quip sufficiently to put it into a comedy about the Depression written in the early 1930s which mocked the discomfiture of the "prosperity decade" beneficiaries. But it was clear soon enough that the whole nation was "taking a beating" along with the bankers, and this was not a subject for comedy.

Aware of the national urgencies, Wilson issued an appeal to "progressives" in the columns of *The New Republic*. He wrote: "Moneymaking and the kind of advantages which a moneymaking society provides for money to buy are not enough to satisfy humanity— neither is a system like ours in which everyone is out for himself and the devil take the hindmost, with no common purpose and little common culture to give life stability and sense." Old conceptions, he wrote, should be "dynamited" and new ones, "as shocking as necessary, substituted." If Edmund sounded ready for revolution, he felt also that Americans needed information. And so he traveled to Detroit, Chicago, the South, wherever there were shutdowns and unrest, to describe and explain and interpret. Of his writings at this time, Matthew Josephson, never an admirer of Wilson, asserted after his death that they were "the most objective description of America in 1932 that we have."

Wilson's assertion that old conceptions should be dynamited was reshaped very early into a manifesto, issued in 1932 by a group of writers that included Lewis Mumford, Waldo Frank, Dos Passos, and others. Its text, and the circumstances surrounding it, can be read in Elena Wilson's edition of her husband's literary and political letters. It is a quiet, sober, rather dry statement, and in a low key. The writers were determined not to be inflammatory. There wasn't a stick of dynamite in it. To read it after half a century is to be made suddenly aware how little the 1930 intellectuals knew what Hitler intended, and what Mussolini was doing: the nature of paternal, dictatorial, capitalistic fascism, or its "proletarian" form under Stalin, was still to be revealed. The manifesto seems now utopian and curiously ingenuous. Free enterprise had proved bankrupt. New social forms, a new social order, new human values were needed. A society stripped of the profit motive and of competition would evolve a changed social philosophy. This was not possible so long as there was "the exploitation of the many for the profit of the few." The manifesto's solution: a "temporary dictatorship of the class-conscious workers." Once nationalization was achieved, and the new society established (one presumed), there would be no further need for this dictatorship. And the manifesto called on writers, engineers, intellectuals, teachers to make common cause with the proletariat, Dos Passos promptly pointed out that the white-collar workers were left out and that certain Communist formulas were being followed in spite of their efforts to keep clear of them. Dreiser, who declared for Communism, issued his own statement.

Revolutions are not often created by manifestos, and the ferment among the intellectuals, their disregard of the "petty bourgeois"—as Dos Passos and Wilson recognized—and their use of a language unfamiliar to rank-and-file America did not carry the writers very far: nor could there be real agreement among them. Wilson's work as a reporter brought him much closer to the nation's realities and he described these with his masterly concreteness. Those who remember him from this time recall the changes that came with middle age. He had ceased to be the slender Ivy League young man of his Greenwich Village days. He had become rotund and ruddy-cheeked. He no longer dressed in a collegiate way, as Scott Fitzgerald described him. He wore business suits, gray or dark blue; he sported a variety of hats, from the floppy to the Stetson. In manner he could be brusque and impatient; in speech he was incisive and he could be rude if foolishly pressed; occasionally he reached for words and a sentence would end in a splutter. His volubility masked shyness, and withdrawal, and depression, which led to hard drinking. But he could be generous and attentive when approached with directness and clarity. His humane sympathies were wide, and no passage in these journals testifies more to this than the record of his trip to the labor "barricades" in the Kentucky coal fields. Here he saw for himself the ruthlessness and cruelty of company officials, businessmen, and professionals, and their hatred of the locked-out and starving miners. This step in the education of his "social consciousness" was completed by his being ridden out of town by a bunch of pistol-swinging deputies.

ll

Edmund Wilson's politics during the 1930s have confused many of his readers and critics. The Marxist penitents, remembering his meetings with Communist leaders, and the utopian manifesto, have called him a "Red." Others have used the word "leftist." Still others have suggested he was either a dupe or politically naïve.

The breast-beaters and name-callers, involved in a constant dance of apology and rear-vision, overlook the simple fact that Wilson was an old-fashioned American individualist. He felt he could vote for "the party of his choice" in any election without carrying a permanent stigma. A passage in these journals written in Provincetown during the summer of 1932 tells us all we need to know. At the height of the Depression, Wilson felt that the helpless and inert Hoover Administration had shown its impotence in calling out the army to drive the bonus marchers from the streets of Washington. Nor was he satisfied with Franklin Delano Roosevelt's platform as the election approached; the time had not yet come for FDR to show his political flexibility and his gift for improvisation. Wilson would always distrust him and accuse him of political duplicities. As for the Norman Thomas socialists, they were like the British Fabians, caught in a dream of some remote welfare state (the term had not yet been invented). Wilson, in later years— or at least up to the time of Adlai Stevenson—voted the Thomas ticket, more in protest than in support. In 1932 he wanted a dynamic platform, "action now," and for one who had seen at first hand the national misery, the Communists offered a program that made sense to him—they would cast out the Washington double-dealers and put the proletariat in the saddle.

Wilson took steps to inform himself. He talked with William Z. Foster, the Communist Party leader. He invited him to his home and invited friends to meet him and ask questions. And he decided, as his journal tells us, to vote the Communist ticket even though he disliked the rank-and-file party comrades. He followed his social and humane beliefs without making permanent party commitments. He was a freewheeling writer descended from the makers of the American Revolution who was not afraid to be revolutionary. He was never a "joiner," and as he remarks, the Communists would never have considered him even if he had pleaded for membership. He had a distinct distaste for stereotyped party utterances and in Kentucky was critical of their maneuvers. What Wilson came to feel was that the nation and the press tended to second-guess history—a common American failing. Wilson's philosophy of history consisted of study and assessment of the past. He was not concerned with prophecy or the planning of national policy on paranoid assumptions of what other nations might do. He was and remained an independent. He would later denounce the tyranny in Russia as he had denounced the muddle in Washington. And he kept an open mind. He settled now to a close study of Marx—almost as if the Marxian text were written by Joyce or Dante. Later he admitted a bias. He had believed the Soviet Union would "put into practice its Leninist ideals" and "this was implied in my whole attitude toward what was going on at home."

We may wonder why Wilson read so intensively in Marx and Engels, Trotsky and Lenin. More than his usual curiosity was involved. He was aware that Marx was too often invoked without much knowledge of what he had written. The Communist Party itself had reduced Marx to a series of slogans and platitudes. Congress was unaware of history—few of its members possessed that kind of literacy. What had Marx really advocated? How were the Russians using him? How did social revolutions begin? Wilson began to see that what was happening in the twentieth century needed to be traced back to Vico's ideas in the seventeenth. But how explain history to a Congress which could only express moral indignation, and a simplifying American press which used only tags and labels? Most persons to whom Wilson talked possessed a derivative Marxism, exception made for philosophers and political scientists. In the fullness of time Wilson himself would sum up his readings. He recognized that Marx clearly understood how workers were exploited and that he had contributed immeasurably to the world's philosophy of labor. But, observed Wilson, "why should we suppose that man's brutal and selfish impulses will all evaporate with a socialist dictatorship?" The welfare state could harbor atrophies and ineptitudes as great as those of free enterprise.

The consequences of Wilson's explorations and self-questionings were far-reaching. He embarked on a book that would parallel *Axel's Castle*. That volume sought the origins of the "modern" movement in literature. Now he would begin to seek out the roots of modernism in politics and revolution. He would show how revolution, rising out of man's misery, gave birth to ideas that flowed and grew within a historic stream, a stream that often became a torrent. He would show how persecutions and massacres and common sufferings, the revolutions in America and France, the years of ferment in Russia, the radicalism in Germany, led to a singular moment in our time: one might call it the turning point in our century—that moment when Lenin arrived in the city that would bear his name: he came with all this history and theory in his head to take command of the floundering Russian Revolution. The title of Wilson's book suddenly occurred to him as he was walking in the street: *To the Finland Station*. Only later would he realize that he had been influenced by Virginia Woolf's title, *To the Lighthouse*. The Finland Station was the little shabby stucco building, "rubber-gray and tarnished pink" (Wilson would travel to Russia to look at it), in what was then St. Petersburg. Here Vladimir Ilyich Ulyanov, otherwise Lenin, arrived from his long exile following his wartime journey through Germany in a sealed train. Clutching a bouquet of roses handed him by his admirers, he had delivered one of his portentous slogans: "All power to the Soviets." His book would show, Wilson believed, how history can determine human actions. It would be, as he subtitled it, "a study in the writing and acting of history."

It was a splendid, a poetic conception and he carried out his plan in the hope that it would enlighten American political and social thought. To write this book, Wilson felt he should visit Russia and study the scenes of his drama and thoroughly document himself. He knew some German. He now began the study of Russian. A Guggenheim Fellowship provided him with necessary funds. His predecessors in this pilgrimage had been fairly numerous—among them his friend Dos Passos, Theodore Dreiser, Max Eastman, and earlier Lincoln Steffens, who had come back saying the much-quoted words that he had seen the future "and it works." They had gone largely as reporters curious about the new supposed utopia in-the-making. Wilson went as a historian and with few preconceptions; he had certain unvoiced hopes that Steffens had been right, that some new form of society was emerging. His ostensible goal was the Marx-Engels-Lenin Institute in Moscow. His journals, however, do not tell us of his researches; they testify instead to his many encounters and interrogations. He had done sufficient "homework" by this time to be able to interpret what he heard—and also what could not be heard: the enigmatic reticences, the deep silences. He sought out his fellow literary historian, Prince D. S. Mirsky, whose work he admired, and we have some notes of their meetings. Mirsky would be one of Stalin's early victims, and Wilson later drew a finely sketched portrait of him, as he amplified his notes. He goes to picnics, night clubs, the

Physkultur Parade, museums, monasteries: he is at the ballet, the theater, the opera, and has an easy familiarity from his readings in America with the plays, the players, the directors. His journey up the Volga, in its singular details, is like a Chekhov tale; and to climax his experiences he finds himself a captive student of socialized medicine in the U.S.S.R.—for he comes down with scarlatina and for some weeks is quarantined in an old, dignified, dirty building in Odessa, a building that went back to the time of Pushkin. There are bedbugs everywhere. The orderlies urinate in the solitary sink near his room. Nurses and patients are cheerful; the patients are mostly children. He has many amusing conversations, is treated with the greatest respect, and at night is permitted to use the operating room as a study. All his bills—including telegrams and cables—are paid by the state. This ends his private adventure in Red Russia. He would continue his Russian studies in all the years to come. The notes of his journeys, printed here in their original form for the first time, served him in two future books and in the *Finland Station*. As we read the later versions, we are made aware how much Wilson remembered beyond his original jottings, and how extraordinary was his visual recall.

In the year before his death, Wilson took a backward glance at the *Finland Station*. He was writing a preface for a new edition and he recalled that he had gone to Russia with "a too hopeful bias." "We did not foresee that the new Russia must contain a good deal of the old Russia . . . I had no premonition that the Soviet Union was to become one of the most hideous tyrannies that the world had ever known, and Stalin the most cruel and unscrupulous of the merciless Russian tsars." However, he believed that his book remained "a basically reliable account of what the revolutionists thought they were doing in the interests of 'a better world.' " He also accepted criticism that he had given too amiable a picture of Lenin. Later documents and much more evidence had convinced him that behind Lenin's worshipped façade one could find all the corruptions of power.

III

Edmund Wilson's wife, Margaret Canby, died two years after their marriage, in an accident while she was in California. She slipped on some steep Spanish-style steps at Santa Barbara and fractured her skull. Wilson boarded a propeller plane for the long trip to the coast; he was overwhelmed and distraught. He nursed anxious thoughts that she might have committed suicide, for he lacked details. His journal record of his stay in California, his visit to the funeral parlor, his talks with relatives, are confined to these pages—a kind of emptying of his grief, his memories, his guilt. The passage is perhaps the most "felt" and intimate of all his writings about himself. If there had been some strain in the marriage, there had also been the love he now expressed. The monologue provided catharsis; but it did not bring total relief. For years Wilson continued to dream about Margaret: she is alive again, they are coming together, he experiences a kind of sublime joy—and always something happens to keep them apart and he races through rooms and corridors but cannot find her. The dreams suggest profound and unresolved feelings, continuing grief and self-blame; he had a strange sense that in dying she had abandoned him; and then the opposite, he felt guilty, as if he had abandoned her. The monologue reminds one of passages in Proust, or the soliloquy of Molly Bloom in *Ulysses*.

Some readers may be startled by this intimate candid record of a marriage. One gains the impression that Wilson wrote the entire passage at a single sitting for himself, without thought of publication. Thirty years later he had it typed up for inclusion here. The candor may seem at times gratuitous; it is a piece of private history; but it is also a search for the truth of personal history. The monologue testifies to Wilson's core difficulty—there were things he could not allow himself to feel. In my introduction to *The Twenties* I discussed his dissociation of emotion in certain human situations. He defended himself against emotional hurt by a kind of curmudgeonly bluntness which sometimes alienated friends. His modes of verbal aggression were in counterpoint with his verbal amiability. One is prompted to say that this problem, which deprived him of certain empathies, made it difficult for him in criticism to deal with writers of our time like Kafka, who explored man's troubled dream-existence. It ran counter to Wilson's concreteness, derived from his ability to look at reality without having to feel it. In the *Finland Station* he tells us that Karl Marx's "blinded and paralyzed side" was his "negation of personal relations, of the responsibility of man to man," and there was something of this in Wilson. For he speaks in these journals, in a moment of insight, of "the dead tissue in my soul—it could never grow back." Perhaps he is thinking of the blocked sensibilities of his childhood. There had been, as we know, a deaf mother and a depressed and often apathetic father. The little boy Edmund had considerable difficulty communicating with those closest to him. In the process there was a short-circuiting of the common articulations and joys of childhood. The distancings were carried into adult life. Certain "social reflexes" were thwarted. We are given a glimpse of his insight into himself during a visit to an old friend:

I was awfully glad to see him, and it was very pleasant at first to talk to him again, with his intellectual range and his cultivation: his history, psychology, literature; but my visit got to be more and more eerie. He wanted to be amiable and hospitable; but he had to make a conscious effort—his solitary and self-centered life had practically deprived him of the social reflexes.

Wilson adds: "I have been that way myself, possibly always to some extent."

There were these sealed corridors in his personal relations, "and it was strange to see it from the outside," Wilson said. He added that it "at once depressed me and made me feel superior." What he could do was to displace emotion from the human scene into his writing. At his desk, the world fell into place. He was free to grasp, explain, sympathize, understand Proust's sensitive childhood, experience Dickens's sufferings and Turgenev's struggles with his mother. Wilson's journals reflect a compulsive and meticulous man reaching out with words to himself and his fellow humans, but allowing masses of fact and detail, and intellectual musings, to defend him against full-face encounter. Perhaps in this way we can understand the use of the bold inquiring front, the value language had for him: there was nothing arbitrary about dictionaries; or about the past. The past was safe—and always confrontable.

Why do authors keep journals? They can be a way of shoring up life and siphoning off a surplus of creative energy. They become, on occasion, a device for dealing with parts of experience not readily useful; in effect, they can be a memory bank. We can see how, for André Gide or Thoreau, or the copious Anaïs Nin—to take three disparate journal-keepers—the personal records became full-length mirrors of the self. In the case of Nin, they seem almost to have become a way of writing her life without having to live it. These are the journals of a profound narcissism. But there are other kinds. Kafka's, as he told us, were a form of prayer. Henry James's were used to solve artistic problems and allay anxiety about his immediate work. Virginia Woolf's enabled her to maintain balance and use her mental iridescence to haul herself up, as it were, from chronic melancholy.

Wilson was not creating on the scale of such writers, and his journals, we may judge, served largely the function of memory and self-discipline. They were the notebooks of a chronicler, a way of tidying the mind for his craft of criticism: no meditations, no prayers, no invocation to the muse, no polished mirrors. He tries rather to be a camera, for this is what he finds most comfortable. A camera, however, doesn't think: and Wilson is using his intellectual powers. His sensitivity resides in his visuality. He has an ear for what (and how) people say things. In this way he also tries to be a tape recorder. The journals are his mental account books and a way of handling unachieved relationships. Even his record of his own copulations has this kind of objectivity—as if he were a naturalist at the zoo of himself, writing a chapter of natural history. Thomas Mann, in his high intellectual way, justified such intimate revelations (when his wife complained) by saying "the most intimate is at the same time the most universal." Erich Heller's response to this seems to me penetrating. Culture is attained, he reminds us, "by a tactful disregard of much that is 'natural.'" When we universalize intimacy, it ceases to be intimate. When we impersonalize the personal, we risk stripping it of its humanity. Wilson wrote down experience often in order to depersonalize it. Once it was written down, he could detach himself from feeling. Yet he couldn't part with it. When I said to him one day (we were talking of his journals) that he was after all quite free to revise and change what he had written and even to trim passages, he rebelled. They had acquired total objectivity; they seemed almost not to belong to him. "I don't want to cut any corners," was the way he answered me. "But they're your own corners, Edmund, you can do what you like with them." My rejoinder did not please him. The text had become a document. He wasn't going to tamper with it. It belonged, unchangeably, to literary history.

LEON EDEL

CHRONOLOGY

The Thirties

1930   Marries Margaret Canby in Washington. Summers in Provincetown.

1931   Visits Detroit and writes on Henry Ford; inspects mine strikes in Kentucky and West Virginia; travels to Southwest with wife and visits California. Publication of *Axel's Castle*.

1932   Brings out *The American Jitters*; visits Pineville, Kentucky, with Miners' Relief Committee and is run out of town. Works on play about the Depression, *Beppo and Beth*. Death of Margaret Canby in accident. To California for her funeral.

1933   Renting house at 314 East 53rd Street. Writes for *New Republic*; visits Chicago. Attends F.D.R. Inaugural. Assorted papers on the new Administration and dawn of New Deal.

1934   Preliminary work on *To the Finland Station*. Decides further research needed and travel in U.S.S.R.

1935   Given Guggenheim Fellowship for trip to Soviet Union. Sails in May, visits Leningrad and Moscow, travels to Volga; after illness in Odessa returns to U.S.

1936   Summer in Provincetown, then settles in house at Stamford, Connecticut. Russian impressions and other papers in *Travels in Two Democracies*.

1937   Serializes portions of *Finland Station*; publishes three plays under title *This Room and This Gin and These Sandwiches*.

1938   Marriage to Mary McCarthy. Continues resi-
       dence in Connecticut. Publishes literary essays
       in *The Triple Thinkers*. Birth of son, Reuel
       Kimball Wilson, on Christmas Day.

1939   First attempt at teaching during University of
       Chicago summer session. Finishes *Finland Station*
       at Truro Center near Provincetown and writes
       essay on Dickens. Plans *The Wound and the Bow*.

1940   *To the Finland Station* published.

1930–1935

NEW YORK AND
WASHINGTON, 1930

[EW's journals of the 1930s begin with his staying,
with Margaret Canby, in the New York apartment of
Lloyd Morris, a man of considerable charm and sophistication who was a reviewer for the *Tribune* and author
of a series of studies of American social institutions and
New York history. Margaret Canby was a Californian
and both she and Edmund had been divorced. Her
former husband had custody during certain months of
their son Jimmy and the boy went to school in California. EW had his responsibilities to his daughter by
Mary Blair, Rosalind, who by now was seven and lived
with EW's mother in the family house at Red Bank,
New Jersey.

EW's work for *The New Republic* and Margaret's
California commitments meant that at the outset of
their marriage they had to face certain periods of separation, EW remaining in the East while she visited on the
West Coast.]

April 4, 1930. When I went out toward Fifth Avenue
on 12th Street, from Lloyd Morris's balconied apartment,

the soft mirage of red, blue, and yellow flowers in a pushcart on its way toward Fifth Avenue, which was the first thing I saw—blurred in the bright April morning light—was like some flowering of the light which rose and walled the sky from the east and poured down into the streets with its firm radiance. I followed the roundish soft insubstantial shapes of the pushcart as they passed across Fifth Avenue toward the east. The gray of New York was soft and radiant, and its firmness was satisfactory, not oppressive—how attractively and solidly Washington Arch seemed to be based! —Greenwich Village, as I walked across to Seventh Avenue and down to the Liberty Street ferry, was flooded with the white sun, rich, for all its clarity, with whiteness—as a quarter, a part of town, the particular shell of shops and habitations where one lived, one hid oneself, in New York; it had ceased to exist—it had been flooded by the tide of light as a little cove is flooded by the tide, till the gullies between the gray buildings, which, during the winter, looked narrow and grim, seemed, with their pigeons fluttering on the roofs and their odd garments flying on clotheslines, as open to the freedom of wind and light as if they had been the virgin hills of the island—the dreadful modern city was gone—on my way downtown, even the rectangular gray walls, with more window than wall, of the loft buildings, had almost, for all their grayness and barrenness, the dignity and freshness of the Apennines, and the streets reminded me of that day in Florence when I heard the sound of the band in the diamond light and saw the pigeons riding the surf of sound. —The wall of March light which shifts in day from east to west.

E. E. Cummings's stories of N. Always used to be going to sleep, always contemplating suicide—"What did you dream about?" "There were many many people, and they were very very angry!"; "I will pay this waiter! I will pay him with my body!—Waiter!"—then took off his hat and coat and ran till he reached the river—didn't commit suicide, however, because the water looked too cold. —On another occasion, "Let's go out and hang me!"

Margaret, May 1930. Cousin Watty [Toby Waterman] said (when Margaret said that she was a very heavy sleeper) that it was a family characteristic—he had always been able to sleep twelve hours himself.

—Hurray for our side!—*post* a letter—*ice chest.*

—The night we went out with Daisy Waterman [Margaret Canby's mother], Margaret looked so beautiful during dinner—with the drinking, conversation, and music—and no doubt with our increasing harmony together—her face lost the impassivity it often wore, and its angular outlines disappeared—her green eyes, always beautiful in a vitreous or lapidary way, became alive and flashed with a vivid green light of animation, enjoyment, and intelligence—and her high and nobly modeled brow and temples were no longer merely Anglo-Saxon, but showed the modeling of a high civilization—and all the lower part of her face had a roundness and softness which responded, which vibrated, as I had never seen it do, to her feelings and thoughts—she has, as I had never seen her have before, the attraction of that sensitiveness which had been immured so long and so impregnably behind her cool, imperturbable, and matter-of-fact Scotch-Canadian shell.

—Her blue-gray dress, flowered in the same shade, that she bought to be married in and which made her eyes look a crystalline gray-blue—like certain kinds of palely clouded opals?—or what?

—delish—cute as a bug's ear—pretty as green paint— (Esther Hartshorne's cliché: funeral baked meats)

—Margaret standing up with her clothes off in the sitting room at 12th Street—her round soft broad bosom (white skin)—the only word [bosom]: the old sort of feminine beauty—and her fair open-eyed guileless-eyed face—as if it were the old feminine look of combined trust and wonder at the male—what next? what was I up to?—her mother's simplicity: she [Mrs. Waterman] couldn't follow movies when they got complicated or developments came too fast—a slight candid untroubled apprehension or mildly bewildered expectancy of light upon what my movements or what my expression meant. —Short little figure, when I'd embrace her without her shoes, standing up nude, fat hips and big soft breasts and big torso and tiny little feet she was standing on and little strong paws of hands (with hard grip)—when lying on bed, little arms and legs, turtle paws, sticking out on each corner.

—Once, when I spoke of her look of constant alert attention, she said that she had just been thinking.

[EW and Margaret Canby went to Washington to be married and stayed with EW's old friend, John Amen (1898–1960), who was then special assistant to the U.S. Attorney General. Amen had won great success by his prosecution of industrial racketeers. In his later days he assumed a professorial tone and wore a perpetual carnation in his buttonhole. Marion, his wife, was a daughter of President Cleveland. An earlier description of Amen is given by EW in *The Twenties*, p. 216.]

Washington, May 8, 1930. [The day of the marriage.] Compartment, drunk on hot night—made love—lay awake and looked out window—liked darkness, lights blistering it (*blistering* with onomatopoetic effect) brightly.

[John] Amen's nice little brick house in Hillyer

Margaret Canby Wilson

Place—little balcony off bedroom in front over the Washington green trees—little sun parlor in back, with the Washington greenery behind the light curtains, blown a little by the air from the open windows. It was hot when we arrived, but became cloudy and cooler and rained a little.

The Strange Death of President Harding. Jess Smith bumped off in the Wardman Park Hotel—the hideous figure of Harry M. Daugherty, the super-racketeer, still haunting the city. [EW must have been reading G. B. Means's book on Harding (1930), an account of the corruption during that President's Administration. It was an "as told to" book, and the narrator's facts were questioned because he admitted complicity.]

The ride through Alexandria to the little shooting box on the Potomac—getting up the nigger caretaker. —Margaret with her head on my lap. The bright moon—the low slightly unkempt woodlands of Virginia—I asked Margaret whether they didn't give her a thrill when she said that the trees were so different—they didn't have eucalyptus and things she said yes, they did, but they were different. —The whippoorwills—their different cry at early morning.

Morning—the green soft lawn above the level Potomac with its level tides. —The niggers who were playing something or other—John had thought it was some kind of insects, then that they were playing on combs—but then he kept on hearing it, and it "seemed to be something a little better than that."

John's sun bath—"I wonder if I spit in that water, if it'll make it dirtier." —There was some reason you couldn't swim in the Potomac. Our attempts to do so—I in pansy pants, John in dressing gown, Margaret with the curse, Marion slender from having trained her figure down and very pretty in red bathing suit (blue pajamas in morning)—we saw why you couldn't swim in the Potomac: no particular reason, but a multitude of annoyances and frustrations—if you started to wade in, you could apparently walk across the river—in the stream which led back—as Marion said, you felt as if you were in some foreign land, way down in Old Virginny—into a sort of semi-swampy series of lagoons, it was a little bit deep sometimes in the middle, but there was mud like quicksands, in which you sank. We pushed the rowboat part of the way back.

Marvelous lunch of shad and shad roe (eggs fresh, pale, and intact) with stewed tomatoes—the shad caught fresh in the Potomac.

The nets on the beach to dry—the houseboat shoved up on the shore, in which niggers seemed to live and sleep. The pleasant slightly down-at-heels but comfortable and rather satisfactory well-to-do look of Virginia. (Typically unmistakably Southern look of houses, already, around Alexandria.) —A sort of pool reminded me that I must buy turtles for Rosalind.

Some unheard-of illustrated social paper in the shooting club and a bound book of circus advertisements—a phonograph with records made mostly on one side—enormous gun over fireplace, used to blow up great quantities of ducks till stopped by law—John's attitude about this: despite respect for the club, ridicule and disdain for the idea of blowing up the ducks. —The (two female and one male) wild ducks in the rather rickety cage down in the water.

Our untimely embarrassing departure. [We had a room next to the Amens, with a door or a partition so thin that every sound could be heard. This was embarrassing to everybody, so we left the next day.]

John's present phase—administering justice: "You don't know what a great thing it is to administer justice!—to rich and poor!"—I said that he was soon going to drop that, however, to go back to his firm. —More bumptious than ever—hadn't been able to argue a single one of his cases—Hoover friendly to movie people—California judges on all sorts of pretexts got out of hearing them. —He was rather stout and ruddy-faced from riding in the open roadster. —I said I understood he was being mentioned as the next President—he said, "They're holding me back, though, because I'm so young." —I asked him whether he'd met any interesting people in Washington: Lots of interesting people but social life very unsatisfactory—people seemed fine at first but then everybody in Washington was there for a purpose and it always turned out that they were preoccupied either with interests they wanted to advance or with responsibilities they felt they had to live up to.

Margaret. Face and head clear as a crystal—when kissed, would look at you interested and alert, but not in the least voluptuously overcome; or she'll look, when I come up to her and caress her face, open-eyed, a little amazed, as if she didn't know just what I was up to.

[We must have stopped over to visit Cousin Watty on our way back to New York.]

Chestnut Hill. Gray stuccoish wall of piazza at right angles with the yellow floor that was level with the lawn, and wrought-iron cornice and trellises (or whatever they'd be called)—general atmosphere of whiskey drinking—butler, sinister, about to be fired (chauffeur more amiable)—oldish respectable-looking bottles—take up whiskey to room—kept Toby policed (Toby was Margaret's "Cousin Watty"). Margaret had described him as "a little man with pale blue eyes—I don't know but I think he's been used by other people all his life." —Dinner jacket, ribbonless pumps on little feeble short legs in piazza chair—what it meant to have French manners—bow low from the waist. —My vision at dinner of Cou-

sin Watty as a drowned body drifting to the bottom
while three women worried him and took bites out of
his face, which was rose-red with drinking and broken
out. —He was shunted off to bed immediately after dinner—no chance to talk to me. —Edith nudging me at
dinner, had heard I was human—her house and her big
white police dog and Pekinese, with which I thought
she probably slept. Large bright phony family portraits
combined with bright and ugly (red figuring prominently) chintz-covered couches and chairs. Her hard
Pennsylvania accent: r's. —The dated nineteeth-century
views from our bedroom windows—charming, perfect,
clear steel-engraved lines and, as it were, cultivated
masses—green—tempered and slightly dulled—grays, the
next day, of coming rain—big mahogany four-poster.

—The house from outside: shiny yellow, new-painted
(it was just being done over inside, too), square cupola
with fancy spikes like the tops of chessmen, as of conventionalized wooden flowers and torches. —The beautifully kept and waxed parquet hallway—the chaste marble
statue of Sabina, with her robe held around her with
one dignified hand—a marble bust of Cousin Watty—at
the opposite end of the hall, a large doorway with round
panes of glass, painted, apparently with flowers, which
looked a little faded now, in spite of the marvelous repair
in which everything was kept—the upholstered grand old-
fashioned rather forbidding-looking furniture—the Sully
portrait—the Japanese vase (in the hall)—the tall carved
sideboard and chairs in the dining room—the Washington portrait which was not a Stuart, the not very good
landscapes—the gilt-framed mirrors.

—Cousin Watty as a beau of the nineties—Crowninshield*—dropped his g's—"Button it up!" to me, of the

* See *The Twenties*, pp. 32–44.

raincoat—"Well, let me see you do it!"—Margaret's solid sinuous woman's young body, as she sat on the arm of his chair on the porch, contrasting with his pulpy thin-skinned decaying flimsiness—she kissed him, put her arm around him. —His pleasantries about trusting women and servants drinking up liquor. Men could do things that were winked at, but if women did them, the other women would talk about them. Margaret said that modern women got away with quite a good deal just the same, and he seemed abashed at this, made her repeat it, as if he hadn't grasped her idea, then dropped his eyes to his plate and began to eat, murmuring without assent, "Yes" . . . He wasn't married but he didn't want Mr. Wilson to think that he'd never kissed a girl—didn't like Margaret's bobbed hair: "I've got a wig upstairs"—couldn't attend to business as he used to. —His blood-curdling shrieks when he had nightmares at night—wouldn't have a phonograph or a radio, although they wanted him to—rheumatism in the family.

[EW went with considerable regularity to his mother's home at Red Bank, N.J., to spend time with his daughter Rosalind. It was a comfortable home and his mother continued to live the life of the American "gentry" to which she was accustomed. EW would be met by the car and chauffeur. He always enjoyed his mother's well-tended and large garden. The affluent home of his childhood afforded him a retreat from the crowded life he led during the Depression years. He was also, as always, interested in the growing up of his daughter, her schooling and education.]

Red Bank, May 23–4, '30. Rode out after supper on bicycle in direction of Seven Bridges—from red motor road, smelling of dust and gasoline. I looked out at the pale blue May waters of the salty shallow inlets from the sea, calm and happy in their summer trance and blurred with the moist air of the coastlands, beyond which some white house with outbuildings shone through the high rank summer foliage, at the same time that its outlines were concealed by them—half-stagnant happy summer Jersey—such names as Manasquan, with its swampy sound of low vegetation, Mantoloking, with its sound of dryer and brighter sands, with waters strung back from the sea in a series of aimless and ineffective (disorganized) but rather pleasure-giving little lakes and ponds—the meadows (still the Seven Bridges Road) also made richer by the damp blurring of evening—past Shrewsbury, a lovely strip of field between two fences of trees, unused for anything, perhaps grown for hay, the long green grass like a panel of fur.

—In the hot afternoon, with a pail and a glass jar, we [Rosalind and I] went to fish in the Shrewsbury River— the rather rank and dirty water, full of mosquitoes' larvae, doubtless, I thought—there was a light scum that looked like it on the water—the soft dirty seaweed, its green clotted with dirt, near the shore, blurred forests of little shrimps, transparent in the gray water, save for their eyes and the structure of their faces—I would wait till they settled on the whiteness of my feet, where they would seem faintly to nibble, then I'd bring the glass jar, blue in the water, down on them—caught four, they were transparent and gray, had legs like little crooked threads of glass and brownish protruding eyes. —There were sallygrowlers in the forests—they were lethargic, would make a short waddling dash along the bottom, then simply rest in the mud—didn't move till I got right up to them and made a plunge after them. —Horseshoe crabs, a smaller one attached to the tail of a larger one, making a deliberate, slow, and rather repulsive progress toward the shore—I pinned the little one down with the pail and turned them over with a piece of rock—they returned, the little one still attached to the bigger one, a little more hastily toward the deep again. [I did not know that they were mating—they go on shore for this purpose in May.] —The speedboats—ripples from farther out would muddy the subaqueous forests and splash against the red gravel of the shore—the summer afternoons in the house hummed with the dim sound of speedboats. —The next day after the day described above was clouded and always about to rain—it was cooler, almost cold, and rather pleasant—all the whitish petals were shaken off the locusts and fell in the grass all around the house.

Margaret's way of touching somebody with her foot or thigh as if she wanted to snuggle against them.

Peninsula House, Sea Bright, N.J. [where Margaret and I stayed]. June 17, 1930—Arrived early in season before there was anybody to speak of in hotel—a drink in the corner room and went in the water, in a rough surf, between the horrid formidable breakwaters, while it was getting foggier every minute—when I came out after a sprawling crawl, standing up out of the surf, I saw Margaret's dark clear trim-though-full silhouetted shape against the misty background in which the bright sun was setting dimly in mist—she looked lovely—I was amazed by her figure and by the mist and the light. —The waitress at dinner was very tanned and broad, quite pretty like a robuster Hogarth's shrimp girl—the manager came up and welcomed us at dinner—a big broad man—the immense expanses of gray gravel, with an oval bed of cockroach-brown calla lilies, and in a corner of the building a bed of small privet balls. —We

walked round the piazzas after dinner—looked in at a
window and saw a jolly party of hotel women guests
playing cards in an otherwise deserted room. —Pulled
down shades in bedroom to make love—afterwards, I lay
and looked at little eyelet of gray light, bright below top
part of flowered chintz curtains—later it was duller—
the light had blurred—the mist was getting thicker—when
I raised the shade and looked out the window, I saw,
across the railroad track, in the fog, the few yellow and
blue and red lights of the movie house and the soda
fountain. —The sound of the surf was almost as incessant
and steady as a downpour of summer rain, but it
swelled and had its emphasis and insistence. —Margaret
said, "Doesn't it ever stop?" —She thought the fog, which
I thought was characteristic of Jersey, wasn't any different from Sandyland—she liked foggy evenings by the sea
when you could sit around an open fire, as you could at
Sandyland.

[Robert] Benchley's sailing for Europe and sending
to each of three girls the message, "Thank you for living"—they all came and told Dorothy Parker about it.

Play? [This evidently refers to the imaginary dialogue
below. Herbert Croly (1869–1930), a founder and editor
of *The New Republic,* had just died. See *The Twenties,*
pp. 495–6.]

Mrs. Croly said that when H.C. was dead and she
had taken him home from the hospital, she had a feeling
of some new birth—as if something had been being
born—not an intimation of immortality, but the idea that,
after suffering and with the body partly incapacitated,
one might see further—get a new light and wisdom,
which one could never live to express. She said that his
faculties, after his first stroke, had been impaired—he

could talk for a while as he had always done, but not for long—nonetheless, in such a condition, one might see things quite differently and in some ways better—with so many natural outlets cut off, with so many faculties arrested, one might attain the supreme illumination which the full possession of one's animal nature had always hitherto hindered—and this tendency toward this other part of human beings, the perception on the part of others of the moments of illumination of the dying, has probably contributed to the notion of immortality.

—You mean that you believe in immortality, then?

—No; but in life even faced by death. It doesn't despair or weaken—why should it? —Perhaps it knows that death doesn't exist—not because there is another world where we silly individuals, we silly Republicans and Democrats, men and women, etc., go on existing to eternity—but because what the dying man says, what the dying man puts into our mind, is remembered by the living—and the living are always alive. They are life, the living—think how many individuals are dead! All the individuals since the Middle Ages—all the individuals since the fall of Rome—all the individuals since the Peloponnesian Wars—all the individuals since the Babylonian Captivity—all the individuals since the Stone Age—many of them no doubt very assertive—all the individuals since the first man made an instrument of the first flint. Think how many individuals are dead!—as the cells in the body die so that the body may grow to maturity—as the molecules in the cell are disrupted so that the cell may keep its equilibrium—as the atoms in the molecule shift their weights that the molecule may adjust itself—as the ions in the atom respond to the changes of life. —All these individuals have died or been changed to something else. Who knows that the maximum energy of the electron wasn't just when it was changing its orbit?—that the

maximum vitality of the cell wasn't just under the pressure that would kill it?—or that the pressure wasn't
broken by the final vitality of the cell—or that the effort
of the dying man didn't divert the raw gushing of life?

[The dialogue above is not my conversation with Mrs.
Croly, but a philosophical fragment inspired by what
she had told me.]

The ocean was quiet now and quite different: gentler
splashings in and longer withdrawings—the rhythm was
more and more like the breathing of a sleeping person.

Margaret.
I busted my boiler to come East for you.
—in the doghouse
—an odd spot
—delish
Swings her arms and shoulders when she walks.
Said her mother used to say, "Over the left eye"—give
     you (something or other) all over the left eye—equiva-
     lent to a wink.
—full of body squeaks this morning [ads for something
     connected with cars used to talk about removing "body
     squeaks"]
—Hooray for our side!

Atlantic. And even when the night and the water were
warm and balmy—walking out before going to bed—
the shore was shallow even when the waves seemed violent and high—even though the night was relaxed—the
storms spent and a warm morning in the darkness—the
sound of the surf was still strenuous and vehement, even
in its comparatively retarded crumbling, sweeping the
beach back and forth slowly but with some steady intention.

June 29, 1930 [Margaret and I at Red Bank, just after we were married]. The night we went out (from Sea Bright) with a little put-put outboard motor, but the engine started going against the current as soon as we turned around—lost in dark, got off and wandered around long dense grass of island (where we had seen big birds— herons and things—on way out?)—rowed, with broken oar, into Monmouth Beach—smell of high thick grass— clover—as we waded up a bank and across the field, while dogs in the houses barked, in the dark—I was thirsty for cold drinks in the lunchroom: lemon soda, sarsaparilla.

—The hedges loaded down with honeysuckle in New Jersey and its smell in the moisture-heavy air.

—The golden light of sunset, in that saturated air, seemed itself a medium of rich density—as if there were a diffused fog of gold.

—Earlier in the spring, I had seen in New York, com- ing toward the Park through the uptown streets of the East Side, a great wedge of white light between the white straight houses (Frick's and who else's), shading below into gold.

—at Red Bank, at night, the sound of motorboats on the river like June bugs buzzing at the screen.

Those blocks of New York neutral yellow, if even that, traveling above the neutral water of the river, neither gray nor blue, slowly on the summer afternoon, when most people must have left town—contrasting, through the window of the boat, a plain enough but flesh-bodied girl, fixes her hair by the reflection in the window, with her tanned and reddish-glowing arms contrasting with those neutral walls, plain but still flesh and blood, black curly Jewish-looking hair—

PROVINCETOWN

[EW had spent a summer in Provincetown during 1927, living first in Commercial Street and later in Eugene O'Neill's Peaked Hill house on a bluff at the edge of the sea. During 1930, the first summer of his new marriage, he was able to obtain this commodious house again. It was an old converted Coast Guard station. Here Wilson assembled his newly constituted family—Margaret and her twelve-year-old son Jimmy, his daughter Rosalind, and her nanny Stella. Jimmy Canby and Rosalind still recall the summer of sun and sea filled with beach life, fishing, and the constant comings and goings of EW's friends and the Provincetown summer colony. The house with its attractive white and blue interior had been originally decorated by Mabel Dodge, the grand lady of Greenwich Village and later of Taos, where her name was linked with D. H. Lawrence. Peaked Hill Bars was a bleak and dangerous stretch of coast; in the old days there had been many shipwrecks along these treacherous sandbars where the wind moaned constantly and the sea, when turbulent, reached in and rearranged the dunes. At certain seasons, schools of whales and porpoises would splash past in the middle distance. The nautical O'Neill had liked the house because he felt as if he were living on a ship. With a big room that used to house the Coast Guard lifeboat opening on the dunes, its large master bedroom and dining room, and a long living room, it proved ideal for the summer during which EW revised *Axel's Castle* but had his ear cocked to the mounting crisis of the Depression. The literary and artistic summer colony was quite as volatile as the sea. John Dos Passos and his wife Katy were at nearby Truro and EW saw much of his old friend. There were the writers and activists who had founded the Provincetown Players a decade and a half earlier, including George Cram Cook and Susan Glaspell; Harry Kemp, the bohemian friend of O'Neill; Niles Spencer, an artist of the "precisionist school," much concerned about industrial architecture; William and Lucy ("Brownie") L'Engle, watercolorists; and Mary Heaton Vorse, the veteran libertarian and trades-union writer. There came also Frank Shay, the local bookseller, who had published the early O'Neill, Edna Millay, and Susan Glaspell, and Hazel Hawthorne Ufford, whom he had met in 1927. She was now doing book reviews for *The New Republic*.]

Provincetown, early July 1930. [Niles] Spencer's upstairs piazza—as if you were sitting drinking cocktails among the treetops—shenanigans on the Harbor for the Fourth of July—yachts, little green oil boat—sailboats against the blue as pretty and light as butterflies—we saw in a little gap left by the trees and the houses—they are built up the slope of the hill, as if in some Italian hill town—a boy going down a long flight of green steps, two green melons in the window of the house next door—story of the old couple who had bought the car, practiced driving it, from directions, in the stable, and then sent it back—the clear air, the white clear light among the fine upper leaves of the willows—after dinner, it was amber and red—then the green of the evening sky, as clear as the white had been—green olives in the cocktail glasses— we threw the pits over the rail.

—Margaret said afterwards that she'd rather be like the Spencers and look out at the world through a little space than live in Truro like the Dos Passoses.* (Their little farm was sunk in a hollow of that gray and dry and abandoned country—the crooked branches and gray stems of the dead birches and the picket fence around it made it look somehow like something in a queer picture by a modern primitive who gave awkward, ugly, or simple things an ominous or simply an intense value.) —The deep blue almost indigo and opaque blue goblets for water—plates with pretty gray old-fashioned pictures— reading of the letter of the old ladies at the library who lived in the house with the figurehead over the door. [The figurehead had been found by their father floating in the Indian Ocean, and the legs had been sawed off to avoid impropriety.] —Niles Spencer's single lithograph of city buildings, a pretty pattern on white of little squares and angles. —Betty's interest in psychoanalysis and in Freud especially—"been lyin' in the sand bare-naked!"— way of coming into the room and landing, in a funny clownish way, on the couch or on the floor—Niles's easy way of talking, easy humor—she had made the cocktails too strong, and he had been "attacking that piece of meat" at dinner, "as if it had been a wild animal."

Idea for Play or Story: Somebody says something about "the first bolt out of the blue"—"You mean, the first crack out of the box." — "No, I don't!" —Drunken argument. —"The first peep of dawn."

* See also *The Twenties*, pp. 205–7, 322–4.

Apartment-house play: bootlegger in one apartment—man and wife sitting around like Clays (the Provincetown bootleggers)—newspapers, drinks, furnished-house furniture—all the other people going up there from time to time.

—The jewelry of the waves at night with little green phosphorus drops—they coruscated like diamonds as they were breaking, sparkling white in the crest of white foam—the sand fleas would eat them and jump around luminous.

Margaret lying on the beach, with her bathing suit off for a sunbath—her back toasted brown around the shoulders and neck and below absolutely white, soft with a coat of down and nicely creased by the spine. —Seen to very good advantage always on the beach—cunning brown legs, thick at the thighs and with little feet. —Would pick her appearance up after swimming with a vivid application of lipstick, which would have been incongruous with her camping clothes and her outdoor lack of make-up, if it had not been becoming. —Enjoyed love-making on chaise longue in the sitting room—naked—she looked in the moonlight, which gave her the pale bluish whiteness of a statue, like a little short plumpish Venus—a sort of Leda—and the Swan effect astride the chair.

Jimmy. Followed Margaret about like a little puppy—"Whoopee!"—"It's O.K." —"Don't pick too many blueberries!" (to little girls when he was riding Bessie [a pony we rented for him] across the dunes)—"Boy! those ———s are good!" —Western cowboy stuff, which has reached him no doubt partly through the movies. —Invented song: "Oh, those half-naked girls, with their big black curls." —"Sat on a rock and tickled his cock" (humorous verse).
Jimmy's clear, though pale, intent blue gaze—like his mother's little-girl-like one.

—Walking up Commercial St. in front of us like a little bear cub: white gob's hat stuck on his head, tawny jersey, blue overall pants, and white sneakers—tilted forward, with his hands in his pockets, broad shoulders shrugged up, head dropped forward—his gait of a miniature burly sailor.

Provincetown, early August 1930. Walking down the beach on a night sultry for Provincetown, but with a wind dully chill—gray and unmysterious night, with a yellowish moon just becoming gibbous, her breasts naked in that gray and dulling air—wondered why women couldn't wear them naked just the same as men—sat down on the sand—I clasped her, my weariness and abstraction—fell asleep in bed as I lay—after my having gone in for a swim in the ocean so warm for the Cape and like burrowing one's way smoothly through plush, as one swam back after the first cold plunge toward shore—as I lay beside her and she told me I was so cool—she had her monthlies, was "unwell"— and I fell asleep—I was never so content, so happy—with desire, but with desire cool and tired, with beauty in my arms, but dimmed to the tints of a photograph—my arms straight around her, not locked or twined tight.

Brown of the flesh of her neck, so rich without rosiness against the white skin of her breast—little feet with their bony toes in New York, when she would take them out of her shoes—more rounded, more cunning, with more sex appeal below her rounded cunning brown woman's thighs.

Margaret, Provincetown, summer 1930. Like a little pony—she said people had often told her so—on the little hoofs of her mules, when she first got up in the morning, standing in front of the stove with her back to me—her firm little hard brown calves—in her brown bathing suit, with its Degasesque cutout-paper angles (an angle in a lighter shade across the front)—her chest always thrown forward—her head, so large, out of proportion to her short legs and diminutive feet, the chin held in and the forehead large and thrust forward like a pony with a martingale in the circus, so as to keep its neck arched.

—When I had quarreled with her one night, I came in and found her in bed, lying toward wall—she turned blue-gray eye toward me without moving her head, like a pony lying and waiting for someone with gentle scared apprehension. —Head handsomest when hair cut short and brushed down close around it—when it was mussed up and stuck out in straight masses, it brought out the long and square aspects of her face.

—Love in mid-afternoon in the remote crater of a sand dune—her solid soft human body after the hard rough grainy sand. – Limitations of nocturnal city love, love confined to beds and couches, I realized for the first time.

—When cross with me, she would roll over toward wall and kick me viciously from time to time, pretending to be asleep when I put my arms around her.

—Pony motif: crunching something or her jaw cracking like a pony, when I kissed her in the kitchen.

—One day, when I was kissing her, on her way through the room intent on doing something, she began to talk while my lips were still on hers.

—delish—simply delish

—swell-o—simply swell-o

Well, I think I'll go to beddo.

Party at Spencers'. L'Engles mentioned—terrific controversy: Betty thought they had their nasty points and their good points—Niles (accused by Betty of "being Jesus Christ") took them just like any other people, came and went without being troubled by all the considerations

which were agitating the rest—Dos had a right to talk that
way, because he'd never been to their house, but the
rest . . . —Mary [Heaton] Vorse thought the attitude of
the others snobbish, couldn't stand Brownie for the things
she did at regular intervals, had come to dinner at her
house once and insisted on carrying all the guests off to a
film which she was the only one who wanted to see—
Susan tried to remonstrate with Dos—after all, the
L'Engles were neighbors, and she treated them like any
other neighbors, she didn't think they ought to be discriminated against because they were rich—but Brownie
had come over to South Truro when Dos was alone in the
house—he had been asleep upstairs, she had walked right
in, and he had come blinking down—and said, "Why, I
don't think this house is so unattractive as everybody says
it is!" —Norman said nothing, his eyelids half drooped as
if he were a sleepy child, as Margaret says—Brownie had
been to call on him the other day, after having "been
down to see Papa" [Brownie's father], had said that Papa's
gardener had said that the big dahlias which he had just
gotten a prize for were quite unfashionable now: nobody
had them, but everybody was trying to raise the little kind
—also something blighting about the other thing he had
gotten a prize for.

Provincetown, early August 1930. [Harry Kemp had a
shack near us and came to see us constantly.] —Harry
Kemp: Mediumistic girl who told him a big black man
with terrible eyes and long hands and nails was following her—one night she got up and grew taller, gigantic,
and her arms got larger, and there was a kind of luminous
aura around her head, and a great deep voice came out of
her, and she said, "I'm a homicidal maniac who died in the
asylum at Trenton, New Jersey, five years ago!"—she advanced on him and made him retreat around the room—

till finally he had the courage to grab her and make her sit down in a chair and say, "You're not going to do anything! You've got no power!"—and she just seemed to shrink up and she came to.

—N. amorously attacked him in a restaurant—leaned over and stuck her arm down inside his shirt—people at the next tables saying, "Oh, there's Harry Kemp seducing that young girl!" —She said, "Olives stand for the testicles and something else stands for the seminal fluid." —After giving his actors a lecture on not making love around the theater: "It's all right to have love affairs, see, but I don't want to find any of you lying glued belly to belly behind the scenery!", N. came plunging in and threw herself astride his lap, winding her legs around him and proclaiming that she loved him.

—His ham account of John Reed's death—but amusing about how the Russians couldn't believe in anything so idealistic—had him watched—couldn't believe that he wasn't an agent of American capitalism.

—He [Kemp] had begun to hear from his religion—had disposed of almost a hundred copies of the five hundred he had printed with the backing of a rich man who had interested himself in it—had just gotten a letter about it from a woman, but was afraid she might be a nut. —He had sent Mencken a copy, and Mencken had presently written and asked for another copy for an intelligent colored girl who was interested in it. —But he was determined not to exploit it—that would be so easy to do! —I predicted that a stream of disciples would come out to his shack on the sand dunes—"Well, I'll just tell 'em seriously what I think!"—the possibilities of the West Coast— he said that the Theosophists were going to be sore—that the churches were going to get nasty when they discovered it was beginning to create interest. —He was afraid some evil demiurge might get into him and make him exploit it—but no thaumaturgy! (Nothing up the sleeves.) —In the afternoons, he used to lie out on the beach, sunburned in his funny mottled way, and read Gibbon—I asked him how he could read Gibbon and still occupy himself with his religion—he said that Gibbon made him feel the tremendous power of religion. —His reincarnations. —(In play, something about his being an old man—to which somebody else would reply that they had always thought of him as being about fifteen.) —His acting out of a wrestling match, in which one of the wrestlers had practically had his neck broken—his impersonation of an old bawd in one of the mimes of Herondas, which he had put on in his little theater— Orestes and the Furies: Orestes says, οἴμοι, οἴμοι.*

Going out to the traps: August 12, 1930. Beautiful night, with light marine blue of sky above sand dunes, with white cloud to the east shaped low and undulated like a sand dune, with the stars sprinkled close around its edges—almost (the stars) as informal and unnightlike as if they were some phenomenon of day—perfect calm night with full moon up. —Moonlit sand dunes: pure and bluish pale soft outlines. —In the town, all the houses, packed full with their large green-blinded windows in their compact white boxes, looked clear and fine in the bluish moonlight, with that New England dignity, one of the only things we have comparable in that line to Europe —a conversation, something in the nature of an argument, coming out of one of the only houses that were lighted. —We had taken along shredded-wheat biscuit and condensed milk and coffee, with orange-peel alky [local argot for alcohol] in it.

Everything was dark on the gray long pier, with its

---

* The familiar cry of "Woe is me" which occurs in the Greek plays.

wooden apparatus overhead and its stink of fish—we sat on the end and had a drink—the moon was so thin, a bright disc placed lightly on the light night blue of the west, and toward Truro, the low gray-pink above the opaque blue of low clouds was reflected in the blue porcelain (a softer zinc) of the water, where the darker dories and rowboats lay parallel to the darker clouds— dark-faced shapeless figures on the wharf—they got down into a dory, five of them, from the other tine of the pier and rowed out toward the traps with regular heavy and funereal rhythm of oars, not saying a word.

We visited a series of four traps—the laborious pulling up of the nets: the butterfish, great flapping silver flakes, making a smacking crepitation of fireworks when they were thrown onto the floor of the boat—the squid would usually be the first to appear, streaming through the water in rusted streaks—they seemed so futile, so unpleasantly uncannily incomplete flimsy forms of life, with their round expressionless eyes, like eyes painted—a white iris with a black spot—on some naïve toy, their plumes like the ostrich feathers of some Renaissance woman of the court in an engraving by [Jacques] Callot,* and their squirting method of propulsion, they couldn't even swim like fish—when pulled up, they would squirt their last squirt, trying to propel themselves away, then expire in- distinguishably in a mixed bluish and amberish carpet of slime, when they would be sold by the basket as bait for trawlers. —Combined squeaking of squids and slapping of other fish, as baskets are emptied. —The first things we saw, however, were little sea crabs, clinging to the meshes of the net, which seemed, with their blue and pink, to match the dawn. —The mackerel, with their little clean-

* French engraver (1592–1635) who specialized in the bizarre and grotesque.

clipped tails like neat little efficient propellers: everything the squids were not—iridescent mother-of-pearl along the bellies and striped distinctly black and green along their backs—a big goosefish: the old Portuguese fisherman held him up for us to see his great gullet with the limp slimy squids drooling out of it, brutally grasping him with his thumb and finger in the fish's dull eyes, then flung him overboard—dogfish with their mean smug sharks' mouths on the white underside and their ugly absurd sharks' eyes with a gray cat-pupil on a whitish lozenge of iris—when you held them up by the tail, they snapped up like springs and tried to bite you. —A few whiting and cod-headed hake—rather prettily mottled sand dabs.

It was cold perched on the roof of the little cabin, but as the full summer sun rose, we could feel its heat growing steady. —A gray warship of some kind farther out in the harbor. —The blue shirts and the dirty yellow oilcloth of the five fishermen matched the sky and the sea and the unseen presence of the sand.

When we returned, the tide was out, and the wharf spindled on the bent stems of its piles, green-slimed almost to the top—we walked into shore on the hard smelly slime of the harbor bottom.

Mid-August. [Edie Foley was about to marry Frank Shay. Bill Smith was living in the Provincetown house.] The moving sheets of water, blue and gray, that one looks out on at Provincetown—from the windows of O'Neill's study or at the Smiths', when one looked out on the harbor, as if one were on the water, but more steadily than if one were on shipboard.

Radio at Clay, the bootlegger's: sentimental song about a nightingale, with an accompaniment of thunderclaps of static.

Saturday, the 16th of August, walked over to town in the rain and got drenched, went to the movies to see *The Unholy Three*—came out to blink amazedly, almost uncomfortably, a minute at finding everything bright with the best Provincetown afternoon sun, the clear shapes of trees and houses, shops and fences, the vivid colors. —Going up the hill to the Spencers', to the right one saw the square monumental dullish-white clock tower of the church and, below it, the smaller green-slated spire, against the softer white of the rounded cloud banks washed of their tarnishment by the rain. I called Margaret's attention to how fine it looked, and she said, "It's five o'clock." —The clear bright liquid crystal sunlight of the late afternoon, as one looked up the mounting side streets and saw it bright behind the houses at the top of the slope—effect, beyond a foreground of the solid white bulk of houses, of a breaking through a crevice of the background of green fine-leaved willow trees of the fires of the clear bright sky, which made the cynosure of the picture and contrasted beautifully with the white of the houses.

—On our way back, at the west end of Commercial Street, one saw through the space between the cottages the plain dense blue, gray, or sepia of the blunt shapes of little boats—and one mast rising gracefully from what, seen from the front, looked like a base as small as that of a toy hurdle—against the pale blue perishable water only distinguishable from the pale blue of the sky by the softly dull finish of the former above the smoothness of the bay's liquid silk—along the horizon lay a row of red gunboats, all pointed in the same direction, toward the town, and with their smokestacks toward the forward end, like the last remaining jagged teeth of the lower jawbone of the skull of some link between the human and the animal.

Picnic in sand crater, etc. The bowl of white sand, steep on the side and with an edge that might crumble when you stood on it—the white sand, the rim bristled with sharp green grass and, above it, the pale pure burning blue of the sky. —We had lettuce-and-mayonnaise sandwiches and sandwiches made of apricot jam, a package of cookies, a little pop bottle of ginger ale, and a flask of clear yellow-green alky and water, which had its affinities with the grass and the sky—flies annoyed us while we were making love. While we were sitting there, a white sand spider suddenly leapt out of its hole and hopped a fly, which it dragged below. Margaret said later it had made her uneasy—she wondered whether the ovum snapped up the spermatozoa like that.

Later on, we walked along the beach toward Race Point to the part where there was a lot of driftwood lying around, some big whitened worm-eaten timbers, the real bleached and picked bones of sea traffic—it was so much more lonely there—they (the bones of wrecks) matched a whitish gray kind of beach weed with roundish blunt-topped clusters of little roundish leaves. —Her brown head floating in the blue ocean. We sat on a big log, and she said she would rather be married to me than to anybody living she knew—"Don't take my outbursts too seriously." We had brought along a flask and drank some more alky and water.

As we were coming back, the sails of a sailing vessel precisely on the horizon, snowy white but blued by their shadows, seemed almost opalescent, and as we went down a little slope, it seemed balanced above the fringe of beach grass on the top of the sandbank in front. —We brought back with us a crate with open slats, a segment of a worm-porous tree trunk, sawed off for some purpose, an old cask, an elaborately twisted limb, and other pieces of driftwood. Margaret, who was a little tight, insisted on dragging some ordinary pieces of board an unnecessarily long distance. When we got home, I, in my enthusiasm, swam out and pulled in part of an old crate which was floating around in the water.

—She stayed in the water a long time with Jimmy, and got a little chill—I lay in bed with her and chafed her and warmed her. —When she got up, she put on a sky-blue wrapper with which her toasted fair rose-brown skin went beautifully.

[EW recalls in the ensuing passage his 1920 visit to Edna St. Vincent Millay, her mother and sisters, at Truro, where he had a glimpse of Miss Millay's threadbare but lively girlhood. See his memoir of Miss Millay, *The Shores of Light*, pp. 744–94, 759–65.]

At the Dos Passoses', Truro. Their big bare fresh brown-and-gray-painted living room, which they had made by knocking a partition out—windows on two sides, screen door on one side, kitchen opening at one end.

—The hollow filling with darkness, the lovely church on the hill—the tarnished rose of the gray sky—a train went by—just like when I had come up to see Edna [Millay], the same train and time of day and impenetrable Truro darkness blotting everything out.

—Supper of cold roast beef, Smithfield ham, potato, lettuce, canned asparagus-tip salad, Dos's special stuffed eggplant, toast made on bottom of frying pan, which gave it special richness and flavor, coffee, admirable cocktails mixed by Bill [Smith] in glass cocktail shaker, through which their orange could be seen.

—The boy Columbus on the stove, the lamps with big bulging chimneys which had been found in the house.

—Frank [Shay] in the chicken house—called in after dinner—"Frank's bittern" [a wounded bittern that he kept as a pet]—all had had "collywobbles"—Frank "with his great sad eyes [as Katy said]."

—Neighbor who had come in, pulled out all the bureau

drawers, and tried to read the manuscript on Dos's type-writer—looked in all the windows of Frank's shack.

Dos's story about the Red soldier who had had one of his balls grafted on a Persian merchant—a counterrevolutionary act—the doctor had to appear before some commission—said it had been done for science—they fined him.

August 17–18. From the window of the shack where I work, there is a little gap in the dune, where the path down to the beach goes, and above the white sand, against the not-dark blue sea, a sand grasshopper, white as bone, will flutter with a dry whir—and then a gull, the white of snow, will fly by on a longer more leisurely more noble rhythm.

Fall begins with the middle of August—the wind, the days headed for the year's end, instead of opening with the summer's beginning—the larger waves of evening, during a sunset of dull rose and dull gray, which finally revealed a bright polished cherry sun, shining, bathed in some molten juice—the larger waves as they opened their maws, lined below the darker blue with the brown leather of the seaweed—the next day, the brown streak along the coast (same as above), the green streaks of the shallows, the bright white cuts of the breakers on the bar on the dark blue roughened water under the sky of fall of low north-moving whitish clouds.

Burning buckets and barrels. The bucket we had brought down from the coast and which was smeared hard inside with paint first gave out smoke, then a thick round column of smoke, then a column of gold fire, which seemed fibrous as if it were woven of roots, then a core of solid flowing molten gold, as it roared up the chimney, the paint spitting glowing sparks out of the fireplace like a package of firecrackers. —Then, as the column of red thinned, became a shell, little yellower clearer flames of a different kind began to pierce bristling through the sides of the bucket, and finally, as the top band fell loose, it opened out like a great black tulip till the charred staves crumbled, unexpectedly flimsy and meager after the ferocity and force of the bucket's furnace blast, into a few blistered and glowing squarish bits among the blackened iron rings and the debilitated crazy floor (bottom).

—Then rougher weather, a terrific undertow—the first time that I've really felt it was formidable—and the waves rising toward you like elephants—deliberate, powerful, crushing. —There was a streaked red and orange sunset, wilder and more remote than any during the summer—it made the sea off Peaked Hill seem, no longer a highway and preserve of man's civilized New England life, where trawlers came and steamers passed, but a waste, uninhabited, almost unexplored.

—*Storm, the first day the Cummingses were here*—the sea came in and devoured the dune on which the house was standing—spray or rain blew in through the windows at night—we started to go in swimming, felt the undertow and promptly went back—the next day we started out for a walk, were drenched in two minutes before we could get back to the house. The gray sea roughened by driven waves not only crushed white on the sandbars but sent sprawling white between there and the shore—and on the shore churning over each other, forcing in and sucking back the gray-white foam.

E. E. *Cummings,*[*] as he heard the crickets when we were leaving the Blue Lattice: . . . "and I always say a town without crickets is not a woman without interstices!"

[*] For earlier references to Cummings, see *The Twenties,* pp. 205–7, 429–30.

—Ann had waked up and asked, "What time is it?"—
Cummings had said, "You know the sea" . . .

The Storm. [The Peaked Hill building had been condemned because the sea was eating away the coast. We
didn't know how close we were to losing the house in that
storm. It went out the next January.] One morning the
rusty metallic twisted fragments of the old wreck, of which
the battered boiler still lay always at the edge of the tide,
were exposed, some sticking out of the water and others
lying closer to the shore—I investigated one and, in the
strong undertow, cut myself on it.

Another morning the beach was covered with fish, cod-
mouthed, brown-smeared haddock, fine-spiny-finned herring, limp squid, soft dog sharks (that rotted and made
an awful stink), grinning skates (Callot's or Brueghel's
devils)—the whole beach silver-scaled along a strip with
sardine-looking spurling, which the bigger fish had lost
their lives gobbling and pursuing till their bellies were
hugely distended and sometimes the tail of a spurling was
sticking out of one's mouth, the wrecked fragments—and
enormous claw or sections of the carapace—of enormous
lobsters lying among the wreckage of the farther shore;
flounders.

—Some old handmade roller in a frame, to roll a rope
around—an old musket found by Bruce [Rogers]*—something with some sort of handle that turned on a nail—
which seemed a little like some sort of seat. —Several
lobster pots, with purple-pink starfish but no lobsters—
one with a red and orange buoy attached with a long rope.

—At other times, crystal-looking things that Wanda
[Lyon] said were sea anemones, like the ones she had seen
in Japan. [She was a friend of Margaret's, once a musical-

---

* Bruce Rogers (1870–1957), the master typographer.

The O'Neill house, Provincetown, after dunes were eroded by a storm

E. E. and Ann Barton Cummings

comedy actress, who came to see us with the San Francisco playboy Stan Gwynn. They were married either then or later.]

—the spray that came in our bedroom window

—the biting away of the bank by the waves up to within a few feet of the house

—a giant cochineal-red starfish found by Stan Gwynn

—the biting man-eating flies on the beach—also waked you up in the morning

The church steeple (it was the town hall, by the way, that was green) as if engraved in stone, gray and accurately square-gouged, against the dull-radiant Cape Cod sky.

The wonderful dense strong eye-satisfying colors of the dahlias, etc., of the little front-yard gardens in the dry air of the Cape, which was always tending to be devoid of color.

All the birds in the fall (migrating)—the fat cunning sandpipers gorging on young sand fleas—flaking sharply with tiny white corners the wide flat blue sea—big brownish birds all deliberately flapping west—the same birds moving slowly and in formation, exactly like aeroplanes over Provincetown bay—the gulls riding and squeaking off the pier whenever the *Dorothy Bradford* docks.

Betty Spencer's story (alone and looking very haggard and masculine on the roof of the house)—had been down to Boston with a beau and took a stateroom and drank cocktails, but hadn't brought enough—"Never dilute them when going to Boston!"—arrived there, thought he knew a speakeasy, but it was all he could do to make the waiter

bring him a little (holding up thumb and forefinger)
glass of wine—they sat in the park and held hands, and he
talked to her about Einstein—"He never talks to me in
New York about Einstein!"—and then he went back to
New York, and she walked the streets with tears streaming down her face—she had spent fifteen years in Boston,
and she was still trying to get it out of her system—
"Fifteen years!"—in New York the people looked terrible,
but they had a sort of nervous excitement and interest in
life—but in Boston all these unbaked faces!—her friends,
married and living in Waltham, still talked about William
Morris—none of them drank except a little claret and
sherry at dinner—in hotel, she woke up and got paper:
"Good morning! Merry Christmas! Wouldn't it be a nice
idea to let us bring you your breakfast in bed?" and then
I picked up the paper and started to read an editorial:
"Well, it's time to put away the old sneakers and to throw
the old summer clothes in the closet and settle down for
the winter." —She was evidently feeling pretty sunk and
probably missed Niles.

[Irving Babbitt and Paul Elmer More had published
essays in a symposium called *Humanism and America*
and for a while some of America's leading writers became
involved in attempts to redefine humanism. See *The
Shores of Light,* pp. 451–67.]

Katy [Dos Passos] said that the humanist business was
like the *Strange Case of M. Valdemar.* [They kept trying
to bring humanism back to life when one thought it had
been dead long ago.]

Harry Kemp. He saw the headline, MESSIAH DRUNK.
Another letter from some woman in California—square
hole beside the door of his shack for Hamlet, his cat—the

cabin smelled rather bad—frowzy bed, red-tranched
Euripides, etc.—Latin fragments, Laevius,* etc.—started
to show me about Eche (Scaliger: *saepe* for *Saeptis*
—Harry: "They try to take the poetry out of everything!"), but his attention was diverted to a Priapean
poem—I read it under the impression that it was going
to be about Eche—I said, "What does *minio* mean?"—"I
think that's the red paint they used to paint the phallus
of the garden gods with."

First day I came to see him: "Did you ever see the
launching of a ship?—sliding along her runway." — "No."
— "This is the beginning of the poem." —He said that he
ought to be dynamited out of the idea that he ought to
earn an honest living.

The night, after an evening with the Cummingses,
when we had such a hard time in getting him out of the
house, he prolonged his being a nuisance by lying down
in the surf when I was taking him home and letting the
water come over him: "It wants me! Don't you see the
sea wants me, Edmund?"

Cummings. His voice began to take on a high slightly
feminine Oxford–Harvard timbre, as we kept on guying
(that's the word) Harry Kemp—great play on Harry's
"dynamited out of" things—"Anybody who says I wasn't
dressed is a cockeyed liar!"—impersonation of an old
Cambridge woman he would occasionally rather eerily
drop in to—he came to the window, as if with some serious
purpose, while I was working in my shack, and said,
simply, "Shit!" —Ann working down her figure.

* Laevius (c. 80 B.C.), a Latin poet of whom practically
nothing is known. He was said to have written licentious skits
on heroic myths. Scaliger refers to one or the other of two eminent sixteenth-century classical scholars, father and son.

Autumn, Peaked Hill, 1930. Coming back from Provincetown, September 8, the blue of the sky so bright and the dark almost cobalt sea beneath it, above the dry sand dunes and dry dark-green moss and the beach grass. —At night, the sand under the moonlight almost freezing cold as one thrust into it one's bare feet. —The cold clear green-blue water in the late afternoon, bracing, full of baby sand fleas and with some kind of a ripish sewage stink—little ladies'-veils of crystal jelly, with larvae of sand fleas or something black and buglike twitching convulsively in them.

An earlier day, when, as we set out to Provincetown, a strange autumnal pink light of sunset made the sand dunes toward the Coast Guard station pink-beige in front of the equally amazing laid-on blue, somewhat unharmonious, of the water, and brought out in the roots of the beach grass, where the gash of the path to the house laid them bare, gray in ordinary light, a ruddy color almost like that of willow roots in a brook. —The shadows, spread out flat on those surfaces of pink sand, seemed strange.

The long white waves on the bar rolling out against the blue at both ends, or two rolling out and meeting. —The new beauty and fresh wilder whiteness of the fringe (hem? border?) of waves crushing their crests on the shore.

The sand lampshades that acted as barometers.

Margaret. Going along toward Race Point on the wet sand, propelling her hardy little breasts protruding through her lemon-yellow sweater above the tobacco-brown trunks, by force of her little strawberry-caramel legs, thick and round and dear at the hips, pushing back the wet sand with her little feet, pointed resolutely in-toed.

—Later, with a splendid fire snapping with all the dis-solved, dampened, and concentrated, the pent-up events of wood in the sea, on the wicker chaise longue in the house, she read *Sweet Man,* with her grave attentive gaze, her largish sober head on one side, her little feet pulled up underneath her full thighs on the staled (or sapped) brown-yellow of the wicker chair, smoking a cigarette, and shifting the brown-and-yellow-jacketed book to the wicker arm, and bracing her head with her hand.

—She talked to Jimmy, when as if alone with him, in a language of intimate low-voiced intonations, which would have been as unintelligible to anyone who didn't know her as the language of a mother bird advising and scolding a young one, who had fallen out of the nest too soon and gone astray by flapping onto the public road.

—Reading like a schoolgirl and yet like a mature per-son as well—the way she held and smoked her cigarette—she lifted her arm to scratch underneath her armpit through her yellow jersey—narrowing her eyes when she took a pull—like a boy—like a dear and naïve woman—one foot hanging off the chair, the other folded diagon-ally across it—she wanted to know what "ginning the cotton" meant—smooth gleaming shanks and knees, scraped of their natural hair, one raised on the chair, one stretched straight out—moving her little toes on the stretched-out foot, as she read—clear cheeks, eyes, mouth, and chin, wrinkled forehead when her eyebrows were raised over her book, under the brushed-back brindled hair.

Profile in front of the fire at Peaked Hill, when she was reading me the riot act—so handsome and so lovely, curved high brow, noble head, cunning nose—little bare feet, crossed legs, coming out from under her blue dress.

[We came down from Provincetown in September. Margaret took Jimmy to Santa Barbara to live with his father and go to school, and I left Rosalind and Stella (her nurse) with my mother. I went back to Peaked Hill and lived in the house for I forget how long, with a young man called Blazy. Hazel Ufford had left her husband, and this was her current boyfriend. I was revising the manuscript of *Axel's Castle*.]

Red Bank after Provincetown, September 16, 1930. Blue at once rich and pale of the river, against which the white or yellow-brown boats and the white blue-starred flag of the boathouse of the near shore showed, in the late light of the sun, in plain solid colors, while the far shore seemed coated and dimmed with the dim rich pale blue of the water.

—Behind our house, to the west, through the dark rich high trees, the clear orange-liquid bright light contrasting with the dull-vivid colors, unharmonious but summer gay, of the red and yellow petals and the leaves of a flower bed to the east—the whole gamut of the New Jersey landscape, the two ends of the scale almost discordantly brought together—the rank, dull, gaudy, and glaring with the luxurious, luminous, velveted, and liquid.

—At night, the thin pulse of the locusts and the whistle of the peepers in the trees seemed the warp and woof of the texture of the rich and dark summer night, the cicadae stitching it with their thin steady throbbing.

September, 1930—Margaret. In apartment in town, in morning, in blue dressing gown, suddenly starting forward, about to stand up, as she was sitting on the bed, at the arrival of the maid in the next room, pink, pretty, promptly and positively moving body, responding to obligations, demands, rising to occasions, firm round breasts sticking out from her dressing gown as it came open in front—her little sharp high-heeled mules.

—Her fine nobly distinguished face, with its fair pink complexion and clear green eyes—her lips seemed more sensual now, no longer narrow but firmly thick—a masculine straightness, firmness, and clearness of outline. High brow, with feminine fineness, smallness, sensitiveness of response—softness with smooth firmness and clear-cutness—as we lay together in bed the last days before she left for Santa Barbara. —Wouldn't quarrel with me even when annoyed—followed my turns in bed all night, when she would probably rather have rolled over and gone to sleep on her own side.

New York all alike after Provincetown—people pale, everything blank and ugly—stuffy oppressive weather—but, walking down Fifth Avenue Saturday night, aware rather agreeably (it gave me for a moment a thought of Paris, quickly lost in the blank dull reality) of perfume-scented urban air, so different from country air where the winds bring in the odors of the natural world, the sea, the fish, the trees—in the city, one smells only the things of man, nothing ever gets in from the outside, it is all man's world: perfume, gasoline—the expensive shops seem to smell, all the finely made things, silver, leather, fabrics, in them, people's clothes, the hot Fifth Avenue pavements.

Provincetown, October 1930. Blazy at Peaked Hill—clam chowder and applesauce—the latter invariably unsatisfactory, even though he'd bought nutmeg for it:

"When I can't do anything else, I can always make applesauce." [He did all the cooking.] He found there were enough plates so that you could have clean ones every day for about a week without washing any—I gave him money to buy paper plates, which he did, but he kept on using china, because it was so nice. —"You don't look down on one for these domestic employments?" —His father's efforts to understand him were pathetic. —Arrangement of goldenrod in yellow vase and segments of big white chairs (he was trying to make a composition of these for a painting)—too big for canvas, had to give it up—a pity, when you'd got up ambition to do something—and it was so hard to get up ambition. —I suggested using smaller sections of chairs, but he said this wouldn't do. When Hazel came in the afternoon, however, he flew at the canvas again, taking smaller parts of the chair arms and legs. —The garbage, the rats. [They would get up on the shelves in the kitchen and knock things off.]

—His brother, who worked with the Rice Leaders of the World—Mr. Rice a social figure, Park Avenue, Social Register. —Business which had just succeeded in "triumphing"—$3,000 a year to belong, you got emblem and could use name on salesman's cards—stood for "Honor, Integrity," etc. —Rice had made the biggest electric sign in the world, then the biggest electric sign on Broadway—big banquet in Cincinnati to celebrate the reception of some organization—had planned only five thousand invitations, but Rice got carried away with enthusiasm when he got to sending them out in his hotel—had stenographers going day and night, hotel filled with them—when one cracked, she was taken away and another brought in, working twenty-four hours a day—finally sent out 105,000 invitations, including one to Hoover, for whom he engaged a special train and whom he called up on the phone, and Douglas Fairbanks—he spent $137,000 on hotel and invitations alone—now working on a new project of allowing worthy individuals to join for $500 a year. —Blazy's brother looked up the records of the companies, had to be run by some family for two generations—was an executive at $44 a week—they took great pains to make sure that employees weren't likely to be ambitious and want more money—were a little afraid that Fred might have ideas of advancing himself. —Chief executive little man who worked for almost nothing and lived modestly on Staten Island.

Walk to Truro. Alternate hot and cold air—bluffs like tomato bisque with lots of milk in it—freckled with some different sort of soil—lichenous green like the mold in Roquefort cheese—man, fishing for bass in surf—unfriendly German police dog coming down high bank—path up cliff at Long Nook Beach—newly painted iron-covered halfway house—brambly path with mosquitoes—views, as one went up hill, of sea with its fishing boats, smooth scrawlings on the slightly rougher surface of the blue water, like the marks of childbirth distention on Margaret's abdomen—the line of white gulls riding on the water all along the earlier part of the walk—occasional banks of decaying soft brown seaweed, among which the sandpipers were feeding on baby sand fleas, which at Peaked Hill were stinking up the water with a marsh-gassy smell—the plundered carcass of black fish, skin stretched like tarpaulin on the scaffolding of the skeleton—row of dull gun-metal summer cottages, all exactly alike and almost all closed. —Long Nook: L'Engles' and Musgraves' houses, hard depressing asphalt motor road, attempt to get across where there was a marsh to the other side of the Cape, amiable and helpful Portuguese farmer—dark among the Truro hills—a lift—

the meetinghouse—the Dos Passoses' house in its hollow—
the dead trees: "the sort of places where people would
drive old cars into the yard and leave them."

—Siamese kitten getting into bed with me at night—
stupor induced by weariness and distillate [liquor made
by Bill Smith with a distilling apparatus]. —Katy had
bought all the things in Macy's basement: cassia, Japanese crabs, birthday cake candles, little chocolate granula-
tions for icing, golden lentils, sage, a cone-shaped German cheese to grate on things, tiny pearl onions.

Election night, 1930.

Taxi driver during 1930 fall depression. Had been
driving a taxi in New York for seventeen years—had
originally been a cutter, but you had to belong to a
union, and the union was always striking, so that you
weren't workin' half the time—so he quit, but before he
got a taxi he was out of work a long time—that was how
he knew how the jobless felt, he had just been talking
to me about them—a guy'll get the funniest dirtiest
thoughts sometimes when he's walkin' around the streets
with no work and nothin' to eat, see. —You ask me, and
I'll tell you, see—I don't know you and you don't know
me—you may be J. P. Morgan, I don't know—but a
guy'll get to a point where he'll commit a crime, steal—
Dan O'Brien had the same idea that unemployment
made criminals—the driver said there'd been an increase
in crime in the last year. —Just at present, he was only
coming home at night with about $3 for his family—hard
to organize the taxi drivers, unstable, overcrowded now.

Dick Wright at Leila Owen's. The full-shouldered
Renaissance bust, the sumptuously bound books in the
bookcase, the lamp with the goldfish-bowl base, with red

coral trees and things in it, but the goldfish were all dead, the imitation hyacinths, the bedroom, old French bed with grandfather's coat-of-arms in middle of green silk pillow, jewels, shoes in pigeonholes in closet—adopted daughters—fairy singing roguish silly-ass jazz songs at piano—large framed picture on piano—silver flowers on dining table, mahogany antique furniture—

Dick Wright thought that the Democrats would probably win, because the people probably preferred the Machiavellian method—"It doesn't seem as if any government could get rid of graft—I don't believe they can even in Russia." —He surprised me (after characteristically catty description about what was going on in the Nast publications) by saying he'd like to go to Russia—had been there before Revolution—would like to do as he'd done before and drift down the Volga and talk to the peasants—wondered whether people who went over there now were really free to go anywhere and see anything—had applied to friend not in Amtorg but the other thing, to go over, and was given to understand he wasn't the type of person they cared to have go. —He'd just like to talk to the people in the country . . .

—Everybody urged to sing—Wright said, "I'll get up and design a garden in a minute."

[I knew Wright from my *Vanity Fair* days—he was editor of *House and Garden*. After meeting him on this occasion, I am not sure I ever saw him till he turned up (1951?) at a tea for the Wellfleet Library. He seemed, I was sorry to see, rather shaken and unsure of himself. He had evidently taken heavily to religion—perhaps even become a Catholic.]

Dewey Martin. Used to preach sometimes—used to be foolish and drink a lot in lumber camp, had spent six months' wages in two days—drafted, tried to fight everybody, didn't know anything about anything then, didn't see why he should fight the Germans, whom he didn't know—if he had to fight, he'd rather fight some of those fellers who were aggravatin' him—they had him up before the officers, told him he was going to be shot at sunrise, and the next morning they came into his cell with sour faces and took him out and told him to get the hell away from there. —He went back to the South and was the only foreman at Gastonia who went out with the strikers and struck—then he went over to the Communists—they had sent him to Russia—he was amazed to find that people there knew who he was and recognized him from his pictures in the papers—the stretch-out in a Russian factory: "You said you had the stretch-out, where is it?"—it turned out to be a question of having somebody else bring the worker's tool over and put it ready to his hand: "That's worth fightin' for!" —He said he'd rather get a job in Russia than do the kind of work he had to do over here. —They were thinking about a strategic strike in the South. —The Southern workers shied at the Communist label of the *Southern Worker*. —He had a scar on his side from a trooper's bayonet at Gastonia—they would probably call out state militia in the future: local police, too, often sided with the strikers. —He was being groomed by the Communists—Workers' School for Marxism.

English People in U.S.A.

Rosanna Driver. The dons at Cambridge didn't get much of a screw—a bishop didn't get much of a screw. —She had worked first in Wanamaker's, then in a modern picture gallery—would like to get books on Early American furniture—had heard so many clever people say that Shakespeare would have been so much better off if he hadn't been an Englishman—this country an awful mess, defects of Central Park—police such a bad lot—had never heard people say *bath* with a short *a* before—the artists who came into the gallery had not been very clean.

—Englishmen who came to the party—they knew there was money around but didn't know exactly where it was.

January 2, 1931. [We were going up to Provincetown to visit the Dos Passoses.] Love-making with gusto just before taking train—she took a douche with Angostura bitters by mistake—in lower berth together sat up till late talking and laughing—conversation punctuated by stopper blowing out of gin bottle to our great hilarity (stopper blew out of other gin bottle in suitcase and saturated clothes with gin, violet border to colorless stain)—Margaret seemed more like a schoolgirl than she had ever been with me—and like one of the Fort girls*— I loved looking out at the Connecticut country covered with snow—dark towns with snow-paved streets, with big squarish houses and here and there a light—rivers flat with snow and ice—roads—reminiscences of New Haven—Margaret: "My heart used to go pit-a-pat when I got to New Haven on the train, but that was a long time ago."

Ted [Paramore]† *in Hollywood.* George Bancroft thought the French and Germans would learn English

---

* Henrietta and Louise were the daughters of a Boston railroad official, Gerrit Fort. They had homes at Beach Bluff, Mass., and Beacon Street in Boston. Louise, a former fiancée of John Amen, later married Peter Connor; Henrietta married a man named Holland.

† Ted Paramore was EW's old disorderly, fun-loving friend. See *The Twenties*, pp. 28–32.

when they heard he was making talkies—he would come into the Montmartre and say, "Well, how's the market today?" when he was playing *The Wolf of Wall Street,* and would put his feet on the table when he was playing *Ladies Love Brutes*—he was a physical coward, and in a picture in which he was supposed to be teaching a three-year-old child to box, the kid gave him a swipe that prostrated him. —His wife said that it upset his nerves to wake him up abruptly in the morning, so she just put a little slice of peach on his upper lip.

The bear that got loose and got into an apricot orchard and got so swollen eating apricots that he could hardly walk—when they brought him back on the set, he had the trots, and they had to suspend the picture for two days.

"The truth is, Alice, you don't practice your pratfalls enough."

The man who played gorillas—originally a sensitive young South American—had come up to Hollywood to paint—a fairy?—helped design a gorilla mask, then got fascinated by gorillas and spent all his time studying them and acting them.

Clara Bow.* "Let bygones be bygones!" (to some old lover); "Henry likes it that way." [She was telling them not to shave off her pubic hair for her costume in some picture.]

Harry Kemp. After threatening to beat up Tom Smith and wreck the Liveright office, he took his book to Macaulay—they accepted it—set Harry all up—hair brushed and shoes shined—hoped he was going to make money and be able to give big parties—they had put one lousy clause in the contract which he'd made them take out,

* The pouting, redhead, "It" girl of the movies.

stipulating that if he gave them (in Harry's words) "an inchoate mass," they would get somebody to rewrite it and then publish it without giving him any royalties.

Had gone down to Boston on bus to see little musical-comedy dancer who was in hospital—says she's a Persian but I think she's a Jew—at last, a purely unselfish love—at least, I think it is—hospital racket—she made him pay her expenses.

Had taken Hamlet—created sensation in bus—Hamlet did his business in bag—it's a terrible thing for a cat to be shut up with its own stink—went wild, tried to bite me when I took him out—only a little undeveloped soul—when bus stopped, took cat to W.C., then went out without paying, because it was only a cat—they'd held the bus for him and everybody cheered when he got back in. —After which, Hamlet got "indurated" to his stink.

Provincetown. Funny soft air and light for January—that pink light on the dunes to the west, which we'd begun to see in September before Margaret left—the whole lay of the land had been changed by the wind, which had been supposed to be blowing seventy-five miles an hour at one time—the [Peaked Hill] house hanging over the cliff—the mild and calm sea, blue with a blue not very wintry—inside, the kitchen end was falling noticeably—handing the stuff out through the cupola—as we came back with the china, the full moon came up like a yellow tea rose or a cinnamon-flavored Necco wafer, and as the sky grew deeper blue, its orange brightened and deepened—dinner in the downstairs dining room (at the Dos Passoses') next to the kitchen and under the stairs—a bowl of oranges, grapefruit, and nuts, with gingerbread men standing up in them. —The Siamese cat, now grown quite large, would drape herself lolling on the steam pipe over our heads. It would crawl along the china shelves like a snake, going over the pitchers and things and never breaking anything.

—In the morning, the water light was playing on the ceiling like Venice, but more sober and mild—the level water outside the window—lovely lead under the moonlight—not voracious, easy to get on with, yet with the indefiniteness of the ocean, the rest of the world lay beyond.

Bill Smith, in our Berkeley apartment, putting cigarette ashes in his trousers' cuffs—when we got back from Peaked Hill, we found him over the casks and pipes of his still, as Dos said, "working quietly for civilization."

Manny Melziner at the Lewisohns' immense New Year's Eve party: "Jesus Christ! where's the W.C.? Jesus Christ! where's the W.C.?"—tried the ballroom, the dining room (suggestion for putting her in a story, could make her try the picture gallery).

The sound of the water outside in the morning like the stirring of a bath—the slight whine of a gull—Dos [Passos] mumbling—humming a wordless chant in the bathroom—Norman Matson's salute when we arrived, firing off his gun like an Ibsen character—oyster stew made by Dos—Katy said the cold day was like the edges of lead when you cut it, glittering—she said the mackerel fleet looked flat. —Long Point light no longer clear and white, as in summer, but merely a few leady lumps on a thin strip of lead along the horizon.

—Coming into Truro on train, the gorgeous green bronzy town, with its gilt top of the enormous white church.

DETROIT, FEBRUARY 1931

[During his summer in Provincetown, EW had been increasingly convinced that his preoccupation with symbolism and the subjective writers belonged to the past: he had finished *Axel's Castle* during 1931 and now it seemed altogether out of tune with the new era. The visible signs of economic distress could not be dismissed and in the months preceding the election of Franklin D. Roosevelt EW began a series of studies of the Depression, many of them written for *The New Republic*. *Axel's Castle* had been derived from his wide readings and his scholarship; the book EW would write at the end of the 1930s would have its genesis in a direct exposure to the slums and the strikes, the politics of the New Deal, the understanding of Marx's "class war" which American liberals derived from the hard realities of the Depression. As Wilson journeyed to the mines and the mills, the desolation of Detroit and Chicago, he published a sufficient number of papers to make up his book *The American Jitters*. At the time, as Matthew Josephson later testified, his writings represented "the fresh observations of a man who had gone 'outside' to

see for himself the scene of economic desolation that succeeded the Prosperity Decade." Josephson added:
"Though he often had the air of an absent-minded professor, he could be a good listener." We might add that
he also could be a shrewd questioner. Josephson, also at
The New Republic during this period, judged EW's
writings on the crisis to be "the most objective picture
of America in 1932." EW seems to have started by visiting the steelworks in Bethlehem, Pennsylvania, as prelude to his descent on the center of the automotive industry, but only a paragraph note of that visit is preserved. He went to Detroit in the depth of winter. The
notes which follow were used by him to write one of the
most searching of his *Jitters* papers, "Detroit Motors."
From Detroit, he swung south, and while maintaining
(as he always did) his interest in the literary scene and
visiting the Allen Tates and John Crowe Ransom, he
paid close attention to the miners in West Virginia and
in Kentucky. Later he would study at first hand a textile
strike in New England.]

Early February '31. *The Empire State Building* bluish-
gray with gleaming silvery edges like a semi-transparent
block of ice against the bluish-gray morning sky. When
I came back [from my trip to Detroit] in the radiant
white air that dimmed it, it seemed partly transparent
like a block of ice, through which the radiance was
showing.

N. visiting Cummings—Aunt Jane asked what a drone
bee was—N. consulted encyclopedia, and first thing his
eye fell on was, "When the queen bee becomes pregnant"—flipped over pages and arrived at Beethoven,
whom he began to read about—but Aunt Jane would
have none of it and demanded to be told about the drone
bee. N. said, finally shutting up the encyclopedia and

putting it back: A drone bee is a vile and degenerate bee!

He and Cummings had drunk some kind of wine that made them pee green. Neurotic impulses on N.'s part to say dirty words with Bostonian Cummingses—one evening they were talking about wine, and he started: Why, I drank some wine once that made— Aunt Jane wanted him to finish. Oh, he said, a mere bagatelle!

Detroit. Two fine black chimneys almost from the ground rising very high against the whitish winter clouds and light—the bulk of some buildings against it not so bad either.

Detroit. Crass—the gray dim monotony of the mudflats, gray and yellow—old-fashioned big square ugly brick houses—small square ugly suburban brick and frame houses—the big Ford hospital, new, yet in an old-fashioned ugly brick style—the white executive offices, plain impressive square ugly, set in the flat dreary winter waste—River Rouge, narrow, winding insignificant waters, mud—jade-green and absolutely still between yellow dry grass and gray bare winter thickets—enthusiasm of gas-station boy over Texaco talked like an advertisement: It's just a clear golden oil—blue-eyed sharp-nosed keen credulous face in soiled white oil-station man's cap and overalls—suddenly interrupted to say: Did you see that?—That has had a blunt nose!—They're new. —Making movies of new Ford models—sent them out in tent shows—man who showed us around, Black, advertizing manager, and guide: undistinguished, cheap, unappetizing, colorless, baldish, keen-eyed (gooseberry eyes) good-natured-eyed types like Ford himself. —Guide embarrassed by [the portrait painter] Roy Gamble's*

* See *A Prelude,* p. 205.

talking about English friend who'd lost his job and questions about Ford workers' owning Chevrolets—wouldn't object to owning different kind of car, but would know about it—no, didn't believe they had any of them (Chevrolets)—

Ford: under obligation to garage man

fairy who made magnetos

Holmes's platform—Are women people?

spy system—service men

the financiers and the Jews

Sorensen and Russia

Christmas party

Ford and Lemare

pursues people relentlessly—also does them kindnesses

publicity department afraid of his making a fool of himself

memories of 999 muskrat dinner

Village—bank account insured

got a man fired from *Times*—service men ironically cheered

Detroit: Frank Murphy and Buckley

licenses put off till March—can't have gas

cars being shipped away so as not to lower price on secondhand cars

banks shrunk from 20 to 5

decline of Highland Park district—overbuilt, men in building trades out of work

riot at Ford's—30,000 rumored to be wanted—men from farms, one with only a nickel—man killed—man impaled on storm fence

Flint strike

metal finishers from 15¢ to $1.05

closed down for Model A

Murphy—free speech, starvation wages for
employed—threw out 800 from public
works
no more relief after March—Royal Oak
bond issue from New York for Detroit on
condition no more public works

Federal Hall on a cement basement and conveyor belt
old-fashioned square dances on the polished
hardwood floor between the new car
models and the collection of old giran-
doles and lusters

—American flag
—thawing water-covered road—dull gray-blue like
Ford fenders beaten flat—beyond it, packed lines of
packed Fords
—From the gallery, one looks out on the flat dreary
plain, gray frozen stains of water on gritty cinder black
in the foreground, and beyond it (tracks) the yellowish
waste, across which dark workmen's figures are moving,
coming or going to or from the staggered afternoon
shift—with, in the background above the tracks, black
silo-shaped ovens, white smoke, the cranes and chimneys
of the furnaces.
—one shift going off in Ford cars—another coming on—
Ford vs. Chevrolets
—black-tipped cigarette chimneys over pale dull thin
pea-soup-green factories, with big darker layers of windows
—croquet wickets over long lines of red freight cars—
disused Ford railway line
—Eagle boats in rusty heaps
Executive offices: concrete and steel, stone-faced build-

ing—cut mottoes above doors, stone that manages to look like concrete

—ugly bluish-gray white-veined rubber-black lino-leum—flypaper-yellow golden-oak furniture, yellow gum-wood panels, white-grained black marble windowsills of reception room. —Simonds: pale-blue buried near-sighted eyes and square-cut blue suit—blue shadows across road like his eyes

—truncated carets and blocks of power apparatus

Detroit. Apartment houses with gray wrinkled rep-tilian limestone skins—the eternal drab—gray and red brick, the slushy gray road—low one-story frame houses of the nigger section—stores and houses For Rent, For Rent, For Rent—old red brick houses with a crass dash of Romanesque—one house with black rock-candy base and columns—old brick machine shops and garages—dreary old long-windowed houses with cupolas and jig-saw fronts—red limestone—diversified by red Christmas-ribbon neon tubes, sometimes with borders of blue-bright script brake service, tire, Hudson, Ford, ice cream, candy, realtor signs—Giant Stove from World's Fair in Chi-cago—old majestic Romanesque waterworks—handsome brick white-trimmed or half-timbered residences of Grosse Pointe.

(Ford plant again.) —Inside the toolroom, the wilder-ness of complex gray-painted machines screeching in the air like monotonous fowls with an overtone of shriek-ing—the steady progress of conveyors and slow cranes sliding overhead—dark overcoats hung up in long bunches—strung up so as not to obscure the light-travel-ing cylinder blocks—dodging the hooks of conveyors going in circles, turning corners, up and down—crawl-ing chains, serpents, carrying joints and bones of the Ford skeleton—another toolroom—smooth-running belts—

smooth gray paint—clean wheels—black iron forest of beams—an avalanche of spilling—whirring and grinding.

—Glass: river of glass 480 feet long—crawls out of tunnel with red glow at end—turbid green—at other end, molten glass comes out of furnace like yellow fly-paper from under roller.

[The notes on EW's conversations with Ford's lieutenants helped him compose his vignette of Henry Ford included in his essay on "Detroit Motors." His essay shows that he also read a considerable number of biographical works on the automobile manufacturer; and his compact little portrait combines the testimony of businessmen, newspapermen, Ford office men and the workers. Granting Ford's industrial and mechanical genius, EW looked into Ford's economics, his Peace Ship—his effort during the war to "get the boys out of the trenches by Christmas," his famous decision that history is "the bunk," and his anti-Semitism, that is, his espousal of the spurious *Protocols of the Elders of Zion,* to which allusion is made. EW described Charles E. Sorensen, Ford's "real" first lieutenant, as "that man of iron." The reference to Leland is to Henry Leland and his son Wilfred, engaged in a bitter fight with Ford over his 1922 takeover of their Lincoln Motor Company. In sum, EW found Ford "a queer combination of imaginative grandeur with cheapness, of meanness with magnificent will, of a North Western plainness and bleakness with a serviceable kind of distinction." He also found that the magnate had "the pettish fury of a temperamental pianist," a phrase he changed some years later to "the petulance of a prima donna."]

Cameron (Ford's publicity man, editor of his magazine [*The Dearborn Independent*], formerly a Methodist or Baptist preacher). Couldn't print anything about

politics, future of world, Russia—Sorensen not sound on
Russia—State Department—we were poor but we weren't
disreputable. —Simonds's efforts to get him away, sent
him note, man who'd only be there till 5:30—"Egoism!
that's it, egoism!"—couldn't get into church to thank God
the war was over—he (Cameron) took me for an Englishman—fixed me with cunning blue gaze—a little round
fat gray-haired man with pudgy little white hands—"Yes,
and it's the Americans who are going to do it!"—What
were they going to do? —"Why they'll just get up on
their hind legs! We'll put out our hand someday and
stop the traffic! . . . They call me a pessimist . . . My
prophecies have come true so many times that I've lost
my reputation." — "Just a plain American home!": he
first took us into his study, then into a hideout at the top
of the house that he said he had arranged since the
Depression, because so many people wanted to see him—
Scotch and rye, with milk—"I've drunk 75 quarts of
that—far too much . . . I do believe in Almighty God!
—do you, Gamble?" etc. (It was Roy Gamble who took
me to see him.) "I believe in God! Light must come from
outside! Inside there's nothing but darkness—inside your
body and inside your mind as well." —Religious books in
the bookcase (in the hideout)—books on the Jewish
question—Rabelais—didn't think Rabelais dirty. He called
my attention to the books on the Jews—which I think
included the *Protocols of Zion*—in a sly and obscure
way—"Do you know what I'm talking about? Do you
know these people I'm talking about?" — "Have you the
least idea of the condition this country's in? Have you
the least idea? The cylinder head has cracked!—and do
you know what happens when the cylinder head cracks?
You've got to get a new car. The system's cracked! I
said to Mr. Ford the other day," etc. —I asked him what
was going to happen. "What's going to happen? Why,

we'll just have to pull our caps down over our ears and
wait, and at the end of about three years"—Roy said
there were a lot of people starving in the meantime. He
answered, pursing up his lips in prolonged dubiousness,
"Oh-h-h-h-h, I wouldn't say that. I believe in human
nature, and I don't believe that human nature will let
people starve . . . You can't do very much for them—
you can pay their rent and their grocery bills . . . And
the worst part of it is that you can't do anything! Mr.
Ford can't do anything—Mr. Sorensen can't do anything! I brought two of the biggest men in the country
here the other day, and neither of them knew anything!
(Pompous, slow, portentous) My boss is a hard man, but
he's not unkind—he's hard, but he's not unkind!"—(Lee
Smitt's stories: fight in saloon—"Do you think God will
forgive me my sins?")—"I'm sorry to be so spifflicated . . .
Do you believe in race? I believe in race! . . . (Pointing
out window at homely view) Talk about art: there's
art!"—brown winter trees and garage roofs.

—Roy talked about Sheridan Ford [Detroit intellectual
and wit] and Leland: "When I first came to this town,
all I had was a pencil." "Yes: when you leave this town,
all you'll have will be a pencil!" Cameron thought that this
last was something that Henry Ford had said to Leland.
"Yes; if you were to throw him out the window tomorrow
(Ford), he could earn his living as a machinist." "Yes: I
didn't think," Roy explained, "that that sounded like the
way Mr. Ford and Mr. Leland used to talk to each other."
—He admired Roy's straightness and goodness—held his
hand and said, "A good artist's hand!"—showed signs of
getting quarrelsome whenever we refused another drink
and started to go—foxy intent blue gaze from behind
drunkenness.

—Mr. Ford wouldn't give the Russians a cent's credit—
there were about a hundred, were there? —"Oh, I could

take you over to the —— Hotel and show them to you—
you and the man you're talking about wouldn't eat with
them!"

—He ran down the Chevrolet people, Chevrolet being
then Ford's rival: Did we know what went on in the
Chevrolet offices? They screwed the stenographers on
the desks, whereas in the Ford offices everything was
open and aboveboard because they have glass partitions
between the rooms and you can see what people do.

—After we had left, Roy was saddened and thoughtful
and said something like, "It's certainly depressing when
you find something like that right next to the Throne!"

—When Charley Walker* later went to see Cameron,
he repeated, Charley said, several times, "Thank God,
there's been no physical suffering!" Finally Charley said,
"What do you mean, there's been no physical suffering?"
and told him about a man who had fainted coming into
a flophouse. Cameron assumed a look of great concern:
"A Detroit man?" — "Yes." — "What company did he
work for?" — "Chrysler." — "Oh!" (As who should say,
"That explains everything!")

Elizabeth and Bill Herbert [Elizabeth was David
Hamilton's† sister]. She had had three children and
grown a little more matronly of figure; his hair had
grown a little brindled since I had seen him at the
time of the war. —Ravel's "Bolero": he thought it didn't
get going till the last part. Hemingway—which she
couldn't seem to read. —Mr. Ford was expanding his
plant to give more people work—Christmas party for

* Charles Rumford Walker, EW's Yale friend and expert on
labor relations. See *A Prelude*, pp. 63–5, and *The Twenties*,
p. 15.

† Hamilton was a Yale friend of EW's and army companion.
See *The Twenties*, pp. 16–17.

children—hunchbacked worker dressed up as Santa Claus. —"I must read your last book, Mr. Ford." — "So must I." —Dances at plant. —The Miss Cadwaladers, who said, "Father never thought that Mr. Lincoln was a gentleman." —Elizabeth said she thought it was fine what Ford was doing, didn't we?—giving his men $5 a day. —People had to learn how to use their leisure. Plays in New York—couldn't remember whether they had seen [Bernard Shaw's] *The Apple Cart* in Detroit. —Other couple were old French family who had gone in for motor business. —Elizabeth thought that Dave Hamilton would never get married again, because Margaret had said once that she knew that he would if she died, and he had sworn that he never would. —Old pieces from her mother's house: china dogs. —Home-brewed wine, served at dinner with towel around it. —Ye Olde Filme Theater with soft armchair seats, an Old World wainscoted lounge and an attendant in knee breeches: Harold Lloyd film, *Feet First*—agonizing gags about falling off side of apartment house. Elizabeth said, "I don't know why it should be so funny, because it's really dreadful, isn't it?" She seemed to me more and more like her mother. Gags: ladder slips through step-ladder, confronts gorilla, gets knockout blow, when he finally reaches roof, from painters, who are discussing Dempsey–Tunney fight, after first getting dopey with ether from rag, as he has climbed over the edge, foot-less nigger, window with bars, etc., etc., as he is suspended over Hollywood traffic. Shrieks and moans of talkies make it all too gruesome.

Roy Gamble said, a little tight on Cameron's whiskey, "Well, Edmund, I never thought you and I would be a party to anything like that! There we were, right next to the Throne! To see that plant and then this drunken old bird!—and then that film on top of it all!—I went to sleep there—when I'm not interested, I go to sleep."

—"People just got the idea, see, that they wanted to put their asses on rubber! —Well, see, I figure that this machinery has run away with 'em." — People had got to improve themselves. On gangsters: "These birds where their eyebrows grows up their foreheads—why, they're just next to dog life!"

—"A person gets into an elevator and the door shuts and the door opens and lets him out and shuts again— Jees, he don't know whether he's going to lose a finger! —I figure man's sold out to machinery."

[It is not clear why EW likens the work of the American painter Frank Duveneck (1848–1919) to the French painter Corot. Duveneck was a graduate of the Munich school who later lived in Florence and was much closer to the Dutch tradition. The allusion to Helen Kane (1904–66) is to the almost-forgotten singer whose high babyish voice and "boop-boop-a-doop" made her lyrics a national hit during the 1930s.]

Detroit Athletic Club. Lightish brown woodwork, coffered ceiling of lobby, shiny bronze shot-putter and wrestlers, well-upholstered periodical room—whorehouse picture of girl in bed, Alexander girls with wide straw summer hats on hill, phony Americanized Corot of Frank Duveneck. Friday-night dance of young people: too much ice in water goblets in dark-oak grillroom with billiard tables, small modernistically furnished room, with John Carrolls and new trick lampshades, as in Fisher Building—triangular lily-of-the-valley leaves, glazed—Fisher Building, orange on top and pale peach below at night— $100,000 laid out on gilt ceiling, part of which got stolen in process of painting. —Mayan theater, where Helen

Kane was playing. —Mulatto elevator girls, very business-like and neat, in D.A.C.

Lee Smitt's household. Chesapeake Bay retriever—one of only two kinds of American breeds: that and Boston bull—light camel brown with gray paws and pink eyes—enormously intelligent, seemed to follow conversation closely, responded instantly to everything it was told to do and had been on trial "a couple of times for biting people, whom," according to Lee Smitt, "so far as he could tell, he had every right to bite." —Barrel of musk-rats sent up from Louisiana—something between rabbit and wild duck—slightly high sour gravy—two bottles of Sauternes. —Pretty young wife from little Michigan town, with long good-looking legs from under unfashionably short skirt—sat around and said nothing, while Lee lay on sofa with coat off and collar open, and ordered her to do things. —His charm and sex appeal—his boy's dime-novel ideas. All the gangsters were so human. When I asked him what Buckley, the radio announcer, had been like: "Why, he was you or me." Had predicted the shooting of Buckley. In the course of our conversation, he was always accusing people of being s.o.b.s. —They had been to dinner at a gangster's house at Grosse Pointe: touching domestic interior—grandfather and grandchildren—the man had shot at his wife the week before. —Smitt's use of the personal reference, along with gift of improvisation, like Crowninshield and Burton Rascoe:* "I might be one of Ford's spies, for all you know," etc. —Apartment furnished without taste—Charles Fort's *Second Book of the Damned* (cat suckling rats, which Lee couldn't get himself to make a story of).

* Burton Rascoe (1892–1957), literary critic and columnist. See *The Shores of Light*, pp. 115–16, 397–402

Elmer Clark's apartment, on the other hand: phony Florentine entrance hall, red-brocade furniture, tapestries, coffered ceilings—his old clock, etching of wild geese, books, Philadelphia *Vanity Fair*-like magazine, full of excellent photographs—great joke about billiard-parlor picture of Tunney, with his short hair and his pug's dip [derby], reproduced with honeymoon picture in tweed coat, white trousers, and soft shirt, with his bride. —Clark was sales manager of Budd Wheels—when he first came to Detroit, he had expressed himself so strongly about living there that he'd gotten in wrong at club on top of Fisher Building—had wanted to write originally—job made him sick at times, but enabled him to make trips to New York—Communists had sabotaged car, scratched up glass and bodies. —Keen amusing eyes best part of flabbyish face—a little like Ted Leisen's regular blue business suit.

—The grown-up kid side of Ford, which would make him start out without a hat and motor all the way to Chicago, then have to dodge around to get one, and things for the night.

—Wide use of spats in Detroit.

KENTUCKY
AND THE SOUTH

[EW's swing through the South revealed to him the exploitation and squalor of the blacks. Chattanooga, which
he visited to write about the Scottsboro case, was "one
of America's most horrible towns." He saw Communism
gaining ground among the blacks who had been laid off by
the mills. For them it was an "exciting kind of revival-
ism." He went to see Sherwood Anderson and talked with
him of the collapse of the industrial system and the rise of
the new left. He spent five days in the coal fields of West
Virginia and called the situation among the miners "the
most exciting anywhere on the industrial scene." He
welcomed their forming independent unions that refused
the Communist solutions and at the same time protested
the inadequacies of the American Federation of Labor. In
these journeys, EW's writings show a sense of exhilaration, a feeling of commitment to "change." What that
change should be, he could not yet envisage, but the 1929
crash came to be welcomed by him as "a rending of the
earth in preparation for the Day of Judgment." In his
work he experienced a new sense of freedom and power
"to find ourselves carrying on while the bankers were

taking a beating." Future events would bring more measured and more sober thoughts.]

Kentucky, February 14, 1931. The last industrial plant to be seen as one goes east on the train from Frankfort is the Kentucky Buggy and Harness Works. There is a mule cart waiting in Frankfort Street, and in the country thereafter there are horses and mules in the fields, galloping and grazing. There are red steers, black and white spotted hogs, flocks of fat-looking sheep with cunning black-footed lambs. The gently rolling meadows washed a firm light green over brown, the wet loose-looking miry Southern soil—it had just rained for the first time since February 25 of the year before, and little muddy streams were running with water for the stock—there were crumbling abandoned barns and houses like Fontaine Fox pictures and a few old brick plantation houses with colonial façades and white columns—big stiff sycamores with white bark peeling and branches sticking out—a sparse slow country—smaller farms with low white houses—

—Near Berea [a small summer resort town in central Kentucky], the country got browner and more barren—more mountainous, mistletoe in the trees—unpainted cabins with outbuildings that stood crooked and did not seem to be very firmly founded—houses without basements propped up on stones from the ground—flat range of hills, shaggy like the horses and cattle.

fish die in streams in Ohio and make a scum on the surface, which produces a poisonous gas

story of shooting

Meal (corn—a mill at every crossroads), meat (pork—ribs and jowl), and molasses made from sorghum—diet produces pellagra? They need money for almost nothing but clothes, and they don't wear many of them. They give them canned salmon, tomatoes, etc., to make a strong gastric tube. Pellagra sufferers get listless and don't eat—their skin dries up. They eat great quantities of pork in hog-killing season. $3 a week for a family of five, raised from $2.50. Moonshine. They sleep on cornhusks, but probably always did—family eating on floor. Eat corn mixture for cows.

Berea sociologist said that it would really be better for the country if they were allowed to starve. Is the radio educating them?—they flock to little stores to hear it. Sometimes there's not a drugstore in the county. Each family is a little unit, self-supporting. They get wild salad the first thing in the spring—don't want to be bothered by outside world—tell workers to get out.

Salvation Army's money-making proposition—will go to a town, make a sentimental appeal, and raise $5,000, a large part of which goes to support the Salvation Army worker or into the Salvation Army coffers—worker gives but only enough for two days at a time very often, so that they have to come back immediately for more. The real work is done by underpaid college girls. She had worked for International Immigration Service—straightened out immigrant troubles. Foundations.

October: 12 to 14,000 (families needing relief?)

They move back and forth between city and country—move thinking weather must be better, move to Detroit hearing that jobs are being given out by Ford.

Wild salad: sorrel, mustard leaves, etc.—cook it like spinach—have been taught to can cherries and tomatoes.

Widow with eight children: six boys, two girls. Boy was wanted for theft—bootlegger?—sheriff arrived, and mother opened door and shot him—sheriff's brother shot widow and two sons—other four sons were put in jail as material witnesses, while little girls were taken care of by the neighbors.

Mean as a snake—so sorry the dogs won't bark at him—a gone goslin'. —he'p—help (old English).

"You're not spending Sunday the way God means you to."—Bible class.

Berea's system of making them work for relief up to what they ought to have.

The tenant farmers supply their own team and seed, and get half the crop; the sharecroppers get only the use of the land and a third of the crop. They get money lent them for seed, etc., and by the time they've paid it back, they have nothing—practically in a state of peonage—little farms in the bottoms.

The Cumberland

Spence, the County Agent [In one county there were so many feuds that they had to get different investigators to take care of the different factions—"I wouldn't he'p 'em, I'd shoot 'em down!"]

Democrats and Republicans

Were the mountaineers Tories who had been driven into the mountains or indentured Virginians?

Badly shaved beards of corn stubble—forlorn dried drooping Indian pipes of corn, uncut—sheep—mules—chickens—red infertile soil.

Children and young people in Sunday best—redheads and towheads of Berea—cotton stockings and blunt shoes—atmosphere of wholesomeness and Christian endeavor.

Coca-Cola drink—orange signs—many chimneys left standing from fires—brown dried-out trees and hills—caving-in houses and barns—shacks on stones—almost all with two doors—creeks running for the first time with muddy green water—old cement works, small soft-coal mines, small company settlements.

Highways had changed mountain life—people no longer went to church—listened to sermons on radios—old personal contact gone—people ought to be made to go to school—bank at Mt. Vernon had failed and lost $280,000 —seventy-two of the members of the 4H Club had lost money in it just when he had gotten them to save— organizations form committees and appoint subcommittees—Berea a fine place, fine Kiwanis, good people, but when it comes right down to a showdown, they won't take any responsibility—Mary hasn't seen John yet— people used to help each other out, neighborly feeling— nowadays they'd shoot you for a dollar—he wouldn't mean to hurt you, but he wants the money—decay of religion— this country has been going wild since the war—other man remembered that in the country he came from, one farmer would lend another farmer corn—never went on a note, pay it back next year—didn't care any more for each other than as if they was stock.

They haven't any feed for the stock and they haven't any seed and they haven't any food and they haven't any job—I tell ye that causes agony and heartaches!

Spence: big-boned, blue-eyed, rural—glasses and cap, new car—rural-featured.

sagging or pinched-in roofs

Children had been so hungry they had been gnawing their fingers.

The devil must have dragged his apron strings along here—miry path, stone-topped quarrylike hills—"I don't see what anybody would want to clear this land for—you couldn't drive a railroad spike in it."—chimney, house had been taken away—somebody had planted potato patch— house which man had moved out of just in time, falling down, had pulled up floor for kindling—sloshing in miry path—river where fish could be caught: salmon and bass and sheepshead—grocer had found the family while fishing—still found in the neighborhood.

The log cabin with crude scalelike shingles—black dog

in a box outside—outbuildings, old churn dasher, much used—two doors, both open, tangled bed, mattresses, covers—Ingram,* brown hat, backwoods-man's hair, profile, mustache, pale blue eyes that water, sweetness and gentleness, thin—wife died of fever three years ago, leaving three-months-old child, he holds it with great tenderness, child with dirty mouth—food? "That's just what we haint got much of"—about two messes of meal, a quart of flour, a half pound of meat—"Now I'm gonta ask ye a question"—had traded quilts for heifer calf in spring—milk—$10 from Red Cross, helped only twice—they heard about his trade and wouldn't give him anything more—How old was the child? —"I don't know. I cain't remember things since I had the fever." —"You ought to find out their ages and learn them." — "I've got it down here." —Boy said in loud distinct voice, "I doan know." —How many children has his brother? "I never counted 'em." —Dishes in corner—blackened kettle on stove, wood under table, one chair, two boxes, iron bedstead with most of white paint scraped off. —Had been sick, hadn't been able to make baskets lately—poured hot water on boneset [a medicinal herb] in pail for most complaints, stalks—had sold two cows for doctor's bills for wife, had sold hog because he couldn't feed it, thought heifer could graze on green things, God knows where she was going to find any—room half suffocating with smoke that stings the eyes—"Don't let the house burn down!" —Spence had seen one burn down just the other day, and the people had just leaned against the fence and watched it. —Yes,

* In the ms. EW writes after Ingram: "something Red Warren (Robert Penn)," apparently to remind himself of something said. Mr. Warren comments: "My only guess is that I had at one time or another said something to EW about the tenant class—I suppose Ingram was a tenant on Allen's place, which did have such a cabin on it."

he'd be careful. —Didn't know where eldest boy was—boy of fourteen could can blackberries pretty well—little girl smiled when he said something to her—boy of twenty, who had been crippled by a rock thrown at him in the back when he was a kid, turned his back when Spence talked about him, couldn't walk, crouched on stunted legs in overalls, held out thin hand to fire—other kids close around it—two, one of them peaked-looking, peeking out from behind stove—told little girl she better move, she doesn't, boy makes inhibited sound and gesture as if to make her move—(dog didn't bark much, probably hungry, too)—their fine clear complexions, blond hair, thin and pale, fine civilized Anglo-Saxon types. —"Don't trade anything the Red Cross gives you again!" —Ingram misunderstands: "No matter what kind of a trade you make, there's always folks that'll talk agin it—and Gillam'll tell ye the same." —Scanty clothes—"You better wrap those children up warm!"—he invited us to stay to dinner—coughed a good deal inside the house—outside, said, "I don't know how it is, but I feel chilly." —Little boy came and peeked out. —"Why don't you move down to Peter's house?—that's a better house than yours." — "Peter wouldn't want me to live in his house." — Spence said that he ought to send those children to school: they were intelligent when they went—but, Ingram said, the other children threw rocks at them on the way home. —The mother had never been willing to let the cripple go, but now they might be able to send him to an institution.

On our way back, Spence said, "The Ingram family make me kind of sad. —He may be a sorry fellow, but they oughtn't to hold it against him that he traded those blankets . . . He'll get traded out of everything he has."

Clarksville, Tennessee. [EW visited Allen and Caroline Gordon Tate.] Tenant sharecropper and wife, little log cabin—complained about inroads on turnip patch. —Gently rolling hills, deep Cumberland River with triple-hooped white iron bridge—town to left. Canebrakes and beech seedlings—mildness and charm of the countryside. Hundred-year-old house (of the Tates) green-roofed, high and compact, with iron stars and curls showing braces, black against white-washed brick—built on the dog-run principle: hall in middle, high rectangular rooms of equal size on either side—big coal in wire-screened grates—the slave cabins which had been blown off the hill, the "office," a little house where the men used to keep their guns and drink. —Corn bread, chicken gravy on waffles, sorghum and maple syrup, big old dark dining-room table with great claw feet and red cover on it—paintings by Allen's mother. —The coal-smoky smell of the South—the fire burning in the big cold bedroom, with its high ceiling and enormous bed. —Police dog—would stick her nose brusquely under your arm for attention.

—Cousin John—little schoolhouse he built for himself to teach children the classics, French, etc.—about fifty niggers—man who came and stayed with him to help him with his syntax. Sitting room, rather bare, homely pinkish magenta curtains on upper part of big windows. Rather attractive daughter, with dark hair not bobbed but done up in old-fashioned way with big knob. Clear thin agreeable wine and fruitcake. His distinguished proud Greek scholar's face—habit of wrinkling up nose. Used to dispute with clergyman brother over Origen and Josephus.* Anecdotes about [Woodrow] Wilson's father—inveterate punster—pun about "malefactor" in connection with male calf's being born, had thought he couldn't make pun about that—told about woman who said, "You can take

---

* Origen (c. A.D. 185–254) was the Christian scholar who pioneered textual criticism of the Bible; Josephus (b. A.D. 38) was the pro-Roman Jewish priest and historian.

away the doctrine of the Redemption, you can take away Absolution, but you must leave me total depravity!"—so that one knew that he was human (Woodrow Wilson's father), though a theological type—like the Roman augurs in Cicero. —Wilson a good deal like Cicero—words, but when it came to action . . . He wrote letters and articles about politics (Cousin John), had pointed out seven years ago that the trouble with the country was that the cities were getting overinflated—Megalopolis, as Spengler said—ought to send the people back to the land and do away with the high tariff. —There was always a living on a farm—he himself had been a dirt farmer, not a white-collar farmer. —Wilson had been a very strange man—he expected you would have to look for his complexes—his state papers had been written in a more classical style than those of any other president. —Mr. Smith would probably have been better than Hoover—he had common sense—definition of common sense: ability to see things as they really were in their right relations. —Will Rogers and Socrates—Socrates had a good deal of humor, you know. "Indulge pueris—indulge senibus."

Caroline's uncle. Had married his housekeeper when her husband had gone crazy—the husband had tried to kill her with an ax and accused him of sleeping with her. For this "act of honor and generosity," the whole community had been down on him—including people that he had done all kinds of things for, and he had remained as sweet about them as ever—had always lent people money and helped them out. —Old house, once fine, now neglected—cypress alley—the niggers had looted it when his first wife died—noble hallway where the children used to dance, stairway at back—avenue of trees—all inside faded, drab, paper discolored and peeling from high upper walls—strawberry plant. —A drink of whiskey all round. —Legge and the Farm Board—he had done just the opposite of what Mr. Hoover had appointed him to do—looks as if Mr. Hoover was going to solve the problem by making the farmers so poor that they couldn't produce. —Tobacco barn—dark tobacco more work, has to be smoked in barn—barn big, losing itself in cross-rafters, from which hung the wrinkled brown tobacco bunches, rich shadows—a nigger woman by a crooked cypress log, the inside of its writhen curve glowing red—she sat in her modern clothes, not exactly sullenly, but paying no attention to our arrival, though she was sitting right in front of the door—niggers breaking off the stalks and binding the stems of the bunches with a leaf—the leaves looked like unexpanded moth wings, not yet unfolded from the cocoon—smelled fragrant like dried rose leaves— he showed us the resilience of the leaves: if you bent one up, it bent back again—the livest plant there is growing— called "dark" because if you put water on it, it turned black—market chiefly among Italians, too strong for other people—farmers auctioned it off to buyers and got gypped —they couldn't get together enough to fix a price—individualism one cause of losing the war. —He had been a cowboy in Oklahoma, when it was Indian territory—the Virginians had come first in esteem, the Kentuckians second, and the Tennesseeans third—old six-shooter .44 gun with long barrel, one of the first made. —He was wonderful with horses and used to have some very fine ones.

While we were driving from one place to another, the Tates talked about Grasslands, the hunt club started by Fleischmann—the only kind of fox-hunting the real Southerners knew was going out at night and sitting around a fire—and they'd say, "There goes (dog's name)—there goes (dog's name)," etc.

Wide spacious hall, as you came in (in Caroline's uncle's house), with stairway scrolling around from upstairs and then coming straight down, so that it must have made possible very impressive entrances by the master or lady of the house—like stairway in Andrew Jackson's Hermitage [trip to Hermitage, his Tennessee home, and description of it]—out beyond the company houses of the Du Pont Rayon Mills, systematically varied as to color, green, yellow, brown, but all exactly alike, flat one-story affairs exactly the same distance apart and with the same chain swing on the porch. —Approach through drive of gray-green cedars—white columns against brick—homely red and yellow big-flowered carpets, furniture already verging on Victorian—big graceful cylinders or hurricane glasses, with candles in them—bright wallpaper from Paris, Telemachus looking for Odysseus and stopping at Calypso's island—the first lovely little red flowers with yellow-dot centers of Japanese quince and another bush fully white-flowered that smelled like lily-of-the-valley— the Japanesy-looking willows here and at the Tates', the lines of the branches falling as fine and as straight as rain and with little pale-green pussy-willow buds—against the gray February air—the song of birds in the woods. — On our drive, one saw a sun dimly copper relieving with an old-engraving touch the gray skies above the silk mills. —Old gray gutted houses with abandoned double verandas, which the Tates could see were "fine."

"I don't guess"

We played Murder.

In John Crowe Ransom's office, there took place a slightly aggressive and invidious conversation about the excited Northern editor of the *Sewanee Review* and the Civil War—Allen's review of *The Age of Hate* in *The New Republic.**

* George Fort Milton's *Age of Hate* was reviewed by Allen Tate in the issue of February 18, 1931. He called the book "one of the great narratives of our historical literature, but intellectually it is muddled, and thus unsound."

Allen's way of adapting his accent to the people he
talked to—in the way of Negroes: "Kin you te'-y me — ?"
—Andrew Lytle's skill at poor-white dialect, etc.*

Cincinnati. There were old-fashioned-looking steam-
boats on the wide muddy Ohio, but they had some high
New York office buildings.

—Between Cincinnati and Xenia, Ohio, a feathery
broom-straw frieze of light-brown sycamores woven in
with thicker blacker trees, the former veining the latter
with white.

—Bank failures—more than a hundred banks had failed
in Arkansas as the result of the Caldwell Company's investment house going up the flue—they had bought up
various industries and hotels and sold people stock in
them. —The crooked banker who had said that he'd always
been an agrarian himself.

—The psychology professor's pretty wife said her
father, who was director of one of the Southern railroads,
got sick every time he got outvoted in New York over
laying off old employees—once they had sent him out to
travel around and fire them, and he had come back and
gone to bed—Why couldn't they do without a little of
their profit?

[This note was made before my trip of February '31]

—The blast furnaces like giants at stool with their intestines wrapped about their bellies, voiding their bowels
with a thunderous hissing and excreting a molten feces
of gold burnt beyond gold to a white ethereal yellow—
shriveling the very autumn sunlight with its supreme
incandescence. It ceased to be something which got light
from the sun but was something which outburned the

---

* EW reviewed the Fugitives, including such Vanderbilt University poets as Ransom, Tate, Warren, Lytle, in "The Tennessee Poets," reprinted in *The Shores of Light*, pp. 191–6.

sunlight, showing through it as if through a consumed white film. Cascades of intense thin sublimated gold pig iron, from which sparks burst like tiny rockets in the air—an explosive spray of fire.

[These notes were carried over from EW's trip to Bethlehem to visit the steelworks prior to his trip to Detroit. The ensuing notes deal with EW's trip to Washington in March 1931 to attend a Progressive Conference. He had issued an appeal to "progressives"—as he described the liberal left, in contradistinction to the Communist left—in *The New Republic,* asserting it was up to the American libertarians to "take Communism away from the Communists," by which he meant that Americans should found a socialistic party with indigenous roots. Two papers in *The American Jitters* deal with the conference, "Senator and Engineer," pp. 105–12, and " 'Still'—Meditations of a Progressive," pp. 113–20, also reprinted in *Earthquake.*]

Shoreham, Washington. Big new buff brick, green-blinded hotel, with as many windows as a fortress or a cheese.

Great big new modern hotel—faintly modern decorations at entrance—all the rooms not finished and elevators not all going—started to push button when there was only electric wiring—very thin pea-soup-colored walls—many closets with mirrors in the doors and crystal doorknobs—two beds for the price of one, with thin pea-soup-colored covers—light pseudo-old-fashioned cherrywood dresser and bureau. With a box of matches and a candle on it, fake lace covers on them—light peachy-pink curtains with flowered chintz of the same peach pink at the side—nice little beds without footboards, pea-soup-green coverlets with simple flower embroidery in the middle—fake Empire lamp between the beds with Greek frieze in fake brass at the base—graceful little mirror—green-striped upholstered low-armed chairs—low narrow doors to hall and bathroom—radiator enclosed in pale pea-soup green, well-proportioned and delicately fenestrated case—little curved spindle-legged green gilt-painted eighteenth-century table—lighter inlay of flowers in dresser—green metal scrap basket with windmill scene—eighteenth-century print in gilt frame—Bébé Chéri in colors: dragging baby in baby carriage, with little sappily smiling girl with little rake and white spaniels leaping around—lace bureau and dresser covers of fleur-de-lis and ferns—pale *cherry*-pink window curtains—bathroom: long tub, white tiles with black border, green shower-bath curtain and green razor-blade cloth, ice-water tap that as yet gave only warm water, green towels and bath mat with Shoreham arms—green blankets on bed—black and white tiled floor—ornaments on white stone gateposts, halfway between a Mayan headdress and a Chinese block puzzle.

Gardner Jackson [journalist and fighter for liberal causes] tight at Bronson Cutting's—four children and wife who didn't like Phelps Putnam, $180,000, old hat and greenish shabby coat with the top button in half and hanging loose—kept falling down on way home—jammed into bus and leaned on elderly lady who protested. —What an s.o.b. Borah was, didn't ask him till they'd arranged radio publicity—in speech, he didn't say that we ought to confiscate the money of those who had it: let them keep it! (At one point he leaned against a wall and kept saying: Oh, Bunny: the two natures in man!)

Books at Cutting's: Alfieri, Metastasio, Dryden, Fénelon—on tables, *New Yorker, New Republic,* Trotsky's *My Life,* Demosthenes on the Crown.

(Paddy Jackson again, I think): The prince who lives in this palace is the American Kropotkin*—it's just a

---

* The Russian nobleman Peter Kropotkin (1842–1921), father of anarchism, was commonly called the "anarchist Prince."

question of whether he can get love enough to give him confidence in himself.

[EW's note: Bronson Cutting of New York was then senator from New Mexico, where the "Mexicans" had rewarded his interest in them by sending him to the Senate. He had a great reputation as a liberal rather further to the left than most. At this time there was something of a crisis going on in his homosexual household. The position of the hitherto reigning favorite was being challenged by Phelps Putnam.]

New York, April '31. At the end of March, a day of bright colorless skies when the sun seemed nearer and natural again, as if the winter had caused it to withdraw—then a dreary winter day of rain.

An early April night—a spring mist, yet cold enough so that one's breath went up in steam—walking along Ninth Street toward the deep end of the Village, 244 West Tenth.

Later, an evening, coming back at 6:30, when a clear luminous rose of sun showed in the sky above the buildings of West Tenth Street and changed to blue through stages of mauve, like the cloth-flower barometers in opticians' shops—at the next side street, Ninth, the new women's jail had blocked out the sun itself and, being shadowy yellow walls with dark purple shadows in vertical lines at the angles, made the sky above simply a lovely and quite different lilac.

Easter Sunday, a mild gray day—coming back to the Berkeley at noon, I saw a tall grouchy-looking gentleman in a silk hat, coffined in a long straight overcoat, coming back down Fifth Avenue from church.

May 1, 1931. Patsy Kelly in *Wonder Bar*—pretty liquid Irish brown eyes and recessive chin—when they asked her if she had a beau, she kissed her forefinger and said, Yes, and no complaints!—gloomy, lived with drunken father, who abused her and called her names—every Saturday night, all her family, taxi drivers, etc., lined up at the stage door to collect—went off alone to movies every night after the show.

Margaret: all kind o' gangrenous (of drinks—cocktails left in shaker from the night before)
—commit sideways (suicide)
—being Pollyanna, the glad girl, all over the place

Dry cattails and scrapped car bodies of New Jersey marshes.

[At *The New Republic,* when Croly was alive, we had all been satellites around him. After his death, we became a group with equal powers, and I tried to get to know the others better. Stark Young, the drama critic, was the only one of them that I had ever seen socially outside the office, and I had not seen much of him. With Bruce Bliven I never made any contact. Herbert had told me the last time I saw him before he had his stroke (when I had dinner with him at the Players just before I went out to Santa Barbara) that he had not made any arrangements for any one to succeed him at the NR and had added something to the effect that Bruce was of course out of the question. But I did see a little more of George Soule and even got him to show me his early poetry, which was disappointingly though characteristically pale. In the summer of '31, Margaret and I spent a day with the Soules in the country, and they took us to see Alice Hamilton.]

Alice Hamilton. Her dignity (on Sacco and Vanzetti meeting, etc.), intelligence, skillful way of talking, wit—her pretty lavender dress and shapely shoes—grayish hair

parted in the middle. —The old house with rooms so irregularly arranged inside, and, outside, the high irregularly level terrace, with the irregular terraces rising behind
it—the lavender and white petunias and the higher white
phlox, like flakes of light in the bright clear afternoon,
and behind the phlox, behind the screen of trees, the
similar bright whiteness of the house next door—in front
of us a tree that expanded at the top into an abundant
fine-leaved sheaf and whose limbs, sprouting from their
stalk, seemed peculiarly organic like the lungs or like
the ventricles or tubes of some sea creature—on the other
side of the house, the little pier, with children and older
girls from the town on it—the old boathouse and the
bright gleam of the river, the Connecticut, just below the
dark verdure of the opposite shore, where we could see
a white Connecticut-looking house half-faint against
a dark wood of which we saw the silhouettes of the stalks
against the brightness of the sky. —There was trumpet
vine thick on the old outside chimney, and all over that
side of the house itself the enormous elephant-ear-shaped
leaves of the Dutchman's-pipe vine, which, in the window, against the white wall inside, showed beautiful
translucent green (almost yellow), on the white sky beyond.

Walter Lippmann. First appearance to Isobel Soule.
She had been reading *The New Republic,* which had
then just started, and had heard about him and admired
him. —One day in the house where she was living in
Washington, on 24th Street, she heard somebody crying
loudly in the hall, and when she went out, she saw
Walter in his shirt sleeves in evening dress but holding
out a small frying pan, with which he was trying to con-
tend with a veritable inundation caused by a leak in the
ceiling. She had always remembered this as a kind of
symbolic tableau.

Isobel's father, John Walker, whom she hadn't seen

since she was eight, had married her mother when they were nineteen and sixteen respectively—when Isobel was a baby, she greatly upset her mother by pretending to turn her into a bowl of goldfish—at the time when rich American girls were marrying foreign noblemen and the young Americans resented it, her father and his friends got a French count tight at a big dance which was being given in his honor—they cut a big heart out of his shirt front and put a piece of red flannel behind it—as a result of which the count challenged John to a duel—John had the seconds remove the ball from the pistols and fill one with chicken blood—so that the count, after shooting, seeing the blood on his coat, collapsed in a panic. John broke up Sherry's one night—he masqueraded as a corpse in a coffin, and his friends carried him around from saloon to saloon, where he would rise up and ask for a drink. Football game at which he was hired to play by some college not his own—made them provide a carriage to transport himself and his friends, who were supposed to be trainers, etc.—they were full of champagne, and he was drunk on the field and ran in the wrong direction, etc., then finally saved the day by beating everybody up terrible.

VIRGINIA AND
THE SOUTHWEST

Mossiness of Virginia. Lushness of the verdure without usual American summer garishness and coarseness—meadows, feathery locust groves and swamps a bright summer yellow-green, with the hills blued under a gray sky of light and shade beyond—muddy yellow streams with bushy willows beside them and little wild tiger lilies—nigger cabins—old larglsh down-at-heels frame houses, yellow or white—men in blue overalls plowing the fields with mules—crude white picket fences around cabins—a vineyard running through the middle of a field—a few longish rows of blue-gray cabbages and light-green corn, following the curve of the edge of a wood—a big transformer, a dingy row of cars, a tiny sausage factory, coming into Roanoke—around the station, old discolored buildings, which have long ago lost most of their yellow paint, and dingy old red brick hotels and stores, with the posters on their walls and in their windows half peeled off—a wider muddy stream overhung with the leafy-burdened branches of bent trees—you can see its winding course through the fields, where the low bushy trees hug it—fields bluish with lupin, chalked with lupin, like a stick of chalk rubbed up and down the blackboard along its whole length—nigger baseball in an open field, a gaunt cow beside the track—sweet smell of honeysuckle thick on the banks beside the track coming in through the screens of the car, and the acrid cindery train smell—the blue hills with a brightening varied sky of clouds and gray-blue above them—forward and in the distance (the hills) dimmer and lost in blue-gray, even the edges of their outlines blurred by the clouds above them—pink boys in bathing trunks paddling little boats in a wider muddy river under a high black railroad trestle—again, you look *down* and see a stream with trees along it, a man following his plow beside it, his fairly large frame house, his children playing around an old car, with a high dark-wooded, thick-wooded mountain in the immediate background—a steep hillside planted with a good-sized patch of corn, green bunches of plumes in rows in the brown soil. [I stopped off and spent a night there, to see Sherwood Anderson. He gave me the proofs of *Perhaps Women* to read. It was interesting to see him living in one of the small towns that he liked so much, and I found that I easily dropped into the small-town way of talking, which was perfectly natural to me. He owned the two town papers, one Democratic, one Republican. Except for the editorials, they seemed to be identical.]

Marion. Neat rather new-looking little brick town, the county seat, with big white courthouse—first day, dampness in the air exquisitely softened and shaded the blues and grays of the round mountains, whose soft curves make the bowl in which the town is situated—in the afternoon, a mild slight fall of rain, the fragrance of the foliage and the ground.

—Walker Mountain—in the foreground, the fine and ferny greenery of the forest—beyond, a succession of slopes rising one behind the other and exquisitely modulated and varied through shades of green and dark green, made where long cloud shadows fell, smoothness of fields, roughness of woods, blue-greenness of the nearer ridge, light blank blueness of the farther one, and above this the blue and white opal sky of roundish white clouds and light blue air.

—Road to Redford—round hill of tender green with a row of white sheep along its top and behind it a larger rounded slope of dark contrasting green.

—From the train, where the New River curves—one shore, nearer, a brighter light green, making a kind of promontory against the dark green background of the other shore looming above it—the muddy yellow river looking suddenly rich with tree shadows making a pale chocolaty-color purple. —People hoeing cabbage patches and corn between the river and the train.

—At night, delicious coolness and fragrance coming through the screens of the train, and nearness of the houses and stations—boys and girls ha-ha-haing the people in the train to attract their attention—the engine softly hooting ahead—

[A. J. Muste's "outfit" was the Conference for Progressive Labor Action (CPLA). The Katherine Pollak article was entitled "Life-or-Death Struggle Looms in Coal Fields of W. Virginia," published in July of 1931. EW's notes were used in "Frank Keeney's Coal Diggers" in *Jitters*, pp. 150–69, and *Earthquake*, pp. 310–27.]

June 17–21, Charleston, West Virginia (where an independent coal miner's union had been organized by A. J. Muste's outfit): Tom Tippett's chameleon tongue—slight lisp—son of a bitch, goddam fool (like Ben Stolberg, he overdid profanity, and on his lips it sounded

inappropriate)—white suit—criticizing Katherine Pollak's article for *Labor Age*—Miss Pollak, who got rattled
while reading it to him, said "West Vagina" for West
Virginia at one point, then corrected herself. He is an
ex-hosiery worker—Chapel Hill student's blue beret and
wrist watch—took out small brown pocket comb and
combed hair before going to meeting—had left white
pants behind, thinking he was going among proletariat,
now regretted it: miners wore them when they could—
Miss Pollak wanted a clean place to eat, Coffee Shoppe,
little pink, blue, and yellow cockades on sandwiches.
—Italian named Chris who distributed bills—let him off
from going to meeting, for fear he'd be slugged; the
superintendent had told him that if he went to the meeting, he'd be "bad man"—had apparently had his handbill distributing interfered with—Musteites thought it
better to let Schear go by himself—then we split up into
pairs.

First speaker: You'll get a checkweighman, you bet
you will!—eight hours, trade at any store—I see a fine
lot of Negro folks—you laugh when I say that: well, I
hope you never did anything like that—because this fellow got into a lot of trouble!—wife asked for money—
operator a fair profit on his investment—Those *brave*
men who don't fear the Devil himself—put women and
children first—tear bombs, nightsticks, etc.

Miss Pollak was a little worried on account of the
hot sun—had just been reading a biography of Debs, and
it seemed that he had a sunstroke in West Virginia.

Enthusiastic Negro with round shoulders and blue
overalls.

Second speaker: two city dudes, little frog—ha! ha!—
everything I am, everything I have—I don't do it for my
salary, Mr. Van B. [Van Bittner, UMW official] don't
care about his salary—I do want to do it for you!—(faint
hurrah for John L. Lewis)

Third speaker: a man or a yellow dog—start as a baby and grow—long-haired men, etc., Bolsheviks—Professor Nutsky, Professor Don't-Know-Nothin', Professor Never-Dug-a-Pound-of-Coal-in-His-Life—also working with non-union employees—and I like to talk to operators—operators are all right, some of them are just dumb—stabilize industry—built with blood of children—(Trains go by)—Questions: I don't know whether they wrote them themselves—I'm glad to have the privilege of summing up these questions—Somebody's just handed me a statement about this circular—I can't spend all day, etc.—operator fair profit on his investment—stretch out arms to prodigal son, but mustn't expect calf to be too fat!

["Mother Jones" was the Irish-born Mary Harris, who died in her 100th year in 1930. A picturesque, passionate labor leader, she was a symbol and activist in most strikes in the United States between 1877 and 1923.]

Chicken houses—possum skins and red and pink ramblers—women in white slips and thin bare legs on porches—company-owned minister and church—sordid creek—old car wheels, and cars—naked, orders—company store, always in debt—owns property—had to go way into hollow to organize them—had to go to oil wells to have speakin's—home brew—evictions and arrests—nine or ten children, birth control—operators never come near them—forty-two years—government corrupt, even the President's against us—wood-hicks, Cedar Grove—superintendent's and storekeeper's houses—operators themselves never go near mines—outside, toy balloon with address—operators, wildcattin', stabilization—$3, $2.60—38¢ a ton—black and whites bathe side by side—cleanup system, ten or twelve hours—two women taken on for Mother's Day—Communists around: real or spies?—Lewis organization—What happened in Kentucky—What happened in 1924—Mother Jones—What happened about hunger march,

where from?—You can look in their kitchens—Governor
read Constitution and ten dollars—Have just been called
Communists—fish without license—courage and independence of enslaved miners compared with panic of owners.

*Visit to Chattanooga to find out about Scottsboro case.**
Old low sordid brick buildings, among which a new
hotel, office building, insurance company, or bank has
been expanded as if with sporadic effort. Business streets
that suddenly lapse away in nigger cabins. —Mill district—Hell's Acre—don't dare go there after dark—a nigger
shot every day—six niggers to one white. —1,500 manu-
factured articles, from locomotives to coffins and snuff.
—Nigger section a vast smudge.

Virginia Price married twice—Ruby Bates younger, in
overalls, dips snuff—drunk at the station that morning,
had come in with boys in car at night—boys worked in
mills?—lived with niggers, arrested. —Black boys: two
Wrights bad little gangsters—going to port—white boys
hoboes from Texas—white stumbled over black boy—
threatened him—fight in gondola—one Negro had pistol,
one had knife—gravel, broad day—boy fell down between
cars—boy with cut head—told telegrapher—telegraphed to
Scottsboro—sheriff and deputies after murderer—colored
boys thought they were arrested for ride-stealing—girls
in good condition—slight bruises from gravel—sperm,
black or white?

Nigger accused of rape, actually wife's lover—lynchers
defended—rivals for attorney general at last primaries—
Chamlee has Negro vote—success of Communists with
Negroes.

Brass band from hosiery mill—28 Ford trucks, phonograph and amplifier—music changing guard.

* The Scottsboro Freight-Car Case," *Jitters,* pp. 175–92;
Earthquake, pp. 334–47.

In Scottsboro, people had to shake hands with their servants in the morning. —In Chattanooga, one lady's cook got so excited she wouldn't stay. —One preacher on jury, mostly farmers, poor whites—judge has to be elected in that county—afraid of a second monkey trial—Communist trial—Chamlee went to Scottsboro with a bodyguard—had to keep Brodsky in courthouse to keep him from mob—interdenominational Ministers raised $50.08—special committee about April 4–5—got Roddy to go about March 30—ILD [the Communist International Labor Defense] showed up about April 10–12—White came down May 1 or 2—broke off with ILD April 20.

Contradictions in girl's story—about men, about mills boy made to lie about being nineteen—fourteen-year-old Wright boy got mistrial—prosecutor didn't ask for death sentence, but eleven jurors in favor of it—one didn't believe in capital punishment—one boy beaten up.

—The blond wheatfields under the long Tennessee mountains, darkish and bluish in the distance, under a pale blue sky.

—*St. Louis.* Industrial, but a comforting disorder, evidences of grandeur and pride—the Unique Building: old black house, with stone-fruit decorations and ram's head over door, harboring studios and manufacturing companies—demolition of whole blocks—big library, civil-courts building monolithic with sphinxes on top, scratched figures of justice on front—vast Romanesque State House and other building, with genuine park around them, luxuriant with grass and psilanthus leaves—loud Harvey lunchroom, Middle Westerners—green electric signs in gloomy station.

—*Kansas City.* Good-looking girl, Fort type [allusion to EW's friends Louise and Henrietta Fort], both robust and well dressed—vast station, place where you take trains with high oak-coffered roof—great display of electric signs, all apparently converging on station: Sherwin's Paint, with its red drip over the world; Coca-Cola in bright red and blue neon; ethyl gasoline, red letters of name in the middle of red circle with blue rim shoot out yellow scintillations, which get longer and longer till they pierce beyond the central circle and make the whole circle go satin-white with thinner red letters on it and a thinner blue rim; sign advertizing neon-tube signs. —Enormous rectangular building with red letters along top: Business Men's Association—a slender illuminated shaft and, farther away, the far tops of celestial castles, illuminated with fine ivory light—contrast to the neon-tube signs.

—*Colorado.** The pale prairie with its palish and dry green grass and its pale-blue sky above—tinny windmills, rare farms with flat houses—rare trees, darker dabs—all the shapes, such as they are on the flatness, are little bunchy dabs, the sage-grass clumps, the trees, the clouds—the dry pale sky, an occasional bank scrolled with erosion—a few fields put under cultivation, a slightly richer brown—the prairie beginning to be dotted with slightly darker clumps—all an even pale water color—a herd of small wild brown steers running together a little distance and raising dust—a sprinkling of orange black-eyed susans, some reddish chunky people that look like Indians—a crease of land rising in the flatness, queer, not hills, a crease of earth with a sharp slightly overhanging edge—wild horses walking together, stopping to graze or stretching up their heads—light and lovely white clouds spread out like woolly suds in the sky and intensifying a little its tender blue—a boy with two goats, the only human being yet seen. —And then two dim blue forms

* See "The Enchanted Forest," *Jitters,* pp. 193–206; *Earthquake,* pp. 348–60.

of mountains outlined on the blue sky as if they were painted there, lightly drawn and washed in with water color, faint heavier blues and light browns—now we have lost them, they have slipped behind the prairie—the sage grass is gray now—now clear lodes of snow in a farther range of mountains which has just come into view—square mud huts, made out of the pale clay: Indians?—a little spread of fresher green, the clay has been dampened here, a water hole—riding toward rugous grimmer cindered hills—mud houses, bigger trees and getting common—big buff dandelion balls in the grass, a harvested field with little low mounds of grass—a clay colored [settlement] up and down on low rises of ground—now we are in the midst of the settlement and the hills—a clay-colored hill, stony and broken as a quarry, with a sign on top of it: Trinidad.

—The thin constant ray of the copper telegraph wire going with us all the way—threading the brown hills and the blue sky—paler against the white clouds, redder against the green banks with their redder rocks.

[EW traveled west from Chattanooga and met Margaret in New Mexico. She had brought Jimmy from Santa Barbara, and Rosalind, with Stella, joined them. Boyd's Ranch was a dude ranch high in the mountains, 8,000 feet above sea level, near Bland, originally a gold-prospecting center of 15,000, now shrunk to a ghost village with only a handful of people and two old prospectors who had never been able to tear themselves away. New Mexico seemed to Wilson the best possible antidote to New York, and he was deeply stirred by the landscapes and forests of a kind he had never seen before. With his interest, from his earliest days, in the American Indian, he explored their villages seeking to discover if their "communistic" way of life provided good government.

He visited the caves of the prehistoric cave dwellers which had earlier fascinated the novelist Willa Cather. In Taos and Santa Fe he looked critically at the artists and bohemians, many living there because they had tuberculosis. The towns were attractive, but his final judgment was they had "about the worst set of artists and writers to be found anywhere." However, he saw something of the poet Phelps Putnam, in whom he was interested; he met Georgia O'Keeffe, and the elderly playwright of another generation, Langdon Mitchell. At Taos he encountered the echoes of D. H. Lawrence's passage half a dozen years earlier, and met Mabel Dodge, the thrice-married "culture carrier" (as Lawrence had called her), and her husband, the burly Indian, Tony Luhan. He also saw the naturalist Ernest Thompson Seton, and Paul Strand, the photographer.]

Margaret at Boyd's Ranch. Good-looking in whipcord riding pants and brown jersey and brown man's-brimmed hat, bestriding her horse with Pool boots too big for her—pretty chestnut horse, with mane and tail of more faded mousy brown, that became her—a biggish horse, she sat it with her solid biggish bottom, legs firmly sticking out and holding on either side.

Ride to ranger's cabin. Deserted remains of prospector's log cabin in high green hollow—the great pines that seemed to rise from the bottom of the valley and rise to the very top of the mountains (yellow pine, blue spruce)—we would pass them along the trail at midheight—(little purple shooting stars—great quantities of white trillium and high lavish-leaved mullein-like stalks, rare red flowers—that marvelous mythological valley, towering white aspens, Spanish names cut horse-high on their trunks—white skulls and bones of horse and steer—pines fallen with branches like skeleton ribs, too, fallen aspens, one broken over the trail, so that we passed under it—a great grove, all the white flesh of aspens like the legs and necks of antelopes—the enormous solid mat? hot-water bag? of smooth gray cloud covering the valley—the bright white clouds against the blue sky—the dark green dentelated skyline along the top of the mountain—the view from the top, with its rich dark greens and greens darkish blue—blue smoke rising from somewhere: a forest fire?—the mist shafts of light from the clouds, when it began far-off to rain—on the way back, the aspen trunks in the shadow of the forest, and, as the sun began to set, they were like some downpour of long thick gray lines of rain—it was strange to be able to climb so easily, to be traveling, as it were, in mid-air and able to look down into the valleys—the tinkling, when we set out and when we came back, of the bells of at first un-seen cows—those clouds and mountains must have given the Indians a grandiose religion—the cunning little fattish horned toad, with his grouchy and sullen look, that we found when we tied the horses and sat down for a drink at the top—a little strange kind of frog that seemed to have orangish markings.

At Boyd's, at night, the moonlight made a sort of mother-of-pearl effect on the uplands to the left behind the house—to the right, the clouds were luminous white against a dark blue sky, with a few stars, from an invis-ible moon—I had never seen such an effect before.

The Indians. Afraid of owls—dignity of squaw, speak-ing occasionally to her husband in a low voice in their language—story of the captured Pueblo girl, married to a Navaho, she cuts his throat, the talking scalp which brings her home. —Buffalo hunt and rain and cloud music to the accompaniment, sitting in the swing, of a well-sustained rhythm on the drum. —Tactless questions of the Albuquerque jeweler on the subject of the Indian who had whipped his son for using modern farming implements. Their sunrise call—singing at night, chant that would end in a strange kind of yelp or grunt, repeated, it seemed, too many times till the stanza or whatever it was started again.

—Little four-year-old Boyd boy to his mother: "Come on, Cattle Kate—do your stuff!" — "This horse is gentle as a kitten already—hey!"

—*Margaret,* when kissed, looks up with clear gaze, as who should say, "What now?"—the way a horse, when you pat it, cocks an ear.

—When we started out in the car for Taos, all the sky was suffused, as if for a storm, with a delicate blue-black ink, in which the Sangre de Cristo Mountains seemed dissolved—then later, when we looked back, the foreboding black had begun to disintegrate, with here and there a white cloud detaching itself from the dark background—*before this, however,* one of the hills showed a queer light green quite different from the color of the others, as if it were a chameleon changing among chameleons that still kept a dark self-protective slate, the pines giving the effect of the little pigment buds of its skin, and the long backs of the mountains the effect of lizards sprawling on top of one another. —In the foreground everywhere, the dry flesh-colored pink of the clay, spotted with dark-green clumps—chalk pink.

—At Truchas, in the morning, as I climbed the hill, the golden uplands in the light, white to the east—the primitive farms, with their irrigation—the shadowy soft pinkish-bluish-tinted mountains to the left.

—The thin and flimsy arroyos, but quivering, clear and alive—surprising, gratifying life and freshness in that dry and desert land.

—Coming into Peña Blanca, the fragrance of the cottonwood—lemon verbena?—and the cotton shreds float-

ing in the air—the smell of the grass and corn, strange
after the dry barren heat.

July 4, 1931. Starting out for Bland about four—sky
blue white mottled with cloud—forest getting darker
and cooler—when you looked up under long stalks of
aspens, you saw the tips lit with sun, and you heard the
leaves always way above—now, on one side, the clear
grove of nude long aspens; on the other, beyond the
gulch, the aspens against a dark dense pine forest getting
mysterious with night—on the high trail, we seemed almost on a level with the tops of the pines across the
valley, where the leaves of the aspens, always [tw]itching,
showed fine against a sky where the sun, white and clean
like the aspens, was setting—Margaret's thick little shape
in its brown jersey and white collar, her hat off, her hair
longish like Greta Garbo's, and booted above the horse's
brown rump—the loud howling of a steer never seen—
the valley dark-green with blue spruce that feather the
great hillside with peaks, like the trough of an enormous
wave—all darker and cooler in the forest, only the brightness above the mountain to the right, then a sudden afternoon brightness when the trail came into the sun—to the
left, a clearness almost of morning of distant bright vistas
hovering in the tops of the trees, which presently became
the mountains toward Santa Fe in faint and exquisite
colors, hanging like a mirage, almost iridescent with pale
green, blue, yellow, and pink like a sunfish, and above
them the faint blue sky and the late sunlit clouds which
seemed stained with the yellow of the desert—later, behind the brown and pink pines, becoming a sandy pink,
and finally, above pink-lined cliffs full of holes suggestive of cave dwellers, softened by distance from the rose
brick of the road and brushed with the dim green of
pointed pine—the clouds, a long flat queer line, were becoming a redder sand-pink—finally (the cloud) solidify-

ing like a pink peak solid (?), then just as it had been a moment ago.

Bland. Old trestle, old rusty corrugated-iron wood-burning powerplant and rusty round tanks—stove in scales—house keeled clean over backwards—front end of roof resting on façade and back end on ground—little cramped boxlike rooms of 1898 hotel that seemed higher than they were long or broad—one long hall with ten bedrooms—tiny steep narrow stair—steer's horns in the dining room—man who had bought it had gotten irritable and nervous keeping books at Phoenix, etc.—old register, names from Lowell, Massachusetts—utter darkness in the gully, but when you went up, you saw, at the top of the notch, a lavish night sky of stars (a slice of the Milky Way) all twinkling in that direction.

—Margaret said, "Well, the bed has good springs, anyway!" and sat down on it, and it sank like dough—wooden bed varnished and with fancy flower perforations at the head, which reminded me of one we had had at home in Red Bank—brownish-yellow wallpaper with indistinct flower bunches, pretty dismal this—plank ends in the ceiling didn't quite come together—bright green, red, and black flowered curtains, evidently put up by the new people who had just bought the place—no chamber pot or slop jar at first—window that wouldn't open and had been broken both above and below, evidently with people trying—utter silence—voices from below, laughter—tall lanky brother-in-law, who talked Navaho and knew a lot about the Indians—explained the legend of the storm (the house split in two and turned away, so that it would not face wrong, storm ensued) on the Navaho blanket on the wall—a greasy pack of cards, a stove, heated—too hot—for the guests?

—Down at the bottom of Bland Canyon, under the perforated cliffs—

—raw pine boards—old saloon, with roulette table and

bar—spittoons, jail, safe—prospector there since 1893—
GOLD DUST IN THE AIR—*Angelus*—cans—paper through
windows—old bakery—$10,000 worth of equipment lying
around—Phelps Dodge or Rockefeller—Ed always had
creased clean blue shirt—would get drunk for days and
point out the weak points of one another's phonographs—
Al gave his to Ed and got a new one—Al looks like Swin-
burne—took a long ride in first speed—sheepherder got
on and showed them how to shift it, but they put it back
again—Al (or Art?), the son of an attorney in Santa Fe—
hadn't been there since his father died—Ed has a mouth
of teeth worn down to the gums—nine in precinct of
Bland (sixteen now)—swung it for sheriff who hadn't
been convicted of cattle stealing—company must have
put million and a half or two million in it (Bland and
Albemarle), only got half a million out—had about 600
inhabitants apiece—most old miners in ghost towns plumb
nutty—Ed is seventy-seven, violating every rule of health—
drank, lived on ham and eggs, shut himself up tight in
winter—stack of matches in spittoon—an old calendar and
a turkey feather—Jenks had same diseases as Fall, cirrho-
sis of the liver, we used to call it hobnails from drinkin'—
no relations, but wouldn't talk about family—hadn't been
to Albemarle for thirty years, said it had changed—thinks
Bland the only place to live—Art (or Al) reads Funk
and Wagnalls Unabridged Dictionary—somebody used to
steal Ed's cattle, and he finally gave up ranching.

Aspens. With trunks that look as if they had been
whitewashed and others like cream-colored flesh and
others that seem flecked with gray ash near the bottom
of the boles and seem to have ashes at the base—groves
of trees so fine and thick that, blurred below by the blue
spruces, they seem almost a whitish mist—as thick as
grass—when the forest drops away into a hollow, they
seem even more insubstantial and mistlike

—black nipples or strange open eyes

—a great red cigar-box-colored pine—the sound of a bird like the frail vibration of the ringing of a silver bell— a sheet of silver shaken and ringing exquisitely in the forest

—little pink, red, or purple flowers disproportionately small

—the trunks of white elephants

—in late afternoon, a cool iron white

—on the top of the hill in the canyon—the green inside, like the palm of the hand of the canyon, was all gold-rusted with small sunflowers (the New Mexican state flower)—galloping through the sunflowers (mid-July)— and up on the hill, another bright rust color of little red bells, to which hummingbirds, tobacco-brown, with heads and throats metallic coppery red, flew with a whir as loud as a distant aeroplane motor, which one mistook at first for some roar of a distant bull, and then away over the green abyss, beyond which rose the beautiful uplands, which, rounded though the mountain slopes were, seemed almost as flat as a tapestry, the white aspen stems painted on in groups too regular not to be a human pattern, and, away, away above the top pasture, smooth, sunlit, tender green, below the tender blue sunlit sky, where smooth white clouds almost rested on the mountain. The bugling and trumpeting of bulls and cows—the tinkle of hobbed brown horses away up on the mountainside. Some rank big-leaved mulleinlike plant that grew in the marsh bottom of the canyon and that since we had last been there, had blossomed in little whitish uninteresting flowers, inconspicuous among the leaves, like the flowers of a century plant.

Weather. Funny variable weather—dark clouds threatening a storm just close above us, then gone, the sun hot and too bright to read, then a breeze that chills you a little—one quarter of the sky always innocent blithe blue and white while raindrops may be falling where one is, rain clouds constantly shifting, disappearing, turning up in a new place darkness, freshness, bright sun, a breeze

—Where the bears hunt honey and the mountain lion drops on his prey—bobcats—an occasional lobo wolf is seen.

—Jemez crater, the Baca location, buffalo caisson (?), that marvelous wide green valley in the sky.

—Spanish names on trees, imperfect hearts, a palm.

—When it rains, the aspens look greenish-yellowish like glazed kid.

—white trunks which become dark above against the luminous sky of white and blue

—fallen pines like dead centipedes, like picked fish spines or red dust crumbling into the leaves

—blue-purple bergamot

—aspen limbs with branches lying on the ground like the crooked yellow ashes of Fourth-of-July "snakes"

—Oriental language written in ash along the base of the trunks—eyes with branches protruding from pupils

Valle Grande—the Baca location, where the cattle look as small as the troupe of bedbugs in the bed of the old man with his burros at the spring, filling his wooden casks with a tin cup, the sheep as small as mushrooms in the road—the shadow of a great cloud swallowed up by the immense crater—the sky with white clouds that look as if they were painted on a blue china jar.

Frijoles. Riding along the spine of the mesa—the immense canyon, you look way down, as if into the depths of a deep lake, at the roofs of the little square houses among the trees—the perforated reddish cliffs—wild grape, hops, and Virginia-creeper vines and mountain

cottonwoods—phlox, bachelor's buttons, tiger lilies, red
poppies, yellow sunflowers in the grass—cabbages and
corn—

They lived in holes in the lava, the spongy rock—
Supreme Biscuits—Borden's Milk, peanut butter, Aus-
tello (?) aux modes de Paris—crude pictures scratched
on the rock.

Dry creamy yellow-pink opalescence toward Santa Fe.
—Splendid grape-juice-colored clouds to the west for a
few moments, as we were flying over the crater, before
they turned black in the night and the full bright moon
of solid silver light came up on the left.
—Blue gun-metal backs and lighter yellowish bellies of
mountains like fish seen through water.
—The Jemez [River] under the light of a moon coming
up out of gray-whitish clouds—you can hear it hurrying
like a person in the dark and when you come up to it
you see it crawling over the stones, then running for all
it's worth where the bed gets narrow—the high meadows
on Redondo look whitish—the grass is wet—the mountains coldish—fresh and wet at night—in mid-summer.
—So high that you can't see the sunset, but only, to the
west, the soft light-gilded gray clouds and the soft thinning light blue of day and, to the east, the upper pines
of the mountain rusted with gilt—only such a stratum
of the lower liquid white and gold as reminds you of
summer furnaces, of colors that glow over the lowlands
and the ocean, so many long trails and roads below.
—Later, the clouds smoke-blue or blue as the blue Indian
meal spread out in thin layers on red-hot stoves, and all
on the underside a light cotton-red-gold of which the
real red lies away below.

Indian dance. Man who discovered American soldiers
in ice cave (prospector impersonation)—[Ernest] Thomp-

son Seton and his Indian-lore village—Mabel Dodge and Tony [Luhan], and the girl who lived with the Indians till they put her out of the pueblo—John Collier and the Cassidys—Mexicans—old Roosevelt Rough Rider ($40 pension—run out of Texas—convicted of shooting man four times with a .38, because the man said, "You think you're tough, don't you?"—boozehound's red face) swindler at pop stand—the Paul Strands and Georgia O'Keeffe—Langdon Mitchell and his wife—sheriff—little girl from Missouri with spectacles and white puttees— T.B. motif—sisters and priest—cutup who disguised himself as Indian—Indians in chicken-pulling contest— Youngs (the father was in the advertizing business)— dude-ranch racketeers—oil motif—Billy-the-Kid enthusiast, made up like him—old doctor with lowdown on Indians—Scotch artist—Jewish cowboy—Harvey House cowboy—Hollywood-looking people in Harvey House car, man with curly hair, spick-and-span puttees and green glasses, woman with pouches under her eyes—drunken Indian with square-cut hair and black suit—man who wants to be Penitente and be crucified—a dream pocket— when they get their money—half-witted boy sent West to get rid of him—boy sent West to cure him of bad ways—Indian sand patterns—crooning cowboy with fancy car—manufacturer of Spanish sauces—Cal Clay, the crooning cowboy—dude ranch: $150—priest who painted horses and angels out—Englishwoman.

1. Crooning Cowboy—3. Dude Ranch Racketeer—6. Remittance Man and Prospector—8. Pop-Stand Gyp—2. Woman Who Went Indian—11. Would-Be Penitente— 5. Hollywood Carload—10. Cambridge Cowboy—7. Old Rough Rider—4. Thompson-Seton—9. Missouri Artist . . . Priest Who Painted Out Pictures.*

* See "Indian Corn Dance," *Jitters*, pp. 206–12; *Earthquake*, pp. 361–5.

Sawmill. Fifty out of work for one that's got a job. Keeping 'em on so that they won't get IWW ideas—in Albuquerque, they're goin' around and wantin' to shoot somebody—they don't know who, but they want to kill somebody. Dabblin' in bootleg whiskey or stealin' somebody's milk cow. —370 people—sayin' that the government's no good—I think that the government could be improved in lots of ways, but I wouldn't want to see things changed so they were Bolshevik. I figure there'll be a third man in the next election. Everybody knew that Hoover was a son of a bitch—that came out during the war, but there was nobody else to vote for.

—Lumber business all right for a while, but mountains get monotonous. —We have our health when we come here—lots of people come out here to build up their health. —Dances every Saturday night—sandwiches paid for out of wages.

—Trucker and family worked for months, earned $11, only got about $7 a week apartment (?)—charged $2 for overalls and for truck part needed (drag rod?)—Sorry, can't pay you—no money, but credit at commissary.

John Boyd. Crack down on him—yelp him down— a bat ranch—I'd never tell ye, though—moanin' like a coyote—shenanigans—we shoot tourists if they get hurt— just too bad.

Margaret
Wines, beers, and liquors
fairly gay about life
Men have more sex than women—organs more exposed—
    have more ideas wafted to them somehow.
Where does the drinking water come from? (The regu-
    lar water was too full of alkali to drink.)
Ogilvie, Ogilvie, Ogilvie—aunt, aunt. (When I had asked

her whom she was talking about, and she felt too tired to explain at length something she had already explained.)

I said there was a cunning little young snail on the door outside, thin, shell and body, head, neck and eyes modeled in an almost transparent paste. She said, on the point of going to sleep, in her hurried half-articulate way: "Don't bring it in!"

Camilla [Margaret's sister, married to a clergyman, Perry Austin] had told her reproachfully that she never saw her old friends any more, and she (Camilla) had made an engagement two weeks ahead for them all to go to Sandyland together—Margaret forgot it. —"All that muggy crowd I hate."

—would feel muggy in the morning.

[Here, and in the following pages, EW uses several Indian terms:

katchina—ancestral spirit bringing rain, or an elaborately masked impersonator

kiva—men's meeting room, round and partly underground

morada—a meetinghouse or chapel of Penitentes

koshare—member of Pueblo Indian clown society representing ancestral spirits in ceremonies invoking rain and fertility.]

Teresita Baca's house. Deep dull rose brick of hematite—sharp, definite, acrid, no cut in stone—threatening Buddy with kitchen knife: "I weell cut your throat!—You see thees knife," etc. —Put her hand on John Boyd's shoulder when she came to greet him—white foam of suds on her arms and in middle of her black hair—white bath towel around her head; later, bright red plaid blanket (red blankets on top of Pueblo houses watching dance—hyenalike, coyotelike dogs—one sat down on its tail and bent over like a spring to chew something it took to be a bone). —Look of agony on her face when she had to leave Boyds—screen door, brown saddles hung up, wool for bedding spread out, pale blue and yellow band below, darker blue woodwork for door, inside: warm, bright, and colorful interior—red, black, and white Navaho blankets on floor—two beds with crocheted coverlets, pillow with "No cross, No crown"—German heilige Maria and Jesus in tin and red- and orange-ribboned frames—commercial calendars, Kewpie dolls, Santa Claus, dolls Teresita and her sister had had, one on either side of the bureau, cushion on chair with the following poem:

> The world is wide and the world is grand,
>   And there's little or nothing that's new,
> But there's nothing worthwhile but the grip of the hand
>   Of a friend that's tried and true.

—Lace curtain with peacocks on it, through which a mechanical monkey on a string between the curtain and the window could be dimly seen, big purple and blue paper ropes with Easter baskets, with yellow chicks and eggs in them, hanging on the end, two sewing machines, the tall cylindrical breadbox—tin roof ladder to upper floor—blue woodwork—white and blue striped screened porch—living room (with beds) all yellow, with low light-blue dado and dark-blue ceiling and beams above— red-brown ceiling and beams in kitchen—porch with colors reversed, yellow dado, blue walls. —She gave us blue wasp's-nest fish-food biscuit, which she wrapped up for us to take in a newspaper—two comfortable thin-stripped green rockers suitable for a summer porch—an all but faceless green katchina, with a matchstick nose, the green spruce sprigs tied around it—yellow dado, sky-blue walls, roof and vigos painted a darker blue (Teresita told Margaret they had lately had them repainted and asked her how she liked it)—roundish ovalish mirror, inlaid in yellow—painted mud of wall—everything on walls symmetrically arranged—on bureau between dolls, an elegant gilded crucifixion under a bell glass, and beside it an iron Buddha from an Albuquerque curio store, scenes from the life of Christ.

—Her proud beautiful eyes, with eyebrows incised, clearly marked and black, in the shape of the strokes in Sanskrit characters or on Babylonian stones, like her no's, her monosyllabic replies, against her skin, olive-pale still from the death of her mother—the mother had been suddenly taken, refusing to go to the hospital at Albuquerque, felt cold in her side, tried to burn it out, had doctor twice, it was evidently her kidney, died, and was buried next day. "My wife was a very good housekeeper, but I lost her," old man Baca said—his fine grinning smile—teeth whitened with grubs?—rather unsteady eye that didn't meet yours long—according to Boyd, he had probably talked them into letting him and Teresita out of dancing—I said I supposed he didn't dance now—"No: perhaps next year." —I said that John Collier worked hard over Indian Defense—"He is very earnest." —Dancing not hard work—they didn't have a leader—they knew—could tell by the— He paused. "Music?" I suggested. "By the music." —When I asked Teresita why they didn't have the Pecos bull [a burlesque bull fight that I wanted to see], she said, "Maybe they are too lazy." —Accuracy of Jesús (old Baca) about figures and dates. —Had the Pecos people (twenty of them) come about a hundred years ago? —"Ninety years: they came in 1838." —Were the bloods of the two peoples pretty well mixed up? —"Yes: they are."

—Handsome rich-brown-colored sister, with little boy

with round black pupils and irises the solidest, roundest, and blackest I ever saw, like marbles made of some polished black metal, but more than this, with light, dark and opaque though it was, of human sight, of the soul, in them.

—The lovely tender inflections in Teresita's voice, even when she was being teased, which contrasted so beautifully, so touchingly, with her laconic mordantly accented answers.

—The dried beef, thin, red and white fat, crawled over by flies, on a line in the kitchen—on the stove, stuffed with kindling and the door left open, a big saucepan boiling two tin cans of some kind of cream for a pudding—buckets of water, with hollowed-out half gourds floating in them—a fireplace, still the hearth of a primitive house, where a coffeepot was set on a charred stove.

—the prickly gray corrals of branches

—the stinking shit-house used by all that side of the pueblo

—the lush-looking big-leaved greenery among the barren hills with their darkish dried green corresponding to the vivid dark but dried blood of hematite—eroded mesa—forms like big primeval altars, or seeming to be consciously shaped without being even so human as that

—Only one candystand at the dance, with big white, red, and black chewing-gum bullets, chocolate bars and shabby peanuts

—Coming down out of the kiva, men forwards and women backwards—squaws all uniform, big-bellied with long black hair and small feet and the high green mesa headdresses on their heads—one wears hers a little bit crooked—they were tied under the chin.

—Teresita: "Mercy!", when it was suggested that she might get a medicine man to say a spell over her

—Her gesture with her hand over something outrageous or funny—probably learned from the whites.

Leaving New Mexico. Between Peña Blanca and Albuquerque—above the speckled brown slope, the dark hard blue hills under the long streak of white clouds that looked conventionalized—whalelike shapes outlined in purple against the other, as if they were on another plane—but strange Indian spirits in them—as if they were painted on a blue jar—Mexican boys holding out cans of plums

—morada across the street from Mr. Boyd's—corpse dragged out every day for three days

—One of the surveyors grabbed him playfully by the head: "Don't do that! I was raised a pet."

—Money that he didn't invest in some land, where there was going to be an irrigation improvement—could have postponed payments on some acres till others had risen in price—"I knew how I'd gotten that money—I didn't want to invest it recklessly."

—"Tiger piss" from in back of Mexican dance hall.

Arizona: the dark hills with the plain bare gold dying behind them.

Flora. All kinds of stars of little asters, white, purple, and yellow—turtle-headed snapdragons (glaucous), maroon beardtongue, and little red flowers almost exactly like beardtongue but ending—(evidently?) a kind of phlox—in stars and painted cup—a light vermilion, so vermilion red among the sunflowers—purple tufts of bee balm—little darkish bluebells—the purple mariposa lily, with its queer speckled heart—ragged drooping-petaled New Mexico sunflowers—purple mints—pale purple-pink needle-tongued onion blooms—fresh flimsy mallow flowers growing beside the little stream, white flimsy, moist after the rain, semi-translucent with reddish-purplish pollen on end of white pistil—a pretty, slightly floozy flower—the big yellow primroses have the same attractive perishable-looking quality, large half-liquid drops of flower.

—little clusters, stars, bells, tufts, and blooms.

—sebizia

—woods sprinkled with pink, purple, vermilion, carmine, yellow, rusty or pale maroon—a simple red and white and blue and yellow

—Strange that a bird and a moth should turn out both so much alike, as in the case of the hummingbird and the hummingbird hawk moth—and that a snapdragon and a phlox should be almost indistinguishable except for the little star of the latter exploding at the end in the New Mexican mountains.

Carlsbad. The cave was opened up, about five or six years ago, by an old cowboy who drank—the government took it over, and the superintendent fired the cowboy—they overdid exploiting tourists—Carlsbad a one-bank town —discouraged new business enterprise—didn't want any there—a car going away had a sign on it saying, "Go to see the Carlsbad cave, but don't stay in Carlsbad."—Fireworks reflected in the Pecos River.

Bland. Lemly comes from Michigan. —Everybody would be delighted in winter if they saw a little bit of sun someday—thought there were other things in life besides making money—father had worked with Ford and thought he was crazy and told him so, could have gotten in on the ground floor of the Ford Company—tried to restore cliff dwellings and got sat on—Lemly can't fish on account of back, which was broken when he fell out of a

tree or was bucked by a bronco or something at the time
he was a forest ranger—gets a pension now—sometimes
forgets about his back and dances or lifts something up—
sexual and ethnological library—had had typhoid twice
and was afraid of the hotel well—appalled by Ed's teeth,
every one of which a dentist would say he'd have to have
extracted—his own teeth bothered him a good deal.

Old Man Boyd said that the Indians' government,
which was more or less the same as their religion, fitted
them to a tee—whereas our laws didn't fit us anywhere—
nor our religion either.

Hewett: "The greatest focus of ancient population in
the Rio Grande drainage was on the plateau around the
Great Jemez Crater, especially that on the east side,
known as the Pajarito Plateau."*
Rio Grande Valley [information from some book of
reference]—great synclinal trough forty miles wide between two imperfectly parallel mountain ranges—on the
east, the Santa Fe range, a prolongation of the Sangre de
Cristo chain of Colorado, embracing highest peaks of New
Mexico, some over 13,000 feet. On the west, the Jemez
range, made up of subranges and spurs: Tierra Amarilla,
Velles, Gallinas, and Nacimiento—broadly rounded contours with elevated valleys between the ranges—highest
peaks over 11,000. On the east slope of the Jemez range,
almost to the Rio Grande, vast sheets of yellowish volcanic tufa full of caves. Tufa deposits laid down as
volcanic ash and are not to be confused with basaltic flows
that border them north and east and in some places
interbed them, comparatively recent. Place of origin of

* EW apparently is quoting from *Ancient Life in the American Southwest* by Edgar Lee Hewett (1930).

the ash deposit was the great Jemez Crater in the west. This enormous oval bowl, with a long diameter of eighteen miles and a short diameter of twelve, Valle Grande, is the largest volcanic crater on the globe. It erupted many millions of years ago and built up around the crater a plateau over fifty miles in diameter, with an average thickness of 1,500 feet. After which, life of every kind must have had to start all over again in the Southwest.

Pajarito plateau between Jemez Mountains and Rio Grande from Choma Valley to Cañada de Cochiti.

—Small single houses preceded communal houses; lava flow 8,000 or 10,000 years ago.

—This country lies between the Continental Divide and the Great Plains.

—Indians had to go into agriculture because there was so little game and wild fruit.

—They started in the foothills, where rock shelters were plentiful, and if irrigation was necessary, it could be had by diverting small streams—large rivers called for engineering skill.

Old Man Boyd looks like Justice Holmes—his shy uncertain way of laughing when he has said something.

Mrs. Boyd drawing down her mouth over "It wasn't a hotel—we just had friends stay with us."

Ted Paramore as koshare (imaginary): fixed shoes, kilts, and headdresses for the dancers—toward the end, urged them on with watermelon—did regular gestures with a banana—raided the pop, cake, and watermelon booths between performances. —[Details that follow are real.] One of the koshares was fat, with a double cornhusk topknot and white circles like spectacles around his eyes: looked like a fat devil. —One of them caught a child's yellow balloon that he saw getting away from her and gave it back, after dandling it for a moment out of reach.

Coming to Santa Barbara. Coming into atmosphere of clean sheets, bright fresh blankets, sun, the little garden and the patio—the smell of a nice summer cottage—bright curtains, ornaments.

Yacht races. New harbor—every two years—Morgan Adams lost and was sore as well, got sore at one of the crew and threw something across the deck—had been down to Guadalupe and the island where the sea elephants were, said they were very tame—people roaming around on the water in a launch, stopping to get drinks, talking about Reggie Fernald's drunk—somebody said somebody else was so low he could wear a silk hat and go right under a snake.

New young Mrs. Adams pretty, something like Louise Fort: blue shoes with silver straps—hard Western accent combined with broad *a*'s evidently acquired at finishing school; "Morrgan said cahzyully, 'He hasn't got a chahnce!' " —Blond man with spectacles, who is Adams's right-hand man in the bank as well as on the boat.

Man named Dalton* who would sail with the mainsail upside down or sail over rocks or anything. Plus fours and melon-striped white golf stockings—face coarse, but rather sharp cut—blond boyfriend in bright blue, with bright-red face, who uncorked an obscene and powerful laugh and seemed to be jealous of Dalton. Told about winning the Indianapolis cup, which got bigger and bigger as he described it and gestured. Like Adams, he is in the loan business—"I do, I don't clip." —No use trying to get money out of the rich now—have to work on the poor—their radio program: If people didn't want to borrow, they'd be glad to advise them—much mirth over this.

* He had formerly managed the Miramar Hotel in Santa Barbara. See *The Twenties,* p. 466.

Dalton's yacht: radio, framed butterflies, brass naked woman on horse, rich elaborately patterned garnet upholstery, gaudy orange lights, whorehouse atmosphere of big cabin, bookcases, *Thaddeus of Warsaw*,* a lot of old-fashioned books—when they asked you what you wanted to drink, it always turned out you had to have a Manhattan, which was served by a Jap, with its cherry, in a big whiskey glass. Merle didn't want to leave, was all curled up on the sofa with Dalton. —The boyfriend had come from Seattle, where they "didn't have anything like this"—the luxury of the yacht.

Had been afraid that, if Adams came to, he'd throw them out—was prostrated in his cabin. He had had an intruder who had gotten in thrown over the side—he had at first been taken for a friend and entertained for some time by the guests.

Dalton is reported to be very brutal: on one occasion, he summoned up his crew of five and told them he'd take them on singly or together, then lashed them to the mast.

The Chancellors. Cacti, two hundred and some species: yellow or green rubber flowers; mammalia with red nipples on pale gray breasts; enormous prickles that were veritable swords; fine invisible prickles that got in your hands without your knowing it and made you very uncomfortable afterwards; hundred-year-old cactus (senilis), with gray hair like an old Indian on top, which got bald in winter, propped up like an aged caterpillar; little ones— a great variety—in little purple or green pots, some with pink waxy pseudo-flowers on pink stems; big cabbages of cactus; agave; sea-urchin cacti balls of needles; black charred-looking cockscombs that bloomed that way; more commonplace cacti like balloon plant; little or big bristling

---

* Jane Porter's novel (1803).

phalluses. —Charlotte had watched one that somebody brought her multiply its leaves and flowers.

Charlotte Chancellor's face: the eyes gentle and pensive, soft, velvety, and dark like the portrait, in a face which suffering and illness had otherwise made sharp and drawn—the nose sharp, sharp lines to the mouth, lines at the corners of the eyes—if it hadn't been for the eyes, it might have been the face of a pinched and sour old maid—eyes without a trace of bitterness.

Phil Chancellor [a retired physician, veteran of the First World War]: the $1 wage cut at Boulder Dam was only the beginning of a general wage cutting—the unions will have to give in to capital—the workers will have to bear the hard times—everybody has had to do without something—committing suicide was weak, meant a lack of courage—he had never, as a doctor, known of the poor getting care any less good than the rich—it was hard to make them do things for their own good, they wouldn't be obedient. —He thought that it was dreadful that in Russia a child should belong to the state—that women should belong to everybody—had read in a book by a Belgian about the immorality among the Russian children: the author had seen two children screwing in the schoolhouse and another looking on and abusing himself. — Flaccid insipid face, florid and fleshy, pale blue eyes— supposed to be a Virginian but has an accent like Paul Dougherty.*

English sealing wax horses on the mantel in the dining room, a medieval knight in chain mail on the sideboard— a red cardinal's cape pinioned like an eagle on the wall.

Poor child confined to his armchair hiding fingerless hands under the table—enormous electric railroad, two

---

* The internationally known painter of marine scenes (1877–1947), who was a member of the Carmel art colony.

glass cabinets full of animals from all over the world,
moving-picture machine—Mademoiselle devoted her life
to him and had everybody else intimidated.

Charlotte's hard loveless not unintelligent black-eyed
half-paralyzed face—as who should bite her lips over life,
which she still aims to enjoy without bitterness against
anyone in particular. She had been pretty as a young
girl—a portrait of her over fireplace.

Kimmy, daughter of friends, visiting them—on her way
to dinner and party at Beach Club—very pretty, like a
cigarette ad: slim arms and dark-eyed face tanned dark,
white evening dress, shoes, blue with silver straps, that
arched her insteps very high—self-possession, shellac of
sophistication—dinner late but she declined milk—but was
glad that Charlotte had made her drink that glass the
other night.

Phil didn't have electricity in his camp, because he had
all that here—only acetylene and kerosene.

Terraces with palm vistas.

Chancellor's Ed Wynn observations on medicine: mas-
toid came from same germ as athlete's foot—we used to
call it eczema; Havelock Ellis got rather pornographic in
his later years.

Family party at Sandyland. Uncle Starbuck Macy from
Nantucket, with his humped back; collected Early American furniture; he told them to peel the fig for him and
take him out and feed it to him.

Uncle Alden Boyd from Albany: had come out on account of his lung; had a ranch which didn't pay any more
but which he still liked to live on, though his wife didn't.
"There are a lot of little pledges of love here"—and more
coming—why did they have to play around the house
when they had the whole beach; he snatched away the
dishes almost before people had finished and washed

them up—had to pay the fiddler—people had to sit and chatter and chatter.

Both of the old gentlemen then went and sat in their cars and read the Sunday paper.

When some hoboes got into the Sandyland house once and left bottles and candles around, they asked Margaret whether she knew anything about it. Mrs. Waterman told Margaret that she was so glad the window had been broken while she (Margaret) was away, so that there was no possibility of her having done it.

Las Vegas [I went to Las Vegas to do an article on the Boulder Dam strike*]. Park full of people in blue overalls and khaki shirts—low flimsy white town with greenery—silver Standard Oil tanks, with sky-blue band around bottom, harmonized, as if by intention, with the blue sky and white hard distinct clouds.

Barren mountains full of silver, iron, gold, aluminum, Aztec turquoise, sulphur, that looked as if they would ring if you hit them with a hammer—they looked like strange animals of some non-human period, lying with their heads down—the landscape "all heaved up and then baked again"—flat basin of deep red, with whitish expanse that looked like water—gray and blue mists—blue-inky clouds, as if for a storm.

—Gambling casino—bar—horse-racing wheel, red and silver, with mirrors and colored pictures of horses.

Setzer (an IWW† at Boulder Dam): efforts of the liberals like Holy Water, couldn't do any harm—reading one of Upton Sinclair's novels like eating a half-ripe melon: the social thesis spoiled the story and the simple-

---

* "Hoover Dam," *Jitters,* pp. 213–25; *Earthquake,* pp. 368–78.

† International Workers of the World, also called Wobblies and mocked in their day—the IWW being expanded to "I won't work."

minded stories spoiled them as pamphlets—the hero is always a rich young man—the Communists didn't deal with American conditions, they demanded too much in strikes—if you'd tell people that somebody got a kick from going to San Quentin, they wouldn't believe it, but they do get a kick out of it—the stool-pigeon horrors. —His conversation with the farmer: "When the fight comes, I'll at least know which side I'm on, but you won't know whether to side with the farmhands who work for you or with the banker who holds the mortgage on your farm"—the farmer medieval.

CALIFORNIA

Santa Barbara. The enchanting great goofy plumes of
the trees, through which the sun was burning a hole—the
hills behind Montecito, with their faint razor edge of a dim
rampart, dulled with the gold dust of a Pacific late blank
afternoon, the blue, more dull and even than they, dulled
with that gold dust, too—the waste dried light-brown grass
in back of the window of the room where I worked, with
its yellow sprinkling of buttercups—and in one corner,
part covered with green creepers, the old faded green
water tower, like the disused New Jersey windmills—the
gold dust glows a little brighter, then night suddenly
comes—a beautifully clipped smooth-topped long green
privet hedge fencing off somebody's ground from the side
of the road across from the unmowed unfenced empty
field—the pines stood up against the flat gold-dust sunset,
unstirring, unmoved by any wind, like ideal ornaments
on somebody's lawn.

—The white walls of the house and the garden like
snow and the blue mountains beyond them, looking as
light and as easily broken through as snowbanks, too.

—Later, in mid-September, as we were coming back

from Mattei's, the ocean looked dark, almost like the Atlantic, between Santa Barbara and Montecito—dripping with honey—yellow honey of sunlight and blue honey of the sea.

Hollywood. Coast road like dead snake in road—Malibu Beach—barbed-wire fence on both sides keeping people out from Mrs. ———'s Spanish land grant—ridge of rocks like iguanodon's back going down to the sea—California horses and cattle on the tawny hills.

—John Barrymore's wife a soft little doughnut

—"You may have a human feeling, but it's not a picture!"

—Sam Hoffenstein: "All the problems solve themselves." — "Will you people leave me now: I've got to pass a stone for the American museum." — "You see that pink thing? [pointing to Lorraine]—that solves all your problems out here."

Santa Barbara. Ted Paramore talking to little girls on the beach: the stock of virginity was pretty low, wasn't it? —"They've even taken it down from the big board and only list it on the curb." —The ants were nipping him pro and con.

—A eucalyptus with long light-gray trunk and light-gray leaves curving out on one side with lines like a silver pitcher

—*Sunday at the Biltmore Beach.* Looking out at the dazzling band of water, liquid blue that burned white-hot, shot with white heat and shifting? shimmering? like silk— the brown figure of a girl, walking along the waves, would pass before it and look lovely, then as she returned along the path in front of the cabañas one would see her retreating—chinned popeyed face.

Stan Gwynn: "Always a guest, never a host!" (Always a bridesmaid, never a bride.) —Forty-five years old—he had been going to work, but got an invitation to go to China. —He had played two games of badminton—had gone out and swum around raft a couple of times (not)—wouldn't it be awful if we got drowned before he got the drink we'd promised him. —"Imagine my embarrassment!" — "Cupid has him!" — "Don't get that faraway look in your eyes—we'll be all fixed up right away." —Lyman Pratt: "Well, Gwynnheim" . . . —S.G.: "Last night I knew something about everybody in the room—gave everybody advice—a great advice-giving evening!" —Advice about what? —"About nothing! everything! I had one woman's eyes hangin' out on her cheeks: 'Not really! Not really!' she kept sayin'." —He always mixed drinks himself—instinctively ordered for himself—in spite of the fact that we wanted to get sandwiches from the bar.

Camilla [Wanda Lyon's sister, not Margaret's sister] impressed by Stan's family, became social about Wanda's friends, used to reprove Stan at parties—Didn't he think so-and-so was rather common? —Didn't know, had never given her a thought. —People in San Francisco talked a lot about their ancestors.

Lyman Pratt on Sam Untermyer, on suicides, on compound cataracts—the three big men in the latter line all in this country—somebody trained up by somebody else to be the big cataract man.

Stan injecting the old California spirit into the party at the Paseo—hard-boiled, banged his fist on the table: "Who the hell are you?"—talking out of the side of his mouth and sounding more like Al Smith—swung the white wine bottle back and forth on the string of his sombrero, yelling at the top of his voice, "The old oaken bucket! the old oaken bucket!" Camilla remonstrated with him: "We're not sure of a social position." —Stan: "Have you got a

crest? Have you got a crest? [singing and swinging bottle]
Oh, have you got a crest?" etc.

*Leon Walker** makes no sense any more, drunk or
sober—had to sign a whole checkbook of checks before
Ted could get one that even resembled human writing—
Camilla thought it was a shame, too, because his mother
and grandmother adored him—now, in his bathing suit,
he looked like a dinosaur: enormous stature and animal
face with no brain—made obscurely insulting remarks:
"You're almost good-looking!"—finally left with unintelligible parting remark.

Janet Fuller, riding on the beach on her polo pony, had
to take insulin for diabetes, and they didn't know if she
could drink at the same time—glorified kept woman?
When you mentioned her, according to Margaret, people
like Bobby Dalton would say, "Janet Fuller: hey, hey!
ho, ho!" —Big blue sunbonnet, long ringleted dyed
golden hair, ugly feet, funnily freckled legs—somebody
had been angry with somebody because she had closed
her eyes when she had danced with the latter, etc.

Frances Paramore [wife of Ted's brother Jim] said she
felt as if she were making the best of the last twenty-four
hours of capitalism.

Fiesta. Kimmy's clothes—at parade, in light-blue overalls, with straps that crossed on her deeply tanned back,
blue shoes and thick blue socks that came down over them.
—Spanish costumes, with short skirt and red shoes for
fiesta party, round things over her ears. —Smart dark-blue
traveling suit, with angular-cut sleeves that came down
over her elbows and a collar that corresponded, when she
came down to the beach to say goodbye to boyfriends the
day she was leaving.

---

* Walker came from a wealthy Minnesota lumbering family.
See p. 722.

—*Parade.* Indians—Drake's sailors—pirates—Spanish—couple on horse, girl riding in front of man, horse dancing and cutting its capers—good-looking women of Spanish families in coaches and calèches—*Cielito Lindo*—wonderful creamy, coffee-colored, black and white mottled Appalachian horses, dancing and doing their stuff, silver-patterned saddles and silver-studded sombreros—some of them had come miles—the Bear Flag—an impersonation of Frémont—men on bucking horses dressed like Aunt Samanthy pioneers—clowns on donkeys—the red and orange (California? Santa Barbara?) banners—Spanish houses, American houses on floats, lots of music—the priests from the Mission marching, some of them very tall and impressive, with their brown robes and Franciscan cords and spectacles—they smiled at each other with irony—the Americans, when they first appeared, were made to look very tough, a good idea—"Jubilo" and "Oh, Susannah!" played by a marching American band.

—The palms, the boats and yachts in the harbor (donated, created by Mr. Fleischmann), the hot early-afternoon sun—absolutely unlike the Spanish to be out at that time of day.

—The party at the Paseo: crowded, loudmouthed, close with awning over the top, tinny gold leaves up the columns—Owen's party—the Americans with their bone-rimmed spectacles, the awful taste of the dresses of the older women—the Spanish costumes made you feel how little of their own the Americans have left—the Spanish were Spanish, the Americans are nothing.

[I looked up the Frankfurters,* who were out there, and took Felix to a party in Hollywood where he was right in his element.] The forest of oil wells—derricks—

* The future Associate Justice of the Supreme Court (1882–1965) was then professor of law at Harvard.

on the way to Laguna Beach—as Felix Frankfurter said, unbenign, like druids of eld with beards that hang on their bosoms—like the ghosts of objectionable insects, dry, transparent—like locust shells—as many as a plague of flies which have descended on the land—the sound of one going on jerking by itself in the dark at night.

—The motors ripping at night past the road that leads up from ——— Avenue like the accelerated roar of rockets.

Phil Chancellor's Saturday-night party. Somebody preferred to stay with her grandmother—That's what they call necrophilia, or love of old people (Ted probably said this)—What the French call *pied à terre*, getting off on the right foot—Different kinds of pneumonia: mental pneumonia and the kind of pneumonia you get from lying in bed—San Diego, it's on account of the climate—like Santa Barbara, the wonderful climate—like Newport and Bar Harbor, fine all the year around—When Charlotte's not here, we have champagne glasses all around those shelves. —Merle: "This library's such a cozy room, don't you think so?" — "Do you think it can be the books?" —Lady from New York, who had been obliged to live in Los Angeles—city completely unplanned, her disgust, dirty cracks. —Jim Thorne, simple-minded elderly gentleman who had fire alarm in his house so that he could go to all the fires—finally his wife had it taken out. He was most interested in the man playing the saw, stood up to see, and very seriously called my attention to the fact that he was using a bow. —"Do you think Arthur Ogilvy is a stool pigeon?" (this must have been said by Ted about Margaret's cousin)—*Kamenoi Ostrov* on the accordion. — Phil on unemployment—didn't believe in it, and to hell with it, anyway!—confided to me that he had taken a drink that day, just one drink, which had given him complete aphasia, he had been dizzy, had to lie down. I asked if it was the first he had had—"Oh, no: I'd been drunk for two weeks." —His gallantry: "The heart of me, the soul of me, the feet of me," etc. —His face, a pale uniform alcoholic pink, looked, close to, like a pale-pink tomato whose skin is shriveling up in fine wrinkles where it is just beginning to rot—pale round blue eyes, no eyebrows, bulbous Roman nose. —Always calls people "old dear."

—His bathroom: black shiny bathtub, closet, and seat—toilet paper in unornamental stained wooden rack recalling the jigsaw period, loosely put in so as not to suggest mechanical devices and processes—frieze of grapes and vine leaves along the side of the bathtub—eighteenth-century rustic engravings suggesting an imitation of Callot, engraving of some noble French character, with his title and his claims to distinction in fine engraved French script under the oval—his large flat sky-blue leather slippers—Persian rugs with square-headed and square-limbed animals and men.

—Merle looked like a lace valentine with a little rose at the top of her corsage—sent me to get her purse. —Big sitting room, rectangular, coffered ceiling. —Ted's songs: the ladies wanted more amusement and went and got Ted out of bed after he had passed out—he came down stripped to the waist and did his stuff better than ever—somebody put a flower in his navel.

[Charlotte didn't like Ted's dirty stories and tried to prevent him from telling them, but with no success.]

Art Carey. Charm, with occasional metallic monosyllabic replies. Had studied physical chemistry at Cambridge, surface tension, but was glad he'd quit: they didn't know where they were at. He had always wanted to get into the pictures—this place was lots of fun. —His sister was extremely fond of him: "Pretty appealing" —

"Make a lion, brr-rrr—No, he's tired—just a good dog." — Standing up naked in the bathroom, reading a German novel while pissing. —Should we see what was going on on the Ambassador roof? (Embassy?). —Felt terrible the next morning—regretted death ride in getting up to (Aimee McPherson's) Temple—"so sophomoric"—played piano for Ted's songs—made him bring key down: "Have you turned pansy?" —Reprise: " *'Cause it's memories, memories!*" —Ted's song: *Many happy returns of the day.* —They had pulled a turkey on North Dakota (*Take me back to North Dakota*)—received with silence—but Jim had picked them up with "The Road to Mandalay." — Movie jargon: mousetrap (man hides by posing among waxworks), menace, heavy dog heavy (son of a bitch, no redeeming features at all), light heavy. —Jap servant named Marcel. —The house, though large and comfortable, had a ready-made look and a look of bachelor's quarters—no woman had arranged the furniture or improved the taste of things—silk coverlets on beds. —Ted's and Art Carey's proposed song: *"I've got to get you into my bed to get you out of my mind."*

Lyman Pratt. It had been so hot at Southampton even on the beach that your cuffs were all sopping wet around your wrists—when I mentioned magic, he immediately said that his late father had been—well, only Thurston and Kellar could do the things he could do—he used to have Herrmann or Kellar perform at my birthday parties sometimes, because I loved it so—and they used to play cards together and see if they could detect the other cheating—Father would follow an ace all the way through shuffling and dealing—could always beat the roulette wheel if it wasn't weighted or had an electric switch or anything, you know—until they got on to it—the Colonel [his father]: he would bet on anything—a redheaded girl or a dog crossing the street or anything, and he'd make the chances large enough so that he'd win—no trick about it: just this astonishing actuarial mind.

Ted's story about Perry Austin. In Kensington, Pennsylvania, Perry had taken Ted through the mill—a strike had just been defeated—he showed him an old cross-eyed woman as an example of the kindness of the company in keeping on their old employees—Ted talked to her and discovered that she was the "old bellwether of the flock": "Yes, I can run sixteen machines"—that set the pace for the piecework.

Mattei's. A stagecoach route till 1900—delightful, mild, and easy—the mild and easy hills, like the humps of yellow camels—even yellow hides like mountain lions (of which several skins were hung up in one of the empty stores)—palms and pines in the little town, all easily dispersed fields, frame houses, stores and garages combined with blacksmith, and chicken yards—dusty-looking white oaks and greener live oaks along the yellow roads—dry and all the streams dried up, the middle of September—the coast range like camels—the Santa Ynes [twenty-five miles from Santa Barbara] dark like dinosaur backs and with deep blue creases.

Bright glossy orange thick-wicker furniture, dark thin walls, great big beds with quilts, bright striped cushions—all in rather bad taste and the chairs mostly more or less uncomfortable.

Big stone fireplace—long room, with simple perfunctory desk for registering—longish windows that came down low and looked out on the vine-covered arcade outside—old Gus, eighty-some, a Swede, had been there forty-five years—extraordinarily sweet face, old blue eyes, beard and slippers. —Fossils on mantelpiece and on table under

arcade—scallop shells, petrified wood and moss, the joint
of a dinosaur, an enormous petrified oyster—the gray remains of the ancient sea floor.

Wild doves, black and white woodpeckers and blue and
white long-tailed shrikes (butcherbirds).

Screen-roofed semi-enclosed porch between bedrooms
with sitting room between.

Tanks and gray windmills, the silver-and-blue Standard
Oil petroleum tanks—the little old-fashioned yellow station, with its tiny tracks like streetcar tracks. —Los Olivos.

A slowly revolving spray that made the grass green and
the roses grow.

—*Perkins ranch.* Woman who talked like Aunt Caroline: "pitty well"—didn't like to be asked how many
horses they had—had come out here a widow and married
man who owned ranch—a small one, by California
standards—interest in Perkins's ancestors—old house in
Burlington, Ohio—president of the Burlington and ?
Railroad—long house built like a Pullman car—didn't
know how many rooms—nice big room open on three
sides—Spanish drape: "It has a name but I cahn't remember it." —She felt relief when the Santa Barbara
season was over—people she ought to have ahsked—picture
of Black Hawk, with authentic tomahawk and rose-and-
gray-stained horsehair headdress underneath—pictures of
race horses—so glad to give away books they'd read—
English groom—feeding the foals—beautiful gray and
coffee horses grazing up high on a dry yellow hill.

Reggie Fernald. He had tried to kiss the hand of the
octogenarian head of the Seamen's Union, who had
hauled off and biffed him—was against Stalin, who suppressed individual liberty—Hoover just a stupid son of a
bitch—What was the matter?—He was ready to grab a
gun any day!—perfectly easy to turn the government out.
Next day: came around in early afternoon, still drunk—

insisted on giving Jack Lawson a card to a man in New
York, an editor of the *American*—"If he doesn't treat you
right, would you mind dropping me a line and letting me
know? If he doesn't, he's a lousy bastard. —People differ
from here up [indicating the ears]; below that, they're all
the same. Do you agree with me?" (The first time he
tried to say this he got it the wrong way around.) —He
had been to see a Russian who lived up on the hill: "He'll
tell you a story that will make you sit up!"—he'd been
smart, he'd been in Russia when the what-you-m'-call-it
happened, and he'd come over here and bought three
places, one at Atlantic City, etc., then he'd sold them and
bought a place at Santa Barbara and had struck oil, and
now he was sittin' pretty—he'd been a smart fellow! —We
laughed heartily, and he showed signs of becoming indignant: "Am I as funny as that?" —On his way out, he
thought I was kidding him for wearing a straw hat so
late in the season; he threw it down and put his foot on it,
then tore it in two.

At his own house (with its front lawn, dark for a
California place, covered with ivy and myrtle): dispensing
sherry, talking about upstarts—the man who comes up
from there (gesturing toward red rug, so that Margaret
said she thought somebody was going to shoot up through
a trap door in the floor) is the man who is boss now!

Fremont Older,* he said, befriended criminals: "If you
commit a murder, he loves you, will do anything for you.
What about the wife and the mother and the children of
the person he murdered? Those are the people I think
about!" (He had gotten into trouble himself for hitting
somebody while driving his car drunk.) —His talk about
taking the rival editor of the evening paper for a ride.

"That's my grandfather [photograph]: he was the
governor of [some Eastern state]. My uncle was president

* Editor of the San Francisco *Call-Bulletin* (1856–1935).

of [the] Pennsylvania—not that that means anything!" —
He drank our healths in sherry. —Shaved, white trousers,
blue coat, red speckled tie—sister furious and disgusted.
Had gone down to Republican Convention in Los Angeles
to try to get Kent Parrot and his gang out—had seen
earthquake fault from aeroplane.

Cop with guns in holster brought car for him: "Did
you see that? I told him to go away and come back for
me! Did you see those guns? that's capitalism!—And
there's something wrong with the whole damn thing!"

His story about the party where the movie men talked
in big figures—he had gone into the next room and found
a friend who had disappeared pacing the floor there. —
"What's the matter?" — "All that kind of talk's damn
embarrassing, you know, when you're trying to decide
whether you've got enough money to get new linoleum for
the kitchen floor!"

Nat Brush's* stories about Portuguese who recommended whirling spray to friend, then found out that his
wife had taken it away from behind picture; and about
palomino colt: he came back home and found his wife
in bed with another man, "And, Judge, I want to find
out who the hell it is!"

Hollywood. [Jesse L.] Lasky: "What do you think of
this picture?" —[Frederick] Lonsdale: "I think it's appalling." —Lasky: "But, aside from that, what do you
think of it?"

—The man who had been hiding behind the sets for
years, drawing a salary and trying to avoid having anybody ask him who he was.

—Everything done through somebody: One man had
his own story read to him and then said that it had possi-

---

* Edward Nathaniel Brush (1852–1933), a psychiatrist who
practiced in Baltimore and wrote extensively on mental health.

Edmund and Margaret Canby Wilson in California

Margaret Canby Wilson

bilities as a picture. Another hired a Mexican boy to bring one in and got $500 for it when it was worth only about $50.

—Horace Liveright, who had been making up to Schulberg's wife, found that he was always being passed over in conference when it came his turn to have his opinion asked, and finally went back to New York.

Two Frenchmen hired to make independent translations of an English play, then an American hired to translate the translations back into English, and another Frenchman to compare the translations with the original. They were afraid that the two Frenchmen might have been working in collusion.

—Ted's idea of organizing writers—only about a hundred and seventy-some and fifty, if you got the right ones, would be all you needed.

Margaret. So cunning with black tan-spotted white hound puppy named Pal, with pale wistful yellow eyes—warmth in her voice: "Oh, look at those great big paws! Are you going to grow up to those great big paws? Are you going to grow up to be such a great big goofy dog?" — "Oh, goodness gracious, look at that fire!" —He finally slipped off the couch head first, when I began to read poetry—then she excitedly turned him out. How did she know he wanted to make water? —"He has that look!" — She had also said to him: "Oh, how would you like those turtles?—goldfish?"

He thought he heard her feet in her mules coming toward the garage across the gravel, but it was only the mice in the wall.

—Toward the end of September, everybody gone, "end of the summer blues," fires built, cold outside, and yet that great soft vacuum there: the void. —The tepid Santa Barbara world.

[The following notes on suicides were used by EW in "The Jumping-Off Place," *Jitters*, pp. 253–60, *Earthquake*, pp. 414–20, in which he also used the Coronado Beach Hotel, described below, as a metaphor for death.]

Notes on suicides at San Diego. January–June 1930: 51; September–November 1930: 20; January–July 1931: 36.

January: insane—gas; despondency, no work or money— ch. [apparently EW's abbreviation for children]; ill health, family troubles, no work—cutting arteries.

February: drunk and desperate—poison; desperate over ill health—shooting; desperate financial condition, worry— shooting; deranged—shooting; seeking sensation—bichloride of mercury; financial worry, illness—found in bay; cause unknown—cutting artery; deranged—gas.

March: shot self after shooting wife; no cause—gas; desperate over health—shooting.

April: cause unknown—gas; desperate over health— strangulation; desperate over health—sulfonal and Barbital; cause unknown—shooting; evidently ill health—gas; desperate and financial worry; cause unknown—strangulation; deranged—gas; deranged—gas.

May: desperate—Lysol.

June: deranged—drowning; no work—strangulation; deranged—shooting; health, and failure to collect money— cutting artery; rent due him from tenants—shooting; health—shooting; deranged—gas.

July: family trouble—ant paste; health—shooting; no work—gas; deranged—shooting; no work or money— drowning.

San Diego. 6% of sickness in whole country—24% San Diego—asthma—queer people—the navy—the bums—the people who take in sick lodgers—sick people who expire almost as soon as they're unloaded from the train—real-estate man who killed himself because he'd lost money in the crash.

—Old people lacking support kill themselves through pride; middle-aged people for ill health or lack of money; young people who have done something; girls deserted by husbands; people who don't fit into communities; people trying to run away from illnesses.

—overadvertized climate

—Stabbed himself with meat knife on municipal golf course—they stuff up cracks of door, jump into the bay, drink Lysol, or eat ant paste.

—Sand-colored power plants and hotels, waterside cafés, Bill's Bait House, rummy and freeze-out, naval outfitters, old spreadroofed California houses with a fine close grain of clapboards, that take in sick lodgers.

—the empty California sun

Coronado Beach Hotel. Old hotel of 1887, a masterpiece of its period, in absolutely white and shipshape condition: the five tiers of railinged porches with long steep flights of steps like a ship, slender pillars, white wood fretwork, superb cupolas, red roofs with little white lace crenellations, rotundas with long windows—white as wedding-cake icing, the quadrangle with tall palms and great bushed bougainvilleas around them—in the middle a grotto of rough bark with a Stock Exchange blackboard inside, the inside (portico) has a suggestion both of the deck of a ship and the portico of a colonial mansion, brass points of the compass (inlaid in the floor), thick red carpets, people quietly playing cards in the card-playing room in the evening, enormous menu on the American plan, sheets about the stock market on the way down the broad thick-carpeted stairs to the barbershop—outside, a dream of little galleries, cupolas, and staircases—red fire ladders and fire hose wound on red carts. —Yellow-latticed windows—white companionway—the dome and cupola (American flag) like an inverted top, with the white railing of an observation tower just below the peg, and little dormers like blinking eyes looking out below all around— wide brass-edged steps, brass handles and bars on white screen doors—some architect of the eighties satisfied his dream—lathe-turned rungs like the banisters in old houses —electric lamps like coronets—brown light-looking cigar-box wood—varnished mahogany mantelpieces with round mirrors—darkish in-between rooms with closed grates and big vases—Ladies' Auxiliary in ballroom, explaining the election of officers, with badges: "Mildred hasn't done anything about the corsages"—should they give them to all the officers or just the incoming ones?—black and white onyx gueridons—soft carpets—yellow lamps and candles in rounded dining room—wealth of dormers sticking out at one place on side—upper part of windows stained glass—mirrors, stained banister rails and yellow stained glass with curlicues—stained-glass window of poinsettias— trees labeled like a botanical garden—fine white texture of shingles—tapestries

—wood vistas of seaside shadows

—magenta begonias, rose-red bouquetlike hibiscus, vermilion salvia, coxcomb, fuchsia (?)

—palms on mounds of fern

—sheets of stock quotations

—wicker chairs and soft plush couches

—slight endearing warping of the floors

—pillars rising straight from flags

Los Angeles (the goozly-floofy beach, flou, floozy, goosy, goozley, goofy, floozent, flooey, floozid, foozled, the floofy goosey beach)

—Scriabin's divine bowl in the Hollywood golden poem

—ye olde yellowe gooffe shoppe

—the red brick Methodist church strikes a note of coarse decorum

—the loan and [trust] building black and gilding national securities cathedral—outfitters robin's-egg blue—the grooves of a great gold business cathedral

—coffee whipped cream—a pink peppermint cabaña

—olde imitation real-estate ruins

—a pink-morocco caramel—a pure-white marshmallow of purest driven snow—a peanut-brittle pagoda—a Moorish nougat with embedded nuts

—those palms with their stiff *tignasses* are like little topsy, they just growed

—stretching away toward beautiful Beverly Hills, the super-riviera of the south, where every wave croons, "Sunkitht California," and the goofs hang like ripe fruit

—a yellow villa or is it an old mossy mance, where they've painted the stone crevices on the walls

—that great big tall office building is made of an inferior grade of lime candy which has gone sugary with the heat

—more beautiful girls scrving sandwich specials than any other city in the world—a black and functional sandwich bar that would make Frank Lloyd Wright, Jr.'s heart go pit-a-pat

—At Hollywood, the grcat big *H* on the brown hills is just the shape of the way the gearshift works

—coast road like dead snake and ridge of rocks like an iguanodon's back going down to the sea

Marathon Corporation

—This? or this?—We must have the Colorado Aqueduct

—Polly van Shoppe—Ladies' Hats

—an olde half-timbered Piggly-Wiggly

—general lubrication—standard lubrication

—a 50-watt electric cross above the Hollywood Bowl

advertizing the importation of the Passion Play to
Hollywood

—Hollywood Mentone Knolls: you'd be happy here, too

—Purr-Pull gasoline

—avoid body fatigue—Puritas drinking water

—a wealth of watermillions—avocado acres

—a new car jacked up like a hat in the window of a
fashionable hat shop

—just the finest chummiest chimp in the world recommending the chummy new tire

—the Maxwell Realty Company is just a broken-down
olde picturesque cobwebby shack recalling the cute old
clockmakers of Nuremberg, who would plan you a little
gingerbread cottage that the oil trailers pass at high speed
on their way up the macadam coast road, for about
$15,000, if you include the cunning sea-lion weather vane,
the Paris-green blinds, the blue-blue floozy sea

—the avocado building with its frieze of cute little
pukids

—the Hollywood movie animal zoo—plaster lions, rubber cobras, a bear that you love to touch, in the bamboo
brake of Wesley Park, a phony gorilla with a man inside,
and a mechanical crocodile, a pair of four-inch ball-
bearing dinosaurs

—barbecue

—Mickey the Mouse

—Aimee's Temple

— a ——— apologetic over earning $——'s rent in hell

—the Ritchfield Ethyl Cathedral—Richlube

—Valmont Acres—H. D. Hunnicunt

—flat houses of the early frame settlers, who spun jigsaw scrolleries, cupolas, and gigolos

—false fronts to shops

—you can buy a chow pup or a small walnut farm for
a song—for a theme song you can buy a little pink

Moorish synagogue ashamed of selling itself in Hollywood for $—— a year, but happy as a bride and with all its problems solved

—blue windmill—brown derby—ice-cream freezer

—Sid Grauman's movie theater*—Aimee McPherson's Temple—Babylonian garage

—a light-green house like a lime freeze

—Ritchfield filed for $54,000,000—looted by directors, who had sent in prodigious expense accounts for taxis, sending their sons to Stanford, and maintaining elaborate private suites at hotels

—a field of high black-eyed susans, a walnut orchard, a papier-mâché bellboy straddled gallantly under his double-armed burden of bags against the brown papier-mâché hills—a million assorted god-boxes of sunny-faced pasteboard chrome or buff—a wee wonderful Swiss shilly-shally—igloo and totem-pole golf course, a hot little hacienda, a little *enchilada con queso*—violet-ray gasoline—a bargain in lovebirds and beach lots—a frozen orange-drink stand gone bankrupt—sandwiches

Distant lighthouse going off and on reminds him of rhythmically expanding penis in vagina.

Mr. Ed [Ted Paramore's father; see *The Twenties*, pp. 160–73] used to sing Heine's "Morgen Rot."

Margaret: "Just love's home."
—She had a lot of cosmetics given her by some friend—all kinds of creams, beautifying creams, etc.—used them all and got pimples all over her face.

---

* The theater builder (1879–1950) who built Hollywood's Chinese Theater in the forefront of which hand and foot prints of Hollywood stars were pressed into the cement. Grauman also originated the "gala première" of elaborate movies.

—She gave birth to Jimmy all alone in Sloan's Hospital next to the Negro ward, where she could hear the Negro women having babies every night—it was like being next to the torture chamber and hearing other people being tortured before your turn came—she had an infected kidney: the doctor had told her, when he examined her urine, that she'd have to stop eating everything—Daddy came to see her every day, and he must have bought out Brentano's basement, bringing her everything from the *London Illustrated News* to the Spanish magazines—Camilla was around, but she wasn't much help—Jim was in training camp—they telephoned for Jim and Mother because they thought she was going to die—the nurse had an aviator lover and used to show Margaret his picture, had her mind on him all the time and used to sleep through Jimmy's nursing time, and then Margaret would nurse him for two hours—she thought that was the thing to do—after Jimmy was born, she couldn't see him, but she didn't ask about him for two weeks, didn't even come to the conclusion he was dead, she was in such a coma—couldn't nurse, then suddenly began to, characteristically—nurse always did everything wrong, which drove you crazy when you were sick, shaving her with a blunt razor—she was six weeks on orange juice, with Epsom salts every morning.

—Daddy had given her a letter for Cousin Watty, which she never gave him, asking him to help out taking care of his daughters—was always a little bitter about Cousin Watty's monopolizing the house—still, Cousin Watty had squatter's rights on it.

[*Margaret and Ted*] overdid making free with the Paramores' house—Mrs. Paramore began to treat them with coldness, but they didn't realize it.

—Man in Santa Barbara who apologized to hostess

morning after party (it was really Frances Paramore, Jim's wife) for not having said good night to her, when, as a matter of fact, he had kissed and embraced her and had slipped and fallen on the rug.

Addenda to *Axel's Castle*. Proust's principal hero is a stockbroker, who is played off against the aristocrats, but he himself is shown to be an excessively unhappy man (he has inherited his seat on the Bourse) and a part of a society which is collapsing. —Proust himself with his private wire through to the Bourse—exaggerates and throws into relief all the diseases of the period.

—[Joseph Wood] Krutch's quotation about breaking glass

—Saint-Simon passage—all depends on breaking down a whole set of preconceived ideas—shows that the society is crumbling—what are Proust's preconceived ideas?—that art is the only thing permanent and worthwhile in life.

—Flaubert and Henry James

—Flaubert and Marx

—Marx

—Zola

—Joyce record [an allusion to James Joyce's recording of a fragment from "Anna Livia Plurabelle" later included in *Finnegans Wake*]

Fire Alarm
Humanism 1 and 2
Thornton Wilder 1 and 2
Chapman and Plato?
Limperary Cripples?
Addenda to *Axel's Castle*
Osbert's Career?

Bob Shuler. A city prosecutor arraigned Shuler over the radio for using inflammatory language against the Julian thieves and was fired the next morning by the mayor.

Shuler attacked District Attorney Asa M. Keyes for booze parties and shady meetings with luscious Julian defendants, and he was sentenced to San Quentin for bribe taking.

On the occasion of the Pantages [theater] case, Shuler and Briegleb were fined 75 and 25, and they compared this to the persecution of Jesus.

—jerry-fixing—1929

Duncan Aikman on Shuler [notation from an article]: "He tells his public where the candidate for the city council, who is not quite strong enough on Prohibition, gets his drinks, and in what suburban apartment house the villain of the latest Hollywood scandal dates with his sweetheart. He tells of the Negro male pedagogue's advances to the white schoolmarms in his district. He tells how and where the high-school students are getting their liquor, and what members of the younger set are experimenting with the vices described in Petronius. He tells of the judge who, when a comely witness fainted in his court, revived her in his chambers with ardent spirits produced from the magisterial desk. He tells how long and profound the osculation was between two members of the faculty of a local school—incidentally married to others—when a speeding trolley-car burst upon their sylvan retirement and reduced the engrossed gentleman to mincemeat. And, in a typical burble of punitive humor, he recommends that the surviving lady be tried for manslaughter for leading another woman's husband on." —Blackmailing jurors.

1,233,000 in Los Angeles ('30)—2,000,000 in county—3,000,000 in circulation of papers

—sale of rubber goods—mayor stuck in trolley track—men who took advantage of straps—rope

—dowdy dry-faced women, old men with sparse hairs, whose heads hung forward, a woman with bone-rimmed glasses and a pushed-in nose—dry skins, pasty flesh, colorless faces, clothes without style

—In front of enormous baskets of yellow and orange chrysanthemums, whose perfume sweetens the Sunday atmosphere of the church, under a dome very badly painted with a dingy and indistinct cloudscape, with one electric-light bulb symbolizing Jesus, and an American flag hanging down

As he steps down to administer the sacrament, a man with a blue coat and white trousers gets up and turns the microphone.

Briegleb. Blue coat and white trousers, handkerchief sticking out of pocket, bone-rimmed spectacles, grizzled hair, his expression when he told jokes

—American flag with gold spike, only one basket of flowers, choir behind him in white, white walls, rough beams, better-class audience

—Yale theological accent—hymn—Yale campus and women

—$2.80 for telegram—if religion isn't for sinners—don't believe Christ was a hypocrite

—Porter Iowan and Klansman—Davis fired

—Aimee bringing up the Devil and chasing him away, after her escapade

BACK EAST

[EW returned to New York during the autumn of 1931; Margaret remained for some weeks in California. He crossed a country morally devastated by the Depression. There were bread lines, soup kitchens, and plant shutdowns everywhere. For the first time in his writing career EW was face to face with the lives of all kinds of workers in America; and his reaction was intense and realistic. Large changes, he felt, had to come about. To him the national bankruptcy seemed clear and he was imbued with a certain kind of reforming zeal, a belief that intellectuals had to find specific courses of political and economic action. In October he visited the textile strike in Lawrence, Massachusetts. From Boston he went to Provincetown to work on a play dealing with the Depression, entitled *Beppo and Beth*. Margaret returned from California and at the year's end the two moved into a furnished apartment on West 58th Street. Their neighbors in the apartment above were Harold Clurman, the theater director and drama critic, and the composer Aaron Copland. In his journals of the time EW interpolated the following passage:

"We rented an apartment on West 58th Street from a

woman Margaret knew called Ethel Hutchinson, who owned the house. She had been a friend of Margaret's stepmother, Daisy of the Floradora sextet, and had been kept in solid comfort by Colonel Ruppert, of Ruppert beer, who was also the proprietor of a baseball team. The apartment got little daylight and for me was embarrassingly chichi. The bedroom was done in a subaqueous green and had the elegant white bed of a kept woman's boudoir. Margaret—who sympathized with her father in his flight from her Scotch Presbyterian mother, though he had left Daisy all his money and her mother was now dependent on what was given her by Camilla and herself—had always made a point in New York of keeping in touch with Daisy. In this way she met some of Daisy's friends, who were all middle-aged mistresses, sometimes equipped with gigolos; they got together to play cards in the evenings. Their conversation, Margaret told me, was stodgy and banal in the extreme. Copland and Clurman and his wife Stella Adler inhabited apartments above us. We entertained many friends, frequented the foreign-language film theater that was near us on the same street, and on one occasion were induced by some of my leftward-oriented friends—the Walkers (?)—to give a party for William Z. Foster, at which he answered questions."

Clurman's memoirs (*All People Are Famous*) provides a picture of certain observed tensions in the apartment beneath his own. EW and Margaret were apparently drinking quite heavily. Clurman writes: "I overheard from my bedroom window, directly above his—quarrels that ended with his tearing the curtains from their rods . . . Both she and Wilson drank nonstop." Stella Adler, of the Yiddish theater acting family, and Clurman were among the leaders of the Group Theatre, one of the liveliest of newer groups on Broadway. EW was eager to have the Group do his Depression play, but Lee

Strasberg, its director, disliked the script and told Clurman it was "disgusting." He would have nothing to do
with it.

William Z. Foster, for whom EW gave a reception in
58th Street "at which he answered questions," was candidate for the Presidency on the Communist ticket. He
had been the Communist Party's candidate in 1924 and
1928. EW wanted to know what the party offered as
solution to the economic crisis. With his customary
thoroughness, he was reading "all of Marx's and Lenin's
political papers." He also read the popular Communist
book of the hour, John Strachey's *Coming Struggle for
Power,* and Max Eastman's translation of Trotsky's history of the Russian Revolution. For EW's discussion of
his position as a pro-Communist in the election, although
he was not a party member, see his journal entries on
pages 207–14.]

The kind of thing people said after the crash:

Bourgeoisie: business with Americans like religion—
can't talk about Jesus Christ—can't tell the butcher
you think it immoral to eat meat

—hoping to be the biggest country that ever was—
between the brake and the gas

What they think: equilibrium—prices coming down
so that money buys more than it did—wages will have
to come down, too—the Americans have been spoiled,
the European countries have had to get along by thrift
and hard work, and the Americans will have to learn
to do it, too—they may have to do without their car and
their radio—

This kind of talk seems obscene and shocking, but it is
mostly quite natural. Kindliness and democracy of Americans. That your guess is as good as mine.

—no responsibility, working for revolution
—the suicides of bourgeois
—end of money-making epoch

virtue of saving

we must depend on private charity because relief raised by taxation is mostly bound to go in graft

the only kind of goverment is a monarchy

go back and live as our fathers did (and die as our fathers did)

that the unions have got to submit to wage cuts now—the American Federation has been too demanding

that we have got to learn new uses for leisure

that the workers will have to do without their cars and radios

that the only trouble is people are scared

—or occupying themselves with thinking and talking about something else altogether—literature, a monarchy, sport

a red flag in the attic

pull out for some island

lost twenty-four hours of capitalism

monarchy

leisure

American Federation of Labor

your guess

equilibrium

our fathers

private charity—the dole

Americans spoiled

car and radio

go back and live as fathers did

—Promises and recommendations—Mencken, etc.—end of money-making epoch, catalogue of panics—strong and bold rich people—uncomfortableness of Mr. Southworth

What we get is a kind of democracy trying to be aristocratic and egged on and exploited by capitalism

a wholly unsound kind of [royalty]

—"aristocratic" headwaiter

—class advertizing—advertizing about what a silk hat will do for you—"a wonderful piece of swank"

Western films

—having fun in Europe, cheap living

—no governing class trained to responsibility—everybody grabbing off theirs and trusting to Business

—leisure brings attempts at culture, sport, distinction, but society so unstable that they never solidify into anything of permanent value

—especially has this been true since war (see Beard) [*Rise of American Civilization*]

—vacuous character of cultivated people not attached to a court and absent landlords to a supreme and unprecedented degree—what to do with themselves—despising the business and industrial world which has made their culture and education possible—and the other intelligent or sensitive people who have had to devote all their abilities to advertizing (a description of this) or to bond selling (description)—unsatisfactory pursuits

—nothing to lift the country along—catalogue of depressions

—sons and daughters of the *very rich*—bold point of view of power with no power—can't run the business, can only give away the money—likable and admirable people some of these but they are not a real governing class

Margaret's little plump legs that bruised so easily, like golden peaches that show purple if you pinch them.

gold red mules and purple-red and green Japanese kimono that [Henry] Eichheim* gave her

* Eichheim (1878–1942) was a composer who lived in Montecito. After twenty years as first violinist with the Boston Symphony Orchestra, he visited the Orient and became a leading interpreter of Oriental music.

—said she had given herself to men only because she wanted to be kind to them. Was that really true? No, dear, it's a great big lie.

Sausages with scrambled eggs, flavored and almost brown with Worcestershire sauce—soft purple avocados with French dressing from a glass jar with pieces of garlic in it—a bowl of cottage cheese with red paprika—peach jam—thin toast—a bottle of California Sauterne—onion soup—tomatoes with poached eggs in them—heart of lettuce with Roquefort cheese dressing.

After we made love in the afternoon, the mountains beyond the white patio wall looked like imagined things, gold-dusted over dark.

—Gold of sunset liquefying the white sky—the blossoms of the red geranium on the front of the house, lit, seemed burning a red-gold like points of flame.

[I left the coast before Margaret to take Rosalind back for school. At Kansas City, I got off the train and could not find it again, and Rosalind and Stella went off without me. I telephoned Louise Connor* to meet them in Chicago. I had to spend the night in Kansas City but went on to Chicago the next morning.]

Chicago. Live electric girls in the streets—husky, bulgy, tight-knit—Hazel Rascoe type—Colosimo's: girl with slightly Negroid cast of features, bright amiable as-if-intelligent brown eyes—came out at first with chorus who lined up arms and showed their breasts, which were practically bare—then did Mexican towel dance with regular music and red-and-blue-and-yellow costume—a combination of Chicago jazz and Mexican stuff—finally

* Louise Fort had married EW's old friend Peter Connor.

master of ceremonies pulled towel back and forth across her hips—she snatched it from him with a fine imperious excited rhythm all in the jigging rhythm.

Pete Connor, enormous sagging stomach, pretense of bantering domineering, redeemed by broad and fatuous smile—they were feeling a little Bolshevik themselves today—a bank had just folded up on them—never watched the show, insisted on having us sit on stool in bar and listen to the cook sing, "Only Make Believe," etc.—man who pounded piano, which was brought in for the purpose, "full of hop"—club supposed to belong to Al Capone, who had bumped off one of his victims there. —Pete's complex about New York. —Louise: there's not really much liquor in this, but we're going to feel awful in the morning. —Pete kept on sitting on stool in a daze—we had to go out and send for him inside when we wanted to go.

Touching scene of Mrs. Cummings and Ann, going through Cummings's new book of poems together—Mrs. Cummings would say, What does that mean, Ann? and Ann wouldn't know. —Mrs. Cummings always pronounced whore w-hore.

(In New York I looked up Anna.) October '31. Al had come out of jail, they had lived together off and on— he couldn't get a job, he had beaten her up and left— her face was in such bad shape she couldn't go to Childs to work. She had had to have an abortion, too, and that had pretty well wrecked her. Finally, at her urgence apparently, he had forged a check at a drugstore—detectives, arrest, courts, Welfare Island—she looked thin, colorless, worn out with life—worried about appearing in court.

(Apropos of my having come back without Margaret)
"You people are so different from us: if one went away,
the other would go with him—would never stay behind."

She seemed to melt in my arms to almost nothing—
unsatisfactory now for that reason.

[I went up to Provincetown and lived in Susan Glaspell's house while she was away. When Margaret came
on, we took a house on the hill and later an apartment
in New York. I got *The New Republic* to send me to
the Lawrence strike.*]

Between Boston and Lawrence. Rather ugly winter
landscape—like a toneless photograph which had only
been partially tinted with yellow, orange, and brown for
grass and leaves, leaving the sky and the tree stems
themselves a neutral photographic gray.

Lawrence. The Common in late October with yellow
leaves ragged on the trees, the pointless pagoda-roofed
bandstand in the middle, two solid New England public
buildings one with a flapping gold eagle on the spire, a
brick mission, old big wooden houses with long windows—they look like skulls today—boys playing football—
a sour-faced tall bent gray-haired bespectacled old gentleman walks through during the strikers' meeting.

The prevailing architecture of three-tiered wooden
houses with a bay window or a balcony with railing and
columns on each floor—some variety, some fancy in various ways, stained upper panes to the front windows,
mostly gray—miles and miles of this—brick churches very
much like the mills—the whole ramparted around with

* "Lawrence, Mass.," in *Jitters*, pp. 270–84, retitled "Back
East: October Again: A Strike in Lawrence, Mass.," *Earthquake*, pp. 420–31.

the brick mills from six to ten stories high, enormous solid fortress windows—all silent, abandoned, only solid cops in dark blue hanging around.

Blakely. Philadelphia, newspaper early years, Young Pioneer, socialist, pocketbook worker, strike called, took active part, meant only shorter hours, higher pay, Philadelphia labor college, Brookwood, eight months, people got along there perfectly—if you wanted to know what life would be like under socialism—admired Muste, had a special feeling about Lawrence because Muste had had his struggle there, heard about what he'd been through, heard him talk about the fine comrades he'd made there—raised fifteen dollars and came up when he heard there was a strike there—Muste had thought it was about time there was one—every seven or eight years. —Had tradition here now—second generation brought up on strike tradition—all you had to do to get them out was start a picket line around the mills. —He was staying with Red Mike, a young socialist organizer—shared what money they had.

An enthusiastic picket line gave you a feeling of strength—an apathetic one dragged you all out.

See all those foreigners down there? They ought to be deported.

—good-for-nothing lounge lizards that live on our backs—squander millions at Palm Beach

American Textile Workers. Employees' representation—board of arbitration. Twenty-five percent wage cut for girls in curtain department—protest—said they were abolishing department—moved it to Malden. —Golden Rule a sliding rule. —Competitive system eliminating gray hairs—passed from one department to another till finally passed out the door. —Ten percent wage cut—told them if they were cut 25 percent, they'd still be 10 percent better off than other mill workers. —Brought it up to arbitration board—wanted cut held up till decision was made, management said they were afraid workers wouldn't abide by decision, they said they could say the same thing about the employers—employers wouldn't promise to make wage decision retroactive if cut didn't go through—finally they had a conference with Southworth:* he gave them to understand the wage cut was going through regardless—gentlemen, I move the meeting adjourn, and left them without another word. —On Friday had "assumed" other mills were going to do the same thing.

—spontaneous walkout—leaders couldn't keep them in.

Strike in March. AF of L good speakers—American Textile Workers—leaders amateurs—black intense hard and frank-staring eyes in strong faces rather yellow from mill work

Communist organization might be all right, but suspicious of leaders

Communists meet in private lot with barbed-wire-topped fence around it while police patrol neighboring streets in car—against concrete blocks of garage—above brown gully with steep bank—women hanging out of windows.

Man born in Soviet Armenia picked up from picket line, couldn't deport him, put him in asylum and gave him spinal injections, then when he came out picked him up and put him in lockup.

Won't let Communists speak on Common—two of them arrested and in jail.

* Southworth, the employers' representative, is described in "The Best People," *Jitters,* pp. 284–97, retitled "Mr. and Mrs. X.," in *Earthquake,* pp. 432–40.

Nine thousand UTW (United Textile Workers)

Four or five thousand ATW (American Textile Workers)

One thousand NTW (National Textile Workers)

Printers and engravers of Pacific printworks notified services no longer required, fifty printers, thirty engravers, highest-paid textile workers—had been receiving half pay. —Hoover: The principle of individual freedom requires the open shop. Editorial reprinted from Boston *Herald*: The Right to Unionize and the Right to Work, with quotations from Taft, Roosevelt, Harding, Hoover, Archbishop Ireland, Cardinal Gibbons, Bishop Malone, Bishop Quayle, Rev. Lyman Abbott, General Pershing, James P. Day.

biggest woolen mills and printworks in world

One day announced in paper that they were moving machinery to Utica—the next that Osgood Mill at North Andover had announced permanent suspension—"the first industrial casualty growing out of the greater Lawrence textile strike," etc.—seventy-five workers had walked out.

—Father Macdonald had said he would give Miss Berkman a free ticket to hell.

—Speaker told Shawsheen workers they were either too damn lazy or they were afraid—didn't picket.

Wiggam of Chase National Bank recently became connected with American Woolen Company.

—O'Hara and wife watched papers in the hope Macdonald would be deported—brokenhearted. O'Hara a scrubber, Yorkshireman.

—Wood built $1,500,000 model village to salve his conscience after 1912 strike—workers more loyal to management than elsewhere—Wood committed suicide in

Florida. Company had had $6 million surplus. Village never completed.

—Red Mike said they had a hard mill to picket—a lot of rat holes to watch. —Riviere said don't call a man a scab—that don't do any good—if he gets a blow in the head and finds himself lyin' on the ground he knows he got it because he's a scab—a scab hasn't got a backbone, he's only got a piece of string, but you've got a backbone because you're fightin' for the union.

—They had tried to send some work out to another mill, but the workers there had refused it because it looked scabby

—The police were takin' care of the scabs—helpin' 'em across the railroad track

—AF of L people said to have written to chief of police offering to help them against Communists

—A death-to-scabs song to the tune of "Hinky-Dinky Parlez-Voo"—and rousing the strikers to fight by reminding them of the American Revolution and Lincoln the Emancipator

—educational squad

—Macdonald's hangdog look in newsreel—mouth sagging down.

—getting people taken to the Shawsheen picket line in cars—couldn't afford ten-cent fare

—getting men to sing as loud as women

—Muste and Foster both coming over weekend

—at Arlington Mill largest demonstration probably ever organized in United States—twenty thousand

Picketing. Gray and drizzly morning—yellow leaves on trees up the side streets give them their only color—motor headlights—rough asphalt sidewalk, rough cobbled road—gray frame houses, brick buildings—two-storied bay-windowed houses, the white curtains looped up in the windows made them look like cross-eyed skulls, the lower windows figuring the teeth. —Dismal New England dawn.

Wednesday they had gone in with smiles on their faces—sneers.

The mills with square four-knobbed towers.

Gruesome booing as the scabs went in. *Solidarity, Hinky-dinky, we're here because we're here, on the pick-pick-picket line.*

Umbrellas—pretty girl with round shoulders—overcoats, raincoats—hatless captain—cops at doors and across street.

Nigger stopped and said, Don't you think them people are right?—whole working class of United States ought to be with them. —Booze on breath—worked in private home.

—call each other brother and sister instead of comrade

—Communists called Sam Blakely labor faker on picket line.

—As I was walking with Sam Blakely, somebody said, Hello, comrade!—he paid no attention—some other young fellow, tight, stopped him for a long friendly conversation.

Bob Linscott's children, tall, long-limbed, large-eyed, like foals or calves—girl with colt eyes, oval and dark, boy with calf eyes, dark with large irises and as if looking in different directions. —Waking up in morning and looking out at first into mist with blurred yellow light behind it (after California sunlight), then into clearer yellow light—the mist faintly wreathing in through the screen.

On the way up to Provincetown, last of October. Sea in big strips blue as the butterfly's shining wing—little bright red leaves in bogs—looking out on a bluish inlet, a compact white house with typical New England windows placed in a queer irregular way, three little square

ones right up against each other in the back part—and
behind, a big square barn with three little square windows, and beside it a white outhouse with one little
square window just beside the door—on the lawn stood
a motionless brown wedge which at first seemed to be
made of wood, but it turned out to be an old lady with a
skirt that made straight permanent folds and one hand
with its back under her chin. —Darkish-blue shiny ponds
with clearly marked off darker section, like mackerel
sides.

Southern wife, who, when husband asked her to press
pants, pressed them the wrong way to show him he
mustn't ask her to do anything.

New England stories. Old man brought in mouse on
dustpan and woman shuddered—What would you do if
it was the head of John the Baptist on a platter?
    Miller Brothers (in Provincetown) wouldn't sell some-
body any more silver paint for his boat because they
thought he had enough—when he sent somebody else
to get it for him, they said, That's for M. ———, isn't it?

Dos's observation about marriage that the organism
would take up as much room as it was allowed. —Also,
that Dreiser was the Trojan horse for the ILD—[John]
Dewey and Dreiser pushed forward on wheels by their
respective organizations (Dos Passos meant that Dewey
was being used by the Trotskyites)—cat mewing in
kitchen closet part of evolution—Kentucky miners part of
class conflict—apropos of Anna Rochester's book about
coal.
    —Cummings "squaring the circle."

Walk with Katy [Dos Passos] *at Provincetown* in early
November—Hawthorne's hilltop lawn, the monument—
queer strong but mild and almost warm wind blowing—

white square steeples down below in the darkness—a night of plain rumpled beauty, shadows dark and white. *Milky*, milk stains.

—winter—big white square churches and white high-keeled houses built like ships

—Katy said it was like something in a book

—Katy's little green socks and untied gray leather moccasins

Murray Godwin. If the ignorant masses hadn't existed, it would have been necessary to invent them! (Got up and went to urinal.)

Edison's death—was reported as saying he believed in a hereafter but didn't know what it would be like! Probably hoped that goldenrod would grow there—so that he could continue his rubber experiments.

Provincetown, mild early-November day. Dry milky light in which the churches and houses stood merely like solid shadows

—gulls scattered in the blue harbor like paper

—sunset next day blue and gold molten but soft, the bare trees and white houses sticking up in it, wintry but felicitous, kindly, too

—walked in the dunes—found unsuspected lakes and glades—tracks of raccoons, rabbits, jumping mice, chickadees, people, snakes, a fox—cranberries, light-green dry moss, brown and red leaves in brush.

November 16: like a great gray blotter absorbing all color from earth, sky, and sea.

Margaret's trip East with Jean (Gorman),* *Ted and Lorraine.* Ted sang bawdy songs—one to the tune of

* Wife of Herbert Gorman, the journalist and critic; see *The Twenties*, pp. 271-2, 342-3.

"Frankie and Johnny" about Carl, Tony, and Jean—so loud that he annoyed the old ladies. Jean got familiar with porter, would goose him, would ring for him in morning and say, Guess what we want this morning? A gin fizz. —Girls growling for a drink and Ted said, You know way back in 1880 there was a woman once who crossed the continent without taking a drink—then he sent telegrams to all his Cloister friends to meet train with Scotch terrier, Gordon antelope, etc.—booze was handed on at every stop—etherized Scotch which had been diluted by cutting out a piece in the bottom of the bottle, and some other whiskey that made them sick so they threw it away—Ted taken for a pimp with the sporting girls. —When they arrived, had gotten thin, very nervous—Carl Van Dant and Bill Jutte turned up at the station—the flimsy, new tricky Tudor Hotel—Procrustes bathtubs you couldn't lie out in—girls sat around for an hour drinking and talking about their drinking on the train. Ted tried to spend the night and got put out.

[E. E] *Cummings in Russia*. Was it true they'd tried to show him a textile factory when he wanted to ride on the merry-go-round? —His final statement was that you couldn't make a man look up his own ahsshole with a pair of binoculars.

—*Ralph Barton* [Cummings's father-in-law] egged his daughter on to be a nun, telling her he was going into a monastery himself—had been to see her at convent, talked to her through bars, just before he killed himself.

Out of my *Provincetown* window in the morning—one glimpse of the harbor a blinding mirror with the sun in it between two houses and behind two bare trees—a little space of grass a little sunken and a little greener, that "greased with green" effect, beyond it a big old gnarled tree—it was a house with an unfenced yard in between the others and had a specimen of ornamental Ionic-looking woodwork up close along under the eaves—in a late dark afternoon the houses would seem to stand, so strongly built and close together, in an absolutely clear gray fluid. —The houses built like ships, the narrow lanes, the houses crowded at queer angles but firmly and stubbornly based.

Margaret—when kissed, gives a single cough, the way a dog sneezes when you make a fuss over it.
—I've got the shiver-shakes—spooking around.
She'd say that I was Old Man Gloom himself.

Coming back to New York, December 22, '31. As if you were going down into the whole great big city or into a subway—people at Scribner's seemed gaunt, gray, unsure of themselves and gloomy. —At *New Republic*: the *Herald Tribune* had to arrange extensions in order to make the drops on the chart go low enough—only thing Amalgamated was buying were short-term government bonds—no bonds at all, not even government bonds, otherwise—$3 million cash in bank—just trying to stay fluid—every bank insolvent except Chase National, and all the other banks were only conspiring to keep that solvent because if that went, the government went. —People looked whiter, more emaciated than ever—dyed brass waves on girls' foreheads like too-pale eggshells— the park from the Barbizon Plaza (where you got your breakfast under the door)—a big blunt-cornered rectangle like a Dennison tag—a threading of lights, asphalt, motor roads so wide that they made it look like a map—their scrolls choked out the rocks and dead grass—all bleak and abstract and town-yellow, but exciting when you first come back to it—but the sky or whatever it was seemed to be shutting the people down into the streets so that they crawled along them more dismally, dumbly, ignobly,

than ever—yellowish, colorless, sharp-nosed men shut up
calling in telephone booths that were lined with that
linoleumlike stamped stuff on the sides—the city so
much darker at night—dismal, dumbly unconsciously
borne-down-on, not itself—economizing on electric signs—
the squeal of the policeman's whistle sounded feebler,
less important in the dark—the life, the excitement, had
partly gone out of the city—the heart had been taken out
of it—they didn't know where it had gone—when the
electric current is turned off, the filament looks pretty
thready. —We heard shouts and saw out the window
at the edge of the Park what we took to be a hunger
march of the park bums being organized by Communists,
but when I went down to investigate, it turned out to be
NYU freshmen starting a snake dance—ominous and
dreary like everything else.

Dream about Anna, early January 1932. She had
turned up at some house where we were living—as servant?—she had seemed unneat, sweet and amiable, smiling, the whole occasion genial—and we went somewhere
with her—then she was a kitten I was carrying—then
something happened to her—bitten by a dog?—and I saw
after I had carried her a little distance farther that she
was bleeding—then I walked into rather a luxurious
house in a more or less crude, ugly, and heavy style,
where I didn't know the people—nobody at home—I began to shave in a bathroom which had green and black
marble—then the people were there and I was talking to
them—a social occasion, cocktails—but the kitten had
been shrinking up—I had kept thinking I ought to put
hot water on it or something but delayed for a long time
till there was nothing left but a little oblong thing like
a cocoon in my hand with a round hole in it—I finally
put it under the faucet and turned a little water on it

gently—it shrank after this all the more—I couldn't do anything about it—finally it was only a little round thing like a cell, which got dropped out of my hand on the floor—I ought to look for it, did look for it, but was absolutely unable to find it—gave it up and went on talking.

Ethel Hutchinson [landlady at West 58th Street]: Good-natured eyes, must have been sweet and attractive though dumb once—now fallen on hard times—dog, French maid, bluish-greenish Victorian ruins in large painting that occupies a large part of the wall—high coal grate—whole room dark and padded—brown carpet. —Afraid to go up and down stairs for fear of being robbed of pearls, etc. —A man who had lived in the house had run up six months' rent and then killed himself—I haven't got any sympathy for people who behave like that, have you?

Fuse blowing out in kitchen when electric heater was attached—put out light in all that side of living room and in bedroom and bathroom— psychological effect.

Cummings. Rapid succession of imitations of fairy— How about Russia?—Oh, darling!—My clitoris is bigger than your clitoris! Englishman—buggery in India—sending a girl under the table and the last man to unbutton his pants won. —Jewish Communist: He's a good comrade, yes (patronizing). —Idea of buggery suggested in connection with going into an elevator first. —Comrade Suksemoff—Buggeroffsky—Twotsky.

Esther Murphy's anecdotes. Soviet ambassador who had said that the Russians were somewhat dismayed to see capitalism going to pieces so fast—"we think it very disobliging of them."

—"Comrade Lenin, here is a book by Comrade X—that

I want you to read—much better than Dostoevsky—
Dostoevsky only dealt with the difficulties of the bourgeoisie—but Comrade X—writes of the life of the proletariat," etc.—Lenin put book under his arm—and, as the
comrade goes on praising up Comrade X and crying down
Dostoevsky, says, "Yes, but Dostoevsky is better reading."

Later entry: Actually, it was Pushkin—story in
Krupskaya.

Wanda (Lyon): Isn't it awful to have to ring a bell to
get a servant?

PINEVILLE, KENTUCKY:
THE COAL STRIKE, 1932

[In February 1932, during the hardest winter of the Depression, when 13 million were unemployed in the United States, EW got his first taste of the labor "barricades." He accompanied a delegation to the Kentucky coal fields on behalf of the Independent Miners' Relief Committee. He had visited this area during the previous year and had written of the miners' attempts to create an independent union. Subsequently, Theodore Dreiser and John Dos Passos publicized the plight of the miners. The coal operators, from all the contemporary evidence, were attempting to isolate the miners and starve them into submission. Groups seeking to bring aid encountered violence from the local authorities and representatives of the mine operators.

The relief delegation was led by the novelist Waldo Frank, and EW joined the party as a reporter for *The New Republic*, accompanied by Malcolm Cowley, his colleague on the journal. Others in the group included Mary Heaton Vorse, the labor writer from Provincetown; Elsie Reed Mitchell, a retired medical doctor; John Henry Hammond, youthful heir to a Vanderbilt fortune, interested in the rights of the blacks, and an authority on jazz music; Quincy Howe, the journalist and broadcaster; and various other liberals and leftists. Already on the scene was Allan Taub, an International Labor Defense lawyer.

The delegation first called on the mayor, a dentist named J. M. Brooks. He agreed to the food distribution but stipulated that it be limited to the miners' camps outside Pineville city limits. He then warned against holding meetings, making speeches, or staging demonstrations or parades. This challenge to freedom of speech was disputed by a subcommittee of the delegation consisting of EW, Dr. Mitchell, Malcolm Cowley and Waldo Frank. The mayor maintained he could not allow any inflammatory situation to develop. He sent the group to the county attorney, Walter B. Smith.]

Pineville. Met Mary [Heaton] Vorse in Pennsylvania waiting room, very sour on the whole thing—Mary: It's different from up here. Those people—are likely to mob you!—she was dispirited about the picture having been taken in front of the WIR headquarters—wouldn't go in and meet the others till the train was about to start— must have seen a dick there because Smith at Pineville knew that Charley Walker had bought some of the tickets—conference in train: Charley's mouth opened, and a program from the *Daily Worker* poured out, making Mary and me very uneasy—insisted on free assemblage and free speech as well as distributing the food—*We'*ll do so-and-so! Where did he get that "we" stuff?—thought [Benjamin] Lieder* was a dick at first—elected Waldo (Frank) chairman—visit to (Sherwood) Anderson—Charley called up Adelaide [Mrs. Walker] and learned that WIR

---

* Lieder was the Paramount newsreel cameraman who accompanied the delegation.

headquarters had been raided—conversation in train—
philosophical side of Communism—Marx and Henry
George—Mary read *New Yorker* and *Redbook*—econ-
omized on berths and meals—beautiful soft hills of Virginia and Tennessee, even in February—a felicity to the
eye—weather warm: I had my train window open—cool
and pleasant air of the country came in through the
screen. —Adelaide met us at the station, much excited and
looking very chic in brown clothes, neat brown walking
shoes, and brown scarf—constraint weighed on this part
of the expedition—Farragut Hotel—nothing much said
about the WIR raid, "just a gesture"—Room 909, where
we had meetings—ugly wallpaper with coarse gray flowers
against dry weak yellow—mystery of non-arrival of Dr.
Mitchell, [Harold] Hickerson, and Way: Way had a
large part of the funds—Liston Oak, with his gray mild
eyes and crinkly hair which made me think he might have
Negro blood, being tense, taut, efficient, grimly exact, and
disciplined—I had been made uneasy, however, coming
up in the elevator, to see that his hands were quivering
with nervousness—discussion of telegram: appearance on
the scene of Doris Parks (Allan Taub's wife), her speech,
full of mass action and demonstration—all I'll say will be,
etc.—that's all I'm going to say! (She had in the meantime made a regulation Communist speech—though it had
been promised to us "liberals" that no Communist line
would be played.) Reaction against using a ruse, defended
however by Charley—nice-looking, nicely dressed, blue
eyes, clear complexion, finally at my suggestion she left—
tensity of evening meetings, hard intense electric light—
Liston Oak's long thin hand along his head—the Jewish
problem, counting noses, Polly Boyden* doubtful, thyroid

* Polly Boyden was the wife of a Chicago lawyer; they had a
large summer house at Truro. Her novel *The Pink Egg* was
described as "vaguely surrealistic and vaguely Communist" and
was read only by her friends.

Delegation for Independent Miners' Relief Committee, 1932
Standing: Unidentified, Quincy Howe, John Hammond, Liston Oak
Seated: Edmund Wilson, Mary Heaton Vorse, Waldo Frank, Malcolm Cowley

type? something wrong with her—John Hammond like somebody who had modeled himself on Proust, then received an injection of Communism. Complained of bad writing of Harlan report, same word used three times in one paragraph.

[Quincy] Howe said at meeting he'd like to visit a coal mine, had never done so—Oak or somebody said we'd come under the wrong auspices for that—Malcolm [Cowley] said, That's just the point at issue.

phony-seeming floozy Mrs. Wright who said she was friend of Malcolm and wanted to go along

Our dismay at handbill about Solidarity Delegation and holding demonstration to demand release of political prisoners.

La Follette. Hammond had missed his directions, didn't stop where he was supposed to and wait for the others and the trucks. Crowd around the courthouse steps: There are our people waiting for us (said probably by Mary Vorse). Bad hour in the town. Hot dogs with Southern goo on them and coffee in a soda fountain where we could see a sign that said Coffins through the open door, into which came a little Jew with an enormous black hound suggestive of the Hound of the Baskervilles and where Mary had great difficulty preventing Hammond from putting a nickel in the automatic player. Our crabbing about Doris Parks and Walkers—Doris kind of girl Mary couldn't get on with. Waited around on street— I was scared for a moment by crowd of children just out of school who were coming down the street—walked around, Mary stopped and patted two enormous brown bloodhounds with bloodshot and innocent eyes, talked to the big Nordic-featured Negro who had them on a leash— had a hard time getting to the point of asking where the fairgrounds was—finally a kid directed us—nothing doing that we could see—a couple of men appeared walking toward the entrances. Drove around—found miners gathered with American flag near one of the mines—went on past. — Back to fairgrounds: good-looking kids, one of their fathers had been a union man and got killed when Sheetrock fell on him—told us the town had refused to let the meeting be held on the fairgrounds—on to Violet's —had a hard time finding way. Hammond wanted to give it up, said that what he took to be miners' houses around there looked very comfortable—if that was what they wanted us to see. Violet with big hat and red scarf— large toothless smile—leaning on his gate: They've been robbing us for years for the upkeep of that fairgrounds, and now they won't let us use it. Went back and met procession coming, then trucks and rest of party—Well, they've got the right flag anyway!—marching with miners —speeches from trucks—nigger speaker didn't get up on truck till it came time for his speech—elderly Communist organizer in black, tinctured with Communism, but sounded more or less like miners—miner who said, As long as I have a bed to lay on, I'll be a NMU (National Miners Union) man till I die!—Comrades—beloved— tyranny—when Doris Parks began to talk about Communism in a loud, clear, resonant voice, the liberals began to climb down from the trucks. We went to visit some miners' houses—paper pasted on the wall—Gertrude Logan, nice-looking red-haired Jewish organizer (they took local Southern names to disarm suspicion)—boss's place, he had a contract, cows and pigs, pretty daughter in red dress—turning car around in the mud—scared young fellow who was a missioner—I'll tell you frank, the superintendent came down when there was some people here the other day and made them go away. Boardinghouse, fire in grate—just as well off with strike relief as when they were working—man with good-looking married sister who had been told that if he went

out on strike and tried to farm the plot of ground he'd
leased, it would be taken away from him. —Houses
along road uphill—straight steep coal-car track, walked
over trestle.

—the liberals' phony role—easy for Communists

Doris Parks: in Russia there was dukes and princes in
the movement—always very much pleased with herself
(she said this when we were on the train)

—That fine old aristocrat: De Voikus [the workers]
(a joke of Malcolm Cowley's on the train)

Conference that night: Charley: They don't take their
criminal syndicalism law seriously, though. Adelaide:
We're not going, you see. (Since Charley, after the first
expedition, had been forbidden to enter Harlan Co., she
was embarrassed at the militancy with which he was
sending us in.) —We tried to admit only one Communist
—but three got in, including Belle—whom some of us had
made a firm attempt to keep out. —Neal, after proving
rather elusive, came and advised us—said it would be
better to get Kentucky lawyer, but if we couldn't, he
would help us. (Sociologist in lobby and Joe Krutch's
brother and his wife. —Also, vulturine detectives watching
us pointedly beside hotel door.) —Sudden departure of
Owen—who had been afraid of a small riot. —Arrival of
Dr. Mitchell, like an ant, flat-heeled square-toed shoes,
socks over stockings. —Long fierce telegram from Mayor
and Smith—our reply. —Malcolm stretching out on bed. —
Jews who never said a word—were they stool pigeons? —
Waldo firmly sat on certain of the comrades' proposals.
—Way with his low forehead egged us on, but more
restrainedly and sensibly than Doris Parks, he had promised Mary he would tell Doris to hold herself in. —The
Christians sapping the foundations of the Roman Empire
all over again. —Oak said firmly that he reminded him of
the conference they had had the night before Ella May

Wiggins was shot at Gastonia. —Malcolm: I'll be very much relieved when I get to bed tomorrow night. —My protests that I didn't want to get arrested. —Oak's and Polly Boyden's retorts. Oak said there would probably be violence.

News the next morning that Way had been picked up and that Simms had been shot. —Johnson in the gray morning—said they probably intend to take jailed relief workers for a ride and kill them. —Start off: sleepy in car—young boy driving had gun, surprised we didn't have any. Liston Oak spoke about Belle—as rather a recent convert—rather leftist—enraged to have her left behind. —Expected to be stopped at Elliott—Oak's slip about T. S. Eliot—bare countryside with sheep looked like Greece—Waldo's indifference to the newspapers—said he couldn't keep his mind on reading newspapers—to Mary's horror (this belongs to the train: someone tried to show him something about Harlan in a newspaper), Dr. Mitchell on her travels—I got a little uneasy: too much Russia—the Kalmucks—their wedding customs—bride usually older than husband—intoxicating drink made out of mare's milk which she had drunk on this occasion—fond of travel, born in South Carolina, had grown up largely in California. —Malcolm thought we were running into rain, but then the sky cleared up—we talked about the beauty of the scenery—a delightful mild day like early spring—we stopped at a little town—had hamburger sandwiches, etc.—send Hammond back to find out about the trucks—Mary and I walked up and down—Mary's troubles with her children—Ellen had come down with her husband and intimated that she wished Mary were dead so that they could have the house, Mary had intimated a little less crudely that she wished Ellen were dead—we discussed marriage, husbands and wives who both did things and competed with one another. —Liston Oak said, What

does this remind you of, Mary? (He meant Gastonia.) —
Finally the trucks came and we went on. —The word had
reached us by this time that the trucks of clothes had been
found overturned.

[Billboard signs.] Get Right with God. Prepare to meet
thy God. Jesus Saves.

Entering war zone—my conversation with Dr. Mitchell
began to falter slightly—kept looking out for deputies,
who, driver thought, would merely stop us—but we got
past Elliott's gas station without being interfered with,
though there were people standing around there. —Talked
about heat of American houses—best thing to do, she
found, with steam heat was to keep turning it off and on.

At Pineville. Miners around courthouse. Stone's office:
Stone said he'd get us lot (to hold meeting in?). You better
not sit with your back to that window—they've got their
machine guns trained on it. We at once went to the
window to see them. —We had the right to do so, hadn't
we? —You've got the right, but you want to understand
that whatever these people want to do, they'll do it anyway! —Old, sallow, unnerved, smiling rather sadly—
evidently of plain stock himself. —The big picture of a
luscious fuckable girl, a brunette with black bobbed hair
and black silk stockings and short skirts—a big sensual
eyeful on the calendar above the desk. —Appearance of
Taub like a New York breach-of-promise lawyer coming
into court with pants creased (spats? smoking cigar?),
breezy, glib, sure of himself, ready for us to wade right
in. What about the machine guns? That's four-fifths
bluff! —Had to turn him off to be on our way. —As we
went out, Waldo asked me whether I felt as if this was
my town.

—man beaten up—bruised, swollen, bandaged, trembling, unnerved

Mayor in his dentist's office—he and another unknown

man, both with kind eyes as they shook hands—discussed warm winter—Mayor first said he had to go to Harlan to see patient, then that it would only take him twenty minutes to finish up patient from Harlan, then waiting in chair.

[Cleon Calvert, who figures in EW's ensuing notes, was the attorney for the Straight Creek Coal Company and other coal operators. "Dreiser's errors" apparently consisted in his having advocated federal intervention.]

We went to hotel, didn't know whether to meet him or not—arrival of leading citizens. —Enormous high-ceilinged grand and gloomy chambers of old-fashioned hotel— incongruous with unpretentious lobby like the cheapest kind of drummer's house—yet the pomp of the place had no flavor or color—far enough South to be stately, not far enough to be mellow—dark old rooms rather crass.—They told about relief work. —Attempts of mayor to put an end to interview, Waldo always able to talk over it. —Big tall fellow with large brown simple eyes who supposed that none of us had ever worked on a farm—he had and had worked for a living and thought that if a man wanted a living, he had to work for it. —Cleon Calvert on Dreiser's errors. —We'd have to see county attorney. —Threats when they got up to go—my conversation in the meantime with the Baptist minister—had sat in trepidation on the edge of his chair and asked to have us hear their side of it. Told me it really was very bad down there—this agitation helped call attention to it—didn't side either with miners or with operators—tried to be for humanity—understood there was unemployment in New York. Calvert said they *couldn't* pay the miners any more. —They had said it was very funny the way our activities seemed to cross with those of the union: first this bill, you see, and we appeared on the scene. —(Soft-spokenness of Southerners: Mary's story—He has three brothers, hasn't he?—I wouldn't like to be in that sheriff's shoes. —As contrasted with a violent wordy quarrel among Jews.)

Waldo running it out a little bit about how well known we were and how we'd publish whatever we found out from New York to California. —Mayor: And that's really what you're after, isn't it?—something you can publish from New York to California. —Waldo had said, The pen, as Shakespeare said, is mightier than the sword. —I'm not scared of a Bolshevik pen any day! —Big brown-eyed man: I think the citizens ought to run ye out of town— we can't do that, but— He had talked about getting something for nothing, and I think you're up to something of that kind. —As far as I'm concerned, this talk can come to an end. —Waldo: Well, listen, brother, don't you see you're doing the worst possible thing for your own case— rights as American citizens. —Asked him whether he'd registered for the draft during war—Waldo said that had nothing to do with it—as a matter of fact, I did—but— Malcolm said, I volunteered! I said, So did I!—Detective standing by door as we went out (flat-heels, Oak said, a race of their own). —Amiable enough woman at hotel desk but didn't know quite how to take us. —People standing around without saying much.

[The notes which follow are EW's record of the committee's talk with the county attorney, Walter B. Smith.]

Smith's office—light suit, polished black shoes, persistent smile and ironic politeness masking nervousness and lack of character—Phi Beta Kappa key. —Herndon Evans [editor of the Pineville *Sun*] wanted us to see relief on floor above. —Waldo began by saying that he assumed that Smith knew who we were and what we had come for. Smith to Waldo—You must be smart enough to know so-and-so if you're such a smart man as you say you are (accused us of working to get a thrill)—All I know about you is that you tell me that your name's Waldo

Frank. —Well, I don't think I can prove it. —I don't think I could prove my name was Smith either. —Criminal syndicalism law, which he reads—if the miners talked about gun thugs, that would be inflammatory. —Waldo's line about how if they had met at a club they would have liked one another. I think you people have got a quirk— and, as you say, since we have no social friends in com- mon—you can distribute food as much as you want to, but as soon as you buck the law, it will be my pleasure as well as my duty to prosecute you. —Why should it be your pleasure? —Because it's my official duty, and I enjoy discharging my duty. —Cleon Calvert came in and sat down by desk—positive, loud, and clear legal voice—What about right to revolution guaranteed by Kentucky con- stitution? That doesn't mean armed revolution—of course! (As if this had already been brought to his attention and he had thought it over and come to this conclusion.) — Calvert declared that the Communists, who were con- trolled by the Communist International (I remembered the Fish Committee), had no constitutional rights what- ever!—had begun by saying that he wouldn't say that he wasn't the best constitutional lawyer in this town. —Our mistakes about the circular: I always said I hadn't seen it, and in the hotel Mary said she hadn't seen it and asked to look at it, and in the county attorney's office Waldo did the same thing. —Smith on red-Reds and pink-Reds and tea-hound Reds. —Who had paid our fares down there? —Girl standing in door looking at us with a closed-up expression which I judged to indicate disap- proval. —Finally, while we were still pleading to be al- lowed to speak to the miners, Smith got a telephone call and said, Yes, if they make any speeches like that, arrest 'em.

I interrupted his reading the handbill—Waldo told me to let him finish. —I guess he knows that much even if

he does come from New York—I feel sort of inferior with
you men—because I've never been to New York. —Where
we come from doesn't make any difference!—I made some
unfortunate reference to "the party," meaning the group—
corrected by Oak (?), Not the ——. —Oh, not the ——!
—Waldo: I assume that you believe in Jeffersonian democracy. —As a matter of fact, I've always been a Republican—I've heard about it, though.

We came out of the courthouse, Evans took our pictures, and found Hammond, Polly Boyden, and somebody
else very indignant over our capitulation to the authorities—It seems so yellow! (Polly). —Then Smith came up
behind us and continually smiling and evidently nervous
told us that he'd have to cancel permission he'd just given
us—then, as if half to himself: You can't see things from
my point of view and I can't see things from your point
of view. —Went on. —Mary and Dr. Mitchell turned up
and told us what had happened with trucks. —Woman
who had picked them up took Waldo and me back to the
scene of action. Waldo: If there's a bad mess, what do you
think we ought to do? I said that I didn't know. Woman
was much perturbed—told about relief work she was
helping with—said radicals were stirring up roughest most
ignorant members of community, and if there wasn't
bloodshed over this, she'd be surprised. Said she'd wait
for us. —What had happened before: deputies had
heckled young miner—You've got a brother that's a law—
ain't that so? —Yes. —You've got a brother that's [a] mine
guard. —That's a lie! —Pulled guns on him—he had fled. —
Paramount man had been stopped from getting pictures,
but Lieder had popped up. —Provocative tactics: deputies
had tried to take down the tailboard and break into the
truck with the sugar—Malcolm had held it against them
with a gun poked in his back. —One stunted-looking
brown-paper-faced boy with his neck bent forward—

sinister-looking, it seemed to me—said, in a language almost unintelligible, that tweren't right the young miner
should have run away when they said his brother was a
law. —Another came up to Waldo and me and said, You
want to look out for that man in the long black coat over
there who'd threatened to shoot the speaker, he's killed a
couple of men. Waldo said that we'd like to see somebody
who'd killed a couple of men. —The blues singer's husband, a funny old coot. —(Mrs. Copenhaver, Sherwood
Anderson's mother-in-law, had accused Aunt Molly Jackson of being really an old blatherskite, had been jealous
of Sherwood Anderson's getting more prominence over
the radio.) —Deputies pretending to be disgruntled
miners: Those men have had some already! Those men are
all workin'! Make 'em form in line and give it to whoever's
worthy! (They were in line.) —Couldn't believe we
weren't carrying guns—when Waldo went back to car
(where woman said she would wait for us for half an hour,
till six) they searched us all, thought he'd gone back for
guns. —Quincy Howe: slightly whimsical look of amazed
seriousness—"This is certainly very instructive!—Don't you
wish J. J. Chapman* could have had some such experience as this?" —As it began to get dark, Waldo began to
think we ought to go—Oak wanted to stay as long as
possible to see that the food was given out properly. —
When we did go, the deputies grabbed what was left. —
On way to car, I asked Lieder whether he had gotten any
pictures: Don't talk about it! —Woman complained of
deputies as curse of community, had license to do what
they pleased—Mary had stayed in car with her—woman
wanted to show her relief and have her meet two men in
town.

* See EW's essay on John Jay Chapman in *The Triple
Thinkers*, pp. 133–64.

—Ebbings and flowings of fear—fear of spies, of being watched, having what one said taken down.

—*At the hotel,* somebody—Herndon Evans?—advised us not to go out alone that night. —Dinner late in the big deserted dining room with the doors closed—Waldo's peevishness with the waiter—announced at the end of dinner that he was going out for a walk around the square. Before that, when I first came down, someone said, We're having very general conversation, and everybody laughed—I was hushed when I asked what had happened to Hammond—I thought perhaps he had dropped off like Owen.

About six of us walked around the square—bought some cigarettes in a drugstore—before this, it had been a question of sending a boy out to get them. —Then Waldo had proposed calling on the people in jail—a couple of people dropped off—Waldo, Howe, Polly Boyden, and I went. —The happiest most cheery place in town—white-washed, unusually accessible, unexpected cordiality of the jailer—shook hands with Hickerson and Vernon Smith through the square window in the pen. —Hickerson said they had a dandy crowd in there—the little Jewish com-rades looked pretty and rosy in their pen (though Clarissa Michelson was sick)—one was small and plump, round little breasts right behind blue rayon (?) waist—another taller and skinnier had black eyes under the line of frowning brows. A big woman wanted us to ask to come in—we said we'd try to do that in the morning. —The visit to the jail cheered us up, made us feel jollier and more normal, but it apparently scared the town because we soon afterwards heard that there was a gang of depu-ties standing around in front of the jail.

Meeting that night. Big thronelike dark-red plush-covered chairs—we pulled down the shades on the street. —Taub wanted to offer suggestions: we had gotten sour on him, didn't want him in—finally agreed to have him in and let him speak ten minutes—he wanted to read the Kentucky constitution from the courthouse steps. —About Waldo's shoes wrapped in the *Daily Worker*—Malcolm spoke of their having threatened to lynch us. —We decided to get food in the morning and take a truck into Harlan County—decided to visit just one place—Wallins Creek, where two men had been shot. —Malcolm, the ladies, and others went to bed and left Waldo, Howe, Lieder, and me there—we loosened up and became quite natural telling each other incidents of the day and laughing. Finally Waldo yawned and said good night. — Liston Oak was just about to call up Herndon Evans, Boyden, etc., to hospital to see [Harry] Simms.* —At these meetings, feeling of gloomy distaste and constraint that came down on you—didn't know the people and didn't like them much—thought them either people like yourself who were going in for the thing out of curiosity, exhibitionism, or desire for drama, or queer equivocal anomalous people—mongrel Negroes and Jews, thyroid women—who didn't make any sense anyway—also Communists, etc., finally putting it over on you—leading you like lambs to the slaughter. —A common feeling, however—solidarity?—would assert itself. This happened particularly when we visited the prisoners.

[While the discussions were under way with the mayor and the county attorney, the food trucks were driven out of Pineville under surveillance of the sheriff's deputies and were parked in a muddy side road well outside the city limits. Here milk and groceries were given to the miners under considerable harassment from the deputies, who confiscated at gunpoint newsreel film taken by a re-

* Simms, a National Miners Union organizer, had been shot by a Brush Creek mine guard and died later that day of his wounds.

porter. Malcolm Cowley, who helped, said that most of the food was distributed in spite of these difficulties. Later, when delegation members went back to the hotel, it was learned the deputies seized the remaining food for themselves. The delegation met that evening in the hotel and decided to purchase more food the following day. Before the evening was over, however, there occurred the events EW now describes.]

Waldo came back, saying there were men around his door: What shall I do? A loud knock. Yes. Come in. Phony warrant without Howe's name. Search us. Gesture of bumping Oak with shoulder:Come along!—demoniacal-looking deputy with gray hair bristling straight up from crown, black peering eyes which seemed to gleam with fiendish delight at his work, and head thrust down and forward, and comically stealthy tread. We were appalled by them at first but they turned out to be quite amiable: We can't talk the same as you. —Lieder in bathroom. Telephoning Taub—Taub demands to see warrant. Waiting for ladies - Dr. Mitchell looked a little taken aback for the first time—her hat on a little bit crooked.

The court: boy who dropped gun getting out cigarette—Taub's attempts to postpone trial—public excluded: niggers at window, white woman complained as window was lifted in front of her face—very few people left room, all the rest deputy sheriffs. Cleon Calvert, fussed Judge, young full-faced smiling prosecutor who moved indictment (?) be quashed for lack of prosecution. —Oak: It's quite possible they meant to beat us up.

Back to hotel: fiendish-looking sheriff told us amiably enough, when we asked him what we were supposed to do now, to go to bed, but that we'd better leave town. — Mrs. Wright, who had turned up taking notes in the courtroom, made Mary Vorse sit down in one of the chairs outside the hotel and, much excited and all quivering, told her that they were going to take the men for a ride, but that the women were an embarrassment to them—they were Kentucky gentlemen and wouldn't do anything to the women, there was a taxi there and they would be glad to have them take it and get away. Mary said she would stick with the party. —Told us to go up and get our baggage and pay our bills—about nine deputies with Waldo—tried to provoke him, looked under his mattress.

Baggage of cars with trucks taken to courthouse—we had to go over to claim it—took all papers, found notes on a lecture on Russia by Dr. Mitchell and a bulletin of the Foreign Policy Association. (By this time she had begun to talk about "a country whose existence we are supposed to ignore.") —Smug little buglike man with blue eyes, red face, light suit, soft hat, and light-brown scarf, who stood around and watched everything in an imitating manner, examined my *Hard Times* and *Progress and Poverty,* looked at newspaper clipping used as bookmark and had cop be sure to put it back in place, said, These books are published all over the country. —Cop asked us in a jocular way whether we had any moonshine whiskey. —Coming out, fell in with man walking across green: That's the curse of this town, they're always searching everybody—it's been the same thing for the last twenty years!—what were they searching you for?—did you run over somebody? —There won't a tourist come here any more. —Good night.

Took us out through dining room: closed doors. Big man said: We're not going to harm ye, but we're going to take you out of Kentucky and we don't want ye never to come back again. Mary and Dr. Mitchell were taken out through the front door. Waldo and Taub were taken out at the back door first—I thought perhaps they were going to beat us up by twos. —When they searched

Quincy Howe, somebody said, Aw, he wouldn't know how to use a gun if he had it!

In our car, they began by asking us our occupation—if we were born in this country—young fellow who had been to school at Staunton, Virginia. —Told us about boycott of Knoxville merchants to make them withdraw advertising from *News-Sentinel*. —Things were so bad in Bell County now (where they had all three been born) that he would have been glad to go away if he had the money—twenty years ago, before the railroad came, life had been different, but then all the foreigners came in—miners from West Virginia and real foreign labor from abroad—so that you could count the decent people in the town—they had never had anything like this in those days. —When car stopped—lights dimmed—the driver offered us cigarettes—had offered to take us to hotel, which they said was much better than the one we had left. Had said that there was a certain person who was lucky to get away without getting hurt—if he ever came back, they'd kill him (Allan Taub). —Big leader in brown suit with colorless sallow coarse face stuck his head in car and said, Get out and don't ever come back to Kentucky again.

In one of the cars, talked about killing them, etc.—then turned around and asked, Don't you believe in a Supreme Being?

You're going to see something you never saw before! Rumor they were going to take us to Harlan.

Somebody reading list by moonlight—it was only the second time I saw Waldo that I noticed the back of his head was swollen and bloody and greasily shining in the headlights. I had heard him saying indignantly: You can beat me up, but that's a lie! —Let's go! Taub's face covered with blood in the darkness—kept talking all the way downhill. White tablet about Daniel Boone, etc.

[In a deposition made after these events, Malcolm Cowley said the motorcade escorted by the "night riders" consisted of thirteen cars. They were driven with their lights out to the state line in the Cumberland Gap and were then told to get out of the cars. "In the darkness," Cowley testified, "I heard someone shrieking about thirteen feet away. When I reached the spot I heard Waldo Frank say that they could beat him again if they wanted to, but he would not swear to a falsehood . . . When the lights were turned on, I saw Taub's face was a mass of blood. Waldo Frank was bleeding profusely from a bad cut on the back of his head. Before releasing us, they forced us to stand in front of the headlights and searched our bags for films." At the hotel in Virginia, to which the party went, Dr. Mitchell dressed the wounds of the two men.

The *New York Times* report of February 12, 1932, quotes the two victims as saying they were beaten and says the officials of Pineville "discounted their reports." Mayor Brooks was quoted as saying "the intruders left Pineville of their own free will"; he suggested that Frank and Taub had probably gotten into a fight. Others in the town also gave out reports that Taub and Frank had difficulties "among themselves." This was not the version given by the delegation a few weeks later before a senatorial subcommittee on a resolution to investigate conditions in the coal fields of Harlan and Bell Counties. The subcommittee of the Senate consisted of Senators Costigan, Cutting, and Logan, and the evidence heard substantially follows EW's account in these journals.

In later years, stories were circulated by Louis Colman, of the Committee for the Defense of Political Prisoners, and quoted by Matthew Josephson in his article on Wilson (*The Southern Review*, Autumn 1975), that during the Pineville events EW "disappeared." This was denied by Taub, John Hammond, Malcolm Cowley, and Quincy Howe, who remembered that Wilson was active in all phases of their intervention in Pineville (as his notes show). "It was logistically impossible for any of us to 'run out' at any time," Quincy Howe wrote (letter to LE, February 24, 1976). The fact that the committee members were dispersed when they were run out of Pineville made it impossible for any one person to know what was happening to the group as a whole during their trip to the state line.

On February 29, 1932, EW wrote to John Dos Passos: "The whole thing was very interesting for us—though I don't know that it did much for the miners." He added: "I came back convinced that if the literati want to engage in radical activities they ought to organize . . . independently—so that they can back other people besides the comrades and so that the comrades can't play them for suckers."]

The Cumberland Gap hotel: glum or sour-looking old man at desk—simple-minded coon porter in plum livery with flat hat and trousers tailored to be fuller at the bottom of his long thin legs. —Trying to get Taub, who was still talking, for God's sake to wash the blood off his face—when he got into the telephone booth talking to Charley, we had to make him come out so that we could call a taxi—that was supposed to be a bad place to stay around there. —Taub told about rolling around on Mother Earth. —Howe and I talked about Beard, I'd seen it in his suitcase when he produced a large chocolate bar. Dr. Mitchell produced a paper bag of dried apricots—on liberals—neither blow hot nor cold and spew them out of the mouth. —Coon on porch, Oh, you people goin' on tonight—oh, you come from Pineville—have you looked at the room upstairs? —Waldo, sitting on the wicker couch, said, Come and talk to me, Edmund. —He was evidently worse upset nervously than he showed. —Oak: Well, this is the class conflict! (humorously). Quincy Howe thought it would be just too much if the gun thugs turned up at that point.

Big fire of warehouse on way home—saw it from long distance—asked boy driving what it was: They're clouds— they're red clouds. —Possum crossed road, little buff-looking animal with bright eyes. Taub's and driver's stories (he's close to us, though, somebody had said of the latter) about shooting it out in court while the judge hid under the bench. I'd drowse off and come to again while Taub talked a continual stream.

The demon killer John Wilson, the old buzzard with the long black coat and black slouch hat, bought Malcolm a Coca-Cola at one point.

—Sheriff Blair to Jessie Wakefield: Aren't ye going to give me any soup from your soup kitchen?

The first time Taub went to Pineville, he wasn't there two hours before they had arrested him for criminal syndicalism—criminal sympathy, criminal scindalism [EW apparently imitates the way someone pronounced "syndicalism"], criminal scandal—in jail they had a judge and held mock trials—floors washed four times a week, showers twice a week, had to hang up towels, every new person who came had to pay a dollar, ministers three dollars— but they had never had a lawyer before—that was a new one, see. Prosecuting attorney's speeches: You brought in these rats and lice and this cell has been lousy and filthy ever since you came!—we want a clean cell! etc. —The miners would come and offer to get them out, but they would say, No, that wasn't the right line. —There was so much solidarity in there, see, that I didn't realize what Pineville was like and when I came out and had a hearing I made a speech that lasted about an hour on constitutional rights and everything—they were stunned—finally they sent the judge a note—you could see it traveling all the way from the back of the room—passin' it along from hand to hand along the seats at the back and up the side— until finally somebody puts it on the judge's desk and he picks it up and says, No more speeches! —The WIR girls who laughed at the lawyer in court—story about Vern Smith, an old Wobbly: he had a weak-minded judge buffaloed: You're a coal operator, aren't you? (pointing at him). Judge denied it: Well, you used to be one, didn't you? —I never bought a vote in my life! — Went to Knoxville one day and when he came back was met by Mayor and Chief of Police (Pearl Osborn) with about eight deputies—Pearl Osborn was holdin' a sub-machine gun against his chest, all ready to blow my head off—they turned my car around and told me to go back to Knoxville. —At first, when they stopped me, I was puffing a cigar—I thought that as long as I kept on smoking a cigar they wouldn't do anything to me—I figured that I've my pants creased and smoke a cigar and be a regular plutocrat and that that would impress them. — After this, Tom Johnson told him he ought to go back. —It's all right for you to say that—you're underground, but I'm way up in plain sight. —But he went and got off the bus and went into the Green Parrot for lunch—the Mayor came in and shook hands with me and said how-d'ye-do— and then a little while afterwards the Chief of Police came in and shook hands with me. They're very polite and quiet and you don't know what to expect—they can smile at you one moment and then bump you off the next. — Stayed with [W. J.] Stone [a Pineville lawyer]—he was shaking in his shoes, they'd threatened to get him—would call up and ask for Taub, when he went to phone there'd be no one there—Stone had been a miner, son of a miner, county clerk, where he'd picked up his law—would pick up *Daily Worker* and hold it out and look at the headlines on the first story and strike it with his hand and say, Well, where can you find anything equal to that?—and he'd say, What's terrible about it?—I don't see there's anything terrible about it!—they try to divide up equal all around!—Jeez, I used to get kind of nervous when I'd be waitin' around in that house all alone—so long as you've got something to do, it's all right—but when you're just hangin' around!—I'd say to myself sometime, you know: the terrah can't be so great—I'd begin to wonder whether it really existed—because I'd say to myself, Here I am walkin' around the streets and nobody interferes with me—but when you lived there day after day you'd feel the pressuah! Taub: Is it wired for sound? (about the truck).

I said, For God's sake don't try to back down there—the men in my car said if you did, they'd kill you!—That's four-fifths bluff!—Hated to admit defeat. —But wanted to go to Washington to get back some morale. —Didn't want to be infantile—as they say in our jargon.

Story about little Young Pioneer during Pennsylvania miners' strikes: Judge: Don't you believe in God? —No. —What do you believe in, then? —Communism. —How am I going to know you're telling the truth? —I'm a Pioneer! —Don't you know the sun rises in the east every morning and sets in the west every night and the universe is full of harmony and order. —The sun does not rise in the east and set in the west—the earth goes round the sun—and as for harmony and awdah—Communist speech on the Pennsylvania coal situation, etc.

Communist telegrams—effect on Southern judges—messenger boy came into courtroom, then another—judge would open telegram with trembling hands—they never get any telegrams down there except when there's a war or the Mississippi's in flood—one judge in Alabama had fainted—they get a telegram that says one thousand Finnish workers in Wisconsin (?) demand the immediate release, etc.—or, We hold you personally responsible for the safety, etc.

—Quincy Howe said that he had "a pretty rugged proboscis anyway"—perhaps trying to think that it didn't hurt much to be hit in the nose.

Hickerson's account of the jail: had stayed half awake all night four nights—warned by miners somebody might come and stick a gun through the door and shoot them. —One man made a club out of tinfoil which he had been collecting for months, another had a bent stove lifter, which made a pretty wicked weapon. —There was a Veronal addict who would get quarrelsome on Veronal up to a certain point and then suddenly go to sleep—they would have to be careful not to fight with him for fear of getting shot on that pretext. (Taub told about stool pigeons in the jail.) No discipline, left to themselves: beans, bad coffee, cornmeal, and bulldog gravy—latter made out of flour and water and grease. No exercise: no sun had been in the cell since they had put the roof on twenty years ago—jail had been condemned several years ago—what were the rights of a jailbreak from a jail that had been condemned?—no ventilation—electric light all day—*Times* every day, *Nation* and *New Republic, Daily Worker* twice a week, constant communication through miners and Stone with what was going on outside—unknown people sent them fudge, which they shared with other prisoners—one man would sit up all night killing rats—in the morning there would be a pile of dead rats in the corner—moonshiners, shooters, one murderer—bunks not too narrow except when two or three people had to sleep in them—cell so full they had to put a springs in one night—thirteen men, cell 19 by 25 (?)—when he was released, they tried to deliver him over to the boys, there was a "delegation" waiting for him, but one of the jailers rescued him and had him get away out back door—

tire that went off just before they reached state line—sang songs—Vern Smith was teaching illiterate rat killer to read and write—doctor who came from Knoxville to look after Clarissa Michelson would not let prescription be filled in Pineville—tried to provoke him to quarrel when he got out. —One prisoner had syphilis, three gonorrhea— were discussing whether gonorrhea, if neglected, would turn into syphilis.

—When it rained hard, the cells would be flooded. —The day that Taub came back to Pineville, there was a regular flood—it was as if the angels had been workin'— there wehn't very many of them around, see—the Chief of Police and a couple of deputies were just standin' there lookin' at the rain—I said, Hello, and they said, Hello— they took a look at me but they let it go, see. Afterwards I went out for a walk with Stone and the houses were floatin' away. —Jeeze, I had a break.

—Young Scotch girl M.P. (very pretty, dark-green dress, black eyes, full lips, tall, well-grown, but not very good figure as far as you could see from her clothes, large feet bulging out of black shoes)—her people had been or- ganizers of coal miners for generations—adventures in Pineville, deputies came to her room, proper toughs—you know how servile the police in England are, she showed them a card to Sheriff Blair—too outrageous to be convincing.

[After the return from Pineville, some of the group dined at a speakeasy, "accusing each other of not being far enough to the left." EW's jottings seem to be frag- ments of conversation, and suggest that John Brooks Wheelwright, the poet, and Dos Passos, who had not gone to Kentucky, were also present. Subjects of their talk ranged from Communist activism to the aborted Russian Revolution of 1905, and in the midst of this EW's three words "Dante on Statius" refer us to Canto XXI of the

Purgatorio, in which Publius Papinius Statius, the Roman poet who lived from 45 A.D. to 96, salutes his master, Vergil:

> *Al mio ardor fuor seme le faville,*
> *che mi scaldar, della divina fiamma*
> *onde sono allumati più di mille;*

("The sparks that lit the music in me came / From that great fire divine whence many another, / Thousand by thousand, fetched their light and flame.")

Bob Minor, who is mentioned, was best known for his Communist cartoons in *The Liberator* during the 1920s. Walter Smith was the county attorney who had talked so blandly and cruelly during the Pineville visit.]

Mary: I always feel that my ancestors were running around and painting themselves blue while theirs were writing the Psalms of David, don't you know.

—We haven't even had our 1905 revolution yet.

—Pulling the Communists' chestnuts out of the fire.

—Mary: You have the same idea about them that they have about the capitalists—they think that they have some deep dark plot when the poor old things are just blundering along and haven't any plans at all.

—Kentucky miners part of the Marxist line-up only unconsciously as cat mewing to get out of cupboard (Dos) was part of evolution.

—Jack Wheelwright at Russian anti-religious movie—saint walking on the water: I did that once on Newport harbor. (He meant that he had been able to walk on the water with the aid of those water shoes.)

—Honesty a bourgeois virtue—all the solidarity on their side.

—Dos (Passos) said that Bob Minor talked like a phonograph.

—Lenin looks like a little East Side Jew.

—Both Communists and liberals must have their moments of feeling insecure.

—Walter Smith with his buzzer that he shakes hands with people with—symptom of defense mechanism he develops.

—Communists smile furtively like bootleggers.

—Dante on Statius

—The Walkers getting bitter about Trotsky and Communism an irresistible thing that swept aside whatever was in its track—at dinner at the speakeasy after we got back all accusing each other of not being far enough to the left—Mary Vorse announced solemnly that she had thought about her Provincetown house being confiscated.

—Deformed people at the Communist headquarters—hunchback running the elevator, dwarf woman with glasses, woman with part of face discolored as if by a burn but with a protruding growth of some kind from the discolored part.

Lyman Pratt on seaweed, which was supposed to swell up inside you and become a wonderful laxative—used to be very cheap, sold for ten cents a package, now seventy-five cents, being put over in a big way—knew all about it, where it came from, what produced it—tried to sell idea of using it in food—man who gave friend a lot in his lunch so as to ruin his golf game.

Niles Spencer. Wrote a note and put it in his pocket at beginning of party saying, I am not going to drink. —Sinking at first—facing all those people he didn't know.

Ethel Hutchinson's. Fortuneteller had told D. (her gigolo) he was never meant to work—his brown suit, long, well-tailored legs with that gathered English effect at the hips—slight lisp after a couple of drinks, hand, fingers bent forward with elbow on arm of chair—mild

and blank blue eyes—Wanda's fortuneteller had told
Margaret wonderful things, he couldn't have known
about her—a great theatrical fortuneteller—Hope Williams and others consulted him every time they opened
in a new play—he was a fairy, of course. —Ethel's
Schnauzer, everybody that went near her had got bitten—
it was sex expression, they said—she'd had him without
breeding him for seven and a half years—had jumped
on Antoinette's back when they were fooling around
the bed and bitten her badly—Ethel knew how to get
a lot of work out of French and Italian servants by being nice to them, taking them to the movies—and whereas
the Italian girl would answer back, Antoinette would
never enter into the conversation, even when you tried to
make her one of the three—and at the same time keeping
them in their place—girl who in April '32 gave her marvelous ravioli dinner—spinach, liver, and rump steak
chopped up to make meat inside the ravioli, which
showed almost like blood blue in veins through white
skin, and salad with yellow tender leaves and balls of
white creamy cheese—and kosher pale unsalted butter
and brown and white bread. —Englishman who owned
furniture—had been in United States most of his life
but often asked of other Englishmen, How long have
you been out? A green-blue-yellow-brown-toasted early-
nineteenth-century picture that you turned on the light
above when anybody took the trouble to do it for a visi-
tor who asked—with a curious embrowned lake and in
the foreground a classical building—it always seemed to
Ethel that the trees ought not to seem to be growing on
the roof—bridge books—his golf clubs on the mantel, one
of them dated Oxford in the '80s—a picture of him on
the table—a big table, a big upholstered couch—marble
and lacquered dark tables for ashtrays and drinks—a
regular bachelor's apartment—where Ethel was living
with his furniture.

—Margaret didn't know what coal was.

—Ethel thought that Monte Carlo was near southern Italy.

—They talked about Betty, who had her face peeled and looked "like a baby lobster," and everybody said that Ethel didn't need to have that done to hers.

—The radio—speeches about Prohibition and about the tax situation in Congress—shut that off!—a little music—*Ooh! that kiss, makes the world go wiggly! Everything is jiggly! Just like this*—nights like this give a swell reaction. That's the big attraction. —Army Day, with Pershing at the head of a big parade up Fifth Avenue, had just taken place the day before—Goethe's *Faust* in red leather on the table, and economize on the lemons by putting only a fourth of a one in a drink—backgammon, red and white men (what were they made of?)—in the middle of the conversation, one of the tenants came through with the rent. —Swans on the shower-bath curtains—mysterious gadgets inside—a great big bed—we changed the big mattress, why?

Ethel at Bridgeport, used to walk out to husband's tire factory, houses like boxes, local society of bankers, etc., stuck it out three months.

André Gide, the old flawed Protestant diamond, still able to make a scratch on the smooth surface of French culture.

Hal Smith's apartment. The front room with dull silver and gun-metal-gray modern paintings, no carpets on the floors, gold curtains of some heavy-looking material looped up on the windows, cocktail-shaker, glasses dull silver cylinders, vase for flowers two shiny silver cylinders fastened together, one bigger than the other, lamp like a pile of big glass crackers, white walls, woodwork of doors and windows black and red, lamp with white stars and half-moons on light-blue shade. —Silver stars and moons or suns on blue on ceiling of one of the rooms. —Dining room with black and white tiled effect and plain dark Early American-looking furniture. —Fancy kitchen, yellow dish towel, eighteenth-century Toile de Jouy wallpaper with bridges, cascades, and groves with ducks floating on the water and period country people fishing (green)—eighteenth-century furniture in bedroom, eighteenth-century wood-paneled elevator with gilded wooden bird done with an imitation of authentically worn and battered age (at Alec Woollcott's* on East 52nd Street overlooking the East River and Welfare Island, barges passing in the foreground). —Elaborate electric refrigerator.

Margaret. Somebody had said she was built like a watch—also a Shetland pony.

—Ass in a pat of butter.

— Some little man in Paris was like a watch charm— but dangerous—girlfriend stopped her being seen with him.

Betty Huling said that somebody or other thought that George Soule was an empty valise.†

Ann, in her blond phase, while acting up over Cummings's escapades, at a party at the Rogerses', in the bathroom with Margaret and Katy, seized the fancy guest towels, such as no one would even think of using, soiled

---

* Alexander Woollcott (1887–1943), the drama critic, poetaster, and radio commentator, the "original" for the main character in the play *The Man Who Came to Dinner.*

† Elizabeth Huling and George Soule were both at *The New Republic.* Betty remained a close friend of EW's until her death in 1969.

them in the toilet, and threw them across the room. Katy's eyes grew round as saucers.

Lyman Pratt. He liked the turns at the Palace, the Trans-Lux, the pineapple-drink stands, etc., in a naïve way—I realized that this was the psychology that had made the boom period, American advertizing, etc.—it was enough for him to enjoy all this—to enjoy it and put it over. Casanova.

Knew all the restaurants you could suggest—walked into speakeasies without challenge—nodded at man in gray suit who passed us on the street and said he was Owny Madden's* pay-off man—used to know him well, I think he would do anything for me, if I went up to him now and asked for five hundred dollars I think he would give it to me! —Mussolini and Lenin—rumors of the collapse of a very solid bank in Chicago—a notorious bore whom he'd seen at a party the night before and who was talking poor, withdrawing gold from circulation—knew all the sets at the Palace—had he seen the black-face monologist?—Yes, (adding after a moment) not for years though. —Vanessi had been kept by a friend of his and had ruined Harry physically and financially—had used to be in spectacles in Winter Garden. —Pornographic ideas about the Chinese contortionists. —Pornographic movie show on Broadway—had seen it in Grand Rapids. —Motorcycles—had had one as a kid—his father had hated to have him ride it—also in army. —Had been one of Franklin Roosevelt's aides when latter was Assistant Secretary of the Navy. —Spoke to little man who was

---

* Madden was Owen Vincent (1892–1965), the notorious beer baron and Prohibition racketeer, nicknamed Clay Pigeon by police (he had been shot at so often). He was born in England.

casting director for musical comedies on street—those two
slick-looking little girls we saw on the corner had probably been waiting for him. —Harlem. —Voyage he had
taken with two other boys. —Stopped and priced Used
Cars. —Genuine pleasure in everything, vaudeville acts
(Trans-Lux)—booths for grape, cherry, pineapple, and
orange drinks—This is a cute little place! clusters of
artificial grapes, artificial cherry blossoms—this Depression had taken the bunk out of a lot of things—you remember there used to be a nickel? —He was disgusted
with this country, would like to pull out, it had grown
up fast and was going down fast, didn't have a drop of
patriotism left—tempted by a man he knew to charter
boat and go on moviemaking trip: fable just erotic
enough, "Most Beautiful Woman in the World."

Nathanael West (Weinstein):* Father a building
contractor—died in the tool house in spite of the fact
his heart was weak and the family'd tried to persuade
him not to go to work—gave him half-Hebrew, half
English service at funeral church, up on Riverside
Drive—West was horrified when he found that they had
rouged the old man's cheeks and cut off his shaggy eyebrows and put a great big white tie on him. He couldn't
see that there was much in the funeral service that could
comfort you very much. The first spadeful of earth that
he had to throw down on the coffin gave him an awful
jolt.

"From shirtsleeves to shirtsleeves in one generation."

"In this business you've got to know the value of
$1.49."

* EW supplied this paragraph to Jay Martin for use in his
Nathanael West: The Art of His Life (1970), p. 228. Born
Nathan Wallenstein Weinstein (1903–40), West is best known
for his *Miss Lonelyhearts* (1933).

PROVINCETOWN
AND NEW YORK

[Margaret Wilson left in early summer of 1932 for California, intending to bring back her young son, Jimmy, and to go with EW to Provincetown as in the past. He in turn would be joined by his daughter and her nurse. On arriving in Santa Barbara, Margaret learned that her former husband had lost so much money that he could give her nothing for their son's expenses and travel. If she wanted to be with him, she would have to remain for the summer in California. EW had in the meantime left *The New Republic* to devote himself to the writing of his play *Beppo and Beth.* In a note inserted in his journals EW said that, in addition to his own shortage of funds, "I recurrently felt [the need] to be quite by myself, sufficient to myself and not responsible to anybody." He added: "I had to do something about Rosalind for the summer—she had come to seem my most important responsibility—and I thought that in the situation it was natural and inevitable that we should each spend the summer with his own child." In this way "I was able to reconcile myself to so long a separation." One gathers that Margaret had no choice.

He added a further note about the period before going to Provincetown: "Till Rosalind got out of school, I alternated between the apartment in New York and my mother's house in Red Bank. I worked on *Beppo and Beth,* drank gin, and played Beethoven on the phonograph. Eventually I looked up Anna and had her come to see me. I would not let her go into the bedroom, but made love to her on the couch."]

Going down to Red Bank on the train when the orchards were in bloom—the green country through a lace of pink and white.

Late June: bicycling on road to Freehold, red soil, heavy greenery of trees and creepers draped on fences— the air charged with wonderful smells of locust, ailanthus, honeysuckle, roses (planted in rows like cabbages in the field of a nursery), cows, manure (?), etc.

Red Bank, mid-July. All day a gray remote rain-shadow threatened the otherwise bright Sunday, then in the late afternoon it grew dark, too dark to read on the back porch, with the awnings down, and the rain fell—I had gotten up early and fell into a doze on my bed in the darkening room—Jenny called from downstairs—I'd been in the house alone—and waked me up—when I came down and looked out the front screen door I saw that the rain was already over—the evening was wonderfully cleared as if one were in a hollow in the middle of a great green and yellow melon. —At night, the ice-cool air on sweaty cheeks was so delicious from the open window in the sun parlor and the full moon looked so cool and fresh and perfect that I went out and stood in the garden—dew on the rosebush leaves—rich air, a smell almost like chestnuts—the spare towering locust trees, their plumes moving in a little night wind, and smoke-gray clouds moving in the west against a sky darker gray—I tried to think how such nights might have seemed to the Kimball girls [EW's relatives on his mother's side] at Eatontown with their beaux—"Roll on, silver moon!"

Harry Kemp (August '32), so dignified and proud and on his good behavior at Provincetown, butter wouldn't melt in his mouth—partly afraid he had offended people with his novel—Betty Spencer's story about his appearing to Ida Rauh* at the end of last summer and putting on a big act about shaking the dust of Provincetown from his feet—orated, rhapsodized, stormed, going to put all that behind him and go away to seek strange shores, refresh his soul with new incarnations. Ida said that she had been having bad indigestion and that after she had listened to Harry it had all gone away. Ida was thrilled, hadn't had anything to stimulate her so for some time—told Betty how wonderful it was to find somebody who had a *faith!* —The next spring Harry turned up as usual—no: it was this summer, Harry had come up to get away from people who would be "after him" in New York as a result of the publication of his book—said he was going to walk to Rome and read his poems to Mussolini—came back to Provincetown after an absence of three or four days.†

Betty Spencer. Her boating friend, gave party while he was staying at her house. Susan [Glaspell], who was splitting up with Norman [Matson], said that she missed Niles giving drinks, didn't like Betty's giving the party

---

* Max Eastman's first wife, described as "languid and wealthy."

† Kemp's novel, *Love among the Cape-Enders* (1931), was a thinly disguised account of the Provincetown Players and other Cape personalities and was criticized for its flamboyance, scandal-mongering, and hyperbolic style.

with him away—Norman objected to the boyfriend because he couldn't talk about anything but boats. —Betty
had been driven to desperation by two weeks of her
mother-in-law, had had to do all the cooking, had begun
spilling the dinner the last day, had scorched herself
badly on the bosom. After mother-in-law's visit, had
tried a little lechery, had found that a little lechery was
a great thing. —Her old maid that they hadn't been able
to have this summer on account of the expense had come
in lately to do the work and that had been fine—she was
anal-erotic like Betty—she knew because she had all the
symptoms: careful, neat, meticulous, not so good in some
other ways, but awfully orderly and neat.

This summer at Provincetown ('32) like fifty years
ago—men on wagon and getting restive, falling in love
with young girls, going to New York and looking for
jobs. —Picnic at Gull Pond—blue little very slightly
wind-roughed inland fresh-water lake—Sambo and Toto,
cocktails in thermos bottle, little chickens, Sunday papers, Dudley Poore—water creamy and warm—a sort of
sentimental swim—I used to crawl all over lakes like this.
—Harbor back of the Dos Passos house—diving raft—
tanned groups with legs standing up on it—sometimes
people (big children) just lying on it like logs in the
sun— the Russian with the narrow-striped jersey who had
brought a water bicycle from the banks of the Seine—
people apparently taking a big police dog for a ride in a
boat—a whole pack of police and other dogs single-foot-
ing around on the sands when the tide was out—a boy in
a boat dragging another boy on what looked like a cellar
door—a row of sailboats like white butterflies—the small
waves from the *Dorothy Bradford* which caused Stella
to think that the tide had gone out as far as it was going
and was now turning back—a boy in bathing trunks in
a kayak, rotating the double oar like a propeller—the

salad and hors d'oeuvre of the garbage—other days absolutely clear—stumps of the piles of the old pier just
sticking up in a rectangular patch like the worn-down
bases of old teeth. —On rainy days and in dreary winter
weather you felt cooped up on the narrow land, however,
like all places where life is so much the water. —A sailboat slipping by at night refreshing the night by a tracing
of silent life across it—the dark church of Truro set high
on its hill on one side of the harbor and white Long
Point light at the end of its sandspit on the other.

—pack of German police dogs on the sand flats

—children in kayaks like water bugs

—Sunset: the oystershell harbor—the water roughened
and shell-blue, the Long Point lighthouse and the buildings behind clear white like bits of shell—then a sail and
the lighthouse sharp white on a uniform dim pink-gray
of sea and sky, the sea now smooth—then the sea delicate pink over blue, silken, the sky a baby blue at the
horizon that deepens toward smoke-blue of night and
above it a layer of cloud a slightly brighter pink than
that of the water—the sailboat and the houses on the
point came out suddenly, it seemed, clear yellow as the
color of the sun struck them—then a pink pale ruby
came out in the lighthouse.

—*Toto* nationalizing the duck, expropriating the kidneys—*that house all built by young people* with no serious responsibilities—they had "outgrown" the alcove in
the downstairs bedroom, abolished it when they fixed
over that part of the house—party the decent and honest
Balls, the highly commendable, always dependable Balls,
finally gave after years of excuses, alleging unsettled
house, etc., couple who had eloped from college, gone in
for being sick rather early in life—Jerry Farnsworth* had
been so apprehensive that he had brought along a bottle

* Farnsworth, the painter (*b.* 1895), lived at North Truro.

of his own distillate—he and the Dos Passoses kept coming over to look at the still—Dos had thought the party
was probably breaking up by now but Katy said no, the
Balls were sitting up like that (attitude of dog sitting up
with front paws)—Dos said that in that case they'd
better go back and liquidate the Balls.

—*Mary Vorse's brother* had brought *Chesco* back from
Italy years ago because he couldn't get away from him—
Chesco paranoiac, would threaten to kill him, hadn't
gotten away from him to this day.

—A speedboat cutting a parabola and trailing its white
comet's tail.

—Young round sturdy girl, skin tanned almost purple,
in dark-blue bathing suit, smooth, round unexpressive
face, snub nose, round white bathing cap with flaps that
came down over her ears and fastened under her chin,
would stand with arms down at her sides and legs close
together on end of diving board—she seemed to be practicing diving in a serious way—or moved about in this
posture on the raft as if she were still thinking about diving.

—Hoarser and louder voices of Portuguese who seemed
to sneak out on the shore when the other people weren't
there, lying on the bulkhead of an untenanted house or
even going out to the raft.

—Boys with mongrel dog went out in boat, dog when
it saw them apparently going away swam out after them
and they had to come back.

—Crime wave: two holdups—White Terror: Russian
movie suppressed—police patrolling beach, on the rumor
of a nudist colony, making men put on their bathing-
suit tops.

—Waughs*—the Wizard—his five canvases in one

* There were two Waughs in the Provincetown art colony,
Coulton Waugh, a "modern," and Frederick Waugh, a marine
painter.

day—his short story—portraits in shells and cement—disused conservatories and aquariums—"nunes," pieces of
wood that looked like figures—Waugh girls who went to
ball won first and second prizes, only ones in George
Washington costume.

—the first brimming back in of the tide, glittering along
the edge

—little loud tough red motorboat like a water beetle

—little tough boy who said in a loud hoarse voice, you
goddam gyp!

—outboard motor

—Whitened horse-mackerel heads that smelled so they
finally had to be hooked by an anchor by young Mayo,
who was tired of coming out every morning and smelling
them, and dropped at sea.

While I was reading something, a song through an
association of ideas began to sing itself at the back of
my mind as if it were heard on a radio as one turns the
dial along past it on the way to some other station—coming out of the dark void, dim, and, still dim, dying away.

The men and boys standing in front of the Provincetown Town Hall reminded me for a moment, as I rode
past them on my bicycle, of Princeton—something about
the fall afternoon light coming through the trees ragged
with fall.

Provincetown. Late afternoon, the white sailboats and
white shell-shaped dories were yellowed like the nautilus
shells and the small clamshells in certain places (certain
species?).

A fine September morning: under a cloud-thinned
sky of thin blue, the sun on the pale gray water makes

something like a hemisphere of quivering silver butter-fish scales.

[Chauncey] *Hacketts.* His anecdotes about his former wife—she had said, Your being sick has upset all my plans!—And, the so-and-so's are so poor they've had to give up two of their houses! —A person who had those ideas only got worse with time—got to be very repellent. —Wouldn't let him have children and he had never fought it out—he couldn't keep on disagreeing with people—had managed to wangle twelve-year-old girl for a week—the best he had been able to wangle so far.

—He had been down to meet her coming over from Nantucket—she had wired, missed boat (hydroplane)—later made it in nineteen minutes in a speedboat—he had been waiting in sun in the car without a hat for one hour and forty-five minutes. —Sunk into stupor when he got back—it must have been the nervous strain of watching Bubs playing doubles—daughter taller and more aquiline, well brought up. (Muffy, little anomalous poodlelike dog who looked like a black toy lion—Frank Shay said he had always wanted to wash him to find out what color he was.)

—As soon as he saw me, said we had better escape into the dining room, left daughter with mother, who had been telling me how mad people got over contract bridge—said they hadn't brought me the mackerel because it had turned out to have lain around in the sun and gotten bad—he'd cleaned it till the kitchen was a shambles, then it had begun to come apart. —I asked about the last brewing—it had turned out terribly, just like vinegar, and had to be thrown away. —Cockeyed tennis racket which had been given him years ago by a pro, but lately they'd left it out of the press at night and it had curled up until it looked as if it had been made that way on purpose and was intended for some strange game. —They said there was something mad about the house—immediately after saying so, Bubs, trying to re-seat herself on the chair, said, Why, I tried to sit down on nothing!—about three feet from the chair!—Chauncey, trying to open the door, hurt a cut which had gotten in-fected from the mackerel and was always getting opened up—nothing serious, just a little slice. Bubs complained that Chauncey had put too much bitters in her drink the day before—she had refused to drink it—he said, You can put that on my tombstone, my dear—He put too much Angostura in the cocktail. —Then he said with sudden insight, I know what's the matter with me! I'm hungry—I haven't had anything to eat! —Bubs offered to get him a chop and went into the kitchen. He sat down and said it was a wonderful thing to have someone to get you a chop when you were hungry. He started to pour me another cocktail, then noticed that he had put in all gin and split it with his own glass. They *were* very pink and spicy-tasting with bitters—he said, You know the way they do—they just put in a few drops, but you soon get so that a few drops mean nothing! —The book-cases with the books of the Hapgood* children in them—it was an awful phonograph and really didn't work. Bare walls and floors, sloppiness (though Bubs had sewed up everything torn that afternoon), rented-looking furniture. —Chauncey's amusing stories several days before about going out with the fishermen at Truro. Today his story about the pro who turned up in the Provincetown tennis tournament—some man in town had evidently fixed it up for him to play with him in the doubles—Chauncey had looked him up and found that he was a regular

* Norman Hapgood (1868–1937), an editor of *Collier's, Harper's,* and *Hearst's International.*

teacher and kept a store for sporting goods and everything—very curious, I wonder what he got out of doing
that—because pros usually have a very high sense of
honor! —Finally he said, I must go in to my mothball in
the other room. She had her hair done in a funny old-
fashioned way. —The kids, when put to bed, would always be calling them back on all sorts of pretexts. They
had been very active in getting up a beach picnic and
many people, so far as I could see, had accepted—but
now that they had heard about the Dos Passoses and
others clustering around the gloomy church, they decided
to go there—they didn't know exactly what to do about
the other thing and finally, apparently, did nothing.
—Bubs had gone in and gone up the tower and rung the
bell and Brownie L'Engle, who was having lunch near
there, nearly had a fit, as she paid money to have it
taken care of and thought it was boys who had gotten
in.

—Bubs tried to turn on electricity in front room and
failed, then tried electricity in back room, with same result, said that all the bulbs in the house had ceased to
work one by one—later tried the dining-room light again
and it went on—simply hadn't found the right combination of things: you turned on bulb and wall switch.

—Katy told me about a picnic given by the Hacketts at
which the only food produced was sandwiches which had
become soaked with water and had to be eaten with a
spoon, the guests came away very disgruntled. The
Hacketts promised them soup, as they had some in the
house, but the soup turned out to be gravy—they said
that gravy was practically the same thing as soup and
put rice and tomatoes in it. This was all a party for
somebody from the German embassy that the Hacketts
wanted to make a fuss about.

—Chauncey, tight, got insulted at Corn Hill when a

lady asked him for a cigarette, and walked home all the way to Provincetown, hiding among the trees beside the road when a car passed, taking care to keep his dark coat in the shade and white trousers in the moonlight— then felt so badly about his surliness that he motored all the way back and stayed at the party till six, telling the hostess what a success it had been.

—Miss Kelly, who lived across the street and knew and disapproved of everything they did—Bubs said they didn't mind her, though; she stood out as a "real personality," you know what I mean.

—Sister and Winky, who had been used to a well-regulated room (house?), got up and came down every morning and waited around till breakfast—Hacketts didn't rise till about ten.

—Bubs thought about her early impressions of Lakewood, New Jersey, Chauncey told anecdotes about Washington.

—Juice of preserved cherries in cocktails, everything in kitchen greasy when you put your fingers on it.

—Trip to go out with Truro fishermen that didn't pan out because too many people had been asked—it was cold and windy besides. Ended up by having a second breakfast at my house—talked about distilling. I told Chauncey that I didn't understand how the trap worked and he began to explain very courteously about the fishermen's nets—Imagine a net with just one hole open where everything can get through, etc. —I listened to him intently for some time—when he began to talk about forty-foot poles (?)—before I realized the misunderstanding. —Sitting around the cold stove and spitting at it, sleeping on the wooden couches—"from this out"— walking to window and door and watching light and weather—Cockeye, the Skipper.

—Morning we went out—calm and warm and stars

very clear—the orange harvest moon hanging low in the
West—the delicate pink dawn, one silver star high up
among the light smoky clouds, the sun came up like a
cherry, the houses along the shore looked light and were
light brown almost like the yellow sand, a little bit dim,
grays and sandy-colored yellow of the delicate and barren Truro dawn. —The first trip, white mackerel gulls
perching on the poles, closing the gate—the fins and tail
of a shark, shiny and black, cruising around inside, not
yet quite light—the dark deep water, mysterious and
pregnant, about to reveal its catch—fight with the shark,
hooked and hauled up and stabbed, head cut off, it still
strained in convulsions, and even when the guts were
taken out—the mackerel, silver and vibrating like the
glass beads of a chandelier—the starfish and hermit crabs
and sea crabs and spider crabs clinging on to the net as
it is pulled up, the whiting of the second catch gaping
up as their heads are brought out of water, sorting out
the fish—the goosefish of the fourth catch, muddy, amor-
phous, ugly, lying on their bellies in the boat, automatically chewing at mackerel which would slip down their
throats as they lay there, hooked up and thrown out
beyond the nets, their big white bellies flapping helpless
through the air—butterfish like thin silver coins, brown
hake dripping long pink tentacles—a bonita, a few blue-
backs, with beautiful blue metallic sections along their
backs.

—The fishermen were nine weeks behind in their
pay—"the help are carryin' the company"—mackerel
worth only three-fourths of a cent a pound—"we're just
poor slaves," though didn't have anybody standin' over
them with a watch, they were left to themselves, somebody over them but they organized the work themselves—we're tough but we're human—Joe King, the old
Portuguese who would bite the head off a live mackerel,

why eat dead fish that you don't know nothin' about?—
live ones, you knew they were fresh.

More Provincetown beach life. Little tiny girl with
the legs of a little brown boy coming back from a boat
ride with her parents and stepping over the thing they
slid the boats down with, her head of long blond hair
down her back and her little pale-green sweater pulled
down over the trunks of her blue bathing suit—balancing
with her little brown arms.

—High tide coming in late in the afternoon—the daylight darkens—the water deepens—the sailboats and dories
come out.

Hacketts. Always stopped car directly in front of gate
so that it was impossible to get in.

—Bubs invited me to lunch, then she wasn't there,
but Chauncey made apologies, explaining that at the
L'Engles' all sorts of disorganizing things had happened,
such as Gwen Waugh getting under the kitchen table
and pounding and Bubs going off in Charley Kaselau's
car and leaving Chauncey without means of conveyance
home—he had said goodbye to everybody and then had
to go back and unsay it—then when he did get home he
sat up waiting for Bubs to come back and finally found
her asleep in bed—it was six before he had gotten to bed.

—His use of "loathsome"—Harvard, no doubt. The behavior of the coffeepot was pretty loathsome.

—Found them that evening sitting around the fire—
the new clothes they had just gotten for the children
more or less strewn around in the middle of the floor—
having one of their dubious cocktails—cunning little shy
children with curious hoarse way of talking, combination of Chauncey's drawl and Bubs's hissing and biting
down on consonants, did a good deal of shrieking, un-

restrained by their parents, and insisted that everybody should put large paper bags on their heads—we continued the conversation, Bubs laughing very hard over the appearance of the people in the bags. —Chauncey's stories about Washington—Henry Adams, frail, malicious, and feminine, had given him the *Education* to read, he had introduced Lord Middleton to H. C. Lodge* when he (Chauncey) was drunk—had gotten them on a couch together anyway and Lodge had asked Middleton to lunch. John Sharp Williams got drunk every day of his life—valedictory to the Senate, left because he had become disgusted with their making politics out of international relations and would as soon be a dog and bay the moon as sit another day in the Senate—left it and never returned—the night they were going to give a farewell dinner for him he went off and had dinner with three or four senators and his favorite bartender. —Secretary of Navy Adams on "colorful lady": "Isn't that whore satisfied yet?"—used to greet visitors with profanity. —Washington "late Roman"—place where you wouldn't be surprised if all the policemen turned out to be fairies—retired army and navy officers, many of them committed suicide, considered all right in the service.

—Strange, obsolete make of portable typewriter—you had better not carry it by the handle, I don't think that case is very reliable we didn't know how to open it at first, it seemed so weird, and then when we did, it proved not to have a standard keyboard, just enough different so that Marcelle Rogers couldn't use it.

Betty Spencer's idea for character in play based on man she had met at party who had begun by inflating himself, then humiliated himself, eaten the dirt—had

* Senator Henry Cabot Lodge, in office 1893–1924.

told her something very odd about himself in exalting himself. He or somebody had played *La Cathédrale engloutie* [Debussy]—"then decided that he'd better go and get englouti."

[During his summer on the Cape, EW wrote out in his journals a statement about his political beliefs at that season of the American economic crisis. His self-communion reflects his recent extensive reading in Marx, Lenin, and Trotsky. It was corollary to the position he had taken in his essay in *The New Republic* in which he had appealed to progressives to face the realities of the Depression. It followed also on the drafting of a manifesto during May with Lewis Mumford, Waldo Frank, Dos Passos, and Sherwood Anderson advocating—in highly theoretical language—a "socioeconomic revolution" to "release the energies of man to spiritual and intellectual endeavor." The literary men recognized "the fundamental identity of our interests with the workers and farmers of the nation" and advocated "a new order . . . in which economic rivalry and private profit are barred; and in which competition will be lifted from the animal plane of acquisition to the human plane of cultural creation." They urged more than "simply a revolt against the economic chaos of today." Dos Passos complained that the language was unfamiliar to the average American. And it was felt, too, that in advocating revolution—or a total change—they were hewing closely to the Communist position.

The statement written into his journals focuses on the election out of which would emerge Roosevelt's New Deal—perhaps a part of his clever manipulation of the semantics and the words "new order" used by the literary intellectuals. In a sense, EW was rewriting the manifesto into a language proper to himself. He believed that this was no time for political passivity. Today, with our hindsight of almost half a century, it might be easy for an ahistorical person to make light of the precise and even scholarly view EW took of the collapse of American society at that moment in the century's history. In effect, he was saying that the system had been shown to be a failure and it was necessary to change it. To someone planning to cast his ballot during the autumn of 1932 with a vivid sense of the economic urgencies EW had witnessed in the coal fields, the mills, and the motor industry, the alternatives offered the American voter seemed discouraging. In a lucid and intelligent way—though one must grant that for the moment EW made no allowance for political expediencies and a patchwork democracy—he saw little hope in Franklin Delano Roosevelt, who was groping for a party platform. To vote the Socialist ticket of Norman Thomas seemed to EW a vote for tergiversation and those errors which Social Democracy had made in Italy and Germany, the kind of vacillating liberalism that seemed invariably to end in Fascism. The examples of Mussolini and the ascendancy of Hitler were in full evidence.

EW's self-examination seems accordingly to be a weighing of acute and deeply embarrassing alternatives. The conclusions he reaches follow logically from his premises. The American Communist Party had not yet had a chance to make many of its later blunders; and Roosevelt's great salvaging effort in behalf of the status quo could not be predicted in 1932. EW's decision to vote the Communist ticket was more than a gesture of protest: it seemed to be a belief that W. Z. Foster and Earl Browder were in the American grain, that an American Communist Party need not follow the Russian line. If EW was wrong in his evaluation of the American party, he at the same time refrained from joining it. And he knew only too well the historical meaning of the word "revolution." His crisis of belief would lead him to Russia and a study of the Russian language and its people.]

I expect to vote for the Communist candidates in the elections next fall.

Hoover stands frankly for the interests of the class who live on profits as against the wage-earning classes. Franklin Roosevelt, though he speaks as a Democrat in the name of the small businessmen and farmers and is likely to be elected by them in the expectation that he can do something for them, can hardly be imagined effecting any very drastic changes in the system which has allowed him to get into office. Whatever amiable gestures he may make, he will be largely controlled by the profit-squeezing class just as Hoover is.

He is like the specter of Woodrow Wilson's liberalism—less forceful, with less rich an unctuousness, and smiling an inhuman Boy Scout smile that fairly makes one's flesh creep. Wilson himself, with a strong will, some imagination, and excellent intentions, was caught and finally crushed by the machine he believed himself to be running and whose defects he thought he was mending when he tried to make it do work for which it was never intended. The more passionately earnest he became for democracy and human rights, the more regimented and censored and enslaved the American people were; and in establishing a League of Nations, he signed a treaty which guaranteed all the antagonisms of imperialist Europe. The old-fashioned southern Democrat never really understood the modern world. And what can one expect of Franklin Roosevelt?

There remain then the Socialists and Communists.

Theoretically they both aim at the same thing: the abolition of the capitalist system. And theoretically perhaps there is no reason why either might not effect it. A false emphasis is often given to the fact that the Socialists hope for peaceful revolution whereas the Communists expect violence. A Socialist government, if it succeeded in voting the nationalization of the means of production, would certainly not refuse to use force if the capitalist owners resisted; and a Communist government which should be fortunate enough to get control of the parliamentary machinery would certainly not insist on violence if the politically vanquished bourgeoisie allowed themselves to be expropriated quietly.

Yet there are profound psychological differences between the Socialists and the Communists—profound differences in point of view. The Socialists, in depending on bourgeois institutions to engineer the transition to socialism, have identified themselves in general, whether consciously or unconsciously, with the point of view of the owning class; and the consequences of this in the cases of the German and British socialists have been far from reassuring in regard to socialists in general. It is true, as W. Z. Foster says, that having committed themselves to the agencies of the capitalist state as instruments for achieving socialism, they find, as soon as that state is threatened by a crisis, that before they can do anything further about socialism, they will have to save capitalism. Hence the behavior of the German Social-Democrats in the war; hence the coalition cabinet of Ramsay MacDonald. They end up supporting the imperialist warmakers, the Tory tax evaders and the bond-bolstering international bankers, and indistinguishable from them.

And the American Socialist leaders during the war went for the most part the way of the Europeans. It is difficult to imagine their present leader, Norman Thomas, in the role of a Ramsay MacDonald: he is an able and honest man who made himself unpopular in 1917 by opposing participation in the war. But the party he represents is the old Socialist Party and it has suffered, it seems to me irremediably, the demoralization brought to the Socialists by the war and the Russian Revolution. Who will expect at this time of day to see the American Socialists occupy even the kind of position that the German and British ones did. The real Marxist revolution in Russia threw the socialists into consternation. The American Socialists have only just succeeded in passing at their recent convention a resolution approving the Soviets; and a great many are still bitterly of the opinion that since the revolution was expected by Marx to take place in a highly industrialized country, the U.S.S.R. is therefore, as I understand them, only a myth. Yet in proportion as the Communists have been manifesting self-confidence, energy, and fervor, the Socialists have visibly been becoming less confident and more confused. They are now torn between their old tradition and a militant left wing. But the net result has been, in spite of the efforts of the latter, that the party has decided to rely entirely upon political action: with the Communists already in the labor field, the Socialists have concluded there is no room for another radical labor movement.

Norman Thomas "clings to democracy," writes his official apologist, Paul Blanshard, "not because he has serious illusions about it but because he feels that it is the only hope left of avoiding a catastrophe which in so complex a civilization as the United States might retard rather than advance the socialist cause." This seems an ambiguous position. If Mr. Thomas has no serious illusions about democracy, why does he continue to cling to it? But he must have serious illusions if it is not plain to him that the democracy of the capitalist system is at the present moment mowing down lives like hay, and by killing off the dispossessed classes through starvation, disease, and despair—to say nothing of the slaughter of soldiers in imperialistic warfare and the assassination of strikers and radicals—rolling up a record of cruelty and waste which makes the Communist revolution in Russia look like a humanely conducted operation. Is not the catastrophe already here and is it not simply a question now how to end it?

The Communists assume, on the other hand, that "the owning class never gives up without a struggle." They have no faith in "democratic institutions," because they believe that the owning class controls them. They insist that the only agency which can ever establish socialism is an organized movement of the classes dispossessed by the crisis of capitalism. This movement must be based on the working class, because the working class is at the bottom of the social pile and has the most obvious interest in having it upset; but the farmers and as many as possible of the white-collar class and the technicians must be shown that their interests are identical with those of the working class and not with those of the owning class.

The Communists distrust the bourgeois—that is, they distrust anybody who is getting anything out of the existing social order, no matter how emphatically he may assert or how sincerely he may believe that he is in favor of having it superseded by socialism. Political history has shown that such people are likely to sell out when the status quo is actually threatened. The Communists therefore go into training for the classless society that they foresee: they renounce the rewards of bourgeois success and repudiate the standards of bourgeois respectability. They school themselves in austere living, in the discipline that makes possible united action and in the courage required to declare openly their revolutionary objects and to lead the working class against the owners.

The Communists, it is true, at the present time, do not invariably pursue these policies with a maximum of wisdom or skill. But their shortcomings are, I believe, due to causes which are temporal and local and have no necessary connection with Communism. The period of the boom in America was exceedingly unpropitious for the Communists. The working class was bedazzled by prosperity; the unions became conservative and corrupt; the majority of the capable leaders in radical politics and labor identified themselves with bourgeois movements or organizations built into the capitalist structure. Those who stuck to the Marxist–Leninist position were a small isolated band, almost universally ridiculed and repulsed. They went so far underground at one time that it was said of them that not only did they manage to keep their activities a secret from the police but the workers never heard about them either. The result of this was both a purification of principle and a weakening of realism in approach. Then the collapse of the capitalist economy came with a suddenness and completeness which astounded the Communists themselves; and the situation which gave them their chance became more acute so rapidly that they have never yet been able to catch up to it. Furthermore, the fact that the Communists in the United States are guided by the Third International and that the Communist International is dominated by Russia has tended to make them at their worst mere parrots of the Russian party and yes-men for Stalin.

Yet they alone at the present time are working in any impressive way to educate and organize our wage-earning classes for the defeat of the capitalist system. There is no reason why, in catching up with the American crisis, they should not modify their methods to fit it—they have indeed begun to do so already. There is nothing intrinsically Russian about Communism—the Communist International announces by its very name that the Russians are to count for it merely as certain units of the peoples of the world. And as Trotsky says, a Communist revolution in Germany would make Germany, no longer Russia, the most important Communist country of Europe because more typical of modern industrialized society and more closely involved in European affairs.

In the meantime, therefore, though I agree with many of the criticisms made of the official party by its rivals and expelled heretical factions, I recognize that what sometimes seem to me its narrow and wrongheaded policies are partly an effect of that discipline, that obedience to a central authority, without which serious revolutionary work is impossible; and I feel considerable confidence in its leaders, men like Foster and Browder, representatives of labor who, in educating themselves theoretically, have not lost touch with the working class and authentic American types who, in making the difficult transition to the international Marxist point of view, have not lost their grasp of American conditions. I shall vote for the Communist candidates because they seem to me to understand the crisis better than any of the other candidates in the field. I believe that they are fundamentally right—that the development of capitalism, by throwing out of work and reducing the purchasing power of more and more people, must inevitably bring society to a pass where the impoverished public has no choice but to take over the basic industries and run them for the common benefit.

We Americans have trusted to our general middle-class psychology, the result of a middle-class revolution, without considering the actual social relations and the economic situation behind it. We have believed that our society was "democratic" because it has in the past given scope to the aims of middle-class people and allowed a certain number of peasants and working-class people (I speak from the European point of view) to succeed in becoming middle-class. But it does not even do that any more. And the Marxist split is already beginning to appear right across the middle-class psychology—the split between the impoverished and the property holders. When the President the other day drove out the petitioning veterans with a brutality not unworthy of the Tsar, he put the first conspicuous crack in the middle-class illusion of democracy.

The truth is that neither the veterans nor Franklin Roosevelt nor Norman Thomas nor anyone else can remedy the Depression by appealing to the principles of the Republic. They will have to organize as the Communists do for the frank purpose of enforcing socialism. When they get to the point of doing so, it may or may not be under Communist leadership; but their aims will be the Communist aims.

NOTES FOR
BEPPO AND BETH

[EW embodied his political beliefs not only in the statement he incorporated in his journals but also in a play at which he worked during his stay in Provincetown in the summer of 1932. It was titled *Beppo and Beth*, and as we have seen, he attempted to have it produced by the Group Theatre. One can understand why it was rejected. Its slapstick and caricature, while dealing also with the serious questions of Marxism and the American Depression, proved a poor "mix." Like many intellectuals in the theater, EW reached for quick laughs and zany characters. This diluted whatever serious intentions he may have had when he sketched the play for himself. He published it with two other plays in 1937 and later reprinted it in *Five Plays*, but his wit, and his ability to write scenes of brisk dialogue, did not coalesce into a theatrical whole. *Beppo and Beth* was described by him as "a comedy of New York 'sophistication' reeling from the Stock Market crash," but none of the characters "reel"—they make light of the Depression—and the central situation of comedy relies on a gunman's failure to "waste" his quarry; it takes two acts of sloppy shooting to finally extinguish the real-estate racketeer. At moments, EW emulates Bernard Shaw by having his characters make long speeches, but these lack the sustained Shavian logic and Shaw's gift of paradox. The party-line views are put into the mouth of a Chinese valet who voices EW's own feelings that capitalistic contradictions resulted in the general crisis. Other views are juxtaposed. The New York "sophisticates" pictured by EW are largely comic-strip types—like the flamboyant capitalist who has built a fortune out of pyramided real-estate mortgages. Beppo keeps in his apartment a little piggy bank, "a fund for collapsed financiers," and he says, in the same vein as EW's article in *The New Republic*: "I think that we artists nowadays can afford to give them a helping hand."

Beppo's daughter marries a shady racketeer; and his divorced wife is involved with a stagy Englishman. EW throws out many vivid ideas, but neither the characters nor the central theme of the play provides that unity which made the social dramas produced by the Group Theatre documents of their time. The notes for this play suggest the surface quality of its humor; the names of the characters given here were later changed. There are many more such notes among EW's papers, but these are the ones he transcribed and expanded in his 1930s journals.]

A Party at Barlo Peet's. A Party at Carlo Bailey's. Beth Gates.

Hurlo Robert's. Burlo Bates—Banks.

Apartment. Mexican things, caricatures on walls, pictures of Burlo himself.

Opening conversation. He: lost job, busted, can't pay rent, gets horribly depressed, his marriages and affairs, Hermann Fay Fairbrother, Napoleon of journalism, reporter who told him pants were unbuttoned. Shall he take job, apartment half-furnished, is it all rather vulgar?

She: maternal, who's his girl now? her Englishman: her family tradition—he says that his is just the other way.

Interchange of inferiorities and phobias.

Gilbert and Beth twit each other savagely about their inferiorities and phobias at one time in the conversation.

His pretensions—get prodigious when the guests arrive —Isn't it awful to have to ring a bell to call a servant?

He tried to sell her attractiveness of life in New York by holding up composite picture of apartments they have lived in—think of this apartment, for instance—well, I haven't lived in it very long, of course—only two years, in fact—but it doesn't differ much from a lot of other apartments I've lived in and in fact it gives a rather attractive variety—the same thing—always the same comforts—with just enough difference so you don't get bored— different views, moldings, kitchen and bathroom fixtures, etc.

Girl he's in love with—her account of eight days or more she spent with boyfriend—heroine disparages her— had conversation with her in ladies' room and found her dumb—had taken her money and disappeared, but now he's turned up again. Was he a good lover? Oh, don't ask me!

Married woman—used to go to Ruth Snyder trial and then come home and hypnotize little alligator in the bathtub.*

Elephant and girl—End of Act II—have come after landlord, who had been backing their show?

* EW recorded this anecdote in *The Twenties*, p. 360, and used it in the play. See also his article on the trial and execution of Ruth Snyder, "Judd Gray and Mrs. Snyder," in *Earthquake*, pp. 161–3.

Drunk anecdotes: woman in ermine—all dressed up like sore thumb—went all the way down several flights of steps on her fanny so that elevator man wouldn't see she was drunk, then got up with dignity and walked out.

—I knew a man who stopped drinking for a month once and he said it didn't make a bit of difference—Niles's note in his pocket not to drink—put five glasses of water on table before going to bed.

Landlord. Tenant who committed suicide—no sympathy with people who behave like that—what was the country coming to—lack of responsibility

Cuthbert note in pocket

Constance tells about Cuthbert putting eight glasses of water by bed

Beth on how Peggy Follansbia was chased by man in park

also mooching downstairs

didn't make any difference

June doesn't drink because she has to watch her step

—little green men

Heroine must be shown not far from beginning to have some unsatisfied maternal or passionate instinct.

Big Smashing Scene: and Uncle Edgar and Uncle Joe who wouldn't speak to him!—they might as well go, too—in fact, they're probably at the bottom of the whole business.

Matisses and Picassos

Orthophonic Victrola and Radio

pulls down tapestry on self from gallery

She: Oh, Beppo: when you go on like that, you remind me of my mother!

Maxchixes and Pischottos

Ends by deciding to go to Mexico and buy some pottery animals and gourds, get away from it all

Before he begins smashing, he tells her how much it all means to him—that he always feels, even when discouraged, that he at least has these—old memories, beautiful objects, a little comfort, a few intelligent friends.

He must appear in very fancy dressing gown—later in trick evening clothes—lavender or purple shirt.

Scene where two people rub it into one another, each referring in an undercover way to the things he knows about the other—ought to be relieved by scene between young people.

—girl must make terrific speech about her domineering mother during which auditors shrink up in their chairs as if waiting for a storm to pass—exaggerated comic business of pulling up coats around their ears—so all through.
—She must be really intelligent, trenchant, brutal-spoken, likable—convince you of her strength and value.

—Entertainment at party while very sour situation prevails in other quarters—old English or American folk ballad—party discourages him profoundly—Chinaman finally shows him story in paper.

Beginning of Third Act. Boring (landlord?) guest who won't go (man who comes in by mistake?)—just about to put him out more or less brutally when he makes appeal to his pity—at the very door—he has gotten up to walk around the room from emotion and hero rising promptly has tried to corner him and get him out the door—there ought to be something else, too.

Psychoanalysis—pants-pressing memory.

My mother who managed a house with sixty servants and the picture of St. Francis feeding the birds—I always think of it as that horrible place where I had to study Latin—no wonder I came to New York and stayed in a cheap theatrical boardinghouse!—

Patisse–Matisse

apartment half furnished

Curtain Third Act? But everything's smashed! —It doesn't matter—it was only half furnished anyway.

Chinese Communists who replace each other.

Just as he is about to kill himself, it turns out that she has tried to kill herself in bathroom—groan—he talks to her, persuades her to live, she has been torn between social father and puritan mother, he denounces puritanism and American middle-class snobbishness (from which he has been suffering himself), smashing various objets d'art and articles of furniture in order to emphasize his points— marries her?

At the end he comes in and says that while he'd been living there in a dull and orderly manner, living on his dividends, a sophisticated and cultured life, entertaining people whom he liked and found amusing, gently satir- izing the stupid, he'd had the most cuckoo dream—the answer is that that was real—the other thing was the dream—and here's Bortschley to see you!

Sees in paper senator's opinion that we could be rescued from the Depression if we could only persuade the Chinese women to wear cotton ruffles on their trousers.

Suicide speech: People used to love life and think it wasn't long enough—they hated death. What's wrong with us? What's wrong with me? —Am I mediocre and middle class? Is that what's wrong with all of us? —Would I live in spite of everything if I were bolder or finer or greater? —Would I live if there were some big idea in society that I could believe in or that could use me?—like the Roman Empire or the Catholic Church or Communism in Russia, like what people used to think America was (rat-catching for the Soviets) or is my quality really poor? —Still, so-and-so's quality is good, I'll swear, and she's the worst off of all. —He goes back over his girls— things that had made life worthwhile. —X when she first took off her dress—I said, Take off your dress, and she said, Yes, I will. —And she did, and now I'm committing suicide just the same! —Literature and art—none of those things are enough. —Well, it seems a shame to leave them cold, but what did the damn booboisie ever do for me? I never liked them—they don't want what I want—what could I do for them anyway? —Perhaps I've got too much in common with them. That's the trouble perhaps—I play the common game and still see through it. —Well, anyway, here goes!

Comedy: Ralph Barton character
sudden lapse of enthusiasm after preparing to go somewhere or do something—what was there in it, after all?
—on the eve of an effort of virtue
—two men who begin with elaborate social pretenses à la Lyman Pratt, then end up by frankly and grotesquely discussing their rackets
—I must remember to make love to ——— tomorrow night.
—killing the Tsar and embalming Lenin gruesome— there's something distasteful about the whole thing!
rat-catching for the Soviets—but I don't want to catch rats!
—But if I lived in some kind of society dominated by

a great ideal, I'd have to submit my will to the majority, and I could never do that, hell no! to hell with the majority, I'm a gentleman and gentlemen are too scarce around here to be able to accomplish anything!—

Is the friend worse off than he?

Go and sleep with your father! Why should I sleep with you?

Isn't life miserable?

First I bought etchings of flying ducks and then I collected Zorns*—lately it's been Matisses and Picassos.

Holden: emotions in the hands of the psychoanalyst and finances in hands of receiver—no responsibility at all—all right if wasn't disturbed.

Kimmy character—
sophistication and naïveté
didn't know you had to get an extra ticket for Pullman
sophistication with grown people
—naïveté with boyfriend—Scotty kennels—bursts into tears when it falls through

The young people play Truth—Physical Phil—Did your relations with Dorothy make any difference between her and your husband? —Yes. —Well, in what way? —In a physical way. —Too formal and sophisticated for it to end disastrously.

Art Carey a born pedagogue: kept teaching this little girl things until finally they knew he'd taught her about life—one day she said she couldn't play tennis and the sisters rushed up and shook her hand—the next day she went back to St. Louis.

* Anders Zorn (1860–1920), Swedish painter and etcher, was chiefly known for his paintings of bathing peasant girls. He had considerable vogue.

Every night they have dates and sometimes double dates.

He's the only man who's never tried to touch me.

Simply want to count the scalps—whereas I used to get worked up in a regular *Ladies' Home Journal* way.

She got all glanded up.

I jumped across the counter—the desk—I jumped across the counter and I shook him like a terrier shakes a rat.

—Put him out—he's getting terrible!

—You can't put me out—I own the bloody place!

—Put him out—he's terrible! —You can't put me out—I'm terrible!

—You can't put me out, you tarts! I decorated this whorehouse myself!

We've been getting drunk in the bathtub together. —It's not clear whether or not she's been trying to kill herself (?)

He asks her during the first scene whether she doesn't think there's something vulgar about the apartment—something vulgar about him. —Don't you think there's something inherently vulgar about that screen, tapestry, bust

They end their first conversation on a note of Ho, for a fine night of revelry and amorous adventure—don't meet again until after it's over.

Van Court character—neat, clean, cultivated, decent, unsuspecting little man.

Visiting Englishman: appears in first act—dialogue with hero—curtain line at end of second act as they are all going in to dinner.

Bootleggers

Ritzy artist and his wife—Billingses, L'Engles—wife keeps saying disagreeable things to the other women like Brownie L'Engle.

Suicide speech: I'm not anybody—bundle-of-mirrors idea—the things in the apartment, what do they represent? Nobody! Nothing! A dozen places and times and personalities, and none of them mine! What am I? Not a farmer's son—not a real cosmopolitan!—not a citizen and not an artist! The phony result of all the stupid money that doesn't know how to spend itself. I don't enjoy making it—I can't buy anything with it that satisfies me—I don't enjoy having it spent on me. —If I was really good, it might be different. I might work for something else I believed in—but I can't get it out of myself. —That Russian girl that X—— was telling me about who got a kick out of being a rat-catcher. She was happy to be a rat-catcher because she was catching rats for the Soviets—she read all the books about rat-catching and studied all the methods. —But hell, I don't want to be a rat-catcher. Lenin and Tsar and those awful names they make up out of the first letters of words. —I want to "enjoy the companionship of civilized people." (Laughs ironically.)

Simple-minded silly-ass character (?)
There's an element of mystery about card playing.
What do you mean?
You don't know what's in the other people's hands.
Character for Mary (Blair)—she stays on after the party and says she won't go.

Gallery of duplex apartment—along which people are seen coming and downstairs—this has its effect in connection with conversations going on below:

Girl who saw man in park—she thought he had taken his pants off, with rape in his heart—and was chasing her—she ran and he ran—and then we were running around the aqueduct—finally he stopped and I stopped— I saw he was out of breath and just a runner—I went up to him and asked him whether it wasn't cold running around late at night like that—he said you got warmed up running—I saw that he was a Jew, then I walked away.

She's banking on the Englishman—he's banking on the mysterious and obsessing little girl—he can't get anywhere with her. —She finally tells him she knows the little girl—nothing interesting or powerful about her— just a dumb little working girl (?)—but he still sticks to his point—she represents something in his mind.

Englishman: You're not a bit like an American, buck teeth—not real—they wobbled.

Interior Decorating: $20,000 for apartment and the result is I land in Brooklyn over among the gefüllte fish where if you lose your way once you have to come back to New York and start over—putting polychrome furniture in for families who will end by living in the kitchen— stinging them on the lampshades

—mulberry, orchid, and blue—somebody else complained that rooms weren't all exactly alike—somebody wanted the rainbow reflector outside the window—husband with long beard would haggle about price, then pay cash. —Run up money with little silk flowers on bed-covers and lamps—Jews like monkeys.

THE DEATH OF
MARGARET

[A brief note inserted years later precedes EW's long passage of memory recording the death of Margaret Canby. The note reads: "I came down from Provincetown, with Rosalind and Stella, in September 1932, and spent the night in New York. Charlotte Chancellor called me up and told me that Margaret had fallen downstairs and fractured her skull and was dead." EW learned later that the accident had not occurred at home. Margaret had gone to a party wearing high-heeled shoes; on leaving she tripped on one of the steep Spanish-style steps of the building in Santa Barbara and was all but dead when she arrived at the hospital.

EW flew out at once on one of the slow propeller planes of the time; it made various stops for refueling. During this nightmare journey he set down a series of staccato notes later transcribed into his journal. We read that he "succeeded in not crying except for a moment or so at a time." He was in a state of shock; and his notes suggest that he tried to bury grief by observing the immediate happenings around him, the people on the plane, the stewardesses, and the panorama of cloud and terrain. It is only after he has reached Margaret's family that his journal becomes a kind of stream of consciousness of memory, as in Molly Bloom's monologue in *Ulysses*: there are moments when EW seems to take over that vein of writing, as if one memory enfolded another. He allowed himself complete freedom—setting down everything that came to him out of his past with Margaret. They had been married two years, but had known each other for much longer.

This remarkable monologue—remarkable for its candor, its deeply felt affection and love, its crudities and uninhibited sexual content—was written in the privacy of the journal. But there is clear evidence that EW intended to publish it, for he had it typed out along with the rest of his 1930s journals, and partially edited it before his death. One recognizes that this was all he had left of Margaret—these memories—and he seems to have clung to them even when they were unflattering to himself. In part, we may see this as reflecting the strong guilt he felt when he remembered some of their quarrels and his verbal brutalities. The love he felt for Margaret is sometimes implicit rather than explicit and never wholly expressed: it comes out in his discontinuous story of their drinkings and beddings and the small talk of their companionship; but also in his picture of Margaret's high breeding and elegance, the complicated terms of their marriage, and EW's own difficulties in accommodating himself to women of his gentry class. Margaret was a gentlewoman, not well-defended against the rough-and-tumble of EW's masculine-predatory world. She seems to have loved him unquestioningly, and was devoted to her son. The turn of fate that suddenly took her from EW came at a moment when he was undergoing a personal struggle, at thirty-seven, to find himself and make his way as a man of letters.]

Motoring to Newark airport in early morning—buy your sweets now, slot machine, chocolate-covered Brazil nuts, reminded me of going to sanatorium (Clifton Springs); waited pacing floor at station, emergency straps for taking off; nervous at first as I looked down on houses and trees, a little bit rocky and seasicky going over mountains in the east, they looked like fairly unimportant creases in the earth covered with trees—fields etc. in clear crude light to left, soft and dappled with cloud shadow to right.

Cleveland spread out on the flat continent—the dull opaque almost stagnant blue of Lake Erie, Detroit, another big flat city out there. —Gas tanks.

Fields, etc.—Rectangles of worn green billiard-table cloth, yellow rectangles, macadam highway stiff and metallic like a wire—white and black horses in a field, delicate, clear, and neat—a freight train, you could see how long it was with its red and yellow cars—coal-mining towns, a blot, a smudge of coal heaps and grimy buildings, a smudge in the middle of the flat country—we were flying most of the time quite low—old square white houses sitting in a rectangle of trees, grass, and bushes in the midst of the great flat wide country, that was all American civilization had been—near Cleveland, what seemed to be an abandoned roller coaster of some kind, very high and steep, taken in conjunction with the plane ride, made me feel a little of the horror of height of a dream—ignoble dingy black cars like bugs rolling alone along the roads.

Excessive cheeriness and politeness of all the air-transport employees in their light-green uniforms. The itineraries stuck into the backs of the seats in front, dials that showed altitude and speed, I suppose, I never examined them—steered clear of what looked as if they might be thunderclouds coming away from Cleveland (reminded me of steering clear of something with Margaret when I was brutal with her by turning away from her, then made it up not long afterwards—why did it? couldn't quite catch connection)—watercourses like simple worms—

Horrible wait at Cleveland: winter grayness of afternoon, walking back and forth on pounded gray ground of airport, two big planes of first section went on first—in little plane with pilot sitting behind, that only held four, squeezed in tight with four other men—nice-looking young fellow said it was old plane made over and could go like a bat out of hell, a little bit rough, that was the only thing—touching fellow passenger's thigh, moving over to keep away from it, did he move, too?—shutting eyes and homosexual fantasies, losing in vivid reality from Provincetown, gray, abstract, unreal sexual stimulus—also thought about coming back with Jean Gorman on train as situation that presented possibilities, but couldn't stomach it—young man too big, not my type—small airplane easy after other—I was braced against fear of falling: not a bad thing if it did—

The shadow of the plane following like a dog on the right—the rectangular cornfields of the Middle West—green carpet samples of different shades, worn out in places—cornstacks like nipples in the fields, or like pegs, sometimes the one, sometimes the other—fields dappled in regular rows with round haycocks—

Coming into Chicago—appalling industrial erection, Packingtown, big plants, high, dark, dirty, dominating gray workers' houses in the rows of straight streets—suburbs of Chicago—there they lived, the Chicagoans, those cottages all much alike set in rows on the flat filled-in swamp were all there was of the buoyant and robust Chicago life—when we left the Chicago airport, we passed over some kind of muddy watercourse with long mud islands in middle, I realized that what I had thought was an insect was really a white bird, that we had come higher than I'd known—succeeded in not crying except for a moment or so at a time—couldn't read papers, couldn't read itineraries much—earth seemed fissured like a sea fan.

It got dark after that—automatic beacons at night— night plane like half a flying Pullman, brown wood- work, little electric lamps, seats with little white head- cloths that tipped back, and they gave you little pillows— big fire-insurance man from Brooklyn who had an apart- ment in New York—stout florid face with white incon- spicuous hair and eyebrows, light eyelashes, no expres- sion much, but positive and immensely satisfied with himself, nothing real in his face, which was basically flabby and betrayed his solid figure—windmills and farms of the West—This don't look very propitious: two fat men together—they ought to pair off a fat one with a lean one—going to Seattle and in constant state of anxi- ety and indignation for fear he wouldn't make connec- tion at Salt Lake and would have to wait over a day—had been held up on previous trip because they said weather conditions were bad, but really, he thought, because there were only a few passengers and they didn't want to send out another plane—American point of view about pride (echoed in ads or echoed from them) in speed, comfort, and completeness of accommodations mixed with rather unbearable impatience at all delays and hitches—woman at one of the Iowa airports who, he claimed, got out of the plane to go back to the ticket desk and buy a round-trip ticket, held the plane there fifty minutes—That won't do!—we never heard the last of it—the stewardess tried to be sympathetic but she had to defend the pilot against the idiotic passenger, said we were lucky to make as much progress as we were doing against the east winds—he wanted to know why

Des Moines?—when we landed in the desert at Rocky
Falls, he said, Oh, *how* I wish I lived here! A woman
would have to love a man an awful lot to come out and
live with him here. The stewardess said, There are
eight thousand people here, you know. What was it,
a mining town? (Iowans and Nebraskans who seemed
to have come to watch the planes land and leave—I had
lost all track of time, never knew what time of night it
was—awful sinking and nervous horror when plane
would come down and I wouldn't have movement any
more but would have to wait at airport—young Jewish-
looking fellow who kept trying to date up stewardess,
changed seats with other passenger so that he could be
on the outside and talk to her. The fire-insurance man
knew all the girls by name—a fine little girl—this one's a
darling—they were all pretty blond Middle Western girls,
very capable, neat uniforms, very neat feet in shoes—did
a lot of professional smiling—pulled out seats, distributed
pillows, papers and magazines in folders—I knew I
couldn't merely desire a pretty girl any more—the most
interesting one from North Dakota with mountain-lion
brows and eyes, serious and as if glaring pursuit of flies
with flyflapper, she would pick up flapper and watch for
it, "an old passenger"—difficult getting around narrow
aisle of plane, her long body lithe in movements inevitably awkward bending over seats and reaching into coat-
racks—started writing letter to father in back of itinerary
and wondered (opening it out) whether she could cover
the whole thing—served supper, little sandwiches, fruit
cocktails, olives and pickle, and cake wrapped up in
oiled paper—she was something beyond me, something
she and her husband would be that I could never know,
faithful to one another, make their home and life together—she would crouch down to get paper cups of
water out of cooler at back of plane—pilot big and fine-

looking fellow, who came through a couple of times to
go to toilet—he was going to shoot over one of the
Rockies just to say he'd done it—technique with stewardess quite different, would put his large palm on her
head and shake it, press her snub nose with his thumb,
to which she responded rightly, naturally, as she had not
to the fire-insurance man. The fire-insurance man said
his work was very interesting—he was going to see a man
in Seattle who was a son of a bitch but after that he was
going to Portland, where he'd see a man he'd have a
good time with—pointed out freight train going through
desert below, had seen several, that meant that *some*
business must be starting up—incident in soft-drink cabin
(the West already—the Coast Highway—Western beef
sandwich) at Lincoln, drunken party with brash loud-
voiced Middle Western woman, who looked through
window, saw fire-insurance man taking out flask of rye
(had Scotch in bag if I'd rather), and wanted him to
give them drinks—I don't know you, why should I give
you drinks?—then she appeared at another window right
beside him: Hey, Foxy Gran'pa!—afterwards he said,
Well, I got kidded, but if I'd given them drinks, I
wouldn't have had a drop left—if I'd had a few drinks
myself, I might have done it!—Sleep in two- or three-hour
stretches, broken by stops at lit-up nocturnal airports—
the livid spark from the motors streaming like some flag
of the Furies—Salt Lake, going up over dun mountains—
the stewardess wanted us to see the beautiful colors, just
like a Persian shawl—yellow of cottonwoods rubbed in
the cuntlike hollows of the mountains—rose-red and coral-
pink of some shrub—yellows and oranges and greens.
The fire-insurance man was very keen on eating—at Salt
Lake there was a little restaurant where you got the best
breakfast you could find anywhere, and kept by the
nicest couple—he had kept telling me the night before

about how he was going to eat a steak when they got to the regular restaurant—Well, now I'll do some telephoning, at Salt Lake—told the stewardess he supposed she'd get a chance to see her sweetheart there—she answered, That's at Cheyenne—here's where I get my rest!—I had never known, I thought, never would know, that—content, resigned to have it shut out—the sterile landscape, speckled hills.

Climbing up out of the Salt Lake amphitheater—plain—earth lined as if by enormous fossils, one could trace pterodactyl heads—more colors of foliage in mountains, darker red smears of hematite—very few passengers in plane, relief of getting away from fire-insurance man—big round dark-eyed Los Angeles woman who went in for looking handsome—more glass, less space between them, freedom, lightness, openness of the coast—one of the ranking pilots of the country—the desert, we flew high above it, the dried-up beds of rivers—a blond and dry color between buff and fawn, a vast waste, the yellow Colorado, the Virgin River—getting over the mountains, strange how we climbed them so close to them—green foliage on the mountains looked like lichens on rocks—hot descending at Las Vegas, I saw it as just a little settlement in the desert—then California, the round trees of the orange groves—the strange climb over the gray round-topped mountain range back of Los Angeles, steering close to the mountains and between the peaks, raising it slightly, lowering it slightly—(then the slide straight down to the airport)—nobody had ever stopped there probably—(almost deaf on arriving, woman passenger's voice sounded like squeaking of a mouse)—*earlier part of trip:* those strange mountains that reminded me of New Mexico, dream mountains that seemed to float among the semi-transparent bluey-whitey clouds, though it's the clouds not the mountains that move—the shadow of the airplane got smaller, followed farther behind.

Man who drove to Athletic Club from airport with me, Los Angelan with big round spectacles and wise-guy look—to my question replied that he wouldn't say things were depressed out there, etc.—didn't I find the climate different from the East—discussed the extraordinary idea of geography and topography that you get from traveling by air. I thought about last summer and about the night we had spent in a hotel, when as the result of one of my jealous scenes Margaret had left me (we had spent the evening with Dorothy Parker and Benchley, and I had been jealous of Benchley)—a horrible night but even that seemed sweet in memory—vaguely remembered taxi man from Texas—new features of drive: signs in the shape of men holding out real flags at the gas stations, Good Humor restaurants, two Hollywood pretties in pink Pierrot costumes opening the cover of an enormous book which said "Harold Lloyd in Movie Crazy," similar blondes in yellow costumes waiting on people in cars at fancy foodstand, where you got pork and beef barbecued sandwiches and mugs of root beer— I got a pork sandwich all wet and gooey with some kind of ketchup that got on my fingers and a bottle of ginger ale—how many times we had stopped to get ginger ale to go with gin—the time she met me at the station and took me up to Santa Barbara—the night when we'd stopped in the dark beside the road for a drink, I'd been telling her about my mother and father, what had there been in it?—silly Los Angeles, cheapness and richness of sandwich—alligator farm, statues of bellboy for Hotel Chelsea, Brown Derby, the dry brown countryside seemed sober, stalks of the small wild Western sunflower leaning over into the road—I asked the driver whether we were going over the Canejo Grade—he said that they were soon going to pave the whole thing—I recognized the bridge and the turnings from my midnight trip down last summer—alternations between grief and fear that she had committed suicide—Montecito: dry gully by my old beachhouse, Montecito riding school, thank God we weren't going to stop there, Montecito Inn—

Jimmy had said it was a gyp, her only staying West a part of her six months. —You old ghoul—Frankenstein—you may have killed me, I don't know—you give me all those complicated ideas, I'm a very simple person really—I'll get out of your life—I'll go back to California with my few poor pathetic little things (I don't want things like that!)—she had left me her house—I said I didn't want it, would give it to Jimmy—I would tell her to go on and cry—she cried Christmas Eve at Red Bank (that she should be spending Christmas without Jimmy) and on platform of train when I was kissing her goodbye (when she was going out that summer to California), afterwards I went in and drank some brandy with her and Jean Gorman (who went out with her), sitting on the berth — Miggs* had made her cry the night she had arrived out there telling her she looked so bad, middle-aged—she had said she was going West and never coming back, would write me a letter when she got out there—I'll crash someday!—why don't you do something about me?—your own suicide at home—how can you worry about humanity and see somebody who's so unhappy?—

I felt for the first time how she'd given me all my self-confidence, the courage that I hadn't had before to say what I thought—all her natural smartness, fine quality, taste—social self-confidence which I'd used to repudiate

---

* A friend of Margaret's who had committed suicide some months earlier. See p. 261.

conventional society and make her uncomfortable in doing so—Your ideas have made one person very unhappy—she had been ready to give up Jimmy for me when she came East, I said I thought that was a horrible idea, I wouldn't have her do that for anything—but that was the way I felt—we'd all be better off if she were dead—she said I always had my base elsewhere: at Red Bank—

Little hotel at Santa Barbara—remembered, as I took a bath, how she used to notice my love of relaxing in a warm bath and lying there indefinitely, in connection with what Cummings had said about a warm bath representing the womb.

—Suppose I should say at the funeral that I'd, etc.— she'd had those impulses, too.

At Mrs. Waterman's house, when I began to cry, she said, I've never broken down. —Would look in her face in vain for Margaret's beauty, in Camilla's in vain for any trace of her—but Mrs. Waterman's voice was so sweet, like Margaret's, and her flurried way of saying things—simple abashed (at a loss) way of saying—when I told her to open letter containing will: But it's addressed to you!—so like Margaret—how Margaret would say, like a child, when I said I was going somewhere: Aren't you going to take me with you?—She'd said, You're a cold fishy leprous person, Bunny Wilson—had said, Well, then, you're a cad—All right then, I am—it was for being so thoroughbred I admired her—even the Scotch-Toronto sense of what was and wasn't done (it was mixed with Philadelphia sporting distinction)— would smoke her cigarette with perfect poise, saying nothing, serious-looking—this really put me at a disadvantage and drove me into asserting my intellectual advantage of her in satire on and comprehension of the social structure, sense of the futility of worldly privileges and distinctions—I had said that her ideal man was a top-hatted morning-coated Canadian walking down the streets of Toronto—she strongly denied it: No, it's not—we never wore morning coats. —She said that I didn't need her, that she was a luxury, something like Guerlain's perfume—You'd be charmed if I were dead, you know you would!—about something brutal I had done to her, she had said that I needn't put any cold cream on either. —When I had said that if only I hadn't intruded, she and Ted might still be "happy and carefree" in Santa Barbara together, she said, Yes, playing battledore in the Paseo all the livelong day.

The house where the four sisters had grown up—they had given it to Mrs. Waterman after Margaret's father left her—she showed me the back room where she and her sisters had slept together—big, but rooms badly arranged, and crowded-together shape generally like our old house in Red Bank, too many doorways on ground floor opening rooms into one another, dark woodwork, no eye for color or arrangement, rather cluttered up with bulky objects, great big bluish and purplish blossoms of hydrangea outside dining-room window—my enjoyment of comforts of house, clean soft beds, ample breakfast, Mrs. Waterman's hospitality, painting of Margaret and Camilla as little girls with long hair—horrible funeral roses and chrysanthemums everywhere—certain attractive richness and amplitude of house and grounds in spite of bad arrangement, lack of logic, balcony outside my room, dark tin-covered floor strewn with dry tendrils and leaves of creepers which almost covered the windows—two big tall palms like gateway on terrace—pepper tree in back, big bush with red berries, mountain lilac, rather rare—window seat in bay window at one side of fireplace that seemed unexpectedly comfortable and light when you came to it—dark closets and crooked halls in back, big pantry, old stables now garage, little pointless reception room to left of door as you came in—Margaret's father by Mary Cassatt—he had been a fine flutist, had pursued Margaret's mother to San Francisco when she had gone there to get away from him—bright little rugs with birds and flowers on them that Margaret had given her mother for bathroom (over oilcloth) for her birthday—ugly tiling (green?) of fireplace, like the tiles in Red Bank—there was a sort of wild garden out back—birds singing, the California fall—maid a country bumpkin from the mountains, the pretty ones all go to the dogs, she'll probably have a beau before long, Let's hope not! (very emphatically). [Margaret had told me how her mother had warned a former maid against letting her beaux take liberties—and it's not very far to Pussy.]

Camilla wouldn't have chosen this kind of life (being married to a clergyman), but she had found that she hadn't just married a man but a job—had to see so much of Long Beach people, had so few friends with any brains. —Perry said she had recrudescences of Paris and Vienna—their father had taken them around and bought them jewelry and had their clothes made at Tappé's and done everything he could to give them champagne tastes (Margaret would say, I have champagne tastes—I have! I have!)—Perry said that for twelve years it had been touch and go, but he'd won. Camilla said that they all felt that Margaret had been the ugly duckling of the family—cousins said she gave them inferiority complex—knew such interesting people. —Camilla twice remarked how much I resembled "Daddy"—when I laughed, she said it sounded like him. —Camilla would say, You have five minutes before dinner, etc. —If it wasn't for me, they would all go down to Los Angeles; Bishop Remington was going to be there, and Perry thought Mrs. Waterman would be interested to see him. Camilla and Margaret's will: it wouldn't be like Margaret to make a

will!—And why I don't think she made a will—question
of fitting Margaret's little box (this must be the box with
her ashes) into Alexander plot, it seemed almost as if they
weren't going to be able to get it in. Camilla's white
dress, plain face, with strong but pale-colored eyes—I
couldn't see anything of Margaret in her. Mrs. Waterman used to remark on how different her daughters were.
Mrs. Waterman said that people couldn't be happy unless they had something to believe in—you don't seem
particularly happy—you must believe in immortality,
Bunny, you must! Camilla waiting on table: Yes, I'll
be maid and butler and all the servants tonight!—Sargent's mural of the white-shrouded Hosea had been put
in front of the picture of Margaret (in the Gibson
period) in my room—they had turned bed back for me
the first night when the maid was out. I said that I
was sorry that I hadn't seen more of the family before,
and Camilla said yes, it was fine the way I'd fitted in,
somebody else might have come and not fitted in at all!
I recognized Margaret's taste in cooking when Mrs.
Waterman got in Worcestershire sauce for the scrambled
eggs—made far too much food for me the first night. Mrs.
Waterman's Scotch phrases: D'ye see?—

Holland's funeral parlors: Mrs. Waterman: Yes, let
him go in and enjoy himself!—Her cheeks were full of
paraffin and hard, they had made them seem too big—
lips cold and hard—also, breasts—a look of pride, almost
of scorn (she had said she dealt with lovers as with
servants, couldn't have any argument—if they behaved
badly beyond a certain point, she simply fired them)—
pink kimono, little freckled hands hard, too—arranging
coverlets—I couldn't remember how they had been when
I came in—smell of flowers again—slight bruise on hand—
cheek, cold, hard, and rather rough, something like
animal's hide, it seemed to me.

Dreams: first night, strange empty dream with dim

figures in it—something about her coming too late to
say goodbye to other people? to me? yet we were all
there. Second night: homosexual wet dream, figures still
rather dim, a boy. Third night: nightmare—the trolls
were in the dark part of the cellar, I went upstairs to
wake up somebody and tell him the trolls were there, he
should have come down and gone after them with me,
but he didn't get up, and with sadistic energy, pent-up
anger, I pulled him out of bed—he was dead and gray,
almost a skeleton, though with some flesh, very long legs
hardly anything but bones—I brutally pulled him downstairs and thrust him down the basement and into a
barrel, in which he doubled up his legs like a dervish
and began horribly spinning the barrel round and round
on its bottom on the floor—I had felt like a murderer at
the funeral—Perry's short but energetic burst of words
about the soul rising again—sounded to me colorless and
confused, though energetic. [They didn't know how to
deal with her.]

Perry's Groucho Marx line: if one of his observations
didn't get over, let it go!—he had studied forestry first
and he talked about the trees on the place—they said
that if the train stopped anywhere in the middle of the
country for a few minutes, Perry would be out and back
with some specimens of flowers in his hand. —Margaret
remembered him as a clown when a kid, and there was
still something of that about him [Cummings remembered him at Harvard as having attracted attention in company by "getting a ripsnorter"]—he said that in his profession you had to use a sort of standardized technique
in approaching people. —A telegram came offering him
an administrative job, supervising religious societies in
the colleges, which he turned down, didn't want an
administrative job—was it on Camilla's account? because
it would take him away from her. —I went around and

looked at the Paseo after lunch, just before the funeral.
—Fussing about where the different people should sit.
—How horrible flowers look all over a cemetery plot.
—Camilla had got for Margaret a corsage of lilies of the
valley and an orchid. —Jimmy had grown and matured,
was wearing long pants.

The town (Santa Barbara) where she had been a little
girl and known everybody—the woman at the florist's—
Diehl's. —But then when I would bring her back in
imagination, the sadistic impulses would come back—at
other times I would begin to cry with grief, my face
would contract in a grimace of grief, how sweet and
pretty and darling she had been, all soft and cunning,
so affectionate and gentle, how we had slept together,
she always turning with me, no matter when or how
many times I had wanted to turn—except when she was
mad, she would be stubborn and lie across the bed so that
I couldn't get in, and couldn't be moved—I thought how
much I had slept with her the last year and not made
love to her, indulging myself in other fantasies. —Movies
or play poster in Santa Barbara: Who Is the MURDERER?
—How she had looked at the Beaux-Arts ball: tiny red
gloves and shoes, so pretty, little strawberry girl, I made
love to her in her costume in the gray armchair—had
hardly been able to wait till Niles Spencer and other
people had gone—we had enjoyed it, it gave a new pi-
quancy—it had been a little hard managing it—had she
put one leg over an arm? The night we had been going
to *Don Giovanni*: we overprepared on drinks, then I in
my evening clothes had put her down on the couch and
made love to her in her evening gown—after which we
had been quite unfit to cope with the opera, she had
become nervous and kept talking to me in a loud
whisper, which annoyed me since I wanted to listen.
—How I had smashed the card table, pulled the shades

down—she had dreamed, she told me the next morning, that I was an ape climbing up the curtains. —How I had said this spring that she hadn't even been able to enter into our trip to Santa Fe—Yes, I did—I loved it! I implying that she was no fun—she had started as if I had given her a deep sudden wound. I remembered how neurotic we had been in New Mexico, I always looking away from her and consequently she from me. —Strain of time we had gone to Matty's. —When I had come back from the trip to Harlan, I found her and Bill Brown* cuddling on the day bed. Bill immediately left. She said, reproaching me, that he was "somebody who likes me and makes a fuss over me." I went to bed on the day bed, but she came in to lie beside me. I asked her coldly why she had come—I want to be with you—I had made her go away. The next day she said, If you're going to be so mad, I'm going away, and she went to a hotel for the night, but called me up next day and I went and got her, brought her back and made love to her. I asked her if she was in love with Bill—You know damn well I'm not!—Couldn't you ever love anybody?— I only remembered all this on the train going back to the East.

I kept instinctively thinking that I'd tell her about things that happened, putting them to her in my mind, as if she were still alive—then remember—discuss Perry and Camilla with her—Perry not really so bad, had, after all, given up chances to have rich parishes in order to work in a mill town—or imagine her saying to me, Are you sorry, dearr? with a hard Western r that she emphasized for fun—I noticed that Camilla said it naturally.

---

* Probably EW's Hill School friend William Adams Brown, a member of the banking family (Brown Brothers) "who showed a strong and outspoken enthusiasm for sex" (*A Prelude*).

—She used to talk about "Mothers and Camillas and people."

Perry dated her decline from virtue to her taking up with Ted Paramore—she had "gotten a sort of sophistication." —Mrs. Paramore had told someone that Margaret was carrying a heavy burden—Camilla wanted to know what she meant—I told her (1926; her difficulties with Jim Canby and part-time separation from Jimmy?)— Camilla was surprised, Mrs. Waterman had always blamed Ted for ruining Margaret's life.

When I had gone down on her, she had tried to pull my body up: I want to do it to you. —When we had made love, she wouldn't go to bathroom for douche, shook her head with her eyes closed. —When we had stopped beside dry arroyo on our way to Santa Fe—I tried to feel it more by a fantasy of a blond Follies girl with a fleshy red mouth. She took down her riding breeches: it was strange and very sensual. The horses were tied to trees. —I said she bit me too hard once, and then she remembered afterwards that she had hurt me and had it on her mind when I asked her not to bite my tongue so hard afterwards—"both ends"—she was sorry. —My sadistic impulses about the horse when I had gone over to the old mining camp all alone. —At the Berkeley we had made love every day for I don't remember how long—she thought then that it was making her nervous—at Boyd's it was difficult, we hardly did anything at all—getting up early in our little cabin, and Rosalind and Jimmy likely to come in—when she came back from Hollywood with Ted and Jean, the whole thing dampened my ardor. —My original feeling of inferiority or unsatisfactoriness at not being able to feel her as much as other women gave me the feeling that I wasn't dominating her but being used as a little gigolo to give her a good time (that gigolo of the old girl we had rented the apartment from had had a psychological effect on me)—Well, you've given the old lady one good time before she dies! —I resented her feeling this, told her later that she was identifying herself with her mother. —Used sometimes to make her get on top of me, which she did self-consciously and awkwardly (my fantasies about this in Clifton Springs sanatorium), though she had dreamed when she was young that she was taking the man's part with a girl—finally, however, one night she got on top of me and did it with some enthusiasm, but this excited me, and I came almost immediately—I told her this, and she said, Oh, that spoils everything!—had never before me done anything but normal intercourse—I telling her she was like a boy—told her that Paul Rosenfeld* had said she was like a little chubby boy, and she had made a face. —Her way of reading with a look of anxiety on her face, as if she believed the story and was worried by it.

Don't you see you're the only thing I've got left in the world?

Mrs. Waterman said to me that we probably ought to have had a child. I have since wanted children, but I evidently didn't—with the problem of Rosalind—want any by her at that time, since I worried about her not taking a douche.

Little tunes that would go through my head in Santa Barbara—waltzes—Perry loudly humming something that seemed to be Wagner. —My damned subsidence into Perry's care and guidance, going around in car, talking to him too long—also, a male friend to talk about it with.

When Ann Cummings had said in Provincetown: Margaret looks about fifteen years old. —It's a terrible

---

* Paul Rosenfeld (1890–1946), music and art critic, a founder of *Seven Arts* magazine and writer of much criticism in the weeklies.

thing when you think about sleep, isn't it?—to think you just lie in a stupor without knowing anything.

How pretty she always looked, what good color she always had, when I saw her in bed in the morning, lips still rouged from the night before—she rarely looked haggard or faded.

Do you ever think about the dunes?—how we used to go out on the dunes?

Oh, don't ever do that again, will you?—when I had said something brutal or caddish.

Uncle Alden wanted to do something, so put himself at my disposal to take me around in his car—he read the paper while I was calling at houses—distinguished, stooped, black mustache, shaggy eyebrows, graying hair— he had originally come from Albany but had come out to the coast for his health and stayed—did he ever go back to the East?—hoped he'd never have to go again, the last time had nearly killed him, cold and raw, the climate —wondered why anybody who didn't have to stay there stayed there—but missed his ranch in the hills, seven years they had lived there, and he would like to go back again—silly sort of life they lived in Santa Barbara, y'know, chatter, chatter, chatter all the time—he used to have some brains but you can't have brains and farm— his wife said the maid they had died, and you couldn't get maids to stay out there—one reason he'd like to get out there was to get away from the telephone, they had oil lamps there, it was quiet (that was where Margaret's mother had escaped to when she was being pursued by her father, and Uncle Alden had stood guard in front of the house with a gun)—he'd never had a regular education, was sent away a year for his health: a year in Switzerland—I said that that was a good way—No: it's not such a good way. He had gone to school with Charlotte Chancellor's uncles, was hesitating about going in to call on the Chancellors. Invasion of Santa Barbara by *nouveaux riches*—told me about various people's beginnings—he made (I forget what), they say, somebody else was a banker—in Albany you were either in or out. —He showed me some little photographs of Margaret, taken when she was a child and now partly brown. —While I was calling at the Eichheims', Camilla came along and sent him home with her mother, so when I came out I was surprised to find Camilla instead—later on he said he hadn't minded waiting, he sat around like a bump on a log anyhow. They said he liked to sit around in the side room and read the paper—he was so honorable, if you did something for him, he had to do something for you right away—I saw tears in his eyes after the funeral— he didn't want to go in and see the Eichheims because he didn't have a decent suit, stopped the car around the corner and read the paper. Margaret used to say that her family were so *worthy*. He had a fine Currier and Ives print of *The Last War Whoop,* had found it in the attic at home—pictures he had in the house there he remembered when he was a child—charming picture of his mother, with a smile well caught by the artist—album of pictures cut off Union envelopes during Civil War. I thought I noticed a slight competitive feeling on the part of the Alexanders when I was admiring Uncle Alden's things—(when anybody admired anything, he had a standing joke: We think it's exquisite!—somebody they knew had once said that when somebody had admired some vases)—Mrs. B. asked me if an old volume of Bunyan was valuable and showed me a framed set of silhouettes of the Alden family (Alexander?)—Alexander family album: uncle still in St. Andrew's, family doctor, their father; Mrs. Waterman: He was a good man, Father. Painting of deer standing in a stream depicting the part of Scotland that their father had come from. —Uncle Alden had framed an eighteenth-century document, a grant of land to his grandfather to build a church on a plot of land in Albany—he showed me these things as if apologetically: You don't have to be bored looking at these things, but— He told me about man from Utica who had spent all his wife's money—he thought that was something that ought to be prevented. Had always wondered how you relieved yourself in a plane. His colorless daughter of forty (Jessie), who had never married. Book of pictures of Paris with descriptions in both French and English, that his father had brought back. Couldn't I come out and work at his ranch?—but I suppose you have to be in the swim. Point of view of the Aldens about woman who thought piece of land wasn't a ranch till its acres were in the thousands. Uncle Alden remembered when land at Montecito had been worth only a fraction of what it was now.

Camilla at dinner told about funeral service of deaf-and-dumb mutes, first saying, I oughtn't to talk about this, especially when Bunny's here.

Mrs. Waterman had a nephew in Toronto who was a curling champion. —Her efficiency about thanking people for funeral flowers—white glads and blue dels.

Camilla on choosing pictures: But we can't decide till we know how many the Ogilvies want (Ogilvys?)— I thought that she had some jealousy of other people's influence on her mother.

Uncle Macy had a big Spanish-looking house, full of an antique collection which he was leaving to the Metropolitan Museum—he had wanted to excel in everything: first he had painted, there was a picture of his in the Union Club in New York; then he had raised Buff Orpingtons, had had a rooster as big as a turkey with which he had hoped to win a thousand-dollar prize, but the rooster had died, and they had all been delighted, be-

cause he'd been so grasping—he always wanted to be at
the top of everything. I said, Always wanted to excel.
Mrs. Waterman in her hurried way: That's it! He had
bred dogs, too, I think—then collected antiques and
prints.

Mrs. Waterman had told Margaret that she ought to
give me a son.

Margaret's things: memory book—old collection of
German postcards—photographs of Paris fairies, one of
them in women's clothes and another with head thrown
back and blood dribbling from the corner of his mouth.
Mrs. Waterman: Is it a man? . . . Tear them up. Half-
gallon bottle of gin (in Margaret's house)—apple sauce
with green spots of mold on it. [Mrs. Waterman gave
me all my letters to Margaret and I burned them up in
the fireplace at her house; but I have kept all hers to me.]

When I hurt her once or twice, she was stunned and
simply nodded with her head, as if it were going to drop.

She had the feeling she was doomed, would not live—
she used to ask me what I'd do, who I'd notify if she
should die.

When they had carried her in and put her on the
bed and asked her how she felt, she said, Sleepy, so low
that they could hardly hear her. Later on the way to the
hospital, she had sat up and said, I'm all right. I'm all
right! I don't need to go to the hospital—take me home!

Perhaps I had gotten more like her father: extrava-
gance, drinking, arrogance and tyranny.

She said to me once, You're the biggest hypocrite! and,
You want to have your cake and eat it, too. —Your great
big beautiful masses—the woman who wouldn't let little
girl play with Jimmy in Central Park because she
thought he was a social superior. —They're the biggest
snobs! —Well, you've won: I can't stand quarrels! (It was
true that she would never quarrel.) —You don't like

Santa Barbara—or don't like me (this summer when we had gone there after Boyd's ranch.)—I used to think, Am I deliberately turning on her, treating her brutally to drive her out. —Just wanted to feel that somebody cared something about her. —Night at Holdens' * when I got sleepy and sat down on the floor beside the couch and put my face against her cunning little "sex appeal" shoe —brown, open like a sandal so that her toes showed. —Change from boyish bob to Greta Garbo style. —She forgave me Anna because she said she'd be hypocritical not to—she'd done the same thing herself. —She thought there was a compensation about these things—other men had been this way about her—she supposed she had wanted Jim Canby to be somebody who'd be always there for her, just as I wanted her to be for me. —She had said, *You* can relax—I'm just like this all the time. I get in and out of a bath as fast as I can, whereas you lie there and read a little—drink a little—contemplate life.

She had told the Eichheims about the letter that I had written her at the end of the summer, telling her that I missed her terribly, and had said that it was nice to know that she was missed.

You mustn't say things like that because I remember them and brood on them.

Going back East on train, I remembered that her father had told her always to tip the porter first. I remembered the trips on trains we had taken with a bottle of gin in compartments—when we had looked out of the window, tight, going up to Provincetown: I had talked about the landscape, she about going to Yale for proms— she got laughing and excited like a young girl, the only time I ever saw her so. —When I asked whether I didn't know her better than Ted: Ted knew me better in my

* Raymond Holden and his wife, the poet Louise Bogan.

younger days. —Her insistence on getting Pullmans and compartments used to annoy me—champagne tastes, but people around her in trains gave her the jitters. —Going back, I began already to imagine traveling West, etc., with ideal and intelligent and devoted girl in bourgeois respectability and comfort.

How all her beauty and goodness and affection fused into something glamorous and magical now that I couldn't have it—and she had gotten all brown during the summer on the beach!—in life it had been her being all too solid and clear, too lacking in "envelopment," that had made me feel she lacked something I wanted.

When I had eaten dinner in silence, made her lose her appetite: Why don't you do something about me? —She told me in connection with shouting at children that she knew I didn't like to have her say so, but it wasn't done. —Folding towels, hanging up coat, putting toilet seat down—leaving the toilet seat up was the only thing she had ever spanked Jimmy for. I always did these things afterwards but began farting rather loudly around the house.

After she was dead, I loved her.

It wouldn't do any good to go to a doctor—I know what I'm all about!

Her snoring—I used to keep waking her up, sometimes I would hold her nose—she was always patient and sweet about this. —Take me out and kill me!

Her way of coming out like her mother (apropos of my not wearing mourning, by association of ideas from one of my shirt-sleeve buttons being off) brusquely with criticisms, rebukes, which had been long on her mind— and her unexpected "gusts" of confidence, as her mother said.

You came home a little bit drunk to your little wife last night! March 16. Postcard she had sent Ted from

Pisa—a bleary-eyed devil by Orcagna, covered with spots and with sinners broiling (blazing, flaming) in his belly: Dear Teddy, here is your old friend the "Heebie Jeebie" himself—We have done so much in two months, and are so full of museums and churches that we long for a beach and a bottle of gin—Leave tomorrow for Santa Margarita, then Paris—I am returning to New York to see your play, if it isn't running I'll wring somebody's neck—but thanks to you I am kept in ignorance—I wouldn't even stop to write you I am that mad except that this devil and his judgment reminded me of your own dear self. This trip has been educational, more than diverting. (This last line written in between two paragraphs, no doubt to break the continuity and not sound so eager to see him.)

Anyway I'll see you in April—In Rome now, leave early that month first steamer I can get—Miggs stays on, hate to leave her, but her favorite brother is in France. Marguerite.

The night she left New York: Ann and friend and Cummings and friend and Jean, Margaret, Dos, and I all turned up at Felix's (favorite restaurant of mine in the Village). She had frog's legs—after she had eaten them all, she said, It seems cruel to eat them, doesn't it? —Hot or cold you leave the house this afternoon! [I would wince at remembering I had said this when I saw her off on the train—it was a quotation from an old joke.] Do we look terrible? (going down in elevator). You look like a couple of tarts! —I had wanted her to leave Felix's early and go back to get her things at the apartment so that we could make love before she left, but this didn't seem to occur to her—I said, We'd better start: we've only got two hours to catch the train. Ann said, Bunny, you're a riot!

Though she would bite my tongue too hard, it was hard to get her to bite my lip while I bit hers, bringing on the orgasm. Don't stop! Keep on! —Strong little hands, would clasp mine so tightly that it hurt, and I would have to make an effort to loosen her grasp.

The time she had fallen downstairs answering the telephone while I had been away over the weekend, and I had found her all covered with bruises.

Her blunt sturdy Scotch-wench quality with all her sensitiveness and distinction. —She would lie with her sharp (bright) clear eyes open while I was making love to her. —The time she took off her dress and her underthings came with it so that she was naked: we both laughed—I'm one of those ready girls! she said. —Once last winter on that lousy old couch, where she seemed to be trying to be swooningly voluptuous, closed her eyes, was she trying to be something she thought I wanted or had I always dealt with her in such a way as to cheat her of something she wanted? —She said that I ought to have engraved on my tombstone, You'd better go in and fix yourself up. At one time she evidently wanted a child—would refuse to get up and go to bathroom, lie heavily as if in a stupor with her eyes closed—Don't you want to go in?—shook head or said no. On the other hand, at other times she used to ask me why I didn't wear a condom so that she wouldn't be put to the trouble of going to take a douche.

On the dunes: the flies, perspiration—her broad white soft flesh—breasts that became flat like jellyfish when she lay on her back—her big brown moles—skin a little wrinkled around neck—it would make her nervous, even hysterical, to kiss her feet, she would pull them away— one that was partly paralyzed by sciatica and didn't have much feeling in it—it gave me a kick to put what seemed to me my large pink organ in her in the bright sunlight

of mid-afternoon—I would come almost immediately,
though I'd try to make it last, and she would usually
come immediately, too—it excited her—I spoke of how
people didn't make love out in the sun enough. —Her
neatness about picking things up after a picnic and
bringing them back in a basket. We had to be on the
lookout for the children. —She would lie on a bath towel.
I would lift the upper part of my body and for a while
slide it in and out that way, trying to remain detached,
insensitive, though it was so delicious—another touch
and my large pink prong would all melt into a pink-
whitish fluid dissolving into momentary bliss—her pink
and white (strawberry and cream) flesh spread out before me. —Fighting the flies. —Stay in me! Keep in me!—
Well, I suppose we'd better be going back—I ought to
attend to myself!—Bare feet and legs through the sharp
beach grass. —De Quincey—which I read aloud to her
(the autobiography, I think)—sounded to her, she said,
like old Foxy Grandpa commenting on it all.

Don't stop!—put your hand down there!

I'll be just a passing thing in your life.

Eichheim (the composer)*—"first-rate man"—Confu-
cius and Plato, but the Sermon on the Mount was the
best of all!—I say Christian: my mother was a Catholic
and my father was a Lutheran. —Wife's death—I would
walk out with my beautiful wife and look at the color in
the sky out there! Mrs. Waterman said that his wife
played better than he did, but she was always putting
him forward—Jeanne Armand—Chinese musical instruments—series of gongs and bells, drums—It's not because
musicians are such wonderful people, most of them are
farts, you know—Two old girls who've never been
screwed, Margaret (he said to her about I forget who out

* See footnote p. 144.

there)—Einstein's visit: It was I who was the artist here—
Einstein was very modest, only with some mathematical
theory so that he'd say, Prove to me that I'm wrong!—He
put his whole place at Einstein's disposal, he told him—
adding, with the exception of two things: my Stradivarius and my wife! Einstein had gallantly replied: How
do you know those aren't just the things I want most?—
so then of course the ice was broken! —Margaret said that
he had been so sweet to her when she had come back
from the East that time and had sciatica. —The studio—
the fountain in the court—you often heard people playing
rather good music in the other rooms of houses in Santa
Barbara.

Man during the war had told her that he'd either be
an ace or nothing—couldn't stand to be in the trenches
or anything like that. Bounderish fellow in Toronto for
whom she'd conceived such an admiration—in the Savoy
in London he was high-hatted (for not dressing in the
dining room) and went upstairs and threw electric-light
bulbs through the skylight so that the people thought
there was an air raid—then he went quietly back to his
room and nobody ever knew who'd done it. She had
said suddenly one night during our first fall in Santa
Barbara: I don't care! I've always liked men that people
thought were bounders!—then told me the above story.
In San Francisco at dinner, I said something about the
Rumson being like Santa Barbara, and she said that she
always thought I was a bounder on account of my frayed
shirts in the Lexington Avenue days. What had put her
off Ted when she wouldn't marry him after getting her
divorce had been evidently his behavior when he was
drinking—especially at a ball to which he had taken her
in San Francisco when she was waiting for her divorce.

Her way of putting her feet against people she liked
or whose attention she wanted to attract when tight,

which used to enrage me at first, then merely annoy me, then I thought nothing of it. She would often have completely forgotten things like that when she woke up the next morning.

Beryl Lord and her dog—she did nursing—clear English eye *à ras de figure* and accent—called Mrs. Waterman Jean: they had been brought up together. There was also an old man that Mrs. Waterman used to mail Sunday papers to—also, her old music teacher.

She looked particularly well in the little hats they had last fall—I hated to leave her last September in front of the elevator at the Hotel Roosevelt in Hollywood.

Night when I left them at Ted's house and went out and got lost and made a pillow of my coat and tried to go to sleep in the dry grass of an empty field next to a large place—the dogs roused me by coming and barking through the fence. I got up and walked a little way and found that I was only a block from Ted's house.

French-pastry architecture.

On another night when I had one of my brainstorms, I took the car that Ted had lent us and drove it to Hollywood. When I had first come out there before we were married and Margaret had met me in Los Angeles and driven me up to Santa Barbara, I had been impressed by the way she and Ted intrepidly drove through the hills along that winding road, the Canejo Grade, with an unfenced precipice always on one side of the car, and had envied them this dashing exploit, which seemed to me very Californian. I now accomplished the feat myself—of course, it was less difficult at night when there were few other cars, and I had only a truck or two to pass; but when I got to Ted's house in Hollywood, I didn't know how to stop the car and kept driving around and around the block. I can't remember what I finally did. When I got back—I can't remember how, I can't have driven myself—Margaret greeted me with, My lone eagle! (that was what Lindbergh had been called). I'm sorry you got so mad at me last night. I ate meat loaf and other things from the icebox, and she made me a drink. I had found Ted's house all lit up and the door unlocked, and drinking equipment all around the sitting room. I had got stalled on the Canejo Grade and started to back off—in the way of other cars.

What are you going to do about me? Why don't you do something about me?

The times I had met her at the Grand Central—the time in the summer when I was living at Ann Cummings's, she had looked hard-faced and middle-aged (how she had hated, after that visit, to go back to Santa Barbara)—then when she was coming back after Provincetown, with her little new hat she looked darling.

Peel shoes—she left one that time at the Hotel Tudor. Ted and Lucille. Margaret's self-disgust afterwards, walking on the Provincetown beach.

How I'd wake up in the night, strained, suicidal, couldn't see any end to it.

Onion soup with cheese and French bread in it, avocados with French dressing—Cheyenne pepper and garlic in it—it always reminded me of a song of my childhood: Cheyenne, Cheyenne, jump on your pony! She used to soak olives in oil with garlic in it.

At the Berkeley, she made the living room so attractive—put up red brocade curtains that she got from Miriam Van Court. —How she would say when I was trying to help her with food, Look out! Look out! Wait a minute! Wait a minute!—like her mother.

At the beachhouse, we tried to make a gin fizz when we heard that the man who invented it had died in New Orleans—even getting orange water—but it didn't work out. —Lentil soup, a meal in itself—spaghetti with cheese—cold sliced meats from delicatessen.

Her cousin Romaine, a rich Paris Lesbian—Margaret was afraid of her. (I met her at some New York party only after Margaret's death and found her very quiet and nice.) Margaret thought that if she were a man, she'd like pale camellialike women—her attitude toward Merle Wilhoyt, a little something in it of the active, protective, possessive Lesbian. Glimpse of her chasing Katy Dos Passos a moment in the front room of Susan Glaspell's house in Provincetown—somehow this glimpse made me feel badly: masculine impulses helplessly, awkwardly, ludicrously in little feminine body—impulse automatic, she didn't know what she was doing or why. She liked actresses because her father had—had danced with a woman once in a Lesbian joint in Paris—That was the only time I ever paid a woman. I imagined her holding herself very stiffly, then saying, Thank you, and soberly letting her go.

She liked gaiety: I'm a very gregarious person— Why don't you take me out and jazz me once in a while?—I like people!—you don't like people.

Her idea that the people at Biarritz and in Santa Barbara constituted the aristocracy—the most elegant, the most sophisticated—those people were the same all over.

She would stroke my fat stomach and say, Oh, oh, oh! We must both get thin!—watch our calories! —Dismissing Jimmy after long walk back at Provincetown: Momma and Poppa are going to have a little drink. —The heartburn we would get from drinking "alky" and water in which orange peel had been soaked and last winter from Dos's horrible alcohol that tasted like kerosene.

Lesbian that she had gone to spend the night with in the country—then when she made advances, Margaret got up out of bed and left the house and walked to the station. (I think that was it).

She used to rinse out my socks and golf stockings. —Not used to having people burst into bathroom while she was taking a bath.

A certain shy matter-of-factness about her body when she was naked—she had no exhibitionistic instincts.

Her orange dress that, as Cummings said, made her look like a ripe apricot. —Her new black low-backed evening gown that made her look very beautiful, last fall. —Charlotte Chancellor and Vonda Case gave her some clothes. —Her mother said, after her death, that she hadn't had much—only some dresses that somebody had given her, "poor thing!"

When I went out to Santa Barbara by plane, I felt as I had when I was about to hear whether I had passed or flunked some examination. (Greek Composition at Hill, which I passed.)

Her big broad shoulders and thick body and little tiny feet—cunning little thick body with little arms and legs on each corner—Don't say that! it makes me sound like a turtle. —I said once that I wanted a tall child—she said that in view of both our shapes, we'd probably have turtles. Ideas of violence about [children]—this so shocked me and made me angry, going into the movies in Santa Barbara, that I could hardly enjoy the picture—impulses she said you had sometimes with animals and children— If I were going to commit a crime, I'd kill somebody like Hickman (I think he was the California chicken-farm murderer), but I'd never, etc.—had felt that she wanted to break things, kill people, say dirty words among the Alexanders—felt just as she always felt before that life was going by her. —Mistake about, if Ted's baby should die. —Ted had promised to divorce Tooty and marry her after the baby was born, and she seemed to have held it against him that he hadn't.

Then you can't support me, can you?

She had never understood about Paula Gates's lack of solidarity with the rest of them—her reading Steve Gates's letters, trimming him, etc.—until I explained it to her (I had assumed she was Jewish, but she told me she was Mexican).

I haven't got champagne tastes, but— A great phrase of hers was "all kind of" this or that. Also typical: "Harrys and Bruces and people," used contemptuously.

At 13th Street (when she came to see me before we were married), when I tried to prevent her from arranging things in my room: You resent interference, don't you? —When we came back from our trip to Montauk, I felt a reaction against her with the dying of my drinks, felt I couldn't communicate with her. I told her about it afterwards: Oh, you must never feel that way about me!— I'm the most inarticulate person you ever knew! (It was characteristic of the Scotch side of her that she combined strong emotion and sexual passion with this inarticulateness.)—But now that you know I am, why do you treat me like that?

So punctual, like the Alexanders—she hated my always dawdling and not being ready—Aren't you ever on time for anything?—little gusts of scolding.

Mrs. Waterman said there was something about Margaret that she never could make out (I suppose that this was what she got from her father).

Other phrases of Margaret's: a self-kidder—around twenty-fivish (Teeny Worthington—I must have meant that Mrs. Worthington at Truro used this locution, too— she is English, and this -ish attached to numerals was, I think, a British usage that was only just coming in over here. It is now quite common, especially in connection with time: five-ish, etc.)—do a Miggs (her friend, who had committed suicide, I think, by putting her head in an oven just before Margaret came East)—Now kill me, but I think so-and-so (some opinion she was going to express that was contrary to my radical views).

Afraid to think about it—Margaret in Holland's room (the funeral "home")—keep mind running on other things.

Had never known any men that worked before she married me—her father, Jim Canby, her uncles.

She had said to her mother that you could drive your car over a cliff sometime so easily and it would look like an accident—but she had told Miggs later on that she would never commit suicide because she wanted to see what was going to happen.

Her nightgowns that I used to object to (I don't remember why—did I think they were not attractive enough?)

When I boasted about my amorous adventures at the beginning, she asked, Ever been a fairy? —Somebody had been telling her that the Roman Emperors kept "hundreds of fairies."

I've found out what that thing over the door is—it's a lentil.

High firmly molded little insteps.

Say that you love me—lie to me!

I could hear her saying, I forgive you, dearr—I don't mind, dearr—but now she was dead.

I brood on things you say—get very morbid.

A cute little trick.

All things to all people—about me and my girls, about her own Lesbian possibilities.

She had never slept with anybody every night before.

Dreams: (1) I thought she was back—nice apartment, room where I could work and not disturb her; (2) I thought she was dying, slimmer, perfectly conscious—but I went somewhere where there were people I knew in New York, there was a movie or some kind of play going on far below, a man fell dying, convulsions of agony, another man finally came and crushed out his life to end it—I had a moment's spasm of sobbing aloud—the hostess gave me to understand that she was surprised at my behavior: it was a perfectly all right film that everybody was going to see—I had to get back to see Margaret, excused myself and escaped—I asked her how she felt, and she said she was getting chilly, I was asking the doctor whether she couldn't be cured, she seemed really in such good shape—I must tell her how much I loved her, I did not love anyone else—perverse reservations even now—the places in both these dreams recalled more or less vaguely the Berkeley; (3) I was in a New York apartment—realized she wasn't dead after all—she was coming back, it would be all right after all—I met her in the hall, so wonderful to see her—she leaned back against a table when I kissed her, so that I saw her throat—but I remembered after waking that her throat and neck had really been different.

I remembered the time when I had said that she hadn't really entered into the Santa Fe trip.

I imagined her coming in—so glad to see each other that we began to cry, she blurting out something practical and irrelevant in her flurried inarticulate way.

[She had talked so much about suicide that when I heard she was dead I was afraid she had killed herself. Her friend Miggs had killed herself. This became a morbid obsession with me. I talked about it with Perry Austin, who drove me around Santa Barbara to question people about her. There was of course no evidence that she had, and it would in fact have been impossible for her to have killed herself deliberately in the way she died. Coming away from a cocktail party, she had tripped at the top of a flight of stone stairs and fallen all the way.* Her

* *The New York Times* in reporting the accident (October 1, 1932) said Margaret had fallen in front of a café and had died of a basal skull fracture.

feet were very small for her body, and she was always afraid of falling when she wore high heels, would always make me stop till the way was clear when we were crossing the street in New York, and then would proceed very cautiously. She had fallen downstairs once in New York. She had known from my letters that I wanted her back. But I should not have let her get into that situation. Not having the money to come East, she had been obliged to live with Jimmy in her little Montecito house. I never thought about how hard up they must be. Her own income by that time from the Pennsylvania coal mines had dwindled to almost nothing. She had almost no clothes, and Ted Paramore told me afterwards that he had found her and Jimmy making a meal on Corn Flakes. I had been getting along on very very little myself. I was writing *Beppo and Beth* and only interrupting it from time to time to raise a little money by doing very inferior articles for *The New Republic*. My mother paid Stella and it may be contributed to the upkeep of Rosalind.]

NEW YORK AND
CHICAGO

November 1932

[EW returned from the West Coast and threw himself into his writing and his work for *The New Republic*. Shortly after settling into an old wooden house he rented for fifty dollars a month, at 314 East 53rd Street, he traveled to Chicago to write an extensive paper on Hull-House, the first settlement house in the United States, which Jane Addams had founded in 1889 and which now became a Depression symbol for active social work. The notes on this trip became the paper "Hull-House in 1932," published in *The American Earthquake*, pp. 447–63.

The wooden dwelling in which EW lived stood next to a similar house in which lived Muriel Draper, a "parlor Bolshevik" of the time, who had a literary and musical salon; she was related to Ruth Draper, the celebrated monologuist, by marriage. EW shared his house with various friends and tenants and so never had for very long the whole expense of the rent. He lived modestly in this way for the next two years, except for the summers, when he went to Provincetown with his daughter and her nurse. The "Rosa's" in the next entry "was a very cheap restaurant not far from where I lived. I ate there often," EW noted, "—if I got there too late, when all the tables were full, I would eat at a long common table with strangers. I took T. S. Eliot there when he spent a night at my house, and he has gently teased me about it since." EW added: "It was a part of my leftist act." EW used the "man in Rosa's" note in his "Election Night" sketch in *Earthquake*, pp. 445–6.]

Man in Rosa's, election night. Making speech in room all alone—had had trouble writing in McKee's name on voting machine—cops hurrying people out of booth before they got a chance to write it in—What's the use? Who cares? It's just too bad!—Turn the bums out, put more bums in!—Hoover and Mellon!—Swine! scavengers!—had been in Argentine six years, just back. —Si, signor. —Things were terrible down there—when he'd first arrived. Sacco and Vanzetti: all over front pages of papers—they asked him about it, and he said that they didn't hear about that at all in the States—they'd have just a stick on an inside page—Swine! scavengers!—they were fiends!—had just bombed Judge Thayer's house—the only thing was that they oughtn't to have kept them so long before executing them—they had Sacco's cap—they were bad Sicilians—it's just too bad!

—Women in kitchen—just give them a kitchen and they're perfectly happy—and (bitterly) that's where they belong!

—Waiter wouldn't bring him any more to drink—his hands seemed to be getting stiff as he made strange fairy-like theatrical gestures with them.

—Talked about religion—did his religious thinking for himself—quoted Scriptures.

Anna, when I told her how good she was, said that when she was a kid and her mother had put out poison for roaches, she had caught the roaches before they had a chance to get the poison and put them in a box out on the fire escape. —Night when gangsters wrecked Fatty's place—hit her in the side of the head—but she thought it was funny. [I went back to her now, and she often came to see me on 53rd Street.]

Between Buffalo and Windsor, mid-November '32: woke up to find flat country all covered with snow—gave feeling of security and peace—brick houses—sheep trying to get at grass through snow—a flock of geese in the snow—a solitary sow with her nose in a mudhole.

—began to sneeze and blow nose slightly—also other people in car

Detroit. Ford's coercion notes—man laid off in August got one—40 percent of Dearborn voted for Hoover—in one precinct Hoover and Roosevelt together only got one vote more than Foster and Thomas.

—Leaving Detroit—the succession of high walls of great brick buildings—snow on the roofs of gray houses, gray snow in the streets and low dingy wooden houses only pricked by a synagogue's bulk—the Clippert Brick Co.— the flat fields with their drab brown weeds bristling through the snow.

—McFee Sheet Metal Machinery Co.

—a great big elaborate old gray house, almost a castle, with irregular high-windowed growths around a steepled tower like fungus on trees or the deposits of a stalagmite, with walled-in snowy grounds full of little irregularly planted pines—an airplane overhead—boys coasting in the street

—then Michigan rivers, no grime, steel-blue—the sun came out on the snow—one stream clear as polished bronze—a park under smooth sunlit snow—Ann Arbor

—finally a fine landscape where the hills begin of white and dark icy blue

—Hoover Steel Ball Co.—Chelsea Division

—snow getting gray like newspapers and sky getting gray like pasteboard—then darkness with just a crack of gray between clouds over Northern Indian Public Utility plant like a fort with one great chimney and an enormous buttress (an enclosed stairway?)

—Darkness—lights at long intervals—a street all of a sudden with a streetcar and electric signs outside stores— then gone and darkness again—a red electric ball above illuminated striped barber pole—dim signboards—lights at long intervals—the dim front of a frame house—darkness— bridges? a shore picked out with lights?

—factories—long streets with lights at intervals losing themselves in darkness

—great movie TOWER with red, green, and yellow lights

cars speeding along the dark lake front with its lights at shorter intervals

Connie at salesmen's convention in Atlantic City, tearing up money, tired of it all, wanted to jump out window.

Dream about Margaret. Santa Barbara: she had only divorced me—met her on a beach—felt so pent-up and badly—took new phonograph record with *Salomé* on one side and went home to Red Bank, where there was a Victrola vaguely associated with our life together and looked forward to getting some little silly pleasure out of playing it—then it occurred to me, Why didn't I ask her to marry me again?—began telephoning to her friends to find out telephone number of the house she was living in—it was all so simple after all!—why hadn't I thought of it before?—I could surely convince her that I loved her—how sweet it would be! —Then I woke up.

Hull-House. —old square house with its high windows— she felt prejudice against private relief workers—German doctor had said organizing workers' committees was dan-

gerous—had found herself marching in parade with Communists. —Said the general situation was like a bad dream
—Jane Addams going out and getting doughnuts and coffeecake

—low drab two-story streets around Hull-House, monotonous, long, the dead civilization of industry, in which human beings live to give the machinery activity—Hull-House had something of this itself—dull red and brown brick—plain and dull, the big rooms with their high ceilings and arched entrances from one to another and doors with impressive moldings—had taken on something of the sober severity, the simplicity, and the barnlike quality of the factories among which it was located, and in these rooms the mahogany sofas and furniture and Turkish carpets of Jane Addams's country home, the Italian primitive pictures and fragments of Greek marbles and modernistic paintings of South Halsted Street—and sets of Ruskin and Augustus Hare's *Walks in Rome* in the bookcases, and the portrait of Jane Addams in the big-sleeved costume of the '90s, pretty and winning, interesting—the walls overlaid with old photographs of admirations or distinguished friends or persons identified with the House—Kropotkin, C. Breshkovsky, Arnold Toynbee, and Jacob Riis*

—copper, pewter, brass, and brick

—her vocation as Mother Superior—tinkle: of a concert of Bach—her portrait of '93—wholesome and sober brick and brass and copper—panes—court and stairs—classical doorways that used to be white and marble fireplaces painted over

---

* Catherine Breshkovsky (1844–1934), the "grandmother of the Russian revolution," was a countess who became an active revolutionary and spent many years in Siberian exile. She visited the United States in 1919. Jacob Riis (1849–1914), Danish-born reformer, journalist, and crusader in New York against oppressive urban conditions.

—a castle—the big house she was going to have among poor people—among the tinsel Greek and gypsy restaurants and the dark alleys where you're likely to be held up, a château where the portcullis is pulled up at night and all is peace and sanctity inside, in the smoky Chicago night—occasional grinding of a streetcar

—old white-mustached man like an illustration by Birch to Frances Hodgson Burnett [Reginald B. Birch, who created the image of black-velvet-suited and lace-collared Little Lord Fauntleroy]

—bust of Dante

—girl with crooked shoulders, colorless, rather a sweet expression, in pale straw-colored dress—old thin lady who had been thus from the beginning

—Jane Addams and the Communist—she found it easy to break him up

—speech she made about one settlement pulling the others up

—Experience with Miss Gates—had come there to do the thing together, then Miss Addams had expanded so that there was no room for Miss Gates—meeting of residents at which Miss Addams had assigned everybody their duties and omitted Miss Gates, and then ended up by saying, And Miss Gates will give her classes in Browning and bookbinding as usual. Miss Gates had said, I haven't given classes for years!* [She would take something like binding and do it very well—Miss Addams was always the administrator bossing in the background.] — Miss Addams went on without noticing.

—Mr. Hooker's room was lined with countless small pigeonholes—when somebody else occupied it, they

* Ellen Gates Starr (1859–1940), co-founder of Hull-House, more emotional, sensitive, and religious than the calm and businesslike Miss Addams. She taught art history and bookbinding.

mustn't be disturbed. —Red necktie and Birch-illustration mustaches waving in the wind.

Boys' clubs—promised them special clubrooms when they got to a certain point—but now there were so many of them and they couldn't give them their special club-rooms, so they were going to turn them all out. —Also, obstreperous boys—Mitchell didn't want to run a boys' club, that was next thing to being a YMCA superin-tendent—but he had seen *The Road to Life* [a Soviet film about reforming wild boys]—he had tried to go in and quiet them once when they were pulling the keys out of the piano and rolling the top of the roll-top desk up and down bang-bang! Just yanking it up and down, and one of them had the bust of Charles Augustus Lindbergh be-tween his legs and was wrestling with it—and they of-fered Mitchell physical violence—began to gang up on him—when he tried to quiet them down—and one of them was calling up a whore on the telephone—completely out of hand, and Hull-House would just have to put them out because it couldn't deal with them. —Not keeping its hold on the neighborhood.

—Miss Gates joined the Catholic Church and went to masses in Santa Fe so that she could confess her hate for Miss Addams.

—Hull-House didn't have much hold on the Greeks— they had their καφφευεια.

—Miss Addams and Norman Angell* (at dinner): Angell said that the extremes of poverty, you see, had been abolished in Great Britain. What about the Hunger March?—that had nothing to do with hunger—the Means Test. — India: Miss Addams said Gandhi had made the high-caste Hindus feel ashamed of themselves—Angell

* The celebrated pacifist Sir Norman Angell was best known for his anti-war book *The Great Illusion*.

said that we only heard about the Indians who didn't want the British—but they were besieged by Indians who entreated them to stay. —Englishman's way of pointing out to Americans that the heroes of American films (gangsters) were assassins. —He was Sir Norman Angell now.

—Miss Addams had said she thought Mr. Hoover was better in foreign policy but Mr. Roosevelt better about domestic affairs.

—When Mitchell said he was going in for relief work, she had said, Well, that's taking up a lot of the technological slack.

—The boyfriend sent a case to Mitchell and wrote, I am sending you a client (that was their name for their cases) who used to be a harp player—if something isn't done about him, he's likely to resume his occupation. —They had a tendency to swap case histories.

Louise and Henri[etta Fort]. Henri in hospital going to have baby—said husband had behaved like perfect s.o.b.—let Louise go to the hospital with her, though it was Sunday—the brokers were amusing themselves in their offices with peashooters—daughter-in-law of Sam Insull—the son had advised somebody in the first days of the Depression to tie a string to it and hang it out the window (his money)—one day one of them had been calling on the Insulls, and the little child had been on the floor playing with miniatures of grandfather—young Mrs. Insull kept saying how worried she was about something connected with the household, while the old grandmother sat there drinking sherry—when the granddaughter went out of the room, the old lady winked and said, I guess she's got more than that to be worried about!—Julie Doan, Dean of Women, for the Insull employees—looked after dirty notes in the toilets, looked through railings—tall, thin, "hawklike," big black eyes, "I just called up my father at the Racquet Club in New York," black dress with high collar—employees had been protesting against giving up a dollar a month to relief fund, and there was a conference being held about it—young man, good-looking but weak-looking, had married rich wife and only thing he had to do with her was give her children— thought there was no doubt Hoover had done a good job—loose brown suit—Julie said he was a wonderful dancer—had met at Atlantic City on the gas convention, had found each other sympathetic—quick and curious questions as soon as I said to Louise that we'd better start for dinner pretty soon: Chicago small-town stuff—arrival of friend with "a couple of cement mixers from the Cement-Mixers Convention." Little mickish-looking man with bright red tie, Sinclair Oil: Ed Prendergast—his made-up story about working with his hands in lumber camp—man who can punch-press and couldn't get him to want to run a lathe—what were you going to do about that?—*The New Republic* wanted to destroy the family as a unit—no constructive suggestions, all destructive, I want to know a single constructive suggestion you've made!—all chaos like Russia!—what about the Thirty Years' War—wanted to give the state too much power— if there was any trouble in this country, we'd be oblit- erated—and there wouldn't be any martyrdom about it— necessary work! —He had been a promoter and now did nothing—Irish, well connected, somewhat pear-shaped, waddled, with long thin shoulders and neck, a low-slung bottom and belly. Third man inarticulately drunk but evidently wanted to be amiable and conciliatory.

—Day which started off clear-eyed losing its outline and contours in cocktails at Julie's apartment and becoming deliquescent, messy, concentrated, wild. Speakeasy, red room upstairs, bar downstairs. Louise wanting comfort, etc., didn't care about anybody—Henri didn't really care about husband's indifference.

—When Louise had been in hospital having second baby, Peter had brought drunken friends who would turn up at two in the morning—made her worse.

—Pretty nurses—round faces, rosy cheeks, which showed when the light was dimmed as rouge sometimes—one Irish with brown-red hair.

—Peter would be sore when he came home after two days and found Louise drunk.

—Bill Blair had started the Petrushka night club, then when it had failed and he had gone bankrupt, had been too proud, being a Blair, to work for anybody else, so had sat skulking at home.

—Insull girl gave Henri handsome bassinets and other things way out of proportion to other things she had. — Louise called Peter a son of a bitch because he said that the Insull diamonds* ought to go to pay the creditors— left the table.

—Louise's comments on how "common people" in hospital wards always talked so low as if they were praying— I said, she'd probably talk that way herself if she were in one of those wards—she said she wouldn't talk at all. —Pretty rouged girl in nursery, slightly hard eyes and mouth.

—Henri, having baby, said, I didn't know it was New Year's Eve. Louise said, Shall I engage a table at the Brunswick? —Henri: No: the American House! (awful old place in Boston). —Before, when she had been under gas, she had done a lot of laughing under the impression that she was the life of the party. —Louise, when she had had baby, had said when it was all over, Jesus, I hope it's

---

* Samuel Insull was the English-born utilities executive whose financial empire, based in Chicago, had collapsed during the Depression, leaving many persons holding worthless stock. See *Earthquake*, pp. 465–72.

not a girl! —Four men got together and pulled, yelling, Bear down! as hard as they could.

—I said, When I next see you, you'll probably have, Henri, been through the woman's Gethsemane. —Don't you know how they talk in Hemingway about the fine big pains beginning. —Afterwards, she told Louise that she never dreamed it was so bad. —When I saw her, however, she joked about the woman's Gethsemane and talked most of the time about how drunk and gay she'd felt— slightly amorous about the doctor.

—Louise and Pat Hurley, Secretary of War—had taken him to drunken party, and they wouldn't believe afterwards that the Secretary of War had been there. —Louise and he had had quite a tussle after getting into the taxi.

—"The Fort girls were just natural-born mothers"— Henri couldn't get the baby to nurse and didn't do anything about it, and when the nurse came back for it, just said she didn't think it had gotten very much—Louise had had an awful time, got almost hysterical about her nursing hours, made her very sore, and they had all kinds of electrical appliances—a regular dairy.

—*Dave Hamilton*: interest in cotton mill with two hundred people—hadn't had dividends for two years— were going to have to make wage cut and that was always difficult—went out there one day a week—about sixty-five miles, and he did it by bus—Mrs. Hamilton had behaved about Hoover's defeat as if it were the death of a friend.

—When Louise and Henri went to stay with the Amens, Marion always complained that they disrupted the household and made regular living impossible—Louise now complained to me that when she visited the Amens she couldn't do what she wanted.

—Mrs. Rockefeller McCormick, "The Death of the Arch-Bitch" [Willa Cather's 1927 novel *Death Comes for the Archbishop*].—That and Insull's failure had brought an era in Chicago to its close—he had had securities adapted to all ages, classes, and sexes—had built the Chicago opera building, then made the opera company pay rent, most of his benefactions, they discovered, had been worked on this principle.

—putting the elastic cord around the unopened yellow talisman rose

—phony vivaciousness of friend—they thought it couldn't be liquor and speculated with great curiosity as to whether it was some kind of dope

—Their mother had asked the Jamaican maid why she devoted so much time to Henri, and she had said: Miss Louise, she so bold she get along all right, but Miss Henrietta, poor t'ing, she have to be help.

—The Duke—took one look at Louise in her bathing suit—she did look very cute, Henri said, and I had on a maternity bathing suit and he thought I was awful—and everywhere Louise went she insisted on taking me and he got positively rude—finally he got frankly rude and sent me to get into the house to get ice for the drinks—and, my dear, no sooner was I in the door than there was a crash and a scream and I ran out and the hammock had broken down—as soon as I'd turned my back he'd made a lunge at Louise!— . . . he'd been making small advances even while I was around . . .

—The doctor at the hospital was gruff and gave her breast a tweak and said, No milk?—he was as bad (the way he tweaked you) as a policeman!—he was amorous (perhaps he hadn't been as amorous with Henri as with Louise)—he leaned down with his face close to hers and he was an old fellow—and she had been very rude—she had said, I haven't halitosis, have I?

—Not seeing enough rich people to get their accounts, only seeing people they liked—Louise would sometimes offend wives of clients whom she didn't like—said social women claimed they didn't get much out of sex any more—Lake Fawrest—somebody talking very Lake Fawrest, talking about polo and so forth.

—I said that, the whole psychology of America was changing! and she said, Well, it's too bad it has to change just as I've gotten settled down to being a broker's wife.

—worried about not getting invitation to Assembly till very morning of ball

—Louise's account of summer suitor: said, I've been in the North five or six months and I find the Northern girls so cold—would say to Henri, You'll have a pretty hard time having a baby at thirty for the first time. — Receiver in bankruptcy, about forty-two—old summer cottage, all sort of crumbling—whole back came off when he made lunge, she fell over spilling highball all over windows—Henri stayed up above and blew up balloon that squeaked when the air escaped—but suitor never understood—he said six or eight weeks was a long time for Louise to be left alone—she got scared of men in front of house, could get up in a tree and shoot—Southerner said, Move on, gentlemen! and keep moving family kidded her about him—made passes at her with practically no preliminaries—Louise gênée by Henri's making boot-legger sit down with us—also, nurse coming in and sitting down and attracting attention with baby.

Chicago. Dark: great banks of square buildings carved out of soft darkness like swamp mud—or dark smoke solidified—all the vistas smoky—enormous black cubes of West Congress Street with snow and then a belt of light—black blind trucks all alike waiting in front of one of the factories—an occasional old one-story wooden house—a long wide deserted street with fairly low-power lights along only one side.

—more of a feeling of latitude than New York, but dark
—the cold bleak lake winds along the big streets
—Vote Red. The people are goofy.

—The green river running the wrong way, itself a piece of engineering, buckled with black iron bridges.

—death for the poor and dispossessed—death for such culture and gaiety and health as the owning class possessed—the former ground down, exterminated, driven finally to fight—the latter disintegrated, the future taken away from them, nothing to hope for, drinking and trying to stop drinking, but when you've stopped drinking not knowing what to do or plan, and getting tight again in a rush, the men killing time in their offices and getting more and more nervous and uneasy, the women not knowing what it's all about, bored and irritated by the gloominess and nervousness of their husbands, more on the loose than ever

—In Chicago they're not sophisticated enough to talk about Communism over their cocktails as they do in New York.

—friends suddenly become bitter—social relations impossible

—brokers and cows

—tug dropping car barge sending jaws of bridges up like peristaltic movement of stomach forcing food along—

—the very coldly rising sun

—darkness merely stamped here and there with red neon light signs: Hotel, College Inn

—Fair Building like an immense red-hot electric toaster

—Merchants Building spread out, corrugated with lights at night, not a town, but a mountain, biggest building in the world as the Empire State is the highest building in the world—

Thanksgiving with the [Robert Morss] *Lovetts.** His frankness and boyish gaiety when he first came to my

* Lovett was an associate editor of *The New Republic* and a former editor of *The Dial*. See *The Twenties*, pp. 149, 419.

room at Hull-House and greeted me and invited me—not
sure about turkey but we'd have a drink anyway—the way
he pronounced "rise" in song [a hard s: this was at one
time a cultured affectation]—You Princeton and Purdue
men—they don't teach that at Princeton—old songs—if
she isn't satisfied with a good-sized lap, let the lydy ride
outside, and, Saloon, saloon, it runs through my head like
a tune!—I don't like café, and I hate cabaret—introducing
Hinky Dink and Bathhouse John—

—Rather plain and tasteless way of living—greenish-
grayish wallpaper, dark woodwork, shelves with miscellaneous books—country place: Well, this is the Illinois
landscape—you'll have to get used to it!—flat fields.—
There's a sort of pathos about a country road—the truth
is they don't build roads any more—they build highways!
—Jovial crew at Golf Club got him in and made him sing
"A Muscovite Maiden" (Bulbul Amir)—among the wine-
glasses, chocolates, olives, half-eaten pieces of pumpkin
pie—son of man who ran the first World's Fair and himself running second, looked thin and worried; Princeton
man, '99, in coal and sand business; man who'd written
book on architecture—Lovett says he used to use the Golf
Club, but now he lived next to it, he never used it—
"typical Middle Western conviviality"—"They're simple
organisms—like an amoeba—when they see me, they think
immediately of that song—it's the only thing I do they
approve of—They got to suspect me of being a Bolshevik."
—Pink and gray winter sky through glass front doors—
bleak inside, too, in a way—you felt Lovett's estrangement
from Mrs. Lovett—the girl had her father's high eggshell
brow, fine brow and nose—proud and Anglo-Saxon—
civilized after Fort girls—attractive legs and figure, though
broadened after bearing children—hair parted in the
middle and with Greta Garbo upcurling bob—Lovett
would sit silent for a long time, and Mrs. Lovett wouldn't

make conversation—daughter called mother sweetheart and darling—mother dropped into silly half-burlesque sweetie way of talking to daughter—clever grandchild who enjoyed the mathematical problems and had drawn up a prospectus for a Saturday day nursery: "To get rid of your child for a day, who would not rejoice at the idea?"—Little boy vigorous and rather quarrelsome. —With the prospect of the wine after we sat down to table, Lovett began to cheer up and be playful with the little grandson. When little girl was putting him to bed he came back with pair of wings—said he was a little cherub—mother said a pair of horns would be more appropriate—Lovett chuckled and said that was premature. —Talked about how Chambertin used to cost two dollars and a half a bottle—Mrs. Lovett said people drank more now—No!—more cocktails then— Why, no! we used to have cocktails!—Only when we were having guests. —Why, I used to have a cocktail every night! —Little grandson came back with wings on head, and I said he looked like Brunhilde, the Walküre—Lovett, affected by the wine, began to hum the "Ride of the Walküre"—sudden burst of merry talk about distilling, etc.—during which Mrs. Lovett seemed a little dismayed— then general subsidence after dinner. Lovett silent again, daughter sewed, son seemed to go to sleep, Mrs. Lovett said little. —He always called her Mrs. Lovett. —After dinner, when we discussed Hull-House, he said he didn't recognize anybody there by name, they were all super-annuated—Mrs. Lovett said, Oh, no, they had five young people.

Unemployed. In schools, factories, warehouses, old jails—whitewashed furniture—factory walls, yellow school walls soiled, blackboards punched through, thin blankets and a sheet, men in holey socks and slit union suits, tattooed with fancy designs and with the emblems of services they no longer served, with fallen arches taken out of their flattened shoes and done up with bandages of adhesive tape, or lying wrapped up in their blankets on their backs, their skin stretched tight over their cheekbones and jawbones almost like the faces of the dead— the smell, peppery-sweetish stink: sulphur fumigations, cooking food, sweat, creosote disinfecting, urinals, one element or the other figuring more prominently from time to time but in the same inescapable fumes of humanity not living and functioning naturally but dying on its feet and being preserved as best one could, venereal disease, Negroes with t.b., lonely as a pet coon, men poisoned with wood alcohol—fifteen cents a pint—two sick and one to the psych hospital—benzine, kerosene, and milk—I say, which will you have, your bottle or a bed?—and they won't give up the bottle—I wouldn't be surprised if a hearse drove up and a dead man got up and walked out and asked for a flop—a cripple drunk again—one man so lousy no one would go nearum and they puttum in the stable with the horse and the horse tried to get away and then the next morning they gaveum a shower and scrubbedum with a long-handled brush. —They fumigate the clothes and if they're moist it ruins them. Chicago is probably doing as good a job as anybody. —Entertainments so that they won't hold meetings and get ideas of revolt—the recreation hall (Hoover Hotel), thick with smoke, men sitting on the steps of the platform and flopping on the floor, newspapers lying around, people sitting in the gallery waiting for the show to begin (Thurston the magician, Tarzan, prize fights in gyms)—honest, good, and capable faces—the floors covered with spit—don't let them into the dormitories till five—humanity being reduced to the grayness or rather the colorlessness of the monotonous streets—lice "crumbs," bedbugs, spinal meningitis, nine cases—the Salvation Army excludes drunkards—razor frays in the basement down with the urinals where the bad characters are sent and the newcomers have to go when there's no room for them yet up above— obscure shootings—less since the four-dollar-a-week ar-rangement—men who run shelters are afraid of losing their jobs, insist that four dollars come back, there's no use in giving them that, they're worthless—old men in showers with thin arms, flat chests, and round bellies— humanity reduced to the primal neutral undifferentiated grayness, even the human glow of life which marks life off from its background extinguished—mess men and officials right out of the line—blue shirts, loose ties, no ties—food—slum, clanking of trays, dumping what was left in GI cans like the army—coughing and colds in the infirmary—a few cuts of meat, the cattle and pigs at the packing houses being killed and cured to feed people— white-collar men with phones in relief offices—tailor shop in basement—playing cards—library—

basements in most shelters only available places for lounging—"bull pens"—

Christian Industrial Union. The Blood of God Can Make the Vilest Clean—Jesus the Light of the World— same smell—men lying with one hand behind their heads or with the sheets pulled up over their faces—the old yel-low oak woodwork and scraped walls of the courthouse— GI can for slops in the mess hall—only two meals a day— fat men, old thin men, men of all nationalities—Commu-nist meetings, entertainers—blue shirts—men pillowed on newspapers—army cots—two tiers of bunks—wooden benches that they slept on with coats—old Cicero police-man who had been saved, they routed them to mess through the prayer-meeting hall so they'd be exposed to religion on the way, prefaced it with waltz to get people to come—people in infirmaries for starvation: weakness, exhaustion, bad kidneys, sores—four of the meningitis cases had tied themselves up in knots and died—sitting under dark bridges—The Shadows.

—the stagnant smell of humanity

—*On Harrison Street.* The snow, big dull dark square industrial buildings around it—blackened weeds old springs, picked bones of old cars and black old metallic junk unsalvageable even for the scaly-scabrous-looking huts that have fastened to the vacant lot like barnacles, made out of old tar paper and tin, with stovepipes all slightly crooked and buttresses of packing boxes—people who can't stand for the shelters—a pole flying a black torn rag, the flag of despair.

"a sense of lost personality—quiet and despair"—"fear"

—young men coming of age during workless period— forced out of their respectable wage-earning class into casual status, associate with confirmed casuals, get discouraged about idea of working

—the abyss of grayness and death—the neutral, the non-human, an undifferentiated plasm that is less than human and then nothing

Jack-rolling, greatly increased since Depression—beating somebody up in a dark street with unnecessary brutality— for thirty cents

Fifty thousand registered at Clearing House during year ending September 30, '32—average age forty-three—49.9% skilled—46.4% unskilled, and 3.7% clerical and professional. —Ten million meals, three million nights' lodging —average number cared for daily, 12,897, largest number 17,381—shelter costs twenty cents—meals between 2.7 cents and 3 cents—only two meals daily—ten thousand men connected up with agencies for service. —Chicago care of family men far in advance of other cities—second city to institute recreation and morale-building activities.

Begun November '30.

—Sent home, poorhouse, veterans' home, giving jobs, asylums, blind pension, juvenile courts, non-residents sent on their way, deported—about 500 a month of these altogether—3,822—"Bread-Line Frolics"—Mrs. Waller Borden invited Mrs. Rockefeller McCormick to join her in promoting recreation—Mrs. Borden sponsored show for society people for one night, and it ran for two weeks—took in $10,445—a profit of $5,214. Marshall Field bought out house for three nights and sent its employees—Sears, Roebuck one night, and other firms bought large blocks of tickets.

—Every able-bodied man must work one five-hour day out of every twelve—sixty-five cents per hour—gets ticket for twelve days and meals and lodging and twenty-five cents. —Communists tried to prevent trucks leaving and led riots against Clearing House. —Also work on grounds around pumping stations and cutting weeds along drainage canal—ragweed control—clearing up unsightly private lots.

—seasonal migratory labor—shoeshining boxes—selling special edition of *Daily News*—selling novelties during political conventions

—clothing appropriation less than $50,000, one dollar a year per man

—problem of young men on the road—50 percent (sample of 6,009) of non-residents younger than thirty

—Median weekly wage—rate $23.97—almost one-fifth are unskilled railroad-track laborers. —Chicago is one of the largest markets for migratory and seasonal labor.

—demand for third meal

—discussion of making them self-supporting in farm colonies

Communist entertainment. Little red ribbons hanging from electric lights and caught up in canopy effect over platform—picture of Lenin that somebody had hung his hat over—child had drawn a worker in collar and chain that looked more like a pet devil on the misted window-pane. —Blackboard with announcements—livid blue lightning from the streetcars.

—Trio including cymbalon—trying, very jolly, of harmonicas and guitar, man knocking harmonica against his shoe before he could start the encore —Young Pioneer reciting humorous little poem—speech telling people that entertainment was all right in its place but they mustn't forget the struggle—raffling off the white-iced cake—it went for a dollar, though one of the kids had misled them by bidding one-ten.

Marian Strobel. Anxious now to be on the right side of Chicago conventions and social prejudices: when I mentioned F.P.A.* (with whom she had once had a great rapprochement), she said that when I had seen her when she had been in New York it had been at a time in her life when she must have been rather unpleasant—had come on to get everything as fast as she could. —She hadn't had it then but now she had a prejudice against (the Jews)—you always come up against something in them that she didn't like, something soft—she felt that they were always trying to get something out of you. —Felt very definitely *against* Sherwood Anderson on account of the way he had treated Tennessee—well, you know, that kind of thing isn't done!—Oh, that sounds awfully snobbish, doesn't it?—married to a doctor—Dick Bentley a "capitalist" with a large nice house—she and Margaret Bentley used to get together once a week and read serious books aloud.

* Franklin P. Adams, who wrote a popular newspaper column "The Conning Tower" in the style of Pepys.

Chicago. Driving out to Calumet City—the morning sun of winter in Chicago is like a forge which has just been started up—gray fog and white smoke—the vast blocks of the buildings seem condensed from the gray fog and white smoke, and the clouds and the sheets of smoke seem walls as solid as the buildings—the asphalt of the road like solidified smoke polished smooth—the Lake: a strange thick pearly liquid, stagnant, faintly luminous, more live than the asphalt and the stone—a faintly luminous viscous pearl just becoming discernible as something which, though stagnant, was more alive (sensitive) than the asphalt and the stone.

Calumet City. The exotic bulbous spires of the Greek church and the sharp spire of the Catholic church among the low houses, two little floors with a Noah's Ark roof, houses absolutely gray, brick houses, relief headquarters a rabbit house—bristling Polish letters and gold crowns of the metallic Slavic saints and Madonnas in ornate gold Byzantine frames—

—Irish brothers—gabby liar, wife nurse, brother knocked out with pneumonia and typhoid—boilermaker

—Good-looking Polish girl, seventeen, who had done housework for real-estate man at two dollars a week, boy who had been laid off at bookbindery when job at conveyor was abolished—wallpaper with large pink, blue, and magenta blossoms (ferns), shrines and Madonnas only things on wall, stuffed (wadded) furniture with orange fruits that looked as if it had never been sat on—oversold on furniture and Victrolas—enormous Polish-speaking mother

—less Americanized family—close sweetish smell of cooking and washing—boy who interpreted for mother—slovenly—she was carrying on with good-humored dismay

—man who had been drinking, wife discouraged or dumb—dirty gray covers lying twisted like old rags on beds—dirty children

—old man dying with no coal, nothing heard in the house but his breath—bloodless, arms skin and bones: tumor—grandmother with cap

—young couple with Kewpies [dolls], very thin, two children in one cot, hated to ask for charity

—O'Connors', domestic situation, drink and going with other men and women, redheaded boy with something the matter with him, he worked in brother's shop but was afraid the union would throw him out for working below union rates, her middle-class dress

—good-looking, pink, clear-eyed, innocent-eyed Polish woman about to have another baby, in neat, modern, beautifully kept kitchen

—good couple, more Americanized than most, in basement which he had fixed up and painted, she had heart trouble, canary and cage

—Swiss couple from Zurich, he had done chemical work, now invented little gambling games, went out and picked up coal on railroad tracks and got chased by detective; she cooking onions, had had breakdown, chromolithographs in blues and greens of Swiss waterfalls and lakes and mountains

—young violinist thrown out of work by talkies

—While sitting at the desk, I saw a bedbug crawling along the wallpaper.

La Salle Street Room. Disinfectant smell—yellow wallpaper covered with ugly leaves, holes burned in chair seat with middle cushion and sections of back that didn't quite match the rest, carpets whose original maggotlike pattern had been worn down to no color at all covered with miscellaneous stains, old and long unidentifiable; little silly pink strips of curtains and pink and blue striped strips laid ineffectually diagonally across the tables; desk; floor lamp; bed with pink curtains: I sat warming my feet at the radiator under its foot with the bed tilted up at an angle during the terrible cold spell; alcove with bureau that you could only get into by climbing across the bed when it was down; when you didn't feel the bed was exactly right, the foot could be bent out so as to let it down even lower; yellow wooden fireplace, bare red tiles—looked tan in the electric light; the little things you took hold of to raise it were off one of the windows—dirty panes—the rain of months had washed down them—all one pane, and when you pulled up the shade, there was a large disconcerting expanse of wood—part of one of the blackened sills torn away—somebody played very old-fashioned tunes—waltzes and hymns on the piano on the floor below—missing notes in "All Over God's Heaven"—rather lame "One-Hoss Open Sleigh"—"Georgia Camp Meeting."

The Fair Store. Cheap toys: idiot-looking doll babies with dot mouths; frog that pulled itself along with its hind legs and that Louise thought was dreadful; dreadful-looking cat with nose cross-stitched in silk and green glass eyes too far apart; round sachet ball that smelled sickening; clothes-brush holder in the shape of a very badly conceived carved-out brown wooden Scotch terrier; try a sample of Heinz peanut butter on a little Educator with a dash of jam; the basement, full of cheap dresses and underclothes and food, smelled something like the stockyards; rings with large glass jewels for a dollar; collar-box dog with small red tongue [Louise sent me this for Christmas, and I may still have it in the Wellfleet attic]; Santa Claus who took children one by one on his knee as they filed in behind a little wooden fence and whispered something in their ear—he wasn't so bad, but the one whom people paid to have their children photographed with on a pony was pathetic—looked as if he had been picked out of a bread line—like the other, for his straight and dignified nose and brow—and hired for practically nothing; child in brown overcoat bawling: Louise: that child is about to attack that ice-cream soda. —Shopgirls kept saying: Can I help you? Louise: Nobody can help us now! —Escalators.

—Henri had had bedbugs in Bank Street—said, Exterminators may come and exterminators may go—but you have to tear the house down to get rid of them.

*Angelus Building.** In the terrible cold, like falling through the ice into the water—the air, the sky—it was dusk—seemed as solid and cold as the snow, the snow as dingy as the dusk, both just the neutral unnatural, unnourishing city medium condensed—the last city dinginess and ghastliness—had a slightly better class of people moved away from it once?—the bay windows of one of a narrow-windowed row gutted like all the houses so that you could see clean through it, one gray old limestone house with a horrid touch of baroque that makes it, with its pointed peaks, look like a black pulled tooth, another with a most ornate brown doorway from under which the steps have been knocked like a lower jaw; dingy red brick, gray limestone, colorless boards, scattered along the long street running for miles and miles, monotonous without being uniform, attempts at one kind of house or another, all looking abandoned now in the winter afternoon; the Angelus Building—seven stories, dark, thick with windows, the windows gloomily dark, covered with fire escapes, built 1852, popular in that part of town at the time of the World's Fair, inhabited by white people then, the Ozark Hotel, darkness in the entrance except for enough light to light an entrance hall with an old smeared and stained and worn and roughened pink and white mosaic, a plaster pattern of molding on the ceiling, fancy ironwork, most of it broken off on the black grille of the

* *Earthquake*, pp. 460–2.

elevator, the last marks of the old hotel, trampled under, abject, surrendered—the dark shaft of the court with its outside iron galleries, truly infernal—the coal smoke—a dulled darkness covered with glass at the top—the top stories condemned, old firetrap, the top stories partly gutted, the Negroes had wrecked the rest before the manager came, doors pulled out, bathroom floors ripped up and plumbing uncovered, public toilets; on one of the lower floors, bathroom with water standing in it—no light, little heat—the heating and the plumbing don't work very well, banging and sounds of breakage in the dark and silent shaft; some families striving for neatness—children in the dark halls—prostitutes, killings and fights—all crammed into the Angelus Building, its darkness filled full of living Negroes—grim and forbidding, ominous, with its irregular ugly knobs on top—drove them out of the top floors, but where could they go?—about four working—Negroes of all degrees of respectability—oil lamps.

St. Louis. A mellow Old World city after Chicago— Nugents and Paramores in those streets—women (in the Italian cafeteria) of an older society: thinner, more civilized, Southern (?)—brown-eyed—bottle-nosed girl in green with big base in cafeteria, waitresses blond, amiable, and obliging in white—old birds sitting around hotel lobby looking out through double glass doors at the snowstorm—a cuckoo nigger passed by, gesturing crazily with his hand and with a crazy smile on his face—all much more human—did the Negroes do something for the Anglo-Saxons?—snow—from the window at night, long avenue looking rather old, old-fashioned lamps close together all along it, much closer together than in Chicago, only one street lighted but looking hospitable, not like Chicago dark; old blackened chimneyed narrow-windowed

half-Southern-looking buildings, a man running across
the snow in the big open place in front of the station
where the avenue seemed to begin, nobody would ever
do that in Chicago—informal, unspeeded-up, leisurely,
deserted, people all gone home for the night and much
happier at home than out, half-like-the-South—satisfying
effect of smooth snow-covered roof of station stretching
below my window, beyond in low complexity of roofs: you
probably couldn't figure out the streets by numbers, you'd
have difficulty getting around—

Hecker (my old friend of the army, now teaching
school in St. Louis).* Wouldn't look at me at first—a
boys' school had done that to him—I kept seeing his snug
cap with the little bow on top (he thought somebody was
kidding him at first when I called him up on the phone
and talked about the Department of Propaganda and the
Department of Exterior Fronts)—then became witty, talk
good prose with prepared sequences—about A. Lawrence
Lowell—thought that slavery, syphilis, and liquor could
get the human race unless superior men, dictators—like
Lenin, the greatest man in five thousand years—could impose ideas upon them, control them—the most horrible
thing in the world, the step of a drunken father, his
father had drunk, he had drunk and had a good head for
whiskey as well as wine till he went to Harvard and saw
in Boston seven saloons to the block—I asked him if he
ever got tired of teaching: he said he'd rather be in
politics—had spent $1,200 on his campaign—if he'd spent
$1,000 more, he might have gotten it—everybody but him
talked about beer—one of the other candidates paid atten-

* Eugene Arthur Hecker, a Latin teacher, had worked with
EW in Chaumont, France, in military intelligence. See *A Prelude*, p. 26.

tion to his talk and began mixing the tariff and the gold standard and unemployment insurance up with the beer—and apparently, from Hecker's point of view, that hadn't worked so well either—kept railing against drinking of members of Harvard Club—

When I came back to Chicago, the pianist in the apartment above was playing "Sleep my little one, sleep," also very lamely—pounding it out slowly and patiently—what pleasure did she get out of it?—was she alone?—was that all she had?

Belleville. The long main street; on the way back, men talking in bus on how Soviet Russia ought to be recognized—[Senator] Borah's statement—it was so to say, as somebody had done, that to recognize it would be Communistic—why should we dictate to them what their form of government ought to be?—strong compact German houses with fine ornamental door—time-yellowed white on red brick. *The Wiecks:* * farmhouse on a little hill with a dip in the ground just beside it, beyond which you saw a field dry russet—color against the snow—and beyond that the thick stacks of corn. The countryside in Illinois is large and flat and calm and covered with snow—a sort of purity and sobriety and distinction: a picture of Lincoln in every home. The house in excellent taste—Mrs. Wieck referred to the overstuffed furniture which had been sold to people during the boom—bare of everything but necessities—George [Luks, the Ash Can school

---

* See "Illinois Household," *Earthquake,* pp. 465–72. Edward A. Wieck worked with the Department of Industrial Studies on prevention of explosions in coal mines; Agnes Burns Wieck was head of the Illinois Women's Auxiliary of Coal Miners' Wives.

painter] picture of a coal miner and two dark pictures of miners in the old days being let down into the pit with a rope, which looked as if they had come out of the old *Harper's*—big stove that gave a lot of heat—the dictionary on its stand—the desk—bookcase and magazines—oilcloth in green and white squares on kitchen table—green stove—rather rich pattern of linoleum on floor—steps leading upstairs, on which it was convenient to sit—blackboard: ethnology, etymology, philology, entomology—Babe Ruth, Cellini, Michelangelo—potatoes, pork sausages, German cheese made out of buttermilk, delicious liverwurst which seemed to me richer than what you get in delicatessen stores in New York—setters, white with a few black, in chicken-wire enclosure, shivering in the cold, jumping up against the wire—Wieck, when in his anecdotal vein, talked very much like Mr. Ed (Paramore), then when he was talking about his adventures as a sailor, would drop into the sailor's accent, then as a coal miner, would have Irish *r*'s, etc.—variations of his grammar. —The way the little boy talked—all in a loud outpouring that ran the words together.

Scotch photographer and three attractive children.

Tippenses—molasses candy—fat dog: that pore dog doesn't get a thing to eat—dog would sit and yelp in front of anybody who was eating.

People thought the Allards* were snooty—she smoked cigarettes—*Farewell to Arms* which Gerry had given her—to my wife Irene—and which had been lent to the photographer's family. —Little yellow house not much bigger than the garage.

* Gerry Allard, chief organizer of the Progressives. See "Illinois Miners," *The New Republic*, June 14, 1933. A Communist, he edited *The Progressive Miner*, leading the rebellion against UMWA.

John L. Lewis. Suite at Bellevue Stratford—had taken room there because Lewis was there, ten dollars and breakfast expensive—had made them let him come on and spend ten days in New York to get city-broke before German delegates arrived—met them at boat—Lewis had been through list and crossed out several modest hotels, substituting more expensive ones—in Indianapolis they had large parlors on the mezzanine—the closet was as big as a room—and he counted the electric lights and there were seventeen—seventeen lights!—ran out of money and got check for $1,000 without any question at all!—got cars blocked off—Lewis squat, long hair, talked without moving his mouth—people go to see him and come away as if they'd had a dose of hop—he never had that effect on me, but he did on some people—walk up and down floor and give vent to a torrent of eloquence—the Mussolini type—Pierce Arrow, big house at Springfield—wonder what it is between Lewis and operators, Congressional investigation—not a poker player, no scandal—what was it about his going to see Lewis in hotel?—hang on to their salaries, graft—labor leaders getting cheaper stocks—did Lewis have Insull stock?

Chicago: tailors on Rush Street. Had been in New York but came to Chicago because he had brother there—wished he was back in New York—Why?—People more fren'ly there. —I expressed surprise. —Oh, the people here—they're wildcats! —But were the people in New York really more friendly? —More fren'ly—more cee-vee*lized!*

Mac, the Bootlegger. Steward on liner, chiropractor, headwaiter on Pullman, undefeated lightweight champion of Alaska when you could always get a meal by getting the pianist to play "Sweet Adeline" and singing. Had kept hotel. Had taken somebody around to see Hymie Levine—he was tough, his hands in pockets and a gun in each hand probably and his hat pulled down over his eyes—man kept looking at him and Hymie came up to um and said, Have you seen me before? —No. —Then, whatchou looking at? —He would leave his car with the key in it and they'd drive it away and fill it up and then come back and say, Your car's around the corner. He started out from there and saw the cops following him in the mirror and he turned up a side street so quick, he almost run over an old lady about seventy-five and he went back to Hymie Levine's and he says, There's a carload of coppers givin' me the tail! —The cop come to the door, a great big fellow, and Hymie bawled him out and said, I pay you $1,200 a year, now what more do you want? Now get out of here and stay out—the cop went away! —Two old people, eighty-five years old, who used to be good for a case of gin and a case of Scotch a month— vice-president of some railroad—now only ordered two pints of Bourbon. —All he wanted after Prohibition was a hotel with about forty rooms and he wouldn't care much if the rooms weren't filled. —Tom Newbury, leader of the Northside gang, a nice kid though—oh, he's not a killer, he's a nice kid— Of course, he knows the killers, he could have you executed, but he doesn't do it himself.

—He was offered vice-presidency of Cleaners and Dyers —$1,500 a month—man who offered it said he would take $750—why should you take $750? —That's for supplyin' the muscle—I have the gang and anybody that has to be removed is removed without your knowin' anything about it. —I called up my wife: Don't even talk about it! Come right home! —They're Jew boys—your own nationality. — The man who accepted lasted four months—first man shot in Valentine's Day massacre—but he had a wonder-

ful time because he'd never had so much money before—
a car, a woman, and an apartment to keep her in. —Cop
who saw him getting out of car with two gallons of alky.
He said, he was in the Frigidaire business now—cop who
held him up for $500—held out, could settle with the
government for $250—cop would accept $200—he had
$200 in pocket but pretended he didn't and went to cigar
store trying to borrow—finally gave cop $10 and paid out
the rest slowly when he saw him, $25 at a time. Cop
who was supposed to be a friend of his but who had
tipped the other cop off was there on one occasion and
asked his wife if she was getting a new dress out of it—
she said no. —Partner with the face of a saint who had
been making a graft on twenty or thirty cases a week of
bottles that he pretended to be paying two-fifty a piece
for when he was really paying only two dollars—Irishman
and Jew who lied about who they were delivering goods
to so as to collect larger prize, but man happened to call
up from hotel and gave it away and Mac told him not
to pay and they came back and he said, Well, you're a
couple o' smart guys! —Goodbye! —You can't trust your
own wife in this game!

[The bohemian crowd in Chicago] *Janowitz and boyfriend* burning incense while Brussels sprouts were cooking, so the studio (made out of a store) wouldn't have
that cabbagy smell—Communist fervor of ex-wife, he
didn't read her mail any more—McKenna's wife perfect
Pittsburgh type, pretty, like Lois, only much taller—
pulled brick-red blanket over her up to her neck, and
face looked very pretty coming out at top—charm of
feminine naïveté in eyes, feminine lisp in voice, coming
out through that spare, sharp boyish appearance. —They
called Negroes in Chicago "bugs" (the *u* pronounced
like *oo* in "food") and used to twit her at the La Salle Ex-

tension College where she worked on showing interest in bugs burning when there was a fire. —From time to time Janowitz would pull himself together and say very loudly and emphatically that Karl Borders was "an enemy of the working class."*

Janowitz said he'd been an only child, had had all the advantages—used to think he'd be happy if he could only get to some place in Italy or on the Riviera with his painting, but then he wasn't happy and he finally came back.

Detroit. . . . Barber who advertized haircut for 25¢— Come in and let me cut your hair or I'll vote for Hoover—Roy Gamble on plants that had depended on people owning cars and being able to get to them that way . . . Hamiltons going in for Buchmanism . . . Roy on the Russellites and the Book of Revelation, the Church lined up with the Devil: the Church, politics and business . . . Diego Rivera painting art museum . . . Margaret Longyear's husband, typical Rotarian on the young-married local-society side, slightly caustic about Rivera, etc., smiled much too much, smile had nothing to do with bulk, or, apparently, with rather heavy personality and mind . . . said goodbye, shaking hands and smiling much too much . . . people disliked modern pictures . . . Roy said he had been laid up for three weeks by his adventures in the Ford factories with me—not the weather, automobile factories—I never liked 'em . . . on a fake Titian in Detroit, all part of big advertizing game—

---

* Karl Borders (1892–1953), socialist and secretary of the League for Industrial Democracy. He appears in EW's *New Republic* article on Hull-House, January 25, 1933, pp. 287–90.

not a pin has been put in the whole thing!—Buchmanism (Rasputin)

Ralph Holmes on Times. Kick he got out of news-papermen who came around asking for jobs on copy desk . . . big buildings imitating New York—in every little city in Indiana, they were so proud of big build-ing—you could spit out of the window on any place in the whole town.

I didn't feel that I ought to go to bed with her so soon after Margaret's death, but she made me, against my better judgment, take her to bed in Hull-House—There's no reason you shouldn't have a little treat, is there? Then I took the horrid room on La Salle Street—Shall we have our little treat? Do you want to sleep with me? I'm a fine whore! Do you think we'll be able to make it? —My comment on her not liking dirty jokes: I take it much too seriously. Liked it, unlike most of the women nowadays, who seemed to be getting blasé about it. —Gaiety reviving, started humming afterwards while lying on bed: *No more dishes in the sink!* —What am I out in the hot sun for?—when sitting on edge of the bed, I coughed and sneezed so long: I was about to write you a note and go home. —She said she had always had the feeling that she didn't fit into life.

Her original fiancé had told her when they broke off their engagement that she had no feeling and her nose was too thick. She had gotten infatuated with Dick Knight after her present husband had practically had her signed up—he slipped the ring on her, told his family, insisted on having her meet them.

When I had gone with her into a store, she stopped to see a woman slap a child and said, I like to see that. At the same time she rather shocked me by telling me that she wanted me to beat her; one of her friends liked to switch his wife. I bought a hairbrush with wire bristles—which she described as "peerless"—and first scraped, then spanked her with it. I found this rather difficult, perhaps because of inhibitions. She said afterwards that she had thoroughly enjoyed it, and explained that she thought she had wanted this because her husband didn't dominate her.

NEW YORK, 53RD STREET, 1932–33

[At some point during this rather sordid period, I formed the project of writing *To the Finland Station*. It was while I was walking in the street in New York somewhere in those East Fifties, I think. It occurred to me that nobody had ever presented in intelligible human terms the development of Marxism and the other phases of the modern idea of history. I saw the possibilities of a narrative which would quite get away from the pedantic frame of theory. I knew that this would put me to the trouble of learning German and Russian and that it would take me far afield of what I thought was my prime objective: a work of fiction made out of the materials that I had been compiling in these notebooks; but I found myself excited by the challenge, and there rang through my head the words of Dedalus at the end of Joyce's *Portrait*.*

The title came, I think at an early stage, and it did not

---

* Joyce's *Portrait of the Artist as a Young Man* ends: "Welcome, O life! I go to encounter for the millionth time the reality of experience and to forge in the smithy of my soul the uncreated conscience of my race . . . Old father, old artificer, stand me now and ever in good stead."

occur to me till later that I was echoing it from *To the Lighthouse.*]

Talk, etc.—Bread is the opium of the people (*Hemingway* at Italian restaurant)

—Thinking Stalin is Santa Claus—Stalin taking Santa Claus for Marx (*Cummings*)

—I'll bet Paul [Draper] is fluttering around like an effing butterfly (Betty Huling night we went to Paul's for dinner—she feared he wouldn't have enough gin, and not only did he not have enough gin, he didn't know how to pick up the shaker and spilled almost all that was left)

—people talked about things "having them down"— and about things reaching "a new low for all time"

(Bronson) *Cutting* told Esther (Arthur) the Republican Party would never come back and had egged Roosevelt on to split the Democrats—said Roosevelt was really pessimistic—he didn't think he himself could do much more than situate the Democratic Party a little to the left of the center—thought civilization might revert to a period like the Dark Ages, had read Marx when Phelps Putnam had taken it abroad with him and his only quarrel with him was that Marx was much too optimistic—he couldn't believe that the working class would produce the leadership to take control of the situation.

Kenneth Simpson used to get drunk at parties and come into the dining room naked after he'd been put to bed and say that he'd only married Helen for her money and now she didn't have that, and she would take it just as sweetly as if he were coughing and sneezing with a bad cold.

—*Betty Huling.* Telephone in *New Republic* office the morning of a hangover "sounded like the last trump to her!"

Slang: a new low
      can't take it
      got me down
      Hello, Keed
      You're telling *me!*

—Fashionable feminine way of using "definitely"—as in hat ad: Easy to wear, but definitely difficult to make.

—Song: *Let's put out the lights and go to bed—No more money in the bank—no cute baby to spank—Leave the dishes in the sink—**

—All hot and bothered. Anna: What's the use of getting me all hot and bothered?

—about '30, people were talking about selling New York back to the Indians for a dollar

—*Betty*: you mugs!—you rat—you mink.

Phil McMaster. With his brown Brooks suit and watch chain through first buttonhole from the top of vest—red face, no very definite purpose in expression, slightly watery-seeming eyes—I thought at first he was just an old Princeton drinker who had gone into business and gone on drinking, but he turned out to be working at the Rockefeller Institute, trying to find the cancer virus—cancer *was* a virus, he held—trying to cultivate a virus in a healthy cell—but still with the mental slant in mind—had gone in for psychoanalysis but couldn't stomach Jews, human lice, in Psychoanalytic Association—I said to Louise that it was like Communism—he said that [Paul] de Kruif used to drink—he kept on having more wine himself—finally invited us all to lunch and moonlight party at the Institute and insisted on paying for the check—if you got licensed by Psychoanalytic Association,

* EW scrambles the lines of a song hit of the time reflecting the Depression.

you had to hang out somebody's sign—Freud or Adler or
somebody—the man who psyched you sent you patients—
you had to string along with his particular school, whatever it was—he didn't want to be psyched evidently—
remarked at the same time that people who were psyched
by Jews wasted a good deal of time denouncing the Jews.
—His wife came from Rittenhouse Square or somewhere
in Philadelphia and thought he was bourgeois. —His
proposal to have an analysis with both the analyst and
the patient drunk—difficult to manage but could get
things out of him faster. —Next time I saw him, he looked
less watery-eyed—Sara Teasdale [the American poet,
1884–1933] has just been found dead in bathtub—If
you had a psychosis, jumping out the window was a
good thing to do.

Scott and Hemingway. Scott fixed me with basilisk
stare the moment I came into the room—he had still
never been able to get over my having been three years
ahead of him at Princeton—wouldn't talk and wouldn't
let us talk. — What happened to you? he asked me—
Where's Mary Blair? —Hemingway took a victoria to
the Aurora restaurant because he wanted to do something for the horse—to make it up to them for bull-
fights—Scott with his head down on the table between us
like the dormouse at the Mad Tea Party—lay down on
floor, went to can and puked—alternately made us hold
his hand and asked us whether we liked him and insulted us—told him he was a good writer—complimented
him on story in *Mercury*, "Absolution," * and asked him

---

* "Absolution" appeared in *The American Mercury* in June
1924 and was included in the short-story collection *All the Sad
Young Men* (1926). See also *The Bit Between My Teeth*
(1965), pp. 521–25.

whether it was part of a novel, and he answered, None of your business. —Said at first he was looking for a woman—Hemingway said he was in no condition for a woman—then that he was done with men—perhaps he was really a fairy—Hemingway said they used to kid like that but not to overdo it. —Hemingway said, We'll have to be careful because some of the best kids are so darn close to insults!—but he lectured him on his over-head—had to cut it down now, but he could have cut it down in Paris and had been so proud of his overhead! —Scott would say to me of Hemingway, Don't you think he's a strong personality? —At the Plaza, I stayed behind after Hemingway left, thinking Scott might open up, but he simply took off his coat, vest, pants, and shoes and put himself to bed and lay looking at me with his expressionless birdlike eyes. —I had asked him what he did in Baltimore—he replied truculently, The usual things! —I said I'd heard the theory advanced (by Dos Passos) that he was never really drunk but used the pretense of drunkenness as a screen to retire behind—this only made him worse if anything in order to prove that he was really drunk—though his answers to questions and remarks suggested he was in pretty good possession of his faculties. —Hemingway told him he oughtn't to let Zelda's psychoanalysis ball him up about himself— he was yellow if he didn't write. —It was a good thing to publish a lousy book once in a while. —Hemingway sang a little Italian song about General Cadorna to the waiter. —Next morning Scott called me up and apolo-gized for things he had said which might have wounded me and called Hemingway up and asked him to repeat something he'd said. —I remarked on the cold eye Scott had fixed me with when I'd first come in—he said, No confidence, eh? Well, you'll have to learn to take it? —He'd also said apropos of nothing, Shall I hit him?

When Scott was lying in the corner on the floor,
Hemingway said, Scott thinks that his penis is too small.
(John Bishop had told me this and said that Scott was
in the habit of making this assertion to anybody he met—
to the lady who sat next to him at dinner and who might
be meeting him for the first time.) I explained to him,
Hemingway continued, that it only seemed to him small
because he looked at it from above. You have to look at
it in a mirror. (I did not understand this.) —It seemed
to me that ideas of impotence were very much in people's
minds at this period—on account of the Depression, I
think, the difficulty of getting things going. I had one
adventure myself when I was unable to get myself going. It was true that I had been drinking and that I had
never before even kissed the woman, who was a fairly
close friend but who did not enormously attract me. I
have the impression that various kinds of irregular sexual
ideas are feared or become fashionable at different times:
incest, homosexuality, impotence.

Hunger march. John Herrmann's* terrible night with
[Edward] Dahlberg† (who always turned up, Adelaide
[Walker] said, and asked completely irrelevant questions)—took ten years off his life—kept talking and
wouldn't let John sleep—then lapsed into troubled slum-
ber, during which he groaned and complained, at the
same time kicking John out of the bed. —Bill Brown
drinking and sending telegrams to Hoover and Congress
all the way to Washington—collapsed—first casualty—
and was taken off to hospital. —Charley Walker losing

---

* Herrmann (1901–59) wrote a novel *What Happens* (1927)
published in France and banned in the United States.

† Edward Dahlberg (1900–77), son of a lady barber, who
wrote novels in a prophetic vein.

the way and driving [Earl] Browder and Stachel through Fort Lee—Browder fascinated by the gambling game in the lunchroom, didn't want Stachel to beat him (Lenin's chagrin over being beaten at cards?) —how Adelaide found them sunk in large comfortable chairs at home of wealthy sympathizer. —Bill Brown and the rest at Calverton's* house in Baltimore.

—They told me that people had been outraged at seeing Negroes not only parading with white women but walking with their arms around them and loving them up—would have been disgusting for any couple— Miss D. intimated that the white women looked like whores—

John Herrmann on right deviations masquerading as left deviations.

Bill Brown's party. Above the antique store—something and a half Bleecker Street—a punch like dry martinis— Dawn Powell† thought she heard somebody say they wouldn't stay if Dawn Powell was there and rushed out, pouring her drink down the back of a girl who was sitting on the stairs—Bill kept directing guests who wanted to go to the can to take the wrong turning when they got to the floor below so that men kept trooping into the room of an unknown girl, fumbling at their flies— I said to Bill, you sent me to the room of a very pretty

* V. F. Calverton (1900–40), Marxist critic and editor of *The Modern Quarterly.*

† Dawn Powell (1897–1965) lived in the Village and wrote realistic novels about Westerners adapting themselves to New York. EW carried on an amusing correspondence with her in which she was supposed to be Mrs. Humphry Ward and EW was a seedy literary man named Wigmore. See *Letters on Literature and Politics*, pp. 397–9; also *The Bit Between My Teeth*, pp. 526–33.

girl! (She had been looking at herself in the glass and I had seen her against the light) —Then she came out and I saw that she wasn't pretty at all—I excused myself and she said bitterly, It's happened too many times! —Bill said she hadn't paid her own rent, which accounted for her being so particularly nasty— Soon the landlady and her boyfriend appeared and tried to get us all back into Bill's room—Bud and I went down into the antique store to meet Maidy (Louise Bogan's daughter), who had had to be telephoned for, and pay her taxi fare—the boy-friend came down and we told him we weren't going to steal his antiques—he explained apologetically that there was "a woman upstairs with the jitters"—I remembered about having failed years ago at Hillsdale to buy Maidy a box of candy I had promised her when I used to go out there for the weekends and rushed across the street to a drugstore and bought one. —Nobody could remember afterwards much about the dinner—Louise remembered a cockeyed scallop looking up at her from the bottom of the bouillabaisse—Bud and I challenged each other to remember old songs from *Little Johnny Jones*; Forty-five minutes from Broadway, etc. —I said that I bet Bud didn't know what it was that was forty-five minutes from Broadway—New Rochelle! (Bronx cheer) —I kept in-viting them all to come to my house and sleep in the soft patches of plaster in the ceiling. —Bill Brown was afraid to go home for a couple of days and slept at the house of friends. —A sordid and deplorable Greenwich Village party of those days, redeemed only by Bill Brown's charm.

Bud, the first time he came to eat with Betty Huling's family, said, The only trouble with the Hulings' seventy-five cent lunch is that there's no choice of dessert! —Her father had been unable to reply.

Betty's parents came all the way to New York because they heard she was having an affair with a married man—her father used old Elizabethan words like "strumpet" that she'd never heard except in books before—finally they put him out and she and her mother had a good cry together, and Betty consented to go away with the family on a trip. —This fall, however, her father (who, she thought, was going crazy) got angry with her at dinner, began to tell her about how he had information to the effect that she'd become a notorious whore in the Village, and went after her with a carving knife. She decided she'd better not go to Larchmont any more, but went out for Christmas, which was pretty sour and strained. —Bud every Friday; insomnia other nights. —I used to tell her she was a model for a new type of human being. —Her father had inherited some money when he was thirty and since then had done nothing. Would talk about the market—fine when they were young because he could tell children's stories, but when they got too old to sit on Daddy's knee and hear about the Indians and the cowboys, it hadn't been so good. Parents had heard that the people at *The New Republic* believed in free love and took drugs.

Betty had been caught one evening down on the floor biting Bud's ankle—a crisis—they wouldn't speak to her for days—her mother met her on the stairs and accused her of drinking: Why, Mother, don't be silly! —Her mother said, If it had been gin—but it was whiskey!

Janet Howard (one of the ladies who lived on the top floor of the house on 53rd Street). Made an unpleasant and nosy impression when she first arrived and introduced herself, making me open the door for her. —Waylaid me at midnight about coal when I was tight. Notes and memorandum. Gasmen about non-existent leaks, etc., till they "thought she was crazy." Worried about colored man, Earl (who worked for Muriel Draper's son Paul), about garbage, about disappearance of garbage pail. When I got ceiling patched, "Oh, Maddy! that old ladder has scratched the paint all up!" (Maddy was her friend the French teacher.)—*tutoyer*-ing like the cooing of doves. Turning out lights—on Anna in bathroom. Piano—keeping Anna out of living room. —Walking in on Anna to see about piano when she was in bed on the couch just in front of the door. —Heroic defense of Griffin (?) against Mary (Vorse?): She's not going to kill you!—She was very menacing! *Avez-vous bien cherché?* —How to get new lock put on door. —How they had searched all over Spain for real Spanish dance but men friends wouldn't take them where they could be seen—finally saw women dance nude, in place where respectable women weren't supposed to go, in dances that required the voluminous Spanish clothes. —No one who wasn't part pagan could appreciate *Death in the Afternoon*. —Didn't want plaster in her room fixed because it messed up things so.

Winter of '32–'33 at Provincetown. Susan (Glaspell) and Knobby living together and drinking constantly: name for female inebriates. —Mary Vorse going around and being friendly for the first time in years with Susan to clear up some points about Norman. Norman in New York in the bosom of eight million Strunskies—Old grandmother Strunsky and Wallace Irwin. —Betty (Spencer's) neurotic decision to kill cat—would just take it to Dr. Hebert and have it given a shot with a needle—just a single shot, wouldn't even have to see the body—had taken it out for a motor ride to get it used to being taken out. Susan scandalized, rushed around and found

a home for it. Betty had thought she could do that with
a different cat every summer. —Niles on "painting out
of desperation."

—Mary Vorse said the dogs all came around when
Tucker was in rut (Katy had said Tucker wasn't in rut)
—they'd open the door and find them sitting on the front
steps, and when they went out to the outhouse they'd
see three or four pairs of green eyes—they bit Knobby
quite severely—this was after she'd set herself afire with
a lamp going down to look after the furnace—earlier in
life she'd had a fibroid tumor.

Hollywood. Dos on impression produced by [Irving]
Thalberg and one of his actresses passing through dining room—a hush fell. —On Don Stewart, lately returned from there: he had said, in exactly the same
words as Ted and Jack Lawson,* that he hoped that
after years of it he might have enough technical knowledge really to do something. Began by offering up his
evening prayer to Thalberg, then after a few drinks went
so far as to kid a little about him—though he looked over
his shoulder as he did so. —Lawson and Ornitz on the
Pat Kearney case.

Louise and Maidy playing piano the night that Raymond (Holden) went out with his mother to Radio
City: Raymond's crawled back into the womb tonight.
—A little piece of the Kreutzer Sonata, a little fragment
of Glück—with a one! and a two! and a three! and a four!
—I was touched and delighted by it—like Margaret with
the bloodhound puppy. She had kept her music and
managed to pass it on to Maidy, in spite of Raymond.
Raymond came back and said we were drunk.

* Donald Ogden Stewart, the screen writer and novelist, and
John Howard Lawson, who wrote plays on social and proletarian
themes.

Dinner at Bertram Willcox's (an old friend from Hill, he and his brother Alanson were lawyers in New York). Just as I should have imagined it, large apartment on Washington Square East looking out on the square— clean, rather bare, though the intention was decorative— red Chinese mandarin jacket or whatever it was on wall— a few mediocre etchings—antique chest with assorted drinks in living room—viviparous guppies whose children had died because room was too cold for them—gas-lighting fireplace that they drew around after dinner. Vague YMCA and social-work connections—she had been visiting Ambassador Schumann when Jimmy Walker* came to Berlin. After a couple of highballs, got more eloquent about professors at Harvard Law: Holmes and Carl Becker [the historian at Cornell]. What do you think of the human race, Dr. Becker? —Why, I'm pessimistic about them, but I wish them well. —Well, I don't give a damn about them nowadays. —Holmes on Wigmore, whose new theory of evidence was expounded in a jargon that nobody could under-stand—on Sacco and Vanzetti apropos of contradictory opinion: Well, Wigmore may be a better lawyer than I am, but I'll bet I'm a better soldier. (Wigmore had been in Adjutant General's department during the war.) —Frankfurter: they were "both pros"—you didn't seem to be learning anything from his courses at the time, but afterwards Alanson realized in dealing with railroads that Felix Frankfurter had taught him general principles which illuminated the subject. The question of Jews: opinions not to be absolutely trusted because they had reasons for wanting to assert themselves—not "because of their aristocracy." Chafee sounder, though it had been said of him that he was so much impressed with the

_____
* The jaunty and popular former mayor of New York.

importance of seeing that there were two sides to a fence that he thought that was the most important thing about the fence. —Man who always brought in Peter and John and dog and "his horse Major"—Peter bets John he can't get to a certain point in a certain length of time, then just as he is almost there the other man comes along in a car and taps him on the shoulder and says, The bet's off! —Roscoe Pound*—phenomenal memory—could look up cases in books in his mind, turning over pages —did he trade on it now?—story of professor who said, I find that nowadays every time I remember a student I forget a fossil fish. —Pound's fits of temper—good scholar, should probably never have been an executive—spoke better on a few drinks, speech on analogy between feudal system and development of big corporations. (Anecdote of [Robert Maynard] Hutchins at Chicago: someone asked him, is it true that you teach your students that opinions of the Supreme Court are unconstitutional? —No: we let them find it out for themselves.) —Judge Staley's decision about having no jurisdiction in con- nection with Walker—just the decision Marshall had been so much applauded for—Dred Scott case? —Alanson Willcox's cynicism about Supreme Court. —Pound on "permanent" fixtures in real estate—criterion of perma- nence of screws—how could certain fixtures be permanent when the man had only taken the house for five years? —Well, they were permanent as long as he was there, weren't they?

—They undoubtedly sat around and got mildly tight every night or so—invited people to dinner, then dis- cussed them afterwards. —I could see everything coming all evening—the courses, the rising from the table, the

---

* Roscoe Pound (1870–1964), for many years dean of the Harvard Law School.

coffee—saying to myself: Here comes the dessert—here come the highballs, etc. —The wood she had been buying in sealed envelopes—you could more easily boil it than burn it—when you put it on the fire, great quantities of water came gushing out from both ends of the log. —They climbed mountains and had photographs of the peaks.

Man who shot at Roosevelt [Zangara]: If you had stomach ulcers and couldn't pay a specialist, you shot the President—"a sign of the times!"

*Tom Matthews** comes back from Majorca with ulcers of the stomach—no drinks, milk, no saltines, crackers without salt—dividends decreasing, seventy-five dollars a week from *Time,* "almost half self-supporting now." Sister, who had always been a sulky silent little girl, had married Montana cowboy and was now perfectly happy, writing no more poetry, but cooking and sewing as head woman, only woman, on ranch. —I thought at first I'd refrain from drinking to be polite, then, thinking of Dahlberg, decided that ulcers of the stomach were silly and ordered a lot of beer.

Max Perkins [the editor at Scribner's]. Chuckling: It's a funny world—it'll really be a shame in a way when they get everything all straightened out. Scribner's press had restored some of their losses by making picture puzzles out of old Maxfield Parrish [1870–1966] pictures— demand so great they couldn't turn them out fast enough. —Jigsaw puzzles on all the newsstands. Would they hurt the market for books? —When drinking, he would expound schemes for ameliorating things—Jews at Harvard, unemployed army.

* T. S. Matthews; see *The Twenties,* pp. 447–9.

[S. J.] *Perelman, Phil Wylie, and Dashiell Hammett all back from Hollywood.* Hammett talked about people being screwy—crazy—When you first got out there they "ribbed" you (kidded you)—sent Arthur Caesar* ribbing notes telling him to go to Perelman and have him look over and correct his script. Man who only held his job by sitting three times in boss's chair that gave you an electric shock. Tripping people into swimming pools: Fairbanks and Chevalier. Man with buzzer to shake hands with: now don't tell—so-and-so's coming in! —Boss who sat at table in restaurant with head in hands, munching crackers, while other people stalled off man coming to see him till he was ready—then he blew crackers in his face—subordinate, who forgot for the moment "which side his bread was buttered on," hauled off and slugged him, and boss hit him back with a signet ring that marked his nose with what looked like a permanent scratch. —Groucho Marx's idea of himself wasn't any you'd ever think (Perelman): he wanted to be an English country squire, keep beagles and wear tweeds—always trying to start serious discussions, had been talking to Chevalier and thought Europe was cracking up—what about the Revolution? Marxes and Eddie Cantor very exhibitionistic: in New York at a bridge game at the Whist Club somebody had said to Zeppo, You haven't got anything! and he said that's a lie and took out his privates and put them on the table—they fired him out of the club. Harpo, being photographed on shipboard, put a dice box over his cock and then took it off just before the picture was taken—Gershwins "wanted something special," so they got a house with three grand pianos in the living room, six mandarin coats over the couch. Artificial moonlight by electric lamps from out-

* Arthur Caesar (1892–1953), a Broadway playwright and screenwriter.

side the windows; busts of Mozart facing out the windows. Barbecue stand where they first put a table in your car, then decided they weren't giving enough service, so they added a movie screen with talkies and a small organ. Want ad for a barbecue hostess.

Stories about movie magnates.

What we want is spontanooity.

It's too insipid (insignificant) to talk about.

I'll tell you in two words: Im-possible!

I stand where I laid.

Buttonhole Bim (Buger): reached over in conference and said, That's a lousy buttonhole!—then, No: I can't give you any more than $250,000.

One man had made shirts in Hollywood.

One had said to Perelman: I want romance (pointing toward his fly), romance! girls in chemises. Go and see the picture!—you'll see a dozen of the prettiest girls you ever saw in less than their shifts—black lace things— sliding down the banisters.

We can't do *The Captive* [Proust]—it's about Lesbians. Well, make them Americans!

A house with the only real colonial mezuzah he'd ever seen. —Mezuzah's the Ten Commandments in a gold scroll that you kissed as you went into orthodox Jewish houses.

Mrs. Perelman had eaten with the Mankowitzes—big fat Jews, swinish, what's really meant by the word "swinish"—pigs!—awful fat boy who sat there with his mouth open—her husband started talking Jewish (Yiddish) and everybody talked Jewish till somebody said something in English—then the daughter said, We come from Riga!—they said his Jewish accent was terrible. Snobbery: Litvaks (good); Galicianos (low). A feud that was obsolete everywhere except there. Big Tudor house they lived in with colonial mezuzah as above.

—Some dealer tried to sell Perelman Clark Gable's old

car—he went around to the garage and they told him
there wasn't a nut or a screw—not a sound part in it.
—Laundryman who was proud of doing somebody's washing.

—Fatigue that sets in after listening for a while to
company of wisecrackers.

—Max Marcin had yacht always just ready to steam
out so as to get girls where they couldn't get away—

—Openings: they made Marion Davies turn the light
on in her car while Hearst and Arthur Brisbane shielded
themselves behind their hats. Would break glass in car
to see people. Would make people show themselves, then
say, Aw, she's nothing—go on!

—Jewish girl in apartment house across from Garden of
Allah—Good morning—Chateau something or other!

—Phil Wylie's seriousness—said he was "teacher's pet"
at California Tech—went into crystals, atoms, etc.—a
picture on the subject—H. G. Wells.

—they didn't buy any football players at the University of Southern California—students majored in physical culture

—Indians who bought hearse and rode in it

—Serious conference on whether they should use
George Olsen's locomotive signature—one of them went
ch-ch-chew

—Rhine wine that cost forty cents a bottle that everybody said was lousy, so he (Pep West) ought to have told
them it was a fine old vintage that his grandfather had
laid down in Minsk.

—Mrs. Perelman smart and fashionably tapering,
though with good full figure—Yiddish, I should pet you!
to dog, etc.

—cold Anglo-Saxons—

—Perelman was working for Royal Gelatine—Fanny
Brice on the radio

—At Sid Grauman's—opening *Once in a Lifetime*—man talking to wax figure in lobby—stooge to a dummy.

Jean (Gorman) *and Veiller*
(her boyfriend in Hollywood)   } rather similar
Betty (Huling) *and Bud*   combinations

Bud's lack of interest in anything on the stage except Broadway stuff

[Nathanael] *West on newlywed people in hotel.* Two old ladies with young girl—girl complained that people next door were making noise like this with bed—had slept next to married people and they had done the same thing—girl had malformed yellow teeth, well to the front—daughter of the historian Fiske

—That great constipation that is New England—only thing pleasant they could remember about Connecticut was that they made peanut-butter taffy there in the winter.

Looking out of window at *snow-removing dinosaur*—head stuck down in dirty snow pile, conveyed up to top of back, then sent down by traveling black brushes into truck pushed up below—hideous interminable clacking noise.

Uncle Charley: Well, the great Coolidge is dead!—showed that isn't always the people who talk the most that have the greatest minds. —He seemed to become narrower and more stupid—at the time, I think, of the Hoover–Smith election, he had asked me whether I thought there was really much difference between the two parties. —Now he said at Sunday dinner that it was a pity they had arrested Zangara—Mother said, Everybody's got a right to have a trial. —They ought to have

garroted him right there. —I said he was insane—they
ought to put him in the asylum. —And I pay to keep
him there!

—The next week he was hoping Cermak would die
so as to give them a chance to hang that fellow—

—My friends in New York thought Zangara was pathetic, good-looking: Don't you think he's pathetic?
—Yes: awfully pathetic. —Uncle Charley a little bit
like Coolidge—Well, an awful lot of people got wet
today!

Going over to Kings Highway on Sea Beach train.
Coming out of tunnel: Brooklyn Bridge: through two
rows of dark girders weaving back and forth like a
mechanical loom, the city in dark silhouette above the
lead water, white hot at the edge—Governors Island, the
great harbor; and to the east, the sordid roofs packed for
miles; I was moved for a moment by a vision of that
immensity of anonymous life.

—Looking down into the sordid streets of the East
Side—climbing up with the bridge: Neptune raincoats,
Castoria, 5¢ something on chimneys—beautiful suspen-
sion bridge light as a cobweb.

Death of Berenice Dewey.

Hazel Rascoe's way of narrowing eyelids in immediate
intimate response to things said to her: female.

The terribly creepy mirth of fairies.

My feeling of naturalness, well-being, again at having
Jap in house, making bed, emptying ashtrays, getting
meals—in spite of his cold and watery eyes, chirping
voice, practically no English, greasy knives and forks,

dumbness and stale foreign smell—explained to me in the middle of dinner that he had bad teeth and couldn't eat the other pork chop. —Cough and nervous limp, kept wiping nose on back of hand. —Blow when I told him he wouldn't do—lower lip dropped. —Reassurance when Tom arrived.

Taximan in downtown delicatessen store. Another man suddenly came in and said: "Look out for your rig; there's a jump; on Carlos!" (Charles Street?) —He immediately got up and left three poached eggs on three pieces of toast. Delicatessen man explained that they had to make five-fifty or six dollars a day now or their cab would be taken away from them in the morning. —Old man eating there kept smiling at me. —I was tight from Betty's (Huling) tremendous cocktails made of applejack, gin, and pink grenadine—and another younger man came in who began smiling at me as soon as he came in the door—I smiled back at him in a burlesque fashion—the whole thing was seeming to me goofy—then it turned out to be Henka Farnsworth's brother-in-law.

Cummings's new girl, Marion. The shape, somewhat exaggerated, of Elaine, way of talking of Ann—did he have the effect on both of making them talk this way?—subdued, low-voiced slightly self-conscious, poking in some modestly, femininely humorous remark. She is pretty, a model, and just like the girls in advertizements: very long tapering arms and legs, pretty hands, Victorian bang over forehead; a lot of facial expression, which Ann didn't have—prettily changing, especially when watched, in response to what was being done and said, but seemed like the variations of the expression of a model in different suits and hats, not spontaneous, not as attractive as it would have been if it had been spontaneous.

Morrie Werner's* *family* were in the kosher-killed
chicken business—his father had always told him and
his little brothers to lift their little straw hats, fastened
with elastic under the chin, when they were out riding
and saw a chicken wagon pass—they knew it was some
sort of a ritual. —But Morrie didn't even know now how
kosher chickens were killed. —His father used to say,
When a man a name gets, he can piss the bed and they'll
say he sweats.—apropos of Kreuger.

Elizabeth Hawes's [dressmaker and later a successful
writer] *party*. White armless and headless dummies
behind bar; Elizabeth Hawes little swart mouse-beady-
eyed Jewess. New type of casual college-girl model—
three tall, one petite—Depression names for dresses
[see program on opposite page]. All the artists, writers,
etc., who got free or reduced clothes for their wives by
doing things for Elizabeth Hawes: Billingses, Seldeses,
Alexander Brook and Peggy Bacon,† Perelmans, Steiners.
Film: Electric Gags by Perelman: Hawes as baby crying
for dress hangers and scissors. Walk Up Five Flights and
Save Nothing . . . Nothing . . . Nothing . . . while with
naked head and shoulders she preens herself below. Displaying her dresses to Patou: at first one, he blushes with
a red gelatine slide; at second, he faints: close-up of his
fainted face. —Mrs. Perelman said that only a few
little places like Redfern had the old style of insipid
model any more. —Ernestine Evans and Sheila Hibben‡
there in plushy blue things—Sheila telling the model to

---

* M. R. Werner, New York journalist and writer.

† Brook and Peggy Bacon, both artists, were married at this
time. They were divorced in 1940.

‡ Sheila Hibben wrote on food and cooking for *The New
Yorker*; Ernestine Evans was an editor and writer.

Spring and Summer 1933

1. FIVE YEAR PLAN — Cotton voile nightgown and Rodier cotton plaid jacket
2. VIVA MEXICO — Serape and bathing suit
3. BADMINTEN — Moss Still wash silk tennis dress and chamois jacket
4. DIEGO RIVERA — Ducharne crepe skirt, Howard & Schaffer chenille blouse
5. GRACIE ALLEN'S BROTHER — Howard & Schaffer bourette blouse, linen skirt
6. REX — Howard & Schaffer bourette suit with tape blouse
7. NAZI — Chatillon faconne street dress
8. RENE CLAIR — Rodier wool coat
9. AMKINO — Rodier silk serge street dress
10. 20TH CENTURY — Nolan crepe street dress
11. THE PEOPLE'S CHOICE — Ducharne crepe suit, Coindrier moire Blouse
12. PUBLIC ENEMY No. 1 — Palm beach cloth suit and Rodier cotton blouse
13. BUY BRITISH — Rodier wool suit, silk serge blouse
14. MANCHUKOO — Moss Still wool coat
15. JEHOL — Ducharne crepe dress
16. R. F. C. — Rodier wool street dress

17. REPEAL — Moss Still wool coat
18. 3 POINT 2 — Ducharne printed crepe street dress
19. E. E. A. — Chatillon silk coat
20. BARTER — Ducharne printed crepe dress
21. CAVALCADE — Haas Brothers serge suit
22. MUSCLE-ING IN — McGuinness & Thomas silk street dress
23. PROSPERITY IS JUST AROUND THE CORNER — McGuinness & Thomas silk afternoon dress
24. THE YELLOW PERIL — McGuinness & Thomas silk afternoon dress
25. STOOPNOCRACY — Bianchini printed crepe afternoon dress
26. TOTAL ECLIPSE — Ducharne chiffon afternoon dress
27. INTERNATIONAL CURRENCY — Ducharne printed crepe dinner dress
28. MACHADO — Chatillon silk dinner dress
29. MUNICIPAL REFORM — Amerin Freudenberg embroidered batiste and chiffon dinner dress
30. FARM RELIEF — Chiffon and Rodier cotton dinner dress
31. REMOTE CONTROL — Bianchini starched chiffon dinner dress
32. GOLD STANDARD — Amerin Freudenberg embroidered batiste dinner dress
33. INTERNATIONAL RELATIONS — Nolan damask negligee
34. FREE SILVER — Racine tulle evening dress and jacket

Elizabeth Hawes's fashion program

35. DISARMAMENT _____ *Ameria Freudenberg embroidered batiste*
              evening dress

36. AUTOMATIC CLUTCH _____ *Chatillon crepe evening dress*

37. THE REVOLT OF THE MASSES _____ *Ameria Freudenberg lace*
              evening dress

38. THE HAPPY WARRIOR _____ *Ducharne printed chiffon evening dress*

39. INFLATION _____ *McGuinness & Thomas silk evening coat,*
              flying squirrel

40. A NEW DEAL _____ *McGuinness & Thomas silk evening dress*

41. STRATOSPHERE _____ *Condurie crepe evening dress, chiffon shawl,*
              cotton cords

42. BATHOSPHERE _____ *Chiffon evening dress, cotton cords*

43. ROCKEFELLER CENTER _____
      McGuinness & Thomas silk evening dress

Collection designed by Elizabeth Hawes

Hats by Hawes

H A W E S
8 WEST 56 STREET
NEW YORK

drape the scarf around her neck with what Mrs. Perelman thought was an "aristocratic" manner. —Hawes herself showed off a couple of the snappy ones: the special
and much applauded appearance of the star. —Fairies;
small Negro women helpers. —Ernestine Evans said of
Hawes, "I think she's going to be a first-rate artist"—
dressmaking was taking the place of children's books in
her interests, she said. —Modernist chairs of bent pipes;
a couch of what looked like white kid with two deep
bright pink (grenadine-colored?) pillows on it. —Mrs.
Billings said she had intended to go to Chicago, but had
read my article and decided not to.

On my way down to *Washington for the Inaugural*,*
I felt satisfaction in looking out the window—everything
seemed sound, American, and distinguished: bridges,
aluminum-silver gas tanks, gray sky, Pennsylvania Railroad, the train gave its tone to the landscape; the cities:
West Philadelphia, Wilmington, Baltimore, Washington,
the Capitol, not undistinguished, the dome polished
glossy gray; after all, the capital of the country, impor
tant.

—Paddy Jackson's: tremendous comfortable high-
bourgeois interior, which I'd never seen before—red-
dressed middle-American painting, little girl with dog
in the corner—the painters used to carry them around
and just paint in the heads—the red dress harmonized
with red curtains in the windows on either side. Mongrel
bitch who had been altered, cross between a Sealyham
and a dachshund, white with dachshund spots of brown.
—His wife, Dody, white-haired, smooth pink face—

* EW's impressions of the nascent New Deal are included in
a series of papers in *Earthquake*, pp. 534–65, headed "Glimpses
of the New Deal."

awfully good taste, sober light-blue dress that matched her eyes. *The Dinner*: strawberries that you dipped in a fig wine, then in sugar (would anybody but Dody ever think of a thing like that?); lamb chops, broccoli and Hollandaise, little hot muffins, delicious wine-flavored jelly, salad with Roquefort-flavored mayonnaise, wine, some kind of near-ice-cream frozen dessert.

—The Federal Reserve man who thought Morris Ernst's plan too shortsighted, but couldn't be induced to divulge his own—thought economic planning "all the bunk"—exercised a repressive influence on the evening— slightly on the belligerent offensive—his wife, graying-haired, looked much older, as Paddy's did—Dorothy Detzer, Indiana accent and face, smart sandal-like shoes, though with insteps sexily revealed, and a red scarf or handkerchief she carried in her hand to set off her black dress—well-made-up red mouth—she had been brought by young man in State Department who was exercised about the danger of the government's inter-vening under the pretext of saving Cuba from Machado to hand it over to the business interests—sympathetic with the Communists in connection with the B.E.F.— small black Massachusetts-looking eyes like Raymond Holden's close together, dark eyebrows almost meeting, thin, close-knit suit shapely and rigidly pressed—Dorothy Detzer was worried about slavery in Liberia and Abys-sinia—her adventures with Assistant Secretary of State. —Great discussion of the banking situation: Morris Ernst looking to the "short run"—giving people milk— Federal Reserve guy telling him that what he proposed— issuing government scrip—wouldn't do any good in the long run—Ernst, when he came, struck a much sharper, more articulate note—stimulated discussion, roused people.

On the way to taking us home that night, Paddy

wanted to go to the Troika restaurant: to Dody, I want to dance with you!—I really do want to dance with you—When I'd been on for the Progressive Conference, he'd gone home from Cutting's house and gone in through the cellar, when there'd been people to dinner, and come up from the coal cellar after dinner was over with coal dust in his hair: a domestic crisis.

—*Party at Drew Pearson's* with co-author *of Washington Merry-Go-Round* and his wife. Evening dress, champagne, sleazy newspaper look of Pearson in spite of his evening dress—general atmosphere of newspaper gossip and looking in on government from the outside—Bob Allen's ranting against the liberals like Felix Frankfurter who didn't want to take any responsibility (he was a fat little blond mutt)—the Haitian ambassador and [Ernest] Gruening, all swollen up in a dress suit, talking French with the Haitian (he hoped to be Governor-General of Haiti)—young man in opera hat who wrote Washington society column, who did a lot of displaying of his French and evidently aimed to look like the diplomatic service—the Haitian minister's attention seemed to be wandering during a long story about himself the young man was telling—he kept facing him but turned his eyes to the side. —Drew Pearson hoped to have his father keep his job as Governor-General of the Virgin Islands, so had pulled his punches on Roosevelt in an article he had written in *Harper's*. —He evidently invited people with a view to pumping them for his books and his column—probably had stag parties because he thought they would talk more freely. —The bogus diplomatic-service type had ridden a horse on the Washington Merry-Go-Rounders and Paddy Jackson for their Bolshevik views—after the Revolution, the lack of service in the collectivized town where they are living makes them very peevish.

The Fitzgeralds—La Paix, Towson.* The house, built in 1886, set in a depression of the low mildly rolling ground of Maryland—*out*side, the shape not easily grasped at a glance, with its large surfaces and balconies and bulges—Pax Vobiscum: the hall and the staircase: the newel posts and fancy bulbed railings, the big landing big enough for the little girl to play, she had a bookcase there with books by Frances Hodgson Burnett, doll cutouts; above it, a perforated cutout piece of woodwork that corresponded to the balustrades making *out* of the whole thing a light-brown *woodwork* jigsaw lace—the clock set into the *woodwork* below, with, in Gothic, Our Times are in His Hand, and below it a tercet ending, "By Love Alone," on a mirror (you expected a cuckoo in the clock, but all there was was a motto instead)—the bed in my room with a frieze on the headboard, daisy, locust leaves, and cattails carved out (perhaps by hand); alcoves and cupboards up high in the rooms; wooden wainscotting in the bathrooms that went a long distance up the walls (Scott's forest of dandruff cures, etc., in the bathroom adjoining his study)—the way the living room opened into the dining room—a frame of light-brown varnishy woodwork—the room looked emptier as they had it furnished than it could have done when the original owner had it—we tended to sit in the corners (Zelda especially, biting the side of her mouth) or along the edges (on modern couches that we sat too far back or sank into far too deep) of the room. —Little girl's little families of animals on the mantelpiece of her room, which also had a bathroom—richness and confusion of houses of this period, at the same time having the draw-

* This was the house on the Bayard Turnbull estate at Rodgers Forge, near Baltimore, where F. Scott Fitzgerald settled with his young daughter. Zelda was recovering from her second breakdown.

back of being centralized in the sense that all the rooms
tended to open into each other, so that people talking in
the bedrooms, people downstairs by people upstairs
(parents by children who were supposed to have gone to
bed), telephone conversations in the hall, could be heard
much too easily—something of the Jersey summer cottage
about it. —The architect who had owned it had, as a
child, the child of the parents who had named it La Paix,
built little models of houses, half mansions, half castles,
on the lawn—among the gentle declivities—the old stable
(the roof slightly sagging, the 1880 pillars that supported
it, the smell of old straw: imaginary. Compare the real
thing). —They had a grape arbor out back (with a sundial in the middle of it from which they'd never scraped
away the ivy) and a tennis court and all the things that
people had at that period—

—*Gerald Murphy* had house where you sat in window
and could reach mint for drinks outside—undoubtedly
one of his triumphs which had given him great gratification.

Zelda very cute in blue sweater that matched her eyes
and light-brown riding breeches that matched her hair,
subdued, a plaintive note in her voice and sometimes a
sort of mumbling as of an old person who had lost her
teeth—not drinking. Scott began by giving me a cocktail for lunch, not drinking himself—a little wine at
meals, one glass to two of mine, a highball before dinner,
and he would disappear from the conversation from time
to time for a moment—finally gave Zelda a little thimbleful of wine—a little treat, honey, in honor of Bunny—
the next day I didn't drink and he was snitching them
regularly—when I refused, he said, It seems so puritanical
somehow, breaking off (entirely) like that!—he gave
Zelda another little thimbleful of wine—when he put
me on the train, he said he was having a hard time with

Zelda because she'd begun stealing drinks. —The next morning he said at our noon breakfast: Drunkenness is an awful thing, isn't it?

Hollywood. —See, the girl comes out of the house and Wham-Socko-Sonk: Wham, the villain lands on the hero—Socko, the hero socks the villain—Sonk, the whole thing collapses, raft on the water or whatever it is. This formula had been used so often that it had sunk into the unconsciousness of the Hollywood people.

—Movie actresses made it impossible for other women, however attractive, in Hollywood.

—Scott seemed more mature, stouter, still talked about being a gentleman—

The Gerald Murphys. Gerald had given up pretending even to paint—he lived on a succession of enthusiasms and created interests for himself—once he decided to walk through the whole of Paris and before he got tired had gone through six arrondissements street by street—would spend a couple of weeks taking people to a new restaurant he had discovered—a new *plage* would set him up for a month. —They entertained clever people—gave them all the appreciation they could possibly want—made them feel important—irresistible.

Connie Eakin's breakdown. The immediate cause, apparently, was Charley Mitchell's confession of wrongdoing before the Senate investigating committee—he had all his money in Mitchell's bank. He got delusions of persecution, said "they'd" been spying on him for months—taxi drivers!—spying on him everywhere!—they were going to get him, they'd found out about him. He'd torn up a check the head of the business had sent him for the expenses of a trip West. —He said the night nurse had kept him awake all night talking. Had sent Mary a note to meet him not at the theater but at a

speakeasy, insisted the play he'd seen had had something
against her—Negro dancing with white woman in it.

Forrest Davis said that nobody had so many friends as
Secretary of the Treasury Woodin—they admitted that
he was light but he was such a nice man, went around
taking a lot of trouble about remembering people's birth-
days and anniversaries. —He had a refined and sensitive
face in the talkies listening to one of his own com-
positions being played—and a lousy and vulgar composition it was. —Also, the Franklin D. Roosevelt march.

Man from Iowa. Almost tropical summers and looking
out the window as a child at a blizzard straight from the
North Pole. Intolerance—during the war, you had to buy
Liberty Bonds or be beaten up; also a woman who was
seen kissing a man was likely to be persecuted—tar and
feathering. —Farmers would go to mortgage foreclosures
and hang a noose over the auctioneer's neck—if there was
a stranger there, they'd all stand and look at him, shake
their fists once silently under his nose. —His theory
of the shift of football prowess from the East to the West
to the South. —The shopkeeping class who used to be
so insolent to the farmer in this part of Iowa largely
cleaned out.

Rosalind's mystery plays with Joan: now she's a lady
and she has a great many lovers! —Rosalind stands in the
background and says, Marry me! marry me! marry me!
—So she faints away —Joan would flop on bed in voluptuous movie abandon—also, movie-heroine way of saying
with great dignity to imaginary villain who is about to
grab her and bind her: Why, what do you want of me?

The long stretch of York Avenue at ten-thirty at
night—like one of the main streets in a dreary small city:

occasionally a lighted drugstore or bakery, a group of young guys standing in the doorway—only three high-swung street lamps to a block, two on the East Side, one on the West—till you came to the big bridge and the gas tanks, which were grand.

Raymond Holden, who had been doing an article for *Fortune* on *obstetrics* lecturing about it like a venerable old authority—telling Mrs. White, who had had a Caesarian, about Caesarians—somebody mentioned something and he replied with tremendous gravity: "Very dangerous! Very dangerous!"

Scofield Thayer, thought art collector in Philadelphia (Dr. Barnes) had paid all the taxi drivers in New York to spy on him. Somebody asked him how much he thought that would cost: "Seven thousand nine hundred and twenty dollars."

Muste (A. J.) gets out of Brookwood for CPLA.

Harriet Stevenson and Margaret's decanters and silver. They had disappeared—evidently stolen—from among the things she left in New York, and I used to look in the antique shops on Lexington Avenue to see whether they had turned up there.

Girls have gotten back to *corsets* in the shape of *rubber girdles* to hold in their hips—they say that garters attached to them make their stockings stay up better. —*Victorian* styles that looked pretty horrible on most New York women. (At some point they began calling them "foundation garments." Getting a woman out of one reminded me of eating shellfish.)

When the Red Bank Trust Company folded up through having invested in too many Peruvian bonds sold them by Charley Mitchell: sourness and gloom of bank employees—telling people they couldn't take their money out—teller who lived next door to us abashed and tired with strain when I hailed him in his car, almost as if he were guilty and expecting to be arrested—asked me to get in—he explained that just as Mother's place had depreciated in value, so their investments, etc. —What were the prospects of the bank's reopening? —"Wonderful?" but as if he had been knocked for a loop and had not recovered, absolutely colorless face— atmosphere of suspicion around town—bad investments.

John Garrett (Dorothy Parker's infatuation)—young man in Chicago who thought Hoover had done a good job—(he ought to end up like this) [I was evidently going to merge them in a character.]

Equinoctial March storm (three or four days, weekend of 19th): nothing but darkness, cold, and rain, had everybody down—I got a cold and finally took to my bed.

Jenny on failure of Trust Company—Well, it seems, if you don't work, they call you a loafer—and then if you do work and save up a little something, something like this happens! —She was sorry for Frank Macahon—an old man, had devoted his whole life to the bank and I suppose he meant to be smart—as honest as you can be when you're dealing with money. The people were disappointed—he'd issued a statement just before telling what a fine state the bank was in, and they thought that he'd misrepresented it.

The rumor that *Zangara* had been hired by the Republicans to assassinate Roosevelt because they knew he was going to start the treasury investigation which would show up Mellon. —*Harriman and Charley Mitchell arrested.* When I told Uncle Charley about this, he replied with the rumor that Tom Walsh was poisoned.

Henri and Louise embarrassed instead of amused by sexual jokes—roused their imaginations, they took it too seriously—more sincere about love than the other more sophisticated-appearing women?—or less gratified in their present situations? —Probably merely the latter.

Gray squirrels bouncing along the lawn like slow tennis balls.

Stan Dell's dream about a black whale and a white whale.

The plays getting thin: *Three-Cornered Moon, The Party's Over*—Depression themes. *Bud Kusell* claimed it was the influence of the movies—incidents strung on a theme instead of the old-fashioned plot.

Effect of the Hitler anti-Jewish activities on social relations in New York, March '33—seemed to encourage latent anti-Semitism, give people courage to be impolite. Bill Troy at party at Aurora restaurant guessing at race of Forrest Davis's wife, who had just told me she had been born in Barbados and was part Scotch and part Spanish ("belonged"—if you belonged to the club, you could do anything, etc.) —Troy said to me: "Wouldn't you say that the difference between a page of Renan and a page of Proust was that Proust was Jewish?" —Paul Rosenfeld got sick—went out and put his supper through the grating in the sidewalk, which I indicated as a splendid place.

Seeing Louise (Bogan) *off* [she had got a *Guggenheim fellowship*]. Beautiful big new Italian liner, the *Rex*—fine little tourist-third staterooms, but they couldn't use the first-class staterooms, etc. —In her new brown traveling suit and round brown hat tilted on one side (Do I look like a Lesbian? I don't look like a Lesbian, do I?) she looked like a Steichen or German photograph, standing behind the glass of a window half slid to the side—shy, self-consciously good-looking and proud, making occasionally gestures and expressions in answer to our signals. —The ship slipped so easily out of the dock—elegantly pinched-up white stern, new modish low-cut funnels with the colors of Italy about them—stood still a few moments in the river, then turned out toward the sea, flying the Italian flag. —How empty the Holdens' apartment seemed when we came back after she had gone—the maid had just cleaned it up.

Perelmans; Hollywood. Jewish girl, very nice and intelligent, not fancy, who had lost her husband out there after three years—her theory that Jewish men thought themselves ugly, so had to keep proving to themselves what they could do in the way of getting Gentile girls—she thought you had to have a permanent relation with somebody but they would go crazy when they got out to Hollywood—any little dumbbell from Indiana—the Jewish situation very important out there—Thalberg and Norma Shearer had nothing for each other—Thalberg just wanted to show what he could do. —Everybody scared—she'd seen prominent Jewish executives break chairs because their wives had used the wrong fork. —When she'd first gotten out there, some other woman had said to her: Oh, do save George Kelly!—who cared whether George Kelly was saved or not?—had no use for writers who went out to sell themselves and then groused about it—Schulberg dignified in comparison, had seen him baited for three-quarters of an hour and come out of it very well. —It was a shame to bait them—it was pathetic—you should see somebody like Schulberg buying first editions!

—Sam Hoffenstein would stand by the piano and say: I believe in Keats!

—Didn't I know how at college the Jew always took the most Gentile-looking girl to the dance?

Jokes: A meretricious and a happy New Year!—Waltham with tears in my eyes. —Conscience-stricken Deutsch.

Reunion of old Brown students—Jew and Gentile—male and female.—Irishman who had been ghosting for Dempsey and Tunney—couldn't stand Tunney—Dempsey was what Tunney wanted to be but never would be—a natural gentleman.

—He was proposing a "permanent pogrom"—he and Dashiell Hammett kidding them (West and Perelman) about the Jews.

NOVEL

Vision of middle-class American families in apartments in summer—young couples—women hanging out of windows—washing stockings—their frankness, used to being free citizens—Florence—hit by hard times, do something to make it possible for them to get along better, be happier. *Vision,* on train coming East from trip West, of whole great American plant as something flimsy, suddenly had grown up to tremendous size and overwhelming aspect, and then been suddenly deflated.

Picture in paper of three Nazis singing the Nazi anthem—all except the one in the middle looked like trolls—in the story about the troll that knocked pieces out of his head for soup against a spike in the ceiling. —Dos said he had seen Hitler and Hindenburg getting into a car together in the newsreel—they had taken Hindenburg's spiked helmet off and put a cap on him. Dos thought they might have him rigged with motors like King Kong.

Second Avenue car line about to be replaced—there had just been an accident when I went to get the plumber, one of the cars had pinned an automobile between itself and an El post and the front of the car was smashed and splintered like a toy and many other cars lined up behind it. The plumber said the Second Avenue hadn't never been no good since the day it was built—"the old Banana Line": you waited for an hour for a car, then they all arrived in "clusters." Also commented on surliness of motormen—always in a hurry. (It was a "railroad" and they considered themselves "railroad men.")

Ted Paramore had let *Time* in its earliest phase go by the board—had had a job there a little while—friends of his?—Tom Matthews's hair-raising story about how the two fellows who started it had had the idea ever since their school days and directed their whole lives to that end. At first they had given a great dynamic exhibition, hiring and firing people.

The Nazis were melting up the life-size bronze statue of Karl Marx in front of the Karl Liebknecht House into busts of Adolf Hitler and announcing that they were going not only to extirpate Marxism but would "tear the word out of every book till in fifty years' time nobody in Germany was going to know what it meant."

—*Dahlberg* came to see me almost as soon as he got

back on the *Bremen*—had been walking in the street in Berlin and a lot of young Nazis dashed by beating people —one slashed him over the head and across the face with a stick shaped like a saber, breaking his glasses. He called a policeman and the cop took them both to the station, the Nazi beating him all the way unhindered by the cop—it was only when they got there that the cop took away the stick and then the Nazi began using his fists— Dahlberg didn't know why but he then hit back for the first time. He didn't understand for a long time what it was about, till the Nazi said *Jude Schweinerei* and he knew that meant Jewish swine. Afterwards complained to the consul and arrived in London along with the news just as his book was being brought out there. —They had been out for men "with Mediterranean complexions"—"I happened to be a Jew," but many weren't. —He accused me of being a social snob.

Did I get in *faked evidence of Communist plot against the banks in* 1932 written in underworld slang? —"This is sure a hot spot" (Chicago) and "yours for the Revolution."

Ted on Boulder Dam: They've got to have some way to get those wages back!

Dos and Charley Walker on National Committee meeting (January). Got to talking about Cornitz and Owen— (Ornitz and Cohen)—Ornitz just off to Hollywood and salving his conscience before he went (when he'd protested about something in a Russian film, somebody had said: You're fanatical!) and Cohen just resigning chairmanship—Ornitz spoke of their trip to Kentucky as if it had been an epoch-making ordeal by fire. We thought when he got out to Hollywood, he deviated quite a little.

Both he and Jack Lawson were sure there had been absolutely nothing in Pat Kearney's losing his job on account of the Boulder Dam business (a little while before, they had told him in the studio that he was "sitting on top of the world"—when he came back to New York, he killed himself). —The Walkers got so involved in committees that Charley didn't get to write the play that the theater was supposed to be being created to produce— they got mixed up with a little girl that the New Playwrights had had, Sophie Feinberg or some name of the kind, who didn't want to accomplish anything but merely to have an office and feel a little important—letterhead, no doubt, with long name. —Melvin Levy had wandered West in a daze like Kalb—Levy's hush-stuff—whispers— "these people we're talking about" (the Communists).

Symposium at Whitney Museum that I went to with *Niles Spencer*: tide had evidently turned away from "abstract form in painting" toward relation to society, etc. A successful Jewish portrait painter had unequivocal ideas about this—Tom Craven spoke, encountering a hostile audience, and what seemed to be Columbia professors. Exhibition of the fruits of the Guggenheim fellowships: man who went to Paris and apparently found a Negro mistress—painted her at cheap dressing table with very solidly and distinctly painted breasts and nipples, which Niles pretended to grab; horses and men: Chirico animal crackers: two loving horses. Oval red-leather thing to sit in, like bathtub. —Niles said that the day of gallery painting had gone by—important work that was being done now would be done by people and put away in drawers and nobody would know about it. —Peggy Bacon with her veil and her little fringe of hair along her forehead looked like something she had drawn. Mrs. Kuniyoshi had evidently busted up with Kuniyoshi.

Manning, the broker Bill (Slater) *Brown worked for.*
About sixty, member of the Stock Exchange, had regal
offices for speculation alone, never did any trading, a
genius, would sit and read the ticker tape as if it were
orchestration, would know that if certain stocks were
going up, certain others were going down—didn't even
know what the stocks were, would say, Buy so many
shares of YZ!—Find out what YZ is. —Everything existed
for him as figures—girls were telephone numbers—he
would say, Let's take that little fat blonde out!—what's
her name?—Oh, Plaza 2546—call Plaza 2546! —Hated
wife, who had inherited a lot of money, and used to give
her bum tips on market—would call her up and say, Buy
so-and-so, when he was selling it short like mad. —His
valet, whom he'd had twenty years, finally decided he
wanted to get out of service and would do a little trading
himself—Manning went to the Stock Exchange, bought
up everything the valet was investing in, sold it short (?),
and ruined him. —Paid Bill first five dollars, then six, a
day—would occasionally give him fifty-dollar bill and say,
Do you like it? —First week he worked for him gave him
a $1,000 bill, hoping he'd go off with it so that he'd have
the pleasure of pursuing him and catching him—said he
wanted to have cash on hand—Bill was several times on
the point of giving it away for a one-dollar bill. —Learned
The Taming of the Shrew by heart on account of his
dislike of his wife—also, the pornographic passages in
Venus and Adonis—when he and Bill were riding uptown
in the limousine, Bill would have to go through a
thesaurus and pick out words—like abracadabra—and
Manning would try to think of a line from Shakespeare
with "abracadabra" in it. —Bill would have to take care
of his girls—buying them tickets to Atlantic City, etc.,
which Manning was afraid to do—they would get $1,000
or so a weekend—beautiful girls and dozens of them, but

Bill never got a chance at them because Manning was likely to come in at any time—he would say he'd be back at five, then appear at three-thirty. —Bill would have to go to Florida and South Carolina and go around the links with him—he could never learn to play golf because he couldn't keep his eye on the ball—finally he hired a colored boy to switch him so he would—the boy was scared to switch a white man so that Manning would keep saying, Switch me!—but he would never keep his eye on it and would slice it. —Would double-cross his best friends. —Bill threw up his job after a year—Manning had fired him frequently but Bill would always turn up as if nothing had happened the next day—once he managed to crush Manning's thumb in shutting the car door and Manning yelled after him as he was quietly walking up the street: You're fired! —When he was engaging him, he asked Bill whether he smoked or drank. Bill said, Both. Manning looked blank a moment, then said, So do I. —He had made a million dollars—finally died just after the stock-market crash as the result of an embolism.

My dream about Hearst. Had just had supper with the Seldeses—Gilbert had been protesting about the attitude of the liberals toward the film called *Gabriel Over the White House,* and I thought to myself, This is terrible that poor old Gilbert should have to think that *Gabriel Over the White House* is good because he works for Hearst! —Then I worried about money (was taking Rosalind and Mary to lunch the next day), went home and dreamed that Hearst had sent me a wire asking me to write him a regular feature—I went out to the coast immediately, not intending to take it—Marion Davies was charming; Hearst as a Jew with a monocle who hadn't really taken her away from her former lover, he walking ahead of them with a large Thurber dog on its hind legs, so as to seem that he was no longer interested in Marion—the ranch—presently Hearst and I went aside and discussed the matter—he was gradually talking me into it when I woke up.

The next night I dreamed I had the American Legion after me for attending a meeting of the ILD (International Labor Defense, a Communist organization) near Pittsburgh—it had taken place in some kind of shack in the country and they (the Legionnaires) turned up in white Sam Brownes and sun helmets something like in the Inaugural parade.

Exhibitionism of Marxes, etc. Harpo told West and his sister to come into the dressing room, asking, Are you decent? when he didn't have a stitch on. —They "took physical advantage" of people—Groucho terribly tiresome to talk to, gagging all the time, terrific vanity—Perelman finally had a showdown with him, said, That's not very funny! about one of his gags—Groucho said, Oh, so you don't think that's very funny, and gave him to damn well understand that he'd better think it was funny. —Then Perelman took a job with Metro-Goldwyn—Perelman had accepted it as a matter of course, but Groucho had said when he saw him, So you're independent now!—sore because he hadn't told him about it. —Cantor pissed in somebody's new hat—put his cock in a girl's hand and then said, I hope you're not unfriendly!—they had to take it and pretend to laugh. —All that shocked Perelman.

[Nathanael] *West* was busy forging bills—he'd sit down and type them off himself, with printed letterhead H. C. Udell instead of H. C. Udell Co., for example—(for new $1,000 ceiling to garden) and other documents (completely faked double-entry accounts) to deceive the Bowery Savings Bank into letting them skip their taxes a couple of years—when a bank began to slip, you could take any advantage of them and they had to take it and he knew that Stenhaus at the Bowery was one of the dirtiest rascals that ever took double interest on a note. When he first used to see his father do this—bribed the banker to redeem the note—he'd said, Why, Pa, this is the same as robbery!—and his father had said, But the note is good, isn't it?—he never would have thought of it from that point of view. —If they should get into trouble over what they were doing at the Sutton, they'd just burn the books. —He thought most hotels were committing sabotage of this kind.

—Talk the businessmen had had—and believed it—during the boom—about the new ethical standards of American business when they were engaged in all sorts of crooked transactions.

—Device of big banks like the Chase inviting presidents of local banks to New York and having them meet Mr. Rockefeller in order to sell them foreign bonds or something of the sort.

The day the Trust Company opened in Red Bank, the desks were heaped with flowers and everybody hung out their flag.

Betty Huling's Piping Rock Club boyfriend, used to get her down on the floor when her mother was out—wrestling matches—perfect gentleman when mother was around so that she thought he was fine—finally called her up one day and said they'd go to Belmont Park and then they'd have dinner and do a little drinking and then they'd come home and have a little nooky. Betty bawled, No, we will not! and hung up on him, never saw him again. An older woman had warned her against him.

Dinner for Harold Laski.* Jumping on Walter Lippmann—Laski made fun of him for giving people to understand that "great changes were going to occur, but not in
our generation"—so that we could sit back and not worry—
then himself remarked later that he could see a Fascist
movement but not a Communist Party capable of accomplishing a revolution for at least another generation.
—Wolman and Frankfurter asking each other why they
didn't accept posts in the government—Laski saying to
Felix, I think the answer to that is, *De te fabula narratur.*
—Wolman had been present at labor conference of April
14—had seen Frances Perkins at station and said, You
better step lively, sister!—George Soule said manufacturers
were worried for fear workers in certain places would
take over factories—Wolman and Laski baited him gently
about his planning—Laski on the fallacy of "the inevita-
bility of gradualness"—George had a hard time explaining
that planning in the future didn't necessarily have to be
Fascist. Rex Tugwell had said in Washington that what
we were getting was Fascist economics without a Fascist
movement—he was thinking of resigning—when the farm
bill had been passed, his job would be done—Laski remarked that it was characteristic of Americans to think
that when a measure was on the statute books, there was
no need to bother about administering it. Laski's capacity
for drawing a curtain or screen in front of his Marxism
and spending the evening on the liberal basis—finally,
however, said that Lenin offered in his writings a program—he was a little more revolutionary than last year.
—Head-shaking over Keynes, also—George said, as if he
had not been doing the same thing for years, that Keynes
had sat there at that table and talked about capitalism

---

* Of the London School of Economics. See *The Bit Between
My Teeth*, pp. 78–100, 520–1.

reforming itself. —Laski's anecdotes, for which he had apparently induced his wife to act as stooge. You remember when we were staying at—? —When Webb and I went to Shaw about renting a building from him for the Fabian Society, Shaw drove a hard bargain with them. —Henry and Brooks Adams—Adams and Holmes: How are your eyes?—hair falling out?—Well, I'll bet your breathing is bad! —Definition of socialism—"I think the best I know"—that Laski always quoted: Taking money away from the rich. —Frankfurter thought that the thing to aim at was to tax the money away from the rich and that it was all wrong to talk against the Sherman Act— it ought to be applied—the concentration of wealth in a few hands ought to be impeded. Berle was all wrong. — Kidding the classical economists. Laski said that he and Wolman belonged to a school which thought the idea that there was such a thing as a balance of trade an illusion. —Wolman said Lippmann had "shot his wad." Why did Lippmann go on the way he did? Laski should have thought it was very simple: Mr. Thomas Lamont wanted a mouthpiece.

Meeting of *League of Professional Groups* afterwards— I never saw such groping—Rorty and Cowley were the only Gentiles there—they tend naturally perhaps to exclude non-Jews—love excluding people, asserting moral superiority (Communism, psychoanalysis). —Lewis Corey with unreassuring face like J. B. S. Hardman's,* rather pale eyes looking in different directions like his—stool pigeon—was just resigning from editorship of symposium on American revolutionists which had first been launched, I thought, six months ago—dispute about John Reed,

* Hardman (1882–1968), otherwise Jacob Benjamin Salutsky, editor of *The Advance,* journal of the Amalgamated Clothing Workers. Deported from Russia in 1908, he spent his life in the trade-union movement.

ending a middle-class intellectual—Ruthenberg and Foster?
—wasn't William Lloyd Garrison a middle-class intellectual, too?—got nowhere for an hour, then Rorty moved to
table the discussion.

Election meeting of Gropers in Cooper Union.
Crowded, people crushed and fainting trying to get in—
Paul Rosenfeld sitting in front row, refused to stand up
for "Internationale"—Rorty on the no end of good it had
done his poetry to work for Communism—Negro who
became very bloodthirsty and said that Major Moulton
and those like him would be the first to be shot when the
revolution was going to be a government by *intellectuals!*
—all the departments in the hands of *intellectuals!* etc.
—Browder not bad analyzing the radicalization of the intellectual—ventured to invoke the Revolution and the
Civil War—Elliot Cohen thought that the party members
present wouldn't approve of that.

Mary Vorse. Always started out, when visiting New
York, by trying to "find a flop" with somebody—Margaret
Larkin and Liston Oak in their new big-roomed second
floor with Corinthian columns across the living room,
where they gave, or allowed to be given, so many radical
parties—then invariably ended by staying at the Madison
Square Hotel—bed made for her, coffee in the morning.
—Ellen (her daughter) had stolen a march on Mary by
stowing away to Europe—headlines all over the papers.
—Mary had left Provincetown in April—said it had been
nice to get home to her own married children (wouldn't
even admit Ellen had left her husband) after Susan and
Knobby (Knobby having, according to the theory, set fire
to herself—and then sat down in a chair, which had broken
down, and she had hurt her thigh so that she had to
stay in bed)—and Betty Spencer, who had been so

"stabbing" to Susan that Mary had forgotten to call on her to say goodbye—Katy and Dos prostrated in Balti-more—Edie with her nose red (worrying?) about Katy all the time and Frank continually on the verge of having to go to the hospital and have all his teeth pulled out—and the Balls' cottage near Pamet River washed away and made matchwood of by the sea, and all the other cottages there having to be set back—and Susan going to pieces for a while over *The Comic Artist* (by Norman Matson, I think) being produced in New York (just the same night that his [Norman's?] wife was having her baby?)—and Phyllis Duganne* had had a breakdown and had had to go to Bermuda—but Eben, no doubt, was still at home with his mother.

—The children—Joe and Ellen—had liked Bob Minor—Ellen apparently too much.

Meeting *Larry Noyes* at the theater with his mustache half-gray.

> *Paramores:* "But fill me with the old familiar juice,
> Methinks I might recover by and by."

Anna (talking in bed late one night: May 1): She thought it was better the way it was—when I went out, she wouldn't know about it and wouldn't be thinking about it—if we lived together, I'd go wild after a few days and would want to be going out all the time—told me not to drink as I was about to take a swig out of a gin bottle: You don't need it!—her absolutely just and sober way of seeing things (as at the circus)—

Meeting Thurber's girlfriend Honnicut in Blooming-dale's when I was buying shoes for Anna and Adele—

* Phyllis Duganne (Mrs. Eben Given), a resident of Truro who wrote short stories for *Collier's* and *American Magazine*.

she thought I was embarrassed. —Were *you* drunk! she said of the last time I had seen her.

—Anna had gotten so "skinny," there were depressions on her hips at the side, and I could feel her little pubic bone—the Oxfords I bought her began to bag—hands always cold—hair turned dull, lost most of its red tinge, got dandruff and began to come out—when her ovaries were bad, she wanted to die.

Bob Cantwell and stool pigeons on hunger march. They said they had had a hard time, breaking through the police lines (he had a police card in his hat, but was hanging around with his group—"not very good under-cover work"), and asked him who was paying for all this—he said, the American Civil Liberties, thinking that was respectable—afterwards, one of them said, There are a lot of foreigners here, aren't there?—the other one said, But they're all workers.

Frances McClernan said that when they were taking down one of the old houses on *West Charles St.*—way over almost by the docks—they found behind the wall-paper a painting of the Black Virgin—and the room had evidently been arranged for an altar. (Perelman said it was probably just these Greenwich fairies.)

After *beer* was legalized, people would drink it and serve it—and it slowed down the tempo and made the *moeurs* milder.

COMMUNISTS
Ed Royce. They used to say to him: "Don't agitate me, comrade, I'm with you!"

May Day, '33. A group of the socialists broke ranks and came over to the Communists.

Man I met coming out of Chaffard's just as I was going in—little man with sharp beak—looked a little bit like Leon Errol—with large woman with eyeglasses who kept winking at me that he was drunk: Are you one of these radicals? —Yes. —Well, what do you live on? Who pays you? —I said, Are you one of these radicals? —No: there's nothing queer about me!—said his mother in Maine sent him a small allowance from time to time. —Understand they want to have labor working five hours a day! —He evidently had being hired by Russia mixed up with Frances Perkins's bill.

Irving Plaza. Sentimental feelings about it going up the stairs between the greasy walls—the windows and the platform hung with red curtains with gilt fringe like a Punch and Judy booth—the white ceiling with unpretentious patterns stamped on it like the dado in a rooming house—the yellow walls, greasy, soiled, with gilt frames painted on them containing nothing, large electric glass candelabra—had resounded to how many Communist meetings, anarchist banquets.

Gropers and Engineers Association. Rauchenbach, the doddering academic technicist, lantern slides of diagrams that didn't work and chalk that broke: Walter Pollak; Shapiro; Lewis Corey got started on Communist rigmarole and couldn't be stopped, couldn't stop himself, engineers walked out.

Hollywood. People like Jack Lawson had been cut to $350 a week—Thalberg was out, gone abroad with a nervous breakdown, too power-loving for them, they had gotten him out. —Helen Spencer said that in the early days, riding around the mountains, you were likely to run into an elephant or a lion. —Perelman complained that everybody was in bed at ten-thirty—no place to see people at night—if you went to the Brown Derby after ten-thirty, you might find Wilson Mizner or one of two or three other people but that was all. —He said they had had the idea at one time of bringing out a great many college boys and they had all turned into pansies except one. —Somebody had said to Perelman, This is the first time I've been kidded by somebody younger than myself!

When *West and the Perelmans* went out to their place in Pennsylvania, they had to fish dead rabbits out of the well—they looked all right when they first took them out, but immediately fell to pieces. West couldn't take it and fled, leaving Perelman to deal with the situation.

Going to see Wendell, the present headmaster of Hill, at the Waldorf. My horror at finding him worse than Boyd Edwards—a big young florid box of shit, an academic salesman—Larry Noyes there, his abject old-Hill-fellow attitude as if butter wouldn't melt in his mouth— the problem of smoking hadn't come up for him, because he didn't know why, but he'd never smoked till his junior year at college. —I said that I thought that in my day there had been a little too much regimentation, understood they had loosened up on it now. —Yes: they left more things to the student committees nowadays. The faculty, calling up every student and questioning him in turn, hadn't been able to fix the guilt for the throwing of hydrosulfuric bombs (he evidently made a point of not saying "stink bombs") in the schoolroom, but the Sixth Form Committee found out right away—some of these little Third and Fourth Formers who'd been very clever about it—one boy buying them, another throwing them, etc. —He would ask the Sixth Form Committee how things were and they'd say, Everything is quiet. —

He'd say you don't know what's going on—you better
find out what's going on—and they'd make a raid and get
five or six boys who'd been smoking or drinking beer—
and then he'd tell them, You want to find out all you
can!—the more you find out, the more wholesome the
school will be! —Larry said demurely, Yes, he was sure
if that had been done in his time, a good many things
wouldn't have gone on that did go on. —He didn't remember he'd seen me outside the theater a few nights
before—didn't even, apparently, remember he'd seen the
play. —I'd come expecting to talk to Wendell more or
less seriously about the school and went away appalled.
—He'd sounded patronizing about the old senior masters—
Lavertun and Rolfe were old—they were letting Lester out
more and more to devote time to his progressive educational researches—he had apparently practically given up
teaching English and become more and more a victim of
the filing catalogues with which, in his small perfect
penmanship, he had in my day kept the data for his
courses and for an edition of *The Jew of Malta* which
was going to prove that Marlowe couldn't have written it
because it was such a bad play. —He was going to the
Chicago Exposition on Oliver Jennings's yacht (this must
be Larry). —I thought afterwards of all those boys, Larry,
Dave, Morris (who had endowed a married friend,
Morris Colline, in Chicago), Stan, Noel, and they all
seemed to me to have petered out—Larry less than the
rest perhaps. —Bill Osborn had at least, I'd been told,
invented a new metallurgical process.

Janowitz in New York. It turned out—explaining that
he hadn't told the comrades this—that he came of a
noble Polish family who had supplied Metropolitans and
other dignitaries to the Greek Orthodox Church for generations—had gone back to visit one of his uncles, found

him wearing cloth and translating some hitherto un-
translated stories of Chekhov's—had made over all his
livings and things to his family—his married nephews,
etc.—because he had no children himself. Lived " 'umbly"
but when they went to see him they were received by six
servants who fell on their knees and you didn't know
what else they were going to do. All the family had been
learned—doctors, lawyers, priests. His father had come
over here at eighteen and made his way, had a job in the
town hall and studied for the bar—they lived among the
Polish steelworkers of South Chicago. His father had left
him quite a little money—had studied painting under
everybody, including [George] Bellows.* —Had gotten
fed up with the ILD, always on the fringes—gone in for
TUUL—hard enough to build a union and building a
Red union just that much harder—would probably get
blackjacked or shot someday, but better than dying of
boredom or drink. —Choice between chaos or Communism—that being so, the little objections people made
were just like throwing pebbles at a mountain—[James T.]
Farrell, author of *Gas House McGinty*—the only thing
that had made any impression on him about the May Day
demonstration was the comrades sucking Eskimo Pies
and pop with banners that said, We Want Bread!

[Israel] *Amter* had told him how they lived up at
Blackwells Island to get their dope, scratching their arms
with stones or pricking them with needles. —Big fight
between the Italian and Jewish gangsters. —Had been
talking about Ben Gold and one of the thugs had said,
Yes, I held a gun in Ben Gold!—at some strike.

—Janowitz's fine thin Polish fingers and finely modeled
forehead. —Nostalgia to take a boat to France and drink
a few more bottles of decent wine before he died. —Used
to talk about things as being "rather decent."

* 1882–1925.

—Count Suffinsky, the head of the Greek Church in Vienna, was a relative of theirs, had visited them for two days when he was in America and it was almost like having the Pope himself.

—Had had six hundred cases during the two years he had worked for the ILD—more than some lawyers have in years of practice.

—Had been in Southern Miners' (when a woman and child had been beaten) to Washington and other places—sleeping on floors and so forth—didn't know he could do it—slept on couch in living room the first night and partly fell off and caught worse cold, very much exhausted —thought he was going to get flu or something but he went out and took a walk in the sun and went to the RKO Music Hall and rallied.

Had gone in for Theosophy and gone through all the experiences of religious illumination—you fasted and that made you specially sensitive to certain kinds of sensations —you could make yourself impervious to pain by self-hypnosis—he could still do it when he went to the dentist's and he could use the same kind of technique to make him indifferent to the danger of his work as a TUUL organizer.

—Had also reflected at one point that he knew nothing about machinery—devoted two years to learning how to assemble and disassemble airplane engines and could run an electric train. —Impressed Weber and another man he was motoring to Gillespie with—something went wrong, they got out and took out every part and looked at it and everything seemed all right and then they started off again and again it presently got stalled—he had been thinking these two skilled machinists must be able to deal with the situation, but when it had happened several times he began to think about it and he said, Just a minute, gentlemen!—and he figured out when the stops had oc-curred and found that they were periodic—that was very strange—about every forty minutes—well, something must stop the flow of gasoline at the same point every time—what could it be?—lack of air—what caused that?—he looked at the cap on the gas tank and he found that at the last gas station they had given them a radiator cap which didn't have something which every gas-tank cap has to have—namely, a little hole—so they drilled a hole in it and sailed right along to Gillespie.

—Had gone to school with the Poles of the steel mills and could talk their own idiom to them—also, enough Polish, Czech, and Serbian to command their confidence—in touch with the masses—talked a certain lingo to us, but when he talked to an audience of workers, would change just like that! (snapping fingers)—Had gotten started on his career as organizer when he spoke so successfully to the shoe workers, keeping Communist jargon out of it, that they asked to have him come back again.

—Lost all his money—the last of it was in mortgages on two apartment houses he'd owned in Chicago which the university had collected—the most he ever got out of the comrades was occasional money for sandwiches—but would rather work for the revolutionary movement than have a job.

—Greatly admired André Gide—his style—had been provincial about homosexuality before reading Gide.

—When he visited the Greek Orthodox uncle, he slept on a bed made of beehives (no doubt with all his effete refined Chicago cigarettes and arty attitudes).

—When I spoke of the deformed people in the Communist headquarters, he said, quoting somebody, Only those who have suffered from injustice will ever put an end to injustice.

Paul Rosenfeld went so far as to make the political gesture of walking in the anti-Hitler parade with Miss Stettheimer—she said that some of the banners were not quite accurate: What Would German Literature Be Without the Jews?—it would be wonderful even without the Jews. —She gave out early in the game and left Paul carrying her coat for four hours. —He said he realized he was protesting for something that was dead: the nineteenth century, but he got a great mystic feeling out of it, which prevented his feet from feeling tired.

Glimpses of figures. Girl seen in New York (mid-May) in the morning in light dress combing out her fluffy blond hair in the areaway in front of a house in the morning, pale, but with her lips made up, and as if contented, as if she had been fucked the night before and that morning and had just gotten out of bed with her lover.

—Boy seen from train on way to Red Bank, standing straight behind lawnmower, the hairs of his blond hair bristling up in back, in blue overalls and a white undershirt, his bare arms held at right angles and his hands grasping the handle of the lawnmower.

—A little farther on, a pretty-looking girl in blue, well dressed middle-class, wheeling a baby carriage—that was the next generation, what would they do, what would they be? in the future that somebody was bringing them into—that future that looming seemed so strange, and they were just an ordinary baby (though mysterious with the future as babies are) and an ordinary American mother (yet these, these days, were slim wisps in a funny way— inscrutable by very reason of there being so little to them?).

—Girl walking with a young man at Perth Amboy, fixing the back of her dress with one hand.

—A man lying down in an areaway, on a newspaper, asleep, strong brown arms, one hand behind his head— in the middle of the afternoon.

—Good-looking boy, well grown and naked except for

loosely worn short pants, sitting on stone seat and watching train go by.

Dawn Powell's story about Dwight Fiske telling mother he would give her son a letter to a charming friend of his in Paris—Dawn felt like saying, Oh, don't let him send him to Oscar Wilde!—the friend turned out to be the innocent boy himself. (Proustian incident.)

Charley Mitchell's trial. The old elevators of the federal courts—going up in the black grillwork cages with large bulky men with wide faces and gray hats—plaster-looking Corinthian columns and ornamental panels and wooden railing of courtroom—bald heads sticking out of close-clinging hair like acorns out of their shells, polished shiny like the seats—the courtroom type, chunky, expanding around the belly and hips, short legs—their sallow faces have known no other light than that of this courtroom, their fat legs had no other exercise than stalking across its floor.

—Max Steuer a shrewd little old Jew; Medalia a weighty obstinate one

—The financial witnesses, the inflated bankers of the boom, enormous, with no necks at all, like hooked frogs or big fish, big bass or giant groupers, hauled out landed gasping on the witness stand—blue suits, brown suits, handkerchiefs sometimes sticking out of pockets—Mitchell in blue suit, big shoulders but short legs, not an impressive man, grizzled hair but basically common face, looking cheap as if he had been caught, not much dignity.

Beer. People had begun doubting seriously (middle of May) whether the beer was real—showed general attitude of mistrust.

Late afternoon, with headache from *hangover,* going to bed. The *children broken out* from the houses and the schools into the streets, their clamor throughout the city, cheers, curses, banging and cries—dying out with the night—when I came to and saw the walls of the opposite building lighted by the street lamps, the clamor was gone—the new life of the city.

Leo Wolmans. Cecil had been sick, seemed a little tart—reaction against marrying Leo, etc., after the first few years? Buffet dinner in the living room—salary from Amalgamated probably going down. Thought Henderson had been fired for incompetence—kept on year after year merely to avoid raising a row. —Howard Kallen and his metaphysics (like Kenneth Burke)—Marx merely a combination of Rousseauist humanitarianism with Adam Smith's economics—unpredictable phenomena such as jumping of elections—Leo inclined to think that Lenin's seizure of power was an accident, Trotsky's history a rationalization—Kallen thought the Russians were worse off under the Soviets than under the Tsar—Leo was always invoking the "facts" about Russia, etc. —*Merwin Hart.* Leo sometimes encountered him—another employees' agent who used to insist that he was just as anxious as they were to benefit the workers, it was just that the proposed legislation was going to do them harm— he would listen to Hillman as if he were hanging on every word he said, when you knew all the time that he was just watching for something that could be attacked as unconstitutional. —Leo had been to *Washington:* perfectly crazy, full of people presenting plans; Stewart, American engineer who had been in Russia, had elaborate plan, was saying that America not Russia was the place to try the Russian idea—Moley a regular academic "political scientist," ambitious, knew he was man of the hour, wanted to be Secretary of State; Tugwell a trimmer; Berle—they said he was queer and neurotic—had been put out but kept coming back. Roosevelt kept smiling and didn't really know what it was all about—didn't understand the bills he signed—they were light-mindedly handling formulas which only a violent upheaval could put into effect—industry was going to be run by the same monopolies that had always run it, concentration hadn't begun yet. —Leo had been offered a job but refused it. —Kallen greatly exercised about *Hitler's* persecution of Jews, why didn't Roosevelt protest as other Presidents had done? —Goering had been put in an insane asylum for sadism—Hanfstaengl was one of Hitler's wives. — Kallen on Marx: social-maladjustment explanation of him. —Discovery by *The New Republic* of Lenin, a bourgeois at bottom (Beard), same ideas as Franklin Roosevelt (editorial). —Cecil on faculty wives—very punctilious— you must never answer an invitation by phone. —Kallen and Wolman had had Bertrand Russell living with them at one time—Kallen adored him, Wolman didn't like him—though the only thing he had against him was the way he treated the colored maid Lottie, neither thanked nor tipped her, accepted her services as a matter of course without human recognition of any kind.

Late summer afternoon in late May, thunder threatening in the copious light green and sun with the birds chirping—the *radio*, turned on, nothing but an ear-splitting rattle of static and the fierce-shrill trilling of infernal birds, the faintest thread of a waltz way behind them—storm kept gathering slowly. Rosalind and I sat out on the lawn and played checkers after supper for a long time—then went in, closed the doors of the back porch, and played Parcheesi with Jenny—the yellow light, none too good, would grow dim, go out for a second, then come on again—when the rain broke, Rosalind opened the door and said how cold the wind was (after the hot day)—it didn't last long, was soon over.

Scott Fitzgerald (Katy Dos Passos told me this). *Man who wrote that he had modeled his life on Scott and his writings.* Didn't come to dinner and they waited for him till ten-thirty, when he appeared, absolutely plastered, said Mishter-Fishgerald-Thishishhonor! and collapsed on couch. There he lay—my creation! His wife had hysterics and they got her to lie down—when they came back, he had disappeared—wife alarmed, they searched house—but he had gone away, overcome by shame, leaving car, which it took seven men to get out of the mire.

Provincetown. Well-to-do lady who owned real estate burst into tears when Howland Smith called her a "bourgeoise"—there had been an embittered controversy between her and Susan (Glaspell) over building a garage under Susan's windows. —Betty Spencer as village vamp (Dos Passos's idea)—Katy, going to see her, was met, when the door opened, by gale of perfume—house full of flowers, Betty with her hair all fluffy—delegation of fiery-eyed wives had called on her.

Dawn Powell's story about Peter Blume hoping to get *Margaret de Silver* to buy his pictures—something was said about a warm rich person—she said, I suppose I'm a warm rich person. —He, with her money in his mind, said, Oh, well—I've got a new suit—I'm a bourgeois, too!

Esther Andrews's going-away party for Dos. Carlo Tresca* made statements that shocked Esther and Mar-

---

* Tresca, an old-time anarchist and colorful figure in the Italian colony, was later shot down, it was said, by New York Fascists.

garet—pointed to scar under chin, Where do you think I got this? —Dawn Powell: Helena Rubinstein! (laughter). What Esther told me about—*Berenice Dewey*: perfect little wife and mother when she first had baby—Jack Lawson had said that when he first knew her, she was a regular little elf. —During the last year, they'd noticed she seemed changed—drank a lot whereas she'd never drunk much before. When she got sick, she was in great pain but got to be like a little girl when they took her to the hospital—not delirious but would look around and talk about the room—a nice room, but I'd like to get new curtains. —She had always refused to take emotional responsibility and perhaps what she had really wanted was to get back to being a pretty little girl—no doubt the strain of carrying on that kind of life was too much for the mature woman—and she was a beauty who was facing getting old. —Esther said she had had a stepfather whom she hated.

Griffin Barry's anti-Semitism with Morrie Werner, whom he was meeting for the first time—first said of Nathanael West that he didn't like that kind of looking Jew—then, that when a Jew insulted you at the opera in Russia, you understood Hitler's anti-Semitism. (Hitler's persecutions, in some cases, instead of arousing indignation, brought out anti-Semitism.) —Morrie later said that you were always a Jew first—that at Columbia the Jews couldn't make the fraternities, so they went in for being students. —Griffin evidently thought he had all Bertrand Russell's ancestors. —Exactly like a woman and yet not exactly like a fairy.

The beginning of the summer, late May, muggy weather, at the little Italian restaurant with Griffin, I felt embedded in the city summer and enjoying its richness,

sluggishness—I tasted it, thoroughly enjoyed it, somewhat
to my compunction—lower part of walls imitation marble
with dark-red and yellow rectangles painted on it like bits
of meat in one of those charcuterie loaves—red wine—
radicals came there, Scott Nearing—chicken livers on
spits, rich, with bits of bacon and grease-soaked toast
between them.

Roosevelt had said, How long will the people give me?
Do you think they'll give me six months?

Movies. Goldwyn had said to West, Give me another
Morocco, my boy—give me another *Morocco!* —Mrs.
Strauss had said to him, when he made some remark
about the behavior of the characters, I always thought
you were a psychiatrist, Mr. West! —Girl who came back
from Hollywood and set up shop in New York with long
white desk and big white electric candles on it—very
snooty accent. —When Sylvia Sidney was Schulberg's
girl, before he was divorced, she gave a party the same
night as Mrs. Schulberg, and people were very much
worried as to what they ought to do, went first for a few
minutes to Sidney party, then straight to Mrs. Schulberg's
and explained that they'd just been to Miss Sidney's and
only stayed a quarter of an hour. —One of the big men
had criticized the Mack Sennett comedies on the ground
that the people laughed when they were watching it but
when they went out of the theater they didn't take anything with them. —Mae Marsh hadn't lasted long in
Hollywood because she had written to somebody who
knew him: You're right—so-and-so is a great big idiot. He
summoned her to his office and said, I think that's a very
mean letter. She was so astounded at having her mail
opened that she could hardly reply at first. You soon
found out that you couldn't send a telegram or a phone

message from the studio. —Goldwyn had given West $300 advance for his scenario and then baited him by the promise of $3,000 when he'd bring in eight pages.

—West's sister kidded him about the hotel's taking more trouble to fake things like chicken salad with veal and celery, mostly celery, than it was worth—also soaking cow's liver in milk so as to make it tender enough to serve as calf's liver. (The Sutton, which he ran.)

Perry Austin trying to raise money to rebuild Episcopal churches of Los Angeles—importance in keeping up the morale of the community—when your property was destroyed, you just went on without any cares about property, everything became communal, a community—had just seen Bill Castle, former Assistant Secretary of State, had had lunch with him at Racquet Club. Perry had said, Wouldn't Roosevelt crack under the strain of dashing off all these bills (which he couldn't have the data to make really sound)? and then we'd have to have Garner. Castle had thought it might be better, just because Garner was slow and practical. —Had also been to see Junius Morgan, who seemed very jaunty.

The Morgan revelations. Walter Lippmann on the bankers "being in a mood to tear away the veils" surrounding their business. —The short editorial in the *Post* headed "A Dull Day"—no possibility of spattering dirt, no hookup.

Dr. Barnes (the Philadelphia collector) had, it seems, persecuted *Scofield Thayer* to a certain extent—Gilbert Seldes said he burst in on them, perhaps hoping to catch them *in flagrante delicto* (he was always scenting homosexuality) in a hotel room in Paris and did what amounted to serving notice on Thayer that he must drop McBride and Rosenfeld, so that Barnes could direct the artistic policy of *The Dial*, and hence of America. —Detectives in various guises used to come to see Gilbert and Kenneth Burke at that time—something connected with some girl he had been going with—had a girl committed suicide on his account? —General craziness of that group at that time—Cummings and his revolver, Cummings and Thayer afraid of getting blackmailed about impotence on account of Paris divorces.

Katy's (Dos Passos) *story about mother and daughter* (Marianne Moore relationship)—somebody finally saw them and asked how they were. Mother replied, We've lost our youth, but we still have our health.—Ogrish.

Hollywood. Your scenario's all right, Miss ———, but it lacks spontanooity—you take it and maul it over in your head awhile. —Zanuck was a young fellow who saved Warner's, so intense about the movies there must have been something to him—neither smoked, drank, nor gambled, got up early every morning—had no vice but practical joking—blew crackers in somebody's face—when old man in picture was supposed to fall downstairs, Zanuck got another old man, picked up off the street, told him to walk on the edges of the stairs, and then pushed him, old man fell and broke a couple of legs—in Cagney picture, shot real machine gun into wall when Cagney was just around the corner—Cagney was ready to quit the lot, but the shot's over, why quit?—West's incipient admiration mingling with ridicule—Perelman, his wife had just read in *Variety*, had resigned after a day of a Zasu Pitts comic—something that wasn't done in Hollywood—radio was worse, little guy they dined with who wanted quartette in night club made into new four Marx Brothers for radio—we could call them Zeppo,

Groucho, etc. —Perelman was so disgusted he wouldn't see him again, an embittered winter for Perelman—West's sister kidding him about talking Yiddish to the movie people, West said he had, sister said he didn't know a word of it. —Herman Mankiewicz resigning, going to Schulberg or whoever it was and saying, I hate Jews, you're a lot of dirty kikes! —Big executive had said, Don't say that: you're a Jew yourself! —Not after today! he replied, going out and banging the door. —They told West they wanted a scenario with a little perversity in it—he had written them a sentimental reminiscence (he supposed) of some old movie he had seen and had carefully stuck in so many clichés as to make it practically unreadable, so that the movie man had said, I want you to write it so that if we don't use it, you can print it as a short story. —His idea for scenario involving D. H. Lawrence stallion (shot of white arms around his neck), clean scientific steely doctor whom woman corrupts (she dances the lewd Martinique dance and beat of drum repeats hoofbeats of stallion—she is in dope ring to keep up stud farm because she loves the stallion so)—but finally the doctor's son turns up, the only lover who has been able to compete with the stallion, she saves the doctor on account of him (wonderful photo montage of hypodermic, the machine, against her white leg)—stallion finally tramples her to death. —West tolerant, Perelman intolerant. —West had sold movie rights of *Lonelyhearts* for $4,000. —Their names! —Gimfel—Lastvogel—West had gotten in wrong for saying to him, And the Lastvogel shall be Firstvogel.

Lovett had attended the meeting in St. Louis of the *Progressives* with *John L. Lewis* when Mrs. Wieck and Lewis had had their run-in. There were tough-looking guys hanging around the hall who turned out to be Progressives. Pearcy and Gerry Allard were scared to death for fear they'd plug Lewis—a wonderful mark, you couldn't miss him, made to be assassinated (had moved from Springfield to Indianapolis). Rank and file always afraid that their leaders are going to sell them out.

The World's Fair. A Century of Progress.

West telling me in his melancholy way how he had said, Why, Pop, that's as good as stealing! but Pop said, But the note is good, isn't it?—shook his head sadly, drooped his eyelids in resignation.

Mary Pickford at Sherry-Netherland. She was little and simply dressed—I was disconcerted at first by the effects of the horrible face-lifting process which she had had performed and which tightened the skin so over all the lower part of her face that she couldn't smile with her mouth, which was nothing but a little stiff red-lined orifice in the face of a kind of mummy, nor change her expression at all. Only the upper part of her face was alive—the eyes, dark agatelike blue which glowed, even flashed, from time to time, with a slate-blue power of energy and will—and intelligent humor coming out in the brows—human and very attractive, while the lower part of her face remained immobile. Her profile was not good— nose common and not straight, somewhat recessive chin, accentuated no doubt by the shrinking of skin which suppressed her cheeks. What had been intended to make her look young for the public had the uncomfortable effect at close range of making her look old. Businesslike, practical, clear in her mind, fairly intelligent—an American small-town girl, probably Irish, who by dint of her peculiar position had become something of a woman of the world. I liked her. —It seemed to me that for a moment when she first came into the room, and for a moment when I was leaving, there was a little despiteful look—

or was it in the tightening of the skin around the mouth—
as of resentment and disappointment against a world to
which she was no longer irresistibly winning.

[Arthur Hopkins, who had read my play *Beppo and
Beth* and who talked about producing it, had suggested
that I might collaborate with her (Mary Pickford) on a
play she wanted to write—I forget about what. She
amused me by talking in movie terms—asking whether
my "options" would leave me free.]

Calling on *Dorothy Parker Sunday afternoon* (June 18,
'33). After was it three years? my depression at finding her
and her circle the same—she still sitting around very
pretty but in slightly dowdy dressing gown, drinking
gin and ginger ale. Philip Barry, Archy MacLeish—she
thought now that Archy was good; Jock Whitney was a
son of a bitch (as Hemingway had said); she and Bee
Ames and Betty Starbuck going through contortions over
people's unspeakable banalities—could hardly keep a
straight face—little intelligent sensitively responsive
cocker-spaniel puppy which keeps peeing on things;
Dorothy's unwillingness to hear anybody else's stories,
wisecracks; Benchley out in Hollywood, what had happened to him? they were vomiting and puking over his
stuff in the *Mirror*—the first one had been headed or advertized by a caricature of Benchley and a little girl saying, Oh, goody! here comes the funny man. —Dorothy
had tried not to see it. —One of their current tricks—the
squeaky little-girl voice: May I use your telephone? —The
Algonquin Circle had grown social, their humor no longer
quite so low-down—but for Dorothy—in comparison at
least to the time when she had been breaking out and
having her first tragedies, the time when she had known
Elinor Wylie—the little humorists' world seemed smaller
than before. —Exclaiming over the lyric of Cole Porter's
"Night and Day" in *Gay Divorcée*—no, Betty Starbuck
said, there was only one place where it really got bad and

that was: "Under the hide of me," "There's oh such a yearning, burning feeling inside of me!" —Dorothy said that "Mr. Benchley" had known how bad it was, but would he say anything about it? no! —*Sew Collins* had gone off, as his mother had explained to somebody, to Italy to see the Nazis. (Years later, when I talked to Dorothy about Seward, I found that she didn't know he was dead. "I don't see what else he could do," she said.)

George Soule in Washington, just after the industrial bill had been signed: old home week for liberals, everywhere you went you met people you knew, the first time they had ever gotten in. But Berle had said that they better pick out places to go in two years' time and not tell anybody where they were. George had said that people like Wolman had "a healthy skepticism" whether industry might not "run away with it."

Uncle Win. Ridiculous this idea of the South and West that nobody should be allowed to have more than $17,500 a year—why, they had to keep up their position, couldn't have a house uptown and take care of a family for that! —Roosevelt trying to handle the situation but had to do things to satisfy all these bums that he brought along with him: Huey Long, Norris, La Follette. —The Scotch firm of James White (my uncle's importing firm) had been underselling the world and doing very well. —Jimmy Walker had created 35,000 new city jobs. —At his Statler Island golf club, there were a good many Tammany Irish Catholics—somebody had said that O'Brien wouldn't reduce the budget and one of the Tammany judges had said, Who the hell wants to reduce the budget? —*The Knoxes:* Mrs. Knox had known the ropes, had been in deals with George Boker and other big men, but Caroline had taken the advice of young brokers who didn't know anything about it—people who lived on tips: Barney Baruch has just bought so-and-so—ridiculous, nothing to it at all!—you ought to get somebody to advise you who knew about it yet was on the outside—the way he pronounced money "moaney." —Said that somebody had bought up all the seats from old-fashioned backhouses and sawed them in half for the half-assed bankers.

Louise Bryant, full of booze or hop, telling Edna Kenton* that she'd always kept Jack's [John Reed] secret but he was simply an American spy.

Lovett arrested for turning up with Tom McKenna at the picketing of a garment factory—he had heard people were being beaten up—and saying, as was alleged, Go right ahead!—You've got a perfect right to picket!—don't pay any attention to the police!—he had spent a day in jail for disorderly conduct—released on $25 bail.

Jenny was taken out of school and put to work in the fields, hoeing potatoes, when she was ten—she was frail and it ruined her health. She was sixteen when she came to us and Mother taught her to cook, etc. —Now jealous of Mrs. Warner, jealous of Stella—forgot everything, and Mother would keep after her, and she would keep after Mother, taking care of her.

Roosevelt's unsatisfactory way of emphasizing his sentences, fairyish or as if there weren't real conviction behind them—in spite of his clearness and neatness—but regular radio announcers, I noticed later, did the same thing. (The remoteness of the speaker from his audience.)

Anna: Just before I went to Boston, conversation sitting on edge of bed and looking out window at night:

* Edna Kenton, a magazine writer, was a friend of Dreiser and Sherwood Anderson; she had been active in the early days of the Provincetown Playhouse and now lived in Greenwich Village.

she was so dumb, didn't know anything—lay awake at night worrying about it—had never met any nice people except me and my friends, wanted to know them, didn't like her own people, but didn't know if they'd want her. She commented on the "beautiful landscape" out the window with the old Ford—it *was* a terrible-looking old Ford, black and hunched up. Then she said she thought she'd better die.

—*Her cousin from Seattle*—steam engineer, stationary engineer—manager of apartment houses and hotels—families who spent their lives in sampans in Japan, cared nothing about human life out there, sold girls into slavery for ten dollars a month—his sister Jane said she'd rather be an American lady than anything else in the world—the Russians were cutting out the white people in the Orient, taking away their jobs and working for less. —After a couple of cocktails, he said that he thought marriage ought to be a partnership, always adding, I don't want you to think I'm henpecked. —He said his wife was a woman in a thousand. —He'd been places and seen people since he left New York—his sister Jane had written him that she envied him living in Seattle, that she often wished for some little country town herself. —Good-looking and slightly superior (the Jewish strain?)—watched his drinks and deliberately moderated his voice—said he didn't mind telling anybody what he thought of them—maybe that was the reason he got along with the family—had chased them all to bed to talk to Anna.

Henri and Louise (July '33). Topsfield: West Indian Annie and Joseph—ma bless!—of Joseph: Everybody speak of his eyes!—thought it necessary to beat him once a month and they wished they knew what day it was so that they could arrange to be away—I saw her threatening him: You see this knife—I'm gonna cut your tongue right out! —Asked me if I thought Louise would ever change. —Louise claimed that Annie didn't know but what we were just drinking ginger ale and lemonade, so she never left the gin bottle around. —Fräulein had studied at the Conservatory and worked for one of the von Bülows—terrible times over her and Annie—Fräulein would get firmly refractory (about putting Mercurochrome on Petie's blistered heel, etc.) and go out for sulky walks, wouldn't help with the kitchen—Annie left the jackets on the potatoes when she boiled them, so as to give Fräulein "a little work to do." —Petie out of sorts, Louise thought he didn't know what to do with himself, away from school and not having his father and mother take him places. —Looked like A. A. Milne drawing, they had evidently dressed him that way on purpose. His father had written her to have him take riding lessons and to take him to Brooks and get him a riding outfit, which she thought was silly. In one of his disagreeable grabbing moods, he began to abuse Joseph for snatching a box of matches: You mustn't grab! You'll pay for this! —Joseph's songs: I want to kiss somebody I like, so I'll just have to kiss myself!—would keep repeating things in talking, as they do in Negro blues. —Petie at the same time sweet and touching, a look of Louise in his brown eyes when he responded to you. —Sissy at the dabbling age—she had said one night when they were out of doors: Let's go in—Dolly's freezing! —Miss Smith and her house—nosy in a refined way, holding a savage Airedale on a rope—smiling, I noticed you got home *very* late. Henri and Louise scared of her and of the town in general, who, they were sure, thought they were the fastest people they'd ever seen. —George Eliot's life in three volumes (which Henri read in bed: after having at first been unable to do anything for the baby, she was now in danger of spoiling him by being too solicitous about him, always going back to him when he cried at night, etc.). Pepys's diary, schoolbooks, standard sets, tinted photographs of Italy, all too thickly set over the walls—but Louise adored the little house and the whole place. —Gerrit's little house—pink curtains and canopy over bed, each flower on the wallpaper of one of the rooms painted by his wife Mabel (Gerrit had a trucking company now), two pictures of frail little lavender-tinted flowers directly over the water closet, lavender toilet paper, a few phony little tinted eighteenth-century pictures, library of American wit and humor, set of little red volumes (house really belonged to parents)—it all looked to me now like a ghastly Boston suburb, ugly bungalows and cottages—the beaches where we had been in those earlier summers now horribly dreary and crass in the Boston way—flagpole sitters, old rickety-looking roller coasters, flimsy scaffoldings of laths, pinched into the narrowest possible space between the roadway and the beach—hard light—the hill covered with gray boxlike houses, the Massachusetts windows and frames too thin, pinched and cramped where it wasn't necessary, merely the mean tradition, a large white summer hotel with the same uninviting aspect, none of the slightly silly seaside-sentimental ornamentation of the hotels on the Jersey coast—the people with their plain pale pinched-in inbred Anglo-Saxonized faces—even the Irish. —Those summer places where the girls had had such a good time only a few miles from the mill towns—a tangle of roads among towns close together and all of about equal importance. —*The House of the Seven Gables,* unpainted, cramped inside with its low ceilings, though large; old Boston ladies to show you around—portraits and handsome antique furniture in the old cramped rooms.

Margaret. —Her death which deprived her of the things we have in life made them seem worthless to me—

I couldn't enjoy them so much because they were things which could be spoiled for her and taken away from her. A loyalty to her had made me less loyal to life itself. I felt toward life in general some of the resentment I had toward the undertaker, etc. (at the same time slight quiet symptoms of sadistic satisfaction). Such things, satisfactions—books, love-making, drinking, talking, enjoyment of sensations—were not serious since they could be cut off from someone as fine and serious as she— as the part of me that had died with her. Scorn of life itself—when someone you love dies, you feel that it does not make much difference having it come to an end. Why should you accept something which has been taken away from someone who deserved it as much—your true comradeship with her, true solidarity with what she represents for you that is noble, is to challenge life, to be proud to take it seriously, to go on paying no attention to its attractions, diversions, demands, toward things of higher importance (life in the sense of such little flash-by of individual sensations as the individual can experience).

—Her books, *Fear, Psychoanalyzing Ourselves*—where I had had a partial outlet in radical writing, etc.—she had had none except sex, which I had shut down on last winter.

—Moving in furniture and little bright things she'd bought, though I'd sent back the red curtains and she'd apparently sold cut-glass decanters (because we had so little money?—in which case they hadn't been stolen)— bright reading and table lamps, lots of them—card table I'd broken—shade in bedroom I'd pulled down—horribly depressed that night—like a strange bright bad dream— green lamp with landscape (on it) that she used to have by the bed when she'd lie there reading with a long glass of green alcohol gin fizz beside her, waiting for me to come to bed—then I'd stay up drinking, with my writing, and come to bed genial-drunk just as it was getting light, when she had had no sleep.

When I sniffed the little bottle of bitters, it reminded me of the Berkeley and I didn't want to use it in the cocktails that night.

—She remembered Richard Carle singing, "I Picked a Lemon in the Garden of Love"—her father had taken her to *The Spring Chicken*—did she connect it with her mother, etc.?

Dream. There she was alive—what was the catch?— that she was supposed not to exist any more—but there she was, and what was to prevent our living together again?—*that* would be just a gap in the past. —The present of her being alive and of our being together again was real—the future could be real, too.

I dreamed again May 13 [1933] that it was merely a question of her being sick and that when she got well, we'd be together—I stupidly hadn't realized that, had thought it would separate us for good so that I wouldn't see her any more—and couldn't help thinking the next Monday, What if she should come in the door?

The two rock hinds in the aquarium, one lying up against the other and on top of her against the rock side of the tank, gave me a sensation faintly gratifying—why? —and then I realized it was because that was the way we used to be in bed together, faced in the same direction and I with my arms around her—one on top shifted up, then back into place, fixed himself better.

Dream. Thought in dim grayish dream I could tell her how silly I'd been about making mistake about not being able to see her again.

Morning of Eliot hangover, I missed her little round body—we used to recover from hangovers together—I used to turn myself around and lie with my face against her feet.

Dream. I went back to her father's room, with the bureau I have now or one like it, in the old house at Red Bank—she was angry with me: While you were doing (something), I've been here all alone!—she was getting dressed.

—But in a sense I could have nothing in common with her any more—she was dead and I was still living.

In spite of the neurotically sadistic things she would sometimes say, she would never bite my lip as hard as I wanted her to or as hard as I would hers.

Even in going back over the situation, I would set certain brutal things I had done aside as outside consideration.

Had she been having a change of life? as Perry suggested.

Dream. I was getting in bed with her—there was no reason after all that we shouldn't be together.

I was glad of an excuse in Rosalind and Mother for staying alive after she was dead.

Dream. I was away with her in the country somewhere and she was getting more and more neurotic, and I realized I had better send her to McKinny (the psychiatrist I went to when I had my breakdown) so that the same thing wouldn't happen to her that had happened to

Margaret—I was looking his number up in the telephone book. —Then I began to come to and had to face it that the woman in the dream was Margaret herself.

Dream. She was ill and supposed not to have long to live, lying on a bed somewhere we had gone to see a woman doctor—as we were talking, it occurred to me that she might get well, and if I could make her believe that I loved her and wanted her to get well, the trouble might disappear—I told her that she must get well, that she wasn't so seriously sick—she said she didn't know whether she was going to like what the doctor would tell her to do—I told her about my dreams, how I had thought we were back at the Berkeley, etc., and then waked up to find she was dead, but now she didn't need to die, there was time for me to convince her I wanted her to get well—yet I asked myself, were the other possibilities of getting some other more congenial, more intellectually developed woman able to tempt me? now that I could have her again, was the same doubt and negative feeling toward her that had kept us apart cropping up again? did I find now that I thought I could have her again that I wanted her less than I had in the dream in the Berkeley when I couldn't have her because she was dead? —I decided I did want her, yes, and I could have her, and persuade her to live. —Woke up among all the green foliage and lovely peace of a slightly overcast June Sunday at Red Bank.

—Ted said that the reason he hadn't been definite about marrying Margaret, after Edith had the baby, was that he wanted to wait till after his father died—he expected him to die soon.

I finally *dreamed* we were back together and not getting along well again—this after I had been talking to Ted and sat up one night thinking it all through.

314 EAST 53RD STREET

[The small talk of Henrietta and Louise Fort continued to fascinate EW, as these notes show.]

Henri and Louise. Henri would always tend to put herself next to Louise so that at the lunch counter in the South Station, for example, instead of my finding myself in the middle, with them on either side, Louise would be in the middle. Martha Blain would say in her social column, "Mrs. Peter Connor was wearing one of the new – – dresses" (Martha hated – – dresses, everybody had them), or, *The New Poor:* * the "so-and-so's have given up their yacht," etc., "Mrs. Peter Connor is doing her own cooking" (Peter had been talking poor—when the note appeared in the paper, his boss had him on the carpet, because brokers oughtn't to give the impression that the business wasn't doing well.) —Louise so lovely when she sang to Petie something that Uncle Eugene Cowles, who had been the original man who sang the Armorer's Song in *Robin Hood*, had sung her—gay and tender, her lovely spontaneity:

* This was the title of a book by Clarissa Fairchild Cushman published in 1927.

Anybody seen mah Lulu?
I'll tell you how you'll know—
Her mouth's chuck full of tulu,
And her shoestring hangin' on the ground
    Doggone it!
Her shoestring hangin' on the ground.

Anybody foolin' with my Lou
I'll tell you what I'll do
I'll play with a razor round his heart
And cut out his left lung, too.
    Doggone it! etc.

When she sang it over again at Petie's insistence, it was actually hard to bear and made me jealous of his attractive children. —I'm jealous of the ticktock on the shelf—I'm even getting jealous of myself. —"Shuffle off to Buffalo": *For a simple little quarter, We can make the Pullman porter, turn the lights down low, Oo-oo-oo!* (train whistle)—from movie, *42nd Street*—popular songs getting more machine-made and commonplace as the movies were taking them over from the musical shows? —Louise loved "Stormy Weather," but they didn't know it—did seem definitely to have gotten out of the habit of singing, no longer broke out with the spontaneity of repressed spirits—they said it had been all taken out of them. —Louise so much fatter but very handsome in white and green negligee with black and silver sandal mules—had bobbed her hair, to Peter's disgust, beautifully scalloped up around the forehead like the curling crest of a wave—blowing out behind as she drove the car, it looked so thick and strongly grown. —Herbert's letter about the radio for his sister—he had picked cheapest one at Macy's, then had wanted Henri to get friend who worked there to get trade discount, then get somebody else to take it to Bermuda—"I shall finance it only temporarily," though a birthday present. —Henri's terse postcard reply. In same mail, letter written him by firm to whom he had been applying for job but to whom he had written such a snooty letter, saying that he was "very well satisfied to stop where he was," that he had provoked a reply concluding with the remark that they wished he had let them know that in the first place. Henri had told their father that Louise had said she thought he was one of the most attractive men she had ever seen, and he had immediately come on to Chicago and finally bored her to death drinking whiskey and telling funny stories. They thought he was "a frustrated man"—he didn't like Gerrit's little girl, thought she was so ill-bred. —Louise has been going to pictures a lot to escape things. —Old $35 car that wouldn't start without your turning on the lights—and she dreaded going through the town and having people say, "Your lights are on!" —Afternoon on beach—Crane house like cement institution way up on hill—Mrs. Crane, they said, having built the house, was taking a trip in a small yawl. —Leaving Boston on train after beer at lunch counter (Louise thought woman beside her, who was eating sandwich, was staring at her because she had never seen a young woman drink so much beer): the factories, (including Crane Valves) dreary and grim, it seemed to me, like no others, each with its plain-lettered sign in its wirelike background, all identical, no matter what they made. —An arbor with green grapes in back of the house—fires in the grates in the late afternoon—an unused well, a show well, rustic with dignity, the house a rather rambling shape—their father had said that the missing kindling wood was in the cushions in the davenport on the (screened) side porch. Henri and Louise had gone to the same camp together as girls, but only Henri had picked up any nature lore. Louise said that Henri would say as they were riding along, "That's pops-a-berry bush!" and Louise would take her word for it, though she had probably made it up.

K. Full lips, smelled like strawberries, almost too rich. In the total dark—began to crawl on me. Afterwards, "Well, that's something nobody can take away from you! . . . I'd like to be married to you." —I asked her if she liked me, and she said, "I must love you . . . Some people can sleep with people they don't like, but I love you . . . This is the last time you ever get such service." Could see different people's points of view. —"Do you want to know a secret?—There's not much fun in the attack tonight" (female troubles). I said that would never deter me. She said, "O-oo!" in not very convincing disgust. —K. was able to make herself believe what she wanted to believe. —Had always felt she could never belong to any group. I said I'd like to have children by her if it were only possible, and she said, simply, "That would be wonderful, wouldn't it?"

Henri and Louise (continued). Henri didn't really get much out of serious verse, though she read it—but Louise couldn't do anything with it at all—this "parade of emotion" embarrassed her. They had had a period of ignoring things, when Henri had been in the habit of embarrassing people telling the story about the man who had hidden under the seats at the movies. —Louise always wanted to sit out on the lawn at night when I wanted to stay inside the porch—she said I was just like Peter in Canada, who had preferred to see the landscape from the window—he would rather look at the picture from inside than be part of it. —Louise said that whenever she lent Henri a dress to wear, it was ruined right away (perhaps she didn't put it quite so strongly as this). Their parents wouldn't give them a cent except under pressure—their mother would say, "Wouldn't you think Gerrit would offer to pay us rent?" (for the little house of theirs that he was occupying). Louise thought, however, that maybe they liked their parents better than if they'd been spoiled by them—she always came to be near them during the summer. —Their great word now was "bemuzzed"—"I'm a little bemuzzed." Petie, having heard them make fun of Joseph, would say to me *sotto voce*, "Isn't he charming!" when Joseph would come up to us and gabble. —The little girl was pulling her mouth out of shape with her fingers. —Louise's backless bathing suit that came up over her breasts in two brassièrelike pockets and fastened with two thin straps over her shoulders. *My dream*: I thought that my play was being done, but that I couldn't go to attend to it, because Mary was having another baby and I had to be at the hospital. I was staying at a hotel and a somewhat disguised Percy Wendell (a sort of more de luxe Waldo Pierce) was the only person among the people I knew there (they seemed to inhabit the whole corridor) who sent Mary any attentions—he gave me some flowers for her. —"Well, s.o.b.!" (Louise said this to me)—John Amen corrupting Louise by making her drink—her husband used to tell her to "eat her soup"—I said that all the young men were offering the young girls gin at that time, and she answered, "And now they're trying to make them stop drinking a little."

Ted Paramore. [Italo] Balbo* had just arrived (Carlo Tresca had sent him a telegram: "I am watching you"— and signed it with the name of some priest who had

* Italo Balbo (1896–1940), head of Mussolini's blackshirt militia and a noted airman, had just made a long-distance flight from Italy to the United States.

tried to lead the peasants and whom Tresca said Balbo had had clubbed to death), and Ted had been to see some friends at the Ambassador or near it (outside which Italian girls and American cuties were waiting)—they had had two Italian tarts there and had said, "These girls were flying over with Balbo but they were forced down here."

Ted had been with the brokers trying to clean up a little something for the future—they said it was the last chance—money not going to be worth anything—sat around offices hilarious and irresponsible—joke about Hoover's coming back. —They had called up and said, "We've got three stale wives here and we've got to do something about them"—took turns being sober and staying in office to attend to clients—one of them ran up a bill of $4,000 in two weeks at the Mayfair Boat Club—they had started off on fishing trip, and the itemized list of expenses told the story: five cocktails; five dinners; five highballs; fifty-five highballs (fishing trip given up); ten cocktails (entertaining the girls in the night club); one champagne cocktail (for the prima donna); one bottle of rye (was going to try to make a girl in the car). Finally, they came back in a plane and the pilot passed out over the controls the moment they landed—one of the party vomited and another took a piss—the girls walked dazedly around the plane.

Ted writing letters in drawers—bending over at basin. Last wave of speculation—but Matey in Philadelphia (Mrs. Roberts, his aunt by marriage) said they didn't take any stock there in the New Deal—Roosevelt was clever: "Let my farmers alone, but you can play with the industries."

Bill [Slater] *Brown in the Industrial Recovery Bally-hoo Campaign*: like putting little blue ribbons around the necks of tigers, testifying that they're not going to eat any more sheep.

Louise or Henri inquired of a passer-by in Boston whether he knew where somebody named Smith lived—he replied that he had lived on that street forty years and knew of nobody but Saltonstalls and Eliots.

Helen Spencer (Rolfe Humphries's wife).* Had hated her mother, had thought she was cheap and shoddy—hysterical and silly, always afraid of finding a worm in the corn—this drove Helen to play with angleworms and in the West to pick up snakes when she was riding and tie them onto the back of her saddle, where they would crawl underneath and make the horse rear. A great horsewoman—had had a Lesbian friend. —When her mother married again and had another child, Helen assisted at the birth, holding down her mother's legs. Had a beautiful sister who went into the movies and whose power of attracting men she envied—they had respected each other for opposite qualities. Now her sister was dead, and Helen, who had been so sickly, was still alive and healthy. It had upset her, but she seemed at the same time to have a sort of feeling of triumph. Helen had been neurotic—had made herself so lame at one time that she had to walk with a crutch—had studied medicine to fight herself and her mother. She had had a good time at medical school—for the first time, male admirers—they used to skip rope in the dissecting room with intestines and throw livers at one another—she couldn't eat meat all that time, though some of the students ate lunch on the cadavers—somebody threw one into the girls' dormitory and raised a lot of disturbance. —In Boston,

---

* Humphries (*b.* 1894), the poet and translator of Lorca, Ovid, and Vergil.

with her aunt who had helped her (but had never given her any money, because Helen would never ask), they were always just outside society, though they always wanted to be in—a hateful state of things—Boston all social climbing.

Her story about the woman with a retroverted uterus and hemorrhagic condition of eye that appeared during her menstrual period and seemed to be due to it—if Helen had examined her at *clinic*, she would never have found out what was wrong with her, but giving her a thorough examination as a private patient, she discovered that one of her lungs was almost gone and that the condition in her eye had nothing to do with her uterus.

Roosevelt is reported to have answered when someone had said to him that he would either be the best President the country had ever had or the most hated: No— that he would either be the most popular or the last. —Perhaps his sailing trip and his message to London referring to stabilizing the dollar had upset him, as he took to his bed while the industrial codes were first being debated (July 1933). Soon afterwards he went for a rest to Krum Elbow (his son at the same time was getting divorced and married again). —Hearst's propaganda in the films—typical Americans listening to his radio talk and saying, "Well, we've certainly put the right man in the right place." —Bronson Cutting was said not to like Louis Howe's humorous radio talks.

—Showdown between government and U.S. Steel.

Provincetown (I was staying in Susan Glaspell's house, with Rosalind and her nurse Stella). *A down summer*— people sick, away, insulting each other—somebody new at one of the L'Engles' parties had just behaved badly about cutting in on Henka Farnsworth—she had said:

"You can have the next dance," and he had then gone over and put a new record on the phonograph—the man she had been dancing with called him outside, and said, "I think you're a son of a bitch," and knocked him down three times—post-mortem afterwards among the combatants and the guests, thoroughly disagreeable.

Chauncey Hackett on the New Deal. He thought they were going on a fallacious theory—couldn't hope to restore the conditions of the Boom, trying to do too much— You and I and the policeman could make an old suit of clothes do for two or three more years. —He wanted the working man to have better conditions of living, but —It soon dawned on me that he and Bubs were living on some little investments which the National Recovery Administration (NRA) was threatening. —He thought it would be much better if all the small companies were put out of business and the big concerns ran the whole of industry. —He took a couple of hard-boiled eggs in a saucepan, an opened can of tomato soup, and a glass of tomato juice out on the back steps and, sitting down, began to eat them. He said they were going to a picnic— I said something which indicated I was wondering why in that case he was eating the eggs, etc.—he replied that he had gotten mad and decided he wouldn't go, but had now changed his mind, but that nevertheless he was hungry and thought he would eat now anyway.

*Joe Freeman and Diego Rivera:** the Communist character.* Joe had evidently convinced himself that he

---

* Freeman (1897–1965), widely read Marxist critic, at this time was commenting on the murals (later destroyed, in Rockefeller Center, New York) by Diego Rivera (1886–1957), the revolutionary Mexican painter who included the face of Lenin in his design. Rivera was at odds with the Communists because of his espousal of Trotsky.

had seen the mangoes and grapes substituted for the worker and peasant in the arms of the figure of Mexico. It is not that the Communist is deliberately unscrupulous about falsifying the truth, but that in a case like this he is honestly convinced that nobody could act except in such a way as to bear out the Communist presuppositions—hence the Communist expelled from the party *must* deteriorate—Judge Horton *must* want the Scottsboro boys lynched. —*The Jew lends himself easily to Communism* because it enables him to devote himself to a high cause, involving all of humanity, characteristics which are natural to him as a Jew—he is already secretive, half alien, a member of an opposition, a member of a minority, at cross purposes with the community he lives in. —The (middle-class) radical must be all those things, he must perhaps lack abnormally (like Rousseau) the kind of sense of solidarity with one's social group which makes the ordinary person defend the interests of his group against humane considerations (toward people outside it) and reason—the radical lacks this kind of human relationship: he can only identify his interests with those of an outlawed minority—sometimes not in any immediate way (like Trotsky) even with these: his human solidarity lies only in his imagination of general human improvement—a motive force, however, the strength of which cannot be overestimated—what he loses in immediate human relationships is compensated by his ability to see beyond them and the persons with whom one has them: one's family and one's neighbors— he can see who and what they are in the larger scheme of life. He is always a foreigner like the Jew who has the foreigner's advantage of being able to see things objectively.

The Jews have the sense of the revolt of the industrial workers in the cities—they have no sense of the American revolutionary tradition created by our farmers—don't know how to talk to people along these lines.

K. Brown round sunburned legs with big thighs and little stubby toes coming out from under brown skirt and burnt-orange jersey (given her by polo player). She said that by the time she left she would know all the things on the top of the bookcase. When I had made her come by manipulating her clitoris and sucking her breast and then twitched my organ against her, she said, "That's the most remarkable gadget—it does everything but have a conversation! —Don't wag it at me—I feel it's reproachful." I had a perpetual erection—drove back in the taxi half asleep, with prick standing straight up. —Her determination, backed by mine, to get rid of other people so we could be together. —Later: black hair and eyes, which, narrowed, looked almost Spanish against skin which now looked white under the electric lamp—"pastimes," "toying." When I woke her up, she was naked under the covers—my knocking had been met by a formidable snore—all opulent, flushed and browned and hot with the sun and sleeping—ready to come over right away—reluctant to withdraw.

Coming into my room after my having scolded her: "I'm furious with you, but I'm coming here partly out of habit and partly because I want to be a good hostess."

(Confusion all through here is due to the fact that Henri and Louise were staying in Topsfield and I in Provincetown, and we visited back and forth. At one point, they visited the Darlingtons somewhere else on the Cape.)

Henrietta, cross-examined by Rosalind about whether she was a contralto or what, replied that she was a female impersonator—which amused Louise. Henri and she went to women's parties and tried to interest themselves in the things that the women were interested in, etc. —My resolution every time they visited me, not to spend so much money on them, not to provide them with so much drink, etc.—a resolution always defeated.

Louise's arrest—the cop who was holding them up in order to be bought off—cleared in court when they found out she was a lady—had been peeing behind car, then weaving from one side of the road to the other. —Mrs. Costello, who was supposed to have poisoned her husband—a popular heroine—we went past the courthouse—the kiss-and-tell cop—she wouldn't leave him alone in the hospital. —Louise had a fur boa and a large hat suggestive of the courtroom scene in *Deep Purple* or *Within the Law*.

Topsfield, Mass. Mrs. Smith, the kleptomaniac [from whom they had rented the Topsfield house for the summer], with the Airedale on a thick rope. She insisted on our walking down the stream through the water—wanted me to dive. Had told Louise that she had reproved Petie for swearing and that another thing was that she thought he played with himself—beautiful cardinal flowers against the green of the banks—Mrs. Smith said, "Why didn't you pull them up and bring them over here?" It seemed that she had planted them herself and that they had then gotten over on somebody else's side—cute boy lying on his stomach on the diving board and spitting into the pool—turtlehead, goldenrod, little Michaelmas daisies growing a lot on a stalk and a few little tiny white orchids—bullfrogs, a fish jumped occasionally—a tree covered with little hard rose-colored crab apples—the ground there was low, seemed to rise all around—full moon with big corona around it at night, when we lay out of doors in the black and gray steamer rug—in the early morning, darkness and mist—Massachusetts, low ground, fruit trees, darkish hedges and woods—big dairy farms—like England—the Fenway with people riding along the bridle path and little lakes and wooded walks, something like Kensington Gardens—what fun we had riding up from Boston at leisure on Labor Day—lunch and Sunday funnies at place where inner tube blew out while we were sitting inside at the restaurant—yellow and white New England buildings standing up on their grounds, very stiff, handsome, and compact—hotels, houses, town halls—old men and women in Boston, grouchy about giving information at information window in station—fresh-water lakes on the Cape, blue and roughened (ruffled) by the wind—when you first see the dunes, low, barren, and white, strange after the dark Massachusetts verdure—the old station at Salem, like England: simply a train shed like a tunnel with an iron fence through the middle and posters on either side and two old smoke-stained wooden waiting rooms— yacht club at Hyannis—big ugly wooden tintless toneless houses of the rich at Gloucester, too big for the grounds, too close together, above the great gray rocks where the waves came in with thunder and breaking spray—"No Parking."

—The morning after her arrest, Louise lost her lunch in the restaurant on her way from the table to the ladies' room—an old man opened the door and when she asked him what he wanted, said, "Sawdust, lady." —Louise and Henri's drinking vocabulary: "whisker" for whiskey—"swigging."

—Warm dry air of moonlit night at Provincetown, after a day of rain.

—[Topsfield] Spookiness of little outhouse at night— triple hole in gable, which made three round spots of moonlight in the wall above the bed, a triple eye which Mrs. Smith developed at night?

—When we were having a conference at Provincetown on whether Rosalind and I should go back to Topsfield with them or not, Petie burst in and said: "You're not thinking but drinking!" —I kept calling him "Jimmy"— Louise, watching him in the kayak, said, "I think he's a very beautiful little boy." —She had so much nerve but was always afraid that people were going to ride her out of town on a rail, etc. —Stella: "Bobby, are you looking for your mistress?"

—Pete Connor still looked back with satisfaction to his life as an officer on the border—when they went out for a walk, would take the greatest pleasure in saying, "Squads right!—Squads left!"—said that if he had her as one of his creatures in the army, he would make her behave herself.

—Louise would almost instantly get up and leave when anybody like Robles or the Walkers came in—got up from table and left peaches.

—Jay would say to Frank Darlington [her husband]: "Don't bother your pretty head about it."

—Row with Fräulein—sent her back to Chicago. Fräulein admired the big Crane house on its hill, with its forest around it and its high iron fence and gatekeeper's lodge, and used to sit on the beach and look up at it— it reminded her of a German castle.

—Henri dancing the rumba with her scarf in the front room at Provincetown, while Louise and I clapped hands and hummed it—then she was suddenly seized by the idea that people, if they saw them, would think they were fast girls, and we stopped, laughing furiously. —Henri riding in the car with my newly pressed pants around her neck. —Her placid friendly unfemininely unresponsive gaze—"female impersonator."

—Henri: "Grandfather Cleary danced the day before he died, more shame to him!"

—Drank whiskey and got so I didn't mind it so much—

she said she minded it more. —After they were gone, went to bed and sank into stupor, from which I woke up to nervous depression.

—I got a definite impression in Louise of the race attempting to improve itself—the grandfather of whom they never spoke, father who "intellectually and socially," said Louise, deserved to have amounted to more than he did, Louise marrying Pete Connor, with his family's high idea of themselves—she thought she'd try to have another child—happy and quiet when she was having them, not restless—John Amen had been in Chicago before Sissy was born, and had thought, she said, that she was fascinating.

—Her rudeness to the Provincetown people. —Said, "Phyllis Duganne is plenty cheap, isn't she?"

—John [when at Harvard Law School] had insisted on staying at their family's apartment all night when nobody but Indian Annie was there—unfortunately Indian Annie came in while he was in the bathroom, so that he was trapped there for some time. She had had her first orgasm that night and burst into tears, and John had cried, too.

—Are you aware the cats have got no tails in the Isle of Man?

All the other cats have tails,
England, Ireland, Scotland, Wales,
Seems a gross injustice, to right it is our plan!
Are you aware the cats have got no tails in the Isle of Man?
Shut the door, they're coming through the window,
Shut the window, they're coming through the floor.
Shut the door, they're coming through the window.
Good God! They're coming through the floor.

An Englishman had *made* Henri's trip (to Bermuda?) and teaches her this song on the boat.

Hacketts. Chauncey had made biscuits out of the whiskey mash—Niles [Spencer's] story about making beer and putting too much of everything into it after putting too little of everything into it the first time—bottles blew up so that glass was even embedded in the ceiling—gave them to ashman to cart off, and they blew up, and the man thought that Niles had tried to kill him (might be attributed to a character). —Children's drawings pinned up in kitchen, with a few by Chauncey which, though less crude, were almost equally child-like. —We sat in beach chairs on little dock out back. The canvas of one of them broke, letting me down on the floor, and Rosalind's was broken and folded up on her. When we told Bubs about this, she said, as if it was totally unexpected and she had to look for a reason, "Well, that's because we leave them out in the rain, and I'm afraid they got in bad condition." —Little children still *farouches*—I asked the boy if he'd like to try the kayak some day, and he answered gruffly, "No!" —Muffy [their little dog] must have missed many a meal, because his temper was rather snappy and peevish—they had gotten him—I suppose when they were married at the Dogs' Friendly Society in Washington.

Louise. Little girl upset by having everybody she knew go away—sister [Henri] horribly down and cheerless when Louise was away—Turtle Woman: "I want to get out of here!" —Caroline would pretend to eat, then spit out food on plate, think it was a great joke—all Louise's most volatile qualities, Louise said Caroline would probably be crazy when I told her this, but thought Caroline fascinating—when Caroline was delighting herself at the table, nodding her head and saying, "Gunk!"—which was soon taken up by the boy (who was older), Louise would be so much amused that she wouldn't think for

some time to correct her. Caroline terribly frightened
by going out in car in thunderstorm—and always made
awful fuss after Louise came back, when she started to
go out of the house, for fear she'd get into a storm—
"Oh, aeroplane! Oh, choochoo train!"—she seemed to be
able to carry a tune, unlike the boy and his father. When
we took our walk in the rain, Louise said that Pete
couldn't stand a drop of rain, afraid it would spoil his
clothes. —"Got another papa on the Salt Lake line"—that
meant they were both going to have the same father,
didn't it?

The Hoover Medicine Ball Cabinet. He hated the
medicine ball, would get up with hangover, hardly able
to find his shoes, and have to go out to the gymnasium—
but there were always so many that you could easily drop
out. —Would look out of window at hotel and see his
dollars going away. Ferryboats on Lake Michigan, in
which he had invested, not running. —Head of Con-
struction Program—laid cornerstone and made a pompous
speech and then discovered he had lipstick all over his
face.

New England. Waking up early in September to
changeable day, with a little rain in the morning and
dark clouds which passed away in the early afternoon,
but brightness and clearness, the first delicious cool air
of fall, still warm enough to lie in the woods in the sun—
a little grass-green snake—the couple in the car—"much
too good for the common people"—waking up and seeing, framed in the white wall, under a green shade with
a blue glass ring hanging from the string and between
white curtains: the stalks of the elms with their branches
and little green leaves so clear and astir with the wind
against the sky, already animated but not yet made bleak

and wild with autumn, small white clouds moving through the blue. —The white churches, white house, deliciously newly white like icing on orange cake—white barns of big dairy farms with distinguished copper weathercocks. —The moon, one night white, another the red harvest moon, another gibbous, another concave and waning and a paler yellow—the stars clear and small as I came back; the night, though inside the house it seemed rather chill, outside seemed rather mild—mists gathering in the sunken meadows—dogs that sounded formidable barking and baying from the dark places— the sounds of streams you couldn't see, beside the road. —All seemed very strange, furtive, underground (going into Lawrence again in summer after my visit of two winters before), exciting and deeply satisfactory.

General freeing and relief of fall, summer's solidity and muteness dissolved at last in wind and cold air— the clouds moving fast in the sky, the trees all alive—and a clear flowing light that breaks up the steady summer sun—bush with aspenlike leaves turned over by the wind and sparkling silver white—almost like sunlight on water, the Provincetown harbor—against the background of white and blue fall sky, now getting windy and wild— while we were having lunch at the restaurant.

K. Burrs from my trousers that I put on her nightgown and the prickles of which got into her skin. —"I think I really like you better than 'most anybody." —She cried when I went, but kept saying I'd think she didn't like me if she didn't get up and take me home. —Her good-humored happy face; and her face at the other extreme, which gets a somewhat narrow self-concentrated expression. Her dirty ears of the afternoon, which she said was soap. Tremors and jitters when I first came; but, "I told you I'd soon get into the swing of the thing . . .

What did you say: that I seemed to respond and enjoy it? But it all seems to me so perfectly simple." Devices used to trap her by girlfriends: they would say that they thought it was a shame to lead a man on and then not sleep with him. But one girl had caused a shock by saying, "Well, I want to tell you I've been sleeping with your husband for months!" The wife had replied, "Well, Janet, it's all right to say that to me, but I wouldn't go around saying that sort of thing to everybody, because you might get into trouble." —When, after my withdrawing, the emission seemed to be all over everything, she said, "I never saw anything so widespread." When she was laughing in bed, her black eyes seemed charmingly a little cockeyed. Her interest in the M.s, with whom I had dined: what did they have for dinner?—when I told her about their Sunday supper of scraps, which sounded like a good deal, because it involved the remnants of so many dishes, she remarked, after some other conversation had taken place: "I think the M.s overeat." Listening for the maid to get back to bed, turning off the light: "Heavens! Murder! If you listen for footsteps in this house, you can always hear them." When I knocked wood about something on the sloping ceiling, she said, "Mrs. Smith may say, 'Come in!'" Her combination of delighted boldness and terror of public opinion. She said that she thought that her father had probably been such a villain himself that he suspected the worst of everybody else. Her cleft recessive Irish chin, almost always cute, though sometimes weak. When I spoke of women who had to be undressed, she said, "That seems to me so silly!" "I must go into the house. Get up!—from your bed of lust."

"I'm used to a life of ease and luxury." It was enough for most men just to be with a woman—she was not used to having to work. "Honeybunch sweetspot" (used jokingly). She and her husband used to indulge in a few mild preliminaries, but had never engaged in any of these pastimes. —Hoover's medicine ball cabinet— thought he was such a sap—lectures on the lack of morality of the younger generation, which she would cut short. —He thought it was all kind of obscene— and when you got started off on the wrong foot with anybody, you never could do anything about it—it was nothing you could do anything about by talking about it. —"You've never said anything about my skin." I told her that I had: I had said, "You've got beautiful white skin, haven't you?" and she had said, assenting, "Um-hum." —When, in the frustrated sensitive state following withdrawal, I began to sigh and whine, she rebuked me, after a moment's surprised silence, "Well, *nobody* ought to go on like that!"

Hacketts. Bubs had gone off for several days to draw when Sister came [Was this Mary Hackett's mother, Ann Moffett, who was a friend of Mary Blair, or Chauncey's daughter by his first wife?]—Sister had some-how (by sudden trick of her mother?) been shipped off to Chicago Exposition—Langston [Moffett] and Chauncey had driven her down to Boston, Chauncey dressed in old paint-bedaubed coat and sneakers—he went to see his respectable lawyer brother. Finally Chauncey had said, Well, he guessed he better be going along, and brother said, "Yes, it's a good thing to keep exercising." —Chauncey couldn't find a place to put electric light in so that they could have light in front room, had at first been in favor of not going in there at all because there was no light—got quite irritated trying to put it in under desk when it really went in up high in the wall—when Bubs showed him, he said, "But you said it was under the desk!" "Yes, I did, but I shouldn't have." In the course of getting it in, the leg of the desk came off. Chauncey was annoyed, and said, though amiably, that he had tried to get the house in order—he wanted to feel that the era was past when people could say that when Bubs asked where her pocketbook was, Chauncey would say, "I think it's in the refrigerator."—Bubs was fascinated by my card tricks, wanted me to do them again and again and kept exclaiming in amazement that it looked so easy. You couldn't see my fingers move at all!—I did it so quickly!

Provincetown (mid-September). Quacking and squeaking cackle of gulls out on water (of harbor), almost like cicadas, but less regular and more agitated.

Provincetown. First day of fall, mid-September, rather pleasant and wet nights but mild, and the town, deserted, takes on a new dignity and peace. —But then a storm: fine rain soaking down all day from a uniform blotting-paper sky—a few fishermen in black oilskins, sloshing around in the streets.

Bubs Hackett and Adelaide Walker went to school together at the Girls Collegiate School in Los Angeles, and they used to have long arguments—had to march into schoolroom every morning and recite the salute to the flag: "I salute the flag and the Republic for which it stands—one and indivisible, with justice and liberty for all." Then they would sing hymns. One day they put toilet paper in the piano so that when the teacher sat down to play it, it didn't make a sound. They got into trouble for this and other things.

Mary [Heaton] *Vorse*. Got back and found the family in a terrible way—Ellen out in Truro apparently living

with somebody in a shack—the children had had the
garage repaired and had moved out under a tree and
left there an old trunk of Mary's which contained a
couple of basques and some petticoats and embroidered
pillow slips belonging to Mary's mother (she and her
brothers had had a certain amount of sentiment and had
burned most of her things, not wanting to have them
worn by scrubwomen—and she had only saved these few
things which were associated with the latter part of her
mother's life)—Mary's wedding shoes, an old garment
with just a spare hole to put your head through that
Joe O'Brien [Mary Vorse's husband] had given her and
an old velvet thing called "the ahssless," because she
had sat the bottom out of it writing, worthless but she
was attached to it. Mary was so furious that she burst
into tears. —The children played bridge all the time.
Ellen was getting thinner, went round in old fisherman's
pants and seemed to have lost her color. —Mary just
back from Germany, etc. —Moscow, where she had been
enthusiastically received by Fred Beal and all the other
people with whom she had taken part in strikes. Her
troubles with her children kept getting mixed in with
her reports on international affairs.

Anna. When I came back from Provincetown, in the
middle of September 1933, she told me that their place
was full of drunks, some of whom were living there,
others of whom were allowed to sleep anywhere. Anna
could put her cot anywhere she could find a place. The
beds made her sick, the drunks vomited and made water
on them. Jane accused Anna and her mother of doing
business with the guests—gin 35¢ a pint.
Lizzie had come back half-unconscious from a fall
which had hurt the whole side of her face, then had
sores in her mouth. Her sister's husband had had her

sister fall downstairs when she was carrying a baby, with the idea of suing and getting $10,000 and the house, but all he got was to get put out. They had had their food ticket taken away from them because Johnny had a small job—and they had squealed on the superintendent, who was getting the food ticket, and he had had them put out.

Anna looked very thin—pale and sweet. —Was not going to see her sister and her family any more; because she felt so sorry for them she would give them her money.

The NRA.* Mrs. Wagner had told her she thought she could get her a job dressmaking where she worked, but as the NRA insisted that the employer pay $15, which he couldn't afford, she would have to give $5 every week to a Mr. Green, who would pass it back to the employer.

"I'm more tired of life than ever!"

Her mother, so strong at fifty, would live to be a hundred. Anna used to have fainting spells when she was a girl, and her mother had paid no attention, just let her lie there. She thought she and her sister were so sickly and imperfect because their mother had done her best to do away with them before they were born (she said that again and again to me). "My father has been [was] sick since he was over here." She had almost died having Lizzie, and she was sure that her mother, if she'd been with her alone, would never have gotten a doctor and nurse or done anything for her. Her mother was cantankerous nowadays because she had no job. Anna had seen a sign outside a silk factory, saying "Help

* Roosevelt's National Industrial Recovery Act, designed to regulate industry through a series of codes, declared unconstitutional by the Supreme Court in 1935. See "Glimpses of the New Deal" in *Earthquake*, pp. 551 ff.

wanted," and it hadn't said anything about experienced help, so she thought she might try it, would take anything so she could learn—but the silk strikes were on now. —A neighbor had insulted her, threatened to have Lizzie taken away from her—she wouldn't take money from a lodger who wanted to pay for her fixing his room.

Raymond Holden entertaining as I had never known him—anecdote about calling on daughter of Rockefeller's pastor at Rockefeller's house—he had been rewriting her pageant for *McCall's*—taxi was stopped every few feet by guards—taxi driver said, "It's always like this," and, "You'd better take my card, you may have trouble getting away"—entrance and steps like the Pennsylvania Station—the old man [John D. Rockefeller] came down the steps with ear muffs and a nose like an oil can with pastor's daughter—she really wanted to write stories, but the tragedy of her life had been that she had gotten a reputation as a pageant writer, having written one years ago for Rockefeller's church. —On the table, Swift's poems in a limited Aldine edition, books on Napoleon and Marie Antoinette in French, side by side with *Motion Picture* magazine, *Woman's Home Companion*, etc. The interior had really displayed taste—had gotten an interior decorator to do it for them—eighteenth-century furniture. Swanky new picture of John D., Jr., and, right next to it, old framed photographs of relatives who were dead ringers for sheep. —He asked her how she liked Mr. Rockefeller, and she said that he was a lovely old man, but her father had never been willing to take anything from him, though he had offered him $1,000 once for his church, because he wanted to be free to say anything he pleased, and she was the same way, though she came up there every year to visit him. He asked her how she liked it, and she told him that if she went a hundred yards from the house, a man with a gun would pop up from behind a bush and she would have to call the housekeeper to certify that she was a guest at the house. —Rockefeller at this time was ninety-four and was reputed to be kept alive by a diet of mother's milk. She said that they played one game of Numero every day and that he greatly enjoyed calling out the numbers. —The Golden Rule Foundation owed her $15 and he strongly advised her to go after them and get it back, he took a great interest in this—after Numero, he would play eighteen holes of golf; he rested a good deal, took great care of himself. —He offered Raymond nothing, not even a cigarette, and when Raymond wanted to go, he didn't offer to call the car to take him to the station. The pastor's daughter said she'd call a taxi. She inspected a row of buttons which said, Valet, Maid, Housekeeper, etc., and finally pressed one marked Service—"I wonder which button I ought to press." Nothing happened, and after a passage of conversation, she pressed it again. Nothing happened, and after another talk, she tried the button marked Housekeeper, and the Housekeeper phoned for a taxi. In reply to Raymond's criticism of the pageant, she had explained that you don't paraphrase the Bible because the ministers objected, and in reply to another of his suggestions, she said, "I see you don't understand conference work."

The Hulings [Betty's family]. Raymond on a visit— coat of iridescent oil on water and under it, "rising to the surface as best they could," worms called blood-suckers—near dump where they were burning rubbish. Mr. Huling, with his high hysterical voice, had just come back from the Cape and unloaded a great cargo of Jolly Jack windmills and all the other things they sell up there. Betty was quite different at home, fighting the family for her liberty, said she had put her foot down about drinks, but answered when her mother asked what they had there that it was ginger ale, but stumbled and spilled some, which her father smelled and said, "That smells very much like gin. That I should have a daughter who's a gin drinker!" Raymond thought he was in a rage, but then he seemed to forget all about it. His fussing over dinner: the family never on time! though they were all right there—but then he disappeared himself when the rest of them were waiting to go in. They quarreled all through dinner—Frances wanted the car: "Oh, all right then! We won't use the car!" —Mr. Huling said in passing somebody on the road who was obviously Jewish: "He looks as if he might be Jewish." Betty: "I don't think he can be because he belongs to the ——— Club and they don't admit any Jews—now at the ——— Club. But then everybody turned out to be Jewish." In the evening, Raymond had met Mrs. Huling snooping in the kitchen in her kimono. —Betty paying for Bud Kussell's meals—when Bud finally got some money, he paid his brother back several hundred but didn't give Betty a cent.

Pennsylvania milk situation. [A man named Moffett was running the strike.]—Moffett's eyes as contrasted with eyes of Norton and other farmers upstate. [He was one of the leaders in the milk strike. I had gone out there to write about it for *The New Republic*, but due to an intervention on the part of the Elmhirsts,* who must have said I was getting too radical, Bruce Bliven

---

* Leonard Elmhirst was the English husband of Dorothy Straight. The Straight family had for some time been financial backers of *The New Republic*, which was now being edited by Bruce Bliven. On the later politics of the journal, see *A Piece of My Mind*, pp. 41–8.

refused to publish my article and it came out in *Common Sense.* *]

—Pretty and self-possessed little girl, who said they had everything that rich children had: school and a pony: wife who was going to garden party, tea, meeting of women's Republican Club, etc.

—Lawyer, son of jail warden, and young wife from Harrisburg—joke about woman going to jail: "I've got to have my Kotex in the morning." "You'll eat cat meal!" His Pittsburgh way of talking; he didn't move his face in talking, only opened his mouth. Husband had a hard time getting them to get meals—much merriment about this—beautiful weather. The women were sitting out in the sun in deck chairs when we got back.

—Well-to-do veterinarian whose house we spent the night at and whose daughter had just been married. Family coat of arms on stairs, four-poster bed.

Francis Biddle† [who was acting as attorney for the strikers]. Complimented me on Proust–Gertrude Stein [articles] when I saw him on my Pennsylvania trip. We later had lunch in New York at the Coffee House. Old Royal Cortissoz [art critic of the *Tribune*] was there, pretty gray, and with shocked indignation told a story about a young sculptor, a monument cutter from Kansas, who found Rodin doing something fancy with his model,

---

* EW's vigorous article "The Milk Interests Write the Milk Code" appeared in *Common Sense* II, pp. 8–11 (December 1933). Apparently, Bruce Bliven did not reject the article outright, as EW suggests, for it appeared in a toned-down version in *The New Republic* 76, pp. 122–5 (September 13, 1933), entitled "The Milk Strike." EW, we may assume, published the original version in *Common Sense* to demonstrate how he had been edited.

† Francis Biddle (1886–1968), F.D.R.'s Attorney General and a judge at the Nuremberg trials.

whereupon he took off his blouse and threw it down and went back to the States, where he became a much-respected instructor at Carnegie Institute in Pittsburgh. Cortissoz ended by saying that Rodin's friends during his later days had had to spend all their time keeping him out of trouble. "What do you mean?" "For unnatural performances." The English actors Philip Merivale and Ernest Lawford took the affair less seriously: "It must have been upsetting to come in and find the *cher maître* upside down." "Just so they don't do it in the streets and frighten the horses." Biddle entered into the spirit of the conversation by telling about the privately circulated number of *Assiette Beurre** (of which he said he had the complete series) [directed against the Germans at the time of the Eulenburg† scandal], and with a picture of two men at a table, one trying to convince the other of "his philosophy of life," and saying, *"Platon l'était— Aristotle aussi,"* Biddle's fruity and refined Philadelphian voice. The milk distributors, he said, were running a fine class. The rich people I could see were glad to have those well-to-do native farmers around. What they were trying to do, I learned, had back of it the socially and economically most influential people.

Lunch at the Colony Club with Mrs. Gifford Pinchot, Oct. 5, '33 [Gifford Pinchot was then governor of Pennsylvania]. She had said to some woman that they had it in common that they had both dyed their hair red. She had asked Moffett over the phone, what about this charge that he had been fired by the Chamber of Com-

---

* An illustrated weekly founded in Paris in 1901 and dedicated to satire, but violently Anglophobe and anti-clerical.

† Eulenburg und Hertefeld, Philipp, Prinz zu (1847–1921), diplomat, adviser and friend of Kaiser Wilhelm II, was attacked in the press in 1906 and accused of homosexuality.

merce for dishonesty. He said that he supposed it came
from the same source as the story that she had been
found drunk in a taxi. She had laughed. (Moffett had
pointed out to me that the Pinchots were millionaires—
where did they get off talking about malefactors of great
wealth? Moffett thought she pushed him—he said he
would rather fish. Pinchot's fragmentary roads—political
debts—only went as far as the country club—five privately
owned toll bridges on the river.)

She didn't know whether Franklin Roosevelt was quite
right in his head—she and Gifford had gone to Hyde
Park, and Roosevelt had talked very earnestly about the
coal situation—Gifford said something about getting
Moses to sign. Roosevelt said, "But he *has* signed." Gifford made him call up Richberg at Washington to make
sure. Roosevelt asked whether the Frick Company had
signed and apparently got affirmative answers—then Gifford took the phone and asked whether he had agreed to
the check-off, collective bargaining, etc., and got negative
answers. (Were they trying to make Roosevelt sign under
false pretenses?—getting it to him late at night? Bruce
Bliven thought the explanation was probably that Johnson and Donald Richberg* were on the verge of collapse,
gaga.) Roosevelt sat there without changing his expression or making any comment. "The house is burning
down, the house is not burning down, don't you know?—
If somebody says there's going to be rice pudding for
dessert, and then they bring in baked apple, you expect
them at least to say, 'Oh, I thought it was going to be rice
pudding,' don't you know? like something in *Alice in
Wonderland*." The wages and hours were also bad, and
it had to be sent back as unacceptable. —The Burgess of
Apollo had tried to prevent her from speaking, and they

* General Hugh S. Johnson and Richberg were running the
NRA for President Roosevelt. See *Earthquake*, pp. 553 ff.

had immediately afterwards tried to bankrupt the man who had rented the hall—but it had turned out to be the most successful meeting of all. —Pinchot's newsreel: "These swine," but they had cut that out—The miners have done everything I have asked them to, and they deserve your sympathy and respect. Picture of man beaten up by deputies and arrest of the deputies, with the announcement they were now in jail. —She had flown to Apollo in a plane—she and Pinchot were learning to drive one. —Apropos of General Johnson, soldiers in politics were always timid. —Her bias against the Administration—she pointed out the indications, such as Johnson's speech, that the NRA was losing ground, and a reaction against it setting in. This bias was perhaps due to political ambitions for herself and Pinchot, and it may be that she counted on a Republican opposition to call the Roosevelt Administration to account or even a more radical, instead of a more conservative, reaction against it, which would put Pinchot in line for the Presidency. She talked a lot, obviously full of it, wanted to keep on talking. I liked her. She thought that enough emphasis hadn't been put on the fact that an economic revolution had occurred, that it used to be that people had to work hard to provide as much goods as they needed, whereas now there was enough for everybody produced with comparative ease, and the question was simply to get it distributed—why should so many people be getting a cut out of the distributing end? —If it could only be arranged so that, etc. I said I didn't think those problems could be solved except through socialism, impossible under the present system—which left her silent a moment and without a direct reply.

Leit Dahl [the Communist in the Pennsylvania milk strike] just out of Columbia, with pretty little wife who had been ill. She sat in front of the typewriter and oc-

casionally supplied some information—he would refer to
her data occasionally. She had just been in the hospital,
he was going to find a farm for her to stay on. He had
the sterile Communist sneer that he had perhaps learned
from Earl Browder and that would curl one side of his
mouth when talking about Moffett and other "milk
fakers"; but his face, in spite of its thinness, grayness,
and wear from his Communist work, was sensitive,
readily becoming gentle and with a charm in his smile
of youth. When I faced him down about his denuncia-
tions of Moffett in his pamphlet (bracketing him with
Allebach) for crimes he hadn't yet committed, he admitted that they had perhaps made mistakes—the ideas
in the pamphlet weren't his own, were what they had
agreed upon. "Don't forget the mass demonstrations
started it all!" John Strachey's *Menace of Fascism* and
other books packed in his suitcase—he was going to
hitchhike to Chicago for the farmers' convention. —Bare-
ness of *Donald Henderson's* apartment—bed, dining-room
table, typewriter, chairs, no rugs, Lenin and Marx on
the table. When I said, "Don't underestimate Moffett's
abilities and character!" he replied, "We don't [criticize
people's characters—we simply see that Moffett does
certain things and gets money from certain sources]."*
I said, "You people get money from whatever sources
you can." "Yes: but [there are no strings tied to it]."
"You've described a careerist." "Some of the most valuable work in the world is done by careerists." "Yes: but
they have the revolutionary aim." The fact that it is a
young boy doing this and making all the mistakes—his
own not so bad as those who were giving him directions.
His way of saying, "I have seen this," instead of, "That's

---

* EW's note: "Brackets indicate paraphrases, not later addition."

something I've seen"—like Earl Browder—does it come from some foreign language, German or Russian?

Griffin Barry [he stayed in the 53rd St. house for a time]. Two things especially that drove me crazy—"good nourishment" over the pancakes and sausages; and Dora Russell was not like Bertrand: "Oh, no: she's lusty!" "Our old Hatty"—Hatty was not particularly old. His unctuous old woman's voice.

Coulton Waugh's story about how "complex" *Province-town* was. He had gone in late to the Kaselaus'—found violence impending—Charley was under the impression that Eben Given was about to take a crack at Langston— or Langston take a crack at Eben?—so he took Eben out and walked him along Commercial Street. Coulton came with his car with three other men in it, offering to pick up Eben and take him home, but Charley kept making incomprehensible gestures. It finally turned out that Charley thought the four of them were trying to get Eben and beat him up, and that Charley was trying to protect him. Once at the height of the evening, Eben had told Coulton to put back his head, and Eben had gotten a grip with one arm around his throat which strangled him— a grip that was so dirty that it was barred from professional wrestling—Coulton had to resort to poking his finger in Eben's eye, and Eben finally fell and cut his head against the corner of the sink. The next morning Elizabeth found every window in the kitchen broken. Last summer Langston was diving over chairs, and Coulton risking his neck trying to emulate him.

When I first came back to *New York* from Province-town after having been driving all day, first in the chill rain, then in the sweltering sun, arriving in a daze, the people in the streets looked like sinister specters—I was

almost afraid of them, looked askance at them uneasily as
if they might be going to bite or slug me.

Raymond Holden, investigating the finances of *the steel
companies* for the Bank of Manhattan, discovered that
labor was included under "sundries."

D. The cunning old-fashioned-girl way she had of
turning her head in toward my shoulder when I was going
to kiss her—and then, when she turned it away from me,
her crossed feet stretched out straight in front of her, she
looked like a little fourteen-year-old girl—her round eyes
and nose.

The thin girl at the party, who stuffed out her bosom
with toilet paper, which other girls, ashamed for her,
reeled out slowly and at length. One girl was low in her
mind and began to cry—people thought she had no husband, and she wasn't sure that she had.

D. Her frank pleasure in being kissed and praised.
"There's really not much to me, you know! I'm not really
very nice—I mean, physically—everything's just a little
wrong." Red blouse, tilted black hat made her look like
an old-fashioned American magazine-cover girl, only
sensually much more attractive. At the cocktail party, she
wore great big brass earrings, the kind of thing Griffin
Barry called "too much dingle-dangle"—very becoming,
though, to her Isoldesque, Guineveresque beauty.

She said that after several years in the shop, she was
"sucker-sour," like freaks in the circus.

"You like?" He [her husband] likes [her] better and
better all the time. He's really very fond of me." He was
against E.B. [?], he would bite him in the leg any time.
—The way she howled at *Let 'Em Eat Cake*—one of the
things I didn't like. —Putting her cheek against mine on

couch, showing how nice she could be after feeling, apparently, that she had been a little forbidding. Of her own capacity for love: "There's gold in them thar hills!" "I'm really meant for love." The handkerchief she gave me at Childs, with its perfume—she had perfume also on her notepaper: Matchabelli, which I misunderstood as Machiavelli and was mystified. As she was kneeling on the floor, looking through the phonograph records, she was very attractive: serious; mouth, as always, half open; attractive black high-heeled shoes, with gray stockings and [then in fashion] dark rectangular patch that came up at the heel behind. —Gorgeous red evening gown she wore to party, one loosely draped-looking shoulder strap, pink and gold, gold high-heeled sandal shoes, with bare feet and legs. —"Women like me grow on bushes." —Women were perishable—at that age, they thought about it—just the age of women in French novels. —Her little girl's voice: "You must be a good boy! . . . You'll get me all mussed! You mustn't get me all mussed!" —Pretty white starched ruff, with silver edge (worn with black dress), made by one of the best ruff-makers. —"Hey?"*

Strange after Margaret's death (November 18, 1933, at Red Bank) to find oneself back under the same bright light of the reading lamp, among the same fine books— same odors, colors, lights, comfort sitting at the little green card table—as if I were revisiting it from death myself—knew that I could not hope to stay, that it was no longer real for me.

Eisenstein and the Upton Sinclairs. They said he was absolutely crazy, indicated that he was homosexual with-

---

* The woman of these notes seems to be at least in part the "original" for Imogen Loomis, in EW's "The Princess with the Golden Hair" in *Memoirs of Hecate County*.

out mentioning it—Mrs. Sinclair said that people like that
were not dependable about money and other things—
I said I didn't think there was any reason why they
shouldn't be all right about money—she replied, "Read a
book on pathology! They're not, though!" Sinclair said
that in Hollywood Eisenstein had had fourteen of these
people around him, in Mexico twenty-seven! [He was
always proving a case by statistics.] Mrs. Sinclair's brother,
who liked women, didn't know what it was all about at
first, then when he realized was horrified. They thought
that Eisenstein had gone absolutely to pieces since his
return to Russia; he had gone down to the Ukraine and
hadn't been heard from since. They didn't know whether
they ought to tell people who asked what had happened to
Eisenstein, that he was—out of his head. He had been
trying to get contracts with South America and other
places, while in Mexico, without letting them know about
it. They had sent the film to Amkino, and Amkino or
somebody had stolen several hundred feet of it. The fairies
had come to Sinclair after Eisenstein had gone back,
demanding all sorts of things which they claimed Eisenstein had promised them: one said that Eisenstein had
promised him $20,000 (?) for his help, another that
Eisenstein had promised him to have his horse exhibited
in Paris. In New York a mysterious man had turned up
who was supposed to be a Russian molasses king but who
people told Sinclair was a bootlegger, and who wanted to
buy the film. Bogdanov said he had never heard of the
man, but Sinclair thought Bogdanov was back of it. Also,
the Mexican government had tried to get the film suppressed by sending somebody to induce Sinclair to show
it without the epilogue, in which case the agreement with
the Mexican government would be violated.*

* See "Eisenstein in Hollywood," *Earthquake*, pp. 397–413.
Sergei Eisenstein, the innovator in film, had come to Hollywood

Ben Stolberg* on Brookwood. Muste would take money which had been raised to get the furnace fixed and spend it on a trip to talk to five workers in Pennsylvania—just because Lenin used to go somewhere to talk to five workers, but whereas Lenin would talk to workers who were important, Muste would talk to workers who didn't amount to a damn. In the meantime, Saposs and the other people at Brookwood would be wanting their heat and getting sore.

Dawn Powell's knock-down-and-drag-out party. George Hartmann [who once lodged with the Gormans] (his hair now grizzled) found in the kitchen snuffing up the gas out of the range. [Carl] Van Doren's reappearance to get Jean—"Time to go home now!" He said to Jacques Leclerc that he was sorry he hadn't had a chance to talk to him and Leclerc had answered, "Yes, but you were talking so much tripe." Van Doren had gotten up, huffed, and said, "Well, goodbye!"

The Cantwells and the Fascists. George Davis used to come and call on them—others, too—one man inquired about apartment in building; another, who had reviewed Bob's novel and written for the *American Review*, questioned him about the movement. Finally they asked her to go to the Theater Union ball with a party. Bob didn't attend. When Betsy went to the designated house, she was presented to a Mr. Smith, whom she afterwards heard addressed as Mr. Apfelhofer or something of the

---

to direct movies, but could not fit into Hollywood ways. He had then gone to Mexico with the help of Upton Sinclair to make the film here discussed.

* b. 1891, left-wing writer on economics and member of the international board of inquiry into the case of Trotsky.

kind—but the Nazi boys couldn't restrain themselves from making dirty cracks about Communists—at Webster Hall, they kept her at the door and tried to pump her about the people who were coming in, which she countered in her flashing Southern-girl fashion—and then, inside, they kept on—and finally, when there was a question (the news of Nazis present having reached the Theater Union people) of photographing the Nazis, somebody tipped George Davis and Betsy over backwards in their chairs—Betsy left after this. —Absurdity of contributors to the *American Review* spying on Theater Union ball. —Reviewer for *American Review* who tried to rent my top floor—Nordic fairy face, high stiff white collar, reader for Macmillan.

Margaret. Dream (December 15, '33): I thought I was telling her about these dreams—but what was the catch? I asked myself when I had finished—there she was. I was talking to her—why should I have waked up and found that it was impossible?—why shouldn't we be together again?—struggled through the darkness of half wakefulness to realization of the truth.

—Dream of which my memory is vague: I happened to run into her in a hotel—why shouldn't we stay together —I was climbing red-carpeted stairs, going up and down in elevators, having trouble about getting the right key, trying to find the right room, the room we had taken together.

—I had gone back to a dream California of springtime, of brown fields and yellow flowers—I had never seen California in spring—was riding a sorrel horse along a narrow dirt road with dry ruts—hard, scared, self-acrid feeling I got in connection with her death beginning to grip me in its vise. I was going to see her mother again, who would be nice to me, pleasant to me, I would be pleasant. There was that lovely, free, and light California in which she had spent her girlhood, which I had never known and of which, all that she had carried of it with her, I, blackening life when she had been with me, sending her back to die, had deprived her. —One jaw of the tightened vise was sadistic—a dry fated sharp sickening feeling about myself was what it came to—self-contempt and self-assertion, grim insolent will to go on living and awful sickening of realizing what had happened. —Homosexual fantasies were a way of living in the grip of the vise, getting away into a different world where those values that pressed me did not function. K. was temporary relief with something gay, humane, hot—abundant, prodigal of life—from the acrid logical emotional vacuum in which I found I had landed myself. —I now, contrary to my old feeling, preferred working to not working—I could get nothing out of seeing other people that fed my fundamental lacks. Idle, I either brooded, going back over our life together and torturing myself, sometimes passing on myself with sickening insight the verdict of suicide (I attached myself strongly, in opposition to this, to the idea of sticking to Rosalind in order to see her through) or giving myself up to the fantasies. —Fear of having the window too far up, going out on the porch of Margaret Bourke-White's high studio in the Chrysler Building, the long steps down the entrance of the Eighth Avenue El and the escalator on the way out, till I got to where it is filled in between the moving rail and the well. [Because Margaret was killed by falling.]

Commonness of *garbage-can scavenging*—I saw somebody after food or old shoes or whatever in our garbage cans in East 53rd Street. Almost every time I went out on the street or looked out the window.

Story about *Communists in Detroit* rapidly pulling down house from which family had been repeatedly evicted.

Esther Strachey said that *Franklin Roosevelt* was a Phil Barry character—also, that his ideas about currency were evidently derived from *The American Boy's Handy Book*: all the things you can do with a dollar.

The lynchings—in Maryland, California, St. Louis, Oklahoma, Tennessee (Scottsboro), and San Jose, and Governor Rolph's statement in connection with the latter —at the same time, the Scottsboro boys being tried by the openly hostile Judge Callahan (Leibowitz and the other defense attorneys, who had asked to leave the court with their bodyguard before the session was adjourned) were singing, "Take me back to New York town!" at the station. —*General feeling of resentment, disappointment*, after the first lift and hope of the Roosevelt Administration, when conditions for many were not relieved and the winter was coming on. —Family quarreling, Christmas party impossible; people at *New Republic* hating each other—my quarrel with *The New Republic*, unpleasantness with Scott [Fitzgerald], etc.—beneath the surface, the tide was going out again. —Relationships, family situations, whose decline had seemed to be arrested, are now plainly getting worse: Louise and Raymond, Provincetown people. —Mary Vorse said that somebody from Washington had told her that any criticism, however casual, of the NRA was harshly razzed as in wartime.

Chauncey Hackett. In Washington, he had had a trick of falling over backwards just as he was putting out his hand on being introduced to some grand social lady—

his legs would go up in the air, he would roll back again to a cross-legged posture and rise up quickly again.

Ghostliness, dreariness, of night of Repeal [December 5, '33]. Not enough liquor, soon gave out—ghostliness of the Astor [hotel], police and locked doors, people locked inside, lobby and corridors deserted. Reubens [restaurant]: couldn't get in after I had checked my coat and hat, crowded with German Jews in opera hats, the type that frequents Reubens. I ended up at Childs on 59th Street, which was now serving wine—uninviting rather crasslooking people. Algonquin dining rooms had been dark and closed—late, 3 or 4 a.m. —Difficulty of getting drinks for several days.

D. After the trying experience of losing her child, which B. had had to break to her after having fainted when he heard the news himself, she had said to him: "We've been happy before and we'll be happy again!"—she thought she deserved some credit for that. She'd had a nurse who was mean to her—then had one who was all right.—

Anna. They had fish the day before Christmas—"baked and fried and boiled"—she was humorous in such a cunning way about the national customs and the habits of her family—they were supposed to fast "or something."

Girlfriend of Sam's in speakeasy where he took her—had on a fur coat and shoes and nothing else—would open the coat and show herself.

She wasn't well, hadn't had the energy to go out and get milk and fruit and vegetables. She had been eating pork steadily, which was what Fatty always got, and had been constipated for three days—yet she seemed very appetizing, cunning and pink, when I came back and

found her sitting up in bed eating the Roquefort cheese—
but when she had taken her clothes off and I began
sucking her nipple, which she ordinarily liked to have
me do, she said, "That don't feel good!" and made me
stop. She felt sick and didn't want to be loved—it was
nice in a way lying naked with her, touching her little
body and with my arm around her, resting in unsatisfied
desire—toward morning I asked her to do something
about me—she said, "What would happen if you didn't?"
I said, "I'd die." Finally she told me to do it the regular
way and afterwards said she felt better. She left in the
chilly morning, got dressed while I lay naked under the
bedclothes. She looked cute in her sealskin coat and her
black hat cocked over one ear. When I got up and walked
around naked, she said, "I wish I could go around without any clothes on like you and not mind it."

Vulgarity of the Poles: all they talked about was sex.
They'd talk about "doin' it two or three hours"—they'd
say, "What you need is a thing a foot and a half long."

Her mother had told somebody that Fatty hadn't
given her any loving since July 4th last—he had a girl he
paid $1.50, and he tells how she plays with him and does
everything. Her mother was now threatening to move
out and take an apartment with Anna again.

Christmas '33. I turned the balance of the Christmas
party by siding with the oppressed classes, Aunt Addie—
and, as a result, a very amicable evening with Uncle Win,
Aunt Addie, Rosalind, Mother, and myself. Uncle
Charley had gone to Esther's Christmas Eve and was
excluded as being too gloomy. Aunt Addie and Uncle
Win reminisced Eatontown characters and the Davises
("Bring on them eats!") [the Davises were vulgar people
who lived across the street from Aunt Addie]; Uncle
Win told the story he has always told about taking Will

Hurley up the Cape on the Fall River boat; asked him what he thought of it and he said: "Well, them that ain't never seen nothin' don't know nothin'!"

Uncle Win said that when he went to college, it was still true that you were ostracized if you went into business instead of medicine, law, or the church, but after he'd been hangin' around in New York two years, one day when Reuel was talking to one of the James White partners, he said that he understood that there was a prejudice against college men in business. "I haven't any prejudice against them," said the man. "I'd take one if I could get him." Reuel declared, "You've got one. I'm sending my brother down tomorrow."

Uncle Win was becoming imbued with Fascist ideas. First he complained about the cheap Jewish comedians on the radio—then said that somebody who had come back from Germany had been telling him, even before Hitler, that you couldn't get a job in a German university, you couldn't practice as a lawyer in Germany, unless you were a Jew. "We'll have trouble with 'em over here, too. Roosevelt's got a lot of Jews at Washington. We can't have them with their ideas." When I said that the persecution of the Jews by the Nazis was a terrible thing, he hedged: "Of course it is, but—" His point was that I had only seen the nice Jews—I didn't know the ones downtown. The Warburgs and the Schiffs were all right [they were among Reuel's patients and friends], but the others!" (He had once spoken to me sarcastically about "your friend Frankfurter.") Aunt Addie asked him what he thought of the state of the world—were dividends going to come back? He hoped so—he hoped that Roosevelt knew what he was doing, but three economists said that Roosevelt was right and all the rest said he was wrong. He deplored Scripps-Howard's attack on Douglas: "I think Douglas is one of the soundest men Roosevelt's got."

Uncle Win on Exeter: old man Wentworth got him up in class one day—he evidently still remembered with horror his shyness when obliged to recite in those big classes of fifty or sixty—and said, "Where are you going from here, Kimball?" "Princeton." "Boys (turning to the class), we've got to get Kimball into Princeton!—we've got to get him there!—the climate up here doesn't agree with him: it's too cold!—we've got to get him into Princeton right away!" —The story about Hibben coming into the Princeton Club, looking desperately worried about losing the track meet at Yale—they said, "Why don't you clean 'em out?"—he replied, "That's just what I'd like to do!" —About the time Uncle Win began refusing to go to the Hartshornes' for Christmas was about the time he began paying for Sandy's asylum expenses. —The story about Father's speaking at the meeting of protest at Princeton about professors' being sent to spy on students (one boy also revealed that he had been paid to spy)— Father made a speech counseling moderation, but they rusticated him for speaking at the meeting and the strike took place anyway. —George M. Cohan: never a dirty line—Fred Stone had said that George Cohan always put on clean plays and he didn't see him having any failures— this was funny because Cohan used to hang around the Hotel Metropole with the worst-looking bunch you ever saw in your life—and the characters in his plays were always people that were around: the race-track tout, etc. —Cohan was taking care of every broken-down actor in New York.

Aunt Addie's late sophistication: wisecracks learned from Tammany circles [by way of her daughter Adeline, who had married Joe Moran]: "Dorothy calls her bed her workbench." Talking of Aunt Laura's late marriage: "You'd think it was last call for dinner in the dining car." —She had attained through Dorothy and Adeline a new dignity [her daughters had married rich men], which made it possible for her to dispense with her attitude of humility toward the rest of the family. She was no longer a poor relation.

Anna. She slapped me on the bare stomach when I had my eyes shut, and it gave me a sudden nervous shudder. She said, "Can't take it, huh?—I used to do that with Sam and it would make-um so sore at me he'd forget he wan'ed it."

"So nervous—like when I'm here—I think I want to get home and I rush away right away." Her aunt who had had her ovaries out said that that was what it was—she'd been the same way before she was operated on.

"You don't know how low and common they [the Polish boarders] are!" Twice somebody had done his business and wrapped it up in a paper and put it behind the closet. That's their idea of a joke!

She came in in her red dress, looking somehow very fine, I thought—less cowed, more sense of her own dignity. I noticed it as she sat on the bed, smoking and leaning up against the wall, her legs showing attractively through the red skirt, as I had never seen her do—even her hair seemed more abundant somehow, more of a coiffure.

Gloom about Margaret—vivid fantasies about Ted—spell of inertia—more satisfactory relations with Anna, yet Ted getting into it.

Muriel Draper, coming back from Taos. She said she had been full of health, but looked tarnished and stale, having been out till seven that morning—hardly a sign of the little 1890 Whistler girl with the blond English bang. —She said that Tony Luhan would stretch his legs out and go to sleep in his chair after dinner; he would be wearing the smartest and most perfect English riding boots and pants and sometimes a button of his fly would get caught back so that it would show—while Mabel [Dodge] would sit there sewing and talking about the decadence and disintegration of the Anglo-Saxon race—those were the words most often on her lips. Muriel stood up for the Anglo-Saxons—after all, with the aeroplane, this extraordinary mechanical thing, they had made it possible to see the whole rainbow for the first time, while the Indians were still regarding the sky as mysterious and awful.

Lawrence Dennis organizing the hillbillies—his paper, the *Awakener*, had just appeared—Muriel was going to organize the Hollywood homosexuals and the Vermont vigilantes, etc., and lead them to the defense of the Republic. —Dennis had begun cultivating a Southern accent after having evidently gotten rid of one. When Esther [Strachey] had handed her the first number of the *Awakener*, she had seen the word "Americanism" in a title at the top of a column and had said, "Why is it, I wonder, that America should be such a beautiful word and that Americanism should be such an ugly word!" —Ridiculing Esther out of her infatuation with Dennis— Esther had suggested her not telling people about the hillbillies.

Muriel seemed old-fashioned like John Bishop, embedded in the nineties and obsolete, though still with the something, the real courage, imagination, wit, which made her likable and interesting—though she looked more tarnished, more of a shell. What was it about her? with all her ready instinct for understanding people, you never felt any warmth—you always had to listen to her talk and she never willingly gave you a chance.

Meeting for A. J. Muste at Calverton's, January 3, 1934.
Max Eastman* lying on his back in the only Morris chair
in the room while his little Russian wife sat up in a
straight chair. He did not relinquish it to her till Muste
had finished and he wanted to take part in the discussion.
When Calverton's girlfriend came in, he got up for a
moment and offered her his chair, but when she declined,
he immediately sat down in it again while she sat up on
the table. He looked florid and soft beside Muste. Muste
had been delayed by having to speak at a meeting of
garment workers—he ought to have remembered, he said,
that New York time is not God's time and that when you
spoke to a garment workers' meeting you would have to
answer questions afterwards about how they were to get
rid of their officers. He looked worn, tense, and hard-
worked, one lock of hair down over his forehead, his eyes
getting round under his pained and dismayed eyebrows
[EW here drew two circles for eyes and put curved eyebrows over them] like those of an amazed old hick, his
cheeks fevered at the cheekbones and showing hollows
below, his mouth dingy darkened by the traces of his
beard (it occurred to me after I came away to wonder
whether he were a virgin) [actually he was married and
had a son, perhaps other children], his shoulders hunched
up and sitting on his hands or afterwards during the discussion with one leg twisted around the other and his
hands clasped in front of him—when somebody asked
him a question which perhaps embarrassed him a little, he
would knock the cigarette ashes off his clothes with little
pats of his rather fine thin fingers or take a nervous pull
on the cigarette.

* Max Eastman (1883–1969) during his trip to the Soviet
Union in the early 1920s had married a Soviet national, Eliena
Krylenko. She was his second wife.

Frank Keeney had "gone very bad"—gone khaki shirt and wore a little cap and appeared on the platform drunk —he had lost the confidence of the miners.

Karl Borders had refused to go left with the Musteites, Trotskyites, etc., at the Second Unemployed Convention—the Workers' Committee had broken up, and he had gone back to the ILD.

Dinner with Muriel Draper. All-white sitting room downstairs: stale white calla lilies in a big white vase, cameo china ashtrays with cupids on them, white skull of a cow hung on the wall. She couldn't believe in John Strachey, but later a little fairylike English admirer of [Lincoln] Kirstein came in, and the conversation, which had hitherto been about politics, instantly changed to the plane of Gurdjieff.* The young man had been in Persia, and after telling us how corrupt the Persians were, with "gray faces," he said that he was going back to Persia. England had changed so that it seemed quite strange to him: this was based on his just having read Spender and Auden—he didn't want to go back to that—Auden had been very hearty and very ugly at Oxford, quite different from the other young men, who had been quite beautiful and more or less aesthetic—he thought Auden was animated wholly by hatred—envied everybody, imitated *Beowulf* because he envied *Beowulf*. —Had been trying to group Gurdjieff's *Tales of Beelzebub*, etc. —Muriel told story of how Gurdjieff had miraculously saved one of her sons when he had been hit by a car—she had gone to his office, and he hadn't seen her, but had sent her a message: "Tell my friend not to worry." She had been so flattered by his calling her "my friend"! When she had

* George Ivanovich Gurdjieff, the Russian guru whose Fontainebleau Institute for the Harmonious Development of Man attracted much attention during the 1920s and 1930s. One of his more celebrated disciples was Katherine Mansfield.

asked him afterwards whether it was miraculous, he had said, "Once it might be a trick, but a thousand times, no!"—which she took, she said, as simple politeness. Her and Esther Strachey's and Suzanne La Follette's* young Jewish friend, son of the elevated man, who had a perfect non-Jewish upper-class New York accent and always seemed to me to think he was Proust.

Barrytown, Chanler Chapman. Referred to the old man [John Jay] as "this mug"—he was a queer mug—had burned his hand off out of self-disgust because he'd socked some fellow and after that went around looking for a fireplace to put his foot in! Hadn't cared anything about the farm, it bored him—he was really disgusting around the farm, his [Chanler's] mother had had to do the whole thing, and she couldn't check up on things because she was crippled—Harris, the farmer, had apparently been grafting: when they'd gotten somebody to build a new barn, it turned out that Harris had told him he could build it for $350—"My father thought that was awful, but I say, it's fine!—a man's a fool who doesn't take advantage of a situation like that!" —They hadn't realized till they read his memoirs that the old man had made that trip to Russia—though Chanler thought he remembered hearing him mention it when he had been moaning and gasping once.

The dumb and stubborn brown hound that rolled in something Sunday morning and howled because everybody had gone to church. Olivia† said that it was Chanler's dog, not hers—she thought, too, that little Jay didn't

* Suzanne La Follette, sister of Senator La Follette, served as editor and as member of the international inquiry into the case of Trotsky.

† Olivia James, daughter of Edward Holton James, a nephew of Henry and William James, had married Chanler Chapman, son of John Jay Chapman, in 1924.

like to be read "The Ancient Mariner" and "The Wreck of the Hesperus," that it made him nervous, that Chanler enjoyed scaring him. The pigs that Chanler had had and killed and against which everybody had protested—he insisted on talking about it at table when we were eating the sausages—you had to push the knife down instead of up, one of the pigs had taken six minutes to die, had been gurgling for six minutes. He got tight at dinner Sunday night and cruelly disconcerted Olivia, whose perfect precision and poise had up to then met every situation: he read "baked apple" on the menu that he insisted on having put before him—didn't he like apple?—he liked it in a more concentrated form—"Chanler, you said you'd be sensible!"—engaged the waitress in semi-jocose conversation about food—"Your running comment is decidedly annoying! Haven't you ever had baked apple?" "Not lately." "Well, you've often had boiled husband, haven't you?" His songs, after dinner: French, German, Italian, Russian. Al Jolson. He said he couldn't sing because his sex life was all shot. "Why?" "Come on, Marie Stopes!"* —When, earlier, the rector and his wife had gone, he relapsed from the authority and social dignity which his father's death seemed to have released in him and came back into the library shaking his uplifted arms and with his shoulders stooped over in the childish carriage which his parents had no doubt inflicted on him. He usually called me "Popsy" or "Guest." He was stimulated by the farm. The old man had once said out of the blue, when he and Chanler were riding around the farm together, "It's funny how wild bulls get when they don't eat anything but hay!"

* Marie Stopes (1880–1958), a pioneering writer on birth control and sex education, who founded the world's first birth-control clinic in London in 1921. A number of her books were banned in the United States.

The house had been built for them by Charles Platt*
about 1903, well proportioned and fine in detail, but, they
said, not so practical as it should have been—high French
windows let in the cold in winter—Bob Chanler's screen
and decorations, big bad bust of one of the Chanlers in
the library, old allegorical engravings, and Italian eighteenth-century water colors. Fine view past the sundial
through the space between the trees to the Hudson. Old
barn with pigeons in eaves, hay presser that was turned
by a horse, and masses of ivy down below where the cows
were milked that had come through and was growing
inside. —Chanler promising the men he would be there
at seven the next morning—they were skeptical.

Rokeby, the Chanler house—which Mrs. Chapman's
sister considered the real big house, the Chapmans' merely
a villa—was built in 1820, white with fine ornamented
doorway and octagonal tower, where the library was and
where J.J.C. had lain for months during his breakdown.
They thought he was really insane, especially his sister-
in-law. He kept saying he had a fire that was burning
him—his wife asked whether it was a real fire or only
felt like a fire—he answered, "Oh, it *feels* like a fire!" After
that, he got well.

Delano house—1870—looked like an institution—
brownish-yellow brick, with scores of narrow windows in
close rows, ornamental squares of dark green inlaid among
the yellow bricks toward the top of the square tower, and
fancy wrought-iron work over front steps that seemed to
descend by a series of landings so that the hood had to
follow it crookedly—a satyr's head incongruously over a
side door—on the grounds, a romantic group of a pair of
lovers embracing, the man wearing tights—"There's

* Charles A. Platt (1861–1933), the famous architect who
designed the Freer Art Gallery in Washington, D.C.

Gothic!" Chanler said and another of an old woman—inside, he said it was all statues and things and over-upholstered chairs—Lyman Delano* had preserved all this with piety—didn't it look like the coal mines it had come out of?—old man Delano, though no doubt a brutal businessman, had otherwise been a fine type, had broken his own horses and managed the whole place himself—they now apparently derived their income from the little railroad which ran up the Hudson there and which hadn't been doing as badly as the other railroads since the Depression.

Coming up, the winter river had been so misty that I couldn't see Newburgh across it.

—When Chanler had felt he couldn't, didn't want to finish college, the old man told him to remember he didn't have to and stuck a statement to that effect in the corner of his mirror, so that he'd see it when shaving every morning.

Olivia didn't seem to know or care very much about her great-uncle Henry [James]—they had tried to read aloud some of his later work and found those long sentences impossible to understand, and his early work was so *stilted!* All the [James] cousins were friendly now, though apparently William and Henry had put Robertson more or less in the doghouse.

They were sending Jay to the district school, because if he was going to live in the community, they thought that was a good way for him to begin. —Chanler didn't like Roosevelt, said he was a radio crooner—his legs were the best thing about him (this was a regular phrase at the time).

Something which had upset his father: the old man

---

* Lyman Delano (1883–1944), the railroad executive. He was a first cousin of Franklin D. Roosevelt.

had "had several litters of puppies and kittens, and became hysterical and nearly fainted!"

Provincetown. Katy Dos Passos's Gilbert and Sullivan song about her neighbors, the Balls: "The highly respectable, hardly detectable, unrecollectable Balls." They had been to college together in the Middle West and had eloped and come to Provincetown, where they had been ever since—leading a very quiet life, but assiduously checking up on their neighbors. They were disturbed by the people who had taken the Perry house—thought that they had introduced the homosexual element—that it "wasn't decent for those two young men to have married that old woman for her money."

All the Provincetowners have arrived in New York this winter almost simultaneously—where many of them continued to see nobody but one another.

Jenny ill. She called me late one night, had suddenly been "sick to her stomach." Her blue Irish eyes were watering and her sharp nose was red. She looked very frail. I thought she might be dying. So did she; I think, because she wanted me to get one of her family. Mother had a sore throat, too, and both went to bed for a day. But the next day, feeling a little better, they both got up: Mother because Uncle Win was coming to lunch, Jenny because she said she couldn't bear to stay in bed while Mother was up. As soon as Mother got up, she decided that Bobby's ear was bad again. [Bobby was her Scotch terrier.]

Uncle Win. They couldn't cook anything in New York, food getting worse and worse—the members had complained about it at both the Princeton Club and the University Club—they'd been sending them in these button onions raw, so that they slipped—you couldn't get your fork into 'em. The man who went into the cafeteria, got a roll and ate half of it, and went upstairs to toilet—an old woman who watched for leftover food came in and got the other half—the man was found dead in the toilet and the old woman died outside. There had been prussic acid in the roll, the man had put it there himself. Now his family were suing the cafeteria in order to prove that it wasn't the fault of the man and be able to collect the insurance. —McCooey, the Tammany boss of Brooklyn, had just died—Uncle Win used to meet him—a great big good-natured fellow—he believed in doing things right— put his son at the head of a big life-insurance company, and everything had to be written through him—"Did you see his appointments to his library committee?: Joe the restaurant man and Tilyou the Steeplechase Park man— Tilyou's his son-in-law—he has one man there who can't read or write!" Somebody who had been to the McCooeys' house said they sat around at dinner and stuffed them- selves like pigs.

Jenny said that *Mother*, bustling frantically around the house, had declared: "That dining room ought to be cleaned three times a day!" Jenny's nice irony over this— she had become the most refined of her family—"I didn't say to her: 'You needn't think I'm going to clean it three times a day.' " The *great thing about Jenny was that she* had really become more refined than we were—her saying to me when I had been irritated over her bothering me when I was writing in my room [Father's bedroom in the old house when I was working on *Lieutenant Franklin* just after the war]: "A man in your position oughtn't to behave like that." Quite true. She had reproved me also, telling me I was disagreeable after Father died, and before that when I was at college (I think) I had hurt her, my father told me. When I got sore this Christmas and walked out of the house, Jenny said, "I get angry sometimes when your mother treats me as though I were simple-minded." When she was sick and I was sitting in the room with her till her sister Susie came, reading, I answered her, "All right, dear," in reply to something she said—then, correcting myself, said, "All right," etc. When *Dr. Sayre* asked me how old I was, she said, in her fever and weakness, that she had taught me to walk—repeating it with the vagueness of fever. When we didn't understand: "I taught you to walk." —The doctor thought that in *The Undertaker's Garland** I had just about hit the nail on the head at that. —Inflation was going to collapse—we were getting ready for another war.

Uncle Charley had at one time been given a great rush by Mrs. Porter, who had designs on his antiques—but he would never let her go up to the third floor, where the old clothes were, and when she finally walked off with a matchbox, he came over to Mother almost weeping and had Mother bring pressure on Mrs. Hoagland to get it back.

Betty Huling's mother, with her sharp eye and her undershot lip and jaw, on her way up to Bennington, Vermont, where she owned some stores and apartments—mostly empty now. A couple of the tenants she evicted had set fires in the basements of the houses. She thought the government ought not to interfere with the railroads or public utilities.

Anna. January 2, 1934. Russian ballet: she was nervous and excited, insisted on drinking to keep herself

---

* EW's first book, in collaboration with John Peale Bishop, published in 1922. See *The Twenties*, pp. 66–7.

up—evidently disappointed in *Sylphides*: I explained that it was an old-fashioned ballet—she thought the man in the blond wig seemed like a fairy the way he danced out after those girls—she said that she and her girlfriend Helen would have giggled at it—if I hadn't told her it was old-fashioned, she would have thought it was funny—wanted me to kiss her in lobby, said to me during show she could love me to death, but when we got home she got sick from her excitement and drinks and threw up and so we just went to sleep, coming to about 5 A.M. —The music didn't seem to her like Russian music.

In the hospital. Anna was scared when she first went into the hospital—"a Hundred Tenth Street"—they had all cried when she left home, and she had given her mother a bawling out for it. The first day I went up to see her, her mother came in—they were cunning together: the mother round and solid, something like a mother pig, round glittering green eyes, rather handsome, round flat face, round flat nose, no neck. Anna asked whether she was treating Lizzie all right—her mother replied: "I beat her—I trow her out the window!" —Anna's thoughtfulness about Lizzie: right food, bring her to the hospital at 7:00 instead of 7:30—was concerned when she heard that Lizzie was going to the movies every afternoon, they didn't change the pictures that often, afraid she was up to some mischief. —Having her mother and me both there made her nervous. —She had wanted to see Mr. Glagolian because she thought he'd be nice to Lizzie while she was away.

When she had first come into the ward, the other women had thought she was a little girl and didn't want to talk to her about what was wrong with them. Afterwards, however, they had a lot of fun together and laughed and talked all the time. —She told her mother that today she had behaved rather better because she hadn't done any crying, whereupon the mother's green eyes immediately became moist. —The nurses were nice, but one of the women had told her about the room across the hall where they took patients when they were dying, and one woman who had been there a month and wasn't well yet came out of her own room into the ward where Anna was and swore and complained and worried her. She had an Italian woman on one side and an apparently educated woman from Connecticut on the other. The room had a nice view. She was delighted when Helen Spencer came in to see her.

The next day her mother brought Lizzie—Lizzie didn't want to go when it was time for me to come up—she had seen the roses which Anna's mother had brought her and said, "Flowers are for happiness and death, but these flowers are for happiness." Anna hadn't been able to remember the part about death and had had to ask the Connecticut lady what Lizzie had said. Lizzie wanted to know whether she was going to have a baby, after all. —They had shaved her from the breasts down and her skin had been tender and they had scratched her, then rubbed her with ether and swathed her with a big bandage. She was frightened, but felt important and had rather enjoyed the rest of being in the hospital and not having to get meals (she had cleaned house and attended to everything most conscientiously during the last day or two she had been at home)—and she looked what was for her rosier and plumper—cunning and sweet with her fine little hands, which she had manicured for the hospital (she had had her hair done, though somebody had said to her, "They won't be looking at your hair, they'll be looking somewhere else!")

A woman from another room looked in, in her dressing gown, and said, "How do you get to be a pet?" —When they had been shaving her, she had said: "It took me eight years to grow that crop!"—and the other women had all laughed and begun joking about "my operation." —She had manicured one woman's nails for her. She used to go to the bathroom and smoke cigarettes, had had to swipe matches from the room where the bedpans were—"I'm quite at home here!" —She didn't want to see her Aunt Milly, because she was "too dramatic." —I told her about getting tight the night before and later said that I was feeling nervous or something of the kind, and she said severely, "Remember that drinking won't help it!" —She had brought nothing to the hospital except a toothbrush and one or two things of that kind in the little zipper packet of her sealskin muff—and now she wanted slippers and a dressing gown. She had gotten her mother to bring over a picture of Lizzie. —Mrs. Bates, the head of the social-service department, tickled Anna's neck with her forefinger while we were talking and after Mrs. Bates had left the room Anna grinned at me, tickling her neck with her finger.

The first time I saw her after her operation, I knew, as soon as I saw her mother, that she wasn't feeling very well—her mother let me know this, but said she thought Anna liked to complain. I found her lying stiffly with her head back, she hardly opened her eyes. She said she had awful pains. It frightened me. I told her that Helen had said she was doing well—she answered, "She don't know!" I asked her whether she didn't feel better: "Worse!" (in a low voice). She didn't like my breath, and when she began having gas pains, it made her nervous for me to be holding her hand and she took it away—her mouth winced and she frowned in agony—she looked so thin (had had only water), I was afraid she might actually be going to die—she looked unnaturally clean and pure, with color delicate and creamy on the white bedclothes under the electric light. She had said, when I had come to see her before, that she lay there, when the curtains of the bedroom were down at night, and imagined she was in a grave just that high. Her little face with its common Slavic nose had an awful dignity and the simple few words of conviction—"Are they bad?" "Terrible"—with which she talked about her pain had the awful seriousness of suffering. I sat silent and didn't touch her, had to watch her as she writhed with new pains. She complained of the "gas" in her throat and put a finger at the back of her tongue—I asked her why, and she said, "The taste." She had gotten my letter and nodded about the bulbs [I had sent her Japanese narcissuses] but couldn't talk at all in the ordinary way. No doubt she was making an effort to be more restrained with me than she had been with her mother. When I went, she was to have another injection. When I kissed her good night, she said in her barely audible little voice, talking impersonally, "I'll die tonight." I said, "What? Oh, no!" "I can't stand another night like the last night!" I felt sick on the subway and dreamed about her towards morning, after getting up in the night at what I thought was a triple knock (I have had the illusion before) to look into the bleakly and bitterly cold night to see whether there were anyone at the door. Before I went to sleep, as I was reading Shaw, I found I kept saying aloud, "Oh, darling!"—if I could only have had that frail and straight little body in the bed there with my arms around her—she had come into that room, coming to see me, so many times smiling and cute and sensible, taking care of all her duties, smoking her cigarettes—had enjoyed love in that bed, closing her eyes and lying on her back, but from voluptuousness and strong positive response of life instead of from faintness and pain—remembered from my early childhood what it had

been like to be operated on, the indignity of having been
put under gas and cut up and hurt by other people, having abdicated one's independent life, almost as if it had
been done to you against your will and you felt resentment against the doctors and family and friends—as when
I told her the next day that the cyst had been in her
tube instead of her ovary, she said, irritated: "Couldn't
they tell where it was after examining me?"

The next afternoon, however, she was much better,
though her mother said she had made her nervous in
leaning against the bed—she looked more natural, though
in the afternoon light the color of her face was flat
instead of having the fragile deathlike beauty of the
night before, and her hair looked lusterless and stringy—
they were letting up on the morphine injections and her
pains were not so bad. She showed me the little note
Lizzie had written her and said, "You didn't know my
daughter was a poet!" All these women were going out
of there soon, she said—she'd be left there all alone—I
told her there would be others coming in, but she said
they couldn't be such a good crowd as these were. She
talked about the bulbs, they had had to put them under
the table. The days were so long, she said—she wished
she could move around, couldn't get up for twelve days.
I said that it had been four now. No, she corrected me,
only forty-eight hours that morning—they counted it by
hours, she told me. She returned the pressure of my hand
from time to time, said she didn't mind being touched,
and moved her head to kiss me when my face was near
hers. The sunlight hurt her little gray eyes—she had only
slept half the night before—they had been giving her
three hypodermics a night, two during the day. She had
had an enema, was hungry—they had brought her that
morning what looked like a cup of hot broth but it
turned out to be pineapple juice. I told her that when her

bowels moved, her gas pains would stop—when the bell rang for visitors to go and just before I kissed her good-bye, she said, "I think I'm going to ask for a bedpan" (perhaps she had been waiting in torture for the bell, she had begun to writhe again). She had said, "It's cold out, they tell me," in something of her old cunning cute humorous way. I felt very much relieved, had dinner with the [Niles] Spencers and talked and drank a lot. I tried to persuade them to admit merit in Sargent, but he was not "in the tradition of painting." I thought about how they dated from the Independents' Exhibition, how exclusively they had lived in *that* tradition.

I had thought of her poor little body with its female apparatus cut up and horribly sore—they had cut a little off the neck of the womb—and her poor little cunt (all shaved) and so far from being ready for any love—I had wanted to look up the ovaries and womb in the Encyclopedia, but had been afraid it would be too much for me.

But the next time I visited her, she was suffering still, and I went home feeling badly about her again—it was night, they had stopped her morphine, she had gotten them to move her over on her side and she made no sign or movement when I came in, simply told me to come around to that side—her little eyelids drooped over her eyes—she was no better, pains just as bad, they gave her enemas, which hurt her terrible, and milk of magnesia—which she refused tonight when it came—but her bowels wouldn't move naturally—she was afraid there were complications, all the other women had been able to move around at the end of five days and now it was nearly a week for her—"I can't stand it!—when my time comes, it's awful! I can't stand it!" She was hostile about Helen and the doctors—Helen didn't examine her or anything, she just came in and said hello and went away. She had gotten the slippers and dressing gown I'd sent her—I told

her if she didn't like them or they didn't fit her, I'd take
them back—she interrupted me sharply, almost hostilely:
"Why shouldn't I like them?"—I oughtn't to spend so
much money on her. —When I kissed her, she didn't
respond. —I saw the doctor, who said she was all right.

But the next afternoon Jane and Irene and young
Wagner were all there, and she had suddenly come to.
She was glad she had refused the milk of magnesia, because her bowels had moved and the gas pains were
much milder. She was laying Jane's mother out, she
knew she couldn't be getting as much as she said, $20
a week, for that work (dressmaking) because they didn't
pay that much for it—her mother was a liar, had told lies
about her (Anna) and made trouble—Anna was soon
going to be out of there and get a job. A complete trans-
formation—she smiled and told Jane what was what in
no uncertain terms. As Jane was going, however, Anna
said that she'd be nicer in the future—because her health
would be better—she wouldn't be so bad-tempered.

Two visits afterwards: she had slept well for the first
time and felt fine—ambitious, wanted to sit right up.
—Her Aunt Milly: handsome, intelligent eyes, good
manners, no accent like Anna's mother, who talked about
"a lonk letter." Her husband had been to the Ukrainian
[company's   performance   of   Tchaikovsky's]   opera,
Mazeppa—we talked about *Boris Godunov*. She thought
there would be a war soon in Europe—unless the U.S.
could stop it.

Anna's mother: "My Anna was always a good girl, but
my other daughter was very bad." Her mother had nice
eyes, a nice face—she really loved Anna, I think. Anna
as she felt better became a little imperious with her relatives, she enjoyed her own importance—I imagine she
was peremptory with the nurses. —I realized, when I
saw her with the rest of her family, that, even making

allowances for her illness, she was probably less well favored, but she had a sensitiveness and sweetness, by reason of her very humility and her fainter less sturdy stock, which made her the most attractive.

The next time, she looked very pretty and cunning, her skin had, for the first time I had ever seen it, lost that tarnished look—it was humanly pink and creamy; her eyes for the first time were lively in a genuine feminine fashion. She had almost keeled over when she first got up, then the next day she was able to stand. She got plenty to eat, but was awfully thin: it scared her. —Somebody had come home and found Lizzie shut out by Fatty, crying—that wasn't so good. —The Irish girl who had just come in, in the next bed, who kept lifting herself up and looking out the window to see whether somebody was coming. —When Anna had first come to the recovery room, there were long windows and she could see she was way up in the air and she thought she was on another planet—the doctors and the nurses fooling with the pans and bandages, talking—then she thought they hadn't operated on her and she'd have to go through it all again. She didn't remember much about the first four days. I asked her if she remembered suffering—yes and no—she had been full of morphine, but it had become acute when they took the morphine away. People had said she looked like a corpse when she first came down from the recovery room—her mother had gone out of there crying, they told her.

Sitting up in a chair: the blue dressing gown and blue slippers brought out the blue in her eyes—both her mother and I noticed how bright and clear her eyes had become. —Lizzie's animation—more energy, perhaps more personality, than Anna—her expression, raising her eyebrows, her movements, thrusting her head forward, which Anna didn't have to the same degree—she wanted to know if the pompons on Anna's slippers were "rab-bit's tails, dyed." —As we were going away, she waved to us from the window—little blue figure, cunningly animated. —Seeing Anna and her family at the hospital, I was struck by something human about them which I thought Anglo-Saxons lacked—their eyes, sweetness, responsiveness, love—also their directness and the natural humorous irony of the way they talked about things. Her mother said that Japanese narcissus bulbs "wanted to be left alone."

The Tammany clerk of the court kept coming to see Anna in the hospital and finally called on her mother at home and made a big hit by playing pinochle with them.

Anna still had severe gas pains after her meals and would double up when she tried to walk. She was ter-ribly thin: it frightened her. She wanted to get back to see that wonderful baby of her sister's, her godchild.

My trip to Brooklyn, the first time I went over to see her when she was out of the hospital: When we finally emerged from the tunnel of the subway, it was in a raw landscape of tracks and garages, gas tanks and cheap little brick houses and little one-story factories. —The low columned cloisters of the subway stations—light brown. —One came out into unexpected freedom, air, sunlight, and space—the attractive equipment of little brick deli-catessen stores, drugstores, kosher butcher shops, beauty parlors, billiard rooms, newsstands with Italian and Jew-ish papers. Many good-looking children taking the air with their mothers and older sisters in luxurious and spring-equipped baby carriages. Wide streets planted with young maples. The ocean air. The little brick houses in pairs—little privet hedges in front, bowls of flowers with ornamental designs on the steps, lattice shades—arched windows and doors, the latter with bricks raying out around them, each with its garage and a little brick yard, and at a distance from its neighbors.

I had been afraid before this trip that her mother wouldn't really call a doctor. The new house—the mother's fur disease. I talked to her mother about operations, and she gave me a "Ukrainian doughnut."

Anna was so weak that when she tried to take a bath she couldn't lift her foot up high enough to get out of the tub and had to get them to drag her out. The Stradivarius she had [I forget how she happened to have it—it was a real one, I had it checked]. She watched the birds out the window (and gave them crumbs) but never could see them at it. The nice little back yards of small houses, covered with snow. Her mother had hung out the laundry, she did it herself to save money—which worried Anna on account of her mother's hands. Mr. Glagolian stuck in his white hair and lined sallow face inquisitively, at once saying "Excuse me" and shutting the door again (we hadn't heard him). He was chef in a downtown restaurant had told Anna's mother, when she went to the hospital, that he was sure she was going to die. Fatty would come in to see her and just manage to squeeze himself into the armchair and then would have to brace himself on the arms to drag himself out. When we talked about the hospital, she said, "I was one sick girl!" She said she would commit suicide if there was still something wrong with her and she had to go back. She was worried by Lizzie's not coming back from school—she had told Lizzie to report to her when she left school, but Lizzie wouldn't do it. Lizzie brought home papers, well written and well spelled and marked 100. —I used to embrace her when she was so thin and her little mouth was so dry, and the dry skin on her cheeks scaling off like cheap powder, taking care not to press against her abdomen, and she still seemed to me so sweet, excited me in her sweet way when I would sit with my cheek against hers or gently playing with her tongue with my tongue tip or petting the nipple of her little flattened-down breast (she said about them, "There's nothing there any more!")—though there seemed to be hardly anything left of her at all. But she had had a dream when she first came home that had been fine, so that she knew she was all right—I asked her about what—"You and me—we had been trying to do something on a bed which had a woman already in it [the effect of the hospital, evidently] and with people all around." She flushed when I held and kissed her, and seemed to like it.

Found her looking very pretty in the evening, she had a little make-up on, and eyes so clear and sharp and bright and green (almost as much so as her mother's) in the electric light. Lizzie was in bed with her when I came in—they looked very cute and attractive, more alike than I had ever seen them.

Two days afterwards, in the late morning, she was pale, depressed by the visit of her cousin Johnny Gilbert. He did look pale and as if he hadn't had enough to eat and had been much worried since I had seen him before—he had gotten a black eye with the Amalgamated at the time of the Orlovsky trouble, though he hadn't been directly involved and hadn't known what Orlovsky was up to, and hadn't been able to get work and had been behind with his dues, and now he hadn't had any work except such odd jobs as he could pick up, for going on three years—till he had lately gotten work for a little over thirteen dollars a week with the CWA—which didn't even pay for food and he had a two-year-old baby (a wife and two children). I asked him what he did, and he confessed with hardly discernible shame and hesitation that he had begun with a shovel: then the boss had told him he seemed intelligent—not like most of these guineas—and now he was a field clerk, but only got the same wages and had worse headaches. He had been a

marker and cutter, he said he was an all-around man.
Now the landlord was going to evict him (he owed a
hundred and some dollars' rent) and he meant it, he was
an Italian, he'd been in plenty of shootings and his wife
had a bullet in her abdomen. Anna covertly told her
mother to ask him to come and stay with them in the
little room next door at the end of the hall, and her
mother said she wanted to talk to him before he left.
He went downstairs after he left us. Anna showed signs
of crying. She had told me, when I first came in, that
she never saw Johnny but he had bad news to tell her—
it was his child who had been bitten by a dog that they
thought might be mad—I had asked what was the matter:
"Guess what!"—her irony, suppressing her feelings, she
thought it was an overpowering tragedy—for her, when
she was still sick. A little while afterwards she said that
she wanted to get up and work, she had felt fine that
morning—I asked her why she wanted to work: "You'll
see!"—so that she could live with Johnny and his family
and pay them board—she reproached me (only the
second time she had ever done it) with the fact that I
and my friends would go out and make whoopee while
her people couldn't even pay the rent. I explained that
some of my friends were badly off and were living on
the artist's dole. Johnny said that he had been to Aunt
Milly and asked her for only a very small loan and she
had refused, telling him how bad the business in the
shop was, and then they (or one of them) had taken a
trip to Europe—but then they went and spent money
on Irene! —If they moved into the room next door, there
would be too many people there and it would be uncomfortable—and Loretta had left Eddie and he was wild!
On the other hand, her sister was all right: she had come
around Sunday and was looking fine, and the baby (her
godchild) was looking fine. —Her mother's operation,

with the consequent horrible scar, which Anna couldn't bear to look at, had been caused by an abortion that went wrong. —Her mother had been sleeping in the bed with her and she (Anna) must have been making love to her—"I felt pretty hot the other night"—that was the night she had loved her mother up—I asked what she meant—"Putting my arm around her"—because she noticed that the next night her mother slept at the foot of the bed—her mother would make her stop. Fatty had taken away the mattress from the chair that opened up into a bed and had been used for Lizzie—when her mother had had them all, in one bed the night before, she hadn't inquired why until this morning, and it turned out that Fatty had taken the mattress away for the Polish boarder, who hadn't been paying his rent— none of the boarders had—that was why Mrs. Wagner was going to move out, Stanley didn't even have a job— Anna hoped that her mother would move away and take her and Lizzie and leave Fatty and the boarders behind. —The intensity of hatred with which Anna observed Fatty—she knew, as she listened, that, if he was speaking English, he must still be talking to Johnny. He had bought tangerines, and this she had never told him to buy—and brought her back almost no change—she had gotten so sore at him when he brought her back the 41¢ change that she had gotten up and run downstairs after him and strained herself so that she felt lousy and had had a pain and she lay in bed for some time afterwards. But she seemed visibly to be getting a little fatter. "Don't kiss my hands"—because she thought they were so thin— but I did. —She had thought Fatty couldn't pay a fine for parking his car on the street and would have to go to jail for a few days—"we think," meaning her and her mother, but probably only she thought it.

Johnny and his wife and child: the wife was well dressed and pretty, very pale and thin, with blue eyes and a fine knifelike profile—a Czech; the nice little girl with her pale blue eyes, much quieter than Lizzie. Johnny played a polka and a part of *Poet and Peasant* on the violin.

Fatty and the whole situation there had been getting on Anna's nerves again and poisoning her. Fatty called her mother "old whore" and "old monkey" all the time, but he was kind of afraid of Anna, because she could tell what she knew about him—she had been brooding on having him deported—he was a Russian and couldn't speak English and was no good over here anyway. She was irritated and depressed by Lizzie, who sneaked pennies and ate chocolates when she had been told not to—she was such a pest, everybody chased her out, Anna chased her away herself and then felt sorry for her. She thought she could finally get her mother to leave Fatty— the boarders weren't paying their rent, and Mrs. Wagner wasn't paying rent, and she (her mother) wasn't going to support him—"but she loves him, damn it!"—Mrs. Wagner, who had been a cook, had slipped at the place she had been working and injured herself internally, and she was trying to collect compensation, which Anna's clerk of the court was trying to help her to do.*

When she finally came to my house for the first time after her illness, she looked much better, and had been feeling better. She seemed so frail, in her little smart brown shoes and the little blue dress I had bought her last summer, with the white thing hanging down at the throat, that she looked as if you could have passed her through a ring (a little touch of make-up)—she only weighed 96 pounds—had weighed 103 when she went to the hospital. She seemed finer and even nicer away from her family—had been so glad to get away from that

---

* Portions of this further sequence of EW's relations with Anna were used by him in *Memoirs of Hecate County*.

house! It made me like her more than ever again to see
her so fine and slight and looking so well in her clothes,
thin and wobbly still though she was. I imagined that I
could notice the loss of her cervix and that there was
an empty space up there.

She saw me cutting pages of a French book and said,
"Sometimes I think you're the smartest man in the
world!" "How do you know I'm not?" "If you were, you
wouldn't be living on East 53rd Street."

Cummings's story of the man with a mother complex,
who thought that every cunt had a fishhook in it.

Taxi drivers' strike, hotel employees' strike. First week
in February '34: on the corner by the Commodore, a
picket relieving another picket—one little man taking
off his hat and unyoking the sign (which made a bib
both in front and behind) from over his head and
another man taking off his hat and putting it on while
the hats and the sign were blown by the cold wind so
as to make it rather difficult.

V. F. Calverton. Born George Goetz—he said he was
not a Jew but merely German, father had never forgiven
him for looking Jewish (perhaps true). Communist
meeting at which Mike Gold* and others had spent the
whole evening debating whether or not Calverton was
Jewish. Somebody had seen his penis in the men's room
and observed that he was not circumcised. The story that
he told me about his having been elected president of
the Jewish Club at college. He didn't try to explain and
accepted.

* Mike Gold (1893–1967), Communist author who wrote a
column in the *Daily Worker* for more than thirty years.

Mother, sick in bed with a lingering cold, more full of anxieties than ever, worrying about Rosalind's going out in the snow, thinking that Bobby had an earache, imagining that she smelled smoke and that the house was on fire. —Jenny's tact, so much superior to Mother's way of handling things, in telephone calls and in interceding between the various members of the family when there is friction.

K. Unexpected visit to New York. She called up to say that "the personal-service department" would be at my disposal after 6:30. Much thinner, but more worn and harder-looking, though very attractive. We soon went to bed after a conversation in which she told me about how she had "almost lived with C.J." on her last visit to New York but he had sent her a telegram canceling the engagement and saying, "I am frightened—I got too tight." She had explained to me downstairs: "I've got a nice surprise for you—I've got the curse." She stuck her thick little tongue as far as possible into my mouth. She made me get a towel and, lying on it naked on her back, invited me: "If you can take it!" . . . "Will you stop a snitch?" ("Snitch" was now one of her favorite words.) I did, she having come but not I, due to overpreparation with liquor; but I later returned to the charge.

We decided not to have dinner, after all, and I dashed down and left a note in the kitchen: "Hatty: no dinner." The atmosphere of disorder that she always brought with her. House cold, coal only just arrived, gray shaving water frozen in basin, with red hair of my beard embedded in it; cries heard from Hatty, clouds of steam from furnace, Earl summoned [a colored man who worked for Paul Draper, at Muriel's next door].

We went up to the Grand Palast dance restaurant on 86th Street—cocktails, she failed to eat her club sand-

wich. She said she wouldn't come back with me, didn't
like to when her husband was there. She wanted me to
go to her hotel, but I refused. She finally gave in and
came back with me. We got another pint of bad
drugstore rye and another bottle of ginger ale. I had been
telling her that I felt tragic about her and me. I said,
"I like you very much!" and she mumbled something
which, when she repeated it, turned out to be, "I love
you." Her great songs now were "And the dream that
was walking / And the dream that was talking / And
the heaven in my heart is you!" and "Without your love,
/ It's a melody played in a penny arcade." She had been
going as hard as she could with all sorts of gaieties since
fall.

We lay on the couch together. I wanted her to come
upstairs, but she refused because she was afraid of going
to sleep: she had to get back to the hotel. We moved
to the couch by the windows and put the Indian blanket
over us; but I was on the edge, it was too narrow for
me to be comfortable. After more arguments, I finally
picked her up and carried her to the foot of the stairs
and made her walk up. We went to bed. I, having the
night before had very little sleep and being weary with
my drinking and exertions, kept tending to fall asleep;
but she was full of interest and ideas—wanted to know
what "funny way" I'd like to do it, kept getting on
her knees and presenting her rump, which I was quite
unable to cope with. She said that she had been liking
it that way lately. She sat up and dangled the nipple of
first one breast then the other for me to suck, which I
did in a moribund manner (they seemed to hang more
now that she was thinner). She kept talking about doing it "funny ways" and I said, trying to calm her, that
there weren't very many things you could do. She finally
got up and dressed, and I, at the last possible moment,

jumped up and put my clothes on over my pajamas and took her home—sometime after four.

The next day, the top sheet was in shreds, my undershirt had rouge marks on it and a spot of menstrual blood, and all the towels had to go to the wash. There were the contents of an overturned ashtray on the bedroom floor and white spattered spots that I supposed were whiskey. The box and chain of the water closet were wrecked. The couches were in disorder. The hot-water pipes were found to have burst, too.

Jenny in Riverview Hospital. Trouble with her colon, and the doctor thought she might have t.b. Mother very much upset. He had said, "If you don't look out, she may slip away from you." She looked reddened in a raw way, not flushed, and eyes redder than ever when she suddenly began to cry: when you were sick all the time, really the best thing you could do was to cash in (she had been saying that they ought to give her poison). But asked me not to tell Mother she had cried, she was sorry to act this way. I tried to cheer her up. She could see the river out the window and the iceboats, and she got Rosalind to pull up the shade: "You can reach it and then pull it down, dear." As we were going, she said, smiling, that she'd be out making whoopee, she supposed —looking for a fellow! When she had been in the house, I said, Mother had worried about her, and that she was now much better, had slept well last night. And I worry about *her* when I'm there, Jenny said.

Dreamed at Red Bank that Mother said she had picked up two men and a girl in the neighborhood of our old address on 58th Street. I asked her what the men were like. "They were fine-looking little fellows, just like well-kept ponies." I tried to imagine her with the woman.

Jean Gorman was also in the dream. I met her and talked to her as I was going into the big glass door of some office building. It was as if she had wanted to see more of me, but I didn't take her up. The whole dream was unpleasant. I woke up with my mouth open and a dry tongue, my arm numb and cold. It took me a long time to move and moisten my tongue, to move my arm and start the circulation.

John Strachey, speaking before the John Reed Club, had *called Archy MacLeish a cad* on account of his baiting of the Jewish Communists in his *Frescoes for Mr. Rockefeller's City*. Gerald Murphy was indignant, made representations to Esther, who made representations to John, who wrote a letter to Archy, who replied in good temper. Esther said John couldn't have it both ways, couldn't be a Communist and at the same time hang on to the code of the public school.

The Gerald Murphys' apartment at One Beekman Place. Living room with big bay window overlooking river—contrast of dingy and misty gray of river. Welfare Island, prison, Brooklyn shore, tugs hauling garbage barges, with clear and light room, so delicately and comfortably arranged, all whites and very light yellows, large ottomans or poufs that looked as if they were covered with white kid, no pictures on the walls, but sprays of flowers and tall slim stalks of plants with fine leaves, in vases, bowls, and pots, that rose and made traceries against the empty part of the room—one of the vases had five specimens of curious flowers, phallic-looking* red thing, and waxy mauve-blue bud-flowering branch, some-

---

* EW had apparently never encountered the anthurium, the tropical American plant of the arum family.

thing which I had never seen, also some kind of white lily; on the mantelpiece was a bunch of artificial ferns of hoary silver, flatly arranged like a sea fan. Little white marble mantel evidently brought from somewhere, with lambs and cupids carved on it. Katy [Dos Passos] looked so smart and elegant and slim, with a high back comb in her hair, sitting, in her black dress, on the light-yellow couch and smoking her cigarettes, which in her thin little hand matched the delicate tendrils of the plants—she had had her toenails painted and was wearing open evening shoes. —Room that Dos and Katy were living in: small four-poster bed, with light-pink canopy, pink silk coverlet, and pink silk pillows in which Katy's pale-pink skin and green dressing gown and green eyes looked very pleasantly fancy, and bonbon piles of little French hatboxes on clothes chest, white, spattered with little red flowers. Cunning poodle puppy, a bitch this time—sherry bottle with special stopper with a little silver plate marked "Sherry" attached to it by a little silver chain, old-fashioned goose-chase quilt, but with rose patches and a little blue pillow that fitted in with the scheme of the room. Agreeable and sympathetic servants—when I came in, in the afternoon, and asked whether Mr. Dos Passos was there, the attractive-looking maid said with an intelligent smile of a kind very rare among servants, as if she had been assimilated to the charming, sympathetic, intelligent world of the Murphys, that he was telephoning.

[The Murphys themselves were out.]

Helen Spencer said a woman had been trying to sell her a *contraceptive jelly* with a honey base.

Dawn Powell on *Dotsy Greenbaum*, the sculptress, who did rabbits for small apartments. Dawn, when she was with Dotsy, found that the side of her that she always hoped was there finally came to the top—and then she became so *bored* with herself! She said that Dotsy's husband was very much excited because the Prince of Wales was wearing a zipper fly, a big thing in the advertizing business.

Season of '33–34. The Gertrude Stein opera; [the films] *Lot in Sodom* [and] *Sang d'un Poète;* [the play] *The Green Bay Tree.* O'Neill and Phil Barry took to religion; Eliot announced that Hardy and Lawrence had been inspired by the Devil. Dos claimed that everything was converging to make Louis Bromfield the great American man of letters: the connection with Gertrude Stein, the back-to-old-American-country-life movement—*Manhattan Transfer* had evidently been back of [Bromfield's] *Twenty-four Hours,* so that, if Dos proved not practical for the Comrades, Granville Hicks could always just quietly substitute Louis Bromfield. He had had a great reception at the boat, to be sure, when he came back from abroad, long featured interviews. He had gone to live at Princeton.

Elizabeth Hawes's spring opening. Not so many people (they said, on purpose), more casually staged, no applause. Gray walls, blue spiral staircase (all very carefully harmonized), horizontal and vertical tubes on the walls giving yellow light. Gowns going further back in periods: Lady Hamilton and Lord Nelson—and Anne of Poitiers, Henry VIII, etc., plain street dress with very fancy hats shaped like three-leaf clovers or electric toasters or tricornes—tall willowy blond model with no hips, in very pretty outfit of white dress with silk swallow-winged wrap, brown with wide red border—Nathanael West's girlfriend smiled at me slightly when she caught my eye, which I assume they are not supposed to do, as Elizabeth Hawes's assistant, sitting next to me,

seemed to glare at her—and she severely asked another
model where she had gotten those rather tarnished white
shoes—the model replied with poise, smiling slightly,
in the fashionable manner, on one side of her mouth.
Elizabeth Hawes herself had on a very pretty evening
gown, not very long, white satin, just caught up over her
breasts with thin white ribbons of shoulder straps, and
showing off by contrast to splendid advantage her rather
dark well-muscled back.

I met Ralph Stirner's former wife, and she turned out,
since I had seen her last, to have been married to the
architect Lescaze—my reflections on the evident difference of certain other people's tastes from mine—she might
be able to talk to him seriously and more or less intelli-
gently, about his work and other things, but how could
he want to go to bed with her?—like some kind of little
city dog. [She did have thick red hair, however, and, in
her mosquitolike way, a certain quality.]

O. Dark bang, polka-dotted black veil on little hat,
green and black fine plaid blouse, tied with little ribbon
at the neck. Fine hands with square-tipped fingers that
could do something, little feet showing a firm well-
rounded form of instep, in black patent-leather high-
heeled shoes, with thin black stockings of a large mesh.
When I came back, she was flattened out on the couch,
with her head against the back and her feet drawn up
under her. How pretty her eyes looked. She suddenly
cried quietly a minute. Unexpected size and beauty of
her breasts inside her blouse. Confused the way she
looked with her work—with a touch of Marie Lauren-
cin,* but sharper darker eyes and more outline. The

* The then fashionable painter (1885–1956), who greatly exaggerated the eyes of her subjects and painted in soft pastel
shades.

upper part of her face is lovely—very small red mouth—
I found afterwards I had forgotten the rest. Her fineness
and distinction. Afterwards, when I saw her, she would
color lightly or deeply, according to the stimulus, with
a kind of delicate sensitiveness that I don't think I have
ever seen before in a woman. Beautiful dignified manners, a little formal—drawling voice—always complete
self-possession and apparent coolness. Subsequent feelings of love and admiration, and happiness over her delicacy and beauty, alternating with horror over other
features of the evening. [I tried to make love to her, and
she was willing, but I failed: too much liquor and too
little real desire.]

Margaret. Dream (March): I was back with her again
and thought it would be good to see her friends again—
I hadn't seen them for such a long time. —I figured that
if I got up early every morning and went to sleep early
at night, I shouldn't have to drink and shouldn't have to
think about it so much when I didn't.

Dreamed of going out with her somewhere in the
evening—danger of someone else I liked.

Dreamed we were discussing paying for her stone
[jewel] as if it were for somebody else—the difficulties
we always had in meeting expenses. —Then it was the
same thing again of my being back with her—she was
planning to go out to California for the summer. —I
dreamed that I was talking to Mother, who was sitting up
in bed—she said sharply, "Nobody will ever love you!"
Then I saw Margaret, who looked quite different and
who was really another and less attractive person. Why
couldn't we be married again? We could: even though
this was a dream, when we waked up there would still
be no reason.

Esther Strachey said that the Constitution was certainly the sick man of America.

Merwin Hart [my cousin from Utica: his mother, Aunt Lucy Hart, was a half sister of my Grandfather Kimball]. He had read me in *The New Republic* and had written that he would like to see me, so I invited him to lunch in 53rd Street. He told me that he and I were really aiming at the same things in different ways: we wanted the best people to take an active part in government. Capitalism had always existed, and we hadn't waited till this time of day to find out how to run society—the trouble was human nature—his idea of a revolution was people who had been found to be mentally so ill equipped that they couldn't even pass school-board examinations voting out of power the great leaders, Rockefeller, Ford, etc., who had made the country what it is—that would be a disaster. He objected to my speaking of classes: where did so-and-so fit?—some big executive who had risen from the ranks. Industries would have to establish agreements themselves to shorten hours and distribute work—example of a company which did without its profits so that it wouldn't have to lay off men. I said that, for every example of this kind, I could give him three to the contrary—"I bet they're Jews," he said with a smile. He also thought the radicals are all Jews. He didn't think we could go on this way between Communism and capitalism, thought the NRA would crash. I asked him what he thought would happen then. Why, the real Americans would get together and do something to put the country on its feet! I said, "Merwin, what is the difference between your ideas and Hitler's?" He replied, "The American people would never stand for a leader with a mustache like Hitler's. He ought either to shave it off or grow a bigger one." He denied that wars were caused by a struggle for markets; it was slogans which aroused mankind. I tried to put the burden of proof for capitalism on him, and he replied that capitalism was working all right—there were only 4 million people out of work, and they were the unemployables. I reflected that if it were not for the NRA, there would be 10 million people out of work, and that then, by his reasoning, those 10 million people would automatically have become unemployable. He objected to the devices of the government for putting people to work, because they discouraged thrift. He wanted me to know, however, that he had no financial interest in the position he was upholding. It had been rumored that he was getting an enormous salary, but at the present time the manufacturers had withdrawn most of their subsidy to the New York State Economic Council, and he was having a hard time to raise money. He was making very little money, and he hadn't inherited a dollar—so, as I gathered, his support of the capitalist system was due to sheer belief in and love for it. He honestly wanted to understand my point of view. One of the other men in the organization had apparently been criticizing him as an old fogy. Roosevelt was having a Harvard class reunion this spring and bringing the class to the White House. Though he protested the deficiencies of the New York riffraff when it was a question of their being allowed to get the upper hand, as soon as I said that they were what they were from having come out of the wretched slums of New York, he denied that there was anything wrong with New York as a place to live, and contended that there were as fine people there as anywhere.

Vico, which I read in the afternoon, contrasted with the shallowness of Merwin. —Drinks after the theater with John and Margaret Bishop and Esther Strachey. All their talk about royalties and whether or not the

Prince of Savoy had consummated his marriage with the Princess—Margaret loved to identify herself with royalties who were having babies.

Visit of K. to New York. I read Dr. Wirt's* testimony until the train came in, feeling very fit after exercises and a single martini in the old Pennsylvania Station bar. —She said to me in the cab that she hadn't looked forward to seeing me enough. —My shaken state of mind as a result of my experience with O. At first, the same thing almost happened. I ceased after a few nervously tense and alcoholized efforts, and she said, "Don't you love me any more?" "What a pity that anything so good should have a rotten foundation!" All right, after that, however. O.B. had taken to his bed again when she was leaving, but she had come away just the same. She was beginning to feel as if she might suddenly kill somebody, just as Margaret told me she used to do. —The ash blonde whom somebody had asked, not knowing she was in the Social Register, "You work for a living, do you?" "Yes," she had answered, "do you?" The polo player who had married a cute little bitch of a movie actress. They had no money, she was through in the movies, and his parents disapproved. She did a dancing act in a night club, and he was humiliated by this. His friends would go to the show and then laugh at him. They thought he liked to see his wife perform as a Lesbian with another girl in the show, and they also suspected him of sadism. In any case, he got jealous of the other girl and beat up his wife, and they separated. Decadence, from her account, of the relations between the A.s.

* Dr. William A. Wirt, a disciple of John Dewey and William Morris in education, had charged there was a Communist plot to take over Rooseveltian Washington. See *Earthquake*, "Miss Barrows and Dr. Wirt," pp. 538–44.

What a lay in the hay is my baby!
What a treat neath the sheet is she!
What a lay in the hay is my baby,
When we lie lip to lip, knee to knee!

Or starting up with all her energy abruptly:

It was only a paper moon,
Just as phony as it could be
But [it wouldn't be make-believe]
If you believed in me!

When I told her how well she looked in bed, she said it was because it didn't embarrass her the way it did some women. She could never see why you should be embarrassed. She said that she ought to be carried around in a bed. In bed, her beauty became fiercer and prouder—her falcon nose, strong white teeth, beautiful white skin, and black hair of an Irish queen. At other times, especially when a little abashed or frightened, she looked Irish in a different way: her eyes and her round cleft retreating chin, someone who had done some low things and didn't quite know what the attitude toward her was going to be. Her little short ineffectual round darling arms, with pretty little hands, tapering fingers, made a contrast with her short square-toed thick-ankled stocky legs and big thighs. The biggest thickest wettest tongue I have ever known, which she loved to stick into your mouth. Fanny Hill chair, etc. Warm animal sweetish smell of her cunt, when I knelt beside the couch. She said, when I moved up to her mouth: "You want to attend to everybody on the couch."

Bad memories of Margaret. I found I was beginning to develop the same neurotic symptoms: turning away from her, lying, and wasting time relieving my nerves by long tense talks on various subjects. The bed showed signs of breaking down. She would look so appetizing when she came out of the bathroom after her bath in the morning, with her little flower-lace brassière making her breasts round, her girdle and panties and her black and silver mules. The bad elements: the money situation, the bad analogies for me.

I tended to keep her in the house, and though she said she didn't want to go out, it got too much on both our nerves. Her depressing story of her final consummation with I.—the tire exploding on the street on a tense jittery morning: "Now a thing like that can't happen!" We would succumb to cocktails late in the morning or in the afternoon and get to feeling better over them: our joke about L. and N. Alternations of attraction and lust and gravitation away from one another, with tendencies to be disagreeable and quarrel. I gave up trying to do anything, and after the first day or two, even the things I ought to have arranged on her account I didn't seem to be able to do. I never even read the papers, and so missed the rest of the Wirt business. It seemed to me at the time my most animal, though most extraordinary, experience of the kind.

At the little Italian cocktail place, the evening she was leaving: "What shall we do now?" "Let's go back," I said, "and you take off all your clothes, and I'll put my arms around you." "You tell them about it!"—she glanced at the people at the next table. I found her, before she took off her clothes, sitting on the edge of the bed, with her face in her hands, crying. I told her she didn't feel as badly as that, and she stopped. We did a great many things, and finally I was at her a long time. Then we lay there. I had been made so sheer and vibrant and delicately sensitive by love that I snapped like a violin string. She said that I was "the best sleeper-with," and referred to D. as "this quince," "this bitch that won't sleep with yuh." I recited to her, though with one's

usual self-consciousness about reciting poetry to a non-
literary person, Yeats's

> When long ago I saw her ride
> Under Ben Bulben to the meet,
> The beauty of her country-side
> With all youth's lonely wildness stirred . . .*

and suddenly found I was crying, with the distorted
mouth of a child. I said, "We don't really mean that," or
something of the kind, and got up and began getting
dressed, walking back and forth across the room.

We finally got off in a cab. At the gate, they evidently
knew we weren't married, because they wouldn't let me
go on the train with her, and I leaned against the wall,
feeling weak and not caring that I must look so pitiable,
till she returned, leaving her bags on the train, and we
walked back and forth under the high marble ceiling behind pillars, till in a minute it was time to go, and in
spite of her apprehensions of detectives, we kissed in
front of the trainmen and other people. I walked back to
the house, not having a cent.

My horrible dream the next morning about the picture
exhibition where the pictures were all practical jokes, one
containing an electric battery, one lighting up from the
inside and revealing a sort of television of the head of
the artist, finally one combination compelling my attention, first from one, then from another direction, flying
out at me with long crowding rocks from the wall. Then
when I side-stepped, I fell over a sort of hurdle that
sprang up, and while I lay on the ground, I heard
threatening noises, which included something like a

---

* EW is quoting from the third stanza of Yeats's poem "On
a Political Prisoner," which has two more lines: "She seemed
to have grown clean and sweet / Like any rock-bred, sea-borne
bird."

Dadaist speech in French. Before that, Betty Spencer had turned up and made invidious remarks, and Cobey Gilman had asked for the $15 I had borrowed from him at the beginning of K.'s visit, telling me that it wasn't like me not to have paid him the next day, as I had said I would; and I discovered that my fly was unbuttoned.

I had sinkings the next day; but, curiously enough, it seemed to me though I had not wanted to see Anna and had wired her not to come, when she did come and I did not want to hurt her feelings by letting her think that I was indifferent or had been unfaithful, she looked to me sweet and desirable. When she demanded, after a little averted hovering around the room on my part, that I should join her on the bed, where she was sitting, I laid her with great gusto and satisfaction so fast that she herself didn't come; and, after that, to my surprise, though my nerves were covered a little thinly at moments, as if by a film that might possibly break, the whole confusion and fear and muddiness seemed to have been wiped away, and I was quite clear when I went to the *Modern Monthly* meeting. Anna was smiling to herself so happily, she said, because she had her little room to herself, nobody knew where she was—she said that she was going to rest. But I wondered whether, after my [not] seeing her, at her request in her telegram, Saturday, she might not have been pleased at this proof that I was not indifferent to her, that I had probably not even been unfaithful to her. The relationship, as I slipped back into it, satisfied and seemed to me natural—it was nice to see Anna again. She was so cheerful about the new place that she wasn't worried about my not having given her, about my not being able to give her, much money.*

*EW's notes here contrasting Anna and K. suggest the central theme of "The Princess with the Golden Hair" in *Hecate County*.

The reporter who came to the *Modern Monthly* meeting that night to interview Max Eastman about *Trotsky*. He didn't know what the Third International was, thought Rivera's getting shot at by Nazis was probably just a publicity stunt, and imagined that we were up to something very deep. The more we tried to tell him what he wanted to know, the more he didn't believe us. He said to Calverton, "Your name is V. F. Calverton, but they call you George"—made us feel as if we were conspirators and actually had Trotsky concealed there on the premises—yet he was evidently the *Herald Tribune's* radical squad. He said that he had written for them several years ago a series of articles on Communism in the United States.

Cobey Gilman's cousin, a former technocrat who was turning Communist. He was full of the ridiculous anomalies of the technological situation—would tell us about them, then laugh "Ha-ha!"—fiendish, a little mad-sounding type of the eccentric old American uncle.

WASHINGTON, 1934

Washington, April 17–May 2 [1934]. [I had a serious nose infection, which must have come from letting a barber clip my nose hairs in a dirty barbershop in the neighborhood of my 53rd Street house.] My nose, entanglements of uncomfortable associations—the mild Washington spring, still a little chilly—tender green grass and red bricks from the window of Griffin [Barry's] place, 1620 P Street, up under the roof—open yards with grass, nice to find the leisure and space. All the smooth young college boys with their Princeton-Philadelphian line.

Griffin and I sat at Gene's Italian restaurant just alongside the Mayflower Hotel, across from a couple of young men on the industrial side of the board, very drunken and jocose, apparently hostile to and contemptuous of Griffin as representing the labor side. They did not recognize each other till just as we were going, and when Griffin said good night, one of them, after saying good night, seemed to mutter something contemptuous as we went out.

Miss Barrows over her garage with a green wooden

hood like a portcullis that folded down and covered the stairs; the front was all dark. Miss Vreeland, rather cunning Mickey Mouse face and rather smartly dressed in a pale way—young economist from Brown who was known up there as a Red. Miss Barrows was wondering whether they ought to have made an issue of Dr. Wirt, declaring their real views in order to clarify the situation. Bulwinkle, who had been against the Reds at Gastonia, wasn't crazy about defending them, but had to. Senator Clark had said that the conspiracy was to put Roosevelt to sleep by taking him to hear a speech by Ham Fish, then convey him to the very secret place where Morgan and Charley Mitchell had kept their incomes to escape the income tax, then to turn on Fess and a couple of others, in order that at the end of a couple of months the country would either turn to Communism or turn on the gas. The Soviet Ambassador Troyanovsky had said in surprise, "Do you mean to say that people in America aren't free to say what they please at private dinners?" [The rumor in Washington was that Mrs. Roosevelt had been present at the dinner.]

In the Investment Building, where the Labor Advisory Board was: good-looking agreeable-looking girls and women who talked humanly and humanely like Southern women—little blonde who decided to go up with the other elevator, saying to the boy in the elevator, "You go up jerky."

Griffin felt the place could be a whispering gallery— felt involuntary qualms when I was talking about capitalism and Communism, that "you oughtn't to use such words."

Gardner Jackson, sitting on the stone rail of the plant-grown court of the Department of Agriculture building, said that he and his assistants were about the last lefts there and agreed to my filling in that they mightn't last long.

Dead tissue in my nose—the doctor told me I was threatened with necrosis if I didn't take better care of it. He had dug out some of it already. The dead tissue in my soul—it could never grow back in again when somebody else was dead. I had brought on the severe infection myself, I suppose, by jabbing the tip with a needle before it had really come to a head.

The Wolmans at the Hotel Washington. Leo had been very much excited by Detroit. He looked fat, but his face was gray. A big movement but no one to head it. He had had to bolster up the AF of L himself to present their own side. The union leaders made demands, they made demands in the morning, they made demands in the afternoon, and they made demands at night. Lots of people to make eloquent speeches—Matthew Smith in this class. Mechanics' Educational Society disintegrating—Communists and other radicals fighting among themselves —AF of L had stated that 6,000 men had been discriminated against, but when Leo had asked for the list, they didn't have any list! They scraped together only seventy-some cases, one man was an epileptic. Ford's, he said, was never mentioned—they claimed he had a spy system which made it impossible for anybody to do anything, but Leo thought this couldn't be true. [Having visited Ford's myself and knowing that this was true, and that everybody in Detroit knew it, I was able to take the measure of the extent to which Leo, from working with labor entirely in a financial way, was ignorant of actual conditions.] He quoted sympathetically employer's statement that he didn't mind giving way but he wouldn't lie down and be trampled on. I said it was the old conflict. "If you mean whether the employers are to own the business or somebody else is to own it," he said, "but anything you can do in a practical way." —He was excited by having come to realize some of the things that the academic mind didn't know—the dingers, indispensable people who could get practically anything they wanted, they dented back dents so that they didn't show. He thought Detroit was a Godforsaken place, didn't like big industrial cities anyway, liked Washington as a place to live. He laughed a little too much over the absurdities of unions, felt himself under fire by people who "thought he wasn't a liberal"— Blankenhorn, for example.

Young Woolston, rich college boy from Philadelphia— also Griffin's Henry Collins from Chestnut Hill, with his smooth line of Princeton '26, nasal words running into each other: "ab . . . ," deliberately absent-minded. "All right" . . . "Do you think Karl Marx would approve of that?"—an aristocrat stronger on the labor side than a good many of the labor people, according to Leo Wolman, though Griffin and [Mary] Heaton Vorse couldn't bear him. He was working on the food codes—amusing about pretzel bending; not a mechanical process so presented a special problem, they had to loop them and throw them over and catch them (illustrating), whereas sticks were entirely made mechanically. Averell Harriman in the restaurant, came over to talk to Leo Wolman: a tall dark suave young man, former reactionary (I forget just in what connection) but has spent some time in a lumber camp and for the first time found himself accepted as something other than a rich man's son, anxious to do and be something, looked like a fellow of small caliber, one of those thin and uninteresting-faced rich men's sons. He had with him another more solid-looking and smiling square-headed man, and we sat on the sort of dais that runs along two sides of the dining room, at the table just in the corner, that dominates the entrance.

Leo on General Johnson. I said he hadn't any brains, had he? "No brains and no guts, but he has remarkable literary gifts." He was dominated by his secretary, Miss

Robinson—very easily influenced and always by people weaker than himself. Leo had told him, when he suggested Leo's being the third member of the Detroit board, that he didn't want to be—the AF of L hated him. Johnson: "To hell with the AF of L!" Then he had called him around after seeing Green and others, and said, "How would it be if you didn't serve on the board?" Leo was anxious to resign—if he didn't serve on the board, he was out entirely. Leo went back to New York, and in his classroom at Columbia was told that the President wanted to speak to him. Roosevelt said, "Hello, Leo Wolman," as if he had been seeing him three times a day, you know—"Frances Perkins* is here with me and wants you to accept the place." It had been a beautiful piece of work! (Yet Leo, although flattered, was not taken in by Roosevelt—though he answered at lunch when I asked him how Roosevelt was on labor: "Fine!" In the evening, he admitted that the reason that there was no general policy was that Roosevelt had no policy.) He insisted that they had secured an agreement that the workers in Detroit could bargain collectively and that the papers had paid no attention to it. "They can bargain collectively, but there's nobody to bargain with."

Cecil [Wolman, Leo's wife] said that Washington was now pure Chekhov. I said that whereas the Ohio gang had played poker, the Brain Trusters talked. Leo said there was very little formality, that people went to each other's houses and didn't dress. Cecil said, Oh yes, they did dress. Young college boys had made the social life much gayer. —Leo, as neutral member of the board, leaned toward the employers' side: it didn't make much difference that he could see whether the workers were bossed by the union

---

* F.D.R.'s Secretary of Labor. See "Madame Secretary," in *Earthquake,* pp. 560–4.

leader or the foreman—but he thought that the presence of the board in Detroit had stopped a good deal of the intimidation.

Johnson: When Leo had been about to resign before, Johnson had written him something in the nature of a love letter, such as Cecil had never seen written by a man to another man—she didn't mean to suggest that there was anything queer about him—but excessively sentimental.

Wolman's nice little house, 2200 Wyoming Avenue, big bare tiled ceremonious reception room occupying whole front part of the first floor, with rather wide curve-railed staircase leading up to dining and living rooms; bright fire in fireplace behind bright brass screen, brass fire things and brass lining of hearth below white mantelpiece. Cecil on a couch at the opposite side of the room in sober small-checked pajamas. Lilies of the valley, Easter lilies, highballs. Leo filled the glass decanter carefully from the whiskey bottle. Pictures of birds as if from books, one large clear one of some long-necked green bird above the couch where Cecil was lying on her back. Leo, after having a couple of highballs, began to sit on one leg of his chair and goddam, evidently a relief to him. He damned all the Brain Trusters. Of [Harold] Ickes* it had been said, "He's suburban." Tugwell he hadn't seen much of—in response to my question: yes, he didn't think much of him—a bootlicker, after a career. I asked about Fred Howe: "Oh, you [know] Fred Howe." Roosevelt had no policy—the whole thing, he had said at lunch, was an imposture, a tragic imposture!—the government's case was weak against Weir: the government had broken an agreement with them. —Weir, unlike Budd, would have been willing to cooperate. When he told me about the situation in Detroit, I said, "Then the NRA will be beaten." "Sure."

* F.D.R.'s Secretary of the Interior.

He thought it was going to be "terrible" when the reaction set in—but I couldn't drive him into any Marxist position, except, once, to admit that Communism was a possibility. Yet he couldn't answer the question of how his immediate prospects for the government could lead to the benevolent control of industry under capitalism. He denied that the industrial situation had anything to do with colonization. When I asked what technological development would lead to, he said, "That's a long story"—and went on to grope at a position something like Merwin Hart's: cut down hours and distribute labor. At lunch, he had railed against the NRA for insisting on their securing collective bargaining. This thing in Detroit had nothing to do with collective bargaining.

The baby had tonsillitis, which was just getting into his ears, and his crying was heard from time to time—Leo would excuse himself and go right upstairs. The class situation, he said, was much more complicated in the United States than it had been in Russia. He knew the bunch at the Barrows-Wirt party and bet they had talked plenty. The headwaiter at the Washington addressed him as "Doctor."

Frances Perkins made her entrance very late, after a party at the British embassy. A sort of English-comedy voice coming up the stairs: "So nice to have you back!—I haven't been here before!" Smartly dressed, black evening gown, silver openwork shoes. I was favorably impressed, had expected one of those demon old maids, but Frances Perkins is quite attractive in a rather feminine way: full body, pretty hands, with which she made a good deal of rather fancy play. She shook hands with me with her left hand (the other was holding a bag), as if she hadn't expected me to try to shake hands with her. They asked her whether she would have a drink. "Not now." They supposed she had had plenty to drink at the embassy. Leo at once began laying before her the situation about the discrimination. He took the attitude that the leader who threatened to strike didn't really know why he wanted to strike. Frances Perkins had asked him, "Why *does* he want to strike?" She said, somewhat in the tone of an intelligent and good-natured rich lady talking about the servants: "*I* know why they want to strike—they're bored and tired and getting discouraged about the NRA's doing anything for them! We're supposed to take the attitude [I wasn't quite sure that she didn't know who I was and that this wasn't for my benefit] that we're against strikes, but in certain situations violent methods are necessary." When I shook hands with her on going, I had the impression that she hadn't expected me to do that either. They said that when she got started, would talk for hours. Mary Vorse's story about the reporter (*Daily Worker,* I think) who had asked her, "What about Ambridge?" (where a number of people had been shot) "Well, what about Ambridge? What is it about Ambridge?" She had made one error of which even Leo disapproved by putting herself on record not long ago as asserting that "There was not a single first-class strike in the whole country" at the moment when the motor strike was impending. She had told Mary that admitting Emma Goldman* had done her a good deal of damage. Harper in the Indian Office said that the Department of Justice was still up to its old stuff (though Frances Perkins had somewhat improved things). A Department of Justice man had said that they had been watching one of the Indian Bureau people as a Red and that they had plenty on him.

I said there was something rather flimsy about Wash-

* Emma Goldman, the old-time anarchist, had been readmitted to the United States after being deported to the Soviet Union, where she had had a difficult time with the Communist leadership.

ington, and Cecil answered, "Yes," and now it was like a show that had been on the road too long—the costumes were soiled and the scenery was getting weak. She had enjoyed it, she said, as a show. Sometimes would get so excited, as after a dinner at which they had debated the crucial Treasury resignation, that she hadn't been able to sleep afterwards, and had gotten a complex, last winter, being torn between doing her sculpture and keeping a diary. Leo wanted to get away and live in the country and write some books he'd had in his mind.

[My infected nose became worse, and I had to go to the hospital. There I added to my discomfiture by reading Hegel's *Philosophy of History*.] Little North Carolina nurse: "I believe 'its' gonta rain after all the pretty day!"

Coming back to Griffin's apartment, after the wine of the brawling and bellowing dinner at the left newspaper-men's club and the highball at Childs: the park with its big bright low globule lamps with tails on top like Prince Rupert drops and dark low clumps of bushes, green and black, cool, almost cold—and in the center the black horse of the statue rearing behind its spiked grating—pleasant after New York, but reminded me somehow drearily of that provincial Washington I had visited as a child with Sandy, when I had gotten sick as I had this time, where there were not so many amusements as in New York. Playing in the brick suburbanlike streets with the nice but not very interesting Todd Ashby [Sandy's cousin]. Poli's "polite and refined" [a vaudeville house] had to be made to go a long way.

The food nowhere seemed to be as good as you would have thought it would be—not a bit like Baltimore, or my idea of Baltimore.

On the way to Cecil Wolman's for dinner: the new leaves and grass smelled like Princeton, and the house reminded me of Prospect Street. Mike Ross; beautiful and smartly gotten-up German girl married to an American husband, and less attractive sister; young German from Santa Fe, suspected by Muriel Draper of carrying on Nazi propaganda; young Englishman, a newspaper correspondent; dark evidently Jewish girl who came in eating peanuts. A general atmosphere of refined tea, it seemed to me. [Leo was away again.] Young Woolston's entrance: he opened the door a crack, so that Cecil could see him but not the rest of the company, and asked her whether she wanted a cat. He brought in a little cat, dirty white with gray spots, and threw it over on the couch in a spectacular manner. The Englishman said he liked alley cats because he lived in an alley. Cecil got somebody to feed it. He offered to make another cocktail when she was about to do so. "You don't know what to put in it." "You can tell me, though." As I had come in, I had thought how, much as I had used to resent Father when he was alive, I had come to value more and more highly his little provincial study, with its books and its stuffed birds—as I left, this all seemed to me more like Prospect Street than ever. I thought it was spinach and to hell with it!

Cecil always wore open sandals, which showed her pretty feet. There was no brass rim to the fireplace. Shell-like concavities above bookcases on either side of the fire—couches covered with something light and flowered, cushions looked stuffed hard and with a slightly metallic finish, but were soft when you sat up on them.

Cecil's stories about going to the White House: importance of procedure, how much people thought about it. The men were handed cards, which indicated whom you were taking in to dinner, and you were introduced to one another as in a Virginia reel. She and Ritchie [Governor Ritchie of Maryland?] had once found themselves left behind without partners, and he suggested their going in together, but a look of horror came over his face, she said, when they got near the dining room and he realized he was going in with a woman of the wrong rank. He was probably the ranking person there—should he have had Mrs. Roosevelt? Wretched dinner: consommé with nothing in it, very tasteless lamb, canned corn with pools of water in it—nothing to drink. A general atmosphere of social workers. A lady writer who sat down on the floor in front of the fire when the ladies went in after dinner— Mrs. Roosevelt said, when she came in and saw her, "Well, I *hope* you're comfortable there!" Ghastly entertainment, embarrassing: Jewish *diseuse* who did Dolley Madison in the White House, trying on bonnets, then a Negro sermon "The World Are on Crutches," looking at the President. Other features of the White House entertainment were a colored girl who had been taught to sing like an Italian diva and did Negro spirituals self-consciously and a little gypsy boy who played an accordion while Mrs. Roosevelt kept time all through with her head. They ended up with some very weak pink punch.

Washington is really a hollow shell which holds the liberalism of the New Deal as easily as the crooks and thugs of the Harding Administration—no trouble to clean it out every night and put something else in the past Administration's place.

The bathroom at Derson's rooming house reminded me of the bathroom at the Keysers', which I hadn't thought of in years. [The Keysers were the relatives of the Knoxes whom Sandy and I visited in boyhood.] Bathtub, extinct type of gas jet. I paid a visit to the Keysers. The sisters were back together [I think they had fallen out]. The family portraits and furniture. Their hair gray now, but vivacious old girls—Bessie going out after dinner to a meeting; Alice liberal-religious; Fosdick–Henry

Sloane Coffin. How Chester [their old-maidish brother] had loved to make people see sights. —They showed me an enlarged snapshot of him, beaming—in Italy, where he had been happiest—he had spoken Italian so well. Their Knox malice, everybody else an outsider. I was depressed at seeing them still asserting their little Washington government-servant gentility by making fun of other people. Was surprised at how much they knew about my family—they inquired about Uncle Win, who was supposed to have nearly married Alice but to have been thrown off by Mrs. Knox's tactless efforts to make the match. He is supposed to have said to Mrs. Knox: "You can lead a horse to water, but you can't make him drink."

Paddy [Gardner] Jackson kept saying: "And I promised Dody this morning I wasn't going to drink!—Oh, the two natures!"

Lunch with Paddy Jackson, Blankenhorn, Griffin, and Rodman—? drinking from one to four; Blank all ready to go out and organize steelworkers, all that was needed was $500 for a paper—Griffin kept asking him why he didn't do it—finally, Paddy Jackson clasped his hand to his brow and exclaimed, apropos of the prospects of the Administration's liberal policies: "Blank! Bunny! Me! —*Jesus!*" (this last coming out with explosive emphatic force). He kept saying, "And I promised Dody this morning I wasn't going to drink! The two natures! The two natures in man!"

The kick I got out of my room at the back corner of the sordid rooming house kept by a blowzy yellow-haired woman with a German accent and glasses and a shirt-sleeved taciturn man with glasses—in spite of the dark and greasy-walled halls, with signs asking that what I took at first to be "rondoes" be not played after ten, and suggestive of stuffy and sordid lives behind the closed doors, occasionally left open and revealing unappetizing interiors (one showed a woman's bed with an ugly fancy coverlet and other stuffy fancy trappings)—the sour, dirty, and repulsive bathroom: the marble of the basin never washed, with toothpowder on it, toilet paper always sticking around the seat, bathtub usually dirty as if people had been trampling around in it with their shoes on, putting their feet on the edge to tie their shoes, long nail used for a bolt and frequently falling out, shade apparently immovable: it could be neither lowered nor raised, scrap bucket befouled with cigarette ashes and, apparently, expectoration, as if it had never been cleaned out but only emptied in the most perfunctory fashion, towel worn thin and largely in rags and no soap supplied, attempts to wash around the closet, which left everything wet and almost more forbidding than before. —But on the third floor in the little room, with a bed of which the sheets seemed to be clean and with windows on two sides which looked out on the backs of low brick houses and through which the morning notes of a few spring birds as well as the monologue in a debased Southern accent of some slatternly-sounding woman reached me— I enjoyed some sort of peace in that place where nobody knew me, where, as had not been the case with the old fool at Derson's, everybody was indifferent to me and where nobody that I knew knew where I was—to be away in the little back room of a house in a provincial Southern city when spring has just definitely come on!— away from family, politics, engagements, even love affairs, where I could lie in bed in the morning and think about pleasantly but coolly at my leisure—read the papers at my leisure by the electric bulb in bed at night— warm enough so that you didn't need covers while reading, yet cool enough so that you did not perspire and were not even enervated (the enervating weather came,

though, soon enough, along with uncomfortable rain).
Clearness, simplification, and peace. [I read there Edith
Wharton's *A Backward Glance*.]

Senator Homer T. Bone of Washington. Shrewd eye
and speech, loose reassuring mouth. He was opposed to
power interests and war—power interests had tried to
frame him at home, would send around blondes with
peach basket hats who would ask him to get (collusive)
divorces for them, and he would take great pleasure in
taking their money and then explaining to them that, if
they did it, they would be guilty of a penitentiary of-
fense; and he wouldn't sleep in a hotel without a newspaper editor in bed with him. Senatorial poetry of his
speech—once when he paused for a flower: "If I had the
logic of a—Plato," Paddy Jackson supplied, "Plato or an
Aristotle." He would occasionally break into verse quotations.

American: Wilkie (Indian Defense man). He showed
the dangers—he pointed out fifty dangers—

Dillinger headlines every day: "Dillinger Forces Doctor to Treat Him"; "Dillinger Halts Four Cops." Dawn
Powell said, "Dillinger is surrounding the United States."

Georgetown: little vivid red-brick houses—more like
the South, wooden Negro houses and sauntering
Negroes—clear sunny afternoon air, light as if of clear
yellow through new American leaves on brick walk,
slightly unfamiliar flavor in the air (beginning of characteristic Southern smell of bricks and cooking?), somehow
seemed to remind me of Lakewood.

"*Little Red Schoolhouse*," supposed stronghold in
Georgetown of the Brain Trust, often brought up sarcastically in Congress.

[I went to call on *Martha Krock*, Arthur Krock's wife,
who had previously been married to Bill Blair in Chicago
and had been a friend of Louise's.] She said that she
missed Louise, but had left Chicago after such effortful

preparations under such disagreeable circumstances that she didn't feel homesick for it—would probably have stayed in Lake Forest all her life if Bill hadn't gone bankrupt. A rather appealing mouth and slim arms, though pale thyroid eyes; pink flowered print dress, with sleeves that gave a glimpse of her upper arms, then was caught up over them again—she said that Krock told her and Louise that their Middle Western wisecracks seemed stale and crude in the East—she complained of the small-town character of Washington—if you said you had another engagement, people asked you what it was—when she had said she was going to Virginia for the weekend, they had asked her where in Virginia. Fleda Springer (from Oklahoma), when she saw my glass was empty, said: "Boy, you want some more whiskey, mister!" She had been fascinated by somebody in Washington because he had kept saying, "By George."

[Peggy Bacon* had come to Washington with Dawn Powell, and I arranged to have her do drawings of Roosevelt and other people.] One of the Listerine Lamberts Peggy Bacon told about who had the radio arranged so that it could be turned on from any room in the house; managed to have all his work done by nine o'clock in the morning and thought that the unemployment problem could be solved by putting all the unemployed on a big raft and sinking it in the middle of the Atlantic. Alex Brook had said, "I suppose you'll be on it." Peggy thought he was stupid and most objectionable, and it was just his money that made people say that he was an eccentric millionaire. I remembered that John Amen had been rather enthusiastic over one of the Lamberts—perhaps, as Peggy thought, this man's brother.

Peggy Bacon flushes with lovely delicacy.

* See "Peggy Bacon: Poet with Pictures," in *The Shores of Light*, pp. 701–4.

Esther Strachey had been to a dinner of the Young Republican Builders—someone had said that they wanted to insist on the sacredness of the Constitution, that they disapproved of the present policy of the Administration in treating it lightly—but someone else warned him that, on the contrary, they ought to be careful about that: it was something that could be used both ways.

PROVINCETOWN, 1934

Beach at Sea Bright (June 3, '34). Were they all really the pretty maids of the people who went in at the Beach Club? Girl in pistache-green bathing suit, very pretty, but surely no virgin, by her lack of self-conscious ness and her way of handling her legs—bathing suit with no back, coming up to cover her breasts and caught up over the shoulders with white strips little more than ribbons that came down over her back—this kind of bathing suit, of which the serious part in back only really began with their buttocks, seemed to show off their behinds—at any rate, in this case, this part of her was beautiful and large beneath a small waist and with legs that tapered down beautifully from the thick thighs to slim ankles and long feet—her hands were long and fine, too, and she moved with a certain looseness as she tickled with her red-nailed fingers the toes of another pretty girl in a blue suit, who, with plumper and fatter less modeled legs, was lying on her back with a thing like a small pink towel half over her face to shield her complexion and with the slit of her cunt, which I lay on the sand looking directly into, showing through her bathing suit—she wagged her toes when the other girl tickled them, and the latter half smiled at me, with her round brown eyes and pert nose, as she saw me watching amused—the tickling and wiggling went on some time— the supine girl shifted her foot slightly, but on the whole seemed to show a remarkably slow defensive reaction— very slowly the development went forward—the girl re- cumbent on her back began patting the sand with a stiffened foot almost more as if in rhythm than as if she were trying to avoid the tickling—then the other girl took a small bit of driftwood, almost frankly amused by meeting my gaze again—the plump girl in blue began kicking sand on the tickler's hands in the same rhythmic unirritated way—and only after some minutes of this, sat up, showing her face from under the pink thing: she was pretty, in a more baby-faced schoolgirl way, simple, plump, and amicable, too. It was hot inland at Red Bank, but when we got off the breeze at Sea Bright, the breeze from the sea was cold, and the water at first was hard to bear.

Dos said that *the Communists* would have a hard time to compete with *Huey Long with his "Every Man a King,"* because the only thing they could promise was a good clubbing a week—nothing like it since the 11,000 virgins: Every Man a Martyr. —That left nothing but the Jews. —*Ernest Boyd's* crack in the *American Specta- tor:* Proletarians of all lands unite. You have *nothing but your chains to lose.* I had quoted it with the chains last. Dos said that when he read it, their missing the right sequence [the *American Spectator* people] showed that they couldn't win.

Morning, June 2, '34, after *Anna* had gone to live by herself in little dormer-windowed rooms at 2430 85th

Street, and Jerry was pressing his suit. She had applied for relief and a widow's pension, and the social workers were coming to see her and asking her about four million questions till she got self-conscious and mixed up. She had had to give the addresses of all the places she had ever lived. Who had paid her expenses in the hospital? Had she ever practiced prostitution? ever been in a house of detention? She had to explain who was who between Fatty and Sam, who had both taken the name of Litwood. They had apparently looked up the jail sentences and wanted to know who had been sentenced for what. —She had left Lizzie under a bush in Central Park because she didn't want to bring her here on account of Lizzie's being so dirty and having just gotten over the chicken pox, which she had had pretty badly, having caught it from Suzanne, so that it had affected her throat and her eyes.

When Sam had ruined her, she tried to commit suicide by shutting herself up in her room and turning on the gas—because she thought he wouldn't marry her and she'd never ask him—but somebody came in. Later on, she drank some stuff that Sam told her was poison—so that she did have the nerve to do it—but nothing happened—he'd put something else in the bottle.

Red Bank (end of June). Sweet, faint, and acrid scent of the white clover in the grass. Mother said, "They miss me (those flowers)—they're used to having me weed them!" She had just sent Bobby to the dog hospital. "You know, I used to be a good dog doctor, but I can't labor with them any more."

Scott Fitzgerald at this time had the habit of insulting people, and then saying, if the victim came back at him: "Can't take it, huh?" [I learned years later from Morley

Callaghan that this was a habit of Hemingway's, from whom Scott had undoubtedly acquired it.]

K.'s visit to Provincetown in the early summer of '34, when I was living in Frank Shay's house.

Sam Insull was a little man, which made him cocky, combined with his father's disgrace. He had got them in a small room and deafened them with the phonograph. When the English secretary got up and turned it down, he went over and turned it up again. He had been going in for low women, who turned up at his father's birthday party (etc.)—a former burlesque queen who said, *"Pardon me!"* Old man Insull had "welcomed the opportunity" to come back and vindicate himself.

Upper room with big wooden bed, into which the sun came through the slanted windows. The Portuguese family in back sounded so nice together, she thought— the mother so nice to the little boy, the father so nice to the mother—they made clucking sounds like a poultry yard. I fell asleep one afternoon trying to understand a word or two of their language, and finally dreamed that I did. The bed creaking in the otherwise empty house, which rather exhilarated me but turned out to have frozen her. I suggested leaving on the *Dorothy Bradford,* but she said, "With two such poor sinners as us on it, it would go down, I'm afraid!" We could hear, in the room upstairs, a boy practicing on some kind of wind instrument—the merry tunes were halting and somewhat off-key, which made us listen to them with a sort of nervous suspense and laugh, and yet it was somehow nice, and we felt friendly toward him, not peevish. Her great word now was "plopse": plopse on the boat, plopse out of the taxi. "Mosquitoes the size of eagles." Her bathing suit which hung around her neck with a narrow white strap to which a narrow white strap from her trunks was tied. When she walked into town wearing it, the authorities told her she couldn't.

On the last night, I told K. that she was the damnedest most inconsiderate woman I had ever known. She had been drinking and I not, interrupting me as I was reading to tell me about Chicago and what she was reading in *Time*. [I was reading Michelet's letters, and about to get the *Finland Station* started.] When she came upstairs to bed, she perched the oil lamp on the edge of the shelves with one leg hanging over, and insisted on smoking in bed and leaving some candles alight on the floor. I snatched up the small sheet and a pillow and my watch and went downstairs and slept on the couch. Perhaps the fact that the gray sheet was one which Margaret and I had had several summers before had something to do with this. But I was touched, after getting her off, to think about her having studied shorthand.

Provincetown, July 4, '34—seemed subdued: people on the wagon, not making a point of seeing so much of one another, rather withdrawing. Susan [Glaspell] and Langston Moffett had united on an alcoholic basis. Charley Kaselau said it was a great thing for the rest of them, because now Susan and Langston could listen to each other where they had previously made other people listen to them—but they had come around one night and Susan had kept saying: "Now you must listen to Langston—he's saying something *beautiful!*" etc. Harl Cook throwing lighted cannon crackers to go off in people's faces—afterwards got into a motor accident with Nilla Cook's little son, both hurt. *The Hacketts* had moved up to the other end of town and were afflicted with poison ivy—empty, a quiet Fourth, which came in the middle of the week, saving up for Sailor Week.

The Hacketts had started to go on a fishing trip, and

Bubs had set off the alarm when she had been trying to set it before going to bed, and waked the children up—nobody had gone to sleep again. Chauncey had lost his pants while frying eggs in the morning and had cut 180 proof alcohol so strong that nobody, not even the fishermen, could drink it. He had finally decided that he felt in such bad shape that he couldn't undertake the expedition, and had gone back to bed. He had been having a recurrent dream about biting the heads off matches—connected in the dream with situations of embarrassment. He had also had a dream of meeting and talking with two old friends whom he had never seen before. One of them remonstrated with him in the most friendly way about the way he was living. They always told their dreams, he said, in that family. He talked charmingly about Washington—he defended the style of the Capitol as something that corresponded to Victorian, and thought that it ought still to have the statue of Washington with his shirt off in front of it instead of being led up to by large boulevards, which made it a sort of anti-climax—but admitted that it was disheartening—you always felt that there were hidden places in it where secret things went on—and there *were* all sorts of things—rooms in the piers that supported the dome, a tunnel which had been discovered leading to the old ——— Creek and through which it was supposed that papers were to have been carried in the event of a threatened attack on the Capitol in war—was there anything under the basement? —Washington was supposed to have been buried under the Capitol, you know—the legislative chambers with no direct opening on the outside, only the lighting from the top, so that the sun made a glare on the papers when you looked down on them—and you looked down on the heads of the people.

New Beach. Glimpse of group—woman in white

sweater and dark-blue trousers, with big-brimmed white flopping hat that drooped mostly down in front, sitting on the sand with two tiny children, and a big black Great Dane, whose legs looked like wrought-iron work against the pale molten blue sea, in which the heads of swimmers made white-shining molten streaks—the whole with an effect at once metallic and of pure dark and light.

Hacketts. Using their bathroom: rusty rectangular white tub and rusty seaside smell like Peaked Hill and New Jersey—I felt affectionate toward it—Chauncey's solitary old large silver military brush with his monogram on it, relic of better days.

Norman Matson. Making $12 a story by writing anti-radical stuff for *The Saturday Evening Post*—he enraged the Kaselaus by calling on them and telling them about the special mahogany paneling he was putting in in his new Wellfleet place and saying, "Don't tell me about your troubles! I don't want to hear about them!" He said that it was ridiculous for people not to make money—no excuse for it! He wrote Susan asking her for a list of things out of the house, including a spinning wheel that they had bought with her money on their honeymoon. I met him in the telephone office—he was developing a big belly and a kind of pale film seemed to have passed over his blue-gray eyes.

Hacketts. Bad situation about Harl Cook—Bubs has the money [I don't think that this is true: they both, I believe, had a little]. Chauncey takes to shutting himself up during day in workroom and trying to do comics— Bubs and Harl take car and go off and leave him fuming at parties. Susan, closely allied with Langston, aided and abetted them.

Waughs. They were getting sucker-sour. Once Coulton had replied to a lady who had asked him how high he had said the hollyhocks grew: "Oh, about twenty-five feet!" Elizabeth would insult the customers devastatingly two or three times a summer. Katy said she had come in and found them like tired spiders in the back room— they would start into life at once at the sound of some- one coming in. They had divided the customers into two classes: nitwits and swankers; they rather liked the former, but the latter were impossible. They saw pre- cisely how the customers were going to respond to a given stimulus—for example, immediately after asking how the ships were gotten into the bottles, they would always say, "O, I see: the bottle is blown around the ship"—so Coulton would always wait for that remark before an- swering the question. Elizabeth wouldn't let me ask any questions when I came in after hours, because answering would start her off on her monologues. I used to come in and ask for "one with red hair and big brown eyes," or a carbon with a typewriter in it. Elizabeth told me very seriously that I mustn't get fresh, because her tenant had been there at the time. Elizabeth finally collapsed with sciatica, and they got in Mary Hackett, who did nothing at all—then Chauncey took her place and did better, was charming to the customers and offered them cigarettes. He promised, at my suggestion, to pull the rugs out from under the customers someday when the shop was full. One day, Chauncey said that there had never been anything more depraved than the conditions in that shop today—the customers had been milling like fish, afraid they were going to miss the boat, etc. Chaun- cey was stimulated by his work, became extremely lively and witty in his silly way—said that my account of my conversation with Marjorie [Niles Spencer's sister] at the Spencers' party, which hadn't as a matter of fact been particularly amusing, was "a gem of purest ray serene." He said he was going to have to go to the bath- room in a minute—his stomach was out of order, but it was very easy to ease it, all you had to do was to drink a lot of rum, and he had drunk some beer, too. He began turning up with liquor on his breath or a hangover, which violated the discipline of the shop, as the Waughs during the day only drank Coca-Cola. Elizabeth, while Coulton was away, had to strain herself more than ever, as Chauncey never helped her to pick up the rugs. He was delighted at his encounters with the customers—one woman had called him Mr. Waugh and he had told her that his name was Hackett—could he tell her where to find Hackett, the artist: "Madame, I am Hackett, the artist." A Pen Rhyn Stanislaws girl from the South came in and gave him postcards to mail, which he read—of *course,* she was engaged to a young man who worked in a bank, and of *course,* she was writing to her girlfriend and giving her the lowdown—and then there was one to her mother. Then there had been old ladies with falsetto voices, who had looked at everything, stayed a long time, and then started to go and came back and bought a postcard apiece. And the old lady who had put her finger on the map and said, "What's a Salem?" —I get irritated with the Hacketts, neglect of their children, I think. They had promised to take them to the drugstore for a soda, and then tried to get out of it because they wanted to stay for drinks themselves, and attempted to fob them off with ice cream—till the little girl began to cry. One winter they had fed them raw vegetables in order to get out of the trouble of cooking them, till the children had gotten sick.

Visit to John Bishop at South Harwich: picnic with a Mrs. Bellinger [no connection with my old friends the Washington, Conn., Bellingers]—mother and boy just out of Yale, who was teaching English and French at Loomis School and quoted long scenes from *Alice in*

Wonderland—picnic on sand, too elaborate: charcoal burner, low table that folded up and could be carried by a handle like a suitcase: steak, hard potatoes, tomatoes—Margaret talked French constantly with the French cook—sand in the food. Margaret very sharp with the children: "Stupid little boy!"—interrupting our sand game in a peremptory way to make us eat—impatient with John, perhaps made impatient by his inability to fathom the game. When Rosalind asked her whether she was going in swimming, she said sharply: "No: Thank you very much!" When Margaret was around, they talked most of the time about fine food—you could get it up there if you took the trouble to send for the things from Macy's, etc. Grocer who had gotten her a larding needle, and somebody else had gotten her two calves' feet, because gelatin wouldn't do—*boeuf à la mode* soaked in a bottle of sauterne and a bottle of Rhine wine for their party. Margaret would say: "But marvelous!" They told at great length about their château and how they had fixed it up—had had six servants. John would revert to literature and art as soon as Margaret was away: Gregorian chants, hopeless invariable fall at the end, a phonograph record from Solesmes; Stravinsky's Dickens, he was sure that Fagin buggered the boys; Archy MacLeish and the rhymes in *Conquistador*; *Chanson de Roland.* Margaret brought one of the twins in to be punished for throwing a stone through the window; to John: "You'll have to do it, I haven't got time!"—so John took him upstairs and spanked him audibly, the child making hateful resisting gestures. Margaret had been told by an aunt, when she was young, that sleeping on a pillow prevented you from carrying your head erect, so all her life she had never used one, and she told with great triumph and something like passion of moral mastery how all three children slept without pillows, and when she went in to look at them, there they were all lying on their sides with one leg up just as she did. She went sound asleep as soon as she laid her head down and never moved all night. She said with the same grim aggressive satisfaction, when John and I were remarking that when we wanted to get up early the next morning we found it hard to go to sleep early the night before, that she could always go *right* to sleep!

Brownie L'Engle on the Fall River boat. She found me in the dining room, told me with what I thought tended to be a gratified smile that her father was dying in a hospital which the boat was passing—next morning, after a wretched night—getting into Newport always wakes me up—I had made the changes involving three trains, Taunton, Middleboro, and an hour and a half wait at this last place, and had just gone to sleep on the train headed at last for Provincetown, when Brownie waked me up brusquely so that I gave a cry and attracted the attention of the other passengers. She was delighted when she discovered that I had had the train trip instead of the bus, which enabled you to stay on board the boat till 8:30 instead of only till 7:00, and told me it was "very comfortable." Her unpleasant and peremptory way of asking me to take her suitcase off the train, or there was something the matter with her so that she couldn't carry it. She had wanted to know whether the textile workers were striking against the employers or the NRA—was wondering whether the NRA wasn't making it impossible for the former to pay any higher wages (her father had been on the Reconstruction Finance Committee)—had been very much impressed by Stuart Chase's* last book and thought it ought to be made into a movie. When I told her about the steel mills, she said

* The writer on economic affairs whose book *The Economy of Abundance* was published in 1934.

that she and Bill ought to go and sketch them. She had once told Elizabeth Waugh that it was a good thing she had never had any children, as she wouldn't have had enough money to take care of them—Elizabeth had retorted in kind and finally gone off with, "Goodbye, Poison Face!"

Opening of Chauncey Hackett's trunk and bursting out of all his old Washington social clothes, which had been made for a slimmer figure.

They (the Hacketts) put together a very good dinner, tender lamb, excellent fresh peas, boiled potatoes, cheese, crackers, lettuce salad, and coffee and King Corn (50¢ for a half pint), which Chauncey served to me a little at a time in a single liqueur glass like Napoleon brandy. This cheered me up very much after the cold, canned, and unappetizing meals which Hortense had been giving me [one of the Portuguese who came originally from the Cape Verde Islands].

Awful summer when Knobby [Stella] had been living with Susan and had come in two or three times a day to depress Chauncey with her tales of woe [she was a hypochondriac who always managed to keep herself ill and spent her last years in a hospital, lived with the Smooleys*—a repulsive girl; told Elizabeth that I probably had syphilis]—finally he had induced her to go to England, giving her a letter to a friend of his, to whom, however, he wrote to tell her that she didn't really need to pay much attention to Knobby. Knobby and the friend, however, apparently got on like wildfire, had been together constantly and were apparently coming back together.

---

* According to Mary Heaton Vorse, the Smooleys was a composite name for a family of friends who lived together in Provincetown—probably the Sm—ths and the F—oleys.

Ozzie Ball [no connection with the other Balls] had had a mild case of shell shock from being in the Graves Registration Service during the war. Once he had been on the subway and had seen one of the men he buried sitting next to him. He began to scream and was taken into the police court—it turned out to be the dead man's brother or something. Chauncey said that the story had curdled his blood the first two or three times he heard it: after that, he got used to it.

They had had the idea at Provincetown of putting on *Hamlet* one winter and had even gotten so far as to provide themselves with books and hold a rehearsal. Ball had been cast for the First Grave-digger—they didn't know then about his past—and he began to cry and say he was too much trouble, and then to vomit loudly out the window, while they were trying to read the lines. Charley Kaselau got hurt and sulky because he wasn't allowed to play Hamlet.

Dr. Hebert applied to Muffy, when the little dog was ill, the same stethoscope he used for his human patients, then took his pulse and told Bubs that he was dying of arsenic poisoning, which acted very slowly. When I told him that the doctor in New York had been giving me tin [I was suffering from boils that summer], he told me that the tablets which he had been giving me had been tin, but that I oughtn't to take more than ten of them, as they might be injurious—hinting, on my inquiry, at obscure and mysterious deleterious effects which they might have on the liver and kidneys and thus attempting to scare you about the remedy as well as the disease. Coulton said that Dr. Cass, who was of the cheerful and reassuring type, was all right if you saw him from the front, but if you went around to the side, you saw that he had no back to his head and realized that he was just a small-town doctor.

Bubs would wake *Chauncey* up in the night and ask him to tell her again how Floyd Clymer had looked when he and Langston had been plunging around like Behemoth and Leviathan in the L'Engles' kitchen.

Chauncey had once gone to the country to spend a weekend with a girl—only she and her grandmother were in the house—he and the girl began playing charades all by themselves—there was a scene in which he was to be assassinated or something, for which she produced a revolver, and she assured him that it wasn't loaded, but he tried it and it went off—if she had actually killed him, nobody could possibly ever have guessed the truth.

The men in one of the fish-storage plants struck because they are getting only 39¢ an hour—Niles overheard the old man in the newsstand say, "Those boys ought to be horsewhipped!"—a woman, I am told, said, "Do you suppose one of those agitators is been here?"

Energizing October day, blowing the winter light about the cubes of the Provincetown buildings—blowing freshly the faded blue and pink and khaki of the fishermen's wash on the line—blowing the fine straggly twiggy treetops on the crest of the hill where I live—beyond, the thinning copper and spreading branches of the bigger trees along Commercial Street, and the gulls above them, blown about, but still active—cut away from all the world in the homely lovely town with its combination of safe felicity and wild sea weather.

On damp days, when the brown of the trees was almost gone and the sea and the sky were gray, all colors neutralized, Provincetown was like being on a boat—for me, living alone, writing during the day and reading at night, the external world was almost obliterated.

The Truro churches on their bare hills, and the inland hollows with little ponds that get so dark at nightfall.

The sad fog signal, carrying a human meaning but

managed by no human hands and with no human quality—empty, dreary.

Susan and Langston and Commander MacMillan.[*] The dinner she gave for the Commander—Langston was handing out drinks made up with alky which he'd forgotten to cut, then he sat on the stairs and delivered a long speech to himself. During dinner, Susan had said that, after all, we all came from the ice: humanity came from the ice—Charley Kaselau pointed out to her that, on the contrary, life had been killed off by the Ice Age: "Well, I don't know: it's an idea of Langston's." Later he intimated to Susan that you don't drink on Arctic expeditions: Langston, on learning this, thought that in that case he wouldn't go—he'd also discovered that he couldn't take his chow and that he couldn't get there in his Packard. Susan called MacMillan "darling." He drinks nothing and left soon. —Eben described another party at Susan's at which the guests had gotten themselves around the room by hanging on to the furniture, like a slowed-up moving picture or an animal act. —Susan and her repetitions, when drinking: I had read her Shakespeare's sonnet about the sessions of sweet silent thought, in which the phrase "death's dateless night" occurs, and then she had asked me to read a sonnet in which "death's dateless something" occurred. I read it to her again, and then she made Betty read it to her several times and would have gone on making her do so indefinitely.

Laura Merriss. Pale yellow hair, sweet round Scotch forehead, light blue eyes, slouching or, rather, tilted-forward walk, large feet, woman engineer's hands of the same general type as Jean Gorman's—regularly recurrent emphasis on certain words in speech, which I think is

[*] Commander Donald B. MacMillan had led the Crocker Land Expedition (1913–17) in the Arctic.

Scotch, too. Her directness and a certain loveliness triumphed over her middle-class aspects: told Betty to come at six because she got so hungry in the afternoon with riding that she *had* to eat. At her house, she had her little girl play rather stumbling little pieces on the piano—the little girl, who had made Tiny Worthington's South American brother get down on the floor to play fishpond and who had very decided views on the relative intelligences of the Merriss dogs: two Sealyhams and a Scottie pup, all very amicable—Betty said they seemed to have no nerves whereas Susan's Tucker was always likely to bite you. Laura exclaimed "Good night!" when the dog made water in the middle of the dining room while we were having a buffet supper—she grabbed him and put him out. I asked to see her poems while she was listening to the returns on the Harvard–Princeton game, and with her usual directness she went and got them at once—"Oh, all right!"—went through them and picked out some that she thought were the best and gave them to me. Also handed me a pencil and asked me to mark the lines that didn't scan. She said that she had written twenty-four sonnets, and the man who gave the course in writing had told her that six of them were good— the one she liked most she couldn't find, thought she had stuck it in some book, as she had a way of doing, could only remember the last two lines—only one she could remember all of was one she had composed in the station wagon, she had said, "Now I *must* write this down," and she had stopped at Hyannis and gone into a grocery store and bought a package of breakfast food and asked for a piece of brown paper and a pencil and written it out—she said that, if it was metrically all right, it was on account of the rhythm of the station wagon and that she probably ought to compose them all that way: "When you're with me again, my love! When

you're with me again!—or away from me!" —I asked her
if she'd been writing poetry long, and she answered,
"Oh, for years! [Though apparently, up to lately, mostly
birthday and Christmas rhymes.] There's a whole
bushel basket full out in the barn, and sometimes when
I'm out there, I pick up a handful and go through them
and think, 'How did I ever come to write anything so
awful!'" When I suggested that she ought to sit down
and work at them and fill up some of the metrical holes,
she said that she might when the weather got colder
so that she couldn't be out of doors.

She really looked lovely the day she came to the
Spencers' in her blond riding clothes and boots, with a
light-blue scarf around her neck. The day I bicycled over
there, she had on sneakers, overalls, and a dark-blue
"hood" which she pulled off over her head with some
difficulty but with direct action like a boy, with her legs
wide apart. —She found the Boy Scout correctitude and
conventionality of her middle boy rather tiresome—liked
the oldest one, who was closest to her, best. —Took Tom
Blakeman and what Betty called other "ginks" out hunting, and they drew blood from one quail, which got
away. Stories about dogs and the horse that went to
neighbor's funeral.

Katy Dos Passos's account of Hollywood. Hollywood
Communists particularly undeviating, bitter against
"social fascists," who ought to be stood up against a wall
and shot. The man who had to work on an anti-strike
film, but was going to arrange publicity urging people
not to go to it. Francis Faragoh saw very few people—
like a man riding a bicycle on a wire, you saw him
start off every morning and sail along over the heads of the
crowd—he would do it every day. He and Jack Lawson
in great secrecy played poker and gave half their win-

nings to the Party. They had to be very careful since the revelations about Mrs. Steffens and James Cagney and others, in connection with the general strike. Jack was more or less in the doghouse—he'd written, under legal advisement, an abject apology to the Alabama judge, who demanded an even more abject one. They were threatening to extradite him, he said there was "no issue involved." When you dropped out of the $1,000 a week into the $800 class, you were in disgrace. Jack had been forced to work for Columbia, the people at RKO Studio wouldn't see him, etc. She had realized, when they finally went out and had dinner with Don Stewart and Dorothy Parker, that the writers had passed out of the phase where they talked about their integrity and said that they wanted a little place in Connecticut to settle down and do something serious—they now said what a wonderful man Thalberg was and how they wanted to try to help him in the new thing that was being done (Technicolor, evidently). Francis Faragoh, who was an ace, became very much upset for fear he was getting out of favor; he threw a great act, went to the studio and told them he wasn't happy, then came home and took to his bed with a nervous headache—great excitement and anxiety at the studio—their ace wasn't happy—they raised his pay.

Elizabeth, a little tight, said of Katy that she was "a stone in fish's clothing."

CHICAGO AND
NEW YORK

Chicago (Dec. 9–15, '34). Blizzard, making taxi trips like Arctic exploration, cars pushing each other out of trouble. —View from big windows above old covered radiator at the Congress: black water towers in the air, which in mid-afternoon became opaque with December dark and smoke; snow-covered roofs black-humped with skylights; great square buildings crammed with windows right up to the top edge—there was a kind of small weave of chicken wire outside the glass of the window, which you looked through—room seemed pleasant at first: freedom; then it got to seem bleak and a little prisonlike; the hammering of the plumber, the water turned off, infinitely discreet chambermaids, dismal oval brownish picture of Arcadian shepherd or shepherdess, with goddess of spring or something scattering flowers on them; eighteenth century, *La Bonne Mère*, woman nursing a baby, above the bed; lake water that smelled of disinfectant, porcelain of tub badly nicked—radiator didn't always work very well, cold would come in through crack under window.

K. when she thought taxi driver had driven past street, sharply: "What happened then?"

Tarts who got into elevator with me: "Well, how are we-all tonight?" When they got out, one of them grabbed a spittoon and went into the room saying: "I've brought you something, Louie!" Hat girl engaged me in conversation on the subject of how it was funny how much better you felt after breakfast. —It seemed to me that the cops, the bus drivers, etc., were polite, because not so hurried, as in New York.

Mrs. B. used to refer to "the cream of Rhode Island."

Day after Assembly: I lay in bed thinking I wouldn't hear from her for some time and kept thinking of "disassembly" (destruction of old Ford cars), and when she arrived, she was wearing a rubber garment which she said was designed for hangovers and which held her hips in and came down over her crotch. She lay on her back on the bed, with her legs straight up in the air. I said that she looked like *La Vie Parisienne!* and she said, "That's what champagne does for you." Phoebe Bentley had told her that she'd been having a good deal to drink (she said that Phoebe Bentley had no humor, acted superior to the other Chicagoans, a little more cultivated)—then later asked her to tea, to which K. had replied that she never took tea, because she drank so much. She had worn gold sandals and a dress which she said was very low in back and about as low in front. I said I was sure she had looked beautiful, and she said she had looked lovely.

C.N. had ceased to caress her, she was glad to say, having decided she'd got too fat, except to slap her on the behind as they were coming out of the dining room. He said pointedly that so-and-so's wife had ceased to be much use to him in the brokerage business, as she'd let herself get too fat. He had made great efforts to get Richard Whitney [the head of the New York Stock Exchange, afterwards sent to jail] to stay with him when he had been on (to back the brokers up?), and they had given him a dinner, but without success. He had gone rushing around the dinner asking people if they didn't want to meet Dick Whitney and saying that he had just asked him to stay with him.

I went to *As Thousands Cheer* and kept feeling as if I were seeing an American show in a foreign country. I wondered how they could understand the lines—they didn't understand all of them: some of the most amusing cracks fell flat.

Pigeons fluttering and futtering on the roof outside the window—a little stroking of the female by the male with his bill, then he got on her and fluttered his wings—pretty brief—the next thing we knew they had turned in opposite directions and the female had flown off. K. said, "That's the way to treat 'em!" I thought that the female had got rid of the male, but she said, "No: he had his will of her and then gave a flirt of his buttoomacks and sent her off." They were smoky-looking pigeons.

My neurotic spells—horrible fit of gloom the first day. Her short burst of tears the third day, after an all-night party. O. had just left her bed, she said, at nine. She had come over about eleven without having had any breakfast. The last day was the best in some ways. She lay on the bed with her skirts up in a most exhibitionistic way, which I enjoyed and reciprocated. She had been sweet the day that she cried, said she'd be all right in a minute, was just tired and was much better soon.

Her hands would be cold and perspire. I told her how much more beautiful she looked when she was being made love to, and she said it was too bad that she couldn't be carried around that way. She was always afraid, she said, that she couldn't conceal her look of eagerness. I thought she had had the black hairs removed from her breasts, but it turned out that it must have been somebody else. This sort of thing amused her.

Old Heidelberg: what I thought were an Irish-Jewish troupe impersonating Germans—also, tabloid Shakespeare left over from the Fair. —Reading about Negro Communist Newton and the girl from Ann Arbor whom he had married—baby, Communist demonstrations, evicted, recognized in police court by someone with whom she had gone to school—picture and big story on first page of *American,* "dementia simplex," jail psychiatrist examining her—the New Freedom—father used to put on bloody bandages to enlist her sympathy.

She said she was leaving her hair down because she looked better that way. I said she looked like the painting of Esmeralda, and she said that she already knew it, she had discovered it at an early age. "Aren't you cute? Aren't you beautiful?" "Umm-hmm."

Her song: "I saw stars! I heard the birdies sing—*so sweet! so sweet!*" She had evidently been saving it for me. I told her and G., when they sang "Forgotten," that they would sing songs to their children, but never to me any more. The picture of their father.

At the party the night of the Assembly, they had played a game of getting somebody to go out of the room, then the people in the room would have to decide on a person and walk like the person, talk like the person, etc. The impersonations of young Sam Insull were unfortunately mistaken for Dave Owen. She had abruptly lost interest in Sam Insull from the moment he was no longer invested with the adventitious interest of his father's trial. After the acquittal, she found that she didn't care about having him around any more—and O. couldn't stand him because he was so common.

Her dream of execution—some sort of sexual thing, she thought. Last swim in swimming pool and with other people (in letter).

"No canoodling," I said. "Not much, I guess!"

My slight jealous resentment of a trick she proposed which I had a feeling she had learned from someone else. In my somewhat drunken state of mind, I accused her of having done it with G. Later on, it turned out to have been O.

Her "come-on" sweater, which would leave a gap exposing her naked abdomen. She began supplying words to me when I would pause for one—significant: it showed that we were tending to think and feel close together.

Making love during menstruation was "such a holocaust."

Somewhat relaxed atmosphere this winter, '34–'35, it seemed to me: people with any money were said to be spending it on amusements instead of constraining themselves to cut down. Parties seemed to have become quieter and cleaner: the Rogerses' New Year's Eve party, intended to fill the gap left by Muriel Draper's when Muriel was in Russia. At the same time, impression of life dragging on without coming to anything. Low state of *Provincetown* that winter: when the Waughs went up and tried to give a party, nobody but Chauncey came: people were "off" each other. Kaselaus sensitive about losing Coulton's dory, etc.

Bob Cantwell standing behind *Betsy* and putting his arm around her at the door just as I left: she had been recently rather sharp or it seemed to me sullenly uncommunicative, and I was touched and relieved to see a look of pure and naïve acquiescence, contentment, and pleasure come over her face in response.

Edie [Shay's] *story of her three months in New York, circa 1924.* The office she worked for in Chicago sent her and others on to New York to handle an account for the

U.S. Steamship Lines: she lived at the Judson, woke up at five o'clock in the morning and wrote advertizing copy—at the office, they drank all day, had a water cooler full of cocktails—went on orgies on the boats, when the state-rooms were put to use—she had to invent a lurid past to explain her non-participation—never got any sleep, burning feeling behind eyeballs. Dr. Rumley, the vitamin charlatan, used to take her out—she enjoyed him, but was scared to death all the time—his secretary was in love with him and came around and made a scene at the Judson and then tried to poison herself. Finally he asked her to go with him on a tour of factories—her boss came on from Chicago and told her she'd have to go but she refused, so they lost his account. The men she knew in the advertizing game at that time, though bourgeois, had completely unconventional minds and much more brains than people gave them credit for. —When they finally got on the train tight to go back to Chicago, she was told that, due to labor troubles, there had been a threat to blow up the train, and she remembered sitting back and thinking that that would be the perfect end to the whole thing.

Waughs' party for Bubs Hackett [in New York]. Barbara Jones, at the end of the evening, discovered that her finger was bleeding and had an idea that Bill L'Engle, with whom she had been talking, had bitten her. Brownie L'Engle told Edie, when Edie said that she was glad to take care of Frank's household but that she hated to shut down completely on her own creative activity, that Edie had done such a wonderful job with Frank and that before she had married him he had been nothing but an old bum, etc., making her very sore. Frank, at the Walkers' suggestion, asked Ann Sayre for $100, they having already given $100 to pay Mary Vorse's debt to Liveright; and Ann simply remarked, "Everybody tries to get money out of me," and immediately got up and left. Elizabeth made Betty Spencer sore by reproaching her for having on a previous occasion bitten Coulton in the shoulder, so that he came home with black-and-blue marks—and asserted that she had also bitten Chauncey through the shoe. They all, more or less, ended up at Ticino's, and as the Waughs were coming back, Coulton knocked Bubs down in the snow. Bubs had made Gwenyth furious by reproaching her for having deserted Floyd in Province-town.

Anna, December 31, 1934. I dreamed about her when I went to sleep in the afternoon at Red Bank, feeling morbid, appalled by the immediate. She had come to see me in an apartment, talked about a Katherine being with her, so that I thought I'd be able to make love to her. She lay down on the bed, talked in an excited moved voice such as I had known her to have: Why hadn't I done something about marrying her? Her skirts were up on her little slender legs, and tragic though she was, I thought I was going to fuck her, but her companion turned out to be her boyfriend, who became apprehensive and truculent, chunky Hunky type, and said, "This can't be kidded!"—whereupon I assured him that I had had no idea of trying to do anything with Anna. —They went, she still referring to her companion as Katherine. —When I woke up, I felt very strongly, as I had already been feel-ing, the necessity of getting a girl.

Old locomotive engineer on train coming up from Red Bank. He was sitting in the seat back of me, a large sparsely built man with keen narrowed eyes, pale and gray, a short Yankee beak, thinned with age, and straight iron-gray hair parted in the middle. He leaned over the back of the seat and asked me if I'd heard Huey Long on the radio—had seen what I was reading, he said (Ryazanov on Marx and Engels), and wondered what I thought about Huey Long and other matters. He thought that if only the seed could be planted and grow up in the right spirit . . . it would have to be slow but if the right seed could be planted. About Huey Long and Father Coughlin he thought that by their fruits ye shall know them. And of Hitler and Mussolini and all the rest that it might be the application to them of the text: "Many, many shall come unto thee in my name." Had been to a meeting where a labor leader had talked about chiselers and had asked, "Ain't we all chiselers?"—had been to a meeting of the ILD, where someone, apparently Jenny Lee, had spoken. If only distribution and production could be straightened out. Objected to Huey Long's obstructing Roosevelt. They criticized him for being paternalistic, but he thought the government ought to be paternalistic if the men who were elected did their duty as the representatives of the people. A bridge is built across a river, and it benefits the community in general, and the men who are thrown out of work in the old ferry—what's going to happen to them?— shouldn't they be provided for by the government? But he supposed there was a bad kind of paternalism. He believed —this at an early stage of the conversation—that if we could only cultivate the spirit of love for men and look for the pathway to God . . . I said that there wasn't much religion in politics: no, but there ought to be, there ought to be. He'd worked for the Pennsylvania Railroad fifty years —showed me the badge on his lapel—and was now at seventy retired. Had driven a train to Camden. Stream-lined trains—he'd never gone faster than seventy miles an hour. Plane going up in the stratosphere and making the coast-to-coast trip in eight hours. He smiled unperturbedly over this. Had started in on the railroad at nineteen—before that, had worked in the marl pits at

Farmingdale. I spoke of the mammoth's tooth, which I seemed to remember had been found in those pits, the shark's teeth which I certainly remembered that Grandfather Kimball had brought home. He said, "Well, there's a lot of things we don't know—isn't there?"

Curious interview with Bill [Smith's] *girl,* asking me not to tell Bill she was Jewish, though the word "Jewish" was never mentioned. She is Joe Freeman's sister: "All the family are Communists except me, so I see as little of them as possible." She had a regular complex about it: used to think as a child that she'd been left on the doorstep. Not even her husband, she said—he was twenty or thirty years older than she—had known.

Pete Sawyer, at her party for Harold Loeb, was *held up* and robbed of the change of a $5 bill as he was coming out of a cigar store.

Toward the middle of February '35, I dreamed that Donald Douglas was around and I treated him rather cordially—Jane [his wife] was married to someone else cottages on the side of a hill: Miramar? Somebody, not Margaret, whom I was thinking about marrying (Elizabeth was behind this) but—it was now more or less the stone house at Talcottville—she had been to see an old bozo friend and had made an engagement with a girlfriend to go to dinner, spend the evening, with him. I was annoyed, jealous, the same thing over again—why marry her and have it all repeated? —I became cross about it. Yet had let myself in for it, couldn't prevent it—I wanted somebody who would want to stay home with me.

My call on Dorothy Stilwell [my first cousin] *with Helen Augur* [my second cousin]. Helen Stilwell was also

there, with a new (black) chow. Helen Augur talking
about family from the pretentious point of view, Dorothy
and Helen Stilwell vulgarly making fun of family, she
and Helen joking about being "whorish." Dorothy on
being impoverished, they were going to have to go back
into nineteen-room apartment. Dorothy on being taken for
Cecil Stewart's mistress at Piping Rock, Miami [actually
she was married to him], etc. Somebody had asked her
about her family, she had said she had a strain of Ethi-
opian, Stewart had rebuked her; one man had tried to
date her, taken her telephone number. Arrival of Stewart:
a little like [Bronson] Cutting [actually it was only in
appearance and manner that he was anything at all like
Cutting]: he thought it would have been an excellent
thing if Germany had won the war, because then the
whole world would have been Germanized, they would
have taken over Russia and attended to that, etc.—then
eventually the whole world would have had Hitler instead
of only just Germany. I argued with him about this.
Helen returned to the family, he told with satisfaction
about this. My cousins seemed to me, in their various
ways, a very ill-bred lot.

Albany. Using O.'s name and signing it to checks; my
collapse; new little Ford roadster. I stopped off at Pitts-
field.

K. in New York (end of March, beginning of April
'35). Her great word now was "holocaust"—she said,
"Now the holocaust (our orgy) is beginning!" —The Z.s:
I.'s note left at the house: "I really think you are both very
naughty, but I miss you." We were touched. L. had eaten
a dinner, including a steak, in the presence of G. and her
friend without offering them any. Our joke about how she
was ordering a turkey for their call the next day. L. had

sent me a letter and managed to misdirect it. —Transparent flesh-colored stockings and gold openwork shoes too much for me, as K. was getting dressed for the [*New Yorker*] party: wonderful. —G., with her escort from an agency, artist-window dresser from Macy's. Their amazement and disapproval at seeing Negroes at the party. It had taken K. a week to get $25 out of her father to enable G. to come on, the family had gotten so to disapprove of her. —The second day, at dinner, we fell out, our nerves giving way, at the Russian Bear: I had thought that K. was disappointed at not seeing I. at G.'s cocktail party (which we hadn't gone to), and she complained, after we got into the restaurant, that she didn't feel like Russian food, had been thinking about a lamb chop (accented on first syllable) and was revolted by Russian charcoal-cooked lamb, with all the parts cut away, that she said she considered the best. —Crying and vomiting, then revival of sex interest. —Next day, we had a very good time at *Roberta* (the picture), followed by vaudeville acts, laughing at them I came to realize that she was afraid of meeting people. Always had been, she said, and would really rather stay with me than be taken around (unlike G.). "Well, I guess we'd better go back to our little cell," she had said to me at one point. In the afternoon, we would go into cocktail bars and sit drinking and usually decide not to go to whatever cocktails in people's houses we were supposed to go to. —She looked so much better in her nightgown and with her hair down than in her street clothes—lovely white nightgown with frills that stood out around short sleeves that had more shape than most nightgowns, taken in around the waist so that it showed her figure.—Her mother, on seeing the contents of her suitcase, had complained that she didn't have many good clothes.

New Yorker Ball. Helen Simpson, of whom it had been

said that she was born with two tickets to everything; Louise Holden's [Bogan] fairy escort, who looked like Roquefort cheese, gray and decayed, eyes, nose, and mouth like the decayed spots. —Dawn Powell was silent, hardly understanding, when G. expressed consternation over the Negroes at the party, asking who they were; on the other hand, the girls hardly grasped it when Dawn said that Thurber had told her that he had a trade-last for her: "You don't belong in the men's room." —Z.s: K. had said in the morning: "L.'s ordering that bird now . . . a little dry old sherry." G. claimed that, as a matter of fact, she had had consommé with sherry in it. On the occasion of a subsequent visit, L. had offered G. martinis, which G. insisted L. knew very well she didn't like; Z. had not turned up at all; L. had had to go to the train to meet her daughter; and for a time they had been there all alone. G. for the first time had been glad to leave New York, because the people had all been so horrid.

K. and G. Their father had said when G. had been sitting around fussing with her hair: "Won't you take off your wig and stay awhile?" —When the waiter on the Pullman had proposed something, he had replied, in the words of a popular song: "No! No! a thousand times, No!" ———

My tongue so "ulcerated" by martinis and hors d'oeuvres that it seemed to me I could hardly taste with it. —The song she kept singing this time was, "Fare thee well, Annabel!" She was afraid she was going to burst into hysterics when she arrived at the ball. She talked about doing what they called in Chicago "walking East till her hat floated." When she was crying and I made some gestures of making love to her, she laughed for a moment and said, "Did you think a quick lay was the solution?" G. keeps making comments under her breath, outside the regular conversation: "They would borrow it, book," etc.

I suppose they were really intended for K., even though she wasn't there, her part in those conversations that they carried on between themselves which other people couldn't understand. She always seems nowadays to be talking to herself; it's very hard to make her hear you when you try to say anything to her, especially when you try to impress anything on her—she instinctively evades any insistence.

After K. had left, she resolved herself as usual for me into a beautiful rich smear of an image: white skin, blue-black hair, violet [eyes?], rich way of talking with thick Western r's due to her fat tongue. —She saw at once how the Shays had made a drudge out of Hatty and imagined that Hatty must scorn me for having allowed myself to be moved up to the top floor. —As she lay in bed in the morning, she claimed that she had been able to detect three distinct odors of cooking with which Hatty had been concerned: coffee, sausage, and toast—"Hatty is throwing up a few sausages." —I was amazed and horrified by the clam cakes that Frank Shay sent up to us and which I afterwards found out to be his own invention, thought they were probably intended as a practical joke, and carefully removed all the parts of the clams. —Managed to flood the basement and the first floor by using the toilet on the second when it was stopped up. —The girls claimed that the Z.s undoubtedly thought that K. and I were over on the East River taking dope together.

Anna's return in March. She couldn't get used to Jerry's face. He had taken her part against her family when they picked on her, and had quarreled with them, so that she didn't see them any more, but it was evident that she missed them. She thought that Jerry was jealous of them, and he was beginning to get jealous of Lizzie. He never took her to a movie, never bought her a drink—he couldn't drink himself, would pass right out. When she would complain of not going to any movies, he would say, "Oh, what can I do? Do you want to go to one now?" She would say, "No, if you can't think of it yourself!" He had promised to do a lot for her and hadn't made good, so she felt she didn't need to be faithful any more. She made a few not very determined attempts to discourage my first kisses and embraces, and before taking off her dress, she sat on the edge of the bed, intensely brooding, staring into nothing a few minutes, just as I had seen her do when I had first known her and she had sat brooding on the edge of my day bed in 13th Street after I had made love to her for the first time. She looked much better than when I had seen her last, but more mature. She had lost some of her pale and soiled freshness. She was still wearing the shoes I had bought her and a becoming brown dress, with a fashionable brown scarf around her neck. We arranged that she was to come at midnight Saturday a week, but she appeared again the next morning before I had got out of bed, crawled in with me and stayed till two in the afternoon. She didn't want to take money from me, but I made her take $3 for taxi fare.

Her sister's two children had scarlatina (her sister was living with their mother), and Lizzie had broken out in a rash. —She thought that she was the first real girl that Jerry had ever had, that he didn't want to admit it, but he'd never been able to get any other girl and that was the reason he hung around her so. He would come to get her after work every day and be there the first thing in the morning when she wasn't working. In the evening, they would play pinochle and read the papers, and Lizzie would tune in on the radio. Anna was working at Childs (Atlantic and Pacific Avenue, Brooklyn), checking up on the checks, which allowed her to sit down but hurt her eyes: $11 a week. He had promised to get her all kinds of good jobs. He made very little money himself, helped his Tammany district leader get people out of trouble.

Saturday night (April 7, '35). She arrived about one, when I had given her up and was trying to get to sleep—looking very pretty, skin clear and pale-creamy, with a little pink on each cheek. The operation had certainly done her a lot of good. Her sister's children had not had scarlet fever. The sister had had a row with their mother. The mother was thinking of moving again—should Anna go back to live with her?—as it was, the place she lived in used up all her salary. She had to get to Coney Island at seven the next morning. She waited on table Sunday and was off at three. People often didn't give tips any more, maybe because they thought waitresses were getting $15 a week as they were supposed to, according to the NRA. Actually, they only got $3. She wanted some beer, and we drank up the three bottles that Frank Shay had left in the icebox. Then I went out to get some more, but it was after three and they wouldn't sell me any. When I got back into bed she said, "I want beer!" and wondered whether we could find some when it got to be later in the morning. Then she thought about Lizzie—suppose she should wake up and not find her there and be frightened. This worried her so that she got up and went back. As she was putting on her dress, she said that she was afraid that she was never going to be able to be quiet, that she'd have to be working all her life.

I was summoned the next morning to answer the phone in the furniture factory next door. (I can't remember why this was—it may be that we had no phone.) It was Anna telling me that Jerry had been there when my telegram arrived. He had started over to Manhattan—he said to see about a job, but her mother thought he was up to something. She wanted to warn me. I decided to go up to

Washington, Connecticut, to see about Wykeham Rise for Rosalind.

Washington, Connecticut, April '35. The Jacksons: Arthur now doing wonderfully, but fine old-fashioned American family. Arthur waked me up for breakfast, then when I didn't appear immediately, knocked again and asked me whether I had gone to sleep—by the time I had gotten down, they had finished and all gone about their various tasks. —Mrs. Will, who was giving the little girl piano lessons, came and sat down with me, and Dorothy appeared—I apologized, Dorothy said it didn't matter: I'd missed seeing the family all together, but then I'd seen that last night at dinner. I said, when the food had appeared, that I didn't want to keep them from what they were doing, and Mrs. Will said that she must go back and returned to her music lessons. Dorothy had acquired something of Arthur's slightly rude middle-class brusqueness—some of her old frivolous humor came out in response to me (though she was a fairly heavy matron now, dumpy and round-shouldered, instead of the volatile and ailing college girl of twenty years ago). Dorothy and her mother had resigned from the DAR. Mrs. Will kept her humor up (Mrs. Will, despite some areas of graying hair, hardly looked a day older than when I had seen her last)— Stan[ley Dell] told me that she and Dorothy tended to combine against Arthur: psychoanalysis and neurology a lot of newfangled nonsense. Arthur was tactless and the Washington people rather stupidly preferred Dr. Wurzby, who was old and had apparently committed some ghastly medical errors—which, however, had entirely failed to prejudice people against him. Arthur was no good at kidding people along when they really weren't as sick as they thought they were; he probably made the neurotics furious. He was convinced that neurology was the great future field. Arthur passed the plate in church, they were both very serious churchgoers. Dorothy, when I was telling them about the Buchmanite meeting, said at the end that it seemed to work for some people, though . . . (aposiopesis). —Nobody could even remember what Alfred Bellinger specialized in, but it finally turned out to be numismatics: he was a complete paterfamilias, who, according to Stanley, presided at the head of the table, and his talk consisted entirely of anecdotes. Mrs. Will had gone somewhere with him on a bus and had had to pay the bus fares because the only money he had in his pocket turned out to be drachmas or obols or something of the kind. Stanley had asked his little girl whether she knew how butterflies were born and she said no, but God was never born. —We talked about Bill Osborn: it seemed that Peggy had gone to Paris and left him for somebody else and that he had retreated to Garrison, where he walked in the woods. He had invented a new metallurgical process while working for Phelps Dodge. Noel Robinson had apparently been gold-dug and deserted by his second wife, and the Tidewater Oil Company had gotten rid of old man Benton [his former father-in-law], and Noel was now one of its vice-presidents. —Robert Jackson had lived near the Green and spent all his time complaining about the narrowness of the people in Washington (of which he himself was only the other side).

Decay of my generation. When I looked back on all these old friends of mine, of whom I had once hoped such great things and about many of whom I had only just seen or learned their present situations, I was depressed at how little on the whole they had done and how badly they had fared. Arthur as the young local doctor, with his fine busy American family, had come off as well as any—and at the same time it made me feel better satisfied with myself— though fatuously: I hadn't been working.

Stanley's sour account of John and Marion [Amen]: they had that magnificent apartment, with sometimes never a dollar in the house—John just a tired businessman, wanted his cocktails and his little girls—they went their own separate ways, he thought. Mrs. Preston had taken over Frances; Dick [Cleveland] had married a bishop's daughter; Frances had gone on the stage; Burnham had been coming to Stanley for neurosis advice. Stanley was devoting himself to his stepsons, each of whom had a room in the barn to devote himself to what he was most interested in: carpentry, birds and insects; little Frances's room had just chairs to sit in and think. Stanley had as a butler in a white coat a model of Robert Jackson, who "worshipped the ground Robert walked on"—he had turned up as he had promised Stan he would at eight o'clock in the morning on a day of horrible weather, after having walked hours and miles in the storm. He was soft-spoken and soft: Robert had, I thought, largely invented the hardness and virility of his portrait of him. Only three miles away from the Washington Green, Stanley's farm seemed isolated and lonely: it was getting dark, we walked into dim woodland, which belonged to the property behind the house. It was queer: I had a feeling of dimness and aridness: how to pick up a man so let down? He had got over his neurotic crisis, but still had discolored flesh under his eyes—forgot to offer me second helpings of things at dinner. He thought that the old man, his father, was coming out more and more as he grew older. He had had a recurrent dream in which he thought he was the hosts of Christianity battling with the hosts of Islam: the Crescent always won: it was the idea of fatality, of just waiting, which, instead of the New England Christian morality which he had taken in his early years from his mother, was now winning in him. In another dream, he had thought he was in Europe, and a beautiful woman had come along, surrounded with great pomp in a chariot —the chariot had broken down, and he had finally gone up a hill and found an American farmer in a farmhouse and gotten him to come down and haul out the chariot. Cut off from his American roots in Europe, when he first came back here to live, he had written a Jungian interpretation of Uncle Remus. At one time, if a car with a radio had gone by, he would have said: "There goes an American, a queer fish!" He had taken up checkers. It was nice to talk to him, though—like seeing John Bishop again, cultivated, intelligent, sensitive, pleasant, as few people nowadays are.

The Washington church has been beautifully kept up, fine view of it as you came up hill. New Gunnery buildings there. The Gunnery was a boys' school. Raymond Holden's boy was there writing poetry—whom his father never saw: another depressing count. No more New Year and other festivities, in which the Gunnery and Wykeham got together.

Bellingers. Ghostly to see the old site of the Bellinger house, all burnt over [It had burned down, with Mr. Bellinger in it, and only his head had been found]—but they were putting up a new house on the same place again right away—as I remember, somebody telling me of the unexpected cheerfulness of Dr. and Mrs. Raymond the day after their only son had died: no shadow of doubt of immortality, of eternal happiness, of the justice and goodness of God. —Alfred and his archaeological colleagues used to have a weekly evening meeting at which papers would be read and after which they would play hearts for relaxation.

I tried to find out from Dorothy whether she had noticed any pronounced symptoms of the disintegration of society, but I don't think she even knew what I meant. Washington had never been inflated to the same extent as other places, so that the Depression had not hit it so hard: she still had her round of duties, neighborly and civic, in the town. Arthur said that it was a meager soil for neuroses.

Esther Strachey's wedding party [she married Chester Arthur, grandson of the President, with a harelip or something of the kind, full of a goofy kind of idealism—had married him, so far as one could see, entirely for his (none too brilliant) historical associations]. I came back Wednesday in time to go to the Strachey–Arthur wedding party: very strange mixture of fine old refined American relics of the Arthur family and Administration with the Seldes cocktail crowd. The President's private secretary, an old gentleman with a trimmed white beard, a quite nice elderly lady with a rather charming well-chiseled faded face and a nice precise cultivated voice, who talked about Southern California and referred herself in my mind to the Helen Hunt Jackson* period. They didn't seem to know what to make of the company and left as soon as they had paid their respects to the bride.

I met for the first time Margaret's Lesbian cousin, Romaine Brooks (of whom she said she had always been afraid), dressed in regular dark masculine clothes but a little shy about being a Lesbian; she would somewhat diffidently look away. —She thought there must be more money in the Kingston Colliery Company [in which Margaret had also had a small interest], so many men were still working there. All of Margaret's Philadelphia family had gone to pieces from drinking. Cousin Watty used to bark at the table (the nieces were contesting the will). She had lived in Paris, where drinking was easier,

* Helen Maria Hunt Jackson (1831–1885), the author of *Ramona*.

Gannery and Wykeham

count). No more New Year and other festivities, in which the ~~Wykeham~~ ~~Jenney and Wykeham~~) got together.

Ballingers Ghostly to see the old site of the Ballinger house, all burnt over--but they were putting up a new house on the same place again right away--as I remember somebody telling me of the unexpected cheerfulness of Dr. and Mrs. Raymond the day after their only son had died: no shadow of doubt of immortality, of eternal happiness ~~for their own~~, of the justice and goodness of God. -)

INERT from preceding page

¶I tried to find out from Dorothy whether she had noticed any pronounced symptoms of the disintegration of ~~events~~ *society*, but I don't think she even knew what I meant. Washington had never been inflated to the same extent as other places, so that the depression had not hit it so hard: she still had her round of duties, neighborly and civic, in the town. Arthur said that it was a meager soil for neuroses.

II Esther Strachey's wedding party [She married the grandson of the President, a namesake with a hardihood with a something of the kinkis full of a goofy kind of idealism--had married him; so far as one could see, ruined his [(now too brilliant) histor]ical ambitions];

~~Esther Murphy's wedding party.~~
~~I came back Wednesday in~~ *for the first time* time to go to the Strachey-Arthur wedding party: very strange mixture of fine old refined American relics of the Arthur family and administration with the Seldes cocktail crowd, ~~Arthur's~~ *the President's* private secretary, an old gentleman with a trimmed white beard, a quite nice elderly lady with a rather charming well-chiselled faded face and a nice precise cultivated voice, who talked about Southern California and ~~referred~~ referred herself in my mind to the Helen Hunt Jackson period. They didn't seem to know what to make of the company and left as soon as they had paid their respects to the bride. ¶I I met Margaret's Lesbian *[of whom she said she had always been afraid]* cousin, Romayne Brooks, dressed in regular dark masculine ~~Lesbian~~ clothes but a little shy about being a Lesbian; ~~would look away~~. *She Colliery* thought there must be more money in the Kingston) ~~Cording~~ Company, *[in which Margaret had also had a small interest]* so many men) still working there ~~all h's~~ ~~family~~ had gone *(were*

⑩*All of Margaret's Philadelphia family) the said,*

and had perhaps for that reason been better off. I had talked to her for some time before I found out who she was. She would begin remarks with "But" in the French way, but without affectation.

Smudge Draper drove up Henderson Place at high speed, in a dashing white racing car. People stood on the balcony and cheered and shouted, "Do it again!"—so he backed down and did it again faster and pulled up at the curb just in time not to go through the wall and the side of the house. —The bride and groom drove up, started to get out, then got back in again and drove away—it was said vaguely that Esther had to go to a drugstore. Then they finally arrived. Friends apparently had decided that they ought to get married, and had succeeded in getting it done the night before Easter. It was all very queer and a little depressing: I got the impression that the bride and groom did not like to be congratulated and changed the subject as soon as anybody began to do so. Chester Arthur, good looking and well set up though he is, leans forward, when he shakes hands with you, with a horrid fairy sinuosity. Reid, the Utopian man [Chester was interested in this movement], buttonholed me and took me into Gilbert's [Seldes] study and gave me a long sales talk on Utopianism which destroyed any remnants of interest I had had in it—purely educational, he explained, no political line, no labor line—and I had a hard time getting away.

I made good my escape from the party early—and had dinner with Louise [Bogan] and Maidy Holden and a girlfriend from the sanatorium, dark and slim and dressed in red and Canadian, who had been menstruating for three weeks. The moderate drinks I had had had put me in extravagantly good humor, and I kept complimenting her and even read with admiration some of Logan Pearsall

Smith's* *Trivia*, of which Thornton Wilder's sister
[Isabel] had just given her the new complete collection.
Maidy, as she gets more mature, makes more serious demands on the attention. I bought them all gardenias at
dinner and in general threw money away like a drunken
sailor. After dinner when the friend had left us and
Louise began showing definite bitchy signs of jealousy
of Maidy, I decided that things were getting too thick
there and left.

Elizabeth and her family. Next day I had lunch with
Elizabeth, and she told me about having been to her
aunt's funeral in Newark, the aunt who had taken her to
Italy as a girl and of whom she was very fond. The aunt's
old admirer of a lifetime, the Princeton professor, was
there and asked to kiss her at the grave—perhaps the kiss,
Elizabeth said, which he had always wanted to give the
aunt. The family seemed to her prosaic and hard: she had
learned at the funeral that the saying that it was unlucky
to light three cigarettes with the same match had been
invented and circulated for the profit of the family match
business. She had had great difficulty extorting from the
other members of the family any money to help her aunt
when she was dying: they had insisted on making an investigation of their own to find out whether she was really
in need.

Princeton, April 20–21, '35. Everything and everybody
terribly let down: [Harold] Dodds† seemed to have done
nothing but try to interfere with the freedom of opinion
of the *Princetonian*—on which [Dean Christian] Gauss

---

* Logan Pearsall Smith (1865–1946), American-born essayist
and aphorist who lived in London for many years.
† The president of Princeton.

had to take issue with him; no money, no promotions. When I said that the college had completely lost its old function, Gauss agreed with me, but when I asked him what the future of such places was, he said he didn't know and couldn't worry about it. They had been expecting something to happen when the new president came in and now nothing had happened. Frank MacDonald complained that there was no longer any Princetonian in the important administrative posts, and it seemed to me that the distinctive Princeton flavor was not there any more. I said to Gauss that I thought that Hearst's anti-Red campaign had left Princeton more or less unscathed. "Relatively," he said, "but it's left people jittery." It did seem to me that people were a little scared—conversation about capitalism, Communism, etc., not quite so free as usual. "The Red Net Work," published by the DAR, had just come out with Mrs. Roosevelt's name in it—the woman who compiled it having been elected head of the DAR over a woman who had protested. That night I had a horrible nightmare. I dreamed I was a chapter of a Malraux novel—I was a riot, with lots of fighting and violence. Mrs. Gauss said the next morning that she had been defying people who were accusing her of something (apparently based on some meeting she had attended, at which she had wanted to speak, but had not spoken), saying, "When any accusations are to be brought against me, I'll bring them myself!" —Frank MacDonald seemed livelier than anybody else, still fuming, indignant, and writhing—but grayer and rather mellowed. He had been away for two years, one in the Orient and one in Barbados —had had serious stomach troubles and had to go up to New York for treatments: "It makes me feel so important!" —now suffering from sinus trouble—and also had Hong Kong foot and athlete's foot, so that he hadn't been able to walk to his classes and had always to take a taxi. He thought they were all against him down there—had never been made a full professor because he didn't have a Ph.D. —was ready to resign—had a nice little house, but they were threatening to sell it over his head. He couldn't read modern fiction, had read *Jennie Gerhardt* and *Sister Carrie* and *Main Street* but had never gotten to the *American Tragedy*. I said that he had probably gone even further back into the nineteenth century, and he replied, "Nineteenth century! I'm back in the eighteenth century —I'm rereading *Fanny Hill!*" His anecdotes: retort to Sam Shoemaker, who had said they were going over to the Graduate College and sell Christ there. "I told him I understood that that had already been done once." I was told that he saw none of his colleagues, only the Ivy boys.

Tom Matthews in a smaller and more commonplace house on a commonplace new back street—Julie had had another boy since I had seen them.

Fire in the lumberyard at night: greedy roaring and crunching of the flames—sagging wire on which the insulation was burning, the current had been running back and forth along the sagging length like a fish caught and put in a tank.

Eisenhart now in charge of the famed humanities of the Graduate School. An unfortunate event which had got onto the front pages of the papers: a football man who had been stealing watches and other things.

Christian came back from the liquor store, embarrassed and as if apologetic, hugging a wrapped bottle of whiskey. He had had to pretend not to see some students who were buying liquor strictly for use in their rooms.

I haven't for some time seen so many people in so short a period as I had during this week, and I have found it stimulating, though the news at Princeton and Washington—and of Hill, which the Gausses told me about—has been mostly in itself depressing.

Elizabeth. At the Waughs' party, just before Gwen's sailing and their leaving for Provincetown, Elizabeth wore a wonderful brown dress with ballooning sleeves and, in her corsage, a bunch of artificial flowers like small white water lilies with orange hearts, and silver openwork shoes that disclosed her reddened toenails, such a combination as only she could wear—her deep-bronze-brown little spit curls on her forehead and rolled-up little copper-red curls above her ears. —I spoke of her feet, when I met her after this, which I'd recognized, as "trotting" along the street, but she marches rather than trots. The people at the project had said, when she left, that they had the impression two people had gone.

Horrible morning we had with Graflex camera, which she had taken out of hock on 14th Street after two years and which she was trying to get fixed—overcast weather after the beautiful days of the first of May. I was nervously exhausted from struggling with perplexities. Stewart's Cafeteria: great jelly-filled roll from which, when I bit into it, the jelly ran all over the table like a menstruation.

Jean Shay and the Smooleys. She told me in the taxi about Jean Shay's running away. Hatty told me afterwards that Frank had spent all the money, $13, on liquor for the Smooleys which Jean was supposed to have had for clothes—she had only had one slip all winter. Edie had complained that Jean was getting sullen, when Jean had asked Edie what she thought of a boyfriend whom Jean had brought home, Edie had said, "I think he's a little common, Jean." Jean had answered, "Well, I guess I'm common, too." Edie had told her that her father was a gentleman and her mother had been a lady, etc.

Knobby had always talked about "the Smith family of America" in referring to their habits, as if they had been the Jukes. Edie said, "You know a queer family when you know the Smiths." Old Benjamin Smith had given his

eldest son, Y.K., the Hebrew name for Jehovah, irony?
mysticism? [I have this wrong. It should be looked up in
the biography of Benjamin Smith.]

Jean had looked quite like a young lady when I had last
seen her, fashionable off-the-face hat and bangs. —Edie
had heard the little German boys in Yorkville crying in
the streets, "I declare war on Italy!" and had been
appalled.

Revolutionary Writers' Congress. When the orders
from Moscow for tolerance came, the comrades inaugu-
rated the new policy nobly by at once throwing out poor
Granville Hicks, who had been trying so hard to comply
with what he had understood to be the previous policy
and who would undoubtedly have done his best to live up
to the new one if they had only given him time.

Sordid house on Bedford Street. Call on Fanny Black at
26 Bedford Street [I can't remember who this was] early
in the morning: horrible old house, where a man with a
glare standing at the door always stopped you and asked
you what you wanted before you went in—painted dismal
green and brown inside, dirty oilcloth-covered stairs, same,
old and greasy smell, old bedsprings set out in hall, stairs
worn in at the middle of the edges, hallways humpy and
sunken. My knock got her up when she had a hangover.
She put her spectacles on. Her little colorless thin bare
feet, nightgown, the old green mattress she slept on with
only blankets. Her pictures, herself without her glasses,
East Side pushcarts (she had told me her father had had
one), funny pictures of horses and cows, a horse stagger-
ing into a stream with a load of hay: yellows, greens, and
browns, with some life but little taste. She had printed on
the wall: "Karl—None Can Be Indifferent"; and on the
glass door into the little room she used for her studio,

there was Christ on the cross, rising out of something like waves, and tilted so as to compose with an almost equally large sickle and hammer.

Father's languages. It rains. —Cataclasm. —It makes no matter.

Slang:
—Do something about it.
—O.K. pal—O.K. keed.
—Can't take it.
—Some fun!—eh, kid?
—Hot pants.

1935–1940

JOURNEY TO THE
SOVIET UNION, 1935

[During the autumn of 1934, when he was still in
Provincetown, EW decided to apply to the John Simon
Guggenheim Memorial Foundation for a fellowship
which would enable him to visit and travel in Russia. He
was encouraged in this by the fact that the Guggenheim
Foundation had from the first invited creative writers
and critics to apply for and hold the fellowships under
the freest possible conditions. His friend Allen Tate,
with his wife Caroline Gordon, had gone abroad under
the Guggenheim auspices; Louise Bogan and Léonie
Adams had held such fellowships for the writing of
poetry. EW felt that the large book he had undertaken
could not be completed without seeing at first hand the
Soviet Union to which a stream of American reporters
and writers had been going since the early 1920s. He
had published some of the early sections of his book in
The New Republic and in his plans for work he told
the Foundation:

I want an opportunity for leisure in order to work on
a book which I have begun. It is to be called *To the*

Finland Station: An Essay on the Writing and Acting of History. There are to be three sections. The first section deals with the decline of the French revolutionary tradition during the 19th century: Michelet, Renan, Taine, Anatole France. (This has been coming out in *The New Republic,* but there is still a good deal of work to be done on it before it will be ready for the book.) The second section deals with the rise of Socialism and centers about Marx and Engels. The third section deals with Lenin and Trotsky and the attempt to apply Marxist principles in actual historical crises. I have not written much of these last two sections yet and want to go to Moscow to work in the Marx–Engels–Lenin Institute.

After providing a list of his publications, EW added: "I have been to Europe a number of times and know at first hand all the countries with which my book deals, with the exception of Russia."

Given his stature as critic and writer, EW had no difficulty in being named a Fellow of the Foundation. The awards were announced in the spring of 1935 and he was granted $2,000, then a sum amply sufficient for the voyage and his proposed sojourn in Russia. He planned to sail at the end of May. His trip was projected in quite a different way from those of his predecessors, many of them his friends. There had been Jack Reed, who had gone to Russia right after the Revolution, had died there and been buried near the Kremlin; there had been Lincoln Steffens, who had returned to the United States with his famous catchword about having seen the future and "it works." John Dos Passos, E. E. Cummings, and Theodore Dreiser had reported on the early Lenin years, and Max Eastman had arrived in Moscow as a socialist *engagé*; but long before the 1930s he had been disillusioned by the post-revolutionary strategies of the Leninists. EW proposed to visit strictly as a historian; he was not involved in immediacies as were the leading American journalists in Moscow, among them Louis Fischer, Walter Duranty, and John Gunther. Dos Passos gave EW a number of introductions and a considerable amount of advice: "Don't believe anything anybody tells you in English or French—there are more lies and more hush dope in Moscow—just as there's more of everything else—than in any capital in the world." Dos Passos suggested EW use German as a language in which it was "damned hard to lie." Since Hitler was broadcasting his lies in that very language, it is quite likely that EW took this advice with a grain of salt. He was sufficiently polyglot to manage; and then he had started studying Russian. He later said he had become genuinely interested in Russian literature on reading Prince Mirsky's history: it had suggested to him that the Russian classical writers had more style than could be conveyed by the widely current translations of Constance Garnett, valuable as they had originally been.

EW ran into visa trouble before his scheduled departure; the Russians were probably conducting a very careful check on him even though he had sided with the American Communists in the 1932 election. The newspapers made headlines out of the delayed visa, and the *Herald Tribune* characterized EW's brand of free-wheeling leftism as being closer to Trotsky than to Lenin. The press was probably right. Sergei Kirov had been assassinated the previous December in the Kremlin. The first great Stalin purge was under way, although few details were as yet known. The Stalin regime was not eager to be observed by a man of political independence—and an American who published so much. However, Moscow finally granted EW a tourist visa and he sailed in May on the *Berengaria*. He was under further investigation in Russia, for he did not receive his three-month residence visa, for which he applied, until the end of June 1935.

The notes which he made during his stay are often brief, simply jottings, to remind himself of things he wanted to remember. These are here published in this form for the first time. In an expanded form they first appeared in *Travels in Two Democracies* in 1936 and then, with further expansions and commentaries, they were published in 1956 in *Red, Black, Blond and Olive*, subtitled "Studies in Four Civilizations." Reading these sparse notes, we can see how active and in what state of well-being EW was: he enjoyed meeting the American colony in Leningrad and Moscow, and in his free-and-easy way had considerable contact with the man on the street. The expansive revolutionary feelings engendered during the 1920s by the Leninist victories over foreign armies and the power Trotsky had built in the army had not yet begun to contract into the restrictions and terrors of the Stalinist regime. As EW remarked much later: "It ought to be borne in mind, in connection with these Russian notes, written in 1935, that this was, in certain ways, the most liberal period ever known in Soviet Russia. Visitors from abroad were welcomed for the valuta [scrip] they had to spend, though they were of course closely watched; contact with the West was encouraged. The political terror had already begun with the first trials of Stalin's opponents; but the writers were still being urged to avail themselves, from bourgeois culture, of whatever it had to offer them."

EW combined his standardized tourism with close observation; he was able to interpret plays, ballet, conversations, behavior, out of his readings of socialist dogma, Russian literature, and his easy familiarity with the arts, including the Soviet stage and cinema. The American journalists depended on informants and translators; but it is doubtful whether many of them had read Marx, Lenin, and Trotsky as Wilson had. Wilson used the facilities of VOKS (the All-Union Cultural Society for Relations with Foreign Countries) and he made free use of the personnel of the travel agency which arranged his voyage. Dos Passos's friends received him with great cordiality and in the notes we can see that his humane sympathies, his endless curiosity, evoked humane response, even if he did not always get full answers, and sometimes found his acquaintances lapsing into deep silences. We can also see, as we follow him, his growing recognition that the great socialist experiment, welcomed by American liberals, contained flaws which, in their idealism, they overlooked. His conversations with Prince Mirsky, one of the old aristocrats who had embraced Communism and returned to Moscow, were revelatory, even though Mirsky was cautious. Mirsky would die a couple of years later in a Stalinist prison camp and EW's brief memoir of him in *To the Finland Station* is vivid and powerful. His notes are almost exclusively travel notes; the delight in keeping Casanovaesque records of his adventures was set aside, although one or two brief references suggest that EW's sexual activity did not flag in the Russian environment. And so we travel with him, through these jottings and glimpses, on the Volga and to Odessa, where in the midst of his far-ranging inquiries he suddenly is victim of an epidemic of scarlatina. But even this is grist to his mill, for thanks to it we have a record of early socialized medicine in the Soviet Union. He was quarantined for a month and a half; and then developed kidney trouble, which further delayed his return. He spent the period of his illness reading and taking notes for *To the Finland Station.*]

Soviet Steamer "Siberia." May 17. When I first saw

England, I was quite moved. The trees and smooth green fields of the Isle of Wight in the soft and moist air under the troubled gray sky made me think of Tennyson, Queen Victoria—and of Shakespeare and the greenwood tree. The last time I had seen it was when we had to wait a day and a night in the Channel for fear of submarines in a troopship during the war (November 1917). I was extremely glad to be able to go where I pleased and not to have to sleep on the shore. We had been embarked from a rest camp at Southampton and had had to sleep on the ground in a lot of water: during the night, I had dreamed that Bernard Shaw, then a great admiration of mine, had brought out a new book of plays in which he had resolved all the agonies of the war into something witty, luminous, and humane. At the same time we were reading little scraps in the papers about the seizure of power in Russia by unknown persons named Lenin and Trotsky. Bernard Shaw was to disappoint my hopes: after the war, he published *Heartbreak House,* and now I am on my way to Leningrad with a biography of Lenin and a Russian grammar. At the rest camp in the south English landscape, lovely even in November, with its knotted oaks and slim beeches, I had run into a boy I had known in school, now a lieutenant in, I think, an infantry outfit. I had always found him rather a bore—I never saw him again because he was killed. —As we were docking at Southampton, I remembered something which I had tried to remember and failed to before we actually arrived: how we had boarded the troopship, now it all came back to me perfectly: the boredom of waiting with our packs on those docks. —On the way up to London on the little fast neat green boat train, green England, all a garden, all park, clipped trees, trees planted long ago to grow in certain ways in certain places, little dark shining streams, soft lawns, seemed to me still lovely and dear.

But London was a shock. I hadn't been here since 1914 except for a few hours passing through in 1921—and I find that I can hardly find my way around. London is now just like Chicago: the same enormous neon signs plastered over the front of all the buildings; the same movie palaces with gaudy decorations and people waiting to get in, in long lines; the same tabloids and cheap newspapers with no news in them—nothing but rather sickish crimes; the same cheap-looking window displays of drugstores and five-and-ten-cent stores—the same men and women sitting in doorways and digging in garbage cans as in New York.—

1066 and All That. Shakespeare seems a long time ago. —A boyfriend —You're telling me!

I found that I had been strangely depressed on the boat at finding that the English illustrated papers were full of American films and other American affairs. Strong as I am for America, I have always thought it was nice for the English to have their own institutions. When I go to the theater, I find that the most successful gags are Americanisms, now already slightly stale, such as—"Oh yeah?" It may be partly the strings of pennons and other festive decorations of the Jubilee, but all the different parts of London which I used to know as quite distinct entities—Leicester Square, Trafalgar Square, the Strand—now seem whelmed in one great traffic nexus and amusement center. The only place I can recognize in Regent Street is Liberty's. Nothing has ever made me feel so keenly that I grew up in one world and am living now in another. It is queer to reflect that the London I knew, which is still so vivid in my memory, was the old London. —Still, the city has a kind of smartness, with its brass signs and well-dressed men, that no American city has. In fact, I believe that during this period it has grown smarter. The English have been through the war, the dole, the General Strike, all the gaiety and hollowness of after the war, since I saw London last.

The gulf between the United States and Europe is already so great that it would take an American his whole life to get readjusted to England, and then he could never get back to the American thing again.

Russian boat. Russian sailor refused my tip when he carried my baggage on board. Nice to see the red flag flying with the yellow hammer and sickle and the one yellow star. Strange to be docked near the Tower—when we started (not on time) the great jaws of the turreted Tower Bridge unclamped to let us pass—past the dark old wharves, coal barges, boats with dark-tarnished brick-red sails. Atmosphere of amiable informality—very curious after the English: captain standing around, all the tea on the table and the man just comes round and asks you whether you want some more tea. Russians in my cabin standing and looking out the porthole and singing sad Russian songs to themselves, man in the cabin next door evidently learning to play the cornet. People talk much more freely, play the piano. Radio that sends us off with old Strauss waltzes and old Sousa marches.

—A new smell on the boat, new soap, towels of a new size and shape, new people, new food, a new language.

—General camaraderie such a great relief after the English—a lot of men came in and organized a jazz orchestra—captain and sailors came in and listened, captain smiling (the boat is run by a Soviet), then the little girls who worked in the kitchen, pretty though rather slatternly around the feet, came in and listened—great proof that everything can get done very well and everybody get along very well without social distinctions. Purser, or whatever he is, with his absolutely clear gaze, contrast to purser on *Berengaria*. Somebody sang "Oi Marie" and other songs; one of the Russian crew sang Russian songs well. Later the Russian boys—an extremely handsome young one, with a boy's sullen adolescent mouth—listening to the phonograph. *I've got the Jitters, I've got the Jitters*, etc., till the English guys took away their records, when they continued to sit up and play Russian jazz records. During the afternoon, somebody was always starting to play things on the piano—from "Chopsticks" to "Donna é mobile"—and then giving out. —American woman married to Negro intellectual off by themselves in a corner—she was putting her head on his shoulder, he was being a little careful—they had a long intellectual sociological argument, in which he was telling her what was what. —Some of the gents went and drank vodka and brandy in the dining room. All rather like a club without distinctions of age, class, or sex. —I have thoroughly enjoyed today, accomplishing my errands in London, in a taxi, having the man with my watch arrive on time, seeing [John] Strachey and reading his *Left Review*, protesting against the Jubilee, in the bus, and looking out the window of the saloon as we pulled out of the Thames, the feeling of a new country, a new life, the loosening up from the English atmosphere in the atmosphere of the Soviets—in the evening I had some of Krupskaya*: *the imprisonment, insanity, poverty, suicide, of the Bolsheviks, the agonies of its birth.* [EW's italics indicate the main subjects to be used in *Travels in Two Democracies*.] Two men who had been in U.S. something like forty-seven and thirty-five years respectively most amiably helped me pronounce Russian alphabet—

* Nadezhda Konstantinova Krupskaya, wife of Lenin. EW drew considerably on her memoirs for *Finland Station*.

crew talked Russian differently from when they had been
in Russia. English ladies retired early, almost immediately after taking a look at the gathering after dinner.
—Haven't felt so at ease since God knows when. —Smell
of boat like hallways of houses with new-painted, or
whatever they are, dados in N.Y. —All the more agreeable because I had been expecting something rather grim.
—Rather like the army under pleasant conditions.
—Toilet-paper roll came off its holder and fell to the
floor as soon as touched. English ladies were very much
worried about fact that none of the catches on the doors
worked properly. The men said, "I've never seen tea
with lemon before." The more naïve lady had thought
the caviar for breakfast was marmalade at first—then
tried it and said it would be good to make sandwiches.
It was remarked that something or other worked all
right, and she said, "Well, we must be thankful for small
mercies, mustn't we?" She said that the Russians were
an artistic rather than a practical race. Politeness of
men in room: I turned off the light when the rest of
them went to bed, and they protested—when I came in to
go to bed, they had turned on another not-so-strong light
with a pink shade. In the morning as they were getting
up, they talked practically in whispers. —Different
degrees of comfort in cabins, but all classes mix in dining
room, saloon, etc. —Little sober but bright saloon with
gray walls and shiny woodwork, decorated with inlaid
pictures of deer on Siberian wastes of snow and wild
lakes and rock formations like Canada and the American
West—furniture with cloth covers—little green-felt-
covered writing desks at either end, with the hammer
and sickle on the inkwells (I remembered that somebody, doodling, had turned a scratch into them in the
telephone booth where I went at the corner of Second
Avenue and 54th Street).

Monday bath. I rang and a gray, thin and anxious-looking elderly woman appeared. I asked her whether I could have a bath, and she said she didn't know and disappeared—then she returned and went back to wherever she had come from in the first place and presently one of the little stewardesses appeared (some of them did their work in high heels, which they tended to push out from under them) and smilingly unlocked the door, showed me how the hot and cold water and the douche worked. That was all there was to it. The bathroom, under the stairway, had no ventilation and was suffocatingly heated by the hot-water pipes. There was no plug and I called her attention to this and she immediately went and got one. It turned out that there was only one for both the men's and the ladies' baths, and she would carry it back and forth from one to the other—roller towel that came off roll when pulled. (Very amiable and accommodating, these little blond girls: the one who came in to take the phonograph away put out the lights in the saloon at twelve, made gestures when I offered to go that I could stay, making cunning little sounds like the language of mice.) I shut the door and began sweating profusely like a Turkish bath. A short spurt of hot water was followed by coldish water. The catch on the door was broken, and I couldn't make the lock work on the inside, so that while I was reclining in the tub, two people, finding the door unlocked, tried to walk in. In scrubbing myself, I leaned against the hot-water pipe on the wall and burned my elbow severely. The douche, when I turned it on, trickled a few drops and then did nothing. The big towel they give you is of the thickness, texture, and non-absorptive properties of a napkin.

English people at table. Man said, "I never saw lemon in tea before." Milder lady said of the bologna slices, "It's a little unusual, isn't it?" and taking the salami,

"This is more like what we have at home." Other lady wouldn't drink vodka but wanted just to taste it. Man, when I said that little side rooms upstairs were probably intended for drinks, said, as if disclosing a horrible secret over which he had brooded, "There aren't any drinks! There's no beer on board!" Great anxiety at first as to whether the sturgeon was fish or meat. —I made efforts to talk to both the ladies and the man, without much success (I gave up and lapsed into reading at table on Sunday). We Americans, in respect to the English, occupy the same position as the Russians in respect to us; but we are closer to the Russians than to the English—we, like them, have had a new deal from the old Europe; they are still fixed in their old hierarchy, maintaining their differences from each other. Americans are in a queer situation in Europe: the only country where we find our language spoken is the country which seems most different from us, and there is always a certain amount of what we say that they don't understand.

—The Russians in my cabin on the subject of the English–Jewish jazz band: the little shaved-headed one said, "Mousika"; the young one in the upper berth said, "Very bad music."

—Third class apparently had rather bad toilet facilities and inferior food. —Book for criticism, which was full of comments on the comradely character of the crew (with the exception of one person, who complained that they were less so than on the other Soviet boat they had been on: hoped something could be done so that they wouldn't be "so stuck up") and complaints about the arrangements in the third class, which somebody said had never been remedied.

Monday—Kiel Canal: woke up to find the porthole divided by a straight line, on the upper side of which was land, grass, glimpses of people and houses. Prussia and Schleswig: flat soft grass-grown grazing ground, in a funny bleak-for-all-the-lushness yellow light—people in German caps, on bicycles, barefoot girl in field, a woman darkly dressed—they all seemed to be dark—walking along road——straight roads, groves of absolutely straight spruce (?)—Kabel, nicht ankern: thick upstanding German letters—houses all alike (contrast with dairy country in Pa. or N.Y.), long corrugated red roof, against the wind, I suppose, like P'town—Kiel: sign forbidding taking photographs from the bridge, the water or the shore of the ships in the Kaiser Wilhelm Canal—out into the Baltic, misty and gray.

Sunday—Afternoon nap in our cabin: I lay on my back reading Krupskaya while the soft irregular reflections of the water traveled along the pale-gray ceiling.

—Strange to find a country in Europe where everything is brand-new—not new from the nineteenth century like Germany.

—Milder but more conventional English lady on supposed Archduchess Anastasia—they were pretty certain it was really she—the other lady's sister knew the nurse who had failed to make an identification or something of the kind.

Monday—English ladies commented on nice friendly atmosphere which prevailed on ship.

—They were studying coke (the boys in the cabin); I was studying Lenin—manners with no formulas of politeness, perfectly simple, perfectly considerate.

—Little boy of nine (Monday night) who had left Russia at five and lived at Tea Gate. Asked me whether I thought Lenin was a good man, whether I was with the Communists, whether I believed in God. In Russia, they cured children of believing in God by locking them up for a day and pointing out to them that if God existed he would help them.

—Englishman at table turned out to be very good scout: had been reading John Strachey and evidently on the radical side. Didn't know what had happened to political life in England—in his youth, a situation like this would have aroused great excitement—supposed it was due to the fact that it had become too difficult, too hard to understand—it used to be that people just took sides on issues in Parliament, like the Oxford–Cambridge boat race. Fabians had died out, and he didn't see anybody to take their place. The English paid a lot of attention to the United States, very little to Russia, wouldn't even print the news about it (this confirmed what Strachey had said). English free speech and justice: you needed money for the courts and you couldn't get a great many things printed.

—English ladies interested in exiled Russian royalty. Of opinion that the poor were very ungrateful when you did things for them. More conventional lady said that no one for whom she had ever done anything had ever shown her any gratitude—woman of education: evidently a lady, with children, whom she had run into, who had afterwards been after her to borrow money.

I thought of the remark of the old man in *The Possessed*, who complained that the Russian country girls got at an early age to look a little like buns, to be sure.

—Lousy English and German radio programs.

—Nervous radio man—very different, this one, from an American.

Wednesday—Talk with Gordon: Black belt and Ukraine. (Gordon was a Negro Communist with whom I had had lunch in New York.)

—The old waltz from *The Cherry Orchard*, German potpourri including, the little German said, a damned war song. —English people at table (day before, when I had asked the man where people got their opinions from if the newspapers were no good: "A good many of 'em haven't gottany."): Milder lady: "Everybody's letting themselves go—it's going to be rather awful"; advised us to keep to ourselves tonight, as there was some sort of cold about. Little lonely island with town and buildings on it: "People take to drink in lighthouses—so that then they're not any good, I suppose." — "Or go mad." —"But maybe radio helps them: they can hear what other people can hear." Woman in lighthouse who'd been bitten by snake and killed three children. —"Couldn't she suck the poison out?" — "It would be in her back or somewhere she couldn't reach." — "Couldn't she hope the husband would come back in time?" — "He would be somewhere very far off." — "Her nerve!" —Woman who kept calling, "Wolf, wolf!" about snakes—till finally she was really bitten by one, and her husband wouldn't go. —"What a terrible thing: I suppose it was too late to do anything." — "Died" (with a look of satisfaction).

—Dark low-mountainous pine-wooded coast of Finland.

—Dessert of vanilla ice cream in pink grenadine juice, with little lump of sugar, set in some kind of cake crust and saturated with vodka and flaming—they succeeded in setting on fire the little wedding-cake paper skirts in which the purple and white flowers on the tables were dressed up, much to the alarm of the English people, but not to the discomfiture of the waiter, who simply, after comment, took it out to the kitchen.

—Finland, which shows sloping and rocky as you get closer. —(Later) It is still light at ten, faint strips of pink in the west on the dimmed blue sky under the dense gray corrugated (boss-corrugated) cloud—the north, clear and clean and rather awe-inspiring, feeling of there being nothing beyond it, the bleak clear top of the world.

—Boy spoke of the "Imperialist War."

—The ladies asked the man if he was an Englishman.

—Tchaikovsky's *Pique-Dame* [Píkovaya Dama] on the radio.

—Baggage tags with no strings—man said life belts in bottoms of closets a secret.

—Later the opaque shreds of the big gray cloud float-ing around in the foreground of the last cold light, hardly distinguishable from moonlight except that it constantly grows less luminous, of the vanished sun of the northern day.

—I told the English ladies about the boys reading Pushkin and asked them whether they thought English-men would do that with Shakespeare. One said that Pushkin was very simple; the other that novels were easier to read. She had read *Pique-Dame* in Russian. I explained that Pushkin had written principally poetry, he was their great poet: "Great for them," they replied. —Collection for the service taken up in the 3rd class: the captain had said it would be given to what the ladies called the International —They said they didn't want that to take place with their money; did I? I said I didn't mind. The woman doctor *sursauta* and said savagely, "Well I do: they can have it in their own country; but they needn't try to make other people have it!"

Thursday, May 23, Leningrad. Intourist sign; porters; long wait like the army. Boat had arrived earlier than announced. Officials all drove away in a bus, leaving us still waiting; crowds, drab-looking, but as if city belonged to them. Touched by Intourist sign—when I first arrived at breakfast: "An old Russian custom: to wait. Are you from the States?" (An American I met in the restaurant.) Complications about [Valentine] Stenich (Dos Passos's translator); VOKS, with Brecht, confused with man in my room named Valentine, I left him note in Brecht's room— Muriel Draper. Tretyakov* spoke to me at desk about Stenich, [I understood him to say] he was Brecht, asked me if I knew his book, then vanished. —*Otello*: much

---

* Tretyakov, author of the play *Roar, China!,* and Bertolt Brecht, author of *Threepenny Opera.*

impressed by audience, never saw such enthusiasm, walked around in a circle in a room under the statue of Lenin: I was moved by it—the hand extended as if he were at once giving the worker what they had made and opening out the future to humanity to make whatever they could conceive. Long intermissions, during which they eat snacks and drink beer and tea. Usher left over from the old regime who asked me for money for the program—I gave him a dollar to change, which was all I had, and he brought me back six roubles—then brought me a pair of opera glasses, bowing with his hand flat on his chest such as I had never seen done—he was like a figure out of an old Russian comedy. Basy (?), who I saw between the acts, confirmed my belief that I had overtipped him. —When I got back to the hotel, I found Muriel [Draper] and Mme Litvinov,* had cocoa, talk with Muriel afterwards. —People going along in slippers, they seem to be particularly short on shoes. —Anti-religious museum as soon as I arrived, malachite columns, lapis lazuli, lots of gold: Greek Orthodox Church Byzantine and creepy, anti-religious exhibit creepy, too—pogroms and religious persecutions, propaganda exhibition, Fascism and Lenin's *Iskra,* quotations from Lenin—pendulum hanging from high dome, mummies of Metropolitan and of Siberian tsars of small tribes, Bruno, Galileo before the Inquisition. (St. Isaac's Cathedral.) —Beggar in street surprised me: people who don't work they won't compel to work (as somebody told me). —*Antiquités des vieux palais.* —Pretty little girl guide from Caucasus, admired *Picture of Dorian Gray.*

$2 for opera glasses, which I declined. —People at opera better dressed than people in street.

* Ivy Litvinov, English wife of the Soviet foreign minister Maxim Litvinov, later ambassador to the United States.

Clever girl guide on recent political events. —Guide spoke of the Imperialist War: it inspires one almost with awe to think how one man, Lenin, has stamped his thought and his language on a whole people.

M. said there had been an exodus from there recently. *May* 24. Peter-Paul Fortress in morning. Old-fashioned prison with big rooms, which didn't seem as bad as American prisons—but everything perfectly quiet, guards wore soft shoes, walked up and down corridors and looked every five minutes through slot in door— Kropotkin's cell, Vera Figner's* cell, cell of woman revolutionist who set her hair afire with kerosene from lamp and killed herself in that way—dark cell where they were sent for punishment and usually went mad. Nobody had ever escaped—the prisoners had numbers, and when their family came to see them, the authorities said they didn't know their names, only the numbers. Little room where Lenin's mother had last interview with eldest son just before he was hanged. Code alphabet: they stood against the wall with their hands behind them, so that the guards wouldn't know what they were doing: Kropotkin told the man in the cell next to him the story of the Paris Commune. —Church inside the fortress and just a little way from the prison: gold altar and columns with gold capitals, white marble tombs of the Tsars, each with a heavy gold cross on top—two made of different kinds of precious colored stone, fraudulently represented at the time as having been donated by loving peasants. Women explaining to children that the Tsars had been appointed to rule, not on account of their ability, but simply be-

---

* Figner (1852–1942) spent twenty years in solitary confinement for her part in the assassination of Tsar Alexander II in 1881.

cause they were sons of other Tsars. Something sinister and desolate about Leningrad: the places and public buildings that seem to go on for miles and miles—the churches like these are horrible—I don't blame them for hating their clergy. And there is something somehow not good even about the Hermitage: the most unpleasing great gallery I have ever seen—enormous canvases plastered on the walls, sometimes in three tiers, Schneyder, Rubens, arranged with no taste, vast high rooms. Catherine's present to Potemkin: cage of glass and gold with gold peacock that spreads its tail and displays it, and gold cock that crows while a little tune of bells is played—also, clock that has an enormous music box and plays eighteenth-century music from vast prickly cylinders on the hour. —*Esmeralda* in the evening. One of the Eisenstein boys estimated, apparently somewhat extravagantly, that I had tipped usher 65 or 70 roubles. That night he recognized me (the usher) and bowed low: I have apparently bought *Bittes* for as long as I stay—thrust opera glasses on me in intermission: "You keep, *bitte*." Beer and cheese sandwich, with only one slice of bread. I kept on sitting in my seat after the final curtain, as if expecting the U.S. Marines to come in and save Esmeralda—M. said it would be funny if Wilson and Baker had sat in those same seats. —On the way back to the hotel, we crossed the street in the wrong place, and the people who were waiting on the curb became indignant and protested, somebody said we were "badly educated" (as Muriel explained to me)—a man followed us, still protesting, but the other people told him he was tight. —Stenich had called up in afternoon, and just as I was about to make an appointment to see him, we were cut off and I never heard from him again. —One of the Eisenstein boys told about how he had gotten into the Winter Palace on the pretense of being with a delegation—when they found he was not with the delegation, they put him out and made him come in again properly. Mrs. Litvinov explained the story to us and said, "He thinks that's a joke!" They had been picked out for their ability and were getting a kind of two-year general cultural improvement. One of them very good-looking in American-looking clothes. —One's feeling toward the Soviets protective—strange effect of abolition of bourgeoisie—still true that it's not possible to be neutral. Proletariat on the signs of classless society. —Women's flat shoes, a few get high-heeled ones, which don't look very smart.

—Competition between Moscow and Leningrad betrayed by Leningrader guide's not being certain, though she had often wondered, whether Red Square in Moscow was bigger than the square in front of the Winter Palace.

—M. and I had late supper at Europa after the theater: when the couples began to dance, she said it looked like the Taft in New Haven or something of the kind. They have only been allowed to dance for about three years, and they learn the steps carefully and perform them very seriously. "Jazz" looks very funny transliterated into Russian: джаз —Her brother-in-law in England had tried to make her take a machine for making cream out of melted butter—wondered how she could go to country which had executed a whole royal family.

—Women working with men on the street; paid the same.

May 25. Futile efforts to get Stenich on phone: they couldn't tell whether his number, as he had written it, had a 9 or an 8—girl insisted on calling 8, which was busy and didn't answer. —Red Flag textile factory: pressure, no doubt, but no such pressure, so far as I could see, as with us—they have Robert Owen's method of keeping the workers up to scratch: they are divided into brigades, each with a chief, whom they elect—the brigades compete and the names of all the members are posted on a blackboard at the end of the aisle with the amount of work each has done—those who fall behind are not punished but their names are posted to make their ignominy public. The best ones get special privileges, theater tickets, longer vacations, their photographs (in the case of the girls) posted on a background of red; skilled workers paid more than unskilled. Propaganda posters: the German working class manacled (a great red giant) and held in a barbed-wire enclosure by a snarling Nazi—to remind them of what they were being urged on for and of the danger to the working class outside. Little technical bookshop; dining room where they seemed to be eating black bread and cabbage soup. An hour for lunch. Woman with her head sunk on her arm at a table. Radio concert during intermission: two girls practicing ballet in the aisle; two more seen through the window outside in the courtyard. Seven hours a day; six hours, in the hot dyeing room—disagreeable work brings special privileges (Fourier). Here they [wear] still rather simple and inelegant clothes which you see the people in the streets wearing.

When I got back to hotel, called up Stenich—girl (Dostoevsky on buns) thought it was 8, which was out of order, so I made her try 9 and I got him: he said, "You are hard to get." Appointment for six. —Conversation with him at six: he arrived promptly—lucid and dressed à l'américaine—confusion, however, again: understood him to ask me whether I had anything to do the next evening—if not, he would take me around—then it turned out it was for tonight he was asking me. I tried to pin it down to one or the other, but he said finally, today is tomorrow. I tried again, but began to get that way myself and said (the base of the conversation had been

English, but with a sprinkling of other languages), "To-day, hier, heute!" — "Aujourd'hui," he corrected me. He suggested eight o'clock; I said, "All right: eight"; but he hastily added, as if things were getting too definite: "Six or nine, if you would like better!" He arrived again promptly at eight and took me to *Peter the Great* [by Alexéy Tolstóy] in the magnificent Empire gold-and-white theater, with the box all over gold for the Tsar. As I watched the expensive and brilliant production, I began to wonder whether there wasn't a political significance, and at last, when the attempted assassination took place, Stenich whispered to me, "Here certain historical parallels start." He said that A. Tolstoy was about their best writer. Stalin admires Peter the Great. Tolstoy and President of Leningrad Soviet there, a short man with black beard and sharp-pointed mustaches. All the writers by invitation in special section. Reflections on the writers; reflections on Peter; reflections on the popularity of Dos— Jimmy Herf (in *Manhattan Transfer*), and Elaine, Stenich told me, as well known as any characters of Pushkin's; reflections on factory. Soviets and U.S.A. both straining industrially for entirely different reasons— the whole thing entirely undesirable. Dos Passos's characters up against industrialism the same as the people in Russia—things that are the same, things that are different—what you can't understand unless you come here. —Walk by Neva—Stenich loved Leningrad—born there and lived there all his life, but soon there would be nothing left but factories and museums. —He was moving out to Moscow. Square of the victims of the revolution—"so quiet here you could sleep." He had been in the Red Guard, present at the taking of the Winter Palace, had known Lenin. Writers still left in Leningrad went around intoxicated by Pushkin and Dostoevsky. We talked amid the desolate long perspectives, leaning against the stone parapet of the Neva. Dark palace of the Grand Duke Constantine, uncle of the late Tsar— "He was a poet—was quite a good poet"—signed himself C.R., Constantine Romanov, he was killed. I asked how they had filled those huge palaces—he smiled, shrugged, didn't know—Constantine had had a large family, many servants. —Of the city, "Ain't it beautiful?" —Writers better off, I am told, even than engineers, the real elite— pretty soft for the writers, but is it necessarily a good thing? —Stenich would love to go to N.Y.—wants to know whether Roosevelt isn't a great man—reflections on interview with W. (?) as contrasted with supposed admiration for Roosevelt. In the midst of all this, every once in a while, old parties likely to pop up with long beards, senile, childlike, and sweet—I suppose the Soviets take the irreclaimable ones and plant them in and around the tourist hotels, making that much concession to capitalist-tourist corruption and the picturesqueness of old Russia—international chambermaids, who speak German and French.

—M. had taken little Intourist guide to opera—girl had demurred at first, because she didn't have the clothes— then, when she went, didn't want to go out between the acts.

May 26. No sightseeing. Walk with M.—M.'s attempt to see Meyerhold's *Dame aux Camélias.* It began with two sailors shaking hands—it was a ship and C.'s lovers began swarming up in groups—she thought it was a novel interpretation, but such was her respect for Meyerhold that she never questioned it—though there were more lovers than M. had ever remembered Camille's having— they seemed to have grouped themselves in factions— no doubt. Those who loved her because she could talk and those who loved her because she could listen, those who loved her because she was virtuous and those who loved her because she wasn't virtuous, etc. —Finally, she came in as if she had been shot offstage, and died. It turned out that it had been *The Optimistic Tragedy* at the Kamerny. —We walked past a number of book-shops—what libraries they evoked, as she said—to Finland Station: statue of Lenin—we sat down in the little park, and a young couple who had been sitting on the bench moved away—M. said they were afraid to have anything to do with foreigners. —Streets always being cleaned with hose—people in streets very nice when asked to direct you, etc.

—Meyerhold's new version of *Píkovaya Dama*—we sat in box—wonderful production, fine fable, which I had never appreciated before, very Russian—old Countess built up to in new production instead of being introduced in the first scene. —Looking out the window of the elec-tric-lighted director's room with its gold Empire sphinxes and classical figures on brown polished wood, I saw the day still light at nine, the cobbled street and an old woman sitting sewing in the doorway of a great shabby yellow stucco building. —Harsh satisfactory trumpets bursting out at the ends of the scenes—mime watched by the old lady. —Harold Clurman. Shostakovich*—shy little sandy-colored man, with unobtrusive glasses—Miss Wright, bad monkey mouth with prominent teeth, which she has compensated for by intensification of eyes, quite attractive in spite of flat shoes—physiologist and translat-ing Mark Twain, had fallen out with Stenich over his translation of Dos, excellent English—on *Peter the Great*. —Mayakovsky's girlfriend sitting in front of me—didn't know about her and didn't notice her. —Afterwards, cav-

---

* Clurman, EW's former New York neighbor, was in Russia at this time; Shostakovich, the Russian composer, had by this time achieved renown in the United States.

iar and vodka. —Went to bed full of Pushkin and the romance of old St. Petersburg—romance of old decanter with cockeyed top full, of water appropriate for biological cultures—story of Gorky going to factory, everything wonderfully efficient and perfect: he inquired what was made there, and was told that they made signs saying: Lift out of order.

—Muriel on her sons—about whom she was perfectly preposterous: If she should find Smudge, for instance, a broker, on the other side of the line, when the great struggle came between capitalism and Communism!

May 27. The Intourist people and I had misunderstood each other about the trip to the Revolutionary Museum* being at 10:30—it was really to be at 2:30, so I got them to give me a guide to take me to the Pushkin Museum—same pretty little girl who had taken me to the Anti-Religious Museum—but we found that the Pushkin flat wasn't open till 4:00, so I got her to take me to the Revolutionary Museum. She had never seen it before and not only had difficulty getting around but was frightened by the gloominess of the Winter Palace (she didn't like the climate of Leningrad, wanted to get away to the sun)—when we would climb a desolate stairway, traverse deserted stone corridors, open a door and enter a darkish chamber, she would say, "Oh, it is so *gloomy!* I am afraid!" —When we came to the waxworks—prisoners in Siberia, in the Peter–Paul Fortress, etc.—she asked if she could take my arm. She had been terrified first by great Cyclops figure of worker, moved in there, I suppose, from some public occasion. We were looking for the Tsar's rooms, and she seemed to be completely misled by the directions given her—we went through a

* An extended account of this visit is in *Red, Black, Blond and Olive,* pp. 170 ff.

museum of the French Revolution, in which she admired an engraving of [Henri de] La Rochejacquelein (the Royalist Vendéan leader) and said, "I like such a face—it is so different!" In the vast empty courtyard of the Winter Palace, little children in pink pinafores (blouses?) were playing. Finally, we discovered that we had to go out and come in at a different entrance—and then we were admitted to rooms of Nicholas I—first, a large bathroom, very queer—it made the little girl guide laugh—with a deep deep tub sunk in the floor and great stove in the next room to heat the water—then upstairs the Tsar's tiny rooms—he had some kind of agoraphobia, it seems—with their ugly nineteenth-century furniture, rather Victorian and middle-class, the paintings by one of his daughters of people in picturesque costumes, and a lot of photographs, slightly faded, of places they'd been to and evidently liked. The little guide wanted to know whether Roosevelt wasn't a great man.

—When I got back to the hotel, I priced the china in the antique store and was told it had come from the collection in the Winter Palace—such a curse seemed to me to hang over the whole thing that I even hesitated about buying one for Mother.

—Muriel's instructor in naval methodology, who had read everything—seventeenth-century English poetry: he had been reading Marvell and Donne to the naval officers, and they had been crazy about it—wrote poetry in French—described landscapes, according to M., and would say, as she told me, "It's like Poussin, except the sky," which was something a little different—recommended many Russian poets, some of them unpurchasable, some of them circulating only in MS.—on Russian films—took her through galleries (she said afterwards that he'd gone through her like a plague of locusts). Some

Russian poet who'd written a poem on the raising of Lazarus, partly under French, partly under German influence, giving it a homosexual slant. Tall, slim in his uniform, pale, a little feminine—a little like Howard Cox—perfect manipulation of cigarette.

—Drank two glasses of vodka and get off on the train [to Moscow], greatly thrilled—Englishman from boat in car, said that the food was all right, the only thing was that there wasn't enough green fruit. At train, Intourist girl impressed on me that I ought to be sure to stay with my suitcases, because one had just been stolen. Traveling "hard": man in bunk above me didn't even get a mattress—official-looking cap, heavy body, heavy inchoate face—but lay down in all his clothes on the bare wood and went to sleep, apparently never moving all night—beer and bread with caviar, sausage and cheese. Man in corridor who helped me out in English about price of food. Childlike tall stooping mustached Pole—had been eleven years in U.S., at Ford's, $5 a day—275 roubles a month—very proud of new Moscow subway, would see nothing like it in America—wouldn't go back to Poland, had come to Russia after Revolution. I told him Detroit was in a bad way. —The northern day that never ends—forests of slim straight pines and birches with their white stems—Russia a hirsute country—sort of disordered and limitless like U.S.—kept sitting leaning on little desk and looking out window, fascinated—reactions, after I had gone to bed, about not finding watch and thinking it had been stolen, then about finding it again.

—In the museum, the figure of the old-regime bureaucrat police officer, braided uniform, beard and pince-nez, with the album open before him of the political miscreants, their photographs and little descriptions in red ink below them, fierce, set concentrated faces—and in a separate album, Lenin and Krupskaya,* in their young days: he already with his white pure young wide high dome, two black shoe-button eyes, intense but not yet concentrated as later when the whole man seemed to become will; she with a full mouth, rebellious mouth and eyes, something perhaps of the gamine, more obviously a fighter than he—exhibit another proof of their dramatic sense (as M.D. says).

—Meeting with Lewis Browne (whom M. had previously referred to as Death in Venice): he said that the people were so much better off than they had been when he had been here last—they have really got going—everybody says this. —B. said that he had previously found nothing but dialectical materialism.

—Correspondence with foreigners.

May 28. Arrived Moscow: Habicht; Dynamov,† with whole upper jaw of gold teeth; other man extremely obliging, nice roundheaded type of Russian, with clear childlike eyes rather far apart under broad forehead; VOKS in old nineteenth-century ugly house with some green to be seen out the window. —Darling little girl from Open Road, same roundheaded childlike type and no bigger than a child—married to an American photographer—reminded me in some ways of A[nna]—people in general a good deal like A. and her family (badly off by American standards as they are, have had all the best of it as far as housing is concerned, if it wasn't that they hardly ever have any work, that they have to depend

* Further described in *Red, Black, Blond and Olive,* pp. 170-1.

† Herman R. Habicht of Open Road travel agency; Sergei Dynamov of the International Literature Office. Dos Passos had given EW introductions to them, saying, "The danger is in Moscow that you'll only meet the official greeters."

on relief, that they are always being forced to move out of their relatively comfortable flats and houses.) —Moscow much more modern, brisk, efficient, and energetic—people better dressed and more prosperous, more like an American city. —Crowded trams we rode on: old people, women with children, and other privileged persons allowed to get on at front of cars—people hang on to outside of cars, as they are not allowed to do in N.Y., fall off and lose legs and arms, hence cripples you see. People push and dispute in trams, but are really more friendly and show each other more consideration than in N.Y.— "I've got to get to the theater." "Well, this isn't the only night you can go to the theater." On the whole, I have found the Russians remarkably natural and amiable people: it is necessary only to smile at them.

Little red-cheeked, freckled, country-girl traffic cop, cunning in her helmet and masculine clothes.

—Alec Waiman from the British embassy and "Mme Litvinova": her flat across from the great former private house where the People's Commissar for Foreign Affairs entertained—four or five rooms, where the Litvinovs and their three children lived—trees and grass here too. —Popularity of Oscar Wilde: they were all reading *Dorian Gray* in English, it seemed. One student had said he preferred it to Galsworthy because it was more idiomatic: they liked Wilde because he had been made to suffer in jail by the hypocritical English. —Petrovsky's house, what would be in N.Y. a moderate-sized middle-class apartment—Petrovsky head of the technical education in the heavy industries—NRA declared unconstitutional*—tea and all kinds of cakes and candies.

* It was the Litvinovs who told EW of the Supreme Court decision on NRA when he was having tea with them.

May 29—Big ugly bulbous growth like mushrooms of the mosque spires of St. Basil's—Red Square: the tomb of Lenin, the Kremlin Wall, the abolition of the Iberian Virgin—city spotlessly clean, I had expected it to be old and musty—only little patches of the old embedded in the modern city. —Green strip with trees in front of modern apartment house not unlike Washington, D.C.

Bookstores, old and new: new a little monotonous, whole stock on shelves as in Workers' Bookstore in N.Y.: all Marx, Lenin, Stalin, and technical stuff; old bookshops full of remnants of pre-revolutionary libraries: French, German, Italian, English, and the classics: man with fringe of whiskers of the vintage of 1880, the only thing of the kind I think I have ever seen.

—Barbed M on wall of Kremlin like that strange Byzantine letter that the Soviets have abolished from the alphabet (ѣ). —Russian lesson: workers' flats: how the people live: extremely nice about showing you the way. Nice-looking officer with his family, uniform contrasting with rather dismal and crowded flat, sent boy to show me the way.

—Buying a stamp.

May 30. *Air Meet*: wet weather—gliders, minuets, turnings around sideways, parachute jumping, woman with two parachutes. Cunning little couples leaning against bicycles, girls with sports socks. Mrs. Litvinov's bum old car—old houses on the outskirts of Moscow with windows with peaked things over them and great fringes of wooden lace under the roofs—made of logs and mud, brown—some of them seemed to have sunk into the earth, their windows were so near the ground —Loudspeaker: the Internationale. —Woman selling little cakes and bottles (of beer, I imagine). —Crowd got out beyond rope; policemen tried to get them back; they argued that if the cars were parked in front of the rope, they ought to be able to be; cop said they could see just as well behind the cars; somebody said that it wasn't that the cars kept them from seeing, but that the psychological effect was bad; the guard begged them to keep back just a teeny little bit; finally the cars were driven off, and the cops told them that now they no longer had any excuse for not keeping behind the rope.

—Walt Carmon: writers the elite, the sacred cows, but they were checked up on: had to appear at workers' meetings, where somebody would tell them they were lousy—every factory had its literary circle, metro workers—Dos Passos and *New Masses* in Siberia—(writers better off even than engineers). I told him about the people I had talked to who couldn't grasp the capitalist crisis in America—and he said that it was very hard to explain to them: he would go before a meeting of Russian workers and tell them how bad things were in America, and they would see he was wearing a pretty good suit of clothes and wouldn't believe him—lots of factories in America meant to them lots of happiness and prosperity, of course that was what they meant in Russia—a new factory meant a new gold tooth or something—when he insisted on the capitalist crisis, they would ask, "The Communist publications aren't illegal?" "No." "Well, then, why isn't there a revolution?" — "Maybe you think that's easy to answer—I thought so at first!"

—An edition of thousands of books like a drop in the sand.

At night, I locked myself out of my room again: nobody at chambermaids' table in hall—elevator boy said he'd see porter, but nothing came of this—I went down myself, and porter who spoke English perfectly, at once summoned boy with box of tools who was standing by—I asked the porter whether he didn't have a key, and he said that this boy was the boy who dealt with situations like this. The boy and I went upstairs—he took out a large wedge and began hammering it with deafening racket in the crack between the double doors—there was nothing appropriate for opening locks—then he took out another large tool and began gouging with it at the lock. I remonstrated, made the old man with the shaved head who had in the meantime turned up at the table look in the table drawers, but he only looked at the keys and shook his head. The boy tried the wedge again—I tried to call the porter at the phone in the hall, and the old man with the shaved head tried simultaneously, but nothing came of these attempts—the boy gave up and we both went downstairs again. Then the porter produced a key, with which we easily opened the door. —I had been trying to think that Moscow was completely efficient.

—Moscow rather dreary—Leningrad the most dramatic city I have ever seen: the short circuit of a society—the Winter Palace, Lenin.

May 31. I met my Englishman again on the steps of the National: when I said I hoped to stay on, "You get along all right, do you?" he said. "I couldn't stand it." He didn't get enough fresh fruit and green vegetables—I said you got oranges, though they were expensive. He said he'd had an orange and a bottle of beer the other day, so he was all right for a time. I said that it was certainly interesting to see it, wasn't it, but he didn't reply.

—*Pickwick* in evening: entrance of Dodson and Fogg . . . Koshchéy the Deathless in the *Firebird*. Wardle's house hung with hunting scenes, man holding fox up by the tail. Men kissing each other à la russe. Sam Weller made strongest character—sits down at table at Wardle's and leads off the polka with Mary the barmaid.

—People at home who spend so much time imagining Russia—one can't imagine it.

June 1. Dinner with Tretyakov and [Louis] Fischers:*
Romeo and Juliet, first classic that the Theater of the
Revolution had put on. Stage vistas very fine; Juliet acted
much better by actress of forty than K. Cornell did it. Too
much rushing around stage, up and down flights of stairs.
—Balcony scene brought laughs, and director explained to
us between acts that it was not made sentimental, as somebody had complained that it wasn't, because it was already
sensual, and sensuality and sentimentality wouldn't do—
it was closer to Shakespeare this way, and was in the mood
of Soviet youth: ironic, tender. —Performance I think the
longest I've ever sat through—7:30 to 12:20.

—The "Black Bread Blues"—diarrhea, reading Soviet
guidebook. Walt Carmon said his had lasted a year.

Muriel Draper's song: the "Moscow Blues."

> "The GPU has run out of glue,
> And I haven't had any mail for weeks."

June 2. Krupskaya on Chekhov.
Interview with Kuliakov.
Talk at Open Road about one.
Visit to Duranty's flat.
—One reason they treat each other so well on streetcars
is that they can be fined for hooliganism, if they don't.
—Lenin's Tomb: Ural marble, black and gray, with
flakes of lapis lazuli like blue butterfly's wing—underground—triangular cover of glass with soldier sitting at the
foot and staring fixedly toward Lenin's face—different
from what I had expected: extraordinarily fine, intellectual, distinguished—square head, with high brow, bald
forehead, gray hair, slanting eyes, features shrunken and
sharpened by death, fine nose, square-tipped effective
figures. —Long line waiting, looping back again and again.

* The correspondent, author of books on Russia and India.

June 3. Call on Umansky*

Dinner with [H. R.] Habicht—Pat Sloan (Englishman); Hazard, young American foundation law student from Yale and Syracuse, had worked hard on Russian since September and made considerable progress with it.

June 4. I found Lily† eating large chocolate candies done up in paper wrappers with bears on them and labeled "Baby Bears"—I don't know why, unless because they were yellowish-brown inside.

—Waking up as if to the tension of adjusting myself to a fourth dimension.

—Ostrovsky's *Talents and Admirers* at Art Theater— Artistic Café afterwards (something quite new, Lily told me), with harsh German and Russian records which made conversation impossible. —She told me how they stayed up till two o'clock in the morning during the white nights of Leningrad without realizing how late it was. Her sister would wake her up because she was still interpreting in her sleep.

—I learned later that the ending of the Ostrovsky play had been changed—the student had originally shot himself—for the same reason that the balcony scene in *Romeo and Juliet* had been given a light tone: in order not to encourage excessively romantic love. —He had said that he would not fight a duel with him because they belonged to different classes. —Never enjoyed anything more than seeing this play with Lily.

June 5. Youssupof estate. —Effects of old-fashioned

---

* Soviet press official.

† In the extended version of these notes later published, EW said Lily Herzog spoke English well, was the daughter of a scientist "of the old society" and "the only really attractive woman whom I have so far seen in Moscow." She worked also for the Open Road travel agency. See *Red, Black, Blond and Olive,* pp. 299–305.

valentine lace in the woodwork around the windows—
countryside flat, the foliage of the slim-stemmed trees
around the house a peculiar bright green I have never
seen anywhere else.

Dinner with Paul Arend and Curtis at Metropole—
Moscow tie strongly developed. Metropole dining room.

—There is what I take to be a solitary prostitute who
hangs around the Metropole—feather sticking up from her
hat and in general resembles an Art Theater character
from Ostrovsky or Chekhov. Like the international
chambermaids, etc., a museum piece.

June 6. Took Lily to ballet—Christmas pantomime
affair, very brilliant.

June 7. Dinner at 2:30 with Alymov and his wife*—
how little even those interested in America know about
American literature—had never heard of Melville—did
not know (Alymov told me) about either Cummings or
Dos in Russia.

Afterwards, talk at MORT by Friedrich Wolf on conditions and the theater in America, 5–8.

—A.: I judge by the Russian classics and the literatures
of other countries.

—Mme Alymov has gray eyes like caviar eggs, only
much more expressive.

June 8—Walk to Russian lesson: center most unpleasing
part of Moscow—outer streets much more attractive with
little strips of tree-planted parts, old houses, walls, and
churches—also Kropotkin Boulevard, or whatever it is,
in afternoon: walking along the river, then long white
street of universities, institutes, and museums.

Trip to Women's and Children's museum with VOKS

* John Dos Passos had given EW an introduction to Sergei
Alymov.

girl guide—bad murals, but beautifully arranged, all olive-green stained tablets, shining nickel rails and glass—wooden tablets with explanations and directions and illustrative photographs—diets reproduced in wax, which the girl interpreter thought marvelous—attitude of girl. —She thought A. Tolstoy their best living writer.

—Dinner in evening with Lily's family: buying caviar and candy at Torgsin store, a man who was also buying something and who volunteered the information that some of the fruit drops were sweet and some were "kind of sour." —Habicht on his adventures in the nut business—sorting out the nuts of various sizes and picking out the bad nuts—but the nut workers of the minor nationalities couldn't see the point of sorting out the various shades of color—so he proposed that they should all be fired—the Soviet authorities, however, wouldn't allow minor nationalities to be fired. Somebody else said that they fired them at will in Moscow, because here they felt surer of themselves politically.

Fine new apartment occupied by the Reisenbords, kitchen, bathroom, and tree-grown stretch outside.

Lily's brother-in-law on political notabilities and events. —Woman in whose apartment Mme M. gave her lessons, whose husband was a geneticist working here: exciting to watch how it changed, although it seemed drab at first —things that you hadn't been able to get anywhere turned up in the store windows.

—Dismissal of Yenukidze.*

—American wife of engineer—he had worked three years for Soviets, wasn't satisfied and went home, then

---

* A. Yenukídze, for seventeen years secretary of the Central Executive Committee, was dismissed while EW was in Moscow, "for political and personal dissoluteness," without further specifications.

couldn't get a job and came back—she didn't become a part of the life, went regularly to the Catholic church, the son couldn't fit in at all, knew nobody.

June 9. Collective farm: trouble about getting there—first going on bus that left every ten minutes, then girl interpreter thought it would be better to take train, got there quicker—no train at Warsaw station for three-quarters of an hour, they had told her one thing at the information window (that the train would go sooner) and something else (the truth) at the ticket window—but she had bought the tickets before she heard the truth, and then we decided a taxi would be better, and she tried to give the tickets back, but the blue-eyed clear-eyed fresh-cheeked little stout girl sitting inside behind the counter wouldn't take them back, they had been stamped and she could only give me my money back if she could sell them to somebody else that day—if we would come back later after she had sold them, she would give us the money back—great argument—I finally took the change and pushed the tickets back—she tried to push the tickets out at me so that I would have to take them, but was hampered by the ticket window. She had been smiling at the interpreter all the time with her clear eyes—no meanness, no ugliness of the employee. (Dostoevsky's characters—the interpreter type—carried through to the present day.) —Yet indulging in comradeship which relieves most friction or strain that I have seen. We decided to wait in line for a taxi—one of the men ahead of us got tired and went over to get a bus—when we were finally first and a taxi arrived, it turned out that he was due at the taxi barn in half an hour to give the taxi over to another man, so he could not take us out of Moscow. The next man behind us got in and we waited for the next—personally I don't mind all this, as my habits are often lazy and careless—the little girl was reading Engels's pamphlet on *Socialism,*

Utopian and Scientific, in order to improve her English
and her knowledge of dialectical materialism both at the
same time, which was just what I would have done under
the circumstances—what I did was talk to the young
Englishman who was in the Ministry of Agriculture. It
had been a question of whether the driver would wait for
us longer than forty minutes, but when we got out, the
girl said it was all right, because he had said he would
wait half an hour and that meant he would wait an hour.
—President of collective who came out of the dining hall,
evidently interrupted in the middle of his dinner, took us
to his office; pretty little girl gave us lilac sprigs and then
a good-looking woman gave us a bouquet. President's red
farmer's complexion, cropped head, cool, straight, and nice
blue eyes—kind of good, easy, and sensitive manners of
boys on ship—explained facts concisely and clearly. —Cow
barn: I inquired about milking machines, he'd never
heard of them—I said to the Englishman that I'd understood that the cows in Ireland had been upset and had
refused to give any milk when the milking machines had
been put on them—but that the American cows were used
to being milked that way: the girl answered, though not
without humor: they are more cultural. —Food in the
dining hall: arrival of another party of tourists—man who
looked like a slightly shoddy Sir Somebody, with trimmed
beard and kindly patronizing English manners. "You
speak English very well," he said to the girl interpreter.
"Have you been in England?" —Did all the people want
to be collectivized? No: they had had some trouble a few
years ago, but none now. (There remain only our own
people.) And if they objected, were they arrested? No:
they were not arrested—but if they were against the Soviet
government, they were arrested. Englishman asked me
whether the slump hadn't been a shock to the Americans—
they evidently take great satisfaction in this—said England

had been that way ever since the war. One practical commercial nation sourly watching another of the same stock.
—Radishes, cucumbers, and that herb they put in soup,
of which the city girl interpreter had never heard the
name before in Russian and didn't know what it was in
English —The girls laughed at the boy and said that he
was a guest and he could have a radish, too—he was very
much embarrassed. —Rutty roads, mussy countryside,
more like America than England. Old brown wood-lace
frills around windows. —On the way back, horses with
their queer collars—asked girl guide about it but she
didn't know—everybody asks, she said. —Like explanation
of straight railroad line from Leningrad to Moscow, finally
found in old grammar. —Beauty parlor. —Blond curled
hair—blue beret on one side of her head—works hard as
hell—homely beauty parlor in kolkhoz headquarters.

Thoughts about Women's and Children's Museum:
America coming to meet (?) all this. — Open Road's gruesome stories of debutantes—on the other hand, the other
kind: Martha Gellhorn.*

Writers caught up in general effort—why not?—collective vision revealed by Lenin stronger than individual's
imagination.

—The first and only (?) thing Cummings found here
was another guy from Cambridge, who was crazy about
it—consequently, Cummings was against it.

Russian women narrow their eyes—I've hardly known
anybody but Hazel Rascoe in America who did this.

—At dinner, from the window of the New Moscow, the
rain is coming—deepening gray of the sky brings out the
buildings of the city so that their colors seem to count

* American journalist and writer, who later became Mrs.
Ernest Hemingway.

more—as the wind blows in the window, all the lusters on the glass chandeliers begin to jingle—red roofs, a few sharp spires, the dry gray-cream-colored buildings with their short rectangular windows in rows rising above the old wall with its slits and its little vines climbing up from the base—and the quiet river below, which ripples quietly without seeming to flow in either direction, with its slow little speedboats and its little rowing parties in rowboats.

—Curious effect of trying to cut off past and starting with dialectical materialism—they are now trying to relieve this impoverishment by bringing back the culture of their tradition: Ostrovsky and Chekhov, Pushkin, pictures of Pushkin all over, right beside Engels and Marx—candy with Pushkin on the box.

They have been whitewashing everything, and the foreigners are usually covered with whitewash and brushing each other off. The Russians seem to know how to avoid it.

—Food tickets for dogs.

June 10—Dreary and shabby inside of St. Basil's, with nothing done to freshen up the angels and lots of quotations from Marx and Lenin to discourage the visitors with religion. Cramped and labyrinthine—a lousy little church.

—Getting theater tickets with Lily—call on Alymovs. L. said they had some good old things.

Russian lesson. Her husband had been a Social Democrat and had had to "fly" from the second Duma. —He had lived in Cambridge in 1918 when Litvinov was in jail. —When one of her pupils spoke Russian at the examination, Nevill Forbes asked her where she had learned to speak Russian—Mme Mitrova taught me. —He asked her about Litvinov, a character in Turgenev—then asked what Mme Mitrova knew about Litvinov—the student went on talking about the character in the book. When she told Mme M. about it afterwards, she said that the student might have failed but she had passed—because if she had breathed one murmur about Litvinov she would have had to fly from Cambridge. —I asked her how she liked Cambridge, remarking that it was a pretty place. She said yes, that she used to say that if she had been Chekhov, she would have found some wonderful material there.

—Things you begin to realize they haven't got: dogs, cats, popular songs, songs that are sung (except by marching soldiers) in the streets (but truckload of children going somewhere and singing some Communist song).

—Moscow *Daily News Office*. Explanations of editor: no reporting apparently, they get all their news straight from the authorities. —Borodin—big straight-standing fellow with clear absolutely fearless dark-eyed Bolshevik gaze—square face, square shoulders, dark square clothes, no vest, white (shirt?)—black toothbrush mustache of proportions that made it look more like a blacking brush.

June 11. хлеб: very stirring, though I didn't understand what was being said.

Alymovs: woman lawyer (Irina)—thought just as many cases came up among the Soviets as with us on *le peuple slave*. —Women trotting to America: Mme A. demonstrated with her fingers. Little phonograph: her talk about men and women, Paris, etc. Oak-leaf vodka, herring, cucumbers and radishes, kidneys, meatballs.

June 12. Park of Culture and Rest: no gaiety, slow quiet crowds—paleness and sadness of the place, great expanses of wide dirt paths, dim grass, sprigs of trees, and, at the bar, cake and chocolate counter at the restaurant, sprigs of purple flowers in pots with white paper around them setting off the bottles of pale yellow wine and the spiral-piled stock of chocolate bars—spiral tower for parachute jumping with a string tied to the parachute—even this rather a leisurely performance—the Russians never

squeal or shriek as we do at Coney Island—frightful paleness and rawness—peculiar effect of nothing having any
color, neither their clothes, nor their faces, nor the signs on
buildings of the park—they have no dyes, I suppose—can't
get them from Germany—except a little indispensable red
for the flag. —"Oi Marie"—"Cielito Lindo"—very poor adventure picture, hardly a trace of imagination. —Park
makes our country fairs look like mad orgies of gaiety and
color.—

—But people allowed to do as they please—not checked
up by petty officials as in Germany and America—feeling
of freedom, lack of self-consciousness—nobody is ever disagreeable or rude, only person I have seen who was since
I came to the Soviet Union was an American. —I found
that I picked up a piece of paper which had fallen from
the chocolate I was eating, which I should never have
done at home—old woman scooping up cigarette butts and
such things with long broom and long-handled shovel
almost as soon as they were dropped.

—Pairs of people standing on rail and trying to knock
each other off by slapping hands—riding on various rather
mildly revolving contrivances—on the other hand, kids
being swung over on their heads on long arms that described an arch.

—Looking at people coming up stairs to movie—the
women's shoes, a kind of flimsy sneaker, all alike, all made
at the same place, and all worn with identical sports socks,
the best that could be said of some of them was that they
were new. —Insipid and tepid soft drinks—loud concerts.
—The whole world is stalled. —Horrors in photographs
and little lighted tableaux which the children looked at
in the building where an exhibition of bad pictures apparently acts as a come-on.

—Lenin and Stalin in tilted flower beds (pansies, etc.)
just below band.

—When I came out of the park, I walked a considerable

distance in the wrong direction—policeman straightened me out: policeman quite unlike grim domineering or stiff cops elsewhere—explain to you in friendly fashion just like anybody else.

—Opening windows at night: Moscow does not seem ever to have any particular kind of smell, as Paris, for example, has.

June 13. Cherry Orchard by provincial company: all the chattering, poetry-reciting, tea-drinking people are gone. —Lily . . .

June 14. Call from Alymovs in afternoon: Alymov tight —insisted on watching billiards, little boys from whom he asked way accompanied him, he said to old lady crossing cobbled street that he ought to help her across (according to editorial in *Pravda*)—she answered that she could manage—he had asked girl in streetcar whether she was taking those lilacs (faded lilies of the valley on restaurant tables) to her sweetheart, she said no, to her mother. But she ought to be taking them to her sweetheart. She said she didn't have any sweetheart, so she was taking them to her mother. —Fischer's evening:* Gunthers, Miss Bach, daughter of the chemist (they referred to him as "the Academician Bach"), Japanese demands to China to remove troops and officials from North China, Umánsky, high politics degenerated into anecdotes about Junius Wood: tipping at Grand Hotel, threatened to stop all tips if bell wasn't answered in four minutes, put Yale lock on door, then locked himself out and had to break down door, apocryphal anecdote about not reporting Hindenburg's death when they told him he had exceeded his

* H. R. Habicht, writing from Moscow June 23, 1935, said: "Louis Fischer had Wilson and Umansky at his home for dinner ten days ago, and although both Louis and I asked Wilson to discuss his visa with Umansky, Wilson never did so." EW intensely disliked Umansky. He did obtain the sojourn visa in due course.

quota of words, buying horse in Mexico and charging it to expense account, "inadvisable sell horse on falling market," then "one bicycle." Umánsky to [John] Gunther about *Chicago Daily News* correspondent (editor?). Umánsky said something unpleasant about the editor, and Gunther at once answered firmly that he couldn't listen to anything against his boss. —While the Americans talked about politics, the Russians made a point of reading Pushkin. —Umánsky deriving force (like Litvinov's son) from Soviet power behind him. Little balcony of apartment looking down into cluttered back yard. Sugared cranberries, little jelly candies, caviar and herring on bread, tea, a little vodka and port. Healthy little boys, one of them going off to summer camp, with head cropped close Soviet-style. —Alymovs came to Novomoskovskaya and drank vodka, wine, cognac—dawn over Kremlin, etc. (2:30–3:30): they thought it was wonderful, though it was gray and uninteresting enough, only a little rather washed-out yellow over the bulbs and government buildings of the Kremlin: Alymov said that he had no use for anything that left the dawn out of account—Katchalov and his dipsomania, wife locked him in, but friends would sometimes lower a bottle down to him from window above —kind of Russian with ineradicable sorrow in his soul. —On the way to the Fischers', Mme Alymov had exclaimed at a little locust tree in bloom and Alymov had invited me to admire the grass between the car line and the Kremlin wall. —Empty smooth gray streets going up the Kremlin hill: at dawn, you could think of the people and it seemed splendid, but when the people themselves came out, there was not one in a thousand who had any romance about him.

—Woman doctors with husbands in the Urals.

—It is not to the credit of the Russians that capitalism wasn't developed here before the Revolution sufficiently to make a strong bourgeois state—collapse due to their backwardness and weakness—their backwardness and weakness also the obstacle to building the social system.

—Call on Mirsky:* through entrance with secondhand bookstall, in second of two cobbled courts, the first one pink, the second one white—door covered with old carpet (or something of the kind)—I knocked, turned the bell the wrong way so that it didn't ring, knocked again, no one came—I visited the Revolutionary Museum for an hour, then came back, turned the bell the right way—bald bearded face, very few teeth, with spectacles, in dressing gown—stood stationary and straight without shaking hands —apologized for receiving me in dressing gown—worked in dressing gown till he went out, he explained—shy, silences, large slightly slanting Russian eyes, dark, human, straight, something the Kropotkin type—good big forehead, with a large brown mole on one side of his bald crown. —Silence, as with Croly, he talked about dinner, and having settled it, I started to go—he said he was in no hurry, asked me whether I was in a hurry, made me sit down again, apologized again for dressing gown. —Slightly silly and what I suppose to be old-fashioned Russian giggle—reminded me of Robert Jackson—over Eliot's *The Rock* (asserted next evening that Eliot was greatest living poet). —Didn't shake hands goodbye and gave me only half his hand. —Unmade bed, door open on bathtub, which was also washstand—(evening of the next day he said the soap smelled badly).

Caviar and vodka in the Metropole dining room—great glass roof which sheds what the French call *un jour blafard* in a big way smeared with big dirty yellow patches of yellowed light from colored glass—four great gilt urns studding the floor, planted with the little loose spriggy flowers, out of which sprout, on enormous gilt stems, heavy glass bowls surrounded with bulbs—flowers along

* Prince D. S. Mirsky, the critic and literary historian.

in front of the orchestra—faded sofa, seats in corners and around the urns—vast but shabby gray gilt and smeary brown marble columns—Egyptian pattern on fresco—false balconies with heavy empty gilt urns—chipped and roughened tessellated wood floor. —On each table, a large lamp with a cloth shade of the same dreary yellow as the glass in the ceiling and with little blobs hanging down, like a gigantic burlesque mushroom—row of zigzagged lights under ceiling—glass above fresco. —Orchestra: the high traps and the opened grand piano—dance floor in front of the orchestra between the four urned pillars.

June 15. Chambermaid, who had been most pleasant and willing and, as soon as she understood, came in and sewed the button right on my shirt, forgot about the laundry and went away and left it. This must have been the one who held up my torn underclothes and said, "Kakou!"

—Dinner at Mirsky's: close-cropped professional linguist, Jewish woman interested in literature and speaking French and English well, Russian girl came in and had just written an article about *poètes de café*, talked and talked and drank tea. —*"Vous êtes terrible, ma petite!"* when she asked about history of revolutionary movement.

June 19. Free day. Park of Rest and Culture and Sokolniki with Herzogs. —Lily's room—couch and wall above it hung with bright red and orange Persian patterns (new, however)—little round bright pictures, with lots of red, of Moscow scenes—little wall cabinet, carved peasant wood, dolls on bed. (She liked dogs and would like to have one.)

June 20. Mirsky. "I haven't the slightest idea who that man was"—of someone who had spoken to him. —He had refused cognacs at dinner—later we went into the Artistic Café, he suggested a bottle of wine, then decided he'd rather have an ice, asked me whether I'd have coffee, I said I'd have an ice, so he ordered an ice for me and a coffee for himself, then brightly and lightly suggested cognacs. —He always gave money to beggars.

June 21. Alymovs': Paul Strand, woman lawyer (Irina), girl from Mrs. A.'s home town of Michurin, who managed artists' models—we couldn't sing on account of neighbors.

June 22—Green-eyed girl but sharp-nosed who stood next to me against the wall during the rain and hailstorm—when a great torrent suddenly began to beat down, so that the arcade we were standing under threatened to be flooded, and I felt for a moment a certain amount of alarm, nobody complained, everybody laughed—as soon as it was over, everybody left, they knew the moment it had finished. —Lily wouldn't let me pick her up to carry her over a puddle—had fights with Frank about that—I'd had the idea first of all that I never ought to refer to her short ness—the Russians are fierce—when she narrows her eyes.

—Bolsháya Ordynka,* with its old white walls and courtyards with some careless Russian greenery seen through gates, old big red or pink (madder) churches closed and dead.

June 23. Habicht party: 2 Russians and wives; 2 Englishmen; English couple; Negro woman and mulatto friend; Muriel Draper; MacGregors; Herzogs, etc. —Sloan's Indian raja and Carmen impersonations; young Englishman who was looking for English novel to make picture and didn't know about Dickens; Pearl, who said that they had no revolutionary literature (like John Reed) in England as we did in America and didn't know about Robert Owen (the way she stood with one large well-shod

---

* EW rented an apartment here at No. 53, a sublet from Walter Duranty, the *New York Times*'s Moscow correspondent, who had gone away for the summer.

English foot stretched out and pointing away from the other).

—After vodka and wine, looked out window, through old white lace curtains rather without taste, the unevenly divided panes, with the drooping pretty silly fern, at the light, pale gray and pale unbrilliant orange (buff?), of the sky, the loose green leaves: Russia.

—Coming back in droshky with Muriel—transparent night with the bright crescent moon in the sky of almost day, clacking over cobbles, droshky shakes from side to side, conversation about Communism, religion, Christ, Lenin, etc. —I hummed "Smoke [Gets] in Your Eyes" all the way home.

—Lily and her maid—maid always sat around with us, and Lily would always become affectionate and embrace her as the evening wore on—maid wouldn't dance, and when Lily had gotten up to dance and maid had sat down in her place, she got up at once to give Lily her seat when Lily came back again.

—Moved into Duranty's.

Younger brother (of Frank Herzog) got tight for the first time and served drinks wildly, was looking for some clouds to lie on (over), had been a corpse for years—"Let's have a necktie party!" lead poisoning, teach 'em a lesson, etc.

June 24—Dinner with Mirsky at Sokólniki: Turk who kept smiling during dinner. —(Mirsky) denied amiability of Russians.

June 25. Ninotchka. —*Je—Où—Je—Allons à la maison.*

June 26. Museums—evening in apartment—crisis with old woman (the Durantys' maid).*

June 27. Went with M. Alymov (Maria Fedorovna) to Greenberg dacha—loose, flat, untrimmed unkempt char-

---

* This was Ekaterina Nicolaevna, who had belonged to the old bourgeois society under the Tsar.

acter of Russian countryside, untidy weedy little garden where they raised big white peonies and a few other things —loved flowers but had very few varieties—crows as at home cawing in the late never-ending afternoon but they were Russian crows and I didn't know what they said— dacha had belonged to rich patron of art theater.

June 28. Maria Alymov and Nina: girl in red dress reading in dark hall (8 families, 30 people), father a Communist—now that she was done with school, she didn't know what to do with herself, sulky because she couldn't afford to go to a dacha, quarreled with parents.

June 29. Dinner at Novomoskovskaya, evening Alymovs' apartment—mischka (мишка) (this must refer to Lily).

June 30—Physkultur Parade: five days for it, a lot of sun with occasional clouds and never too hot: Lenin and Stalin, buildings draped in red, Lenin as a child—for Young Pioneers: Stalin the best friend of Physkultur: bad pictures of men jumping and running, wouldn't do in U.S. for ads. Before the line-up of little round Soviet legs in white athletic shoes and socks and white shorts, the head of the Physkultur Department, standing up in the car with his arm raised, and Stalin and two other officials, two of them in plain white in back seat, ran slowly in a fine plain black car along in front of the ranks while a cheer went around like a wave. —Music: first, the Internationale, then afterwards about three strange but attractive Russian tunes, very simple in structure, the same thing always repeated, which they played over and over again. —Everybody had to stand up because the officials were standing. —115,000 people in parade: greetings to Stalin, "Thanks to Comrade Stalin for the good life." —Simple, very different from anything American but more sincere and impressive than any American parade I remember—as the hours went on and the clubs kept marching by with unabated freshness and vigor, the impression became overwhelming and remained with me all the rest of the day, during which they still seemed to be marching through my mind—I left after four hours of it, at five, and they told me it would probably last another hour—but I was glad to go, and so was the Intourist guide. —Room for many more people. —Airplanes that spelled Stalin. Beelike fighting planes that loudly and dynamically passed overhead in threes. —Floats, always carried, with prize fight, tennis match, volley ball, people running up incline, bicyclist (men turning over in wheels), young men and girls posed in more or less awkward and unsteady postures, toward the end a balloon that threw down wreaths attached to parachutes, sharpshooters, one graceful and very pretty girl who smiled all the time, miners, mountain climbers on top of a mountain, hunters with imitation birds, huge boxing glove that kept flapping in an uncanny way in rhythm with the pace of the people who were carrying it, like one of the dolls in the Macy parade, men with shaved heads, bare chests, and fixed bayonets, I'd already come to realize that the whole thing was more or less of a military demonstration—hosts of bicycles—bicycles here are taken with the greatest seriousness. —Red, white, and blue, hardly varied with other colors, the combinations and costumes showed some taste. —In going to M.S.'s house afterwards, was held up in crossing street by band of kids, in dark-red shirts, white shorts, etc., singing very earnestly, led by their teachers—deeply touching, the costume made everyone look attractive, though when you got close to them their faces were rarely good.

The cadres decide everything, instead of the technique deciding everything.

Ate sturgeon, omelette, and cheese at Maria Alymov's, ravenously hungry. —Afterwards, went out to Greenberg dacha—serious little stocky round contrôle with her jaw tied up on the train—(also woman who hastily and snappingly shut doors on us as we tried to get into the wrong coach).—Tall light Corot-like birches and loose lacy screen against the still bright so slowly waning light—we sat on a bench in front of a fence, behind which the people in the next dacha were dancing to the music of the radio. It was getting cold, and we got up and began to walk, met the Greenbergs, the evening became gay—woman who kept singing and acting snatches of song—finally the master of the dacha played the piano and she sang: song from the Caucasus about the girl who was bathing on the seashore and met a dark Caucasian, when baby was born the father was very pleased but didn't see the resemblance, *pazhalsta* (пожалуйста),* this was the refrain—gypsy songs, gypsy, Ukrainian, and Russian dances, with a touch of ballet—the music of the radio came faintly in from the flimsy lacy wild trees and the slowly drooping light. The man in the white blouse gave us some of his white peonies as we were leaving. Insisted on my eating a second dinner.

At station, when train finally came in, it seemed to be starting to leave again almost as soon as it had stopped, so that we had to leap aboard without a chance to say goodbye properly. Then it stopped again, backed a little, seemed to start—this went on for some time and the gaiety-loving lady was much amused, kept bowing as if acknowledging applause, and humorously saying goodbye every time we seemed to be starting. —"*Notre technique magnifique—illustration pour vous!*" —Two cunning little thick round girls who had been seen off by two boys—conversation all "she said" and "I said"—prettier one leaned forward (I looked at the clean and fresh little scarf

---

* "If you please."

effect which she had tied around her head) putting her hands in her earnestness on the lap of the slightly more dignified one, who sat up straight, and told her a story about a fortuneteller to whom she had given ten roubles to read her palm—the woman had said a lot of things but told her nothing practical—finally, she had said that she had told her nothing about whether or how soon she'd get married, and that she wanted her money back, and started to take it: "You'll get married! you'll get married!" the woman had said.

—I spoke of the quietness of the people on the streets even on that gala day. Maria Fedorovna said that it was the discipline.

July 4 or 5. Gypsies: trip on tram car with Jewish columnist: man said to him, "Please don't crowd against me. I've got a sore knee!"—and, repeating an old Russian proverb: "Nobody can feel the sufferings of others." The columnist replied: "If we felt the sufferings of others, we'd never be able to live: it's hard enough with our own." And the people in the car all laughed. —Gypsies looked to me at first too respectable: thin dark girl in high-heeled shoes and uninteresting dress who danced in a sharp stiff staccato way. (Duranty: "They have gypsies that howl like dogs.")—Big stuffed bear on grand staircase standing on its hind legs and holding one of their little plants with purple flowers in one of their white-paper-pantied pots.

*July 6. Tro*í*tsko Serg*é*evsky Monastery.* Stopped off and got Irina, who had been having a horribly boring and depressed day in country and was overjoyed to go with us—at Zagorsk, walked in miry road and up hill, where rainbow delirium of monastery appeared to us—blue and gold and red and pink and yellow—to little green hotel (where lovers used to come) of exceedingly primitive character—little room looking out on monastery and street, narrow bed, dirty colorless couch with holes from which the straw stuffing stuck out. Laughed about it, sent for a samovar—ate some sausage and hard-boiled eggs and drank some vodka, then, just as the samovar arrived, discovered that the museum wouldn't be open very much longer, and left. —Little house for holy water, like pastry, pink and with twisted breadlike columns, angels' faces not unlike cupids (also in Metropolitan's chapel)—columns on other building with vine leaves painted spiraling around them—five-tiered red and white church, long straight stiff phallic-looking steeple, not so much less thick than church, given by Catherine the Great—sad gray-eyed contracted Slavic icons, cramped and inured to suffering—ignoble tomb of the Godunovs, in terrible disrepair—a hole had been broken at one corner of the lid, apparently from curiosity —the big church behind it was now used to store cabbages and other vegetables—old woman who was shocked at the desecrations and kept rolling up her eyes. Peasant's isba [a Russian peasant log cabin] reconstructed, with pictures of floggings and executions, to offset effect of Metropolitan's palace—gorgeous vestments and icons on cloth, pearls and amethysts—enormous wine boat with kind of wild dog savagely biting neck of savage wild hog at one end and kind of horrible insect-bodied animal at the other —so much that is deliberately ugly and disagreeable in their art, yet sentimentality of later saints, as depicted—heavy gaudy clumsy jeweled miters—whole thing had a certain effect of Coney Island—church built by Ivan the Terrible to atone for murder of son, plastered all over inside with pink pictures that covered even the thimble cups of the domes, horrible taste. —Return to hotel, very pleasant and gay, reflections on pity of wasting the room, which we'd paid for till four o'clock tomorrow. I looked out at cobbled street slanting uphill, on which the sun had come out—bright blue sky, for Russia, bright not dazzling light (after the rain) on the smallish white clouds —the needle point of the big phallic dome was sharp against it, and below the red roof, the white building with one row of square windows, the red fence, the cobbled sloping road along which I saw pass a little gray foal running in front of a horse and cart, a low collarlike carriage with little kids sitting in a succession of seats in it—I asked A. what it was, and he said it was a charabanc and began singing a song which he said had been popular at the time of the Civil War: "Oh, charabanc, my chara-banc—If I don't have any money, I must sell you!" —On the way back, barnlike gutted big station with no benches —suggestion about lying in baggage racks, opened little door and discovered conductor's room, where we sat very pleasantly till we were driven out by little woman con-ductor, who said she had been on the train for five days. —Swimming at Marmontovskaya, but mustn't let mother know. —Little boys at monastery who shouted: "Moskva! Moskva!" at us, as we went up the hill to the gate: "Amerikansky Bar." —Blue bulbs painted with golden stars. —On the way back on the train, we spoke of possi-bilities of room we had left behind. —Working for the future; the past; but we had this vodka, these eggs, this room—"they are now!" Old woman who fell asleep on M.F.'s shoulder on train coming back—when there was later a vacant seat beside us, M.F. didn't want to wake her, but finally decided to.

July 7. Impromptu party at Alymovs': Python bought in Germany for Moscow Zoo—the boy who was bringing it in a car got his sweetheart and began making love to her, and the python got excited and began to think about a mate and got out and got away at the rate of 50 kilos an hour. They knew where he was but they were waiting till he ate something solid.

—A. a night or two before on Ivan the Terrible and Peter the Great: I asked whether the people hadn't loved Ivan in spite of everything. Yes, in the Russian fashion those who were not killed were thankful to be alive, and they thought that Ivan was an able man—a little bit strong, but able—and the people he had tortured and killed were not there to protest. Peter the Great and his crusade against beards—he thought that all the old Russia was nesting in those beards—he didn't merely cut off one beard to make an example, he went on cutting them off for something like two months and seemed to take great pleasure in it.—A. impersonated Peter hiding around the corner with the "squeezers" and saying: Ah-h-h! when he saw a man coming with a beard. —Then M.F. woke up and told her dream.

Carnival: Tretyakov, Saroyan, New York Russian Jew who had been to Writers' Congress in Paris—we lost T. looking at horse and made another man who spoke Russian but who didn't drink get us vodka and sandwiches at restaurant. Later on, seeing gigantic dolls, he commented on Russian taste and design—even the name "Gay Wheel" showed imagination. —Saroyan on Armenian Russia. —People strolling quietly with false noses, scrap caused by little stocky woman at cashier's window. —Two men who engaged us in conversation and who seemed to me very phony. —"A good time was had by all" (said Saroyan at the end of the evening).

July 9. Marmontovka: Mme Greenberg; ravine with white goats on opposite bank; waiting at station for Irina —little kids singing about train which went by night and went by day, also about forest and field and birds which went cuckoo—before they had sung only revolutionary and war songs, but now they had stopped that—then soldiers began singing a very sad song which was apparently a marching song: they were very sad before, now they are sad. —Had read Dostoevsky when she was young, and it had seemed to her fantastic, had nothing to do with life the people had lived then shut up in their houses, knowing very little of what went on around them. Then when the Revolution had opened everything up, she saw all the types that D. had described—he was very modern.

[At opening night of National Café, several days before: pretty bar with bottles spread farther apart than in our bars, but too glaring light overhead and no room to dance. People looking in from street over curtains.]

—No swell parts of city, but no degraded parts: after a while, you get to like it better: no shocking sights, no horrible disease or poverty on the streets, you get to like the little women with their little socks and flat sneakers, with their babies all so nicely wrapped up and delivered to them by the hospital, they seem to be much surer of their babies than the poor people in N.Y.

—You don't feel very much like telling the bourgeois people that they ought to keep a stiff upper lip or like complaining about the sadness and quietness of the other people.

Nicolaevna (the Durantys' old maid): "Ah, les jeunes mariés—moi aussi, j'étais jeune! —Le lit va à Leningrad!" (when she found me in the morning in bed with a woman).

July 18. Rowing on the river at Marmontovka, Free Day—little curling river with grass-green banks, with people, largely naked, on the banks: they look better without their clothes because the clothes are no good—very nice to see them (Vladivostók Express*)—blond girls with white skin, thick round legs, and big round breasts, boys

---

* EW inserted reference to the train to remind himself that he saw here the express, "very trim for a Russian train," cross the railroad bridge and "toot away to the east."

burned brown except around the hips, where they had been wearing trunks, where it was comparatively white— bathing suits seemed to be becoming more and more perfunctory, they seemed more and more to be leaving them off—the factory, where a very rudimentary little swimming dock of planks had been built; at the end a dam and falls, beyond which you couldn't go any farther, a flock of white goats; two men in a pup tent, a man in a shack; an elderly man and woman sitting on something, turned away from each other reading the papers; phys-kultur exercises in a field; a militiaman who made the rounds without "seriously incommoding anybody"; a girl blowing a whistle in a boat, a kind of thing that was rare, and she did it only at fairly long intervals; a short fat man rather heavily and inexpertly fishing; rain shower which briefly passed; gulls, crows, and pies; wry trees of light effect (birch leaves as light as fuzz) leaning askew—she called my attention to them as curious, in that mild and even landscape even such slight distortions showed as strange. —Little restaurant where man with small pale face and trembling hand played accordion and wanted to know whether we preferred something sad or something gay, played only for us. —House near station built by rich man in the early 1900s—little cupola and all covered with lace-valentine wooden lace, pale almost unpainted-looking yellow-brown.

July 19—Lying in state of Pudovkin's scenarist at Writers' House.

July 20. I dreamed that I was asking questions about the anomalies of Russian grammar: "Why do you ask these questions?"*

* The dream is described in detail in *Red, Black, Blond and Olive,* pp. 265–67.

Moscow Zoo

Greenwich Village side of Moscow

The women. Feet without those sneakers—wading through water among the cobbles in the rain—a girl, very cheerful, smiling or joking with somebody, barefoot with pretty feet.

July 29. Kremlin bells: I finally heard them playing the Internationale, so haltingly, so lacking in the adequate scale, that if I had never heard about it, I should never have known what it was.

Argument about Black Belt, evening in Sam Darcy's room.

Russian wastebaskets, vodka, dinners (formless and too heavy), drinking tea out of glasses too hot to hold.

Ekaterina Nicolaevna (Durantys' maid) as product of bourgeois society.

—but Russian suspicion, also: Rukeyser's experiences.
Little Comrade Schoer on Red Army peasant number as "so characteristic of the collective farms."

The Communist use of "this," where we should say "that"—stands for это (this habit had been picked up by the American Communists, along with the Marxist jargon).
Russia and the death of Bergotte. Proust in his way a great moralist.

The impress of Lenin.

The Volga. Enormous, passive, wide open and smooth; a female river. Another pleasant boat trip. The boat seems to wander all over the river. Flat banks—fields of yellow grain—the occasional sharp steeple of a church—the sandy shores, a formless river.

Trip from Moscow to Gorky. Student who wanted to know whether I was an engineer—boy who designed glider models eager for information about American designs, kept holding out book open to pictures of gliders. Two young boys in blue uniforms, with round well-fed Russian faces, who lay stretched out on bunks, listening as if spellbound.

Gorky. Sprawling provincial town with old white-washed fragments of Kremlin and crowded marketplace. Street, such as that where Gorky was born, all gone to seed, still squalid—grass growing up the middle of one cobbled street worn down like a ditch—wooden fretwork of lace on the houses. An old woman who limped carrying a gray goat horizontally in her arms; another younger woman carrying a little pig which squealed. A young sorrel horse, all alone, walking to the drive along the park with the apparent intention of taking a stroll there. People, without the city blight, looked better than in Moscow. Old state bank, nineteenth century, white and grimly ornate, now turned into Soviet Govbank. Very incompetent and lackadaisical Intourist. Slow old provincial town, dating from thirteenth century—population, since Revolution, increased from 100,000 to 500,000.

—Hotels all have stuffed bears with arms extended in welcome in lobby.

Mania for renaming things: Gorky, Zinovievsk, now Kirovsk.

Story about theater director who produced play about Lenin based on book by Zinoviev.

The unpronounceable name of Jehovah.

The Leninist conscience. Duranty on this. Stalin legends of Lenin's reappearance.

Ulyanovsk. Traveler's house, mud, when I woke up I saw that the little girl who was making the other beds was pretty, blondinka with reddish hair, different shades in different places, when I came back she began strumming a guitar which belonged to one of the travelers, came near me and went on strumming after I had spoken to her, we played checkers, her game had different rules from mine, so that I was a little disconcerted at first, but as we went on playing game after game—we were about equally matched and neither of us was very good—I got to feel that we understood each other so well that when we would have finished a game it would be with something of a shock that I would find it was still difficult for us to talk to one another. Pale rather weak green-blue eyes. Talked about the bad weather—I went and got some beer and bread and sausage and candies, which she shared with me—so far as I could see, if it hadn't been for my bringing her these things, she would never have eaten anything during her twenty-four-hour shift—strong arms and hands sunburned from swimming, she would sit with the guitar, with one foot, in its kind of blue sneaker, turned in—she was twenty-one, said she had no man, quite a little yellow mustache on upper lip. —I liked her—little sister, seventeen. Came in and wrote down songs from *Moscow Laughs*, all the verses, signing it with her full name at the top and a monogram at the bottom—she had on an old dark dress, which was long for her and had evidently belonged to an older sister, and what were practically men's shoes—rather pretty, too, in a smaller way, spots of cold cream on her lips where they were chapped—their names. —In the late afternoon, I was waked by Claudia, playing and singing all alone in the dark, playing one of their wild sad high-spirited cheerful songs—she came and stood near the bed, and I took her hand—her plucked eyebrows—people who asked me questions—they asked me where I worked, they always ask you in Russia where you work, never where you live—was life in America better or not?—girl who looked like a Komsomol—strong dark eyes, capable—she was wearing some sort of medal or badge—wanted to see my foreign silver money, was a little bit abashed when I pointed out the head of the English Tsar on a florin. —In the evening, she was reading D.'s *Crime and Punishment* for the first time, I got her to go through the song with me—she was impressed by her sister's autograph at the end and practiced writing it and writing her own—I took her hand and told her that all Soviet girls were very strong—she said she didn't know, but said that she was strong because she'd done a lot of work, and she made me feel the muscle in her right arm—I tried to kiss her left hand but she took it away and said, Nyet. I took a nap, and woke up when a young man and woman came and went to bed in the beds across from me—the man stretched his hand across the gap between beds and held the woman's hand till they fell asleep. —I got up, went into the little front room and found Claudia about to start a book, reading *Crime and Punishment*, she said, for the first time—when I found Claudia lying down with a blanket on her on a wooden couch, without a mattress—she had left the light on, and I sat there reading Lenin while it got colder—she went straight to sleep and snored loudly—finally it got so cold that I went back to bed, woke up at 2:15 and went out to see about the boat. The gate to the dock was locked and I went back and C. called up the landing manager, and he answered that the boat wouldn't arrive till two o'clock the morning of the next day, so I could go back to sleep. I was a little provoked at this, but sat there looking at her and began petting her—I stroked and patted her face and she sat there without resisting but without any visible response—I finally began to feel as if I were patting a horse (colt or a calf) and went back to bed again. (Her light-minded Russian sudden bursts of energy in talking, her sometimes shy pale-blue eyes.) In the morning the weather was wonderful, the sun was out, the mud was largely dried, the mists on the Volga were cleared away, and you could see the wooded further bank. We leaned on the rail outside the house, looking out at the river. It was her free day and I asked her what I should do all day, and she said another girl would come and I could talk to her. —The little brother and sister turned up—she told me that she had just telephoned and that the boat was coming at one that afternoon—I asked her what she was going to do, she said that she and her brother and sister were going to the Cino and dance in the evening. —At the dock, I was told by the landing master that the boat would be there at ten, and even before ten. The little sister who was hanging around took me up to the upper deck of the floating dock and showed me the distant white steamer, which had just come around the bend. We sat there, and she went through the song with me and asked me to read her some English so that she could hear how it sounded. I asked her what she was doing on the wharf, she said that she had come to help with the landing. —They were two very nice little girls, and I was extremely glad to have known them.

—Man who smelled sausage before eating—other man thought there was going to be war—Germany and France.

—They had one of their gusts of animation.

—I said "До свидания" and kissed her goodbye on the cheek.

—but kept looking at me with her straight unselfcon-scious eyes
—her gentle and candid eyes

—Old Bolshevik driver who drove me around—cobbles, rain, carriage with no back, shook till the scenery would seem to be shaking like a bad old-fashioned film—in the fine rain. Restaurant where they had no butter and after some demur brought me for an omelette a thing like a kind of unsweetened custard. Ulyanovsk must be very much run-down since the days of the Ulyanovs and the Kerenskys, the Karlamyins and the Goncharovs. They were busily demolishing a large church—no factories there.

Claudia Dmitrievna again. —Did nothing about giving me a towel, when I was wiping my hands on my handker-chief—though she got one out of drawer and used it herself. —The next time I asked her for one, and she cheerfully produced it. Just hadn't thought of it before: no effort to please, but very agreeable, no professional psychology of housekeeping, acknowledging, just attend-ing to the place while the comrades came and went. —At once cool and girlishly shy.
—Explained *serdtse* [heart] by putting her hand under left breast—"He understands!"
—combination of something like stolidity with quick coming to life in response when she spoke—throwing away checkers when she thought she was going to be beaten
—pigs
—flurry of animation when she spoke

The Russians say, "sie chass," "neechivo," and "what? what?"—this last as if they were not in the habit of attending very closely to each other. —Bolshoi scandal!

A "bourgeois prejudice": that was what waitress on *Spartak* said when she was asked for lemon for the tea.

I remembered what A. had said about "You see how my people live," when I had taken her to Gorky's *Mother* in N.Y. I have really come to understand for the first time on this trip why Poles, etc., come to America, and their psychology about being Americans after they get there.

Communoids. [EW explained: "A person who is not a Communist but who tries to talk and act like one.]

Volga. White clouds which seemed painted on the blue something as in New Mexico, and cloud painted in gray ink on gray surface of sky—flat green shores—the third day there were low pelted hills reflected dull green in the muddy water—one town with thatched roofs, none of the towns painted—*Volsk* dreary manufacturing town, boys diving and swimming, not very well, in the muddy river— cement and cement dust—trip gets monotonous the fourth day. —German republic. —Fifth day: livid gray scattered wooden village with no human form or color on the liver- colored cliffs, and after we had left it, liver-colored cliffs, cut into chunks, and the chunks cut into slices, by the rain, above the browner liver-colored water.

Aviation students on boats. Off on two-month holiday— fine specimens, he blond gray-eyed Russian, she Rouman- ian—"contrast, black and white"—"love, affection," he held up one finger to indicate they were as one—did they have love in America? —I spoke of Lenin's birthplace: L.

was a great leader, loved the people very much, every peasant had his picture in the house. He and his wife had only been registered one year. —Gave me cakes which she had made herself, candy, apples, and boiled milk.

People sleeping on baggage and floor in third class did not look badly—little half-naked boy playing balalaika. —Men and children who played piano in first-class saloon—would go on a long time and card game would go on a long time—*Hiawatha* with all the wrong emphasis—tinkly without the American rhythm.

Boring old lady from Springfield, but heart in the right place—old-fashioned veil tied under chin and some little rouge on cheeks, eyeglasses. Had been in hot spot of Illinois, what with miners, etc. Somebody at the Capitol had turned a machine gun on the crowd and they never would tell who it was—Hoover a great disappointment—a revolution in fifteen years unless the Republicans would nominate some good clean man that the people could trust. —People at home had opposed her going to Russia— if Abraham Lincoln could see Springfield now! —When Roosevelt had them throwing the hogs in the Mississippi! —Her taking the guides to task for losing some of the party—I liked her in spite of the fact that she was so tiresome—other American woman in bus who insisted on its stopping so that the little boy who had jumped in wouldn't be carried too far—American attitude of taking action contrasted with Russian *nichevo*—I remembered my efforts the day before to get the bird out of the saloon.

Tractor plant at Stalingrad: pace seemed much more leisurely, people taking it easier than at Ford's, seven hours a day, six for drop forges—latter better ventilated. —Fine-looking women, taller, handsomer than stunted race of Moscow—attractive in working clothes, big round breasts displayed by tight-fitting shirts, often pink. —75 percent peasants from the surrounding country—had had a hard time learning about machinery at first, now better at it—produced 47,000 tractors last year. —Conversation between Turk, Czechoslovak lady, and myself on train— she was using her vacation, I took it—only a few days— to come to Russia—when would the other countries learn that they had to straighten out their affairs—things very bad in Czechoslovakia—people afraid of Fascism and Czechs throwing Germans out of their jobs—she was rather like the Englishman on the Сибирь—rather like the old lady from Springfield herself—extraordinary gentleness and consideration of the Turk, who was a good advertisement for his country.

—At Rostov, we went in the morning (at noon) to a collective farm—kids being brought back from swimming, girls and tomatoes—view of steppe, as flat (level) as the top of a table and as enormous as the sea, the Don moving slowly between flat banks—Jewish girlfriend of fruity New Yorker pretended to break down over the old lady in the kitchen of the collective farm—boyfriend, to save the old lady's noticing it, said that he had hurt her feelings: Now, let me tell you something, honey-love, I'm an old lady and I'll tell you that you'll get a lot more out of life if you don't let those things upset you!

—old man who talked to Alaskan—the Don, flowing level, between its flat banks

—*first camels*

—The farther south we went, the easier, the freer, the better-looking the people seemed. —The little public parks of Rostov were extremely attractive and resembled in no

respect the Park of C. & R.—shiny classical statues, fountains, "cadres decide everything," in flowers, little walks
with lovers on benches, fragrance of large red flowers,
little lighted restaurants, bands playing gaily old Viennese
waltzes.

—Reformed prostitutes and lying-in hospital, delivery
room.

—Went with Czech lady to plastic ballet—Jewish
woman who came and talked to us the whole of every
intermission: the Jews much better off than before, everything wonderful, had heard of no discontent—afterwards
began obviously to divagate in saying that it was a shame
that some dancer couldn't be there, who it seemed was
one of Pavlova's pupils. Plastic ballet a physkultur version
of many old chestnuts of Grieg, Liszt, *Red Poppy*, etc.,
with tough muscles and almost complete nudity.

—All this time I had been getting sick—
Began to be seriously sick on train morning before
getting to Kiev: Kiev itself attractive, bluffs over Dnieper,
people seemed happy, more animated perhaps but just
as low-voiced as at Moscow: in park, though they were
all talking, I could hardly hear it unless I strained to
listen.

—Rostov Intourist hadn't let them know I was coming.
Languid Intourist girl: I am so tired, it is so hot, and
there are so many people! The manager is always here—
he is just out for three minutes—in a half hour, in an
hour, it is all the same thing. —After I had got on the
bus to go to the station, she appeared and told me she was
very sorry, they had not been able to get me a "soft"
place. —It turned out on the train that they hadn't even
arranged for me to get bedding "hard." —Conductor insisted he hadn't prepared for me. Finally he took it away
from somebody else. Horrible night; broodings on the

Russians—language, food, capitalism. Of course, they closed all the windows in the car—I would get up and go to the sole open window outside and breathe in the country air—I got sickened by the eternal sunflowers from which they make the confounded sunflower oil with which they make their unappetizing omelettes. Smart Jew explaining philosophical background of Marx incorrectly to two big unshaved roundheaded louts—they also discussed literature, the drama, the next war, saying, as far as I could make out, all the expected things.

—Groggy arrival at Odessa: room without toilet. —The doctor was an extremely genial man (in white trousers and white Russian shirt) who hadn't brought any thermometer —told me it was nothing—he and old international *femme de chambre.* Gay exit: *Je vous dis au revoir, monsieur.* One of his prescriptions impossible to get. *Femme de chambre* was going to do something about it, but turned out to be off-duty the next day. Half-Polish housewife who had only been working for Intourist a month: much disorder, they needed people who could speak languages. Hotel orchestra, Gibbon. —Doctor's second visit: had been in every country but America—Scandinavian countries, had even been to North Pole. My temperature seemed to be way up, and we decided that I had forgotten to shake the mercury down—but still up. When he saw spot on my arm, his whole manner changed, became intensely serious, told me it was scarlatina—when I asked him what I ought to do, he shrugged his shoulders and threw out his hands in supreme expression of being at a loss—"Go to a hospital, I suppose"—he rushed out without goodbye or explanation, saying, "It's scarlatina! It's scarlatina!" After that, nothing—(behavior of *femme de chambre,* whom I finally got on the phone)—till little woman with red-visored cap appeared and took me in ambulance to hospital. —Young doctor and pretty blond girl: team of Jewish comedians—perfunctory bath by old woman—did me up like mummy and put me on stretcher on floor—the question of money and watch arose: comedy by Jew, reaching out clawlike hands, till girl shut door on him—I had to burst from my shroud to count the money. —Jews carried me to another building, setting me down at one point and discussing whether or not I had got a receipt for my money. —They put me in doctors' and nurses' room: I called attention to bedbug on tablecloth; nurse changed tablecloth. The young doctor had the windows opened at my request, though nurse seemed to demur over opening second one. The lights hadn't been turned out two minutes when I became aware of the myriad teeming bed life. I summoned nurse: two Russian types, sad one and cheerful one, both resigned, both taking all for granted—gave me new bed and bedding. When I had got into this new bed, I remarked two more bb's crawling along tablecloth on night table and evidently planning to drop on me. I showed them to sad old woman and as she caught and killed them she made pathetic deeply grief-stricken sounds of one who had seen many little children die and who knew there was nothing to be done about it. (While fixing up my new bed, she had knocked over the wine bottle of gargle, and then the other nurse had knocked over the medicine glass.) Then she began polishing the floor with her foot in that sort of dance they do: she would stop and rest, hand on her back, they seemed to pick on her—her eyes always looked as if they had just been crying, or rather they looked as if they had gone dry long ago. —I fell asleep and went into my fever dreams, I dreamed that I had written a play called *A Bit of the New*, which was about to be produced by some organization like the Guild as *Quite a Lot of the Old*—I was determined to go in on the second act (which took place on an old-fashioned American porch) made up as a stranger with side whiskers, bowler hat, watch chain and fob, etc., and deliver a long speech vitally affecting the plot, which I hoped would break up the play. I woke up repressing hysterical laughter and tears. I thought, "I mustn't let Russia get me: the Russians must have dreams like that!"

—Dramatic entrance of old doctor—"clear office, *to-varishchi!*"—they stood without doing anything at first, as they always do, and only got all the furniture out by stages and after hours. Straw cap, umbrella, black coat, white vest, dark eyebrows, spectacles. —When he had gotten them all out, he closed the doors, as if he were about to commence a big scene in opera, and coming over to me, told me he was giving me his office so that I could have a room to myself and that he would have me well in no time—ending with an improvised aria on All right and хорошо. Everything always ended with a comical amiable smile. —Tennyson: daughter who knows English, now in Paris.

meeting trainman

Polish border

children's toothbrushes

Platón Kréchet*—sign on Volga—flower bed at Rostov,

lack of prudery—delivery room at Rostov, love-making,

no publicity and scandals

the Russian comic sense—Dost. Chek. official in valuta department

---

* A play EW had seen in Moscow described in some detail in his expanded version.

espionage

suppression

fascination of Russia

[These brief jottings terminate EW's Russian notes in his journals. He had a retentive memory and much that he had experienced remained vividly with him, so that he was able to add considerable detail when he wrote his account of his journey, keeping the diary form. In his later memories he amplifies his six weeks in quarantine in the old Odessa hospital for contagious diseases—which had been built when Pushkin was still alive. He describes the ubiquitous bedbugs, the total lack of sanitation, the epidemic of which he was victim, and the good-natured easy way in which doctors and nurses handled the patients. He was surprised to discover that he had to pay nothing for his hospitalization and treatment (such as it was). Even his telegrams and cables were charged to his account, as a patient under socialized medicine. During his convalescence he was permitted to use the operating room at night for a writing room, and here he read much in Marx, Engels, and Gibbon. At the same time he studied the way in which the hospital was conducted—as a Soviet institution. He was about to be discharged when he suffered an acute kidney attack. His cable to Henry Allen Moe of the Guggenheim Foundation is still extant: "Can you lend hundred six weeks hospital scarlatina nephritis cable money American Express Paris." Moe added the $100 to EW's stipend, and he journeyed home via Warsaw, Berlin, and Paris. These capitals seemed tame and unexciting after Russia. He had a sense of many things hidden from view; but this only stimulated his curiosity: he had felt strongly that a new kind of society was in process; and he was also aware of the way in which the Russians had learned to focus on immediacies and avoid talking about past or future. By the end of October he is visiting his mother in Red Bank, N.J., and writing to thank Moe for his help. "I had an extremely profitable trip—the most interesting, I think, I've ever taken, invaluable for my book and illuminating about the world in general."]

CHICAGO AND
NEW YORK

(When I first got back from Russia, I lived for a time in the Fyodor Mansvetovs' apartment in New York for the purpose of learning Russian. He was a big blond man, the son of a priest. She was a tiny little bun-shaped woman whose father had been exiled to Siberia and who had been born out there near where Lenin lived. He had acted as a sort of supervisor for the children of the other exiles, and she had seen something of him in her childhood. She had also seen a Siberian shaman working his spell in his tent. She said she loved the country, which was beautiful. When I asked her once whether her husband had been a right or a left SR, she bridled and replied, "A left: if he had been a right, I should never have married him!" Their son Gleb was then in Czechoslovakia. He was a poet and married a granddaughter of Tolstoy's. Eventually they came to New York. She was a capable girl, who was able to make money by lecturing.

I once spent a night with the Mansvetovs at ROVA, the Russian colony in New Jersey, for some occasion over which Mansvetov presided. The problem was to

handle the somewhat difficult relations between the Old
Immigration, the bourgeois who had come over before the
Revolution and who mostly lived on Riverside Drive,
and the New Immigration, which consisted of non-
Bolshevik radicals who were likely to be inacceptable to
the well-dressed and well-mannered bourgeois. Mansvetov was supposed to be good at this. I slept in a big
dormitory for the men. I went to bed very early, before
the others came in, and since it was a suffocating New
Jersey summer night, I opened a window or two. But as
soon as some young boys arrived, they ran true to Russian
tradition by exclaiming, "Who opened the window?
We'll all catch our death of cold!" and shut it.)

Chicago: H.'s new apartment. —End of October
[1935]—rooms opening out of each other—dull rose walls
under white upper wainscot and ceiling—big wide light
—brown wood (what kind?) entrances, with Ionic yellow
wooden columns, from one room to another, ending in
the dining room with a phony fireplace, with the same
Ionic pillars under the mantelpiece, on which a cocktail
shaker and an empty glass-stoppered decanter stood.
—View out on Oakdale Avenue: brick apartment houses,
with their trees stripped in front of them, a few leaves
wagging on top—brick with tapestry, brick towers—the
pearly dull dense and somehow mysterious sky—in general, the few trees, the dull air and sky, the heavy bulk
of stone and brick—the big bay window, lined with the
same light woodwork, of the big roomy informal-seeming
apartment with the expressionless scrollery over the main
part of the window, over the loaf-shaped glass at the top,
the cockroach-brown furniture, the frog-belly white-tile
fireplace, the radio gutted and empty . . . [I can't read
the rest of what I wrote. Drinks and making love had
been too much for me, I had fallen into a stupor on the
couch. I awoke with difficulty with what I thought was
the first soreness of a cold in my throat.]

—I asked about K., how she was getting along with her sex life, and she said, "Terribly: I fell out of bed one night"—she had kept edging over.

March. This time I got a suite, which had a slightly more cheerful aspect, as the windows looked out on the back and shabby side of the auditorium. Sort of bow-window effect in bedroom, and lust-provoking red plush divan: two red pillows and two sort of golden pillows—no regular arms, as with ordinary couches—the sides were so low that with a pillow or two they were perfect for a woman to rest her head on. The constraint I always felt at first soon melted away, and she wasn't under nearly such a strain as usual, so that we got better and better during the thirty-six hours I was there. She hadn't been drinking, had been having dinner at six with the children, so that she looked slender, sober, serious—and older: lines in her face and signs of flabbiness in parts of her body where she had shrunk (she wore one of those confounded girdles which it is like eating shellfish to get off women and which leave the warp and woof of their texture stamped into their skin); but as things went on, the color came into her face and her eyes became bright, live, and hard as agates. Having lunched with C.N., who was trying to disparage O. to her (her husband) with the idea of making her—poor O., entirely dependent on her!—he had announced that he was going to maintain his own standard by stepping on other people, and then had cut O. down to $60 (K. had gone into the real-estate business and made $200, was quite good at selling people things)—he would read her passages from letters that women had written him—begged her to meet him in a bar late in afternoon, as it would be his only chance—she had felt like asking him for what—he was a rotter, but she sympathized with him—his wife had been all right for the first three years, when he had been giving her a swell time sexually—after all, he said, he'd been in the Social Register when he'd been married to her and had been through Harvard—at least most people thought he had, he added. —O. had tried to fill the bill of sex satisfaction by quantity instead of quality, but she thought that after a while he'd realized he didn't like it and had gone back to his twice a week. It was all very brief, neat, and clean—he didn't want to sully his hands by touching it, would always make her put it in—she had made up a rhyme for G.: Of all sad words of tongue or pen, the saddest are these: "Put it in." He said that love was merely a matter of friction. The morning after their wedding night, he had told her she had "bled like a stuck pig"—which had upset her so she never got over it. When she reminded him of it on the verge of her breaking down, he had accused her of making things up just to be disagreeable. —Whole family—O., children, and maid—doted on her: she was the center of all attention. O. would get peevish because he wanted to talk to her when the children were talking to her: the little girl had said, "Let's divide her up." —C.N. had called up and been angry because she hadn't called him at five, wasn't used to being kept waiting—she had waited to get out of the hotel to call him because she was afraid he was the kind of man who would trace the phone call. —Inferior sweetish fresh-yellow-grape-tasting California champagne, with rich-tasting chicken sandwiches with green pickles—comedy of opening champagne bottle—boy was afraid of cork popping—it finally came out, after much twisting and tugging, with only a very feeble explosion. Semi-transparent curtains that enabled you to do anything without pulling down the shades—also deep low armchairs that seemed suitable to fuck in. —Sweet unpleasant powdery smell in elevators that went up opposite that place where they sold candy and Easter rabbits. Tall brass cylindrical spittoons half-

filled with sand at the elevator stops. —She was supporting G., she said. G.'s household worse than ever, though
she had made the apartment more cheerful by putting
green curtains up. G.'s lying in bed with light on. They
were afraid that G.'s husband would be hurt because he
wasn't asked to join us—I went in to see him and was
depressed by his situation, didn't know what to tell him
to do—he didn't get enough of the country, couldn't
bicycle out as you could in England—was hoping to get
sent off on a trip. K. wouldn't see him any more because
he would always take her aside and complain about G.
—After drinks when we were at G.'s, K. expressed
[pleasure] in being beaten. She mentioned it in a perfectly natural way, and I was rather shocked. But I tried
it in the hotel room, spanking her with my bare hands
and slapping her in the face, always afraid I wasn't doing
it hard enough. At one point she began to cry—I saw how
feminine she looked, with her little head and black hair
tight around it. —This spanking made my hands sore—
I at last injudiciously came when I thought I was doing
something else. —Next day we had lunch in a restaurant
—I said that I didn't like peas and carrots and set it over
on the side of the table—she said, "Let's throw it at the
waitress—I'm trying everything this weekend and I've
never made a scene in a restaurant." I told her it was
lots of fun and an exhibitionistic person like her would
enjoy it. —Later on, more divan—I had bought a little
hairbrush—she said afterwards she thought it was darling.
—C.N. was trying to take her to dinner—the maid had
had to go to church at eight, so she thought she knew
she had her in the palm of her hand. (E., another of her
lovers, had a lot of boudoir patter, talked all the time,
asked her how she liked it, said he was going to keep it
up all day—carried kimono with him—only for her, he
said—he didn't want to get tangled up with women in

Washington, though he said there were plenty of opportunities.) —She said that the feeling was inside—a throbbing, about six times. I asked her why she liked to be beaten. "Because it makes me feel that you—"—she stopped. She said later that this would always bind us together. She could always tell when she had had it, because she felt subdued. She had told me about a man she knew—a rather futile little rich boy I had known at Hill—who "swished" his wife with twigs that he got in the woods. I felt that we had passed into a new phase—as if she were resigned to her life out there, as if her breakdown had aged and matured her, and as if we were getting used to our periodical meetings and were becoming less desperate about them—we found that we could walk out on the street on Sunday afternoon almost like a married couple. —I believe, though she was so much less slender, her figure and her skin now seemed to me less attractive. —Picture in hotel room of a rather rakish-looking French lady with drink, big hat, and cigarette. —The theme song seemed to be "Alone." —I liked the city—its blond girls with hard but attractive Western accents, smiling at you in the cloakrooms and bars. —Meeting XYZ in restaurant—she thought he was with an inferior set of hangers-on, with whom he was not himself: they did nothing but make smutty cracks. —Parody of "The Music Goes Round and Round": "Oh, you push the little blonde down, And her bottom goes round and round"—that's all the words they would tell her. —There was a blue spittoon, which I pushed with my foot under one of the armchairs. —I asked her how the children were: "They're probably wondering where their mama is." They were having their teacher to dinner and had been told to offer her sherry. K. wondered afterwards whether the teacher had expected her to be there. —She went to a fashionable fortuneteller at $5 a throw—the woman played up a foreigner (a Polish chemist) this time. She told all the young Chicago matrons, apparently, that their husbands didn't satisfy them and that they were going to get nice lovers. —The hard look of lust—I felt that she was feminine when she cried, but was afterwards sorry I had slapped her. —She didn't want to get up yet, wanted to "lie there and talk and wriggle around." —I felt our situation had changed—in a way, not for the better: my desire to give her a child—perhaps, her desire to have me give her one—had turned (for the time, at any rate), blocked by withdrawals and condoms, into a desire to get more out of passion some other way. —O. had told her she was living in a doll's house.

When we went in a five-and-ten-cent store, she wanted to linger when a mother, a few aisles away, was scolding her child and slapped her. "I enjoy seeing that, too," she said.

April. Drive out to Lake Forest—unexpectedly heavy and depressing—something like Grosse Pointe—in the bleak April: big brick houses, not set off by lawns and half-concealed by hedges and trees, as at Rumson, but quite close together and all plainly visible—perhaps, as K. suggested, so that everybody could see them. Big gray-shingled church with a steeple at one end so that it looked something like a head—the whole building resembled an armadillo. We tried to get out of Lake Forest so that we could have lunch, but she took the wrong turning and we came back past the same conspicuous heavy houses, the same church that looked like an armadillo, with a dreary blue round stained-glass window that made me think about how they must have raised the money for it. The day had been rather stuffy, but suddenly a blast of cold air which soon became much too cold came in from the lake. I felt a need to get out of

Lake Forest. She had been telling me that if she ever lived there, the only place she would want to live would be on the lake. We had a rotten lunch for a dollar—she wondered if it was all going to be as pallid as the chicken broth—in a fancy roadhouse where there was a party of elderly ladies in black hats going on at a long table and where she sat with her back to the room and was afraid to turn around for fear she would recognize somebody. She had been telling me of the scenes of agony which took place at the Lake Forest station: when other people had moved in, the other people had got a club car, which only they could ride in, and while they were waiting at the station, they wouldn't nod to the other people. C.N. had bought a Minerva car (or some foreign make) in order to impress. There was terrible snubbing and gnashing of teeth. —Her husband would lie on the bed feeling gloomy because Charley Wiman had just been to town and given a big party.

—I showed her the hairbrush I had bought, which had wires instead of bristles. She said there was not time and that she had to go home and face O. afterwards. She laughed after she had lain there thinking about it for a minute, and said, "That's a peerless hairbrush!" She submitted, but said afterwards she'd been too nervous, she hadn't been able to enjoy it at all. —She was looking unusually beautiful, had just had a massage, which had, however, left some bitter stuff that smelled like camphor on her nipples—this was a great shock to me—I stuck it out for a while, but finally went and got a wet towel and wiped it off. Dieting now had improved her figure—her breasts seemed round and firm, instead of rather fleshy as they had before, her bottom, also, round instead of, as before, rather flat. —At one point, after coming, she cried. "That was very exciting," she said when we left.

—Next day she started out, as she told me, deciding

not to go to the hotel, but at G.'s she changed her mind and decided she would have "a short sex rally." I felt her up with my fingers while G. and the little boy were in the next room, and then the salmon fish cakes at dinner made me think tenderly of her. —G. was really pretty bad with the kid—too languid and spineless to make him mind. He would grab for things on the plate at table when he was standing by while the grown-ups were eating and whine when he couldn't get them. His father could do more with him than his mother. G——s was likely to sulk and go to his room if he came back and found G's friends. She had had grippe—K. thought she was torn between the desire to get up and go to the theater with me and the reluctance to give up her strong position of being unable to do anything about the household because she was still sick. —Dodie and her Omaha accent, like the girls'—Peggy Cunningham in her little apartment, full of coarse cracks: "There's more tea in them there balls!" —The next afternoon, our party in G——s's study—pulled the double doors while the child was having his nap, and G. went to bed—once she called K., and K. thought she probably shocked her by going naked with her coat around her. It was, I suppose, like them when they were girls, back in the Boston days, and the students from Harvard Law School liked to come to the house. She shed the Chicago social stuff so easily (would have to make conversation when she got back). The brown couch seemed very becoming to her. Her cunt between her closed thighs seemed darling and her little black bush well-proportioned. I sat at the other end with her foot held in my armpit. She lay there looking so beautiful, her hand looking rather fine and tapering, with the thin gold wedding ring on her finger, resting on her opulent breast, and the other foot, too, making a nice contrast with the opulence of her belly and hips. —I felt

very happy afterwards—affectionate toward G., too, calling her "darling"—I told them Alymov's stories about the
Moscow Zoo.

—She had been going to a numerologist, who seemed
to be convincing her now that her role was to stay with
O.

—She told me—what she had not told me before when
she had spoken of O.'s amorous activities as being "a very
neat and clean little performance"—that he would say, "I
love you so!" At one point, she said to me as if rather
belligerent, "Who's a better husband than O.?"

May 8, on her way to Europe, when they were going
through New York: I told her to make O. go out in the
public square in Rome and shout, "Viva Haile Selassie!"
"Don't tell him what it means." She protested that he
was not that stupid. —G. had said to her, just as she was
leaving, that they oughtn't to go to Italy at all, they ought
to boycott the Italians. —(The Italians around me [on
East 52nd Street] had been making the night hideous
firing off guns, and back of me, the Italian family in the
top floor of a tenement had hung out Italian and American flags and a picture of Mussolini.) —The day ended
kind of badly and in chaos—she was supposed to have
gotten back at three, but didn't turn up till seven. I.Z.
came to my house and took her back to the hotel. —She
told me later they stayed up in the room while O. was
waiting in the lobby. She said she had spoiled his trip.

[It is certainly very hard to write about sex in English
without making it unattractive. *Come* is a horrible word
to apply to something ecstatic. The French *jouir* is much
better. I have occasionally heard men of the older generation use the word *spiced* (?) in this connection. Is this
one of those American financial metaphors, like not
taking stock in something?]

Anna. When, about the 1st of December 1935, I found out from her aunt that she was working at the 34th Street Childs, opposite Macy's, I went in and saw her right away. When I went up to her, she said, "When did you get back?" (from Russia) in what seemed to me rather a hard-boiled way and without batting an eyelash, though she afterwards told me that seeing me again had upset her. I had some difficulty at first in getting her to come to see me. She adopted with me a sort of hard tone that I'd never known her to use before. She thought that she oughtn't to. "Why?" "Because that's not the way I want to live." "But it wouldn't do Jerry any harm because he'd never know." "It might do me some harm, though." He was a revenue agent now. She was living with her sister. Fatty and her mother had a restaurant in the Hotel St. Paul on Ninth Avenue. That Childs was a terrible place, they'd let anybody get away with anything, because it was so hard to get girls to work there. The Macy shoppers were terrible people, they gave very poor tips. The girls got $3 a week when the money for their meals had been taken out. And the food was terrible: leftovers given them in the guise of chicken croquettes, with chopped carrots, which the chef told them had been kept in the icebox for days. They worked the girls till they had nervous breakdowns. One of the girls had fainted the day that Anna came to see me—they had to faint in order to get let off. She was very amusing about the Russians—didn't I really think they were stupid?—and dirty! They didn't eat anything but potatoes. I told her about my experiences with potatoes in the hospital in Odessa [They kept them in the bathtub there], and we laughed about it. She wished that she didn't have to go back to Childs. I told her how unembarrassedly the girls went to it in Russia. Yes, she said, at Fatty's place, they used to go in the back room for $2, with just a basin of water and a towel. I said that the

Soviet girls didn't do it for money, though. Didn't they do it for wine or anything? No: they did it because they liked it. "You're telling me?" she said. She was thin from working so hard, but otherwise seemed all right. She had been feeling very virtuous with Jerry, she said.

They charged her 50¢ a day for two meals. The Macy shoppers sometimes didn't tip at all. You would sometimes get 75¢ from waiting on seventy people. The people were horrid to the waitresses, in a hurry to get back to the suburbs. The man who liked her and had sent her flowers and given her candy. He was one of a group of businessmen who ate lunch together. He had picked her out, though she hadn't served him.

She helped her mother with her work at the furrier's during her day off. Her mother was getting old, fifty-six. Her sister's husband was getting $21 a week, which was good pay for him, from the PWA—he was a foreman. Jerry was getting $40, but he had lots of debts to pay off—that was the reason they never went anywhere. She had for the first time in years a bed to herself, which her mother had provided.

She would get so tired at Childs that she would wish she were back in the hospital again, so that she could just rest.

Getting out of an elevator in some office building—I must have been nervously exhausted—I saw a man in a darkened hall—he was in his shirt sleeves with open neck, had evidently been working around the building— his eyes were wide open, and there seemed to be no expression on his face: he looked, not like an ape, but like some kind of primitive man—and his staring face, as I stared at him, appalled me: humanity was still an animal, still glaring out of its dark caves, not yet having mastered the world, not even comprehending what he saw.

I was frightened—at him, at us all. *The horrible look of the human race.*

Another day when I was suffering from the bad nerves of a hangover, in the Pennsylvania Station, I had just asked about trains at the information desk when suddenly I heard a violent insane outburst ending with, "I'll tear you to pieces!" —I looked around and saw *an elderly woman,* evidently fit to be locked up, face livid, hat on top of her head, *in a white-hot frenzy of fury all alone.*

Muriel Draper in her Communist phase. She would wrestle with the souls of her retinue, scold them, exhort them, make them feel cheap—she would say that Leonard Amter had been ill and that his illness was simply due to the fact that he knew he ought to be a Communist on account of the Nazi treatment of the Jews, and that Chester Arthur, she thought, would eventually join the Communist Party. Finally, Chester Arthur developed rectum trouble and had to go to the hospital to be operated on—before going in, he made a will, leaving his money to the Communist Party. —At her New Year's party, she high-hatted somebody who wouldn't stand up when somebody else was singing the "Internationale" and at the same time rebuked somebody else for not being considerate enough of Chavchavadze, who was "a man who had been trained for a certain position in life which it was impossible for him to fill and who had to live in exile from his country," etc. There were the Russian consul, a lawyer who represented Soviet interests, an elderly girl whose parents had come from Moscow, etc.—L., I was told, had been a Fascist and worn a black shirt before Muriel came back from Russia.

News from Santa Barbara. Livermore affair in Santa Barbara: divorced woman who had son's former tutor around as a lover. Son objected to mother's drinking and drank down a lot of gin one night to show her what drunkenness was like. As climax of scene, he handed her a rifle and told her to shoot him, which she did. He was taken to the hospital, and for some time they didn't know whether he would live or not. She was taken to the hospital, too, and arrested there. Divorced father came on.

Grandfather Kimball. Grandfather Kimball was a homeopath and, when he first came to practice in Eaton-town, encountered considerable opposition on the part of the orthodox doctors. One of them tried to crowd him off the road one day, and this was one of the only times he was ever known to get very angry. He and Grand-mother at first were sometimes down to rock bottom—on one occasion, a Negro with a toothache saved their lives. —He used to doctor the Negroes, and he had a horse named Fanny Temple who would take him home by her-self when he was so tired that he fell asleep coming back from the Pines.

Princeton. I thought it had reached a new low—every-body seemed to be let down. Paddy Chapman's wife had gone back to France more or less for good, it seemed, taking one of the children with her and forgetting to send the rest of the family Christmas greetings. Gauss, who had struck me when I had last been down as not having come to an understanding with Dodds, had evi-dently found himself in opposition to him over the question of free speech for the *Princetonian*—now, being much more intelligent than Dodds and in his quiet way quite a powerful personality, seemed to have emerged from one of those ectoplasmic wrestling matches such as Thurber depicts in *The New Yorker,* with his tentacles wrapped all around the president—he was even feeding him his speeches, I was told; and the new policies—a new library and more scholarships for poor but able boys—seemed to me to bear the earmarks of having been originated by Gauss. Gauss, at the suggestion of Dodds, was apparently going to abandon the direction of the Romance Language Department in order to have more time for his executive work as dean—I imagine that he will now have more influence than he has ever had before. But he is being landed in awful contradictions— on the one hand, censoring the *Lit.* for an article that advocated that Negroes be admitted (and he had handled this in the most disingenuous way, as he revealed when he was trying to explain to me that he hadn't exerted censorship at all: he had told them that there were so much more pressing problems which demanded their attention, etc.)—and he had induced one of the poets to change *testicular* to *terrestrial* in the phrase "Trenton's testicular triumphs" (or something)—and, on the other hand, writing an article which he said he would have to publish anonymously, provoked by J. P. Morgan's assertion at the hearings of the Senate Committee that the world was indebted for culture to the leisure classes—an essay which had ended with something in the nature of a knell for upper-class culture and an assertion that this culture was unable to command the confidence of the working class. He was also extremely regular, as it seemed to be the thing to be, on the question of Hauptmann's guilt [in the kidnapping and murder of the Lindbergh baby]. Dodds, a little while afterwards, was one of the signers of a sort of manifesto censuring Hoffman and saying that Hauptmann ought to be executed immediately. Gauss assured me that they had had evidence to the effect that the nails in the ladder had been Hauptmann's—evidence which they hadn't produced in court because the jury would have been too dumb to understand it. —Mrs. Gauss told me about the scandals of the jazz age at Princeton and what seemed to me a very depressing series of deaths, serious illnesses, and defective children—with a certain amount of the smug gusto which even the most intelligent and kindly married ladies seem to develop after a certain age when they have been living a certain length of time in a community (I noticed that Dorothy Jackson had the same thing). Paul Elmer More had been very ill, looked thin, and his profile, she said, when she had last seen him, had strikingly resembled Goethe's. —Dinner at the house of a Canadian physicist who had married an Englishwoman, to which Dodds, his wife, and the Gausses had been invited to meet a visiting English physicist from Cambridge. Whole evening on terribly low level—and the Englishman, by contrast with them, brought out the small potatoes of the Doddses. Dodds himself, the son of a small-town Pennsylvania minister, who had gone to one of those small Pennsylvania colleges, nobody could seem to remember which, had taught municipal government eleven years at Princeton and had attracted the favorable attention of the trustees by preparing some kind of report recommending political reforms in New Jersey. The only good thing people seemed to be able to say for him was that he was hard-boiled enough not to get all torn up, as the more sensitive Hibben had done, in his position, between the faculty and the trustees. His wife, who was a pretty, slim, and reddish-haired Canadian, with features a little on the small and sharp side, but more smartly dressed than most professors' wives, wearing open silver-and-something evening shoes, talked very little, and Paddy Chapman told me that she had said to him she suffered from a feeling of inadequacy to her position—the *Princetonian* had just been complaining that the students weren't received at Prospect and that they had no opportunity to meet the faculty—which, it seems, had hurt her feelings: their attitude had been compared unfavorably to that of the Conants at Harvard—actually, the Doddses were supposed to be at home every Thursday afternoon. —The talk was of a babbittry beyond belief. They began with track and football, went on to some ineptitudes about George Borrow and Dickens, the former of whom Dodds enjoyed, the latter of whom he couldn't stand. He had a flat-footed and slightly sullen way of banging down his Philistine opinions: wanted to know when you fellows, the physicists, were going to get down to doing something that had some practical value. Had been reading Santayana's *Last Puritan*—because it was a book that one in his position ought to read, I suppose. Committed one or two pieces of jocular boorish rudeness: somebody had made some joke about how they couldn't get along without the Physics Department and he had said, "You'd be surprised!"—or something of the kind. They asked me one or two gingerly questions about Russia. —No attempt whatever to talk to the Englishman about anything he might have been interesting about. Long conversation about starlings and other migratory birds and insects, about which the Cambridge physicist had quite a lot of exact English information—always referring to the starling as "he." —On this visit, I would poke and kick the people, turn them over, push them around, but I couldn't get any sign of life out of any of them. Gauss's growing schizophrenia [I used this word wrongly, as if it meant split personality] distressed me. —In May, Tom Matthews told me that Frank MacDonald was retiring and leaving Princeton and that they were giving him a farewell dinner at the Ivy Club.

Visit to Stanley Dell. He had urged me to come up to see him, then when I had written him after Christmas, I hadn't heard from him for a long time—until finally I had gotten a letter which said that he hadn't had a chance to write me until the last weekend, when somehow he had "missed it" and was only getting around to it now—the snow made it pretty difficult to meet me, to get supplies, etc. —Nevertheless, if I wanted to take the chance— —So I went up, spent the night at the Jacksons', as they told me it would be impossible to get to Stanley's that night—next day, a cousin of the Jacksons took me over, nice clean cultivated horsy New England girl, whose mother painted and they had always gone abroad, especially to Italy in the winter, until their money had given out and now they missed it—had never known anybody, she said, "from Russia" before—thought it hadn't sounded very attractive, "full of Communists and things." Clean, straight, and attractive she was in her riding breeches, puttees, and cap when she got out to lead the horse through the drifts at those points at which the road was no longer anything but a valley between two mountains of snow and the sleigh was tipped up on its side. She was so cool, so even, so clear. It turned out we had taken the wrong road—were finally shoaled on a snowy waste (after we had left the road) in a farmer's back yard. (It had been nice to hear the bells in the cold air— we had talked about how rare sleighing had become, almost nobody kept horses any more, first time she had been sleighing in years.) It was late afternoon and going to get dark. She started back, and I borrowed a child's Flexible Flyer from a most friendly Swedish farmer and started out with my suitcase tied to it. I had called up Stanley from the farmhouse, and when he had heard that we had landed in difficulties, had immediately assumed I was going back. —At first, I had an awful time, as I kept falling through the crust and cutting myself and having to climb out, and the suitcase kept slipping around on the sled and toppling it over on its side.

But farther on, the crust was harder and I was able to make progress on it. Presently I saw Stanley coming down the hill on skis. We ascended the hill, saying little, as I was too much out of breath with my efforts.

Finally we arrived and had a highball. I envied him his place, with his land and his books. He had been doing a lot of work on it, breaking his own stone for the road and putting in—what was quite a triumph of engineering —a pipeline with a special kind of valve which made it possible to get water from a well that was situated some distance back of the house without its remaining in the pipes and freezing. He had been reading a large work on plumbing—had also arranged so that it was possible to turn off some of the bathrooms without turning off the others. And he had all sorts of little conveniences such as a bottle opener fastened to the wall just inside the cellar door, and all kinds of barometers. Unfortunately, he had put me in a room of which the bathroom had been turned off and the window nailed down, and during the night I went downstairs and slept in one of the rooms on the first floor. —I was awfully glad to see him, and it was very pleasant at first to talk to him again, with his intellectual range and his cultivation: history, psychology, literature; but my visit got to be more and more eerie. He wanted to be amiable and hospitable; but he had to make a conscious effort—his solitary and self-centered life had practically deprived him of the social reflexes. I have been that way myself, possibly always am to some extent, and it was strange to see it from the outside—at once depressed me and made me feel superior. He would rush to put his bottles away in the cupboard as soon as he had given anybody a drink, and on one occasion, at a later phase of my visit, sat drinking, glass after glass, a large part of a bottle of sherry without offering me any. His great idea about Rosalind and her

friend Ruthie seemed to be that they were well-behaved
little girls because they washed their dishes. [I had had
them come down from Wykeham Rise, Rosalind's school
in Washington.] Francie, he was afraid, had "unattractive" traits because he himself was too self-centered.
His vicarious accomplishment in Arthur's neurological
activities, in the naturalistic interests of his stepson. He
was reading the publicity for a small new kind of tractor
which was being made in one of the Scandinavian
countries. —Unconsciously, he sabotaged my literary
activity, removing the card table on which I had been
working and putting it downstairs, and finally—the climax of my visit—saying that he was sorry to interfere
with me, but if the snow kept up, they would soon be
out of oil for the electric-lighting system and as long as
there was a single light burning, the engine was going—
they weren't all like that, but this one was—and that if all
the oil was used up, it would be a lot of trouble to get
more from the barn and would involve, as I understood,
cutting a path through the snow. As a matter of fact, the
snow began to melt the next day; but I had decided to
leave. His reluctance to have me try his snowshoes—
he would always say that the snow was very slippery or
something of the kind—so that I finally gave the idea up.
—When I left my pen on his desk after writing a letter,
he said rather sharply, "Is that your pen?"

It was pleasant when Jean and the boys, and the little
girls, were there, though Jean and Stanley didn't do
much for anybody and always spoke in such low voices
that presently everybody would be talking in a whisper.
—Jean tried Ruthie on little McCormacks and other
people in Lake Forest, but it didn't seem to come out
right. —Awful silences at table that grew on you and
were difficult to break. —The little girls would go off by
themselves snowshoeing while the little boys did other

things. —I had two marvelous walks on the frozen crust— down the tree-lined lane, along the road—when I was looking for the girls and finally found their names and addresses written large on a bank covered with snow (the little boy, with his quaint rather literary language, pointed out that this was conclusive proof that the girls had gone this way); on a day when the sun was out bright, with no thaw, up and down the wooded hill, avoiding the ice-covered pools in the hollows, and looking at the tracks of animals.

After our families had gone, things became queer and uncomfortable: the butler, a favorite punk of Robert Jackson's and one of his nude models, had gone off on a bat Sunday night and went off to his room and flopped, in the middle of getting roast beef ready for dinner. The result was that we had practically nothing but roast beef, which at my suggestion we ate in the form of sandwiches and whose grease congealed quickly on the cold plates— after that, canned peaches. We began talking about Jung, and when we had moved into the other room, Stanley complained, a little gothically, I thought, that he had felt a chill, it had seemed to get colder, when the subject was raised. (It was just before dinner that he had drunk the sherry.) —Now he expatiated on the sad case of the butler—he worried, Stanley said, about his old father and a wife he had left behind him—I imagined that he tried to play up to Stanley's psychoanalytic interests—he ought to be psychoanalyzed, but Stanley felt that it was hard for him to do it himself. I said that lots of people went on periodic sprees, why wasn't it all right? —Stanley, after a moment's thought, took this up rather sharply, said that for people with a certain amount of money and position back of them it didn't make any difference, but that this man could never hold down a job behaving the way he did—"No!" he concluded, "it's far from all right. —He'll never accomplish anything this way!" —Stanley had worked with him side by side and they had talked to one another about their lives. Yet the master-and-servant relation still came between them: "I'm always the boss," Stanley said. —The man, when he came to, asked for his pay and threw up his job. —Stanley was exhibiting that rather disagreeable trait of people who have just been psychoanalyzed of liking to point out, in an insidious tone, the complexes and things from which other people were suffering. —We talked of getting Arthur Jackson over—after a highball or two (he immediately hid the bottle and didn't produce it again), I was very keen on seeing the Colby girl who had brought me over in the sleigh—he told me how solitary she was: she had had a beau—he was an instructor somewhere—who came to Washington in the summer and with whom she would read philosophy, but aside from that, she only seemed to care about her horse—she did a lot of riding. —But when it turned out that Arthur couldn't come, Stanley wouldn't hear of having the girl, though I offered to send a taxi for her: She'd probably faint away, he said at first: probably nobody has ever sent a taxi for her in her life; but then later, when I kept urging immediate action, he said: "No: that wouldn't be a good thing to do, I don't think." I was all at that moment for getting Dorothy Jackson over and getting her cockeyed; "Try and do it!" he said. —I felt that we were headed with neurotic fatalism for another flat deflated evening—he was going back into his burrow. He had told me incongruously during an earlier conversation that something or other he had done was due to the fact that he thought that all effort ought to be seriously purposive—was it his lack of interest in games? —On another visit, he had mentioned that Cecil always got sick in such a way as to prevent her from working at her sculpture (just as he had done himself about the various professions he had contemplated). He hadn't wanted to marry her, he said, because he felt that she was headed toward being a rich man's wife, the implication being that this would make him simply a rich man.

—I was afraid I'd have to borrow money from him, because he seemed to be so exceedingly unenthusiastic when I suggested it—"I've only got $11," he said—but my check fortunately arrived.

—The house, very pleasant, reminded me vividly of the old days at Greenwich—amiable amenities, cleanness, brightness, friendly bathrooms, pictures of cats in children's room, the house of a young household in spite of everything—was it Stan's personality? a reminiscence of Marion? or simply the way a certain kind of people lived?—after all, a good many of the things were Jean's and her children's.

The strange areas of loose skin, of ceasing to function, lying abed, morbid dreams and introspection, still around his eyes. —When he was beginning to get better at Zurich, he had gone in a little for optics—on which he also had a solid Macmillan volume—doing some microscopic photographing—now he was "passing it along to John."

—The difficulties which the girls and I had about finding out where the light switches were—this irritated him and involuntarily he would show it—irritated all the more, no doubt, because he hadn't shown us about them in the first place. "Haven't you found out how to turn the lights on yet?" he said when the girls were fumbling around in their bedroom, with nervous sharpness and a kindly smile that was verging on a sneer.

—Thick foggy dirty atmosphere of the thaw after the beautiful cold sunny days.

—I had a feeling that his preference for Jung over

Freud was due to the former's, through his concept of the "common consciousness,"* allowing him to escape partially from the Freudian sex mechanism—probably, in his case, of a mother fixation—he had, I noticed, a large photograph of his mother on his bureau. [At Princeton, he had written a diary, which went off to his mother in her t.b. sanatorium in Switzerland—so, in a sense, he was never out of her sight.] —He had been investigating Marxism a little—his ideas on this subject. —His mother's New England family had made hardware.

[It was this visit to the Dells that convinced me that I ought to live in the country, so that eventually I bought the house in Wellfleet.]

Visit to Carolyn Link† at Scarsdale. They had more money now; but the relatively magnificent sitting room showed the same lack of care and taste—though they had hung up the Holbeins and the eighteenth-century French print which I had given them for wedding presents. —Carolyn had broken down and developed tuberculosis—now she had been in bed a year and looked healthier than I had ever known her. —Henry was now the guiding spirit of the Psychological Institute, which included Angell of Yale among its sponsors. The object apparently was to make a big racket out of neurology. He began by telling me what a terrible racket psychoanalysis was, then when I asked him how they handled their cases: Well, for example, a man had come in and said that he had fits of exhaustion. "I said to him, you go out and get a job and hold it down two months—don't come back to me again till you've done that!" The man

---

* EW is wrongly formulating Jung's speculation about the "collective *unconscious.*"

† The former Carolyn Crosby Wilson had married Henry Link in 1917. He wrote *The Return to Religion* in 1936.

went away and got a job assembling radio parts—at the end of two months, he came back and said he still had fits of exhaustion. "Tell me how you spend your week— what do you do every night? He told me, and he said, 'Every Thursday night my wife goes out to a bridge club'—so I told him, well, now you take every Thursday night to have your fit of exhaustion." I asked him what they did about Freudian complexes: he said, "We'd like to see the Freudian complexes all obliterated!" —I asked him what they did about praecox cases, and he said that they sent them into the army or the navy. —They charged only $25—they had questionnaires which the patients filled out and the diagnosis was apparently made from this—the great idea seemed to be to get them to go to work: he described that as the "normal way" of handling such cases, as opposed to the abnormal way of the psychoanalysts. Sometimes, he admitted, if the patients were very badly off, they would send them to the Medical Center—adding, however, that even the Medical Center couldn't do anything for some of them. I thought he was probably trying to relieve his conscience for leaving a lot of semi-lunatics at large without proper attention. —The Psychological Institute had also been making a study of the readers of *Esquire*—four men and two and a half women to a copy, or something of the kind.

—Going away, I thought about Carolyn, was touched by her and felt tenderly toward her, as I had always done—keeping up her poetry through those years when she had been submerged by their dreary suburban life, imparting to her children her own fineness of quality, which she had preserved inside her thin body and her sometimes tasteless clothes.

Pittsburgh. The ghastly approaches: the houses on the steep hill, with their wretched scabby gardens fenced off down the cliff, in which a few things had been made to grow and in which you could hardly see how the people managed to get up and down without slipping down the (what looked like) cindery soil.

—Ed Blair's family were living in a hilly part of the city full of little middle-class residences, where the great mansion had stood once of some associate of Frick whom Frick had ruined completely. —Lois to one of Venita's children, who had just lost a tooth. They were telling her that she must put it under her pillow with a dime and that would mean she was going to get money. Did the fairy take the dime as well as the tooth? Yes: if the fairy came back with just the tooth, they held her for the dime.

Peggy Bacon, May 5. She had on a new shirtwaist and a large cameo with a dove and some roses which Alex had given her for her birthday. The shirtwaist was white dimity peppered with little specks: it was very round and bouffant all around her and had an enormous jabot in front, so that she looked like some kind of beautiful nautilus or Portuguese man-of-war, with lots of meat in it like a mollusk: it made one think of her breasts, which must be large and round. As she was sitting on the couch with her drink, I saw how extraordinary her arms were: they were very long in proportion to the rest of her. Her hands were craftsman's hands, rougher and redder than her arms. As she sat with her drink on her knee, she held the glass with her first and middle finger, which were long, square-tipped, and strong-looking. But farther up, beyond the elbow, her arm grew soft, white, and round and rather pleasantly plump, and where it was sheathed at the shoulder in the puff of the little white speckled sleeve, it looked feminine and toothsome, the arm of an old-fashioned woman.

—She told me about Joe Gouché's attacking her one

night at a party and trying to tear her clothes off. She said, "Nice men don't do such things." I suggested that Joe had perhaps simply thought that this was the thing to do in Dawn's set. She said, "Yes: he thought it was a social obligation."

—After she had been telling me what a fine soul her mother was, how nice she had been about Alex, etc., she sounded so wholesome and smug that I told her she functioned on two planes. Afterwards, when she said somebody was "very nice," she suddenly burst into wild laughter so that I could see her little crooked sharp teeth.

Muriel Draper. When she came to dinner at the penthouse [Helen Vinton Augur's on South Stuyvesant Square, which I rented from Helen at the time she was divorcing her husband], there was a fire at the German Masonic Temple a few doors away, and after it had been put out, she exclaimed with gusto, Wouldn't it have been funny if the whole place, with that furniture and henna ceiling, had just gone up in smoke!—except for the books. She had been somewhere, she said, where she had looked at somebody fixedly and said, "Sometimes I feel such a force within me!"—and one of the walls of the house had fallen down. —Esther and Chester [Arthur] and the Communists—an appointment with Hathaway had been made for Esther—she had waited but nobody turned up, and Chester had written them an indignant letter.

Maria Michelaevna [a handsome Russian woman who was hat girl in a Russian restaurant on Lexington Avenue—I was unable to operate in Russian, so I got Fyodor Mansvetov to come there with me and explain to her that I wanted to make her acquaintance]. Her father a military contractor at Riga, brought up with machine guns rattling and bombs exploding in the streets, women and children lying dead, men hanging to lamp-posts, children called in to see a man fixed with a bayonet to the wall. She liked war, would like to see another—would like to see the airplanes come and throw bombs on New York and see all those big buildings fall down—it would kill millions of people and the wages would go up and the rents come down. What the Russian muzhik needed, she said with great ferocity, narrowing her eyes, was *a good beating!* Then he'd go back to his black bread and be satisfied with it.

The next time, she put on a show about her love life: liked to tease men. Misha used to live with her and her husband, he was so much in love with her that sometimes he couldn't stand it and would say, "I am going away!" —White Russians who sponged off the rich and racketeered the Russians on the pretence that they were going to bring the Tsar back. The count who had invented the machine for turning dollar bills into $100 bills and got $25,000 in dollar bills out of a night-club magnate in Brooklyn, which were supposed to be transformed when they were run through the machine. He had the machine explode and a waiter come into the hotel room and steal the money. I laughed, and she said, "Yes, it is very amusing, isn't it?" as if she'd never thought of that aspect of it before. One army officer whose apartment she had gone to in Riga had torn off her dress and beaten her with a Cossack's whip with a lead thing on the end—she had had to conceal it from her mother—afterwards, he had had himself transferred. Another whom she wouldn't kiss bet a brother officer a large sum of money that she wouldn't kiss a man in the navy, so she went and kissed the other man. I said I should think people would have tried to kill her and she said, "Somehow they always miss!" —Had she ever been in love? No. Didn't she want to be? "I don't know: they say it's miserable." —The first day she had arrived in New York (when I took her first to the penthouse), she met her husband in a drugstore (she had apparently sent him here), and she had said that she didn't like it and she wanted him to take her back—and now she had been here ten years and she still disliked the Americans. I asked her whether she didn't like the people she lived with (also first visit, as above) and she replied, "I detest them!"—but weren't they pretty fond of her: "They think I am a nasty person." —Her husband, whose heart was bad, had gone in and lain down and died one day when he had come back after being out hunting a job, and she had been unsympathetic with him after he came back—about which she was apparently being coldly exhibitionistic. When I was taking her back this first time, she said, "I have been talking all the time and I bored you." I said, "Oh, no: not at all." "Yes, I do: I bore everybody!" —Count Zubov, who was supposed to help White Russians in New York.

The third time, I asked her about her toe dancer's feet and legs (the thickness and neatness of her feet and the way she had carried herself on her strong legs, as well as the agreeable voice speaking Russian, had been, I now realized, what had attracted me about her in the restaurant)—she admitted having danced in the ballet, but not professionally, only for charity—I thought for a moment she seemed scared after this—but after this she became very nice—I realized that her previous impersonations had really been acts which she thought that I wanted, and that I had really fed her the cues with my questions—and she sang me "Ухарь купец" and other songs.

Her story was that she couldn't speak French, that she didn't know who Nijinsky was, and that she had never been in Constantinople, though I'm sure in my earlier conversations with her she had revealed the fact that she had. "The Russians say I was chased out of the ballet in Constantinople," but she had really never been there. —When I would try to pin her down about something she didn't have an answer for—such as why she and her husband had kept their marriage secret—she would look at me and say, "I don't know!" —Angry at the proprietor in the restaurant because they let the orchestra play the Tsar's Hymn at the request of a drunken man (first conversation). —She was not normal, she knew it. —(Second conversation) Misha had come in *so tired* after being out all day in the heat looking for a job, and he asked her for a glass of milk, and she had not wanted to give it to him because when people asked her for things, "I don't know: I don't want to give—but sometimes I do things for people when they don't ask." —She irritated me by always ending her statements with, "Right?" —When she found out I was sympathetic with the Soviets, she said that she thought the Communists had good intentions, though they were vindictive. —Her stomach ulcers and bad health. —Always dressed in quite chic way—first time, little blue hat with blue polka-dotted veil that came down over her forehead and eyes. —Blue shoes, well filled—she always made somebody else buy her shoes for her, because the men in the stores always said, "You are a dancer!" —I noticed that when I would try to hurry her up to get to the upshot of one of her stories, she would say, "I'm going to tell you," and go on repeating the boring conversations with her mother, her husband, etc., as if she had to make it up as she went along. —She had earned pretty good money teaching girls from Eastern Europe to read and write English for a steamship line which brought them to America, had gotten in herself as an actress.

Ballet dancers. She said that it was a funny thing that

when the music would stop, she couldn't stand up any longer, would flop right down.

[She was living at that time with a blond little Baltic Baron Tarnow, who made me a present of a book he had written about his regiment. When I later asked Paul Chavchavadze if he knew him, he said that he thought he did—"I think he lives with a woman who doesn't treat him very well," but he didn't want to talk about him. (The Chavchavadzes, I found out later, were always cold, if not actually *méchants,* when they talked about Baltic barons. For all their affability with everyone else, they excluded the Baltic nobility, because they didn't want to recognize them as belonging to the Russian aristocracy. They were quite horrid about one who had lodged with them and had thought that they "might be interested" in some historical work that threw light on noble genealogy.)]

One day Maria Michelaevna spent an afternoon with me at Trees. The Dos Passoses unexpectedly came by in the afternoon. They were evidently terrified by Maria, who must have seemed to them an extremely suspicious character, and almost immediately went away again. It was true that she had all the appearance of a woman spy in a melodrama or a wicked queen in a fairy-tale ballet. I was surprised when I went to her apartment and met her highly conventional companion—she put on a neat little apron and began getting dinner for him in a businesslike domestic way.

I got her to help me with *Evgeni Onegin* when I was living in Helen Vinton's penthouse, and she behaved as if it were a prelude to seduction: "Pushkin is sometimes very free!"

It was closing time in the Lafayette Grill, and Cobey Gilman was being swept out from under the table. Niles

Spencer had been stuttering for five minutes, and Dawn Powell gave him a crack on the jaw and said, "*Nuts* is the word you're groping for." The voices of vulgar refugees were being quenched one by one. Soon the chairs would be piled on the tables, and the waiters would be counting their spoils. Twenty minutes later, the customers had left and were trickling away to other bars. Peggy Bacon roamed University Place alone in the guise of a stringy black cat.

K.'s visit on her way back from Europe. I went to the hotel late, she had left a message that she would be in the bar. I propelled her straight into a taxi and brought her back to the penthouse, where I found she was uncomfortable and a little sulky, then back to hotel, then to Zs'. At one point they said they found a pair of glasses, and as I didn't have mine in my case, I told them to bring them along—it turned out to be O.'s pince-nez. —I.Z. called her up the next morning and said that things had gotten to a pretty pass if he had to entertain her husband while she was with me. He said at lunchtime that he had such a hangover that he couldn't come, so Miss F. met us and handled the situation. —I tried a little violence the first day, but she couldn't give herself up to it. I asked why she thought she liked this, and she answered that she thought it was because O. had never subdued her. Although I enjoyed it myself, I had some sort of inhibition about hitting her and could only seem to do it clumsily, not landing my blows squarely. I used to look forward to it and wonder how and where to buy a whip; but after this we had little opportunity. The next day, tenderness, which went much better. She thought that if she let herself be whipped regularly, she would lose all her personality. I had stopped taking any precautions by this time—she thought she might have a tilted womb. —O. came in and found her asleep and slapped her, she thinks, and called her a bitch, and he got up and left the room the next morning before she was up. It turned out, when the hotel people produced his eye-glasses, that she had never noticed he wore them. So she came down to my house to lunch—said afterwards she couldn't do anything, would let me "relieve myself" but couldn't enter into anything. When we had finished lunch and were still sitting at the table, I picked up her foot in my lap, took her shoe off and kissed her foot, then put my hand up her dress and my fingers in her cunt. Afterwards, I kept thinking when I got my hand near my face, that we had been eating fish. She rubbed my member in my trousers with the tip of her foot. After that, went upstairs.

Hatty's daughter. Paranoia, apparently—perhaps due to birth of baby, which the doctor had told her she oughtn't to have—they had used birth control till he couldn't afford it any longer. —Hatty broke down and wept as she was telling me about it after they had had to send the daughter to Bellevue. The baby, whose name was Dolores, had never seen white before and was scared of the nurses in the hospital, and Hatty had to take her away. The social worker said the other two children made a good impression in school.

June 1936. In New York, as I came along 59th Street toward Central Park, the sky beyond it was lemon just deepening into a summer warmth of peach, and the buildings before it, growing sandstone (?), seemed light: I saw that new evergreens had been planted along the Park and the line of victorias waiting.

It rained and rained day after day till the leaves and plants and flowers and trees burst into furious foliage and

bloom—the darkness of rainy indoor days was heavy with
gestation of the country being forced into exuberance.
The leaves waving outside the window in the dark afternoon on a rainy day. One morning, when it was fine, I
saw the dawn so easily and evenly first making me aware
of it as a blueness in the sky without emphasis or dramatic (or picturesque) contrast, then as rose just as smooth
and just as unsurprising. —A nursery of irises among
their green reeds white shading to blue through lavender
to purple—like some new spectrum of silver. On the
same ride, I noticed that the tips of the feather grass (?,
don't know real name) were dried, their faint tinge of
yellow to the fields showing that the midpoint of
summer had just been passed (if this is true as Helen
Vinton says). —When we went out to Jones Beach, I
saw in a back yard a girl with bare arms in a kind of
blue jumper leaning back in a chair with her legs
stretched out but not crossed and her arms behind her
neck. —The hedges heavy with honeysuckle. —The 29th,
a beautiful June day, not hot, with the wind blowing the
leaves and the shadows and the grass in the fields around.

—*Hudson, July 4*—The waves, granite gray showing
the mud in the small yellow choppy waves—the banks,
first bare cliffs, then green-wool-wooded rising unexpectedly wild and august to be so near the crowded
apartments and powerhouses of uptown New York—
the sky a pale flat blue in which the white of the clouds
seemed merely a discoloration as the blue seemed to ex-
tend to the banks below, blurring, discoloring, and flat-
tening them—later, the little waves sparkled, the clouds
were dense and white and in relief against the blue in
the regular grand New York State way, the hills were
green-wool-wooded, it was prettier—West Point.
    —The silent and somnolent Hudson Valley, heavy

with plenitude, dark with verdure (hot between its ramparts of hills).

Visit to the Osborns at Garrison—July 4–5. —I was somewhat chagrined to be met by Josh Billings and to find his wife and Lewis Galantière* at the horse show. —We went to the house—it had been built by Bill's grandfather in 1857—later he·had built for himself, on the top of a wooded hill, a sort of castle with a pointed red tower and a long red gingerbread-house roof (which Fairfield Osborn's children were "sharing with each other"), which dominated everything below—inside, there were few pictures, no elegance, almost nothing had been done to relieve the crudity of the badly carved big dark banister posts, the old hall floor in alternate dark and light strips; only a small sitting room seemed to have been fitted up for comfort and use—the dining room, which was directly across from it, had a big arched embrasure for long windows—there was a porch, which I liked, with no roof and level with the lawn, in which from a distance one saw green summer chairs, two earth-colored bowls of white flowers set on a stone wall along one corner and against the windows a light green cage, in a triple arch like the arched windows, in which variegated green finches matched the dark peacock-blue blinds and a canary looked very much yellower than the straw-colored sides of the house—from the smooth uneven lawn which heaves so easily and daringly into a hillside. It was attractive and rather quaint. —Yes, Bill said, it was rather amusing—with its dormers on the second story and protruding around a kind of tower at the opposite end from the chairs on the porch—its blinds which opened out like

* Lewis Galantière (1895–1977), banker and amateur in letters, translator of Saint-Exupéry and the Goncourt Journals.

wings, its roof striped with violet and blue-gray slats, and its funny paler-straw-colored chimneys that looked something like castles in chess—a huge tulip tree beside the house—flower beds on either side of a gravel path that ran up the hill (to the greenhouse, the vegetable garden, and the tennis court), a mixture without selection of hollyhocks, columbine, zinnias, and those little veined morning-glory-like blue and pink flowers—an enormous tulip tree at the tower end of the house, the puffy brownish surfaces of smokebushes—old trees, of which there was great talk about planning them a couple of hundred years ahead, so that they wouldn't be a nuisance to one's descendants, some of the trees Bill's grandfather had planted they now considered a nuisance, nineteen sheep in a field below the house, quite a variety of trees, two big dogs, one black, the other a red setter named Kelt, colorless unpampered country dogs such as I remembered so many of in the other house.

—The horse show had been held on Bill's place, and he had done most of the work laying out the ring and setting up the jumps. —When Billings had complained about the way somebody was treating a horse, spurring and beating it, Peggy had said that some horses had to be treated that way—Bill had won a blue ribbon, Peggy a blue—she had ridden for the first time in five years, had had an operation on her back. —Mrs. Billings, her deafness, her attitude about servants and the young men who had been staying with them, "two Communists," one of them Kenneth Patchen, the poet—they hadn't had very good luck about having people like that there, perhaps they weren't very good at having them—one of the fellows created a difficult situation because they hesitated to give him orders and yet, after all, they were paying him, don't you know—their rude way of managing polite remarks, were afraid they'd been horrid about the bathroom, were agreed they'd stayed in there a long time, but it wasn't as if they'd used it separately—Josh's remark when they were talking about the hotness of the weather: "It was fine waiting at the station!" Then hastened, when I said I was sorry, to assure me that he hadn't minded it—Peggy had gotten the train 3:27 instead of 3:47. When the Osborns asked at the table who Cobey Gilman was, about whom Gladys and I had been talking (she dwelling on his unhappiness with gusto, his unfortunate early life, his being "scared," the probability that he would be better off with rather a conventional woman who would condone his occasional sprees, rather than with Dawn Powell —Peggy Bacon had told me how Gladys had once asked her in her loud deaf voice at a party how much she thought Dawn Powell had to do with Cobey's disorganized state): "Why, Cobey Gilman's a very entertaining . . . gentleman, who," etc.—because, I suppose, he hesitated over "fellow," which was one of their great words—but as to which he was no doubt seized with a fear that in this case it would mean the wrong thing, seeming to belittle Cobey, which "gentleman," of course, did, too—their way of talking about my book, the Billingses saying that Cobey had brought it out to them and they had intended to read it in order to be up, you know, but they hadn't gotten around to it, and Peggy told me how much she liked my *New Republic* articles on Russia, mixing two of them up. —Gladys Billings's blond getup—bare feet in red-strapped sandals, white dress with big skirt hung over the shoulders with straps—when Billings went to get her up to go to bed, he came over to her, took her hands, and lifted her up—she had, middle-aged as she was, a sort of sickening pseudo-young-girl blond bonbon mask and getup over her snobbish and disagreeable Bostonian personality. [I said "Bostonian" because I knew she had been married to a Saltonstall—

actually she came from New York.] —Peggy said of her
after she was gone that she was after all "fundamentally a
social person"—they said of him, when I said that he was
not so limited as most artists, that, no, he was not limited
at all, that his difficulty was precisely that he flowed out
in too many directions.

—Bill came back in his (doeskin?) breeches and riding
boots, the boots making his legs, as he stretched them out
from the chair, look very thin, the sweat making his
roughened hair look very black—with the smooth and
sophisticated way of talking which he had acquired since
I had seen him, he had also gotten something of upper-
class arrogance, though, representing on his part as it
evidently did a weakness which had allowed him to succumb to the interests and point of view of his class in
spite of his seriousness and simplicity and intelligence,
there was certainly nothing nasty about it as there was
about Gladys's, for instance. He had learned Peggy's
patter, I thought, the patter of the Muriel Draper–Helen
Simpson world, but was more intelligent with it than she
was. She was clever in a fundamentally tiresome way,
playing on words, etc., like the characters in the early
Henry James, which went back, I suppose, to the Tom
Appleton* tradition at Newport—and I thought she was
merely the commonplace member of a traditionally tal-
ented family [the Lafarges], who had the aptitudes—she
played the piano and composed music—without any real
vocation to exercise them. She was better-looking, though
[than when I had seen her last], without being really attractive, fine-featured, knife-blade nose, gray eyes, still
rather French.

—He had something of his early charm, often his

* Thomas Appleton (1812–1884), brother-in-law of Long-
fellow; amateur poet, and Boston conversationalist.

clumsy way of moving when he got up from a chair or came into the room, but his coltlike eyes no longer had their clearness, they seemed blue instead of, as I remembered them, brown, and with the way his eyebrows (bristling now) came down over them, seemed rougher, or as if rough things had happened to him. He kept telling me about the changes, the deteriorations, in the faces of old friends whom he had seen at the Princeton reunion: Noel Robinson's face had "coarsened," there had been a change in him, he had turned into a business executive of an ordinary type, etc.

—The fireworks. I went out to where they were setting them up on the rise on the ground. I heard Bill speak to Earl, and I went to shake hands with him. I saw a portly man with gray hair. I said, "Oh, I thought you meant your brother Earl!" But it was Earl. He was still a bachelor, he told me, and lived with his mother and father—he still had the quaint boyish-pompous way of talking. Bill pointed out his father in the dark—he had told me that the old man was keeping up with things pretty well, considering he was nearly seventy-five he didn't like some aspects of the New Deal, things bewildered him now. He stood on the porch, he seemed thinner, and his head had dropped forward a little, but he still had his old urbanity and his ready social interest in everything that was going on: when the bombs went off, he said: "That's what I like!—the good loud crack of a bomb!" He stood looking down while the flares were being set off, said, "I can't stand to look at that, can you?" "Look at that row," he said, indicating the young people sitting along the edge of the porch (the girls had looked very pretty and elegant, in the long wraps in which they were going out later to dances, as they came across the lawn). The rockets, he said, seemed "headed for those sheep." Billings wondered whether they still sent up paper balloons—"Oh," said Mr.

Osborn, "there's nothing so much fun when you're a boy as sending up a fire balloon." In the midst of our conversation about politics, he called my attention to the moon just rising over the hill—he wondered later in his quiet way whether it were really normal for it to rise in the place it seemed to, since from the house it rose in a different place. There was a new and very pretty kind of firework that sent out things like little comets, yellow stars with comets' tails, amid the trailing rain of gunpowder, had a sparkling-diamonded effect. —When, after the fireworks were over, everyone else had sat down, he still remained standing up till Peggy made him sit—he would sit down for just a moment, he said, then he would have to go. His mixture of sophistication with feeling for and enjoyment of life: when Lewis or somebody claimed that Peggy had let one of his bon mots fall flat, he remarked, "It's an awful thing when a fellow says something very witty and somebody else doesn't appreciate it!" Finally he got up, saying that he would look in at the club and then see what was going on at Forest Farm, and he made one of his appropriate little speeches such as I remembered his making to Bill at the time of the war: "Well, there have been a good many Fourth of Julys and a good many generations have managed to survive them, so I guess you'll survive this one." —He had told me how they had liked, at one time, to have fireworks for everybody in the village, but there had been boys who had taken cannon crackers and thrown them into groups of girls, etc., so they had had to give it up, they had been sorry . . . Josh Billings had said earlier, when Peggy and Bill were not present, that you "just let Osborn *père* talk."

—Bill, when he had got back from the horse show, had said that there was a man in town who owed him a day and half of work and he "thought it would be just about his style" to pick up the horse-show grounds. [The whole attitude of the Osborns was characteristic of the feudality of the Hudson Valley.]

—I thought of Peggy's tirades of snobbery when she and Bill had first been married: on the Jews—"but they want social equality—and that's just what we won't give them!" [The last time that I had been to dinner with Bill and Peggy, just after I got back from the army, convinced me that it would be impossible for me to have anything in common with them.]

—Bill and I, on Sunday morning, went out and herded the sheep from their meadow, past the house and across the road to another field, then had to mend the fences so that they wouldn't get out. On the way back, an Italian gardener, who commented on my sweating and winked at me. The house had burned down where Benedict Arnold had stayed before he fled to the British, there was nothing but the cellar and some fragments of the brick wall. Very beautiful among the trees: the clear yellow sides of an old stable, the clear shade among the high locusts and with the dense green background of the valley. A field dull morocco leather with red top, studded with occasional clusters of black-eyed susans—neighbor who had used up land till it was useless and put nothing back in. Roosevelt: the Tory community of Hyde Park took joy, Bill told me, in voting against him. The Bourbons around there were raging and irrational on the subject: it was worse than about Wilson after the war.

—We took a nap after lunch, got up about four. Bill and I took a walk—he wanted to see where he had had a tree cut down for fence posts—also showed me wood cut by people from the village, which he was going to sell— the people had been on relief—he knew the ages of all the trees—there was a tract he would give to the village for a cooperative enterprise, but they would rather have the taxes—he paid $2 an acre, 300 acres. Village drunkard who was to pick up the horse-show grounds, he was getting worse—if you shaved him and cleaned him up, you could pass him off for a foreign nobleman—evidently had some very good French blood. The Hudson Valley was certainly the most "somnambulant place"—unmistakably the origin of the Rip Van Winkle and the Sleepy Hollow stories. The people in the village—he didn't think anybody knew exactly how many there were—were pretty poor stock, the Dutch migration had gone along the other side (?) and up the Mohawk Valley. There had been families that barely got through the winter. —It was a kind of a feudal community up there. We went in swimming in a fine little lock, completely embedded in forest. The water was dark, warm with veins of cold where the springs were—a wood thrush gave its liquid note with the exquisitely shifting flute stops. There was Indian pipe in the woods and the smell of wintergreen berries, long white steeples along the road which I thought were pepper bush. Two fine cold springs, one of them piped down to the house—his grandfather had first come there, he said, because he had caught dysentery in the Philippines (?) and the water there was constipating. He told me about his work: he was the head of the research department of Phelps Dodge, probably knew more about copper smelting than anybody else in the country, had invented a new process which they had finally found the money to install and which made it possible to produce copper cheaper—which he supposed, though a little skeptically, was a good thing—he had said before, after I had told him of Stan Dell's plumbing activities, etc., and his saying that they were an "escape," that he supposed his metallurgical researches were also an escape. He had lately been testing tin, about which he didn't know a thing—trying to extract tin from the tin ore of a Bolivian coal mine which had been sent all over the world and baffled everybody. The British with their tin mines in Cornwall and Malaya practically controlled the tin supply, and Phelps Dodge [his mother had been a Dodge]—this wasn't to be repeated—were thinking of going into it. There were two kinds of South American ore involved: on one of them they were going to make a killing—after the complicated process of other metallurgists had failed, he had solved it, apparently, by some perfectly simple principle which he had found in the chemistry book; the other, a tin oxide, was very tricky and might take three years.

—We stopped at the tennis court, where Lewis (in his tight-fitting shorts and his blue sweater) and Peggy were having a rally. The pressed ruddy earth of the court was becoming to her sunbrowned legs and arms and head in the dark-blue shorts and shirt. Bill said that Peggy had a nice figure and confided to me that he was just as glad not to have had to play, as his game was better than Lewis's, and Peggy, who was just learning, would put him off it; but he took off his shirt and played with her with his long arms and his yellow sunbrowned torso. Buz Law —who, it seems, after killing a man through drunken driving and a lot of other escapades and misfortunes, has ended up as a tennis pro—had given her lessons at Newport. Bill lectured her, though quietly, for having drunk two cocktails at lunch, didn't know how she could expect to have all her senses about her. He and his father had grown more alike, it seemed to me, as they had both grown older, Bill much more urbane, very upright, a little sententious.

—While I had been reading before taking a nap, I heard Peggy's voice raised in what seemed to be a flying at one of the children: "There's been nothing but a continual series of stories, excuses and lies!" . . . very disagreeable. I seemed to hear Bill's deeper voice mixing into it later. When I came down, she told me that Katy the nurse wanted to leave because she said she couldn't control the children—but all that was wrong with her was sexual repression—she wished that Katy and Domingo, the Filipino butler, would have a love affair: but Katy, who was Irish, was full of race prejudice—as Peggy said with the scorn of a superior. Peggy later decided to take Katy to the movies in the evening. (How extraordinarily objectionable rich people can be about their servants.) —Now, at the tennis court, when Peggy had uttered some piece of profanity I didn't hear, Bill said that she used awful language—and with the children.

—When we sat around on the porch before dinner the castle on the hill stood up, with one window which had caught the sun shining as brightly as a lighthouse, against the vast piled-up solid white clouds with their edges so distinct on the blue of the sky.

—At dinner and after dinner, Peggy tried to draw me out on Russia and Communism. She thought, of course, that I was a Communist, wanted to know. I said I wouldn't last as one half an hour—she had been hearing about Communism from Muriel Draper, was reading a book by Taussig on economics to find out, as Lewis said, what words like "amortization" meant. People like this are always strangely silent and turn the discussion off when working-class movements and organizations, which are what Communism is all about, are brought up. Bill said that he thought John L. Lewis would have a better chance of persuading the employees to let him organize the steelworkers if they didn't threaten to decrease the production per manpower—asserted very lamely later on that Oh, he thought the working class ought to be well organized. Peggy wanted to know what would be a good book to read about Lenin, he must be an extraordinary man.

—Vincent Astor's Fourth of July party, which, having no evening clothes, I didn't attend—I went to bed, but the Billingses went. Apparently Peggy's interest in Communism had induced her to invite me out and take me to the Astor party.

—Bill's father and Red Lamberton's father had put an end to boxing at Princeton by staging such a bloody exhibition—Bill's father had gotten a broken nose but, being light, had given Lamberton two broken ribs—that the audience and authorities were horrified. I had just the day before seen Red Lamberton's wife, a very nice German girl, who had been Carolyn Wilson's roommate at Vassar, the daughter of an editor of newspapers in Minnesota, who had just been on to Philadelphia as chairman of the Democratic Committee from there. There had been a big argument in the course of which everybody broke glasses —she had broken some, too.

—My old-fashioned professional-man country-squire reaction of solidarity with Bill stimulated a certain resentment at Peggy's going in for literary and artistic phonies. They had had an American sculptor staying at their house one summer—Bill on the subject of this sculptor and his wives: "Just a mick with a talent for sculpture, you know"—his present wife had had a regular servants' quarrel with the caretaker, and both she and the caretaker had written Peggy letters, and they had never heard from them since. The wife had social ambitions, but did everything she could to make it impossible for him to see his friends.

—*Bill Brown's wonderful broker*—Billings remembered more details about him. He used to go to performances of Shakespeare and hire the whole row and sit there and recite the play about four lines ahead of the actors. Was cuckoo outside of his office, but perfectly all right as soon as he got inside.

In this connection, might use Alex Brook's reply to some friend who had said that the unemployed ought to be put on a boat and sunk: "Well, you're unemployed."

—Gladys Billings said that Alex Brook didn't approve of her because he was a Communist—on account, it turned out, of something harsh which he had said to her at a party one night: what did she want to be happy? certain jewels and two lamé dresses—or some dialogue of the sort.

—Painters are certainly much more prone than writers to acquire the manners and the patter of the rich.

—Bill's grandfathers had not gone to college, they had gone into business—one of them had been president Illinois Central.

—Talk, after Billings had left, about his illustrations to Stuart Chase's book [*Rich Land, Poor Land*]—someone said he or she didn't care for them: you can describe social injustice with words but you can't draw or paint it. Peggy liked the one of the woman being hit by the policeman. —But how about Goya and Daumier? When you saw their pictures, said Lewis, you admired the pictures, you didn't think about the social subject. One of Bill's great expressions: "Makes a lot of sense."

—The conversation about comebacks that one hadn't had the presence of mind to make: Bill said the only time he'd ever made the right retort had been to a railroad conductor—which somewhat deprived him of the satisfaction. He had climbed on the train with two big bags and shoved the conductor aside as he was plunging down the aisle. The man had run after him and said, "What do you think I am, a dog?" — "Well, I certainly am not a pack mule!" — Reminded me of John Amen's story about Dewitt Howe's (?) driving the trainman out of the private car.

—He had acquired something of the regular rich man's attitude toward artists, etc.—partly no doubt out of a more or less natural reaction to Peggy's rather goofy attitude toward them.

—Joyful feeling, when I had come back from Garrison and come down to my mother's in Red Bank and ridden around a little on my bicycle, of being back in the American summer instead of cooped up in Moscow.

New York—Sea Bright, July 6, the 4:57 train from New York, daylight-saving time. The water along by Bayonne the same bluish toneless gray as the tops of the tracks beside the train—the old dingy brick Singer Sewing Machine plant partly grown with some green vine—a yellow roadside lunch wagon glaring in the summer sun—before that, shacks, factories, and oil tanks—brick buildings of Elizabethport, double green verdigris steeples (the Statue of Liberty, its flat old-bronze green)—the streets of saloons and old wooden houses that need repainting, with rank green of the summer trees—from the pale-green salt marshes, below the big red gas tanks . . . (the people on the train: partly workmen, clean shaved with their collars open, partly white-collar men with spectacles and soft hats with here and there a panama or straw—the former with their hats tipped back sleeping, the latter reading the afternoon papers)—soon after, the first country cottages in white and dark boards with ornamental eaves as windows, surrounded by overgrown weedy fields with ailanthus or other shrublike trees—a bright new car going over a bridge across blue water that made an inroad into the swamp—Flor de Cumbal Cigars painted in black and white against the brick side of a house—(Perth Amboy)—the town around its junkyards (rusty iron), with its rank immense trees and its clothes hung out on lines across the streets—Raritan Bay opening out blue and refreshing with its little white lighthouse out in the blue, just before you got to the Jersey Light and Power plant—coal cars on sidings (lunch wagons), clothes in the back yards—the Bay again, a white sail, the shallow reddish-yellow pebbly beach where a few cheap-looking people were bathing or sitting in the sun with their shirts off—opening out to sea past even Staten Island now—bait, hot dogs, cold soda— the flat green marshes smoother and fresher, the country now, the trees, wilder stretches, the red soil (sky much the same as on Hudson), corn growing in a little back yard, a small orchard (Matteawan), a field under cultivation of corn sprouts in the red soil—Matteawan Tile Co., red brick, locusts, ailanthus—old rusty rails of sidings with peppergrass grown between them—swamp with cattail rushes, Maurer Fishery, Raw Bar—Keyport, light-green umbrella trees on a mandolin plucker of turf—the water again in the distance, a rowboat in the back yard of a shack—Union Beach, dingy little gray or reddish stations, a cheap-looking girl or two waiting for somebody—weedy fields and salt marshes the main thing—the little bunga- lows with screened-in porches that mean the sea, to which the view is now clear across the sickly tender-green marsh, in the distance Staten Island—the Natco Tile Co.—a few darker poplars, shabby waxen crests (?) of century plants beside a house—(the train: mock turtle soup? oxtail? old cigarbox woodwork, and blue plush seats)—two little girls in pink dresses gathering daisies in a field—a small field of grapevines strung on wires—Port Monmouth, very bat- tered little station with shingles, and paint knocked off— a pretty little white house, the first pretty one, with white wood lace along the top of the screened porch—a chicken farm, white chickens, white century plants—a white ship in the water, a silver-gray oil tank seeming to float above the earth like a blimp—(the train was pretty well empty by this time, from now on a new stage of the journey, the shore)—Leonardo—the last slight industrial touch was a small sign which said Nazareth Cement—Atlantic High- lands now the gray sea (color of tracks as above), the gray unpainted trestles, pines, and bridges, the rock embank- ment as along the Hudson—Sandy Hook, a strip of beach

and dark verdure (look up map)—a sunburned boy standing up in the water, his warm torso making the water
blue—now the little cottages, community lawns, American
flags (the Fourth?), delicatessen, series of tiny white
bungalows, hedges trimmed to balls at the ends, pink and
red hollyhocks, a gas station white with a bright-red
roof—sea food, fishing tackle, candy, soda—Highlands—
the *Yankee Doodle*, a small raffish launch almost like a
tug—Thrill Ride—the telegraph poles along the sand—
yellow and lettuce-green flimsy pleasure buildings of
Highland Beach on spindly-looking piles in the water—
the Atlantic proper with a large and black-smoking
freighter out at sea—American flags streaming counter to
the direction of the train in a good little wind on the
shore—on the other side, the cottages with privet clipped
in balls and seaside rocking chairs on the porch—a bather
pink in a dark-blue suit in the glare—the bigger cottages
some of them all closed, above the strip of water on the
right dazzling like a mirror in the sun the more grandiose
dark verdure, the bigger more august cottages already on
the summer-residence side, the old white drawbridge—the
little station with its long benches and its weighing machine corroded by the air of the sea. —The Beach Club
low, long, and palatial, with its row of smart cars in the
drive and its smart-looking summer girls coming out.

—*Sea Bright, July 7*—The old brick corner drugstore
with its two comic little seaside turrets—the old summer
seaside hotel spreading over quite a stretch of the shore—
gray-shingle with its myriads, close together, of small
windows framed in white and the slim branching pillars
of its balconies and porches rather elegant in effect like
graining—two main buildings and an annex strung together with bridges and walks, rather pleasant, labyrinthine, lovers lurking for summer-privacy effect—the white
drawbridge, the asphalt road, the tennis club, the smeared

and illegible houses—the lawns were so soaked with July afternoon light that they seemed almost a kind of yellow. —No, the point seems to be that the late light itself is yellow. He (I) turned into one of the cross lanes (from the Rumson) under the hanging branches: everything was silence and shade, there were so many trees that one could not even see the white houses that stood quite close to the road—some kind of a stucco gardener's house covered with vines—even the dust of the road here was gray instead of red, bouncing—but this time of year, like pink that has faded in the wash. Then, the wide lawn in the sun with its tennis net behind the trees and the shrubs under which they (we) used to hide. The privet in bloom, the garage where Mrs. Knox's chauffeur had built a glider, the muddy pond where he (I) used to catch turtles—and where one of the Knox boys was always fishing for perch (?), about which the rest of the family used to kid him.

PROVINCETOWN, 1936

New York to Provincetown, July 31–August 1, 1936
Connecticut. A small white house with two dark trees
in front of the door.

Getting out of New York—a lot of trouble: we got and
strayed way over on the East Side when we were trying to
reach the Grand Concourse: the Triborough Bridge with
its two great gray chalk white castellated (what-do-you
call-ems?)—the apparently infinite stretches way uptown
of little apartments in little stone apartment houses;
garages, corner drugstores, signboards, girls walking along
the street, the pace a little more leisurely there—then we
succeeded in cutting across to the Bronx: the Grand
Concourse—all a revelation to me, largely grown up in
the last fifteen years—the miles of apartment houses—
tasty blocks of cells which the real-estate people have tried
to varnish with elegance (make tasty), but intervals between them, getting into the suburbs—a million Jews with
some Irish—splendid smooth road easily curving out of
the city, past Poe's house, oldish church, big cemetery
with much grass and imposing marble mausoleums, a
pond almost rural, suburban outskirts of the city in sum-

mer, somewhat muffled and slowed down like the country in hot weather, but with the hardness of the town in the apartment houses, the glaring August light all the harder for the great plain flat fronts and angles, emphatic beyond flimsiness of verdure. —White Plains and Mt. Kisco, the kind of places that people are going through all summer going somewhere or getting into New York: summer soda fountains, billboards bright in the sun with the giant pretty beaming American girls of cigarette advertisements, their new post offices aiming at impressiveness and beauty with their colonial masks of brick and marble (?), their country clubs which aren't hard to belong to. Their news-stands with the colors bright in the sun of the Western and movie magazines, of the women's magazines with wholesome bright-eyed girls on the covers, of the funny papers on Sunday. The Kensico reservoir: great dams, viaducts, bridges: white granite, black asphalt, painted steel.

—Connecticut: a pond when the country had begun, with a sheeny surface more beautiful than the sides of a mackerel new-caught, Connecticut's grassy and weedy and feathery not-imposing foliage, the great houses, with lawns kept clipped around them, that look as if they had been iced with white icing, pure and a little shiny, the churches, the little summer homes, mixing their im-permanence with old churches and farms—the main arteries now so well laid out, so easy to follow, so handy from the point of view of gas and refreshments, where everybody can tell you how to go to get to any destina-tion—summer camps for girls and boys, where they are learning expert tennis and fancy diving, the head coun-selors teaching the younger children.

—Fine motor road from Hartford to Providence, curving in large swift asphalt sweeps around and over the mild hills: Providence all traffic, a crossroads, waiting for

traffic and dodging motors to get over to the little park
where there were cutout dolls of Roger Williams, in
celebration of the tercentenary, illuminated in the niches
of a kind of specially erected booth and a fountain, illuminated from below, of which the jet at the top was orange,
looking, from a distance, like Nedick's orange drink, but,
close to, giving an effect more golden, where the spray,
falling, seemed to flake to gold, and the flattened-out
streams which petaled in from the bottom were varied
from green to blue (the indigo tint was the most satisfactory) to pink to a sort of bad rainbow pink and purple.
Up the old hill past the capitol (?), the museums, Brown
University, the old houses wadded with vines, old and
brown, old and white—then, as you are getting out of
town, the fancy and rather curiously attractive erections
of the seventies and eighties, yellow and ornate, quirks
of woodwork, columns, cupolas, fringes of jigsaw lace,
banister newels elaborately turned, special cornices, wood-
work-webbed gables—now suburbia is growing up around
them, the motor roads are swallowing them out, the gas
stations, the road to the Cape, all so clearly marked out
now for tourists, that leads through Fall River and New
Bedford, with their gray wooden houses, their grim textile
mills, their pale slaty expanses of water, with a dingy undistinguished shipping, along which rather gloomy-seem-
ing men are digging clams in the dark slimy mud: the
streets lead downhill to the water, but even the water now
seems stripped of the freedom and romance of the past.
    —Great trucks, big enough, Betty [Huling] thought, to
contain some new engineering development (what was it?
I forget), cars with some middle-aged couple dragging
their dismal closed trailers, new motor models mounted on
trucks which dragged another truck behind them and
which looked, Betty said, as they approached, with their
loads and headlights, like snouts and eyes towering down

on one, like black overpowering monsters—a man in a cracker-box Austin, painted red, new brown Fords with the rumble inside, very doggy-looking.

—Swampy inlets from the water: the Cape Cod Canal— from a distance, the high square structure of iron, less like a bridge than a gigantic gate, the dug-up sand and clay of work still in progress—a ditch in the sand—the new bridge (the approaches not quite completed), a graceful arc of fine pale steel stretched between the crude pale yellow (straw?) banks: soda fountain—gas station—rest room—varied ice-cream flavors, double row of lids of iced cylinders: ginger, chocolate, lemon, burnt almond, pistachio, strawberry, etc.—varied kinds of motor oil—names on signboards for the Cape: Dennis, Falmouth, Hyannis (Harwich, Brewster, Orleans), Provincetown—the holiday atmosphere of the Cape, played up systematically of late years, the old dry and fine quality now being smeared with a Coney Island sugared butter (big papier-mâché pink ice-cream cones, red catsup bottles, fancy restaurants, like the road out of Hollywood)—comic postcard maps of the Cape—but past Sagamore, a view of two church steeples, one plain, one flanged, chalk-white, sunken in the small-leaved trees, the green marsh grass of near the sea, which meant that the East Coast proper had changed into something quite different: the Cape.

—After that, the alternation between the bare white sandbars and dunes lying low on the soft and almost mother-of-pearl summer blue-gray of the sea and the comparative richness inland of towns like Plymouth and Yarmouth with their high white many-windowed houses with grass deep-green and garden flowers and century grown trees around them—broad high-peaked eaves of these houses—the smaller Cape houses with most of their windows only on the lower story—the pale gray roofs built low against the wind—the other windows crowded up under the gables at the ends. —Betty kept sniffing—without much satisfaction—for the rank salt smell of the sea.

—*Hatty* had wanted to be sure to come down to the house for starting instead of letting us pick her up uptown, because, it turned out, she was afraid we might miss her and she be left behind. —When we talked about stopping for a bite to eat, she immediately produced lunch in a handbag. —When her hat was blown off, she let it go and did not tell us, not wanting to be a nuisance.

Connecticut, etc.

Peculiar combination of griminess with massiveness of big houses and factory buildings in cities like New Haven.

The Croton chain of reservoirs—artificial lakes like those near Katonah which would be drained into uninviting mud flats.

Post Road: new gray stone churches, old mansions in Elizabethan and Georgian styles, with carefully tended landscape-gardened lawns, that would suddenly crop up (old gray houses here).

Provincetown, August 1, 1936. Old life all finished: people working now, not drinking so much, not giving so many dissolute parties, but with much less relation to one another, no longer a real community—two boatloads of Boston trippers a day—the *Romance* and the *Steel Pier*—we arrived in town with the Stutz [an old car which I had bought for this trip with Betty Huling] just at the moment of the irruption—a herd of dumb clucks with sordid faces wandering in the middle of the streets, hooked into the tourist traps. —Poor Carl Van Vechten had been up there looking for the Provincetown of twenty years ago, wanted to photograph O'Neill's house, the Wharf Theatre. —Anti-Red feeling—Ernest Meyer of the *Post* had been arrested on the lawn of the Vernon Inn as he was coming out of a meeting of the League Against War and Fascism—the cops had previously frisked it for minors—they put him in jail for a night. —Dos thought that it had practically reverted to the status of an ordinary small town, the town boys were all in the night clubs.

The L'Engles' [daughter's] *wedding* in Truro, which had taken place before I arrived: the Provincetown people, who had knocked together what old ceremonious clothes they could find, were confronted, when they arrived, by much smarter guests, the L'Engles' Long Island friends, in morning coats and striped trousers. People reflected that it was the only wedding they had ever been to where it was easy to see what was going on, then realized that Brownie had turned it around so that the bride and groom were facing the audience and the minister talked into space, to which he directed his "Dearly beloved's." But a worse realization came when the bride and groom disappeared and, instead of the general mingling and refreshments—they had been promised champagne—which usually takes place after the ceremony, the Provincetown guests seemed abandoned and were presently brought big thick locally made sandwiches filled with mouse-trap cheese and pink jelly and with the crusts on and a freezerful of orange sherbet, into which was poured, with feebly popping corks, a few bottles of California champagne. Presently Betty Spencer became aware that something was going on in the studio, and when she tried to investigate it, she found Brownie L'Engle with her foot in the door, saying, "This is only for the family!" —Bill L'Engle reached out a glass of champagne, saying, "Try this! —Pol Roger, Vingt-et-un!" —but she replied, "No, Bill: I don't want it! I'm beyond the pale! I don't want it!" —All the people with morning coats were inside clustered around canapés of caviar, buckets of champagne, etc. —The Provincetown guests soon went home. On the way back, Charley Kaselau said, "I never saw such a separation between the sheep and the goats! It makes me want to vomit." The sheep and the goats were separated along lines of the rich and the poor—so that the Princess Chavchavadze ate mouse-trap cheese.

—At Pete Sawyer's wedding (with his Australian girl) Bill L'Engle made a point of tasting the California champagne and saying, "It's perfectly all right—yes, it's perfectly good!"—trying, Betty thought, to set his conscience at rest. —Brownie had asked old Mrs. Duganne how much chicken she thought she needed for the salad—Mrs. Duganne had asked how many guests. Seventy, said Brownie—do you think two chickens will be enough? —The chicken was undiscoverable in the salad.

—It seems that, at an early period, one of Brownie's ways of insulting her guests had been, first, to make them use paper cups, then to make them write their names on their paper cups, so she could keep them for the next time they came—Betty said that Wilbur Steele's cup was still there.

L'Engles. When Brownie met Judy Wolman on the street, she said, "You didn't get an invitation to the wedding, did you?—I sent you one but I didn't know your address!"

—When I saw Brownie at the Pete Sawyers' houseboat party, I thought she looked much older: her hair was partly gray. They told me that she had been dyeing it for years, but had now ceased. —Later on, she had a kind of collapse, due, apparently, to nervous exhaustion, and had to take to her bed for a week or so. Elizabeth Waugh went to see her and found the room in rather awful shape, with cigarette butts lying around on the floor. When Elizabeth saw Bill somewhere afterwards, he said, "You did Brownie a lot of good." "Much he cared!" said Floyd Clymer, who told me this. —Floyd was deeply disgusted with Provincetown—had just brought Jeannie down and got her off to school—"a pretty heavy business!" He had an almost Joycean way of talking, as of a man who had been so long alone that he could still only talk to himself: queer words like "skidamerink" and "cockalorum," such as may remain still drifting around from childhood in the shadows at the bottom of one's mind, would turn up in his conversation. "Too many people": he had had his own family there. "Too many details" — "All the details."

Betty Huling and the Stutz. Her enthusiasm, energy, and affection, which have no proper object (Bud away in Hollywood). She would go into spasms about trivial things: a new pair of colored glasses was perfectly wonderful because it enabled you to see things in real color— the Wolmans were *so* nice (Adele and Judy had taken her on at tennis first, leaving Margie, the best player, till the last, but Betty had beaten them all). She had lain awake for nights before our trip. —Something, though always something inessential, would go wrong with the Stutz every day: a flat tire, the steering wheel loose, the battery dead (so that, in order to start, we would have to get another car to push us), the seats would slide out, etc. But Betty was as loyal to the car as to Bud or *The New Republic* and would be indignant with me if I expressed any apprehensions. —[Betty stayed with me a few days, then went back to New York. At the end of the summer, her sister Frances came up and drove Rosalind and me back.] When Frances came to take us back, she was in rather a sullen mood and told Betty in private, when we got to New York, that she would be lucky if she could sell the car and get $50 for it. She told her that she could feel the back part dragging and that it was likely to come apart like the horse with two men inside. But Betty was as enthusiastic as ever: she had been dreaming about it at night. She drove it up from the Pennsylvania Station and said it was so wonderful to handle it again. Their own car had seemed like a tin can after the Stutz—and it worked for her so wonderfully: "Why, it's going to say 'Mammy' in a minute!" —After we had left Provincetown, wrenches had kept falling out, like the knives and forks of Harpo Marx—which had apparently been left hanging on it by Jack Connell. "Now, if we only had some works!" said Betty. —She decided to call it Lambie. —She was putting all her energy into games and such things—played cards with the utmost seriousness. She would keep catching people up at Provincetown on trivial inaccuracies and inattentions, as if we were playing a game—feeling, apparently, that the conversation was over her head, so that she would want to score and bring down the town: "I'm one up on you," etc. —Indignant at Katy Shubert's indications of anti-Semitism at Irvine's expense.

—Betty said that Frances had been the spoiled darling of the family, and that she always insisted on her right of way in a car and was always running into people— she was always bumping back fenders. On one occasion, she had knocked three children out of the back seat of a car she had run into behind and had been sued by the mother. Betty said that she had gone out and earned her own living—worked as a floorwalker at Macy's.

STAMFORD, 1936

[In the autumn, I went to live outside Stamford in Margaret de Silver's house (called Trees), which was isolated in the woods. Hatty first sent out a young mulatto woman named Celeste to take care of me, but she couldn't stand the loneliness and left. Then Hatty came and presently smuggled in without asking my permission several of her little grandchildren, whose mother was in the hospital insane. But I didn't mind this. The house was admirably designed: I lived in one of the little wings and Hatty and her family in the other, next to the kitchen. There was nothing but the big living room between them, so the two halves were quite independent. I relapsed into my old habit of working at night. I would go to bed about four—putting myself to sleep with slugs of gin—and get up for lunch about noon. There were many days when I never saw anyone but Hatty, though I quite often had people out from New York for lunch or for a night or two. In many ways, I much enjoyed this life.

I read *War and Peace* in Russian, and I was struck by Tolstoy's genius as a mimic—something which does not

come through in translation. He is one of the greatest
impersonators in literature—in the same way that Dickens
and Proust are. The narrative is all in a vein of his own—
very aloof and ironic. You usually cannot tell, in the
case of any given incident, whether he means it to be
tragic or comic, and it is possible for different people, or
for the same person at different times of life, to get quite
different impressions from *War and Peace* and *Anna
Karenina*. But the voice of Tolstoy himself is in itself
a kind of impersonation—of an aristocrat, away above
everybody, writing with a certain indifference, as if
talking in complete self-possession with a negligence of
the niceties of style. But the characters have a life of
their own. I seemed, in that winter silence, alone in the
solitary room, actually to hear their voices—Prince André,
Natasha, the old Kuragin, the old Bolkonsky. The epi-
sode in which the old Bolkonsky obliterates the traces
in the snow of Anatole Kuragin's carriage when he had
come to ask for the hand of the Princess Maria has
ever since been merged in my mind with my house in
the woods where I read it, when there was also snow on
the ground.

I made at the time the following notes:]

Tolstoy:* on father-son relation—in early scenes of
War and Peace, something we don't usually feel until
after our fathers are dead, and then we shouldn't be
able to write them because we know that the reality was
quite different. But Tolstoy's father had died when he
was nine.

Tolstoy did not put his whole self into his books as
Dostoevsky did. Dostoevsky was either the author of
Crime and Punishment and *The Brothers Karamazov*

* For EW's later view of Tolstoy, see his "Notes on Tolstoy,"
in *A Window on Russia* (1972)

or he was nothing. Tolstoy was always a nobleman and a landowner. It may be that the greatest novelists are men caught between the social classes, like Dostoevsky and Dickens.

Tolstoy could not be comfortable as he was, yet could not give up his responsibility—he merely transferred it to his wife, whom after all he had married at a mature age and the first part of his married life with whom he had spent writing that "heroic idyll of the Russian upper classes" (Mirsky), *War and Peace.* The short circuit between the upper class and the peasantry is beginning to be acutely felt in Tolstoy—his peasant mistress, by whom he had had a son—this son afterwards worked for one of his children. He gave his wife his diary to read before he married her, and she afterwards disguised herself as a peasant to see whether Tolstoy would take an interest in her.

That he couldn't, that he worked at his peasant schools, that he worked for two years to relieve the peasant famine, and that the Church would have had him in jail if his aunt, who was a Maid of Honor of the Empress (look this up),* hadn't intervened with the Tsar and saved him—certainly Tolstoy went further before the Revolution than any other articulate Russian had done. Lenin devoted more attention to him (*International Literature*) than to any other great Russian writer. *But* his relations with [Vladimir] Chertkov and the other pro-early-Christian religious characters, are something of which the later parody was the relations of the Tsar's family with Rasputin. Lenin, who was a middle-class man, technically a noble from the bureau-

---

* Tolstoy's aunts Elisabeth and Alexandrine were maids of honor to the Grand Duchess Marie Nicolaevna, daughter of Nicholas I. It was Alexandrine who used her influence in high circles and the court to help her nephew.

cratic rank of his father, but not from the point of view of land or power, and yet had no great estate dependent on him, no three hundred (male? look this up) souls. His mother and he had lost caste in Simbirsk through Alexander's execution—and they had lost Alexander.

Russian literature. Permeated with comedy and with comedy of a classical kind. The reason it seems wild, hysterical, extravagant, and mystical to Western readers is that it comes out of a feudal society, a society more primitive and with social contrasts more violent than ours. A classic point of view working in feudal material.

Russian language. Gibbon in his *Autobiography* on the difficulties of writing a history of Switzerland because he couldn't think of learning the barbarous German dialect. People used to feel the same about Russian. Karamzin got rid of German–Latin syntax and substituted French. Tolstoy, in *War and Peace*, makes a fool out of the French language. Out of the German he makes an oaf—an oaf wound up in the barbarous rituals of a crude Latinized language.

Between the study and the bed,
Liquor stands me in good stead.

But while we talk and scratch and grub about,
The silver rocket passes.

This morbid sleep—during the day—escape

Dreams about Margaret—I have begun having these dreams about Margaret again out here in the Stamford house—it is as if I kept trying to make the thing more probable, put up more obstacles to surmount between myself and the reality. Last night, October 29 (I'd gone to bed about twenty minutes to four and had lain awake in the complete silence and solitude), I thought that I had met a man—an editor in New York who looked something like the director of the Odessa hospital, but bigger, thicker-set, dark-haired and American, who was said to be madly in love with her. Why didn't I look her up? it suddenly occurred to me to ask myself. I heard that she was staying at a seedy little hotel—I asked Cobey Gilman about it, and he said that he had stayed there once when he was broke and gave a humorously depressing account of it. I went there, asked for Waterman, Canby, Wilson—I went upstairs, had a glimpse into the halls, it seemed almost like the ladies' equivalent for a Mills hotel—she had stayed there as Mrs. Edmund Wilson, they said this as if imitating her accent when she had given the name, as if they had thought she was snooty. —I could see her with her Scotch-Canadian dignity and her shyness, how she must have hated staying there. She was now at the so-and-so, a much bigger and better hotel uptown. She might be having a love affair with the editor, but she couldn't marry him, she was still married to me, she probably didn't want to marry him. I would telephone the hotel at once—if she wasn't there, I'd telegraph Camilla and find out where she was, and if Camilla didn't know, as possibly she wouldn't, there were other people out there from whom I could find out. I went into a large bar with a lot of rather well-to-do-appearing old bar habitués sitting around, and I called up. —There was no booth around the telephone, but I thought that that didn't matter, I was sure that she would see me, go back with me—the first time I had the wrong hotel—with the usual difficulties one has in dreams, but, finally succeeding, I looked up the right number—it was Wackham 95—a strange small number, but due, I knew, to the fact that the hotel was in an old rather exclusive section, which had a small set of numbers of its own. An old drinker with a red face and a white mustache made way for me to get to the open telephone, and I knew the number was going through and I should speak to her, when I woke up. —In this dream I had tried to safeguard myself: I didn't see her as I had before—there were obstacles, an attempt to do away with the impossibility of reality, but they were obstacles which could be overcome: I kept telling myself that I had never seen her dead, that there was no real reason for believing she was dead, that it was obviously not true that she was dead, as people told me of her being around—and even after I woke up I had to recall to myself that I had certainly seen her dead in the funeral parlor at Santa Barbara— that I had seen her pale and smooth and hard and rigid in death and now could never see her talking and affectionate, a little live human girl, again in New York, as I had thought I was going to in the dream. —Shy and warm, inarticulate and lively.

Election, Nov. '36—I found that I was quite cheered and stimulated, as I'd been depressed by the bad news from Europe. Went to cocktail party at Studin's and saw that other people had been affected the same way: Sherwood Anderson had, he said, begun celebrating early in the day—maybe we didn't have to have a dictator, after all. Studin said to Max Ernst, Well, what do you think of your country—and mine?—the only thing he regretted was those two states (Maine and Vermont). Ernst said that Roosevelt was going to demand a recount. Big two-page spread in *Daily News* (one of the early Roosevelt papers) showing the Roosevelt family frankly delighted, old Mrs. Roosevelt looking up at her son with proud, pleased, and shining eyes, which seemed to have come to life for the occasion—with some caption with the phrase, Your President. I felt for the first time in years that the President who had said that, if elected, he would be "President of all the people," had a real warmth of popular support behind him. They had voted, as someone said at the party, directly opposite to the way the papers had told 'em to. All the bugaboos raised by Hearst, the *Herald Tribune,* etc., did look very spectral the morning after. I found myself brooding with delight over the feelings of Hearst, Walter Lippmann, Betty Huling's mother, Al Smith, etc., taking each one up separately. —But then when I read Roosevelt's little messages and went over the record of his past Administration, I felt that the popular enthusiasm for him had more warmth and force than he. It had seemed for a moment to magnify him and vitalize him—but could it really? I should think that such a mandate would give anybody pretty solemn pause as to what their responsibilities were. How much was he moved?—how much merely gay at winning the college boat race? —At the very least, however, he exerts some kind of beneficent influence.

—Reports circulated by the opposition: his real name was Rosenfeld and he was the tool of a big Jewish conspiracy, who had been committing sacrificial murders, killing off Roosevelt's opponents, such as Cutting—Al Smith wouldn't dine at the White House for fear of being poisoned there.

—Father Coughlin* had said that if he couldn't raise nine million votes, he would stay off the air—all he had gotten was 900,000.

Provincetown—While Bubs Hackett was in the hospital in Washington having her baby, Brownie L'Engle

* Father C. E. Coughlin of Royal Oak, Michigan, whose broadcasts and journal, *Social Justice,* used the familiar anti-Semitic phrases of the Nazis.

got into the house—Chauncey, as Katy said, was putty in her hands—and redid several rooms, including Bubs's bedroom *à la moderne,* painting the floor orange, etc. —Bubs spent her first evening weeping.

Dos—Rosalind and I had taken the rowboat out and had had a terrible time with it: I asked Dos what the mysterious force was which, no matter how you rowed, kept bringing the boat back to shore—in spite of the fact that the current was going in the other direction. He said, You don't think it could be Trotsky, do you?

The King and Mrs. Simpson during November and early December '36. I played Edward's speech for Hatty, and she said he sounded "right pitiful." She said that she hoped she'd be faithful to him after he'd given up being king on her account.

Hatty. Her quietness, poise, soft-spokenness—the way she would pause a moment before replying when anything embarrassing or difficult came up—seriousness with which she stood a moment and studied the oil furnace when I explained it to her—easy mastery of anything, always knew what was wanted and could produce it: beds, china, silver, food from Muriel Draper's and Mr. McMullin's iceboxes, tablecloth with Yale Club on it when K. was there. —Perfect tact about Scottsboro boys, Harlem riot, etc., until she knew what we thought— intelligence and desire to better herself showing occasionally through deference of old-fashioned Southern colored servant. She had apparently come North after her husband died in order to better herself, but had never been able to, because, though she worked hard, she didn't have the right psychology—contrast with the mulatto girl Celeste, who wrote little poems and missed the radio, whom Hatty sent out here with me at first. Hatty tended to think that she belonged to the people she

worked for—used to try to lend me money when I was
hard up, didn't want to take over $10 when I offered
her more, when she came out to Stamford to work. On
the other hand, would occasionally take things she liked
or found useful—Helen Vinton insisted that she went off
to Provincetown with one of her best table napkins
pinned on the baby for a diaper.

Daughters' families used up everything she had so
that she guessed she never would get ahead—guessed
she never *would* have nuthin. Daughter who went insane after birth of baby—couldn't afford any more birth
control. Her conversations over the phone from Stamford
with her son-in-law, who had the landlord and the duns
closing in on him: "Just stay there and stand up to it
like a man!" —Gentle, soft, and sweet voice over phone
ordering groceries—always said "please" a good many
times. —Sensitive very refined face—when she was nervous and hard-taxed I always knew because one corner
of her mouth would twitch, or rather, she would seem to
be biting it. —Would always say, "Yessuh, Mr. Wilson."
Helen claims that once, when she had stuffed potatoes
in their wrappers for dinner, I said, "Those stewed pears
are good, Hatty"—she said, "Yes, Mr. Wilson." —At
Stamford, when I was bilious, she turned out to have
epsom salts when I expressed a wish for some one morning. On another occasion, when she thought I had been
drinking the night before and would need it, she appeared with some without my having asked for it. —I got
to feel a deep sympathy and affection for her at Stamford. She was very sweet talking to Dolores [her little
granddaughter, the child of the insane daughter]. Always
remembered everybody's telephone number and what she
had had for dinner the last time they were here and tried
not to have the same thing again. If I told her an Englishman was coming, she would know that beefsteak was the

right thing to have. Decided that Mrs. Draper was real nice—"I mean [a favorite expression of hers] she's real nice. —You mightn't think so at first, but she's real nice." Thought Maria Michelaevna would be a good person for me to marry—"She has such nice manners 'n' all, you know." Dan Mebane was such a nice little gentleman. —She took *The Big Money* away and read it. She thought that Harlem was hell—only the whores and crooks made money—some of the girls got $100 a night from white men. On our ride to Provincetown, she would keep remarking, of any pretty little town we passed through and called her attention to, that she wouldn't mind living there. Had never lived in the country before, liked Provincetown, left it with reluctance, had stayed up there as long as possible, hoping I was coming back. Baby, who wasn't used to white people, grabbed a colored child in a passing car, so that they couldn't go until they had detached her. —When she prospered, she would apparently lay in rather gaudy furniture and decorations, which she would pay for on the installment plan, but which, when she wasn't doing so well and wasn't able to pay the installments, would invariably be taken away from her. There were always people trying to garnish her wages. She put bright green curtains of hers in my bedroom on 53rd Street, thinking I needed them. —Her mastery of the stove that heated the water at Provincetown—wouldn't have men to fix pipe, just bought the joint and fitted it herself. Tailoring my evening clothes at Stamford. [I hadn't worn a dinner jacket for years, and my old one was now much too small for me, but I found that I had to dress for a party at the Soviet consul's.] —She is strong—long arms, big hands—helped me get sailboat up on bulkhead at Provincetown, would carry beds around at Stamford. —Her tight black wool around her oval African head beginning to turn white in patches.

Mary Updike's baby. [Mary Updike had been my secretary at *The New Republic,* and she was living not far from me in Connecticut.] When I went over to Mary Updike's and used the bathroom to shave, it woke up the baby, who had been put to bed next door. She began to cry and went on almost all the time I was there—the most feminine and appealing crying I have ever heard a baby do: it was really more like warbling; she would repeat a phrase, as it were, as if she were singing, and it didn't sound distressed or distressing, but as if she were engaged in a kind of recreation which enabled her to express herself. —Later on, I saw her in their car—she was a homely but cunning little blond pale-eyed thing with a kind of flat button nose.

Dream about Margaret, early December 1936*—at Stamford.* My subconscious mind had invented a new device: I thought there was another woman who resembled her exactly and who was still alive. She resembled Margaret so closely that we even had memories in common of our earlier life together. I saw her, and we arranged to marry, but then she was dining with somebody else that night, and I let her go without getting her telephone number or her address. Then I realized that if I could only find out, I could be with her that night— could love her and sleep with her. I saw her in my mind in her slip. As I was trying to think of someone who knew where she was, I woke up.

Reading late at night after work, I found myself correcting the sentences of the author to make them read the way I wanted mine to. [I made this into a poem.]

My hand on a book—At Stamford one day, when I had long been absorbed in reading and writing, I looked at my hand on the page of the book I was reading and suddenly saw it as an animal's paw with the fingers lengthened to claws and become prehensile for climbing around, in strange, in incredible contrast to the detached and limitless life of the mind: that was what we were, we still carried with us those animal paws, those were what we had to work with: stubby fingers with nails at the service of the dreaming horizonless mind: a shock to me then in my detached and dreaming literary life.

Trip to Pittsburgh, December 27–30, 1936. [I went on to see Mary (Blair) in the hospital.] The stony hills bristling with the leafless sticks of trees, the greenish muddy river, the bleakness and the grit—a row of eight big square and grimy houses, desolate with broken windows, and between the last of them and another smaller house a great long line of Monday washday clothes, shirts, and counterpanes pink and red—the first ridge of the Alleghenies (?) —You look down on industrial towns, castle (?) like wooden houses, which have not had enough paint, that spread away from the base of brick chimneys— a stubble field looking poor enough with the wry topknots of corn sheaves—the railroad gashed through a kind of livid purple soil and pale brittle-looking rock— (the stumps of broken stone piles of a ruined bridge in the Susquehanna)—big dairy barns, which need paint, too—bristly ridge hills like a starved stoat's back—tombstone-pebbled graveyards on hillsides—in the river there were little rowboats half sunk or lodged in the mud— the landscape is brown in shades without warmth, bristling and bleak—that friable-looking unpleasant-colored rock—a wretched house, with milk cans on the porch, on a wretched creek that runs down the meadow and trickles away in the mud—on the outskirts of one of the more dismal towns, a baseball field which, though it was only December, did not seem to have been used for so long that the weeds had partly won it back (reclaimed it) and the wire backstop was leaning flimsy—a few Christmas wreaths lurking in the windows—Altoona: now we get to the blackened houses—good God!—people love and feed their living bodies in them!—just outside the city, the cliff of a big tin-can dump, where two men stand, looking out at the view or looking for possible salvage?—other men below seem to be digging in the dump—black hillsides—totally black town above a great blackened sweep of hairy country, lit up only by the gay red front with gold letters of a five-and-ten-cent store— hillsides soggy with the wet of melted snow—and now great gray opaque stalactite clusters were dripping down the dark rocky cuts, and the gray families of identical company houses no longer made any pretense of the normal social organism of a village, making a line below the gray slag (or cinder?) mountains, varied only by churches just like them, which seemed to be neglected or unused (the front steps had been knocked away from one of them—stratified rock easily chipped—a sudden red ribbon of slag burning from a car down a gray slope)— and now an all-black town, really black, with its hills behind it, the whole thing an unbroken mask of black, a mask for nature and for life? I was surprised to see, farther along, that a house we passed had blue shades, drawn slatternly to irregular lengths (Johnstown)—a great square dark industrial building of some kind out-bulking everything around it, a cluster of blast furnaces, dusty, wound around with their intestinelike pipes: Bethlehem Steel—dense and yellowish clouds rise from behind the hills that are not the clouds of the sky—the sun went down, red, distant, and dull, beyond the gray thickets of the foreground (through which the train was going)—(striated livid rocks)—double family houses with pairs of chimneys sending out double streams of smoke. —Then it got too dark to see the most wretched Pittsburgh environs.

Pittsburgh. Old Stevenson Building at corner of Ellsworth and Center, where Roy and Lois lived in their penthouse [Lois is Mary's sister] (cigar-store wooden girl with cigarette in her mouth, merry-go-round wooden house rigged up on ventilator on roof, big board with everybody's signatures written on it, Dali Christmas card with shaggy shoulders, drawer coming out of head and buttoned-down breasts with little brass nipples, mural land- and seascapes painted by Roy, one or two paintings and pieces of sculpture in Roy's study, old oval-topped windows and American encyclopedia in very old shabby calf toppling off the edge of a desk which was stuffed with papers in the old-fashioned pre-office-routine way, and his dance posters and autograph books)—the Italian music teacher with his large Dutch painting, sick and thin, the second time I was there, and sitting up on a kind of army cot—stairs you had to walk up, old grille-caged elevator chained for the night, special little stair to their penthouse, wide lobby, wide stairs, large elevator—Duquesne Beer signs alternating with Iron City Beer, in bright-orange neon—I always located the Stevenson Building by one of these—that spot in the city looked old and like the first part of the city that had been built and worked in and used by machines and serious Scotch-Irish (whose names began with Mc) sitting over their desks full of papers, talking short and pungent when they met each other in the halls.

—The smog (as they called it) had settled down, what with the smoke and the dampness of winter, in that valley, and made the air damp and gray and flat—when, coming out of the Stevenson Building and going for

Roy's car, we went through an auto showroom which had a garage behind it, the smell of leather and rubber and new paint was refreshing, I breathed it with gusto as one breathes the smell of earth in a cellar, after that flat and thick air. —Those pretty and thin and sometimes little scrawny-necked Scotch-Irish-looking women—to which the West (Pittsburgh) had added sex appeal: coat girls, sales girls, waitresses, nurses in the hospital, women in the street.

—Pittsburgh a mill town already dying, no longer a mill town on the rise and on its way to be a big metropolis, as Chicago is now becoming, the neon signs not so many or so high in the sooty air and the people on the streets (after all, much more like small-town people on the streets than like the crowds of a great city; Mary spoke of the freedom of New York), only the movies, only the crass department stores, only the old turning-cheap hotels—and the cinders sifting down on your hands, so that you had to be washing them all the time— the streetcars starting or stalling along, trying to prevent the taxis from passing them—the millionaires who had built the great palaces and had very soon moved away— gone crazy in New York or Paris and left the palaces dead—and they no longer tore up the William Penn Hotel, with people under the bed and everything, with the terrific parties they gave—streetcars (from my window in the hotel) lumbering home with people and tooting—the whole of a winter night of rolling-scraping wheels and tired sirens subsiding (growing fainter) toward some destination.

—Ride in the afternoon with Roy: so dark, air so opaque, on the hill that looks down into the valley, that I couldn't see a thing: only the flat cutout shapes of big factory buildings and bridges, flat as if cut out of gray pasteboard against the mountainside of flat even gray. —Old sharp and steady-eyed sarcastic German Seibel who had just been fired from his twenty-five-year job as literary and dramatic critic on the *Sun-Telly* for, as he believed, his pro-Roosevelt activities on the air during the campaign—had been on a tour of the German Turnvereins throughout the country and had found only about three percent for Hitler (except in New York and the Atlantic ports), had evidently had his troubles during the war. —Store and studio for Catholic statues, where we went to see Italian sculpture, but found instead his factotum, strange Negroid fairy (whose father, nevertheless, had been a professor of chemistry at Northwestern and whose sister had married a white man in Chicago) who had worked for Arthur Brisbane (just dead). Brisbane would receive hundreds of letters every time he dug up an old 1906 special Sunday article and published it in a slightly refurbished form, and this maintained him in his conviction that he was one of the greatest men in the world—would do nothing at all all day, then wake his secretary up at four in the morning to get something out right away.

CONCORD

D. Telegram, which went wrong, forwarded to Red Bank when I was at Stamford—I had spent a strange serious industrious day, full of a coexisting confidence and suspense, waiting for a telegram or a telephone call—finally took a six o'clock train for Boston—went to Bellevue, called up Hatty and Gloucester, where there was only one hotel and she was not there; then looked up hotels in Salem. I took a hot bath, still vastly contented, read myself to sleep with Gibbon's *Autobiography*. In the morning I called up Hatty and got her to read me the mail: Trotsky Defense Committee, letter evidently from somebody who had read something of mine in *The New Republic*. Called up Gloucester again: no luck. Called up Salem: yes, but she had gone to Gloucester. Lunched with Bob Linscott, talked about Russia, and got him to cash check—walked around Boston a little, thinking that she wouldn't be back in Salem till late afternoon. The weather was quite crisp and clear: it seemed nice to see the old Common. I finally took the half-past-three train—thought about John and Louise and me that summer at Swampscott, tried to identify the

North Station as the one where we had done our gin swigging but couldn't retrieve it so as to make it fit. At Salem, I checked my big suitcase at the newsstand: they said I'd have to get it before 6:45, as the newsstand— this characteristically Boston—closed then.

At the hotel, to which I walked, killing time, I was surprised to learn that she was there. I gave my name— which made the hotel impossible for us—and went up to her room. I found her white and travel-prosaic, energetically charging around the room and packing. She didn't want to let me embrace her, had been about to run away in a panic. She had called up and traced the telegram and written me a letter, she told me—had thought at first I didn't want to come. We set out for Concord, after a nervous bill-paying and cocktail: dreary bleak pinched and commonplace industrial suburbs— when the train had pulled out of the station at Lynn, she remarked that we ought to have gotten off there— I had thought of it, too, but the notion had chilled me, also. I was still constrained by the long time, now four years, during which I had been unable to prevail over her. I had bought two bottles of Mt. Vernon Rye, and we left all our belongings on a seat and went into the smoking car, where she smoked several cigarettes. On the way back—another Boston touch—the elderly conductor would not let us go through between the cars, because the train was rocking and the car ends were not enclosed—until we stopped at a station. The whole thing was rather awkward and conversation somewhat difficult—we should not have had to travel together. In the North Station, we had discussed Boston as a possible place to stay, but she was afraid of seeing people she knew, and I could see she preferred Concord, where she had known the Colonial Inn as a child—when the little Boston children had asked her how she liked it, she had answered, "I've seen better and I've seen worse"—where we could "live on the Square like a true married pair," she had said. She had been somewhat unnerved that day by having passes made at her by the lawyer in Gloucester—he thought she was the best thing he'd seen in a long time, she explained—then she reverted to the subject after a lapse of time, during which other things had been said: "There's not enough for the rats up there!" —In the Concord train, she said suddenly, "You won't frighten me, will you?"

Concord had completely changed since I had visited it that May in the early twenties. The square was more built up—new buildings, a regular tourist stop now. I signed the register Mr. and Mrs. Edgar Watson. B.'s wrapped-up canvas dragged along. We had to wait to be shown the room, old ladies going up and downstairs, over whom we looked at one another. She was nervous, we looked at the postcards. She sat down, but as we finally started upstairs, she indicated that she thought that a room on the ground floor was one in which she and B. had stayed. When we first went into the room, she felt the softness and resiliency of the bed, out of bravado, bending over it and bouncing it with both hands. I ordered ice, we waited nervously and awkwardly for them to bring it, but we started in on the whiskey simply with water from the tap. She unpacked some things from her suitcase, including a sort of dull rose-red or maroon dressing gown. She said, "I've got beautiful clothes." (She had bought them, I learned afterwards, especially.) Then she sat down in a big arm-chair, and I sat down beside her. "So what?" she said. When the ice came, I said, "Let's get on the bed." She complied, but asked whether I didn't think it would be piquant to have dinner with the old ladies first. I told her to take off her dress; I took off everything but my underclothes, looking the other way, then lay down on the side of the bed, turned away from her. When she came to me in the luscious dressing gown, I was surprised to find her completely naked. I went to her breast, which was lovely—she said that they had been spoiled, something about their having been held in at the time she was having milk before her baby had miscarried—she tried to direct my attention to the right one, though I had started on the left, because she thought it was better than the other—confessed that she was afraid they weren't pretty, that was why she had never let me kiss them, not knowing how firm and round (and rather low) they were, how tender and white and with darling little pink nipples. But when I looked at her lower down, I was really amazed at her beauty—I had always supposed that her claim to classic beauty was one of her compensations for her bad jaw, but now I could see it was true: she was the only woman I had ever known who really looked like a Greek statue—her waist was beautiful, and it also made her back extraordinarily beautiful—though she thought she still had too much flesh on her stomach—her legs were straight and beautifully proportioned—her toes were round and very small in proportion to her feet, she had had them made up red, in spite of the fact that, as she said, she knew that I didn't like it—although they were so pretty in themselves that it seemed to me all right, I had never seen anything like them—and her sex was, I had to recognize, the only genuinely beautiful, as distinguished from sexually stimulating one, that I had ever seen—she had the lighter hair of a blonde, and it was coppery so that I had to admit that her hair was, after all, that color naturally—I accused her of having said that she had dyed it, but she replied in her dear little-girl way, "I never said I dyed it," adding, "I put henna on it, that's all." She was rounded like the mons

Veneris of a statue—round and smooth, feminine, plump, and her vagina did its female work of making things easy with a honey-sweetly-smooth profusion which showed that I had misjudged her again in supposing her unresponsive to caresses. Indeed, it was so smooth and open that after the first few moments I could hardly feel it. She had begged me again not to frighten her—she had jumped a little when I had touched her clitoris, which was also very feminine, deeply embedded—the most embedded, I think, I had ever known. She made me stop my movement and did something special and gentle herself, seeming to rub herself in some particular way— and then climaxed with a self-excited tremor which also seemed to me strangely mild for a woman of so much energy and passion. I went on, trying to come—but she was all the more slippery now for the brimming of female fluid. I stopped for a while, then went at it again and came, though not feeling it very acutely. —Her back was classically beautiful and almost unbelievable—her buttocks were at once lovely-looking and hard and tight, instead of soft.

She got up and began to dress, and I lay and watched her. She looked at herself in the glass all the time with her big eyes and her mouth half-open and a little horsy with teeth, as it became when she relaxed from the gaze of others. Her clothes, I could see, were new from the store, and at every stage of the proceedings she looked exasperatingly attractive: she had a slip which was green and blue and flowered and which looked almost like a dress, and her legs and feet in her (gray, I think) stockings were attractive almost in the way that women's legs were in stocking advertizements and as I don't remember seeing any woman's look after she had been made love to, before. She was paying so little attention to me, I thought, and regarding herself so intently in the mirror that I accused her of being narcissistic. She said wasn't it true that every woman who wanted to please men had also to please herself. I said yes, I supposed so. I beckoned her in my brown bathrobe from the bed, and she said, "Now you want me to make love to you!" and added that I looked "like one of those monks in Boccaccio"—which I resented a little, and it tinged our dinner.

There was almost nobody left in the dining room. I accused her a little peevishly of having married E. off to F. when he was actually in love with her, and then having become annoyed with him when he went stale on her (F.). We walked out. I said, "Is this your coat?" as I got her black sealskin coat from the coat rack. When we were out of doors—one of the silent but prying men who seemed to be running the hotel had been standing around—he said, "Don't you know your wife's coat, Mr. Watson? Those are the things husbands pay money for and remember." On the way along the square, she felt sick—we went to the drugstore, where the town boys were standing around, and she got a prescription filled for Mercurochrome. The old druggist said, "Do you know how to use this?"—and in his severe and fatherly New England way, like the old conductor on the train, explained to her that it was strong and that she ought to dilute it.

We went back and got undressed. When she went into the bathroom with the Mercurochrome, I told her to be careful with it. She said, "Don't you want me to be all eaten inside?" in a cute and darling way but, it seemed to me, also in a way that was rather narcissistic, as if adopting the man's point of view about herself for her own satisfaction. I lay on the bed, but she held me off again and sat down in the armchair, and we had another one of those conversations—till I made her come over to the bed. The second time, I climaxed first, and she said, "Are you angry with me because I didn't love you when you loved me?" I worked her with my finger till she did come. She said, "I usually love right away with great abandon," and, "I never saw such virility— you're so masculine!"—whether to flatter me or not, I don't know—"I'm only used to once." She said that I hadn't frightened her. "It's all new to me!" —I never knew precisely what she meant by this. She said she liked the hair on my chest—an admirer of hers had shaved himself in order to be like B.—he hadn't known that this was just the wrong thing to do. She wouldn't take hold of my penis. I moved the two single beds together, and I thought about how Margaret and I used to do this in order to be together when we were staying in hotels—I had never thought about this since. We had all the usual difficulties about sleeping with this arrangement. I was all waked up—she had expected me to go to sleep—I told her that it always had that effect on me—she said that must be because I wasn't satisfied. I said that it always made me talk, read poetry, sing foreign-language songs. She said she would like to hear me read poetry. I was thinking—it was the kind of thought which always seemed to me dramatic and beautiful just after making love—that, after all, nothing was perfect, nothing the final satisfaction one had hoped for: there she was so incomparably beautiful and her vagina was so wide and wet that I hadn't been able to feel her. She asked me whether I had noticed the two little pink butterly buds up the front of the bodice of her new pink nightgown. I lay and talked for a long time. When I would peek out one side of the window shade, I would see the cars all lined up at the curb in front of a big white church, where there was evidently a prayer meeting or a sociable going on. When we were trying to go to sleep, she would turn over very obligingly backwards and forwards with me. We heard almost all the hours struck by the church that was right outside the window, and I conceived a great distaste for that church and for the shiny cars lined up in front of it and for the drugstore and the whole town of modern Concord. She told me that it had hurt her, that she was having cramps, that she hadn't been supposed to make love while her cervix and her tubes were being attended to. Later she seemed to feel better. Later, when it was getting light, I began to stroke her mount of Venus, of which I was greatly enamored, and had an erection and turned and pressed on her. She said, "Do you want me?" She lay still and seemed to feel it in some particular spot— not her clitoris—in her curious special way, and climaxed with her same mild tremor. Then I made her close her legs—she looked lovely, with disheveled red hair and her great open liquid female brown eyes—then I made her open her legs and came. I had wanted, in order not to hurt her, not to put it in too far, but she had told me to. When the evening before I had been making her come with my finger, she had uttered little low incoherent phrases, which seemed to come out of her inmost woman's nature—I wish I had been able to understand them, but cannot even remember them except something like, "You were in deep, weren't you?" I think she half hoped that I would get her pregnant, that that would decide the thing for her.

Then she got up and took a thorough bath, and when she came back, I could see from her changed manner that she was suffering a revulsion. She wouldn't stay another night. I was irritated, and I felt, when I went into the bathroom and saw myself in the mirror, that I probably looked pretty cheesy, with the bump on my chin where I had been hit [by O.—I find that I have omitted this incident], which I had cut while shaving and which was hanging down like some unpleasant growth from my all too fat and debauched face. "Let me go back into my shell now!" she said. I watched her put on each garment and noticed with slight exasperation how attractive she looked at each stage. She packed her bag with her usual efficiency.

We went down to breakfast. My nerves were pretty strained—though with the strain of excessive love-making and sleeplessness, which involves a certain satisfaction and which you know will be certainly and progressively relieved, rather than with the hellish torment of a hangover—we hadn't drunk much of the whiskey. There was nobody in the dining room except one of the Concord-bred managers with spectacles and a brown mustache. When we made for the table which we had the night before, he said, "Do you know where you're going?" D., in her bold and masterful way, answered, "Yes, we know where we're going. We're going to the table we had last night!"—and, just as she had the night before at the time of the incident of the coat, burst out with some remark about how it was getting colder.

A man who looked like Thoreau and charged us $10 drove us into Boston—the smooth road: a good thing for our nerves—I thought that I was able to identify, and I pointed out to her, Emerson's house. We sat looking slightly away from one another.

I met her for lunch at the Parker House. I had walked up there from the South Station, had lost my way and rambled up behind the State House through streets I didn't remember to have seen before. I began to feel better and content and elated: the day was bright and cold—Boston with its English streets and buildings was almost like being in a foreign city. I stopped in at a bookstore which sold foreign periodicals and bought the

New Statesman and Nation and the *Saturday Review of Literature,* and read them while I was waiting in the Parker House lobby. She was late. The lawyer had talked to her a long time, had convinced her that the property would be valuable again, that she oughtn't to surrender her claims, but on the contrary get the other heirs to give up theirs to her. I told her how I had felt on my walk—(had been feeling less fine while waiting). She said, "I suppose this must be a great moment of triumph for you." But as she was leaving me to take the train before mine, she gave me what was, I thought, the most affectionate look I had ever had from her.

When I saw her again, she looked—as I have never seen a woman do—as if she felt she was one who had sinned.

March 8, '37. She got over the guilty phase later. When she came in to meet me at the Amen corner, she asked, "Do you like me as much as I like you?" B.'s subconscious, she said, had been coming to life: he hadn't been able to sleep for three nights after she had come back, but had said it was the Spanish situation. Later he had dreamed that he was going to kill me with a glass lamp, but thought that she cared for me, so didn't. Then she went away, and he decided that the glass lamp was not a very good weapon for suicide, and she came back. He asked her where she was going whenever she went out for an errand. When I stopped at the Washington Square Bookshop to get a check cashed, she got out on the other side of the cab, as I had had premonition she would do, but I caught her and brought her into the shop. Afterwards, when we were riding uptown and through the park, it seemed to me that she liked me better and that we had come closer than ever. I kissed her a lot and she liked it. I would cover her eyes with my mouth and lick her eyelids, which I found excited me. Then I put my hand inside her dress and held it over her breast and she made no resistance as she used to do. When I took my hand away, her breast looked so lovely and round and small, just one side showing in her blouse—she started to cover it up, but I told her to leave it, because nobody could see it but me, so she did. I told her in detail how lovely her body was, and she was pleased so that she laughed—almost like giggling—at the compliments, like a little pleased embarrassed girl, as she had done when I first looked her up at her job. When I said she was the prettiest woman I had ever seen, she said, "Really? the very prettiest?" When I talked about 14 East 60th Street, she said, "I can't bear that place! You have a streak of the most awful New Jersey vulgarity—just like my family!" This for some reason delighted me, and I thought about it with gratification afterwards—and reflected that Helen Vinton's criticisms, usually along psychoanalytic lines, irritated me. Perhaps I liked this streak in D. herself— perhaps I like to be thought vulgarly ostentatious; but primarily it was the fact that she said it so lovingly, perhaps because she loved me for it—whereas Helen is sharp and spiteful. She told me that at the time I had first known her, she had told B. that I thought she looked like a Greek goddess. He had said, "You look half like a Greek goddess, half like one of those dolls you put over a lamp." "There's something sort of cheap about me," she added.

NEW YORK AND
STAMFORD, 1937

[EW continued to divide his time between New York and Stamford during the next couple of years; he was deeply immersed in work on his *Finland Station* book; however, he saw through the press in 1936 *Travels in Two Democracies* and in 1937 brought out three unproduced plays under the title *This Room and This Gin and These Sandwiches*. He also gathered a number of literary essays of the past few years in the volume *The Triple Thinkers*; these included his study of Flaubert, his important essay on the "ambiguity" of Henry James, a paper on Pushkin, a tribute to Bernard Shaw at eighty, and an essay on "Marxism and Literature." This book appeared in 1938.]

Fairies in the room next to mine at the Lafayette. Deep rather mellowly gruff and pleasant English voice. He had just come up from Washington, was arranging a passage back to England—and a lighter softer voice, evidently Harvard, because he called up the Harvard Club and wanted to know if he had left something there. I was interested to observe the English and impressed by the sang-froid, dignity, and ease with which the elder man seemed to carry it off, matter-of-fact, friendly, only occasionally dropping anything in the way of affection: "I like you, you know." The younger man said that if something or other hadn't happened, they would never have met. The older man: "You don't feel any worse than you did an hour ago, do you?" Younger man: "I feel better." He seemed to be the complete university punk, always supinely assenting to and playing up to the other man. When the older man was evidently pissing in the washbasin, the younger man said, "It's long." The older man, letting the water run, presently said, "Easy!" but in the same quiet, friendly, matter-of-fact way. The older man was packing to leave the next day. I finally got sick of listening to them and yelled to them to shut up—whereupon the older man began to whistle "God Save the King." He kept on packing, however, and the conversation continued. When I yelled again, the older man whistled "Drink to me only with thine eyes." After I had yelled for the first time, he began telling the younger man about how he had seen a beautiful girl in Washington.

At the Soviet consul's. At the party I went to at the Soviet consul's to celebrate the new constitution, I ran into George Soule, who, from his early slim and unobtrusive self, had swollen up like a balloon—then Joe Freeman appeared, dressed in a sack suit though everybody else was in evening dress, as if he had slipped in underground through the butler's pantry—and he, too, had swollen out to the same middle-aged convexity. It surprised me: it gave both of them a new mildness, a new uninterestingness, for all their bulk a new insubstantiality. Their faces, now also puffed out above their puffed-out persons, seemed themselves a little surprised at having lost their lean and earnest character—like puff-fish blown up by children. Then I reflected that I myself had filled out and did not perhaps look so very much different. There we were all bumping together like toy balloons which have been allowed to float to the ceiling; and we were perhaps floating above the proceedings—the situation of the Soviets at that time in relation to the bourgeois world and the radicals—in very much the same fashion. —I had never been able to go to one of these parties before, because I had never before had the pants to my evening clothes—which had finally been dug out of an old suitcase and marvelously enlarged and patched up by Hatty.

Dream about Margaret. This time I thought I had found somebody different who looked exactly like her—so that I couldn't be deceived again by finding out I couldn't have her.

Visit to Betty Huling at Larchmont, Aug. 5–6, '37. The Shore Club; Betty and Frances on Rosalind's diving; their tennis, which they had to have; the players looked pretty in a vivid but severe and dry way in their white clothes against the clay courts; footbath for athlete's foot; men compelled to wear tops.

Larchmont, peonies, phlox, hollyhocks, snowballs, and greenish-blue hydrangeas, white sails on the Sound, Long Island quite near, seven miles.

Larchmont with its neat and bright and wonderfully equipped Shore Club—with its cockscombs, salvia, dahlias, snapdragons, elephant's-ears, calla lilies—with its dark green foliage and garish red flowers—houses, a funny mixture, new stucco and fake Elizabethan cottages and new colonial houses with bright whitewashed brick façades and furniture on the shallow front porch brightly covered in reds and blues—in a confusion with the old wooden houses of the eighties and earlier, with wooden fretwork of icicles dripping from the roof of the piazza or many decorative newel posts appearing in all sorts of places—or a few old bare gray faded unpainted frame houses from the day when all these places were just small towns, maybe with a thin-haired and colorless old lady sitting alone on the porch and looking out at the traffic on the Post Road—the houses close together on their lawns with such bright flowers and heavy greenery, but the people not knowing each other, as little neighbors as in New York, along the concrete avenues—Jews (iron dogs, an enormous pair of white griffins guarding the entrance of one of the larger houses)—Jews next door to the Hulings—lots of radio and howling children, one family had rented the house, but several others came to spend holidays in it—a sultry day in suburban Larchmont with the greenery thick around the piazza—I was stupefied by sun on the beach, steak for dinner and drinks.

The sultry, almost suffocating day, house enclosed by greenery, old fancy but clumsy houses of eighties or nineties—porch that ran around in an arc considerably more, I believe, than a semicircle, screened in by vines—all kinds of knickknacks: flowerpots hanging by chains but without any flowers in them, rocking chairs, little stands for cigarette trays and things, with only three legs, so that they fell over—Betty leaned one against the arm of my rocking chair, so that I could set my cocktail on it, but whenever I forgot and rocked, the little stand would topple over on the side where it had no leg. Little windmill weather vanes and cutout wooden figures of little women with sunbonnets and watering pots stuck in the flower beds by Mrs. Huling's rather sloppy phlox.

Big living room (high, thin, ugly radiators and hot-air pipes from the floor to the ceiling), around which the

piazza curved: at front end, two very bad and crude
large family portraits of a woman and a man, in whom
could be seen, however, quite distinct resemblances to
the Hulings. A fine old mahogany claw-legged table, but
with some kind of dreary rug spread over it. Betty's gigantic tennis cup on the floor; and more of her cups
standing on a little table; a miniature of Kay in a case
propped open; old upholstered rocking chairs with upholstered footstools in front of them and straight upholstered chairs with a variety of coarse lace tidies on
their backs; old mirror with heavy gilt frame; grandfather's clock. A great lot of knickknacks: clocks that
looked Chinese and Chinese pagodas, an enormous
brown glass German beer cylinder, with a towering ornate top and a lot of German verses on it; one of those
(ecclesiastical) things you can open and close, with
Raphael's panels of the Sistine Madonna in it (?); glass
candelabra; a small bookcase, with a pair of bowls of
glass flowers on top of it and full of thick volumes on
genealogy, the *Mayflower*, the symbolism of the American flag, etc.; a great chart of the barons of England
spread open and thumbtacked to the mantelpiece, with
rather decorative bright-red coats of arms (something
else of the same kind on the wall in the hall); an immense crockery turtle which Mrs. Huling had carried
back all the way from somewhere and had given Frances
to keep her door open, but it had given Frances the
willies, so that she couldn't sleep; a carved camel from
Egypt. They always kept the bow window at the front
of the room closed—the girls didn't even open them
that hot night: only the windows at the other end when
we were playing anagrams—and it smelled like old-
fashioned shut-in parlors: there was a sort of miniature
mahogany horsehair couch at this end of the room, too.
—On the floors a variety of rugs, fitted in so as to leave

none of the floor bare: one or two old red Oriental ones, like the one we used to have in the hall at Red Bank.

The dining room was full of ornate silver and luster-ware pitchers and things in whatnots. Mrs. Huling had at one time had three complete silver tea sets out, but the girls had made her put two of them away. The first time I went there, there was a most elaborate display of bottles—wines and liqueurs and liquors—on the side-board and some of them in bottles which looked pre-Prohibition, and Mrs. Huling, when I commented on them, had asked what kind of wine I would like for lunch, but I had declined. Betty said that the old bottles were still there, because her mother had never offered anybody anything. But when I came when her mother wasn't there, they had all been put away.

Beyond this, there was an enclosed porch, all glass, in which they ate in summer, and it was rather like eating in a greenhouse, with all the plants outside instead of inside. They had obtained an old lady whom they called Deanie—such as only a Vermonter could have dredged up—who cooked and waited on table with a certain amount of assistance from the girls in the way of stacking and carrying out the plates. Also, they didn't have butter plates, in spite of the elaborate sets of things on display: Betty explained that they didn't have them— "I think those things are going out, anyway." The great staple seemed to be a certain kind of meat loaf with slices of cold tomato, which they had for both the lunches I ate there. For dinner, they sunk us on that hot night with beefsteak, boiled potatoes, peas, cold consommé, salad, and peach shortcake with whipped cream. Deanie had a figure straight down in front—in fact, a little concave—she was so thin and flat and straight that she seemed hardly to have a human body. She had a nice blue dress and a bow tied under her chin—she was very quiet and mild—a slight look of amazement through her spectacles. Betty told me that Deanie had belonged to quite a good family—they had had servants—a good-for-nothing brother, I think, had squandered all their money. Betty's mother had a hard time keeping servants, because she always made terrible scenes with them over all sorts of breaches of proprieties which they had never been instructed to observe. —Mrs. Huling used to trim vines out on the porch in order to overhear when Betty and I were eating in this room. After having listened for some time to more or less confidential matters, she would take up the conversation emphatically and coolly.

The kitchen was wonderful: everything was hung with little pink-checked muslin curtains—frills like panties along under the china closet, of which Betty explained to me the purpose was concealment of pots and pans that looked "ugly" on the shelf underneath. The kitchen was big and high-ceilinged, so that the hangings looked silly and strange—also, oilcloth hangings, I think.

The garage and the side lawn, walled off from the neighbors with hollyhocks, peonies, and phlox, exuberant but rather blowzy and unkempt, were also cluttered up with junk. I noted, under the windows of the outside pantry where the enormous refrigerator was kept, lying on the ground a sort of plaster window box with an Italian frieze of cupids.

The hall: there was an arduous and turning staircase, with a desk at the turn on a large landing where Mrs. Huling had her headquarters and ruled the house. Immense photographs of the Acropolis and the Castle of Sant'Angelo, I guess, on the Tiber.

My bedroom was the one where Mr. and Mrs. Huling slept: basin with running water in room; little bathroom with closet with pink toilet paper and shower which Betty said she didn't think worked. Family pictures all over walls and on mantel and tables and dresser. Fireplace—in sitting room, also—made to look rather machinelike and bleak by leaving deep cracks between the bricks and painting white lines in these. Beds of rather cheaplooking finish of a kind which Mrs. Huling must at some definite moment have decided to substitute for old ones— twins instead of the big double bed—with a matting effect in spaces at the bottom and lights to read by with shades that you had to take off and that were just at the height to hit you in the back of the head. Ceiling white with a raised design of some kind of fancy but unattractive squares. A big water bottle and glass on a tray which belonged to the set, which Betty warned me against, as the water probably hadn't been changed for ages, if there was any. Photographs of Betty on her beautiful horse; and of all the girls with their mama when they had just become young ladies—quite appealing. Mrs. Huling not yet so hard-faced. Pretty schoolgirl picture of Kay, who had gone to Farmington. Sort of inlaid-with-fancy-wood bureau. Shabby old dark painted screen. On the mantel, a glass jar with very large elaborate chocolate candies, which were discolored and had evidently been in there a long time. A picture of one of the girls as a baby—one large head against a blank white background and underneath a garland of smaller heads like a chorus of cherubs. A framed sampler behind the door. More fancy clocks that didn't go.

Otis Ferguson* always had to drive up to the back door, because Mrs. Huling wouldn't have him in the house—I was summoned once to see him and Dinah

---

* The movie critic of *The New Republic* during the 1930s and a staff writer.

from a conversation with Mrs. Huling on the front porch. [Dinah was a spaniel that I had given Frances when she had come up and driven me back from Provincetown.] —Frances's sulkiness and jealousy about Betty. She would play the radio all night in her room. Betty would talk about her as if she and Rosalind were about the same age. Actually, she was thirty.

Their efforts to do us all the honors. [Rosalind was with me.] Couldn't refrain from the tennis rally, however, and wouldn't play with us. Enormous dinner. New England drudging politeness—redeemed, however, by Betty's good heart.

—Their attitude toward Dinah—Frances had seemed to think she was too small at first—as if she were afraid I was palming off on her something inferior. Dinah had got lost in one of their motor accidents and been badly scared—and one always felt that the girls despised her a little because she was so timid and that they handled her so roughly as to make her more so.

Betty's story of their trip to Europe with their mother. When they were leaving Venice, the old lady, who was terribly close (had sent Kay off to Farmington without any adequate wardrobe), retrieved the bottle of wine from their table—they had paid for but hadn't drunk it all—and proposed that the girls should drink it so they should be sure to get their money's worth. When they refused, she drank it herself and got a little tight. It affected her, not by making her more generous, but by elevating her to an ecstasy of thrift. She wouldn't let them go to the station on the fast motorboat, though they had very little time and had engaged reservations on the train to Milan; but insisted on going on a local, which stopped everywhere but cost less. They caught the train by the skin of their teeth and got into the first-class carriage, though Mrs. Huling always traveled

in the second. The girls insisted on staying there while
their mother went back to the second. She was furious
and refused to give them any money for meals, but they
had a little and spent it with great joy on all the things
to eat that people brought to the windows at the station.
Betty's delight in everything—babbling along about
Lambie—when the car would backfire with one of its
short dry farts, Betty would coax her along, speculate on
what was wrong with her—thought she hadn't wanted
to go up to New Hampshire, thought that was why she
had acted up at once. When talk of the trip had been
dropped, she had behaved again. Betty would howl
along, heading off the cars and trucks on the Post Road,
and exclaim, "Oh, summer's so wonderful!"—or, "There's
a pretty church!" or "a nice house!"—over most unattractive specimens.

Arthur Jackson's wedding anniversary [at Washington,
Connecticut]. I went up there with expectations, if not
exactly high, at least cheerful, thinking that it would be
nice to see them all again and that I would endeavor to
be the life of the party. I got there about twenty minutes
to six—six was the appointed time—and was shunted off
by Arthur to his office. The tables were spread on the
lawn, and it all looked very pretty; but the Jacksons
didn't know what to do about people who arrived before
the hour—as a few others did: they couldn't turn on their
cordiality and hospitality till precisely the stroke of six,
so merely greeted the early guests in passing and rushed
off to attend to something in such a way as to make them
feel that they oughtn't to have arrived so early. Then
when the party finally broke, it turned out to be three-
quarters women and no drinks except thimblefuls of
brandy were served. I sat at a table with four women
for the buffet supper. When I came back from a call

on Mrs. Bellinger, they had been driven into the house by the rain and Alfred and I found the living room packed with women, who were clustered around the piano singing. They said something, with a great deal of laughter, about all the men being out on the porch, and we thought we were not supposed to be there and went out on the porch, too, where we found all the men with Gertrude Hinchman and Stanley Dell's wife, the only women who had the usages of modern society. It turned out, on the contrary, that the ladies inside had believed that they were trying to get the men to join them—which some of them were intimidated into doing. Almost everybody left about 9:30. They brought Dorothy and Arthur presents, but nobody drank their health, nobody made a speech, nobody sang them a song. Nobody except me, so far as I observed, kissed Dorothy. I heard no one wish them long life and happiness.

The Bellingers. The house rebuilt where the old one had burned. Lou still pretty and sweet, though with incipient signs of the spinster; she was curator of old musical instruments at Yale—tuned the old spinets and things. Charlotte was in some ways prematurely aged—her hair was perfectly white, but she looked all purified and beaten out fine—very quiet, submerged and subdued by her years of children and trying times with the Bellingers. Mrs. Bellinger seemed to have changed surprisingly little. She still subscribed to *Punch* and thought it was still good, and had gone to the trouble of getting another set of the old bound volumes when the set they had owned had been burned up in the fire.

Stanley being snooty, when I first saw him at the party, about not remembering that he had been an usher at Arthur and Dorothy's wedding: "I didn't know I had been, did you?"

Alfred more tolerant than I had expected about

Charley Walker and Phelps Putnam—and more intelligent, too—I think it was partly that he thought they were Bows men, so that whatever they did must be fundamentally all right. I saw his sensitivity as in the old days, but thought that it was almost as if he had compelled himself systematically to become academic about his archaeological work. When I threw out, in the course of our philosophical conversation, my theory about the superiority of the dynamic qualities of English, German, and Latin verbs over Greek and Russian verbs, he said, "I don't think I know what you mean." Still, I can see now that with superior intellectual qualities he combines very commonplace ones.

Crisis at The New Republic. Before the CIO, it had been only the editorial staff proper who had been eligible for the Newspaper Guild. But now the Book and Magazine Guild was to merge with the Newspaper Guild; and E. G. Wood [of the business department] suddenly turned up in Dan Mebane's office with a CIO contract. Dan's immediate impulse was one of violent opposition. He took the all-one-great-big-family line; then, at Wood's further insistence, said, "Why, you've changed, E.G.! You wouldn't have behaved this way a few years ago!— And, you're part of the management here, E.G." —Wood said: "What have I got to show for it?"—and he asked what had become of the NR's enthusiasm for organized labor and the CIO? Why, Dan said, "That's educational." —And as Wood still persevered: "Now let me tell you, E.G., that if you persist in this, you may find yourself in trouble!" Dan's line had been that they didn't want themselves checked up on, punching time clocks, etc., to see that they worked eight hours a day. Afterwards, Dan was heard in Bruce [Bliven's] room talking very loudly and emphatically: "If they're going to be hard-boiled, we'll show them that we can be hard-boiled, too!"

The word got around, and one morning Dan came in to find the four Weird Sisters from the subscription department waiting for him at the door of his office. They said, in a fluster and with indignation, that they had heard about this union business and that they wanted him to know that they were loyal. John Irvin [the elderly Irish office boy], always prone to grouches and rages, flew into a permanent fury: he went around fuming and threatening to crack the head of anybody who tried to bring pressure to bear in the direction of unionization, and talking about the damned foreigners in the office. The boy who was working for him was supporting himself and a mother and sister on, I think, $17 a week. Miss Gabriel, the telephone operator, had been working for eleven years and had never gotten more than $19. When this was brought to the attention of Dan, he said that, well, he had expected her to get married any day. In the case of another girl, he explained his not having paid her more on the ground that she was married. (*The Nation* was 100 percent organized—even the copyreader's job was paid $40 a week.) Dan and John Irvin spread a terror; everything in the office was very tense; people whispered behind doors about the union. The point was that Dan, unhappy in his home life, had come to get his chief satisfaction out of the feeling of benevolent power which he got from his paternalistic relation to the *New Republic* employees. He had worked Miss Simpson to death—maybe she had been in love with him, too—and now she was in a t.b. sanitarium. He went around outside the office talking wildly to people: the proposal to change the Supreme Court hadn't been put right, etc. He told me one day that he had seen the same unionization movement in Indiana around 1910, that people had in the same way expected great things and that they hadn't materialized. Another day, while the conflict was still raging, when I had gone in to see him about my book [of plays]—about which, from the point of view of business arrangements, he had made and continued to make no sense—he had left me alone in his office a moment and during that moment Wood came in. I was used to his aspect of light colorless untrimmed hair, colorless eyes although glasses, pasty face, un-natty clothes, and general demeanor of gentleness and humility. But now he was animated with some of the initiative and assurance of a new class rising to power. He suggested that it might be a good idea to advertize my plays by printing some of the long speeches—suggested my taking it up with Dan. When Dan came back, I mentioned this to him. He cried, "Wood? When did you see Wood?" —He was jittery, more unsure of himself than ever.

Betty and Otis Ferguson set out to organize the office. Betty agitated the old ladies in the subscription department, pointing out to them the advantages—of old-age insurance, etc.—which would accrue to them under the contract and of which they had never dreamed, till, so far from being loyal workers, they became enthusiastic CIO supporters. The editors of *Antiques, Theatre Arts,* and *Asia* [all subsidized by Mrs. Elmhirst] called meetings at which they told their employees that if they didn't drop the CIO, the magazines would immediately shut down. Betty and her supporters insisted that Dan should call a meeting—which he did his best to get out of—and then, when he had finally agreed, he apparently tried to pull a gag by setting the meeting for eleven and then calling it at half past ten before Betty and Otis Ferguson were back from the press. Their supporters, however, prevented this. Bruce Bliven spoke to them

and said that they knew the *New Republic*'s attitude
toward labor and that he thought they might like to
have him leave the room, so that they could discuss it
among themselves. When asked what the *New Republic*'s attitude was, he answered, "Benevolent neutral-
ity." Dan thought they wouldn't be able to get a majority,
but Betty arranged it by having Otis and herself resign
from the Newspaper Guild and join the Book and Magazine Guild, so that they had twenty-one members.

During the hot spell that followed, John Irvin fell
dead. Then it was found that all those years he had been
lying to people about living with his sister. He lived
by himself in a single room and had hardly a friend in
the world—he had only wanted to seem to have a family
like other people.

—Dan Mcbane soon accepted the situation, turned
sweetness and benignity themselves, and came to think
he had thought it all up himself. (His evading showing
Bruce and George the books after Croly's death.)

While all this was going on, nobody could ever discover whether or not George Soule even knew about it,
till Betty told him one day at lunch.

First of autumn. Stamford, September 3, '37. There
was a horribly muggy day, like the deepest of August,
when I was sunk and spent most of the day in bed
with a headache—then I woke up early the next morning
to realize that the autumn had come overnight: I could
see some dead leaves in the bushes and later I saw a leaf
or two drifting down from the high trees. Suddenly one
was aware of the first tarnishing of the green with
autumnal rust and what was no longer the haze of
August and had turned to September mist—there was
a distinct scent of fermentation—"all that richness passing to decay." —Dead leaves in the tennis court.

K., *September 9, 1937* [in Albany]. Contrast between that saddest blankest sitting room of a suite—the only one, the room clerk had said, that they had in the hotel—with its settee, its window shades (on the corner, looking out two ways on the street), its wallpaper of neutral color and inconspicuous pattern, its carpets and its lamps, all equally devoid of color or even of the least attempt at meeting any kind of human situation—I couldn't even imagine political conferences taking place there. On the corner by the hotel, rather bleak: Albany in the fall. But then, on the other hand, you weren't likely to disturb the people next door. We decided to go at once into the bedroom, which had at least a bed and had the bathroom next door. We sat first on the plush-bottomed chairs and talked—then we went to bed. Contrast between all that and K., all voluptuous and ripe after sunning herself for two weeks and a half on the beach, with the white strips of her bathing suit brought out by the burn as if they themselves had been burnt into her shoulders as scars, and her figure which had naturally expanded—she thought she was disgustingly fat—not flabby as it had seemed to me in B. more than a year ago now, but all rich and big and soft like Venus in those Renaissance paintings of Titian *et al.,* when she pulled off her rubber shell and her hat and her brassière. She was marvelous, monumental, with her lovely little feet (with a corn on one of them, where her shoes—though these were much better-looking—never did fit her very well) and hands. If the hands and feet don't puff up, the women can get quite fat and still be all right—as in the case of Margaret de Silver. She kept wrapping the old bedcover about her—it was a kind of dull tan with an Indian-pipe design, it had probably, as she said, been bedraggled already by many migrations of traveling salesmen. Her darling long black hair, which she said had begun lately to fall out—it would get tangled in my hands when I put my arms around her under her. When I looked down on her face, making love to her, it would have changed in the instant from that Irish and humorous to that black-haired and white-skinned Spanish look, with the eyes closed and looking so different, serious, and slanting and the eyes of a beauty. She tried to keep me with her when I was leaving to put on the condom. The second time, it lasted a long time: she was dry at first. I thought it hurt her on account of her having had an inflamed vagina during the summer. Then we resorted to other methods, and finally, when I had made her come, I rubbed in some Vaseline to make it easier. It was wonderful, and I thought that, in spite of having just come, she seemed to enjoy it, too. My penis went in and out so beautifully sensitively, caressing (me) each time so sweet-smoothly (silkily), until I had to take it out [not to get her pregnant] and told her to take hold of it, but she jerked it with her fingers in too rapid a rhythm, which hurt me, and I told her to let go, and worked it back and forth on her belly and felt pleasure and wonderful satisfaction— much more, curiously enough, than the first time. She began to cry, and I knew that we loved each other still.

After that, I was tired, she talkative. She kept gird- ing at me because I wasn't brighter. Later she threw up and then felt apologetic, thinking she had made things unpleasant; but I didn't mind a bit except because I thought she was upset: she looked so warm and sun- burned and luscious, an unspoilably appetizing repast of flesh. But then she drank some more—I thought that she ought to get back [to her room in the same hotel]— and was beginning to get numb and drowsy. I felt that the whole thing was over—she would say that it was but we neither of us quite wanted it to be. This time she drank whiskey and I only Liebfraumilch, so that I was able to get away in fairly good time in the morning. I accused her of infantilism in going back to her family

[her parents] and behaving as she had during the summer—though I knew that the whole thing was my fault—
we should never be the same again. Her talk against
another marriage, more children—Lesbian talk; Betty
Cunningham—her father's jokes—Betty Cunningham's
letter—her letter to the woman at camp, which she
thought scathing but which seemed to me polite. Her
father was telling her now that the B.s were only vulgar
people varnished over, who had never had any decent
ideas and had never cared about anything but money.
The California girl she had met at a party: her husband
had said about somebody: "He's a big shot out on the
Coast!" His wife had said, "And don't forget to dot the *i!*"

Pittsburgh, September '37 [I went out to see Rosalind's
mother in the hospital]. Pittsburgh: arriving early morning, the glitter of pearl and silver (in pearl light?) of the
houses on the other side of the river on that barren and
gritty hillside.

Venita [Mary's sister] had had a farm girl, who had
come into the city, to help her, and invited her to sit
in the living room. The girl took off her shoes and
stockings and put her feet up on Venita's chair.

Andrew Wilsons [my Cousin Carolyn's parents]. Contrast between the Wilsons as I used to see them in Newark, where they were living in a part of the town which
had gone and where everything seemed dark and rather
sordid, and in Scarsdale, where they seemed dignified
and distinguished, very solid among the changing American fortunes. —Portraits of Captain Andrew Wilson. The
legend was that he had come over here from London-
derry in the eighteenth century, with nothing but a
trout rod and a silver onion watch, made in London.

Susan Wilson. Her trip to Labrador: she had gone on
an expedition where they hadn't wanted to take a

woman, had cooked for the men and never regretted having gone. Her Anglo-Saxon translations. Thought maybe the Anglo-Saxon race was played out and that the healthier "foreign" stock was coming to take its place. She likes to set herself forbidding and difficult tasks: Labrador, Anglo-Saxon, therapeutic work in the insane asylum. This is like her grandmother Wilson, not like her Virginian family. Hallucination—such as she sometimes had while lying down—of herself, pale, weak, spidery, and odious, coming into the room. Dream in which she found her father, still alive, in Greenwich Village. —How her mother with the children had ridden through the snow in the stage when her father had died at Spring Lake during the blizzard and had heard the people talking about how John Wilson had died and left his poor young wife with three children. —My ideas about their life in Pittsburgh. —Susan talked about how good Venable Minor had been to her at the time of her mother's death in such a way as to make me think he had probably been pretty cold blooded. Minor, she said, had done quite a lot of drinking after he had been practicing law in Lewisburg, and this probably had something to do with his death—he had not been very happy. She had always hoped to live with Minor someday.

Holidays, 1937–8, Red Bank. Mother invited the Kimballs and Hartshornes for Thanksgiving, served cocktails; they talked about the favorite boy ad nauseam, denied he was good-looking in such a way as to make us feel they really thought he had everything; Bobby and I, after a few lame attempts, did not talk; Aunt Addie flourished her diamond and amethyst ring which she had been given by Adeline and when Aunt Caroline said, "What a lovely ring, Addie," at once took it off her finger and handed it over to be admired. As soon as they were gone, Mother said thank heaven we had liquidated the problem and shouldn't have to do anything about it at Christmas. Rosalind and I went for a walk.

But on Christmas Eve Rosalind went to the Hartshornes', and Mother weakened and went, too. The next day, when we had Aunt Addie and Uncle Charley over for Christmas dinner, it seemed to me that she was rather silent and sour. Rosalind told me later that at the Hartshornes' they had given her a couple of highballs and a couple of glasses of champagne, and that she had become the life of the party, making wisecracks and slapping Aunt Caroline on the back. Uncle Charley, also warmed up by a few drinks, had come to with morose cracks about Kimmy. When they had had Kimmy play the piano, he had said, "I can do that, too!"

Gausses. It was just after Paddy Chapman's death and the death of Gauss's grandson, and they seemed much to have aged since I had seen them. Gauss had, besides, just had to have a tumor—which he said was not malignant—removed from the back of his head. After Coindreau (a little bright and appreciative, but probably not profound, coffee-colored Frenchman [whom Gauss had installed at Princeton]) and I had talked about André Gide's recent assertion that he had ceased to write "from disgust," Gauss said, later, that he felt the same way; and it seemed to me that it was true that he had less aim and direction than usual, but he was in a way not any less impressive: he gave somewhat the effect of a radio, which you shift from feature to feature. There was the journey during the Middle Ages of a traveler from Rome to Avignon or Nîmes—he wouldn't have any feeling of having entered a different country. This, at a turning of the little knob, would give way to the contemporary subject of mental disorders among the students—8 percent, he thought, needed the psychiatrist, and he told me about a boy who had threatened to saw off his com-

panions' heads but had afterwards gotten married and
apparently worked out all right, of a boy who had
thought he had worked out a prescription for the salvation of all mankind—Reconciliation Peace, mathematical
formulas, etc.—and had gone down to Washington to get
it patented—had thought people were after him to steal
it from him and had sat up all night in the pay toilet of
the station—Gauss described his adventures with the same
precise imagination with which he had recounted the
journey of the traveler from Rome to Nîmes—then the
boy had attracted the attention of someone as he prowled
around the capital in sneakers and was eventually sent
back to college. Another boy was apparently a potential
sex criminal, had attacked several women and finally a
little colored girl. Then he would shift to the question of
"historicity," greatly overemphasized nowadays—he
thought; people devoted too much attention to dating
things rather than appreciating their general importance.
There was a man at Yale and there were others who "had
a stake in" establishing the idea that there were more
Giorgiones in existence than had previously been supposed
(only sixteen), so they had moved up Titian's birth
twenty-five years in order to make it impossible for
Giorgione to have studied in his studio (the old tradition
was that Titian had died at ninety-nine), but Gauss
thought that a face and certain other things in some of
Giorgione's pictures—he seemed to have them right before
his eyes—had probably been painted by Titian. Or it
would be Hutchins at the University of Chicago or contemporary French fiction or the *Aoi* that set off the
stanzas in the *Chanson de Roland*. I had never seen so
clearly before how he lived in an intellectual world of
which he was perfect master, which included many
centuries and countries, the past and the immediate
present, but where he wandered rather than worked, one
thing leading to another, ideas leading to trains of

thought which carried him without effort through the ages, but not giving rise to definite lines of inquiry or the establishment of definite principles on which he should act—like the physicist's continuum of time and space—from which he never emerged, absent-minded about daily matters for all his grasp in such detail of the administrative affairs of the college—on the cold day, after putting on his coat, he started to go out without his hat. But it was what made him such a wonderful teacher —he seemed to have infinite learning, infinite range of interest, infinite intelligence and sympathy. He suggested all kinds of lines of thought, was always sprouting fresh ideas, which, though he himself never far developed them, provided leads for other people. And at the same time, in connection with his duties, he had succumbed to some of the stupidities of Princeton: signs of anti-Semitism; the knowing glance and smile which he and Nat Coindreau exchanged over the prejudice against Jews which they shared—many Jews seemed to love coming into the scientific side at Princeton, especially since the ascendancy of Hitler. Gauss seemed to have seen little of Einstein. Gauss said that in the teaching profession there was no criterion of competence, as in medicine or the bar. He gave as an example that some reactionary man in the History or Economics Department had a panacea for all the ills of society—as if I were supposed to draw the conclusion that this constituted an incompetence for which he ought to be fired. —When I asked Walter Hall about academic freedom, he replied: "You know what Conant says—if we want to preserve our academic freedom, we'll have to watch our promotions."

Isabel—Susan [Wilson] and I went over to see Isabel in the Old People's Home at Trenton. Mother always got into a fight with the head woman when she went. If you told her about Isabel's complaints, she would always snap that they were imaginary, but I think she was always afraid that Isabel might not be being treated properly—as when she was so convinced of the guilt of Sacco and Vanzetti. It brought back my Wilson grandparents' house —even the parsonage at Shrewsbury—how it smelled when the copious dinner was being prepared on the rather bleak Sundays; how Isabel's voice sounded when we first came into the house and she greeted us, her tall-ness. Now I saw other things about her: her Irish intelligence and accent—she told us that she came from—I think—East Newtown, about ten miles from London-derry. (Grandmother Wilson was supposed to have found her sitting on her trunk at Castle Garden, after the first person for whom she had worked in America had put her out, having no further use for her. She had good-for-nothing daughters, who got her drunk and took all her money away from her. Mother had to watch this. Grandmother Wilson had left her a small pension. She had turned up once at Evie Valentine's drunk and with her clothes in such condition that they had to burn them. Mother felt that she had to manage not to let them let her go into town, so that her daughters wouldn't get hold of her.) She still seemed tall, but no longer upright as she used to be, her rather stiff figure collapsed forward. She peered up and out at us from her confident light-brown eyes as she first came in the door—very clean, though with large blackheads in her face and hands—she said that she was ninety, but mother thought she was not so old—her brown eyes, as she would turn to fix her gaze on us, would still take on, in the collapsed and wrinkled face, the critical near-ironic look with which I had since become familiar in other Irish people I had known, as she remarked that I looked more like my mother, who had used to be so pretty, and that Rosalind

resembled me. She got to telling us how the Duke of
Hamilton had taken a fancy to a girl he had seen working in the fields and had asked her mother to bring her
to see him. When she had done so, very much excited
and thinking the duke was going to marry her daughter,
he had said, "The mood is off me!" —I asked her how
they treated her, and she stopped short for a moment
before replying: they didn't get much but cereal for
breakfast, she hadn't seen an egg for a year—but she suggested it was "as good as most of 'em." It was an Americanized phrase—it might have been one of the Wilsons
speaking.

Phil Littell, winter '37–38. Called me up at Stamford,
voice so faint I thought it was a poor connection. —Met
him at University Club, had simply wanted to see me
and, I think, write something for *The New Republic.*
He said that he was now so old that, when people asked
him how he was, he told them. He had suffered from
asthma for years, so that he couldn't go out and write;
then he had had a kind of heart attack. It was very funny
—instead of prostrating him completely, it had actually
cured his asthma—so that now he was getting around
again, taking quite a lively interest in things. He was
well enough again now so that, though it was a lot of
trouble to write, he was nervous if he didn't. I found
him walking stiff-leggedly, limping, in the carpeted, ugly
upholstered room. We sat down on a couch and ordered
lunch—then he said in his faint voice, which it cost an
effort to catch, something about a "cocktail." That would
be fine, I replied. —"I said what kind of a cocktail." We
both decided to have martinis. He walked over to the
bell and banged it with his palm in a decisive and masterful fashion. As we were going into the dining room, I
told him what Ben Stolberg had said about *The New
Republic,* which he had politely said he found rather

dull, didn't read—sometimes read Stark Young, when he wanted to be made indignant: All the other journalists, Ben had said, established some sort of contact with the reader: Mencken had made the reader feel that Mencken and he were making fun of some third person, Villard wept on the reader's shoulder, involved the reader in his grief; but *The New Republic* excluded the reader altogether—they seemed to convey the impression that, if the reader could only have lunch with them, he would understand all about the subject—but the reader didn't want to have lunch with them. —Littell liked this very much: "One of those frivolous things," he said, "which may be profound." As soon as we had sat down at the table, he said firmly: "Now the question is—what shall we drink? The alternatives are wine or hard liquor." I induced him to compromise on beer. We talked about Harold Nicolson, John Jay Chapman—Arthur Platt had told him how Chapman used to go to the Porcellian and keep complaining about how rotten and snobbish it was. On the way back from the dining room, he told me that all his old friends whom he used to see in the club were dead—he had lately been talking to men he had never met. "Do you ever despair of the Republic?" he said. All those men in the dining room there had stayed away from the speech upstairs (political speech by Roosevelt or somebody, which had been going on in the dining room upstairs). —His Bill Nye bald head and spectacles; his coat and pants of different colors. He had been born in Brookline, Mass., "with all that implies." We went to his house because it was easier to talk. I asked him what he thought of Edith Wharton. He said that he had stopped reading her at an early stage—there had been *The Valley of Decision*, "two vols."—he had remembered it as being rather good. Later on, he reverted to the subject and said that now he remembered what it was which had made him stop reading Mrs. Wharton. There had been a character whom Mrs. Wharton considered a "prime s.o.b.," and one of the things she had told you to show you how dreadful he was was that he liked to go out in the street on a windy day and look at the women with their clothes blowing around them in such a way as to show their contours. "I never could read her after that because in my youth—and in fact through my whole life—looking at women having their clothes blown around them in such a way as to show their contours has been a continual source of pleasure." —He asked me whether he should read Thomas Mann's *Joseph*; I said that I hadn't read much of Mann, didn't care much about German fiction. "Fanny and I read *Wahlverwandt-schaften* together." I asked him how it was. "Why, it has a certain sporting interest—because, at the end of every chapter, you wonder whether you can possibly get through another." He had produced a bottle of brandy and poured us both out enormous slugs in brandy glasses. I think that he had his heart set on going through the whole bottle and was disappointed when I had to go. He had become a little senile, but not un-pleasantly so. I remembered what Croly had told me about his shutting himself up to write a novel sometime in his early days: he had always fallen asleep. Also, he had started a review of some book by Hamlin Garland (Hamilton Mabie, perhaps), but had never been able to get beyond the first sentence: "Mr. Garland (?) leads the young lady into the outskirts of literature and leaves her there." He was very pleased with this. Almost eigh-teenth-century wit, sophistication, cultivation, worldly tastes, but all cultured on a Boston background: sardonic common sense, nipping of pretentions, sometimes silly verbal jokes, echoes of Oliver Wendell Holmes; Boston-ian coolness, dryness, *nihil admirari*.

STAMFORD AND
PROVINCETOWN, 1938

[During 1937, EW met Mary McCarthy, who was working as an editor in the publishing firm of Covici Friede. She was in her twenties. Born in Seattle, she had been reared as a Catholic. At this time she was much involved in the *Partisan Review* and was a particular friend of its editor, Philip Rahv. That phase of the journal has passed into literary history; she moved in a group whose view of literature and society was colored by exposure to earlier forms of American Marxism, with the later repudiations, disillusionments, apologias. Mary McCarthy would depict these with great wit in her fiction. EW's courtship seems to have been rapid: he had led for so long an unsettled sexual life and he seems to have craved a stable marriage. His first wife, Mary Blair, the actress, whom he had divorced at the end of the 1920s, was now dying of tuberculosis. His second marriage with the jovial and social Margaret Canby had been cut short by her death. He now married a literary woman with strong opinions, and quite as immersed in literature and society as he was. But seventeen years divided them. They were seeing much of each other at

the end of 1937 and the wedding took place at EW's
mother's home in Red Bank, New Jersey, on February
10, 1938. Mary was about twenty-six; EW was forty-
three. They lived in Stamford until early summer and
then moved into a house nearby at Shippan Point. By
this time Mary was pregnant. She had a difficult time
and was much in the hands of doctors. EW's only son
was born on Christmas Day of 1938 and was named
Reuel Kimball, old family names.

EW would later note: "I made fewer entries in this
journal during the years I was married to Mary, and
this usually about other people." Apparently he could
not write about a marriage as strained and often as
stormy as this one. There were also the pressures of the
new war; and his need to complete *To the Finland
Station.* A retrospective note says that he found his wife
"an amusing and provocative companion and I really,
till the very end, never ceased to be extremely fond of
her." He said she had "a child-like side" which tended
to make him "sorry for her" and he invariably wanted
"to rescue her." He adds: "I suppose that I reacted neurotically, too, as I usually do with women I live with,
in rebelling against her at intervals, as I used to do
against my mother. Our life—though we had also a great
deal of fun—was sometimes absolutely nightmarish." The
marriage ended in divorce eight years later. Mary
McCarthy was given custody of the son and EW was
accorded visiting rights.]

Stamford, February 1938 [*just after coming back here
married*]. It seemed to me about the only really attractive
February I had ever known to occur: beautiful bright
clear days, some of them cold, but not too cold—on one
perfect afternoon, we walked into Stamford—and some
of them so warm that the birds began to come out. Then
there was a gray day, then a damp and dreary day—then,

Mary McCarthy as a student at Vassar, 1932

Mary McCarthy and Reuel Kimball Wilson, 1939

that night, the last hot one of the month, a big wind like those of March came up, and it was pleasant to feel it blowing through the bedroom between the two open windows, after we had gone to bed—one felt that it was sweeping the mists and the damp and the grayness away. Next morning it was very cold, bleakly clear and bright, frost on the fallen leaves, flakes of snow in the air.

On the afternoon mentioned above, a red setter followed us almost into town. Mary amused me by saying, when I finally made him go back, "Do you think he repents of his adventurism?"—an echo of the Marxist jargon she had picked up at the *Partisan Review*.

(Last April: the early days before the spring has really broken—lying at night in that end bedroom—the woods, the utter quiet and calm, in which nothing seemed yet to be stirring; but there was something wonderful, deeply satisfactory about them: they were full of the assurance of summer, of all that was going to happen and in the immanence of which one lay entranced.)

Bruce Bliven's Museum of Clichés, as compiled by Malcolm Cowley and myself.

> the man-eating shark
> the sacred cow
> flogging a dead horse
> style stripped bare like an athlete
> pulling one's oar

He regarded the word "fatuous" as libelous.

Buddy Kissell—when he got back from Hollywood, he called Betty up and said, "This is the fatted calf!" He actually had grown very stout out there. —Before that, he had sent her a postcard which said, "I wish you were here, you rascal, you"—addressed to himself and signed with her name.

Birds, etc., at Stamford. While I was looking at a beautiful pale moth, fluttering against the bathroom window, a bird sprang out of the darkness, grabbed it with its beak and was gone back into the darkness in an instant. In my study at the corner of the house, I used to sit working late at night, and all kinds of moths— including Luna and Cecropia—would come and adhere to the screen. I would go out and get them and put them in the little screened porch that looked out on the Mianus River. They would sleep during the day and come awake when the sun went down. The peeping tree frogs also stuck to the window: jewel-like little green things that blow up their throats. I kept one for a while in a jar, but I didn't know how to feed it and let it go.

In the mornings the ovenbirds used to drive me crazy with their harsh reiterated rattle, always the same. Then I saw one one day giving its call on a branch, and it looked so cunning, vibrating with its plump little body as it pumped out its raucous call, that I felt rather affectionate toward it. —One day in May when we went out for a walk, it seemed as if all kinds of lively and bright-colored birds had arrived suddenly: yellow orioles, cardinal birds. Blue and brown wild duck that flew past us, up from the water, with a flapping and rush, when we were fishing by the big rock out in the water at the gorge.

Communists. Before the Popular Front phase, they had sent down a shy young man, who wanted to join up, to agitate some girl glove-makers. He bought a large bag of candy and offered it to them as they came out after work. They probably thought he was some kind of sex fiend.

Provincetown—Early August 1938. Going back into the Dos Passoses' house with Mary while they were away—we stayed there a night or two—the past in that house of my two summers there suddenly came back on me, bringing unexpected nostalgia. It may be that visiting places only really brings back the past when one comes upon them unexpectedly. For the first time, I really took account of the break that going out to live at Stamford had made in my life—everything I had ever done before in that house now seemed such a long time ago, though it was only two years since I had left, and Mary's being there no doubt made it possible to enjoy the thought of a past when I had actually been much less happy than I now was. I had forgotten how dreamlike it was to have the harbor right outside the back living-room windows.

Susan [Glaspell] seemed much better for her years in the West, seemed to have resigned herself to become an old lady, but took to her bed with a sinking (evidently based on real illness) while we were there. Frank and Edie [Shay] seemed most depressingly sunk in the Dos Passoses' Truro house, which had been stripped of most of its ornaments and furniture: they had just started in with their characteristic rather kitcheny afternoon drinking. Jean Shay and Jane Ufford had a room in Provincetown together, waited on table at one of the restaurants, snapped a candid camera at tourists on the street. Mary Vorse's Joe O'Brien was also waiting on table. Mary herself was still indomitably lying in bed and dictating to a secretary: her house was so full of summer lodgers that the family lived in the dining room and kitchen; and there was a tourist sign on the lawn advertizing the house as the original old one which had belonged to somebody or other. Heaton had married an extraordinary new wife, who seemed to be about six feet tall, wore spectacles, and had a great frizzy head of hair, parted in the middle and sagging down over both temples—so that she looked like a member of the sixth form playing *Charley's Aunt* in a school play. She was on the way to having a baby. Heaton seemed to have been very much set up over having been shot (?) during the CIO disturbances, and talked more than usual and more animatedly in rather a feeble-minded way. Ida Rauh, too, had got over her rather serious illness and seemed to have resigned herself to growing old. Dan Eastman had married the youngest of the beautiful Walling girls. It had been a bad summer for the honky-tonk tourist trade, so that the town looked both sordid and dead. But we had one lively evening of conversation at the Walkers' with Manny Gomez, a relapsed Communist, whose real name was Charley Phillips, and a local evidently well-to-do young composer—a regular college conversation about whether each art can be judged by whether it works—writing music, building bridges, etc.

*The Bishops.** New colonial-plantation-château at Chatham in which they had invested $30,000 to the worst possible purpose. Blue and white living room, bleak with no pictures, buff dining room. While John had been in France selling the Tressancourt château and bringing the furniture back, Margaret had cut his study in half in order to enlarge her bathroom, which was handsomely done in silver and had an Oriental rug on

* EW's friend from his Princeton days, John Peale Bishop, and his wife had settled at South Chatham, on the Cape. See *The Twenties.*

the floor—so that you had what Mary said resembled a kept-woman's boudoir filling practically the whole of one wing, with a little narrow cell behind it containing a small cot and a tiny desk and room for just a few shelves of John's books. His other books were all stored out of sight in an awkward and anomalous little cubbyhole, which could not be described as either a hallway or a room, between the bedrooms and the living room.

We gave away the fact that John had been planning to visit the Tates, whom Margaret doesn't like. She hadn't even known they were in the neighborhood and was very cross and grim about it. John said, "I told you, but you were probably spanking one of the children." She beat the dachshund (she spoke French to the poodle) because he had followed us when we went to the beach, and shut him up in the car, where he vomited. John had also vomited the night he had lain awake worrying whether Jonathan, who had won a scholarship at Middlesex, should be sent away to school so young. There had been a Portuguese man-of-war and a pearly nautilus seen there that summer, and Margaret was gloating over the children who had been stung by the Portuguese men-of-war and brought to the doctor *"in agony!"* The twins were evidently combining against their parents. They talked with a fisherman's Cape Cod accent. There had been a house robbery and Margaret at once suspected them. They said they knew but wouldn't tell who had done it. While I was there, I heard Margaret say to one of them in a loud and sharp voice: "You go and tell Robert you're sorry you stole his cigar. I'm going to ask him to see that you did. Now go." When I put eighty-five cents on the mantel for a long-distance phone call I had made, I noticed that John quickly took it and slipped it into his pocket. He had identified a rare "extirpated" bird, the long-billed something, and an ornithologist at Harvard had trusted him enough to come up after it and shoot it. Margaret was rather impressed by this, since she regarded it in some sort as success. Under the influence, he explained, of Dos's drinks, he had discovered in a stuffed bird that the Dos Passoses had on their mantel an example of some rare species which the museums would pay them a thousand dollars to get a specimen of, but it turned out to be something quite common. Margaret got us late to the train at Hyannis—though we couldn't quite figure out why— and we had to go back and have dinner with them.

Second visit to the Bishops, end of September. Margaret managed so they wouldn't be there for lunch. Skimpy omelette for dinner. The dachshund would automatically retreat under the couch when it heard Margaret's angry voice: I could see it, standing under there— it could stand up, didn't have to crouch. Next morning, Margaret parked me with a tray at the end of the long dining-room table, while she ate at the little table next to the window. As soon as John appeared and spoke, she declared that he had a cold and began to bawl him out, told him to go back to his room. He sat down opposite her, tried to eat, but she sent him back to his own room. It was too bad he couldn't go up to Provincetown! [as we had intended he should] She went herself and seemed to enjoy herself more for his not being along— remarked on the way that if she hadn't been firm with him he would have been naughty and come. Her splendid behavior during the hurricane when they had been taking Jonathan to school. A tree had fallen right in front of their car, and she had gone back—although she hadn't wanted to do it very much—to warn the people at the school. John had taken Jonathan to his first Princeton football game: much to Margaret's pride. Was he to go in for football or baseball at school? Her moments of humorous Middle Westernism: "I don't like these high-falutin things!" (Allen Tate's novel). She had had the time of her life over the hurricane, as she loved to see things smashed and people hurt: there had been a minister on Long Island who had left his house for just a few minutes and came back to find it destroyed and the *eight people* in it killed. —She told us again about the Portuguese man-of-war. When I came downstairs, I found the twins dressed up as girls: one, Margaret said, was the Tsarina, the other a peasant girl. It had apparently been her idea—in an effort to un-man them young, I thought.

Floyd Clymer. They were late to lunch, and Floyd apologized, saying that so much circumstantial evidence seemed to pile up! As we got up from the table and were leaving the restaurant, he muttered in my ear: "Look out for those Caucasian horsemen!"

Provincetown, end September 1938. Picnic at Gull Pond: cold water took my breath away while swimming in it; afterwards, tingling and whiskey; that night, slight rheumatism.

Shimmering pearly background to the Dos Passoses', of Provincetown harbor—white gulls floating on the soft electrical gray that seemed rather a magical medium existing beyond the house like a backdrop than a geographical body of water.

—The water—cold from night and washed clear by the dark. —Against the gray and shimmering sea—the white gulls floating quiet against the light—the shifting, bright, and shimmering floor. (Is it too still to be described as shifting?)

Scott Fitzgerald. [He came to see us at Shippan Point, Conn., with Sheilah Graham.] —Sober, industrious, completely transformed—just like a well-meaning Middle Western businessman who takes a diffident interest in the better kinds of books. Serious about problems of "technique" in movies and *Saturday Evening Post*. Innocuous sometimes inept little jokes.

He told about Benchley fighting with a waitress—something, it seemed, he had been wanting to do all his life, but had always been too cowed before he became a big shot in Hollywood. Don Stewart went around radiating a consecrated glow—apparently going to marry Ella Winters.

Scott had taken up with a little blond English girl, who wrote a syndicated movie column. She apparently allowed herself to be more waspish than most of them— when Connie Bennett had said to her: "Is this the biggest bitch in Hollywood?" she had replied, "No: the second biggest."

[I read him "The Omelet of A. MacLeish,"* and he helpfully explained it to her.]

Washington, Conn. In the wonderful October weather: all around a sea of yellow leaves—children's playhouses built in the high trees—a wasp with its golden markings eating an autumn apple crushed in the driveway among the yellow leaves—in two days, one could see the turn of autumn: the yellows and oranges and reds were already a little spoiling and tarnished as we went back to Stamford.

---

* Originally published by EW in *The New Yorker* and later in *Notebooks of Night* (1942).

CHICAGO and
TRURO CENTER, 1939–1940

[The period of EW's remarriage and the birth of his son was one of considerable literary fertility. EW's journal keeping dwindled to sporadic entries, some of them undated, so that years later, preparing them for this publication (shortly before his death), he could no longer find the correct sequence. Time had telescoped his stays at Shippan Point, Conn., his trips to Provincetown, and his general sorties along the Eastern Seaboard. He was feeling an acute money pinch, and he left Scribner's, writing to Maxwell Perkins that he saw no reason for giving them *To the Finland Station*. He felt they had not sufficiently supported his *Axel's Castle* and other of his books published with them. The historico-political book had been appearing in various journals, mainly in *The New Republic* and *The Atlantic Monthly*, and he had also published certain of his literary essays which would form *The Wound and the Bow*, another volume for which he now signed a contract.

In the margin of this serious work he relaxed by writing satiric verses and an amusing playlet, "Karl Marx: A Pro-let Play," mocking the pseudo-Marxists and

Stalinists in the United States. To Muriel Draper, who had been in Russia when he was there, he wrote that "the Stalinist regime in its present phase is pretty hopelessly reactionary and corrupt." He could not see why the American leftists should not be as critical of this regime as they were of other tyrannies—Hitler's, Mussolini's, Franco's. His vein of satire and mockery could not be contained; it bubbled forth and caused a stir in literary circles with his poem mocking the high-seriousness and poetic stance of Archibald MacLeish, who in 1928 had published a poem called "The Hamlet of A. MacLeish." Now, a decade afterwards, EW called his contemporary to task with "The Omelet of A. MacLeish," which appeared in *The New Yorker*—this was the poem he had read to Scott Fitzgerald, as recorded in the preceding pages.

Also to this period belong two of EW's most significant essays (one was a lecture given at Princeton) on literary criticism and dialectical materialism. Both appeared later in *The Triple Thinkers*. The essay "Marxism and Literature" is a kind of overflow from his work on the *Finland Station*. These are dense and thickly woven papers, drawing upon his wide readings, but their message may be summarized as a belief in historical criticism—this was the subject of his Princeton lecture, and was a kind of answer to the ahistorical and aesthetic New Criticism. He felt that Marxism could throw light on the origins and social significance of certain works of art; rare were the works of literature which did not contain within them some attachment or reflection of the society in which they were produced. But he also accepted the need for another kind of historical approach—the biographical-psychological. These were, inevitably, given his education and experience, the "procedures" for his own writing: in a word, "man and society." And he warned, too, that "no matter how thoroughly and searchingly we may have scrutinized works of literature from the historical and biographical point of view . . . we must be able to tell the good from the bad, the first-rate from the second-rate. We shall not otherwise write literary criticism at all."

During the summer of 1939, when the consequences of Chamberlainism and the Munich agreement—with its corollary of the Hitler-Stalin pact—threw the American left into consternation and panic, and the Second World War arrived almost as if it had been scheduled, EW embarked for the first time on his flirtations with Academe. He needed money; and he had discovered that he could earn occasional honorariums by reading in the colleges from his writings. He was not sure he could lecture extemporaneously. He wrote explaining this and inquiring of his old friend Christian Gauss whether it would be possible for him to do some teaching at Princeton. Allen Tate had recently taught there for a term. But before anything could be worked out, EW received an invitation from Chicago. "I'm going to teach —God help me!—at the university summer school," he said of his Chicago plans. EW and Mary were warmly received and spent a summer filled with friendly encounters and talk, amid the tensions of the coming war. It was during this period that EW established certain friendships—among them with Morton Dauwen Zabel—that would endure to the end. He considered the Chicago mix of Aristotle and Aquinas "fantastic," but he told Gauss: "I got used to talking on my feet and could hold them all right through my double classes of an hour and a half." But he was never comfortable on a campus, disliking college politics and professional pedantries; he had a strong feeling that writers lost some of their integrity by having to think consistently on the level of students. EW's later seminars, given at discreet intervals at Princeton and Harvard, were "prima donna" affairs in which he usually talked only of work in progress.

He was back with his family in Stamford that fall during the beginnings of the war. He decided to withdraw from the stress of those days and finish *Finland Station*, a book long overdue. The war made its historicity seem obsolete—and it would take time for its enduring qualities to be appreciated. But EW persevered to the end. He was able to obtain, from Polly Boyden, a winter rental on the Cape at Truro Center, where he had often visited Dos Passos. Here, during the short winter days and the long nights, he completed the section devoted to Lenin in the *Finland Station* and made notes for a novel tentatively titled "The Three Wishes." A late note recalled: "If the weather was good enough, we went out for a walk with the baby and pushed the carriage up and down the hills. We had a drink every day at five, and some nights we kept on drinking in the evening. At noon we went for the mail. We subscribed to a number of magazines and read them all very carefully and sent for things that were advertized in them. Whenever there promised to be anything a little better than Charlie Chan, we went into Provincetown to the movies."

In this life of monotonous regularity, Wilson not only rounded out his largest book but wrote also his famous essay on Dickens, the finest example of his psycholiterary methods. His existence was in a minor key, but he was in his "major" period: and the journals of the next few years are almost blank. The war pressed on everyone; it was the second in Wilson's lifetime; and it would not be until the end of hostilities that he would find himself finally in the position of a critical sage in America.]

Provincetown, March '39—Betty Spencer and Ernest.

[She had formerly been married to Niles Spencer the painter, but after his death took up with a man from a Portuguese fishing family.] This relationship shocked and sickened us [as she was probably glad to hear it do]: we went to dinner there and found Ernest. It was all like a bad dream, in which you go to some familiar place and find familiar people, but in the midst of them there is a little green devil, with a face like a lizard. He was wearing a bright green suit, said very little (he was janitor at the bar of the Atlantic House). Eben Given said that he had said something about somebody's having committed suicide, and Ernest had said, "I knew a couple of fellows who committed that once." Betty (looking rather puffy-faced and -eyed)—her attitude was one of proud defiance, tinged with a feeling of having declassed herself: she said they were a couple getting dinner for us, and she did treat him a little like a butler. When I would thank him for passing me something, he would thank me like a steward on a ship. I talked to him at the table, and he spoke quite naturally about his return to Provincetown—he was a bookkeeper and this was about the first year that he hadn't had a job—it was almost as if he were explaining that he had picked up this little job as a gigolo to tide him over a bad year.

Betty Huling, late winter '39. Had made a final break with her family and never went down to Larchmont any more—over her rival DAR organization [I think that the point was that she had joined a newly organized leftist DAR in order to annoy her mother, who was a zealot of the regular one]. The Christmas before, she had found in her room a note from her mother, which said, "Please don't give me any Christmas present, as, under the circumstances, I am not giving you any" (or something of the sort)—and Betty had just bought her an expensive reading lamp. I asked if she had taken the lamp back with her. "No," said Betty, in a tone of hard-boiled contempt ("Naw!"). "I kept it there. I'd bought it as much for myself as for her, anyway."

Chicago, summer of 1939 [I had a job in the summer school]. *Picnic with Gerry Allard*. The Allards, Sam and his wife, Lillian Symes and her husband (he was working on the *Call*), a red-haired coal miner with bicycle, a more or less Marxist professor of economics from the University and his wife, the Allards' boy, Mary and Rosalind and I. The food and beer, of which there was a lot, on high trestle tables. The setting of Hyde Park: figures in bathing suits and shorts on the green grass. The parks in Chicago are not so well policed as in New York, so that people are more likely to get robbed or murdered, but on the other hand they have a much better time, seem completely natural and at their ease. There was a fine-looking couple—the girl blond, with nothing on but a blue bathing suit, in a beautiful embrace, she on her back, her long and handsome tanned knees up, he sitting beside her and bending down over her—right out in the middle of the greensward, where there was a sort of hollow coming down from the path. The children went out with Irene [Gerry's wife] in a boat and rowed around the island with the Japanese gardens. The baseball game—Gerry's wonderful faculty of making everybody feel at ease and mixing different kinds of people—consummate French tact, so natural that it was almost as if he didn't know that he was doing it. A motley baseball turnout: Mary playing ball with the others, in her pink flowered bathing suit (she had taken off the red skirt and blue top [?] of her beach dress), long legs, straight figure, olivish skin; the little tiny boy with squeaky voice, who tried to get into game and was easily handled by Gerry in his stride; the man who wandered up at one point and asked us if we were the Spiritualists' picnic: he seemed to be so reluctant to accept the fact that we weren't—he kept on standing there, saying that he knew they must be around there somewhere—that we almost felt as if we ought to ask him to join us; Irene had taken off her shoes and was batting and running around the bases barefoot. She was getting rounder as time went on, as people from around that part of the world (Finland) seem to do, but she was still very attractive, with that beauty of fair flesh and light pigmentation, a skin that seemed almost transparent, which was almost like something delicious that would melt under your kisses. At the beach, to which we later went, she put her arms around Gerry in her bathing suit—she was even shorter, without her shoes, than he—in a spontaneous and charming gesture of affection, pressing her body against his. People tried the red-haired man's bicycle.

Organizers at Allards' house. He [the red-haired man] told, on a later occasion at the Allards' apartment, what seemed rather a sadistic story about beating and killing a mine mule. Powers Hapgood's participation in this conversation—Stalinist reservations, conscientious anecdotes about mules, etc. Hapgood drank a great deal— which they deplored, and had come, after his Apollonian youth, to look rather like some businessman of local good family, whom you might meet at the Indianapolis Country Club. Steel organizer (of partly German extraction) on his way up to Bethlehem, gray eyes, grizzling hair, close-shaven, regular product of that steel country, hard and true as a piston—asked Gerry when he was going to stop educating himself and start educating the workers—called him up the next morning, Gerry told me, and offered him a job organizing steel. Gerry told me he would feel he had to do something like that if the *Call* didn't really succeed. Their anecdotes about

Lewis—which always seem to appear when mine organizers get together—told as if they were somehow proud of him, in spite of his ham oratory and despotic methods —how he had waited an hour at a meeting in the face of a hostile demonstration and then quelled it with a quick and decisive crack.

Gerry Allard—Gerry's picture of his family. His father, after his many troubles, had recently died just when he had finally succeeded in getting a really comfortable job as a gardener. "Marat and Robespierre," (say) his brothers, had turned into successful American businessmen, who thought that Gerry was crazy. The sister, named after a heroine of the Commune, had died recently, too; she had never married, had always worked so hard that she had not had much chance to enjoy life. Irene's father had been a Communist almost since the beginning, and the family situation was strained, because he was now inclined to think that Trotskyists ought to be shot. Irene said that the Finns were funny people—she had never realized that her father really cared about her until the time when she had gotten married. She had felt terrible when she went to school, because she was the only Finn, and they made fun of her—they talked Finnish at home. It wasn't until she met Gerry that he had persuaded her not to feel ashamed of it. Gerry talked about the various nationalities in the mine fields— remarkable the amount of knowledge of national characteristics that he had acquired in this way. The Finns were good people—they didn't say much, but were unflinching fighters; the Russians, he said, were terrible, their standard of living was low and they beat their wives. His humorous point of view on everything. Our bicycle rides around Hyde and Jackson Parks: he always wanted to go where there were signs up forbidding you to ride on the sidewalks, thus braving the police. Jackson Park had been taken over by the Negroes. Along the lake there were strips where the Negroes were allowed to bathe. In revenge against the treatment they had had on the beaches, there had been feeling against the whites in Jackson Park.

Ted Paramore, beginning December '39. He was no longer in the stout smooth and slightly smug and pompous phase in which I had last seen him two years before at Trees—his being black-listed as a result of his activities for the Screen Writers Guild had apparently had the effect of keeping him from getting work. He had the Hollywood jitters, couldn't sleep, would get all nervous and tense about scripts, etc.—had felt that he had to come East to get away for a while. He seemed somewhat demoralized, face showed some sort of ravages. It turned out that he had been doing some drinking—had been drunk the day of Yale–Princeton game, to which (I think) he'd taken his boy (eleven), who was living in Cambridge with Edith and her girlfriend (for whom Edith slaved, as I take it she'd done for Ted). He was also in the early stages of being psychoanalyzed: Hollywood analyst apparently tried to work such traps on him as inveighing against Louis Mayer, speaking of his beautiful young wife—Ted was telling him that he had a racket. Visit to his mother at Santa Barbara—would quarrel with Felice before he went or quarrel with his mother when he got there or go out and get drunk. Kind of thing that drove him crazy: "Did I tell you what Aunt Vi said when she was dying?" It was at dinner that I realized first that he was a little off the track (he'd had a shot in the arm of some drug to help him to cope with a hangover, and he got very nervous, kept shifting his feet in the car when we drove over to Provincetown in the afternoon). [We were then living in Polly Boy-

den's house in Truro.] He took up the whole dinner telling a long story about Leon Walker. Leon Walker used
to haunt the house—Ted's all too graphic description of
this. He had never really known before the meaning of
the phrase "booze fighter." Leon had got started at a
party at Ted's house and had been drunk ever since—
they had finally got him out, then he'd called up from
a hotel, didn't know the name but gave Ted the room
number. Later Ted rationed him. Leon would come
around for his drink every so many hours. At the hotel,
he was in terrible shape—dirty, hadn't changed his
clothes—had a black eye which he'd given himself trying
to put out an eyebrow that he'd set on fire trying to light
a cigarette. When he came home after these binges, his
mother would never admit that anything disreputable
had happened. His family are very rich and he is the
only child: dopes from Minnesota who'd made money
in lumber. Ted dwelt a good deal on drugs, gonorrhea,
and such things: Hollywood-decadent. His general tone,
I thought, had gone down: began talking right away
with Mary about doses of clap, etc. Told us his wife was
Jewish—he was evidently getting sensitive about it with
his brother and his Paoli ("Main Line") relations. (At
Paoli somebody had said to somebody else who had been
denouncing Hitler: "I think you're going too far: you're
talking about him as if he were Roosevelt!") John O'Hara
had said to Felice one day: "You know, Felice, I ought
to have laid you that day I had the chance." "When was
that?" "That afternoon at the country club," etc. "Oh,
that was the day!—I had a dose of clap." His father, Mr.
Ed, would rather have died than talk like this before
ladies—in fact, this roughneck vein hadn't been invented
yet. They had evidently been associating a good deal
with the Jewish comic writers out there. Story about
script which he had at first proposed to re-create, then

found he couldn't do anything with—he said that he'd decided they might as well go ahead and use it the way it was in the first place, they said they'd come to the same conclusion: this seemed to prey on his mind, a defeat which he insisted on telling as if it proved something or afforded him some satisfaction. Compromise measures for the Screen Writers Guild—the writers could be disciplined for gypping the producers—John Emerson and Anita Loos had been paid a big sum of money by Goldwyn for a job that they had actually turned over to a $50 ghost—and then writers who sat around Hollywood for months, drawing big salaries and not doing any work.

Santa Barbara. Jim Canby had died—his kidneys flew out the hospital window, etc. —I asked how Reggie Fernald was holding up: I think he gets along with innards. The Chancellors' little boy had died. Clarence Matty had spells when he was pretty seriously out of his head—due, Ted thought, to the dumbness of Merle. Morgan Adams had lost all his money

The old Hill-and-Yale boy and Western gentleman contrasted with the Hollywood side, then his tone had been lowered and he was not on top but rather helpless.

Hollywood, movie lingo, explained to me by Ted Paramore: Comic—old-fashioned gag man: spread-eagle (throws arms out and feet up behind), and scram; does a Ford Sterling (looks first one way, then the other, then sees policeman), a Bobby Vernon (same business of looking, then business with hat); prat fall (prat pad), 108 (more complicated), high gruesome; the heavy goes into the gauze (the villain is hit on the head and staggers around). Marc Connelly had "embroidered" some careful dialogue for one of his shorts: "Why don't you just have him palm his cane and holler?"

Boy, Girl, Menace or Heavy, Mrs. Rich Bitch. Muff is

girl interest: "All right, but where's your muff?" Weenie: denouement. A take: a strong reaction: Boy finds Girl in arms of another and takes it big. Also, a delayed take—doesn't register it till a moment later—to give a take or a takem. A drehd'l (German–Jewish *drehan*): twist to a plot. The Heavy keeps quilling the girl—throws a quill into her. Grand Oh: surprise of husband making love to the French maid when he finds his wife in the room. Mounted actors: cowboys. Goona-goona is exotic; ouchamagoocha: Mexican exotic.

Most of this jargon belonged to the silent days, now there has come in a phony language of the drama brought out there by Kenneth MacGowan, etc.—"conflict." "Put more epical into it." "Well, we'll take it in" —meaning, "We'll take the idea under consideration." Meaningless phrases that drive the scriptwriters crazy: "This scene hasn't got enough bottom to it"; "It's too episodic." Stretched out like a rubber ball. "It's not wieldy" (from unwieldy).

Lighting. Lupe-big phallic-shaped bulb (Lupe Velez is supposed to have said "Oh-la-la!" or something when she first saw it); ash can (looks like one). Camera: panning (panorama) is moving the camera past something; tracking is pulling it back so that we get a larger view— also called a dolly shot from the little rubber-tired rolling stand on which the camera is put.

"It hasn't got enough spontanooety: take it away and maul it around in your mind." —"This muff hangs around his neck like a milestone" (Zanuck—he fired man who corrected him)—also, "He feels the blood triffling down through the top of the cab."

Thursday night of March 23, 1940. Full moon, on night of terrific wind, we looked at it through the panes on the upper story of Polly Boyden's house, and saw the inky clouds driven rapidly across it, showing their silver hems as they passed, and then the bright complete white (blinding) moon showing through the dark gauze fringe and swimming clear, complete and bright again, with the wind all the time, the wind of March that meant, after all, that summer was over, blowing past us, no longer pounding at the walls. The moon remained fixed and supreme. Mary said she always thought it was moving—I always thought it was standing still.

Stark Young in New York, April 1940. Outburst in taxi—he was pretty tight after our visit to the Lewisohns. If he ever had a child, he hoped it would be a boy: girls would begin to swell up somewhere, and then they'd swell up somewhere else—and then their bellies would all swell up, and there'd be a baby and there'd be a mess! —All this apropos of the Tates' little girl, who was bursting into womanhood at Princeton and getting a great many beaux, who were constantly calling her up and sending her telegrams. His mouth drooped: it was as if he'd given in completely to being a homosexual and yet wasn't really comfortable about it—more defiant than I'd ever seen him.

April 1940 [this must be Polly Boyden's house, too]. Here at the top of the house I lie alone—glad to hear only the wind in the window frame—or silence, silence—of the dullness of neighbors who do not know one another—of friends who have slid away down the other side of the mountain while still, if a little estranged, we seemed within calling distance—of death, of a person who never again can reach one, that one never again can reach—you cannot hear her voice because it is no longer there—she is not somewhere far away now, even sitting alone, writing you a letter—she is no part of this house, of these houses, of any houses of people—she cannot make, cannot hear, a sound—all around there is nothing and I lie alone with silence sloping on every side, slipping (sliding) away to nothing, and I, as it were, content. If I cannot hear or hold that person, I would rather have silence alone.

Margaret. For years, I have been like a spring, uncoiled with difficulty and kept straight with effort, that snaps back into its twisted state as soon as sleep begins to relax the effort: the images that disguise reversion to the past, the convulsive twitching that wakes me up and represents the reassertion of the effort that keeps me straight by day.

The Bishops' wedding anniversary party, June 18, 1940. Old stuffed shirts from Chatham: none of us went except Mary and Nina Chavchavadze. Mary and man she sat beside at dinner: anti-Semitic, joke about many cats in the Bronx, also many Katzes—asked her whether she didn't think that was funny; she said she couldn't find it very funny, since her own maiden name was Katz. Everybody became silent, people didn't talk to her after that. Nina, in the meantime, had paralyzed her table by praising Franklin Roosevelt and saying she was going to vote for him.

It seemed to me that people like Margaret Bishop and Jack Phillips and his wife, who probably thought they were anti-Fascists, were becoming more aggressive in response to the Nazi successes.

[undated entries]
[The first part of this is lost.] And I, too, went home along 8th Street, where I remembered the evenings I had

spent, already such a long time ago, with Louise Bogan and Maidy in the rather nice little apartment they had had. It was pleasant—I was an uncle who took a sympathetic interest in Maidy's schooling and read Heine with Louise after dinner. We divided the work of looking up the words, she insisting that I should look up all the ones that began with *sch*. After twenty minutes or so, she would say in a childlike tone, "Would you like some cake? I'd like to eat some cake!" and I'd have a hard time keeping her to it for half an hour before I went out to Ugobuona's for cake. And she and Maidy would make me good little dinners and afterwards play piano duets. Raymond, from whom she was now separated, was setting her up to the apartment.

Dos Passos. The novel [*U.S.A.*] gives almost the thrill of the great Marxists—historical insight—he sees where the people are going without their having any idea of it themselves—excitement of perceiving the drama of which the characters are unaware, through their unawareness—quite different from Henry James's idea of the importance of perceptiveness on the part of the central character (there is no central character), James's complaints about *Madame Bovary* on account of the limitations of the central character. The shift from a historical purview to following the lives of the characters, job by job, town by town, dollar by dollar. He leaves out a good many things (pleasures of love, exhilaration of the whoopee period) that we get in the books of other novelists, yet he does not cheat in his presentation of life, because he does not pretend to find purpose where there is none. No doubt the things that are left out have to be left out: the vision he is trying to impose could not be brought home to us otherwise.

A sourness which becomes satire.

He resembles Bernard Shaw in always holding his characters at arm's length.

Ward Morehouse in Chicago—Jo Williams and his sister. All his sympathy is with people who are trying to get along and for the moment landing nowhere in particular. He sees the social forces that swoop upon Ward Morehouse pick him up and land him somewhere where he may not find himself at home and where he doesn't want to live: contrast of this with highly intelligent purposive cosmopolitan mind makes the poignancy of Dos Passos's work and creates its form. He is probably one of the least provincial writers in the world. When you have accepted his conventions, including this holding of people at arm's length, you must recognize that he judges social phenomena on the basis of people rather than on that of the abstractions of theories.

The end of *1919*: contrasting colors, poetic intensity.

Dante.

Dos Passos is the poet of the middle class, did not write the works of Gorky.

Dos Passos's novels illustrate the tendency of history to connect with fiction (the French historians of the nineteenth century, in whom, however, history predominated—the cheap fictionized biographies of historical characters, in which the whole thing is practically a work of fiction)—and the tendency of both to connect with politics.

And where does Goethe on being either the hammer or the anvil come in here? This book gives us both—though it is true that the eminent Americans of the interpolated thumbnail biographies are never allowed to figure in the narrative. In real life, as a matter of fact, they would certainly in some way have impinged.

He probably speaks more foreign languages correctly than any other American writer. [I don't know why I thought this. He spoke Spanish and French and some Italian.]

Footnote on his non-hyphenated words [which sometimes result in misreadings. Why imitate one of the worst features of German?]

He bolsters up the weak and mediocre by taking a higher view of their importance—sees them from the point of view of Europe and the great world at a time when America was further from it than it had been at the beginning of the Republic, and when Europe, including Russia, was going in for the most inflamed and hysterical nationalism—so that he means more to Europe, too.

Father's language.

Weltering around in a Dead Sea of mediocrity.

It rains. It snows. It makes no matter. Cataclysm.

Making some sort of fist of it (doing what one could with some job).

He thought that Grover Cleveland was the most overrated public man of his time and made fun of his style: "innocuous desuetude," etc.

Beauties of the Poets:

bird song: Whitman, Aristophanes, Milton

The fascination for me of combined opposites:

Going to bed as the world is waking: *Onegin*, *Tears*, idle *tears*, Joyce's endings where someone goes to sleep: *Ulysses*, *The Dead*. The stillness and trembling of the sea: Martial, Dante (Purg. I. 115–17)

Dante and Gray: Purg. VIII. 1–6, the knell of parting day. Dante betters Vergil, Gray lets Dante down.

Landor's verse (I think I meant that it was deficient in this kind of beauty.)

Dante's dramatic cues from the Hades of Vergil

Farinata and Coriolanus

Sophocles and neuroses

Comparison of the fabulists: Aesop, La Fontaine, Krylov, etc.

Swift on money, *The Drapier's Letters*—his feeling for certain homely things, the street cries.

Lenore in the different translations?

Dreaminess of the Palinurus passage in Vergil—Proust

Dreams: Joyce, Lewis Carroll, Strindberg

Watts-Dunton on Matthew Arnold and Sainte-Beuve on Baudelaire

(Baudelaire's imagery *is* rather banal, as Sainte-Beuve said: that is why he is better on the sordid and commonplace aspects of the life of the modern city than he is on the luxurious, the splendid, exotic.)

INDEX